AREA 51

AREA 51

*An Uncensored History of America's
Top Secret Military Base*

A N N I E   J A C O B S E N

Little, Brown and Company
New York   Boston   London

Little, Brown and Company
Hachette Book Group
237 Park Avenue, New York, NY 10017
www.hachettebookgroup.com

First Edition: May 2011

Little, Brown and Company is a division of Hachette Book Group, Inc. The Little, Brown name and logo are trademarks of Hachette Book Group, Inc.

The publisher is not responsible for websites (or their content) that are not owned by the publisher.

ISBN 978-0-316-13294-7 (hc) / 978-0-316-17807-5 (large print) / 978-0-316-19724-3 (int'l ed)
LCCN 2011925205

10 9 8 7 6 5 4 3 2 1

RRD–C

Printed in the United States of America

For Kevin

Time will bring to light whatever is hidden; it will cover up and conceal what is now shining in splendor.

— Horace

CONTENTS

CONTENTS

PROLOGUE

The Secret City

This book is a work of nonfiction. The stories I tell in this narrative are real. None of the people are invented. Of the seventy-four individuals interviewed for this book with rare firsthand knowledge of the secret base, thirty-two of them lived and worked at Area 51.

Area 51 is the nation's most secret domestic military facility. It is located in the high desert of southern Nevada, seventy-five miles north of Las Vegas. Its facilities have been constructed over the past sixty years around a flat, dry lake bed called Groom Lake. The U.S. government has never admitted it exists.

Key to understanding Area 51 is knowing that it sits inside the largest government-controlled land parcel in the United States, the Nevada Test and Training Range. Encompassing 4,687 square miles, this area is just a little smaller than the state of Connecticut—three times the size of Rhode Island, and more than twice as big as Delaware. Set inside this enormous expanse is a smaller parcel of land, 1,350 square miles, called the Nevada Test Site, the only facility like it in the continental United States. Beginning in 1951, on the orders of President Harry Truman, 105 nuclear weapons were exploded aboveground at the site and another 828 were exploded underground in tunnel chambers and deep, vertical shafts. The last nuclear weapons test on American soil occurred at the Nevada Test Site on September 23, 1992. The facility contains the largest amount of weapons-grade plutonium and uranium in the United States not secured inside a nuclear laboratory.

Area 51 sits just outside the Nevada Test Site, approximately five miles to the northeast of the northernmost corner, which places it inside the Nevada Test and Training Range. Because everything that goes on at Area 51, and most of what goes on at the Nevada Test and Training Range, is classified when it is happening, this is a book about secrets. Two early projects at Groom Lake have been declassified by the Central Intelligence Agency: the U-2 spy plane, declassified in 1998, and the A-12 Oxcart spy plane, declassified in 2007. And yet in thousands of pages of declassified memos and reports, the name *Area 51* is always redacted, or blacked out. There are only two known exceptions, most likely mistakes.

This is a book about government projects and operations that have been hidden for decades, some for good reasons, others for arguably terrible ones, and one that should never have happened at all. These operations took place in the name of national security and they all involved cutting-edge science. The last published words of Robert Oppenheimer, father of the atomic bomb, were "Science is not everything. But science is very beautiful." After reading this book, readers can decide what they think about what Oppenheimer said.

This is a book about black operations, government projects that are secret from Congress and secret from the people who make up the United States. To understand how black projects began, and how they continue to function today, one must start with the creation of the atomic bomb. The men who ran the Manhattan Project wrote the rules about black operations. The atomic bomb was the mother of all black projects and it is the parent from which all black operations have sprung.

Building the bomb was the single most expensive engineering project in the history of the United States. It began in 1942, and by the time the bomb was tested, inside the White Sands Proving Ground in the New Mexico high desert on July 16, 1945, the bomb's price tag, adjusted for inflation, was $28,000,000,000. The degree of secrecy maintained while building the bomb is almost inconceivable. When the world learned that America had dropped an atomic weapon on Hiroshima, no one was more surprised than the U.S. Congress, none of whose members had had any idea it was being developed. Vice President Harry Truman had been equally stunned to learn about the bomb when he became president of the United States, on April 12, 1945. Truman had been the chairman of the Senate Special Committee to Investigate the National Defense Program when he was vice president, meaning he was in charge of watching how money was spent during the war, yet he'd had no idea about the atomic bomb until he became president and the information was relayed to him by two men: Vannevar Bush, the president's science adviser, and Henry L. Stimson, the nation's secretary of war. Bush was in charge of the Manhattan Project, and Stimson was in charge of the war.

The Manhattan Project employed two hundred thousand people. It had eighty offices and dozens of production plants spread out all over the country, including a sixty-thousand-acre facility in rural Tennessee that pulled more power off the nation's electrical grid than New York City did on any given night. And no one knew the Manhattan Project was there. That is how powerful a black operation can be.

After the war ended, Congress—the legislators who had been so easily kept in the dark for two and a half years—was given stewardship of the bomb. It was now up to Congress to decide who would control its "unimaginable destructive power." With the passing of the Atomic Energy Act of 1946, a terrifying and unprecedented new system of secret-keeping emerged. The presidential system was governed by presidential executive orders regarding national security information. But the newly created Atomic Energy

Commission, formerly known as the Manhattan Project, was now in charge of regulating the classification of all nuclear weapons information in a system that was totally separate from the president's system. In other words, for the first time in American history, a federal agency run by civilians, the Atomic Energy Commission, would maintain a body of secrets classified based on factors other than presidential executive orders. It is from the Atomic Energy Act of 1946 that the concept "born classified" came to be, and it was the Atomic Energy Commission that would oversee the building of seventy thousand nuclear bombs in sixty-five different sizes and styles. Atomic Energy was the first entity to control Area 51— a fact previously undisclosed—and it did so with terrifying and unprecedented power. One simply cannot consider Area 51's uncensored history without addressing this cold, hard, and ultimately devastating truth.

The Atomic Energy Commission's Restricted Data classification was an even more terrifying anomaly, something that could originate outside the government through the "thinking and research of private parties." In other words, the Atomic Energy Commission could hire a private company to conduct research for the commission knowing that the company's thinking and research would be born classified and that even the president of the United States would not necessarily have a need-to-know about it. In 1994, for instance, when President Clinton created by executive order the Advisory Committee on Human Radiation Experiments to look into secrets kept by the Atomic Energy Commission, certain records involving certain programs inside and around Area 51 were kept from the president on the grounds that he did not have a need-to-know. Two of these programs, still classified, are revealed publicly for the first time in this book.

One of the Atomic Energy Commission's former classifications officers, Donald Woodbridge, characterized the term *born classified* as something that "give[s] the professional classificationist unanswerable authority." Area 51 lives on as an example. Of the Atomic Energy Commission's many facilities across the nation—it is now called the Department of Energy — the single largest facility is, and always has been, the Nevada Test Site. Other parts of the Nevada Test and Training Range would be controlled by the Department of Defense. But there were gray areas, like Area 51 — craggy mountain ranges and flat, dry lake beds sitting just outside the official borders of the Nevada Test Site and not controlled by the Department of Defense. These areas are where the most secret projects were set up. No one had a need-to-know about them.

And for decades, until this book was published, no one would.

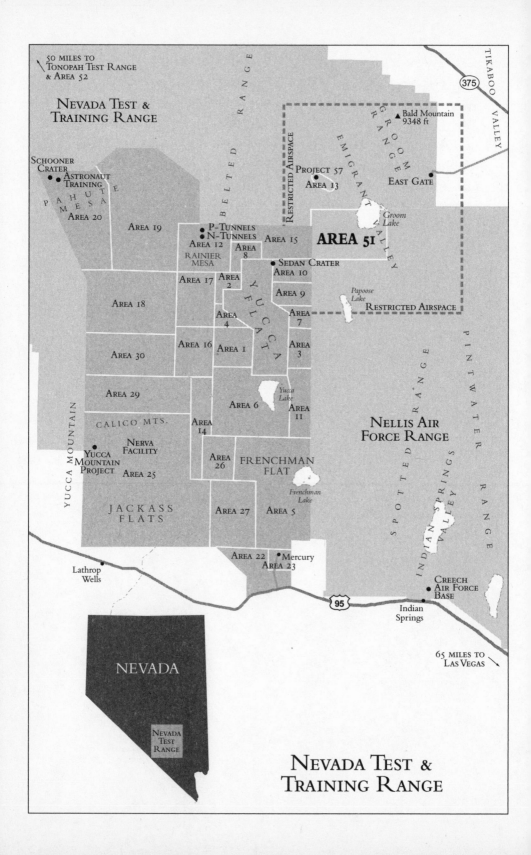

50 MILES TO
TONOPAH TEST RANGE
& AREA 52

NEVADA TEST &
TRAINING RANGE

TIKABOO VALLEY

375

▲ Bald Mountain
9348 ft

SCHOONER
CRATER

GROOM RANGE

RESTRICTED AIRSPACE

EMIGRANT VALLEY

ASTRONAUT
TRAINING

PROJECT 57

AREA 13

EAST GATE

PAHUTE MESA

AREA 20

AREA 19

BELTED RANGE

Groom
Lake

P-TUNNELS
N-TUNNELS

AREA 51

AREA 12

AREA 15

RAINIER
MESA

AREA 8

AREA 17

AREA 2

● Sedan Crater

AREA 10

Papoose
Lake

RESTRICTED AIRSPACE

AREA 18

AREA 9

AREA 4

AREA 7

YUCCA FLAT

AREA 16

AREA 1

AREA 3

AREA 30

AREA 29

Yucca
Lake

YUCCA MOUNTAIN

CALICO MTS.

AREA 6

AREA 11

NERVA
FACILITY

AREA 14

NELLIS AIR
FORCE RANGE

SPOTTED RANGE

PINTWATER RANGE

YUCCA
MOUNTAIN
PROJECT

AREA 25

AREA
26

FRENCHMAN
FLAT

INDIAN SPRINGS VALLEY

JACKASS
FLATS

Frenchman
Lake

AREA 27

AREA 5

AREA 22

● Mercury

AREA 23

LATHROP
WELLS

CREECH
AIR FORCE
BASE

95

Indian
Springs

65 MILES TO
LAS VEGAS

NEVADA

NEVADA
TEST
RANGE

NEVADA TEST &
TRAINING RANGE

AREA 51

CHAPTER ONE

The Riddle of Area 51

Area 51 is a riddle. Very few people comprehend what goes on there, and millions want to know. To many, Area 51 represents the Shangri-la of advanced espionage and war fighting systems. To others it is the underworld of aliens and captured UFOs. The truth is that America's most famous secret federal facility was set up in order to advance military science and technology faster and further than any other foreign power's in the world. Why it is hidden from the world in southern Nevada's high desert within a ring of mountain ranges is the nexus of the riddle of Area 51.

To enter Area 51 requires a top secret security clearance and an invitation from the uppermost echelons of U.S. military or intelligence-agency elite. The secrecy oath that is taken by every individual who visits the base before arriving there is both sacred and legally binding. For those without an invitation, to get even the slimmest glimpse of Area 51 requires extraordinary commitment, including a ten-hour block of time, a four-wheel-drive vehicle, and a pair of good hiking boots. Through binoculars, from the top of a mountain called Tikaboo Peak, located twenty-six miles east of Area 51, one can, on occasion, see a flicker of activity. Daylight hours are bad for viewing because there is too much atmospheric heat distortion coming off the desert floor to differentiate airplane hangars from sand. Nighttime is the best time to witness the advanced technology that defines Area 51. Historically, it has been under the cover of darkness that secret airplanes and drones are flight-tested before they are sent off on missions around the world. If you stand on Tikaboo Peak in the dead of night and look out across the darkened valley for hours, suddenly, the Area 51 runway lights may flash on. An aircraft slides out from inside a hangar and rolls up to its temporarily illuminated runway. After a brief moment, it takes off, but by the time the wheels leave the ground, the lights have cut out and the valley has been plunged back into darkness. This is the black world.

According to most members of the black world who are familiar with the history of Area 51, the base opened its doors in 1955 after two CIA officers, Richard Bissell and Herbert Miller, chose the place to be the test facility for the Agency's first spy plane, the U-2. Part of Area 51's secret history is that the so-called Area 51 zone had been in existence for four years by the time the CIA identified it as a perfect clandestine test facility. Never before disclosed is the fact that Area 51's first customer was not the CIA but the Atomic Energy Commission. Beginning in 1951, the Atomic Energy Commission used its parallel system of secret-keeping to conduct radical and controversial research, development, and engineering not just on aircraft but also on pilot-related projects—entirely without oversight or ethical controls.

That the Atomic Energy Commission was not an agency that characteristically had any manner of jurisdiction over aircraft and pilot projects (their business was nuclear bombs and atomic energy) speaks to the shadowy, shell-game aspect of black-world operations at Area 51. If you move a clandestine, highly controversial project into a classified agency that does not logically have anything to do with such a program, the chances of anyone looking for it there are slim. For more than sixty years, no one has thought of looking at the Atomic Energy Commission to solve the riddle of Area 51.

In 1955, when the Central Intelligence Agency arrived at Area 51, its men brought with them the U.S. Air Force as a partner in the nation's first peacetime aerial espionage program. Several other key organizations had a vested interest in the spy plane project and were therefore briefed on Area 51's existence and knew that the CIA and Air Force were working in partnership there. Agencies included NACA—the National Advisory Committee for Aeronautics (NASA's forerunner)—and the Navy, both of which provided cover stories to explain airplanes flying in and out of a military base that didn't officially exist. The National Photographic Interpretation Center (NPIC), the agency that would interpret the photographs the U-2 collected on spy missions abroad, was also informed about the area. From 1955 until the late 1980s, these federal agencies as well as several other clandestine government organizations born in the interim—including the National Reconnaissance Office (NRO), the National Security Agency (NSA), and the Defense Intelligence Agency (DIA)—all worked together behind a barrier of secrecy on Area 51 programs. But very few individuals outside of an elite group of federal employees and black-world contractors with top secret clearances had confirmation that the secret base really was there until November of 1989. That is when a soft-spoken, bespectacled, thirty-year-old native Floridian named Robert Scott Lazar appeared on *Eyewitness News* in Las Vegas with an investigative reporter named George Knapp and revealed Area 51 to the world. Out of the tens of thousands of people who had worked at Area 51 over the years, Lazar was the only individual who broke the oath of silence in such a public way. Whether one worked as a scientist or a security guard, an engineer or an engine cleaner, serving at Area 51 was both an honor and a privilege. The secrecy oath was sacred, and the veiled threats of incarceration no doubt helped people keep it. With Bob Lazar, more than four decades of Area 51's secrecy came to a dramatic end.

That Bob Lazar wound up at Area 51 owing to a job referral by the Hungarian-born nuclear physicist Dr. Edward Teller is perfectly ironic. Teller coinvented the world's most powerful weapon of mass destruction, the thermonuclear bomb, and tested many incarnations of his diabolical creation just a few miles over the hill from Area 51, in the numbered sectors that make up the Nevada Test Site. The test site is America's only domestic atomic-bomb range and is Area 51's working partner. Area 12, Area 19, and Area 20, inside the test site's legal boundaries, are just some of the parcels of land that bear Dr. Teller's handprint: charred earth, atomic craters, underground tunnels contaminated with plutonium. Area 51 sits just outside.

Bob Lazar first met Edward Teller in Los Alamos, New Mexico, in June of 1982, when Lazar only twenty-three years old. Lazar was working at the Los Alamos Nuclear Laboratory in radioactive-particle detection as a contractor for the Kirk-Mayer Corporation when he arrived early for a lecture Teller was giving in the lab's auditorium. Before the lecture, Lazar spotted Teller reading the *Los Alamos Monitor,* where, as coincidence would have it, there was a page-1 story featuring Bob Lazar and his new invention, the jet car. Lazar seized the opportunity. "That's me you're reading about," he famously told Teller as a means of engaging him in conversation. Here was an ambitious young scientist reaching out to the jaded, glutted grandfather of mass destruction. In hindsight it makes perfect sense that the ultimate consequences of this moment were not beneficent for Lazar.

Six years later, Lazar's life had reached an unexpected low. He'd been fired from his job at Los Alamos. Terrible financial problems set in. He and his wife, Carol Strong, who was thirteen years his senior, moved to Las Vegas and opened up a photo-processing shop. The marriage fell apart. Lazar remarried a woman named Tracy Murk, who'd worked as a clerk for the Lazars. Two days after Bob Lazar's wedding to Tracy, his first wife, Carol, committed suicide by inhaling carbon monoxide in a shuttered garage. Lazar declared bankruptcy and sought advanced engineering work.

He reached out to everyone he could think of, including Dr. Edward Teller, who was now spearheading President Reagan's Strategic Defense Initiative, or Star Wars. In 1988, Teller found Lazar a job.

This job was far from any old advanced engineering job. Edward Teller had recommended Bob Lazar to the most powerful defense-industry contractor at Area 51, a company called EG&G. Among the thousands of top secret and Q-cleared contractors who have worked on classified and black projects at the Nevada Test Site and Area 51, none has had as much power and access, or as little oversight, as EG&G. On Teller's instruction, Lazar called a telephone number. A person at the other end of the line told him to go to McCarran Airport, in downtown Las Vegas, on a specific date in December—to the EG&G building there. Lazar was told he would be flown by private aircraft to Groom Lake. He was excited and followed orders. Inside the EG&G building, he was introduced to a man called Dennis Mariani who would soon become his supervisor. The two men went to the south end of the airport and into a secure hangar ringed by security fences and guarded by men with guns. There, EG&G ran a fleet of 737 airplanes that flew back and forth to Groom Lake—and still do. Because they flew with the call sign Janet, this private Area 51 commuter fleet had become known as Janet Airlines. Lazar and his supervisor passed through security and boarded a white aircraft with no markings or logo, just a long red stripe running the length of the airplane.

Fly to Area 51 on a northerly course from Las Vegas and you'll see a Nevada landscape that is classic American Southwest: snow-capped mountains, rolling hills, and desert valley floors. Bob Lazar would not have seen any of this on his approach to Groom Lake because the window curtains on his Janet Airlines flight would have been drawn—they always are when newcomers arrive. The airspace directly over Area 51 has been restricted since the mid-1950s, which means no one peers down onto Area 51 without authorization except satellites circling the globe in outer space. By the time Lazar arrived, the 575-square-mile airspace had long been nicknamed the Box, and Air Force pilots at nearby Nellis Air Force

Base know never to enter it. Distinctly visible at the very center of Area 51's Box sits a near-perfect six-mile-diameter endorheic basin, also known as a dry lake. It was the lake bed itself that originally appealed to the CIA; for decades it had doubled as a natural runway for Area 51's secret spy planes.

Almost everything visible on approach to Area 51 from the air is restricted government land. There are no public highways, no shopping malls, no twentieth-century urban sprawl. Where the land is hilly, Joshua trees and yucca plants grow, their long spiky leaves extended skyward like swords. Where the land is flat, it is barren and bald. Except for creosote bushes and tumbleweed, very little grows out here on the desert floor. The physical base — its hangars, runways, dormitories, and towers — begins at the southernmost tip of Groom's dry lake. The structures spread out in rows, heading south down the Emigrant Valley floor. The hangars' metal rooftops catch the sunlight and reflect up as the Janet airplane enters the Box. A huge antenna tower rises up from the desert floor. The power plant's cooling tower comes into view, as do the antennas on the radio-shop roof, located at the end of one of the two, perpendicular taxiways. Radar antennas spin. One dish is sixty feet in diameter and always faces the sky; its beams are so powerful they would instantly cook the internal organs of any living thing. The Quick Kill system, designed by Raytheon to detect incoming missile signals, sits at the edge of the dry lake bed not far from the famous pylon featured in Lockheed publicity photos but never officially identified as located at Area 51. Insiders call the pylon "the pole" — it's where the radar cross section on prototype stealth aircraft is measured. State-of-the-art, million-dollar black aircraft are turned upside down and hoisted aloft on this pole, making each one look tiny and insignificant in the massive Groom Lake expanse, like a bug on a pin in a viewing case.

As a passenger on the Janet 737 gets closer, it becomes easier for the eye to judge distance. Groom Mountain reveals itself as a massive summit that reaches 9,348 feet. It towers over the base at its northernmost end and is rife with Area 51 history and lore. Countless Area 51 commanding officers have spent weekends on the mountain hunting deer. Hidden inside its craggy lower peaks are two old lead and silver mines named Black Metal and Sheehan Mine. In the 1950s, one ancient miner hung on to his federal mining rights with such ferocity that the government ended up giving him a security clearance and briefing him on Area 51 activities rather than continuing to fight to remove him. The miner kept the secrecy oath and took Area 51's early secrets with him to the grave.

At the southernmost end of the base sits a gravel pit and concrete-mixing facilities that are used to construct temporary buildings that need to go up quick. Against the sloping hills to the west sit the old fuel-storage tanks that once housed JP-7 jet fuel, specially designed for CIA spy planes that needed to withstand temperature fluctuations from −90 degrees to 285 degrees Fahrenheit. To the south, on a plateau of its own, is the weapons assembly and storage facility. This is recognizable from the air by a tall ring of mounded dirt meant to deflect blasts in the event of an accident. Behind the weapons depot, a single-lane dirt road runs up over the top of the hill and dumps back down into the Nevada Test Site next door, at Gate 800 (sometimes called Gate 700). Old-timers from the U-2 spy plane days called this access point Gate 385, originally the only way in to Area 51 if you were not arriving by air. On the Area 51 side of the gate, the shipping and receiving building can be found. In the height of the nuclear testing days, the 1950s and 1960s, trucks from the Atomic Energy Commission motor pool spent hours in the parking lot here while their appropriately cleared drivers enjoyed Area 51's legendary gourmet chow.

In December of 1988, had Lazar been looking out the Janet 737 aircraft window just before landing, off to the northwest he would have seen EG&G radar sites dotting the valley floor in a diagonal line. Part of the Air Force's foreign technology division, which began in 1968, these radar sites include coveted Soviet radar systems acquired from Eastern-bloc countries and captured during Middle East wars. Also to the north lies Slater Lake, named after

Commander Slater and dug by contractors during the Vietnam War. Around the lake's sloped banks are trees unusual for the area: tall and leafy, looking as if they belong in Europe or on the East Coast. This is the only nonindigenous plant life in all of Area 51. Move ahead to December of 1998, and five miles beyond Slater Lake, across the flat, dry valley floor, an airplane passenger would have seen a crew of men dressed in HAZMAT suits busily removing the top six inches of soil from a 269-acre parcel contaminated with plutonium. Set inside Area 51's airspace but in a quadrant of its own, this sector was designated Area 13. What the men did was known to only a select few. Like all things at Area 51, if a person didn't have a need-to-know, he knew not to ask.

The airplane carrying Lazar would likely have landed on the easternmost runway and then taxied up to the Janet terminal, near the security building. Lazar and his supervisor, Dennis Mariani, would have gone through security there. According to Lazar, he was taken to a cafeteria on the base. When a bus pulled up, he and Mariani climbed aboard. Lazar said he could not see exactly where he was taken because the curtains on the bus windows were drawn. If Lazar had been able to look outside he would have seen the green grass of the Area 51 baseball field, where, beginning in the mid-1960s, during the bonanza of underground nuclear testing, Area 51 workers battled Nevada Test Site workers at weekly softball games. Lazar's bus would have also driven past the outdoor tennis courts, where Dr. Albert Wheelon, the former Mayor of Area 51, loved to play tennis matches at midnight. Lazar would have passed the swimming pool where CIA project pilots trained for ocean bailouts by jumping into the pool wearing their high-altitude flight suits. Lazar would have passed the Area 51 bar, called Sam's Place, built by and named after the great Area 51 navigator Sam Pizzo and in which a photograph of a nearly naked Sophia Loren used to drive men wild.

In December of 1988, Lazar had no idea that he was stepping into a deep, textured, and totally secret history. He couldn't have known it because the men described above wouldn't tell their stories for another twenty years, not until their CIA project was declassified and they spoke on the record for this book. But Lazar's arrival at Area 51 made its own kind of history, albeit in a radical and controversial way. In making Area 51 public, as he subsequently did, Lazar transformed the place from a clandestine research, development, and test-flight facility into a national enigma. From the moment Lazar appeared on *Eyewitness News* in Las Vegas making utterly shocking allegations, the public's fascination with Area 51, already percolating for decades, took on a life of its own. Movies, television shows, record albums, and video games would spring forth, all paying homage to a secret base that no outsider could ever visit.

According to Lazar, that first day he was at Area 51 he was driven on a bumpy dirt road for approximately twenty or thirty minutes before arriving at a mysterious complex of hangars built into the side of a mountain somewhere on the outskirts of Groom Lake. There, at an outpost facility Lazar says was called S-4, he was processed through a security system far more intense than the one he'd been subjected to just a little earlier, at Area 51's primary base. He signed one document allowing his home telephone to be monitored and another that waived his constitutional rights. Then he was shown a flying saucer and told it would be his job to reverse engineer its antigravity propulsion system. All told, there were nine saucers at S-4, Lazar says. He says he was given a manual that explained that the flying saucers had come from another planet. Lazar also said he was shown drawings of beings that looked like aliens — the pilots, he inferred, of these outer-space crafts.

According to Lazar, over the following winter, he worked at S-4, mostly during the night, for a total of approximately ten days. The work was intense but sporadic, which frustrated him. Sometimes he worked only one night a week. He longed for more. He never told anyone about what he was doing at S-4, not even his wife, Tracy, or his best friend, Gene Huff. One night in early March of 1989, Lazar was being escorted down a hallway inside S-4 by two armed guards when he was ordered to keep his eyes forward. Instead, curiosity seized Bob Lazar. He glanced sideways, through a small, nine-by-nine-inch window, and for a brief moment, he says, he saw inside an unmarked room. He thought he saw a small, gray alien with a large head standing between two men dressed in white coats. When he tried to get a better look, he was pushed by a guard who told him to keep his eyes forward and down.

For Lazar, it was a turning point. Something shifted in him and he felt he could no longer bear the secret of the flying saucers or what was maybe an alien but "could have been a million things." Like the tragic literary figure Faust, Lazar had yearned for secret knowledge, information that other men did not possess. He got that at S-4. But unlike Faust, Bob Lazar did not hold up his end of the bargain. Instead, Lazar felt compelled to share what he had learned with his wife and his friend, meaning he broke his Area 51 secrecy oath. Lazar knew the schedule for the flying saucer test flights being conducted out at Groom Lake and he suggested to his wife, Tracy, his friend Gene Huff, and another friend named John Lear—a committed ufologist and the son of the man who invented the Learjet—that they come along with him and see for themselves.

The group made a trip down Highway 375 into the mountains behind Groom Lake. With them they brought high-powered binoculars and a video camera. They waited. Sure enough, they said, the activity began. Lazar's wife and friends saw what appeared to be a brightly lit saucer rise up from above the mountains that hid the Area 51 base from view. They watched it hover and land. The following Wednesday they returned to the site. Then they made a third visit, on April 5, 1989—this time down a long road leading into the base called Groom Lake Road—which ended in fiasco. The trespassers were discovered by Area 51 security guards, detained, and required to show ID. They answered questions for the Lincoln County Sheriff's Department and were let go.

The following day, Lazar reported to work at the EG&G building at McCarran Airport. He was met by Dennis Mariani, who informed Lazar that he would not be going out to Groom Lake as planned. Instead, Lazar was driven to Indian Springs Air Force

Base. The guard who had caught him the night before was helicoptered in from the Area 51 perimeter to confirm that Bob Lazar was one of the four people found snooping in the woods the night before. Lazar was told that he was no longer an employee of EG&G and if he ever went anywhere near Groom Lake again, alone or with friends, he would be arrested for espionage.

During his questioning at Indian Springs, he was allegedly given transcripts of his wife's telephone conversations, which made clear to Lazar that his wife was having an affair. Lazar became convinced he was being followed by government agents. Someone shot out his tire when he was driving to the airport, he said. Fearing for his life, he decided to go public with his story and contacted *Eyewitness News* anchor George Knapp. Lazar's TV appearance in November of 1989 broke the station's record for viewers, but the original audience was limited to locals. It took some months for Lazar's story to go global. The man responsible for that happening was a Japanese American mortician living in Los Angeles named Norio Hayakawa.

Decades later, Norio Hayakawa still recalls the moment he first heard Lazar on the radio. "It was late at night," Hayakawa explains. "I was working in the mortuary and listening to talk radio. KVEG out of Las Vegas, 'The Happening Show,' with host Billy Goodman. Remember, this was in early 1990, long before Art Bell and George Noory were doing 'Coast to Coast,'" Hayakawa recalls. "I heard Bob Lazar telling his story about S-Four and I became intrigued." As Hayakawa toiled away at the Fukui Mortuary in Little Tokyo, he listened to Bob Lazar talk about flying saucers. Having no television experience, Hayakawa contacted a Japanese magazine called *Mu,* renowned for its popular stories about UFOs. "*Mu* got in touch with me right away and said they were interested. And that Nippon TV was interested too." In a matter of weeks, Japan's leading TV station had dispatched an eight-man crew from Tokyo to Los Angeles. Hayakawa took them out to Las Vegas, where he'd arranged for an interview with Bob Lazar. That was in February of 1990.

"We went on a Wednesday because that was the day we'd heard on the radio they did flying saucer tests," Hayakawa recalls. "We interviewed Lazar for three or four hours. He was a strange person. He had bodyguards with him in his house who followed him around everywhere he went. But we were satisfied with the interview. We decided to try and film some of the saucer activity at Area 51." Hayakawa asked Lazar if he would take them to the lookout point on Tikaboo Mountain off Highway 375. Lazar declined but told them exactly where to go and at what time. "We went to the place and set up our equipment. Lo and behold, just after sundown, a bright orangeish light came rising up off the land near Groom Lake. We were filming. It came up and made a fast directional change. This happened three times. We couldn't believe it," Hayakawa says. At the time, he was convinced that what he saw was a flying saucer—just like Lazar had said.

Hayakawa showed the footage to the magazine's bosses in Japan, who were thrilled. The TV station had paid Lazar a little over five thousand dollars for a two-hour segment about his experience at Area 51. Part of the deal was that Lazar was going to fly to Tokyo with Norio Hayakawa to do a fifteen-minute interview there. Instead, just a few days before the show, Lazar called the director of Nippon TV and said federal agents were preventing him from leaving the country. Lazar agreed to appear on the show via telephone and answered questions from telephone callers instead. "The program aired in Japan's golden hour," Hayakawa says, "prime time." Thirty million Japanese viewers tuned in. "The program introduced Japan to Area 51."

As Lazar's Area 51 story became known around the world, Bob Lazar the person was scrutinized by a voracious press. Every detail of his flawed background was aired as dirty laundry for the public to dissect. It appeared he'd lied about where he went to school. Lazar said he had a degree from MIT, but the university says it had no record of him. In Las Vegas, Lazar was arrested on a pandering charge. It didn't take long for him to disappear from the public eye. But Bob Lazar never changed his story about what he saw at Area

51's S-4. Had Lazar witnessed evidence of aliens and alien technology? Was his discrediting part of a government plot to silence him? Or was he a fabricator, a loose cannon who perceived what he saw as an opportunity for money and fame? He sold the film rights to his story, to New Line Cinema, in 1993. Lazar took two lie detector tests, and both gave inconclusive results. The person administrating the test said it appeared that Lazar believed what he was saying was true.

"The odd part," says Norio Hayakawa, "is how in the years after Lazar, the story of Area 51 merged with the story of Roswell. If you stop anyone on the street and you ask them what they know about Area 51 they say aliens."

Or they say Roswell.

To the tens of millions of Americans who believe UFOs come from other planets, Roswell is the holy grail. But Roswell has not always been considered the pinnacle of UFO events. It too had a hidden history for many years.

"What you need to remember is that in 1978, the Roswell crash registered a point-zero-one on the scale in terms of important UFO crashes," explains Stanton Friedman, a septuagenarian nuclear-physicist-turned-ufologist often referred to by Larry King and others as America's leading expert on UFOs. "Until the 1980s, the most important book about UFOs was called *Flying Saucers— Serious Business,* written by newsman Frank Edwards," Friedman says. "In the book, thousands of UFO sightings are discussed and yet Roswell is mentioned for maybe half a paragraph. That is not very much compared to now."

Until Stanton Friedman's exposé on the Roswell incident, which he began in 1978, the story was limited to a few publicly known facts. During the first week of July 1947, in the middle of a powerful lightning storm, something crashed onto a rancher's property outside Roswell, New Mexico. The rancher, named W. W. Brazel, had been a famous cowboy in his earlier days. Brazel loaded the strange pieces of debris that had come down from the sky into his pickup truck and drove them to the local sheriff's office in Roswell. From there, Sheriff George Wilcox reported Brazel's findings to the Roswell Army Air Field down the road. The commander of the 509th Bomb Group at the base assigned two individuals to the W. W. Brazel case: an intelligence officer named Major Jesse Marcel and a press officer named Walter Haut.

Later that same day, Frank Joyce, a young stringer for United Press International and a radio announcer at KGFL in Roswell, received a telephone call from the Roswell Army Air Field. It was press officer Walter Haut saying that he was bringing over a very important press release to be read on the air. Haut arrived at KGFL and handed Frank Joyce the original Roswell statement, which was printed in the paper later that afternoon, July 8, 1947, and in the *San Francisco Chronicle* the following day.

> The many rumors regarding the flying disc became a reality yesterday when the intelligence office of the 509th Bomb Group of the Eighth Air Force, Roswell Army Air Field, was fortunate enough to gain possession of a disc through the cooperation of one of the local ranchers and the Sheriff's Office of Chaves County.
>
> The flying object landed on a ranch near Roswell sometime last week. Not having phone facilities, the rancher stored the disc until such time as he was able to contact the Sheriff's office, who in turn notified Major Jesse A. Marcel, of the 509th Bomb Group Intelligence Office.
>
> Action was immediately taken and the disc was picked up at the rancher's home. It was inspected at the Roswell Army Air Field and subsequently loaned by Major Marcel to higher headquarters.

Three hours after Haut dropped off the statement, the commander of the Roswell Army Air Field sent Walter Haut back to KGFL with a second press release stating that the first press release had been incorrect. What had crashed on W. W. Brazel's ranch outside

Roswell was nothing more than a weather balloon. Photographs showing intelligence officer Major Jesse Marcel posing with the weather balloon were offered as proof. The story faded. No one in the town of Roswell, New Mexico, spoke of it publicly for more than thirty years. Then, in 1978, Stan Friedman and his UFO research partner, a man named Bill Moore, showed up in Roswell and began asking questions. "Bill and I went after the story the hard way," says Friedman. "There was no Internet back then. We went to libraries, dug through telephone records, made call after call." After two years of research, Friedman and Moore had interviewed more than sixty-two original witnesses to the Roswell incident. Those interviewed included intelligence officer Major Jesse Marcel and press officer Walter Haut.

It turned out that a lot more had happened in Roswell, New Mexico, in the first and second weeks of July 1947 than just a weather-balloon crash. For starters, large numbers of the military had descended upon the town. W. W. Brazel was jailed for almost a week. Some witnesses saw military police loading large boxes and crates onto military trucks. Other witnesses saw large boxes being loaded onto military aircraft. The local coroner received a mysterious call requesting several child-size coffins that could be hermetically sealed. Townsfolk were threatened with federal prison time if they spoke about what they saw. The majority of the stories relayed by the sixty-two witnesses to UFO researchers Friedman and Moore all had two factors in common. The first was that the crash, which included more than one crash site, involved a flying saucer, or round disc. The second assertion was jaw-dropping. Witnesses said they saw bodies. Not just any old bodies but child-size, humanoid-type beings that had apparently been inside the flying saucer. These aviators had big heads, large oval eyes, and no noses. The conclusion that the majority of the witnesses drew for the UFO researchers was that these child-size aviators were not from this world.

In 1980, a book based on Friedman and Moore's research was published. It was called *The Roswell Incident*. The lid was off Roswell, and the floodgates opened. "By 1986 a total of ninety-two people had come forward with eyewitness accounts of what really had happened back in 1947," Friedman asserts. Ufologists elevated the Roswell incident to sacred status; that is how it became the holy grail of UFOs.

When Bob Lazar went public with his story about flying saucers and a small, alien-looking being at S-4, just outside the base at Area 51, it would seem to follow that Stanton Friedman and his colleagues would champion Bob Lazar's story. Instead, the opposite happened. "Bob Lazar is a total fraud," Friedman contends. "He has no credibility as a scientist. He said he went to MIT. He did not. He called himself a nuclear physicist and he is not. I resent that. I got in to MIT and could not afford to go there. You can't make something like that up and expect to be taken seriously." Friedman says he does not care what Lazar says he saw. He can't get past the false statements Lazar made about himself. It was not like Friedman didn't try to have a face-to-face with Lazar. "I spoke with Lazar on the telephone in 1990. We arranged to have lunch [in Nevada] but he never showed up," Friedman explains. "Scientists normally have diplomas. They write papers, they appear in directories. I wanted to ask him why none of that applies to Bob Lazar. I tried to believe him. I was not antithetic to his story. He's obviously a very smart guy and not just because he could put a jet engine on the back of a car. But my conclusion about him is that he's a total fraud."

It is unfortunate the two men never had lunch. In talking, they might have realized how close to the truth—something far more earthly and shocking than anyone could have imagined—they both were. The true and uncensored story of Area 51 spans more than seven decades. The Roswell crash is but a thread, and Area 51 itself—the secret spot in the desert—has its origins in places and events far outside the fifty square miles of restricted airspace now known as the Box.

It all began in 1938, with an imaginary war of the worlds.

CHAPTER TWO

Imagine a War of the Worlds

On Halloween eve in 1938, mass hysteria descended upon New Jersey as CBS Radio broadcast a narrative adaptation of Victorian-era science fiction novel *The War of the Worlds*. Listening to the live radio play, many people became convinced that Martians were attacking Earth, in New Jersey, and killing huge numbers of Americans. "Ladies and gentlemen," the show's narrator began, "we interrupt our program of dance music to bring you a special bulletin." A huge, flaming meteorite had crashed into farmland at Grover's Mill, twenty-two miles north of Trenton, listeners were told.

Frank Readick, playing Carl Phillips, a CBS reporter claiming to be physically on scene, delivered a breaking report: "The object doesn't look very much like a meteor," Phillips said, his voice shaky. "It looks more like a huge cylinder. The metal casing is definitely extraterrestrial!" Things quickly moved from harmless to malevolent and Phillips began to scream: "Ladies and gentlemen, this is the most terrifying thing I have ever witnessed! Someone's crawling out of the hollow top!" Phillips explained that extraterrestrial beings had begun wriggling their way out of the crashed craft, revealing bodies as large as bears' but with snakelike tentacles instead of limbs. The woods were ablaze, Phillips screamed. Barns were burning down, and the gas tanks of parked automobiles had been targeted to explode. Radio listeners heard wailing and then silence, indicating the newsman was now dead. Next, a man solemnly identified himself as the secretary of the interior and interrupted the report. "Citizens of the nation," he declared, "I shall not try to conceal the gravity of the situation that confronts the country." Scores were dead, including members of the New Jersey police force. The U.S. Army had been mobilized. New York City was under evacuation orders. Interplanetary warfare had begun.

Although the 8:00 p.m. broadcast had opened with a brief announcement that the story was science fiction and based on the novel by H. G. Wells, huge numbers of people across America believed it was real. Those who turned their radio dials for confirmation learned that other radio stations had interrupted their own broadcasts to follow the exclusive, live CBS Radio coverage about the Mars attack. Thousands called the station and thousands more called the police. Switchboards jammed. Hospitals began admitting people for hysteria and shock. Families in New Jersey rushed out of their homes to inform anyone not in the know that the world was experiencing a Martian attack. The state police sent a Teletype over their communications system noting the broadcast drama was "an imaginary affair," but the hysteria was already well beyond local law enforcement's control. Across New York and New Jersey, people loaded up their cars and fled. To many, it was the beginning of the end of the world.

The following morning, the *New York Times* carried a page-1, above-the-fold story headlined "Radio Listeners in a Panic Taking War Drama as Fact." Across the nation, there had been reports of "disrupted households, interrupted religious services, traffic jams and clogged communications systems." All through the night, in churches from Harlem to San Diego, people prayed for salvation.

In the month that followed, more than 12,500 news stories discussed the *War of the Worlds* broadcast. The Federal Communications Commission (FCC) opened an investigation but in the end decided not to penalize CBS, largely on the grounds of freedom of speech. It was not the FCC's role to "censor what shall or shall not be said over the radio," Commissioner T. A. M. Craven said. "The public does not want a spineless radio."

The 1938 *War of the Worlds* broadcast tapped into the nation's growing fears. Just two weeks before, Adolf Hitler's troops had invaded Czechoslovakia, leaving the security of Europe unclear. Rapid advances in science and technology, which included radar, jet engines, and microwaves, left many Depression-era Americans overwhelmed by how science might affect a coming war. Death rays and murderous Martians may have been pure science fiction in 1938 but the concepts played on people's fears of invasion and annihilation. Man has always been afraid of the sneak attack, which is exactly what Hitler had just done in Czechoslovakia and what Japan would soon accomplish at Pearl Harbor. The weapons introduced in World War II included rockets, drones, and the atomic bombs—were all foreshadowed in Wells's story. Advances in science were about to fundamentally change the face of war and make science fiction not as fictional as it had once been. World War II would leave fifty million dead.

From the moment it hit the airwaves, the *War of the Worlds* radio broadcast had a profound effect on the American military. The following month, a handful of "military listeners" relayed their sanitized thoughts on the subject to reporters with the Associated Press. "What struck the military listeners most about the radio play was its immediate emotional effect," the officials told the AP. "Thousands of persons believed a real invasion had been unleashed. They exhibited all the symptoms of fear, panic, determination to resist, desperation, bravery, excitement or fatalism that real war would have produced," which in turn "shows the government will have to insist on the close co-operation of radio in any future war." What these military men were not saying was that there was serious concern among strategists and policy makers that entire segments of the population could be so easily manipulated into thinking that something false was something true. Americans had taken very real, physical actions based on something entirely made up. Pandemonium had ensued. Totalitarian nations were able to manipulate their citizens like this, but in America? This kind of mass control had never been seen so clearly and definitively before.

America was not the only place where government officials were impressed by how easily people could be influenced by a radio broadcast. Adolf Hitler took note as well. He referred to the Americans' hysterical reaction to the *War of the Worlds* broadcast in a Berlin speech, calling it "evidence of the decadence and corrupt condition of democracy." It was later revealed that in the Soviet Union, Joseph Stalin had also been paying attention. And President Roosevelt's top science adviser, Vannevar Bush, observed the effects of the fictional radio broadcast with a discerning eye. The public's tendency to panic alarmed him, he would later tell W. Cameron Forbes, his colleague at the Carnegie Institution. Three months later, alarming news again hit the airwaves, but this time it was pure science, not science fiction.

On January 26, 1939, the Carnegie Institution sponsored a press conference to announce the discovery of nuclear fission to the world. When the declaration was made that two German-born scientists had succeeded in splitting the atom, a number of physicists who were present literally ran from the room. The realization was as profound as it was devastating. If scientists could split one atom then surely they would be able to create a chain reaction of splitting atoms—the result of which would be an enormous release of energy. Three months later, the *New York Times* reported that scientists at a follow-up conference were heard arguing "over the probability of some scientist blowing up a sizable portion of the Earth with a tiny bit of uranium." This was the terrifying prospect now facing the world. "Science Discovers Real Frankenstein" headlined an article in the *Boston Herald* that went on to explain that now "an unscrupulous dictator, lusting for conquest, [could] wipe Boston, Worcester and Providence out of existence." Vannevar Bush disagreed with the popular press. The "real danger" in the discovery of fission, he told Forbes, was not atomic energy itself but the public's tendency to panic over things they did not understand. To make his point, Bush used the *War of the Worlds* radio broadcast as an example.

Atomic energy, it turned out, was far more powerful than anything previously made by man. Six years and seven months after the announcement of the discovery of fission, America dropped atomic bombs on Hiroshima and Nagasaki, essentially wiping out both of those cities and a quarter of a million people living there. President Roosevelt had appointed Vannevar Bush to lead the group that made the bomb. Bush was the director of the Manhattan Project, the nation's first true black operation, and he ran it with totalitarian-like control.

When the Japanese Empire surrendered, Vannevar Bush did not rejoice so much as ponder his next move. For eighteen days he watched as Joseph Stalin marched Soviet troops into eastern Asia, positioning his Red Army forces in China, Manchuria, Sakhalin Island, and North Korea. When the fighting finally stopped, Bush's response had become clear. He would convince President Truman that the Soviet Union could not be trusted. In facing down America's new enemy, the nation needed even more advanced technologies to fight future wars. The most recent war might have ended, but science needed to stay on the forward march.

As Americans celebrated peace (after the atomic bombs were dropped on Hiroshima and Nagasaki, public opinion polls showed that more than 85 percent of Americans approved of the bombings), Vannevar Bush and members of the War Department began planning to use the atomic bomb again in a live test—a kind of mock nuclear naval battle, which they hoped could take place the following summer in the Marshall Islands in the Pacific. There, in a deep lagoon at Bikini Atoll, dozens of captured Japanese and German warships would be blown up using live nuclear bombs. The operation would illustrate to the world just how formidable America's new weapons were. It would be called Operation Crossroads. As its name implied, the event marked a critical juncture. America was signaling to Russia it was ready to do battle with nuclear bombs.

In less than a year, Operation Crossroads was in full swing on Bikini Atoll, a twenty-five-mile ring of red coral islands encircling a clear, blue lagoon. A July 1946 memo, one of many marked Secret, instructed the men not to swim in the lagoon wearing red bathing trunks. There were barracuda everywhere. Word was that the fanged-tooth fish would attack swimmers without warning.

The natives of Bikini, all 167 of them, were led by a king named Juda, but in July of 1946, none of them were on Bikini Atoll anymore. The U.S. Navy had evacuated the natives to Rongerik Atoll, 125 miles to the east. The upcoming three-bomb atomic test series would make their homeland unsafe for a while, the natives were told. But it was going to help ensure world peace.

On the shores of the atoll, a young man named Alfred O'Donnell lay in his Quonset hut listening to the wind blow and the rain pound against the reinforced sheet-metal roof above him. He was unable to sleep. "The reason was because I had too much to worry about," O'Donnell explains, remembering Crossroads after more than sixty years. "Is everything all right? Is the bomb going to go off, like planned?" What the twenty-four-year-old weapons engineer was worrying about were the sea creatures in the lagoon. "Let's say an octopus came into contact with one of the bomb's wires. What would happen? What if something got knocked out of place?" The wires O'Donnell referred to ran from a concrete bunker on Bikini called the control point and out into the ocean, where they connected to a twenty-three-kiloton atomic bomb code-named Baker. The men in the U.S. Navy's Task Force One gave the bomb a more colorful name: they called it Helen of Bikini, after the legendary femme fatale for whom so many ancient warriors laid down their lives. A nuclear weapon was both destructive and seductive, the sailors said, just like Helen of Troy had been.

As a leading member of the arming party that would wire and fire the atomic bombs during Operation Crossroads, O'Donnell had a tremendous responsibility, especially for someone so young. "Five years earlier I was just a kid from Boston with a normal life. All I was thinking about for my future was a baseball career," O'Donnell recalls. In 1941, when O'Donnell was in high school, he'd been recruited by the Boston Braves, thanks to his exceptional .423 batting average. Then came the war, and everything changed. He married Ruth. He joined the Navy, where he learned radio and electronics. In both subjects he quickly excelled. Back in Boston after the war, O'Donnell was mysteriously recruited for a job with Raytheon Production Corporation, a defense contract company cofounded by Vannevar Bush. What exactly the job entailed, O'Donnell did not know when he signed on. The recruiters told him he would find out more details once he was granted a security clearance. "I didn't know what a security clearance was back then," O'Donnell recalls. After a month, he learned that he was now part of the Manhattan Project. He was transferred to a small engineering company named for the three MIT professors who ran it: Edgerton, Germeshausen, and Grier. Later, the company shortened its name to EG&G. There, O'Donnell was trained to wire a nuclear bomb by Herbert Grier, the man who had invented the firing systems for the bombs dropped on Japan.

"The next thing I knew I was asked to go to Bikini in the summer of 1946," says O'Donnell. "I did not want to go. I'd fought on those atolls during the war. I'd seen bodies of young soldiers floating dead in the water and I swore I'd never go back. But Ruth and I had a baby on the way and she said go, and I did." He went on, "I missed Ruth. She was pregnant, thank God, but I wondered what she was doing back in Boston where we lived. Was she able to take out the garbage all right?" Forty-two thousand people had gathered on Bikini Atoll to witness Operation Crossroads, and

O'Donnell could not sleep because he felt all of those eyes were on him. Thinking about Ruth was how O'Donnell stopped worrying about how well he had wired the bomb.

Elsewhere on Bikini Atoll, Colonel Richard Sully Leghorn cut the figure of a war hero. Handsome and mustached, Leghorn looked just like Clark Gable in *It Happened One Night*. Commanding officer of Task Force 1.5.2, Leghorn was one of the pilots leading the mission to photograph the nuclear bombs from the air. Leghorn spent afternoons with Navy navigators rehearsing flight paths that, come shot day, would take him within viewing distance of the atomic cloud. At twenty-seven years old, Richard Leghorn was already a public figure. He'd been the young reconnaissance officer who'd taken photographs of the beaches of Normandy on D-day. "In the face of intense fire from some of the strongest anti-aircraft installments in western Europe, Richard Leghorn photographed bridges, rail junctions, airfields and other targets," the U.S. Army Air Forces was proud to say. Leghorn, a physicist, had a degree from the Massachusetts Institute of Technology. He loved the scientific concept of photography, which was why he went to work for Eastman Kodak after the war. Then, in early 1946, the Navy called him back for temporary duty on Operation Crossroads. He trained at the Roswell Army Air Field in New Mexico and flew the military's best photographic equipment across the Pacific. Now here he was on Bikini. Soon, Leghorn would be soaring over the mushroom cloud taking pictures of what happens to warships when they are targeted by a nuclear bomb.

At central command, Curtis Emerson LeMay stood chomping on a cigar. LeMay was going over procedures and protocols for the Crossroads event. Just thirty-nine years old, LeMay had already graced the cover of *Time* magazine and was known around the world as the man who'd helped end World War II. By the time he was forty-five, Curtis LeMay would become the youngest four-star general in the U.S. military since Ulysses S. Grant. Dark, brooding, and of legendary self-will, LeMay had led the incendiary bombing campaigns against Japanese cities, including Tokyo. When the napalm bombs didn't end war in the Pacific, President Truman authorized LeMay to lead the 509th Operations Group, based on Tinian Island, to drop the Hiroshima and Nagasaki atomic bombs.

Curtis LeMay rarely smiled. When he spoke, it was described as "not much more than a snarl." Critics called him a coldhearted military strategist and attributed his calculated vision to a troubled upbringing. His father was a violent drunk, and LeMay was forced to help support the family when he was a child. At the age of seven, he was shooting sparrows for an old-lady neighbor who paid five cents per bird. Though journalist I. F. Stone called LeMay a "Caveman in a Jet Bomber," his men adored him, often noting that he was not someone who sent his men into battle but one who led them there. During the war in the Pacific, LeMay often flew lead on bombing raids. But now the war was over and LeMay was thinking about a military strategy for the future. Beginning at Crossroads, he would shape the U.S. Air Force in a way no other individual has since. As deputy chief of air staff for research and development of the U.S. Army Air Forces, LeMay was at Bikini to determine how effective the bomb could be in nuclear naval battles against the Soviet Union.

Operation Crossroads was a huge event, described as "the apocalypse with fireworks." To someone who didn't know World War II was over, the scene on the lagoon at Bikini that day might have seemed surreal. An armada of captured German and Japanese warships had been lined up alongside retired American cruisers and destroyers. These were massive, football-field-size warships whose individual might was dwarfed only by the combined power of them all. Eight submarines had been tethered to anchors on the ocean floor. There were over one million tons of battle-weary steel floating on the ocean without a single human on board. Instead, thousands of pigs, sheep, and rats had been set out in the South Pacific sunshine, in cages or in leg irons, and they would face the coming atomic blast. Some of the animals had metal tags around their necks; others had Geiger counters clipped to their ears. The Navy wanted to determine how living things fared against nuclear bombs.

Forty miles west of the lagoon, Alfred O'Donnell stood below deck in the control room of an observation ship watching the control bay. Above him, on deck, Los Alamos scientists, generals, admirals, and dignitaries waited in great anticipation for the bomb. Shielding their eyes were dark, 4.5-density goggles, necessary measures to prevent anyone from being blinded by the nuclear flash. O'Donnell worked the instrument panel in front of him. There were sixty seconds to go. He watched the auto sequence timer perform its function. With less than a minute remaining, the firing system moved into automation. The bars on the oscilloscopes moved from left to right as the signals passed down through the DN-11 relay system. There were ten seconds left. Then five seconds. The light for the arming signal blinked on. Two seconds. The firing signal flashed.

It was zero time.

O'Donnell kept his eyes on the control panel down to the last second, as was his job. In the event of a malfunction, it would be up to him to let the commander know. But the signal had been sent without a problem, and now it was moving down the underwater wires, racing toward the Baker bomb. If O'Donnell moved fast, he could make it onto the ship's deck in time to see the nuclear blast. Racing out of the control room, he pulled his goggles over his eyes. Up on the ship's deck he took a deep breath of sea air. There was nothing to see. The world in front of him was pitch-black viewed through the goggles. He stared into the blackness; it was quiet and still. He could have heard a pin drop. He listened to people breathing in the silence. Facing the lagoon, O'Donnell let go of the ship's railing and walked out farther on the deck. He knew the distance from the button to the bomb and the time it took for the signal to get there. In a matter of seconds, the signal would reach its destination.

There was a blinding flash and things were not black anymore.

Then there was a white-orange light that seemed brighter than the sun as the world in front of O'Donnell transformed again, this time to a fiery red. He watched a massive, megaton column of water rise up out of the lagoon. The mushroom cloud began to form. "Monstrous! Terrifying! It kept getting bigger and bigger," O'Donnell recalls. "It was huge. The cloud. The mushroom cap. Like watching huge petals unfold on a giant flower. Up and out, the petals curled around and came back down under the bottom of the cap of the mushroom cloud." Next came the wind. O'Donnell says, "I watched the column as it started to bend. My eyes went back to the top of the mushroom cloud where ice was starting to form. The ice fell off and started to float down. Then it all disappeared into the fireball. Watching your first nuclear bomb go off is not something you ever forget."

Mesmerized by the Baker bomb's power, O'Donnell stood staring out over the sea from the ship's deck. He was so overwhelmed by what he'd witnessed, he forgot all about the shock blast that would come his way next. The wave of a nuclear bomb travels at approximately one hundred miles per hour, which means it would reach the ship four minutes after the initial blast. "I forgot to hold on to the rail," O'Donnell explains. "When the shock wave came it picked me up and threw me ten feet back against the bulkhead." Lying on the ship's deck, his body badly bruised, O'Donnell thought to himself: You damn fool! You had been forewarned.

High above the lagoon, Colonel Richard Leghorn piloted his airplane through the bright blue sky. To the south, in the distance, cumulus clouds formed. The U.S. Army Air Forces navigators had sent Leghorn close enough to ground zero to assess what had happened down below on the lagoon, but far enough away so as not to be irradiated by the mushroom cloud. What Leghorn witnessed horrified him. He watched Baker's underwater fireball produce a hollow column, or chimney, of radioactive water six thousand feet tall, two thousand feet wide, and with walls three hundred feet thick. The warships below were tossed up into the air like bathtub toys. The Japanese battleship *Nagato,* formerly the flagship of Admiral Isoroku Yamamoto, the man responsible for planning the attack on Pearl Harbor, was thrown four hundred yards. The retired USS *Arkansas,* all twenty-seven thousand tons of it, was upended against the water column on its nose. Eight mighty battleships disappeared in the nuclear inferno. Had the armada floating in the lagoon been crewed to capacity, thirty-five thousand sailors would have been vaporized.

From up in the air Colonel Leghorn considered what he was witnessing in the exact moment that the bomb went off. It was not as if Leghorn were a stranger to the violence of war. He had flown more than eighty reconnaissance missions over enemy-controlled territory in Europe, from 1943 to 1945. On D-day, at Normandy, Leghorn made three individual passes over the beachheads in a single-seat airplane without any guns. But like O'Donnell, Leghorn was able to recollect Operation Crossroads with precise detail after more than sixty years. For Colonel Leghorn, this is because he remembered exactly how it made him feel. "I knew in that life-defining moment the world could not ever afford to have a nuclear war," Leghorn says. The only sane path to military superiority in an atomic age was to spy on the enemy so that you always had more information about the enemy than the enemy had about you. Leghorn says, "That was the way to prevent war and that is how I formulated the original idea of overhead."

At the time, in 1946, America's intelligence services had virtually no idea about what was going on in Russia west of the Volga River and absolutely no idea what was happening west of the Ural Mountains. Leghorn believed that if the United States could fly secret reconnaissance missions over Russia's enormous landmass and photograph its military installations, the nation could stay ahead of the Russians. By spying on the enemy, America could learn what atomic capabilities the Russians had, what plutonium- or uranium-processing facilities existed, what shipyards or missile-launch facilities the Soviets were constructing. And because Leghorn was a scientist, he could imagine precisely the way the military could accomplish this. His idea was to create a state-of-the-art spy plane that could fly higher than the enemy's fighter jets could climb or than their antiaircraft missiles could travel. In that moment during Operation Crossroads, Leghorn committed himself to developing this new philosophy of spying on the enemy from above, a concept that would come to be known as overhead, or aerial, espionage. Leghorn's efforts would take him from the halls of Congress to the corridors of the U.S. Air Force Strategic Air Command. There, he would be at odds with a third set of eyes watching the twenty-three-kiloton Baker bomb at Crossroads. The eyes of Curtis LeMay.

LeMay's perspective could not have been more diametrically opposed to Leghorn's spy plane idea. LeMay believed that atomic bombs, not conventional explosives, won wars. Japan did not surrender after the firebombing of Tokyo. The empire surrendered only after America dropped its second nuclear bomb. During the atomic tests at Bikini, LeMay knew what only a few others knew, and that was that the Joint Chiefs of Staff had recently reversed America's long-standing national policy of only going to war if attacked first. The JCS's new and top secret first-strike policy, code-named Pincher, now allowed the American military to "strike a first blow if necessary." A single effort could include as many as thirty atomic bombs dropped at once. The new and unprecedented policy had begun as a planning document less than one month after the Japanese surrendered, on August 15, 1945. Ten months later, on June 18, 1946, the policy legally took effect. No doubt this influenced LeMay's perspective at Crossroads.

When it came time for LeMay to present his observations on the test series to the Joint Chiefs of Staff, he narrowed them down to three succinct points. "Atomic bombs in numbers conceded to be available in the foreseeable future can nullify any nation's military effort and demolish its social and economic structures." In other words, LeMay would argue, America needed lots and lots of these bombs. LeMay's second point was even more extreme: "In conjunction with other mass destruction weapons, it is possible to depopulate vast areas of the Earth's surface, leaving only vestigial remnants of man's material works." But it was LeMay's third point that would fundamentally shape the future U.S. Air Force, which would come into existence the following year: "The atomic bomb emphasizes the requirement for the most effective means of delivery in being; there must be the most effective atomic bomb striking force possible." What LeMay was arguing for was a massive fleet of bombers to drop these nuclear bombs.

LeMay got all three wishes. Three years later, after he was promoted to commander of Strategic Air Command, the Joint Chiefs of Staff would raise the number of bombs that could be used in a first strike against the Soviets from 30 to 133. LeMay was also one of the most powerful advocates of the creation of a new and thousand-times-bigger nuclear bomb, called the hydrogen bomb, the plans of which were being spearheaded by Dr. Edward Teller. Over the next forty-four years, seventy thousand nuclear weapons would be produced by the United States. LeMay was definitely not interested in spy planes or overhead. Spy planes didn't have guns and they couldn't carry weapons. Military might was the way to keep ahead of the enemy in the atomic age. That was the way to win wars.

Halfway across the world, in Moscow, in a military fortress called the Kremlin, Joseph Stalin saw what was going on at Operation Crossroads but with an altogether different set of eyes. First excluded from but then invited to the Navy's nuclear tests at Bikini Atoll, the Soviet Union had two representatives observing, one physicist and one spy. The physicist was with the Radium Institute, and the spy was a member of the MBD, the Ministry of State Security, which was the precursor to the KGB. The cover story for the spy was that he was a correspondent for the newspaper *Pravda*.

To Joseph Stalin, the atomic tests at Bikini were America's way of signaling to the rest of the world that the nation was not done using nuclear bombs. It also confirmed for the already paranoid Stalin that the Americans were ready to deceive him, just as Adolf Hitler had four years earlier when Stalin agreed to a nonaggression treaty with Nazi Germany and then was double-crossed in a deadly sneak attack. Unknown to the Americans, as Stalin watched Crossroads he did so with confidence, knowing that his own nuclear program was well advanced. In just five months, the Soviet Union's first chain-reacting atomic pile would go critical, paving the way for Russia's first atomic bomb. But what has never before been disclosed is that Joseph Stalin was developing another secret weapon for his arsenal, separate from the atomic bomb. It was almost straight from the radio hoax *War of the Worlds*—something that could sow terror in the hearts of the fearful imperialists and send panic-stricken Americans running into the streets.

Ten months passed. It was nighttime on the Rio Grande, May 29, 1947, and Army scientists, engineers, and technicians at the White Sands Proving Ground in New Mexico were anxiously putting the final touches on their own American secret weapon, called Hermes. The twenty-five-foot-long, three-thousand-pound rocket had originally been named V-2, or Vergeltungswaffe 2, which means "vengeance" in German. But Hermes sounded less spiteful—Hermes being the ancient Greek messenger of the gods.

The actual rocket that now stood on Test Stand 33 had belonged to Adolf Hitler just a little more than two years before. It had come off the same German slave-labor production lines as the rockets that the Third Reich had used to terrorize the people of London, Antwerp, and Paris during the war. The U.S. Army had confiscated nearly two hundred V-2s from inside Peenemünde, Germany's rocket manufacturing plant, and shipped them to White Sands beginning the first month after the war. Under a parallel, even more secret project called Operation Paperclip—the complete details of which remain classified as of 2011—118 captured German rocket scientists were given new lives and careers and brought to the missile range. Hundreds of others would follow.

Two of these German scientists were now readying Hermes for its test launch. One, Wernher Von Braun, had invented this rocket, which was the world's first ballistic missile, or flying bomb. And the second scientist, Dr. Ernst Steinhoff, had designed the V-2 rocket's brain. That spring night in 1947, the V-2 lifted up off the pad, rising slowly at first, with Von Braun and Steinhoff watching intently. Hermes consumed more than a thousand pounds of rocket fuel in its first 2.5 seconds as it elevated to fifty feet. The next fifty feet were much easier, as were the hundred feet after that. The rocket gained speed, and the laws of physics kicked in: anything can fly if you make it move fast enough. Hermes was now fully aloft, climbing quickly into the night sky and headed for the upper atmosphere. At least that was the plan. Just a few moments later, the winged missile suddenly and unexpectedly reversed course. Instead of heading north to the uninhabited terrain inside the two-million-square-acre White Sands Proving Ground, the rocket began heading south toward downtown El Paso, Texas.

Dr. Steinhoff was watching the missile's trajectory through a telescope from an observation post one mile south of the launch-pad, and having personally designed the V-2 rocket-guidance controls back when he worked for Adolf Hitler, Dr. Steinhoff was the one best equipped to recognize errors in the test. In the event that Steinhoff detected an errant launch, he would notify Army engineers, who would immediately cut the fuel to the rocket's motors via remote control, allowing it to crash safely inside the missile range. But Dr. Steinhoff said nothing as the misguided V-2 arced over El Paso and headed for Mexico. Minutes later, the rocket crash-landed into the Tepeyac Cemetery, three miles south of Juárez, a heavily populated city of 120,000. The violent blast shook virtually every building in El Paso and Juárez, terrifying citizens of both cities, who "swamped newspaper offices, police headquarters and radio stations with anxious telephone inquiries." The missile left a crater that was fifty feet wide and twenty-four feet deep. It was a miracle no one was killed.

Army officials rushed to Juárez to smooth over the event while Mexican soldiers were dispatched to guard the crater's rim. The mission, the men, and the rocket were all classified top secret; no one could know specific details about any of this. Investigators silenced Mexican officials by cleaning up the large, bowl-shaped cavity and paying for damages. But back at White Sands, reparations were not so easily made. Allegations of sabotage by the German scientists who were in charge of the top secret project overwhelmed the workload of the intelligence officers at White Sands. Attitudes toward the former Third Reich scientists who were now working for the United States tended to fall into two distinct categories at the time. There was the let-bygones-be-bygones approach, an attitude summed up by the Army officer in charge of Operation Paperclip, Bosquet Wev, who stated that to preoccupy oneself with "picayune details" about German scientists' past actions was "beating a dead Nazi horse." The logic behind this thinking was that a disbanded Third Reich presented no future harm to America but a burgeoning Soviet military certainly did—and if the Germans were working for us, they couldn't be working for them.

Others disagreed—including Albert Einstein. Five months before the Juárez crash, Einstein and the newly formed Federation of American Scientists appealed to President Truman: "We hold these individuals to be potentially dangerous... Their former eminence as Nazi party members and supporters raises the issue of their fitness to become American citizens and hold key positions in American industrial, scientific and educational institutions." For Einstein, making deals with war criminals was undemocratic as well as dangerous.

While the public debate went on, internal investigations began. And the rocket work at White Sands continued. The German scientists had been testing V-2s there for fourteen months, and while investigations of the Juárez rocket crash were under way, three more missiles fired from Test Stand 33 crash-landed outside the restricted facility: one near Alamogordo, New Mexico, and another near Las Cruces, New Mexico. A third went down outside Juárez, Mexico, again. The German scientists blamed the near tragedies on old V-2 components. Seawater had corroded some of the parts during the original boat trip from Germany. But in top secret written reports, Army intelligence officers were building a case that would lay blame on the German scientists. The War Department intelligence unit that kept tabs on the German scientists had designated some of the Germans at the base as "under suspicion of being potential security risks." When not working, the men were confined to a six-acre section of the base. The officers' club was off-limits to all the Germans, including the rocket team's leaders, Steinhoff and Von Braun. It was in this atmosphere of failed tests and mistrust that an extraordinary event happened—one that, at first glance, seemed totally unrelated to the missile launches.

During the first week of July 1947, U.S. Signal Corps engineers began tracking two objects with remarkable flying capabilities moving across the southwestern United States. What made the aircraft extraordinary was that, although they flew in a traditional, forward-moving motion, the craft—whatever they were—began to hover sporadically before continuing to fly on. This kind of technology was beyond any aerodynamic capabilities the U.S. Air Force had in development in the summer of 1947. When multiple sources began reporting the same data, it became clear that the radar wasn't showing phantom returns, or electronic ghosts, but something real. Kirtland Army Air Force Base, just north of the White Sands Proving Ground, tracked the flying craft into its near vicinity. The commanding officer there ordered a decorated World War II pilot named Kenny Chandler into a fighter jet to locate and chase the unidentified flying craft. This fact has never before been disclosed.

Chandler never visually spotted what he'd been sent to look for. But within hours of Chandler's sweep of the skies, one of the flying objects crashed near Roswell, New Mexico. Immediately, the office of the Joint Chiefs of Staff, or JCS, took command and control and recovered the airframe and some propulsion equipment, including the crashed craft's power plant, or energy source. The recovered craft looked nothing like a conventional aircraft. The vehicle had no tail and it had no wings. The fuselage was round, and there was a dome mounted on the top. In secret Army intelligence memos declassified in 1994, it would be referred to as a "flying disc." Most alarming was a fact kept secret until now—inside the disc, there was a very earthly hallmark: Russian writing. Block letters from the Cyrillic alphabet had been stamped, or embossed, in a ring running around the inside of the craft.

In a critical moment, the American military had its worst fears realized. The Russian army must have gotten its hands on German aerospace engineers more capable than Ernst Steinhoff and Wernher Von Braun—engineers who must have developed this flying craft years before for the German air force, or Luftwaffe. The Russians simply could not have developed this kind of advanced technology on their own. Russia's stockpile of weapons and its body of scientists had been decimated during the war; the nation had lost more than twenty million people. Most Russian scientists still alive had spent the war in the gulag. But the Russians, like the Americans, the British, and the French, had pillaged Hitler's best and brightest scientists as war booty, each country taking advantage of them to move forward in the new world. And now, in July of 1947, shockingly, the Soviet supreme leader had somehow managed not only to penetrate U.S. airspace near the Alaskan border, but to fly over several of the most sensitive military installations in the western United States. Stalin had done this with foreign technology that the U.S. Army Air Forces knew nothing about. It was an incursion so brazen—so antithetical to the perception of America's strong national security, which included the military's ability to defend itself against air attack—that upper-echelon Army intelligence officers swept in and took control of the entire situation. The first thing they did was initiate the withdrawal of the original Roswell Army Air Field press release, the one that stated that a "flying disc...landed on a ranch near Roswell," and then they replaced it with the second press release, the one that said that a weather balloon had crashed—nothing more. The weather balloon story has remained the official cover story ever since.

The fears were legitimate: fears that the Russians had hover-and-fly technology, that their flying craft could outfox U.S. radar, and that it could deliver to America a devastating blow. The single most worrisome question facing the Joint Chiefs of Staff at the time was: What if atomic energy propelled the Russian craft? Or worse, what if it dispersed radioactive particles, like a modern-day dirty bomb? In 1947, the United States believed it still had a monopoly on the atomic bomb as a deliverable weapon. But as early as June 1942, Hermann Göring, commander in chief of the Luftwaffe, had been overseeing the Third Reich's research council on nuclear physics as a weapon in its development of an airplane called the Amerika Bomber, designed to drop a dirty bomb on New York City. Any number of those scientists could be working for the Russians. The Central Intelligence Group, the CIA's institutional predecessor, did not yet know that a spy at Los Alamos National Laboratory, a man named Klaus Fuchs, had stolen bomb blueprints and given them to Stalin. Or that Russia was two years away from testing its own atomic bomb. In the immediate aftermath of the crash, all the Joint Chiefs of Staff had to go on from the Central Intelligence Group was speculation about what atomic technology Russia might have.

For the military, the very fact that New Mexico's airspace had been violated was shocking. This region of the country was the single most sensitive weapons-related domain in all of America. The White Sands Missile Range was home to the nation's classified weapons-delivery systems. The nuclear laboratory up the road, the Los Alamos Laboratory, was where scientists had developed the atomic bomb and where they were now working on nuclear packages with a thousand times the yield. Outside Albuquerque, at a production facility called Sandia Base, assembly-line workers were forging Los Alamos nuclear packages into smaller and smaller bombs. Forty-five miles to the southwest, at the Roswell Army Air Field, the 509th Bomb Wing was the only wing of long-range bombers equipped to carry and drop nuclear bombs.

Things went from complicated to critical at the revelation that there was a second crash site. Paperclip scientists Wernher Von Braun and Ernst Steinhoff, still under review over the Juárez rocket crash, were called on for their expertise. Several other Paperclip scientists specializing in aviation medicine were brought in. The evidence of whatever had crashed at and around Roswell, New Mexico, in the first week of July in 1947 was gathered together by a Joint Chiefs of Staff technical services unit and secreted away in a manner so clandestine, it followed security protocols established for transporting uranium in the early days of the Manhattan Project.

The first order of business was to determine where the technology had come from. The Joint Chiefs of Staff tasked an elite group working under the direct orders of G-2 Army intelligence to initiate a top secret project called Operation Harass. Based on the testimony of America's Paperclip scientists, Army intelligence officers believed that the flying disc was the brainchild of two former Third Reich airplane engineers, named Walter and Reimar Horten—now working for the Russian military. Orders were drawn up. The manhunt was on.

Walter and Reimar Horten were two aerospace engineers whose importance in seminal aircraft projects had somehow been overlooked when America and the Soviet Union were fighting over scientists at the end of the war. The brothers were the inventors of several of Hitler's flying-wing aircraft, including one called the Horten 229 or Horten IX, a wing-shaped, tailless airplane that had been developed at a secret facility in Baden-Baden during the war. From the Paperclip scientists at Wright Field, the Army intelligence investigators learned that Hitler was rumored to have been developing a faster-flying aircraft that had been designed by the brothers and was shaped like a saucer. Maybe, the Paperclips said, there had been a later-model Horten in the works before Germany surrendered, meaning that even if Stalin didn't have the Horten brothers themselves, he could very likely have gotten control of their blueprints and plans.

The flying disc that crashed at Roswell had technology more advanced than anything the U.S. Army Air Forces had ever seen. Its propulsion techniques were particularly confounding. What made the craft go so fast? How was it so stealthy and how did it trick radar? The disc had appeared on Army radar screens briefly and then suddenly disappeared. The incident at Roswell happened just weeks before the National Security Act, which meant there was no true Central Intelligence Agency to handle the investigation. Instead, hundreds of Counter Intelligence Corps (CIC) officers from the U.S. Army's European command were dispatched across Germany in search of anyone who knew anything about Walter and Reimar Horten. Officers tracked down and interviewed the brothers' relatives, colleagues, professors, and acquaintances with an urgency not seen since Operation Alsos, in which Allied Forces sought information about Hitler's atomic scientists and nuclear programs during the war.

A records group of more than three hundred pages of Army intelligence documents reveals many of the details of Operation Harass. They were declassified in 1994, after a researcher named Timothy Cooper filed a request for documents under the Freedom of Information Act. One memo, called "Air Intelligence Guide for Alleged 'Flying Saucer' Type Aircraft," detailed for CIC officers the parameters of the flying saucer technology the military was looking for, features which were evidenced in the craft that crashed at Roswell.

> Extreme maneuverability and apparent ability to almost hover; A plan form approximating that of an oval or disc with dome shape on the surface; The ability to quickly disappear by high speed or by complete disintegration; The ability to group together very quickly in a tight formation when more than one aircraft are together; Evasive motion ability indicating possibility of being manually operated, or possibly, by electronic or remote control.

The Counter Intelligence Corps' official 1947–1948 manhunt for the Horten brothers reads at times like a spy novel and at times like a wild-goose chase. The first real lead in the hunt came from Dr. Adolf Smekal of Frankfurt, who provided CIC with a list of possible informants' names. Agents were told a dizzying array of alleged facts: Reimar was living in secret in East Prussia; Reimar was living in Göttingen, in what had been the British zone; Reimar had been kidnapped "presumably by the Russians" in the latter part of 1946. If you want to know where Reimar is, one informant said, you must first locate Hannah Reitsch, the famous aviatrix who was living in Bad Hauheim. As for Walter, he was working as a consultant for the French; he was last seen in Frankfurt trying to find work with a university there; he was in Dessau; actually, he was in Russia; he was in Luxembourg, or maybe it was France. One German scientist turned informant chided CIC agents. If they really wanted to know where the Horten brothers were, he said, and what they were capable of, then go ask the American Paperclip scientists living at Wright Field.

Neatly typed and intricately detailed summaries of hundreds of interviews with the Horten brothers' colleagues and relatives flooded the CIC. Army intelligence officers spent months chasing leads, but most information led them back to square one. In the fall of 1947, prospects of locating the brothers seemed grim until November, when CIC agents caught a break. A former Messerschmitt test pilot named Fritz Wendel offered up some firsthand testimony that seemed real. The Horten brothers had indeed been working on a flying saucer–like craft in Heiligenbeil, East Prussia, right after the war, Wendel said. The airplane was ten meters long and shaped like a half-moon. It had no tail. The prototype was designed to be flown by one man lying down flat on his stomach. It reached a ceiling of twelve thousand feet. Wendel drew diagrams of this saucer-like aircraft, as did a second German informant named Professor George, who described a later-model Horten as being "very much like a round cake with a large sector cut out" and that had been developed to carry more than one crew member. The later-model Horten could travel higher and faster—up to 1,200 mph—because it was propelled by rockets rather than jet engines. Its cabin was allegedly pressurized for high-altitude flights.

The Americans pressed Fritz Wendel for more. Could it hover?

Not that Wendel knew. Did he know if groups could fly tightly together? Wendel said he had no idea. Were "high speed escapement methods" designed into the craft? Wendel wasn't sure. Could the flying disc be remotely controlled? Yes, Wendel said he knew of radio-control experiments being conducted by Seimens and Halske at their electrical factory in Berlin. Army officers asked Wendel if he had heard of any hovering or near-hovering technologies. No. Did Wendel have any idea about the tactical purposes for such an aircraft? Wendel said he had no idea.

The next batch of solid information came from a rocket engineer named Walter Ziegler. During the war, Ziegler had worked at the car manufacturer Bayerische Motoren Werke, or BMW, which served as a front for advanced rocket-science research. There, Ziegler had been on a team tasked with developing advanced fighter jets powered by rockets. Ziegler relayed a chilling tale that gave investigators an important clue. One night, about a year after the war, in September of 1946, four hundred men from his former rocket group at BMW had been invited by Russian military officers to a fancy dinner. The rocket scientists were wined and dined and, after a few hours, taken home. Most were drunk. Several hours later, all four hundred of the men were woken up in the middle of the night by their Russian hosts and told they were going to be taking a trip. Why Ziegler wasn't among them was not made clear. The Germans were told to bring their wives, their children, and whatever else they needed for a long trip. Mistresses and livestock were also fine. This was not a situation to which you could say no, Ziegler explained. The scientists and their families were transported by rail to a small town outside Moscow where they had remained ever since, forced to work on secret military projects in terrible conditions. According to Ziegler, it was at this top secret Russian facility, exact whereabouts unknown, that the German scientists were developing rockets and other advanced technologies under Russian supervision. These were Russia's version of the American Paperclip scientists. It was very possible, Ziegler said, that the Horten brothers had been working for the Russians at the secret facility there.

For nine long months, CIC agents typed up memo after memo relating various theories about where the Horten brothers were, what their flying saucers might have been designed for, and what leads should or should not be pursued. And then, six months into the investigation, on March 12, 1948, along came abrupt news. The Horten brothers had been found. In a memo to the European command of the 970th CIC, Major Earl S. Browning Jr. explained. "The Horten Brothers have been located and interrogated by American Agencies," Browning said. The Russians had likely found the blueprints of the flying wing after all. "It is Walter Horten's opinion that the blueprints of the Horten IX may have been found by Russian troops at the Gotha Railroad Car Factory," the memo read. But a second memo, entitled "Extracts on Horten, Walter," explained a little more. Former Messerschmitt test pilot Fritz Wendel's information about the Horten brothers' wingless, tailless, saucerlike craft that had room for more than one crew member was confirmed. "Walter Horten's opinion is that sufficient German types of flying wings existed in the developing or designing stages when the Russians occupied Germany, and these types may have enabled the Russians to produce the flying saucer."

There is no mention of Reimar Horten, the second brother, in any of the hundreds of pages of documents released to Timothy Cooper as part of his Freedom of Information Act request — despite the fact that both brothers had been confirmed as located and interrogated. Nor is there any mention of what Reimar Horten did or did not say about the later-model Horten flying discs. But one memo mentioned "the Horten X" and another referred to "the Horten 13." No further details have been provided, and a 2011 Freedom of Information Act request by the author met a dead end.

On May 12, 1948, the headquarters of European command sent the director of intelligence at the United States Forces in Austria a puzzling memo. "Walter Horten has admitted his contacts with the Russians," it said. That was the last mention of the Horten brothers in the Army intelligence's declassified record for Operation Harass.

Whatever else officially exists on the Horten brothers and their advanced flying saucer continues to be classified as of 2011, and the crash remains from Roswell quickly fell into the blackest regions of government. They would stay at Wright–Patterson Air Force Base for approximately four years. From there, they would quietly be shipped out west to become intertwined with a secret facility out in the middle of the Nevada desert. No one but a handful of people would have any idea they were there.

CHAPTER THREE

The Secret Base

It was a foggy evening in 1951 and Richard Mervin Bissell was sitting in his parlor in Washington, DC, when there was an unexpected knock at the door. There stood a man by the name of Frank Wisner. The two gentlemen had never met before but according to Bissell, Wisner was "very much part of our inner circle of people," which included diplomats, statesmen, and spies. At the time, Bissell held the position of the executor of finance of the Marshall Plan, America's landmark economic recovery plan to infuse postwar Europe with thirteen billion dollars in cash that began in 1948. Being executor of finance meant Bissell was the program's top moneyman. All Bissell knew about Frank Wisner at the time was that he was a top-level civil servant with the new Central Intelligence Agency.

Wisner, a former Olympic competitor, had once been considered handsome. An Office of Strategic Services spy during the war, Wisner was rumored to be the paramour of Princess Caradja of Romania. Now, although not yet forty years old, Wisner had lost his hair, his physique, and his good looks to what would later be revealed as mental illness and alcoholism—but the true signs of his downfall were not yet clear. During the fireside chat in Richard Bissell's Washington parlor, Bissell quickly learned that Frank Wisner was the man in charge of a division of the CIA called the Office of Policy Coordination, or OPC. At the time, not much was known about America's intelligence agency because the CIA was only three and a half years old. As for the mysterious office called OPC, only a handful of people knew its true purpose. Bissell had heard in cocktail conversation that OPC was "engaged in the battle against Communism through covert means." In reality, the bland-sounding Office of Policy Coordination was the power center for all of the Agency's covert operations. All black and paramilitary operations ran through OPC. The office had been set up by the former secretary of the Navy James Forrestal, who was also the nation's first secretary of defense.

Seated beside the fire in the parlor that foggy evening in 1951, Wisner told Bissell that the OPC needed money. "He asked me to help finance the OPC's covert operations by releasing a modest amount of funds generated by the Marshall Plan," Bissell later explained. Mindful of the gray-area nature of Wisner's request, Bissell asked for more details. Wisner declined, saying that he'd already said what he was allowed to say. But Wisner assured Bissell that Averell Harriman, the powerful statesman, financier, former ambassador to Moscow, and, most important, Bissell's superior at the Marshall Plan, had approved the money request. "I could have confirmed Wisner's story with [Harriman] if I had any doubts," Bissell recalled. But he had no such doubts. And so, without hesitation, Richard Bissell agreed to siphon money from the Marshall Plan and divert it to the CIA's Office of Policy Coordination. Largely unknown until now, this was how a significant portion of the CIA's earliest covert black budgets came to be. Richard Bissell was the hidden hand.

Equally concerned about the nation's needs in gathering intelligence was Colonel Richard Leghorn. For Leghorn, the mock nuclear naval battle called Operation Crossroads in 1946 had spurred him to action. Leghorn presented papers to the Joint Chiefs of Staff arguing that overflying the Soviet Union to learn about its military might was urgent business and not just something to consider down the line. He walked the halls of the Pentagon with his papers immediately after Crossroads in 1946, and again in 1948, but with no results. Then along came another war. The Korean War has often been called the forgotten war. In its simplest terms, it was a war between North Korea and South Korea, but it was also the first trial of technical strength and scientific prowess between two opposing teams of German-born scientists specializing in aviation. One group of Germans worked for America now, as Paperclip scientists, and the other group worked for the Soviet Union, and the jet-versus-jet dogfights in the skies above Korea were fights between American-made F-86 Sabres and Soviet-made MiG-15s, both of . which had been designed by Germans who once worked for Adolf Hitler.

When war was declared against Korea, Colonel Leghorn was called back into active duty. As commander of the reconnaissance systems branch of the Wright Air Development Center in Dayton, Ohio, Leghorn was now in charge of planning missions for American pilots flying over denied territory in North Korea and Manchuria to photograph weapons depots and missile sites. American spy planes were accompanied by fighter jets for protection, but still the enemy managed to shoot down an undisclosed number of American spy planes with their MiG fighter jets. In these tragic losses, Leghorn saw a further opportunity to strengthen his argument for overhead. Those MiGs could reach a maximum altitude of only 45,000 feet, meaning that if the United States created a spy plane that could get above 60,000 feet, the airplane would be untouchable. After the armistice was signed, in 1953, Leghorn went back to Washington to present his overhead espionage idea to Air Force officials again.

One man in a position to be interested was Lieutenant General Donald L. Putt, the Army commander whose men had captured

Hermann Göring's Volkenrode aircraft facility in Germany just before the end of the war as part of Operation Lusty. Putt had smuggled one of the earliest groups of German scientists, including V-2 rocket scientists Wernher Von Braun and Ernst Steinhoff, out of the country and into America. Now, Putt was overseeing the fruits of the scientists' labor from inside his office at the Pentagon. Putt had been promoted to deputy chief of staff for research and development at the Pentagon, and the three stars on his chest afforded him great power and persuasion about America's military future involving airplanes. But Putt listened to a presentation of Leghorn's spy plane idea and immediately said that he was not interested. The Air Force was not in the business of making dual-purpose aircraft, airplanes that carried cameras in addition to weapons. Besides, Air Force airplanes came with armor, Putt said, which made them heavy. Any flier in the early 1950s knew heavy airplanes could not fly anywhere near sixty thousand feet.

Richard Leghorn was undeterred. He went around Putt by going above him, to the commander of the Strategic Air Command, or SAC, his old antagonist from Operation Crossroads General Curtis LeMay. In the winter of 1954, LeMay was presented with the first actual drawings of Leghorn's high-flying spy plane, conceptualized by the Lockheed Corporation. Whereas Putt was uninterested in Leghorn's ideas, LeMay was offended by them. He walked out of the meeting declaring that the whole overhead thing was a waste of his time.

But there was another group of men who had President Eisenhower's ear, and those men made up the select group of scientists who sat on the president's scientific advisory board, friends and colleagues of Colonel Richard Leghorn from MIT. They included James R. Killian Jr., president of the Massachusetts Institute of Technology, as well as Edwin H. Land, the eccentric millionaire who had just invented the Polaroid camera and its remarkable instant film. The president's science advisers had an idea. Never mind the Air Force. Generals tended to be uncreative thinkers, bureaucrats who lived inside a mental box. Why not approach the

Central Intelligence Agency? The Agency was made up of men whose sole purpose was to conduct espionage. Surely they would be interested in spying from the air. Unlike the Air Force, Killian and Land reasoned, the CIA had access to the president's secret financial reserves. All the overhead espionage program really needed was a team captain or a patron saint. As it turned out, they had someone in mind. It was February of 1954. A brilliant economist who had formerly been running the financial office over at the Marshall Plan had just joined the CIA as Director Allen Dulles's special assistant. His name was Richard Bissell. He was a perfect candidate for the overhead job.

At least one of Richard Bissell's ancestors was a spy. Sergeant Daniel Bissell conducted espionage missions for General George Washington during the Revolutionary War. Generations later, on September 18, 1910, Richard Mervin Bissell Jr. was born into a family of Connecticut aristocrats. Severely cross-eyed from birth, it was only after a risky surgery at the age of eight that Richard Bissell could see clearly enough to read anything. Before that, his mother had read to him. As a child, Bissell was obsessed with history and with war. His parents took him on a visit to the battlefields of northern France when he was ten years old, and it was there, staring out over barren fields ravaged by firebombs, that Bissell developed what he would later describe as an overwhelming "impression of World War I as a cataclysm."

Despite great privilege, Bissell struggled through his formative years with intense feelings of inadequacy, first at Groton boarding school, then later at Yale University. But behind his low self-esteem was a great willfulness and burgeoning self-confidence that would emerge shortly after he turned twenty-one. On a weekend trip with family friends at a Connecticut beachhead called Pinnacle Rock, Bissell fell off a seventy-foot cliff. When he woke up in the hospital, he was suffering from a mild case of amnesia. But as soon as he was well enough to move around on his own, which took months, he secretly ventured back to the site of the fall. There he made the same climb again. "My hands were shaking," Bissell explained in describing the second climb, but "I was glad to have done it and to know that I didn't have to do it again." He had gone from unsure to self-assured, thanks to a death-defying fall. Immediately after college, in 1932, Bissell headed to England, where he received a master's degree from the London School of Economics. Then it was back to Yale for a PhD, where he wrote complex financial treatises at the astonishingly prolific rate of twenty pages a day. Bissell's colleagues began to admire him, calling him a "human computer." His mind, they said, functioned "like a machine." Soon, the classes he taught were filled to capacity.

Eventually, his talents as an economist caught the eye of MIT president James Killian, who recruited Bissell to join the MIT staff. Now, in 1954, here was James Killian recruiting Richard Bissell again, which was how just a few short years after the fireside chat with Frank Wisner, Richard Bissell found himself in charge of one of the most ambitious, most secret programs in CIA history, the U-2 spy plane program. Its code name was Project Aquatone.

The following winter, in 1955, Richard Bissell and his fellow CIA officer Herbert Miller, the Agency's leading expert on Soviet nuclear weapons, flew across the American West in an unmarked Beechcraft V-35 Bonanza in search of a location where they could build a secret CIA test facility, the only one of its kind on American soil. Only a handful of CIA officers and an Air Force colonel named Osmond "Ozzie" Ritland had any idea what the men were up to, flying around out there. Bissell's orders, which had come directly from President Eisenhower himself, were to find a secret location to build a test facility for the Agency's bold, new spy plane — the aircraft that would keep watch over the Soviet Union's burgeoning nuclear weapons program. Accompanying the CIA officers was the nation's leading aerodynamicist, Lockheed Corporation's Clarence "Kelly" Johnson, the man tasked with designing and building this new plane.

Johnson sat in the back of the Beechcraft with geological survey maps spread out across his lap as the men flew from Burbank, California, across the Mojave Desert, and into Nevada. They were searching for a dry lake bed called Groom Lake just outside the Nevada Test Site, which had had its boundaries configured by Holmes and Narver in July of 1950 during the top secret Project Nutmeg that resulted in Nevada's being chosen as America's continental atomic bombing range. Legendary air racer and experimental test pilot Tony LeVier was flying the small airplane. LeVier had a vague idea of where he was going because his fellow Lockheed test pilot Ray Goudey had taken him to Groom Lake on a prescouting mission just a few weeks before. On occasion, Goudey had shuttled atomic scientists from California to the test site and once he had even set down his aircraft on Groom Lake to eat his bag lunch.

"Descending for a closer look, we saw evidence of a temporary landing strip," Bissell later recalled, "the kind of runway that had been built in various locations across the United States during World War Two for the benefit of pilots in training who might have to make an emergency landing." The large, hardened salt pan was a perfect natural runway, and LeVier effortlessly landed the plane. The men got out and walked around, discussing how level the terrain was and kicking the old shell casings lying about like stones. To the north, Bald Mountain towered over the valley, offering cover, and to the southwest, there was equal shelter from a mountain range called Papoose. According to Bissell, "Groom Lake would prove perfect for our needs."

Bissell was acutely aware that Groom Lake was just over the hill from the government's atomic bomb testing facility, which meant that as far as secrecy was concerned, there was no better place in the continental United States for the CIA to set up its new spy plane program and begin clandestine work. "I recommended to Eisenhower that he add a piece of adjacent land, including Groom Lake, to the Nevada Test Site of the Atomic Energy Commission," Bissell related in his memoir, written in the last year of his life. Four months after Richard Bissell, Herbert Miller, Kelly Johnson, and Tony LeVier touched down on Groom Lake, Area 51 had its first residents. It was a small group of four Lockheed test pilots, two dozen Lockheed mechanics and engineers, a handful of CIA officers who doubled as security guards, and a small group of Lieutenant Colonel Ritland's Air Force staff. There was a cowboy feel to the base that first summer, with temperatures so hot the mechanics used to crack eggs on metal surfaces just to see how long it would take for them to fry.

Originally the base consisted of one airplane hangar and a handful of tents, called hooches, constructed out of wooden platforms and covered in canvas tops. Sometimes when the winds got rough, the tents would blow away. Thunderstorms were frequent and would render the dry lake bed unusable, temporarily covered by an inch of rain. As soon as the sun returned, the water would quickly evaporate, and the test pilots could fly again. Power came from a diesel generator. There was one cook and a makeshift mess hall. It took another month for halfway-decent showers to be built on the base. The men could have been at an army outpost in Egypt or India as far as amenities were concerned.

Residents were issued work boots, to defend against rattlesnakes, and hats with lights, to wear at night. When the sun dropped behind the mountains in the evenings, the sky turned purple, then gray. In no time everything was pitch-black. The sounds at night were cricket song and coyote howl, and there was barely anything more than static on the radio and definitely no TV. The nearest town, Las Vegas, had only thirty-five thousand residents, and it was seventy-five miles away. At night, the skies at Area 51 glittered with stars.

But as rustic as the base was as far as appearance, behind the scenes Area 51 was as much Washington, DC, as it was Wild West. The U-2 was a top secret airplane built on the covert orders of the president of the United States. Its 1955 budget was $22 million, which would be $180 million in 2011.

Each U-2 aircraft arrived at Area 51 from Lockheed's facility in Burbank in pieces, hidden inside the belly of a C-124 transport plane. The pointy fuselage and long, thin wings were draped in white sheets so no one could get even a glimpse. "In the very beginning, we put Ship One and Ship Two together inside the hangar so nobody saw it before it flew," recalls Bob Murphy, one of the first Lockheed mechanics on the base. From the moment the CIA began operating their Groom Lake facility, they did so with very strict protocols regarding who had a need-to-know and about what. All elements of the program were divided into sensitive compartmented information, or SCI. "I had no clue what the airplane looked like until it flew directly over my head," recalls security guard Richard Mingus.

Getting the U-2 operations ready was a dream job for the daring experimental test pilot Ray Goudey. "I learned to fly an airplane before I could drive a car," Goudey explains. As a teenager, Goudey joined the flying circus and flew with Sammy Mason's famed Flying Brigade. After the war, he became part of a daredevil flying team called the Hollywood Hawks, where his centrifugal-force-defying outside snap made him a legend. In 1955 he was thirty-three years old and ready to settle down, in relative terms.

Getting Lockheed's tricky new spy plane ready for the CIA was not a terribly daunting task for a flier like Goudey. Still, the U-2 was an unusual airplane, with wings so long their ends sagged when it sat parked on the tarmac at Groom. To keep its fuel-filled wings from tipping side to side on takeoff, mechanics had to run alongside the airplane as it taxied, sending huge dust clouds up from the lake bed and covering everything in fine sand. The aircraft's aluminum skin was paper-thin, just 0.02 inches thick, which meant the aircraft was both fragile on the ground and extremely delicate to fly. If a pilot flew the U-2 too slow, the airplane could stall. If he flew too fast, the wings could literally come off. Complicating matters was the fact that what was too slow at one altitude was too fast at another height. The same variable occurred when the weight of the plane changed as it burned up hours of fuel. For these reasons, the original flights made by the test pilots were restricted to a two-hundred-mile radius from the center of Groom Lake. The likelihood of a crash was high, and the CIA needed to be able to keep secure any U-2 wreckage.

"In the beginning, all we did was fly all day long," Goudey recalls. At Area 51 "we'd sleep, wake up, eat, and fly." Soon, the base expanded and one hundred more people arrived. Navy Quonset huts were brought in and two additional water wells were dug. Commander Bob Yancey located a pool table and a 16-millimeter film projector in Las Vegas; now the men had entertainment other than stargazing. By September, there were two hundred men on base from three organizational groups: one-third were CIA, one-third were Air Force, and one-third were Lockheed. Everyone had the same goal in mind, which was to get the U-2 to sustain flight at seventy thousand feet. This was a tall order and something no air force in the world had been able to accomplish.

Every Monday Ray Goudey would fly from Burbank to Groom Lake with Lockheed's gung-ho young mechanic Bob Murphy beside him in the passenger seat. All week, Murphy worked on the U-2's engine while Goudey worked with the other test pilots to achieve height. The pilots wore specially designed partial-pressure suits, tight like wet suits, with most of the tubing on the outside; it took two flight surgeons to get a pilot into his suit. Pre-breathing pure oxygen was mandatory and took two full hours, which made for a lot of time in a recliner. The process removed nitrogen from the pilot's bloodstream and reduced the risk of decompression sickness at high altitude.

In those early days at Area 51, history was being laid down and records were being set. "I was the first guy to go up above sixty-five thousand feet, but I wasn't supposed to be," Goudey recalls. "Bob Mayte was scheduled to do the first high-altitude flight but he had a problem with his ears. So I went instead." Which is how Goudey ended up becoming the first pilot to ever reach that altitude and fly there for a sustained amount of time—a remarkable fact noted in the Lockheed record books and yet kept from the rest of the world until 1998, when the U-2 program was finally declassified. Goudey explains what the view was like at sixty-five thousand feet: "From where I was up above Nevada I could see the Pacific Ocean, which was three hundred miles away."

Ray Goudey was also the world's first test pilot to experience engine failure at sixty-four thousand feet, a potentially catastrophic event because the delicate U-2 is a single-engine airplane: if a U-2 loses one engine, it has lost all of them. In Goudey's case, he glided down four thousand feet and got the engine to restart by using a tactic called windmilling. "Then it quit again," Goudey explains. He let the plane fall another thirty thousand feet, more than five miles. Down in lower air, Goudey was able to get the engine to restart—and to stay started. Once Goudey was on the ground, it was Bob Murphy's job to troubleshoot what had happened on the engine. Of course, in 1955, no mechanic in the world had any experience solving a combustion problem on an engine that had quit unexpectedly at sixty-four thousand feet.

Bob Murphy was a twenty-five-year-old flight-test mechanic whose can-do attitude and ability to troubleshoot just about any problem on an aircraft engine meant he was promoted to engine mechanic supervisor the following winter, in 1956. "The romance of the job was the hands-on element of things," Murphy recalls of those early days at Groom Lake. "There was absolutely no government meddling, which enabled us to get the job done." There was only one man with any kind of serious oversight at Area 51 and that was Richard Bissell, or Mr. B., as he was known to the men. Most of Bissell's work involved getting Area 51 to run like an organization or, as he put it, "dealing with the policy matters involved in producing this radically new aircraft." Shuttling back and forth between Washington and Area 51, Bissell seemed to enjoy the base he ruled over. "He moved around the facility somewhat mysteriously," Bob Murphy recalls. "He would appear briefly out on the dry lake bed to say hi to the pilots and mechanics and watch the U-2 fly," Murphy remembers. "Mr. B. always expressed enthusiasm for what we were doing and then he'd disappear again in some unmarked airplane." But for Murphy, the concern was rarely the Customer, which was Lockheed's code name for the CIA. Murphy was too busy working with test pilots, often finding himself in charge of overseeing two or three U-2 flights in a single day. "My job was to help the pilots to get the aircraft instruments checked out, get the plane to fly to seventy thousand feet, get it to fly for nine and ten hours straight, and then get it to start taking pictures. There was no shortage of work. We loved it and it's what we did day after day."

The job of the Lockheed test pilots was to get the U-2 ready as fast as possible so they could turn it over to the CIA's instructor pilot Hank Meierdierck, who would then teach the CIA mission pilots, recruited from Air Force bases around the country, how to fly the airplane. Bissell's ambitious plan was to overfly the Soviet Union inside of a year. The Communist advances in hydrogen bombs and long-range missiles had the CIA seriously concerned, as did the hastily hushed Soviet overflight of—and crash in—the West. Human intelligence, or HUMINT, behind the Iron Curtain was at an all-time low. The great news for the Agency was that there was no such thing as an Iron Ceiling. Overhead was what was going to keep America safe. The U-2 was the Agency's best chance to get hard intelligence on the Soviet Union, considering that one photograph could provide the Agency with as much information as approximately ten thousand spies on the ground.

President Eisenhower put the CIA in charge of the overhead reconnaissance because, as he later wrote, the aerial reconnaissance program needed to be handled in an "unconventional way." What that meant was that President Eisenhower wanted the program to be black, or hidden from Congress and from everyone but a select few who needed to know about it. He also wanted the U-2 to be piloted by a man who didn't wear a uniform. Before the U-2, there was no precedent for one nation to regularly spy on another nation from overhead during peacetime. The president's fear was that if a U-2 mission was exposed, it would be interpreted by the Soviets, and perhaps by the whole world, as an overtly hostile act. At least if the plane had a CIA pilot, the president could deny the U.S. military was involved.

Despite his apparent elusiveness, Mr. B. maintained absolute control of all things that were going on at Area 51. Remarkably, he had been able to set up the remote desert facility as a stand-alone organization; he did this by persuading President Eisenhower to remove the U-2 program from the CIA's own organizational chart. "The entire project became the most compartmented and self-contained activity within the agency," Bissell wrote of his sovereign territory at Groom Lake. "I worked behind a barrier of secrecy that protected my decision making from interference." The Development Project Staff, which was the bland-sounding code name for the secret U-2 operation, was the only division of the CIA that had its own communications office. Bissell saw government overseers as unnecessary meddlers and told colleagues that Congress and its committees simply got in the way of getting done what needed to be done. In this way, Bissell was remarkably effective with his program at Area 51. Each month he summed up activities on the secret base in a five-page brief for the president. But Bissell's long leash, and the extreme power he wielded over the nation's first spy plane program, earned him enmity from a top general whose wrath was historically a dangerous thing to incur. That was General Curtis LeMay.

While the CIA was in charge of Project Aquatone as a whole, U-2 operations were to be a collaborative effort among the CIA, the Air Force, and Lockheed Corporation. Lockheed built the airplane and provided the first test pilots as well as the program mechanics. The Air Force was in charge of support operations. It was there to provide everything the CIA needed, from chase planes to tire changers. But Richard Bissell exercised his power early on, making Lockheed, not the Air Force, his original Project Aquatone partner. Bissell worked hand in hand with Lockheed's Kelly Johnson to get the U-2 aloft with as little Air Force involvement as possible. In fact, the Air Force was almost entirely left out of the early planning stages. The first U-2 was built by Lockheed and flight-tested at Groom Lake by Lockheed test pilots before the commander of the Air Force research and development office had ever heard of an airplane called the U-2 or a test-flight facility called Area 51. This overt slight ticked off many top generals, a number of whom developed grudges against the CIA. And yet, by the end of 1955, dozens of active-duty Air Force personnel had been assigned to the U-2 operation. Air Force air expertise was absolutely necessary now that pilot training had begun and multiple U-2s were flying multiple practice missions every day, as the CIA readied Project Aquatone for assignments overseas. Richard Bissell, not Curtis LeMay, was now the de facto base commander of a whole lot of Air Force officers and enlisted men. LeMay was, understandably, enraged.

In early autumn of 1955, a conflict erupted between the two men, and President Eisenhower was forced to intervene. LeMay had been raising questions about why he wasn't in charge of the program. It was now up to the president to decide who was officially in charge of Area 51 and the U-2. Bissell desperately wanted to reign over the prestigious program. "It was a glamorous and high-priority endeavor endorsed not only by the president but by a lot of very important scientific people," Bissell wrote in his memoirs decades later. LeMay argued that the Air Force should be in charge of all programs involving airplanes, which was ironic, given the fact that LeMay had disliked the U-2 program from the get-go. In hindsight it seems as if LeMay wanted the U-2 program simply because he wanted the control.

Ultimately, the president's decision came to rest on one significant quality that the CIA possessed and the Air Force did not: plausible deniability. With the CIA in charge, if a U-2 were to get shot down, the government could claim the spy plane program didn't exist. Air Force fliers flew in uniform, but U-2 pilots working for the CIA would wear civilian garb. The cover story for such a mission would be weather-related research; at least, that was the plan. And so, in late October of 1955, the dispute was settled by President Eisenhower. He directed Air Force chief of staff Nathan Twining to give the CIA control over the spy plane program and Area 51. The job of the Air Force, Eisenhower said, was to offer all necessary operational support to keep the program aloft.

One of the Air Force's designated jobs was to handle flights to and from Area 51. Because the project was so secret, Bissell did not want personnel driving in and out of the base or living in Las Vegas. As far as Bissell was concerned, men cleared on the project were far more likely to draw attention to themselves driving to and from Sin City than they would be if they lived out of town and came in and out by airplane. Locals had friends in the area, whereas out-of-towners did not. This meant that each day, a C-54 transport plane shuttled workers from Lockheed's airport facility in Burbank, California, to Area 51 and back. Ray Goudey and Bob Murphy had enjoyed four months of Goudey's flying the pair back and forth between Burbank and the Ranch. Now they would have to commute on the Air Force's C-54 like everyone else.

Bob Murphy was well versed in the mechanics of the C-54 aircraft. He'd been an engineer on that aircraft in Germany during the Berlin airlift of 1948–1949, the first major international crisis of the Cold War. From a military base in Wiesbaden, Murphy serviced the C-54s that ferried coal and other supplies into Berlin. Flying back and forth between Burbank and the Ranch, Bob Murphy would often chat with George Pappas, the experienced Air Force classified-missions pilot who flew the shuttle service. Pappas and Murphy spent hours talking about what an interesting aircraft the C-54 was.

On the night of November 16, 1955, Pappas flew Murphy, Ray Goudey, and another Lockheed pilot named Robert Sieker from the Ranch to Burbank so the men could attend a Lockheed party at the Big Oaks Lodge in Bouquet Canyon. For Bob Murphy, it would be a one-night stay; he was scheduled for the early-morning flight back with Pappas's C-54 Air Force shuttle the following day. But Murphy drank too much at the party and overslept. As Bob Murphy was sleeping through his alarm clock, eleven men assigned to Richard Bissell's Project Aquatone walked across the tarmac at the Burbank airport and boarded the C-54 transport plane where Pappas, his copilot Paul E. Winham, and a flight attendant named Guy R. Fasolas prepared to shuttle everyone back to Area 51. The manifest listed their destination as "Watertown airstrip." A little over an hour after takeoff, Pappas broke his required radio silence and called out for assistance with his position in the air. It was snowing heavily where he was, somewhere north of Las Vegas, and Pappas worried he had strayed off course. Nearby, at Nellis Air Force Base, a staff sergeant by the name of Alfred Arneho overheard the bewildering transmission. There was no record of any flight, military or civilian, scheduled to be in his area this time of day. Arneho listened for a follow-up transmission but none came. Puzzled, Arneho made a note in a logbook. Just a few minutes later the airplane Pappas was flying crashed into the granite peak of Mount Charleston, killing everyone on board. Had Pappas been just thirty feet higher, he would have cleared the mountaintop.

Back in California, Bob Murphy awoke in a panic. He checked his alarm clock and realized that he had missed the flight back to Area 51 by three hours. Murphy was furious with himself. Getting drunk and oversleeping was completely out of character for him. He had never missed a single day of work in his four-year career at Lockheed. He'd never even been late. Murphy knew there was no sense going to the airport; the airplane would have long since departed. He got himself together and went out to find some breakfast. Bob Murphy was sitting in a restaurant listening to the radio playing behind the counter when the music was interrupted with breaking news. A C-54 transport plane had just crashed into Mount Charleston, north of Las Vegas. The newscaster said that reports were sketchy but most likely everyone on board had been killed. Murphy knew immediately that the aircraft that had crashed into Mount Charleston was the C-54 he would have been on had he not overslept.

Overwhelmed with grief and in a state of disbelief, Murphy went back to his apartment. He paced around for some time. Then he decided to locate a bar and have a drink. "As I opened the front door to my apartment, this guy from Lockheed was raising his hand to knock on it," Murphy explains fifty-four years later. "I looked at him and he looked at me and then he turned white as a ghost. I had been listed on the CIA flight manifest as having been on that airplane. The security officer on the tarmac had marked me off as having checked in for the flight. This man from Lockheed had come to inform my next of kin that I was dead. Instead, there I was."

Two hundred and fifty miles to the east, on top of Mount Charleston, the wreckage of the airplane still burned. Smoke from the crash was visible as far away as Henderson, ten miles south of Las Vegas. That afternoon, a CBS news team was halfway up Highway 158, headed to the crash site, when the newsmen met a military blockade. Armed officers told the news crew that a military plane had crashed on a routine mission heading to the base at Indian Springs. The road into Kyle Canyon was closed. Meanwhile, Bissell had U-2s dispatched from Area 51 to help pinpoint the exact location of the Air Force airplane—an impromptu and unorthodox first "mission" for the spy plane, triggered by tragic circumstances. But there were briefcases full of secret papers that needed to be retrieved, and the U-2's search-and-locate capabilities from high above were accurate and available. It was Hank Meierdierck, the man in charge of training CIA pilots to fly the U-2, who ultimately located the remains of the airplane.

The crash was the first of a series of Area 51–related airplane tragedies that would occur over the next decade. Airplane crashes, sensational by nature, risk operational exposure, and between crash investigators and local media, there are countless opportunities for leaks. That first airplane crash, into Mount Charleston, set a precedent for the CIA in an unexpected way. The Agency did what it always does: secured the crash site immediately and produced a cover story for the press. But an interesting turn of events unfolded, ones that were entirely beyond the CIA's control. Hungry for a story and lacking any facts, the press put together its own, inaccurate version of events. One of the city's leading papers, the *Las Vegas Review Journal,* reported that the crash was being kept secret because the men on board were most likely nuclear scientists working on a top secret new weapons project at the Nevada Test Site. Reporters stopped asking questions and the speculative story quickly became accepted as fact. The CIA would learn from this experience: it could use the public's preconceptions as well as the media's desire to tell a story to its own benefit. Civilians could unwittingly propagate significant disinformation on the CIA's behalf.

In Central Intelligence Agency parlance, there are two kinds of strategic deception: cover and disinformation. Cover induces the belief that something true is something false; disinformation aims to produce the belief that something false is in fact true. In other words, cover conceals the truth while disinformation conveys false information. When the CIA disseminates false information, it is always intended to mislead. When the press disseminates false information that helps keep classified information a secret, the CIA sits back and smiles. The truth about the crash at Mount Charleston, the single biggest loss of life for the U-2 program, would remain hidden from the public until the CIA acknowledged the plane crash in 2002. Until then, even the families of the men in the airplane had no idea that their loved ones had been working on a top secret CIA program when they died.

As a result of the crash, the Air Force lost its job as the air carrier for Area 51. For the next seventeen years, commuter flights in and out of the base would be operated by Lockheed. Starting sometime around 1972, the CIA began turning control of Area 51 over to the Air Force, and the Department of Defense took charge of commuter flights. But rather than running military aircraft to and from the clandestine facility, the DOD hired the engineering company EG&G to do it. It made sense. By 1972, EG&G had gotten so powerful and so trusted in the uppermost echelons of the government, it was even in charge of some of the security systems for Air Force One.

CHAPTER FOUR

The Seeds of a Conspiracy

As soon as the U-2s started flying out of Area 51, reports of UFO sightings by commercial airline pilots and air traffic controllers began to inundate CIA headquarters. Later painted black to blend in with the sky, the U-2s at that time were silver, which meant their long, shiny wings reflected light down from the upper atmosphere in a way that led citizens all over California, Nevada, and Utah to think the planes were UFOs. The altitude of the U-2 alone was enough to bewilder people. Commercial airplanes flew at between ten thousand and twenty thousand feet in the mid-1950s, whereas the U-2 flew at around seventy thousand feet. Then there was the radical shape of the airplane to consider. Its wings were nearly twice as long as the fuselage, which made the U-2 look like a fiery flying cross.

In 1955 the UFO phenomenon sweeping America was seven years old. The modern-day UFO craze officially began on June 24, 1947, when a search-and-rescue pilot named Kenneth Arnold spotted nine flying discs speeding over Washington State while he was out searching for a downed airplane. Approximately two weeks later, the crash at Roswell occurred. By the end of the month, more than 850 UFO sightings had been reported in the news media. Rumors of flying saucers were sweeping the nation, and public anxiety was mounting; Americans demanded answers from the military.

According to a CIA study on UFOs, declassified in 1997, the Air Force had originally been running two programs. One was covert, initially called Project Saucer and later called Project Sign; another was an overt Air Force public relations campaign called Project Grudge. The point of Project Grudge was to "persuade the public that UFOs constituted nothing unusual or extraordinary," and to do this, Air Force officials went on TV and radio dismissing UFO reports. Sightings were attributed to planets, meteors, even "large hailstones," Air Force officials said, categorically denying that UFOs were anything nefarious or out of this world. But their efforts did very little to appease the public. With the nuclear arms race in full swing, the idea that the world could come to an end in nuclear holocaust had tipped the psychological scales for many Americans, giving way to public discussion about Armageddon and the End of Times. In 1951, Hollywood released the film *The Day the Earth Stood Still,* about aliens preparing to destroy Earth. Two years later, *The War of the Worlds* was made into a movie and won an Academy Award. Even the famous psychiatrist Carl Jung got into the act, publishing a book that said UFOs were individual mirrors of a collective anxiety the world was having about nuclear annihilation. Sightings continued and so did intense interest by both the Air Force and the CIA.

At Area 51, the reality that the U-2 was repeatedly being mistaken for a UFO was not something analysts welcomed, but it was something they were forced to address. The general feeling at the Agency was that CIA officers had more important things to do than handle the public hysteria about strange objects in the sky. Dealing with UFO reports, the CIA felt, was more appropriately suited for pencil pushers over at the Air Force. According to declassified documents, the CIA did open up a clandestine UFO data-collecting department, albeit begrudgingly. Seeing as the CIA could easily clear its own analysts to handle information on the U-2, this made sense. This attitude, that CIA officers were above plebeian affairs such as UFO sightings, was endemic at the Agency and trickled down from the top. CIA director Allen Dulles was an elitist at heart, an old-school spy brought up in the Office of Strategic Services, the World War II espionage division of the Army. Dulles preferred gentlemen spy craft and disliked technology in general, which was why he'd delegated control of the U-2 spy plane to Richard Bissell in the first place. As for the UFO problems, Dulles assigned that job to a former OSS colleague named Todos M. Odarenko. The UFO division was placed inside the physics office, which Odarenko ran. Almost immediately Odarenko "sought to have his division relieved of the responsibility for monitoring UFO reports," according to a CIA monograph declassified in 1997. And yet the significance of UFOs to the CIA could not have had a higher national security concern.

The case file regarding unidentified flying objects that Allen Dulles had inherited from the Agency's previous director, General Walter Bedell Smith, was, and remains, one of the most top secret files in CIA history. Because it has yet to be declassified, there is no way of knowing how much information Bedell Smith shared with his successor. But Bedell Smith himself would more likely than not have had a need-to-know about the Army intelligence's blackest programs, and that would have included the flying disc retrieved at Roswell. When the crash occurred, in July of 1947, Bedell Smith was the ambassador to the Soviet Union. During the search for the Horten brothers under the program known as Operation Harass, Bedell Smith was serving as commander of the First Army at Governors Island, New York—a locale from which Project Paperclip scientists were monitored, evaluated, and assigned research and engineeering jobs. And when the crash remains left Wright-Patterson Air Force Base in Ohio to be shipped out to the desert in Nevada, Bedell Smith was the director of the CIA. The degree of need-to-know access he had regarding secret parallel programs set up there remains one of the great riddles of Area 51.

Walter Bedell Smith served as director of Central Intelligence from 1950 to 1953, and there were few men more trusted by President Harry Truman and five-star general of the Army Dwight D. Eisenhower. Years earlier, when General Eisenhower had been serving as Supreme Allied Commander of Europe during World War II, Bedell Smith was his chief of staff. A handful of Smith's closest colleagues affectionately called him Beetle, but most men were intimidated by the person privately referred to as Eisenhower's "hatchet man." So forceful was Bedell Smith that when George S. Patton needed discipline, the task fell on Bedell Smith's shoulders. When the Nazis surrendered to the Allied Forces, it was Bedell Smith who was in charge of writing up acceptable terms.

From the earliest days of the Cold War, General Walter Bedell Smith fought the Russians from America's innermost circle of power. He had served as President Truman's ambassador to the Soviet Union from 1946 to 1948, a position that uniquely qualified him to be the second director of the CIA. Intelligence on the Soviet Union was the CIA's primary concern in the early days of the Cold War, and there was nothing the U.S. government knew regarding what the Russians were up to that Bedell Smith did not have access to. The conundrum for Smith when he took over the role of director of Central Intelligence on August 21, 1950, was that very few people at the CIA had a need-to-know what the general now knew regarding unidentified flying objects. The record that has been declassified thus far suggests that Bedell Smith demanded that all his employees accept what his personal experiences with the Russians and "UFOs" had taught him: the Communists were evil, and this idea that UFOs were coming from other planets was nothing but the fantasy of panicked, paranoid minds. General Smith summarily rejected the idea that UFOs were anything out of this world and he spearheaded CIA policy accordingly. "Preposterous," he wrote in a memo in 1952. Unlike Dulles, Bedell Smith personally oversaw the national security implications regarding UFOs at the CIA.

To a rationalist like General Smith, "Strange things in the sky

[have] been recorded for hundreds of years," which is true—unidentified flying objects are at least as old as the Bible. In certain translations of the Old Testament, a reference to "Ezekiel's wheel" describes a saucerlike vehicle streaking across the skies. During the Middle Ages, flying discs appeared in many different forms of art, such as in paintings and mosaics. In British ink prints from 1783, favored examples among ufologists, two of the king's men stand on the terrace of Windsor Castle in London observing small saucers flying in the background; researchers have not been able to identify what they might have referenced. Smith could offer no "obvious... single explanation for a majority of the things seen" in the sky and cited foo fighters as an example, the "unexplained phenomena sighted by aircraft pilots during World War II." These, Smith explained, were "balls of light...similar to St. Elmo's fire."

Like the president's science adviser Vannevar Bush, CIA director Walter Bedell Smith was primarily concerned about the government's ability to maintain control. Toward this end, he saw the CIA as having to take decisive action regarding citizen hysteria over UFOs. During Bedell Smith's tenure, and according to declassified documents, it was the position of the CIA that a nefarious plan was in the Soviet pipeline. It had happened once already, at Roswell. Fortunately, in that instance the Joint Chiefs had been able to cover up the truth with a weather balloon story. But a black propaganda attack could happen again, a grand UFO hoax aimed at paralyzing the nation's early air-defense warning system, which would then make the United States vulnerable to an actual Soviet air attack. "Mass receipt of low-grade reports which tend to overload channels of communication quite irrelevant to hostile objects might some day appear" as real, Smith ominously warned the National Security Council. The unending UFO sightings preoccupying the nation were becoming like the boy who cried wolf, the CIA director cautioned.

To work on the problem of UFO hysteria, in 1952 Bedell Smith convened a CIA group called the Psychological Strategy Board and gave them the job of putting together recommendations about "problems connected with unidentified flying objects" for the National Security Council—the highest-ranking national security policy makers in the United States. Bedell Smith's Psychological Strategy Board panel determined that the American public was far too sensitive to "hysterical mass behavior" for the good of the nation. Furthermore, the board said, the public's susceptibility to UFO belief was a national security threat, one that was increasing by the year. From a psychological standpoint, the public's gullibility would likely prove "harmful to constituted authority," meaning the central government might not hold. Any forthcoming UFO hoax by Stalin could engender the same kind of pandemonium that followed the radio broadcast of *The War of the Worlds*.

Bedell Smith's CIA told the National Security Council that for this reason, the flying saucer scare needed to be discredited. According to CIA documents declassified in 1993, the Agency proposed a vast "debunking" campaign to reduce the public's interest in flying saucers. The only way of countering what Bedell Smith was certain was the Russians' "clever hostile propaganda" was for the CIA to take covert action of its own. The Agency suggested that an educational campaign be put in place, one that would co-opt elements of the American "mass media such as television, motion pictures, and popular articles." The CIA also suggested getting advertising executives, business clubs, and "even the Disney Corporation [involved] to get the message across." One plan was to present actual UFO case histories on television and then prove them wrong. "As in the case of conjuring tricks," members of the panel suggested, "the debunking would result in reduction in public interest in flying saucers," in the same way that those who believe in magic become disillusioned when the magician's trick is revealed.

What action was actually taken by the CIA remains classified as of 2011, but one unforeseen problem that Bedell Smith's CIA encountered was an American press wholly uninterested in going along with the wishes of the CIA. The media had an agenda of its own. UFO stories sold papers, and in the spring of 1952, the publishers of *Life* magazine were getting ready to go to press with a major scoop about UFOs. Reporters for the magazine had learned that the Air Force had been keeping top secret files on flying saucers while insisting to the public it was doing no such thing. It was a big story, likely to sell out copies of the magazine. One week before press time, the Air Force got wind of *Life*'s story. In a move meant to deflate the magnitude of the magazine's revelation, the Air Force decided to reverse its five-year position of denying that it had been actively investigating flying discs and to attend, of all things, a UFO convention in Los Angeles, California.

To understand what a radical about-face this was for the Air Force requires an understanding of what the Air Force had been doing for the past five years since it had began the simultaneous and contradictory campaigns Project Sign (to investigate Air Force UFO concerns) and Project Grudge (the public relations campaign intended to convey to the nation that the Air Force had no UFO concerns). Of the 850 UFO sightings reported in the news media the first month of the UFO craze, in July of 1947, at least 150 of the sightings had concerned military intelligence officials to such a degree that they were written up and sent for analysis to officers with the Technical Intelligence Division of the Air Force at Wright Field. Six months later, in January of 1948, General Nathan Twining, head of the Air Force Technical Service Command, established Project Sign; originally called Project Saucer, it was the first in a number of covert UFO research groups created inside the Air Force. For Project Sign, the Air Force assigned hundreds of its staff to the job of collecting, going over, and analyzing details from thousands of UFO sightings, all the while denying they were doing any such thing.

In Air Force circles, behind the scenes, officials were acutely aware that "the very existence of Air Force official interest" fanned the flames of UFO hysteria, and so the public relations program Project Grudge needed to officially end. On December 27, 1949, the Air Force publicly announced that it saw no reason to continue its UFO investigations and was terminating the project. Meanwhile, the covert UFO study programs steamed ahead. In 1952, the Air Force opened up yet another, even more secret UFO organization, this one called Project Blue Book. That the Air Force clearly kept from the public what it was actually doing with UFO study would later become a major point of contention for ufologists who believed UFOs were from out of this world.

The UFOs being reported seemed to have no end. In addition to the flying disc sightings, bright, greenish-colored lights in the sky were also reported by a growing number of citizens. This was particularly concerning for the Air Force because many of these sightings were in New Mexico near sensitive military facilities such as Los Alamos, Sandia, and White Sands. Witnesses to these "green balls of light," which had been reported since the late 1940s, included credible scientists and astronomers. These sightings were put into an Air Force category known as Green Fireballs. In 1949, the Geophysics Research Division of the Air Force initiated Project Twinkle specifically to investigate these various light-related phenomena. Observation posts were set up at Air Force bases around the country where physicists made electromagnetic-frequency measurements using Signal Corps engineering laboratory equipment. In secret, air traffic control operators across the nation were given 35-millimeter cameras called vidoons and asked by the Air Force to photograph anything unusual. All work was performed under top secret security protocols with the caveat that under no circumstances was the public to know that the Air Force was investigating UFOs. As the files for Project Twinkle and Project Blue Book got fatter by the month, Air Force officials repeatedly told curious members of Congress that no such files existed.

For Air Force investigators, the UFO explanations trickled in. One group of scientists assigned to Holloman Air Force Base, located on the White Sands Missile Range and home to the Paperclip scientists, determined many of the sightings were observations of V-2 rocket contrails. Other sightings were determined to be shooting stars, cosmic rays, and planets visible in the sky. Another study group concluded that some responsibility fell on birds, most commonly "flocks of seagulls or geese." But the numbers of sightings were overwhelming. By 1951, the Air Force had secretly investigated between 800 and 1,000 UFO sightings across the nation, according to a CIA *Studies in Intelligence* report on UFOs declassified in 1997. By 1952, that number rose to 1,900. The efforts were stunning. Data-collection officers met with hundreds of citizens, all of whom were told not to disclose that the Air Force had met with them and asked to sign inadvertent-nondisclosure forms. Classified for decades, these investigations have resulted in over thirty-seven cubic feet of case files—approximately 74,000 pages. But for every one or two hundred sightings that could be explained, there were always a few that could not be explained—certainly not by Air Force data-collection supervisors who had a very limited need-to-know. Seeds of suspicion were being sown among these Air Force investigators and in some cases among their superiors, a number of whom would later famously leave government service to go join the efforts of the ufologists on the other side of the aisle.

Ultimately, the Air Force concluded for the National Security Council that "almost all sightings stemmed from one or more of three causes: mass hysteria and hallucination; misinterpretation of known objects; or hoax." The sightings that couldn't be explained this way went up the chain of command, where they were interpreted by a few individuals who had been cleared with a need-to-know. In the mid-1950s, this included the elite group over at the CIA working under Todos Odarenko, analysts responsible for matching the CIA's U-2 flights with Air Force unknowns. But no matter how many sightings were explained as benign, there was still the unexplained mother of all unidentified flying objects—the nefarious crashed craft from Roswell. Everything about that flying disc had to remain hidden from absolutely everyone but a select few. If Americans found out about it, or about what the government had been doing in response, there would be outrage.

For CIA analysts and Air Force personnel working together on the UFO problem, one concern was made clear: the public was not to learn about the government's obsession with UFOs. These orders came from the top. Why exactly this was the case, the rank and file did not have a need-to-know. Underlings simply followed orders, which was why two Air Force officials from Project Blue Book, Colonel Kirkland and Lieutenant E. J. Ruppelt, were sent to sit on a panel at a UFO convention in California, side by side with men who were convinced UFOs were from outer space. These men, some of the nation's leading ufologists, were part of a group called the Civilian Saucer Investigations Organization of Los Angeles.

On April 2, 1952, just one week before the *Life* magazine UFO story hit the newsstands, Kirkland and Ruppelt sat in a conference hall at the Mayfair Hotel with the leading UFO hunters of the day. It was a huge media event, with people from *Time, Life,* the *Los Angeles Mirror,* and Columbia Pictures in attendance. The Air Force officials placated the ufologists by saying that they too were concerned about UFOs and offering to "bring them into the loop." In return, the Air Force said, they would "throw" Civilian Saucer Investigations certain "cases that might be of interest" to the organization for their review. When the scientists pressed for security clearances so they could access top secret data, the Air Force began to squirm. "I see no reason at all why we can't work together," Colonel Kirkland said, deflecting the question. "I think it would be very foolish if we didn't." Ruppelt offered up an Air Force perk: CSI members could call the military collect.

On April 7, 1952, *Life* magazine published its cover story titled "There Is a Case for Interplanetary Saucers." The sixteen-page feature article began with the exclusive Air Force reveal. Above the byline, it read "The Air Force is now ready to concede that many saucer and fireball sightings still defy explanation; here LIFE offers some scientific evidence that there is a real case for interplanetary saucers." The article made its case well, with the takeaway being that UFOs really could be from out of this world. But there was a second reason the Air Force participated in the UFO convention. The CIA's Psychological Strategy Board had urged the National Security Council to "monitor private UFO groups [such] as the

Civilian Flying Saucer Investigators in Los Angeles," and because of this, the Air Force officers had been placed at the UFO convention in Los Angeles through backdoor recommendations at the CIA.

The CIA was particularly interested in one specific individual on the Civilian Saucer Investigations panel, and that was a German Paperclip scientist named Dr. Walther Riedel. Seated front and center at the UFO conference at the Mayfair Hotel, Dr. Riedel was a study in contradiction. When Riedel smiled, a close look revealed that he had fake front teeth — his own had been knocked out in 1945 at the Stettin Gestapo prison in Germany. Riedel had been a prisoner there for several weeks with fellow Peenemünde rocket scientist Wernher Von Braun, and during the war, Riedel had served as the chief of Hitler's V-2 missile-design office. The American soldiers guarding Riedel at the Stettin Gestapo prison roughed him up after Army intelligence agents passed along information stating that in addition to designing the V-2, Dr. Riedel had been working on Hitler's bacteria bomb. It was in the harsh interrogation that followed that Riedel lost his front teeth.

At the end of the war, Riedel, like Wernher Von Braun, desperately wanted to be hired by the U.S. military so he could work on rocket programs in the United States. Germany no longer had a military, let alone a rocket research program, which meant Riedel was out of a job. The Russians were known to hate the Germans; they treated their pillaged scientists like slave laborers. An offer from the Americans was the best game in town, even if their soldiers had broken your teeth first.

In January of 1947, Dr. Riedel became a Paperclip. His past work in chemical rockets and bacteria bombs was whitewashed in the name of science. The caveat for Riedel's prosperous new life, as opposed to his possible prosecution at Nuremberg, was that he would comply with what the U.S. military asked of him. But Riedel's rogue UFO-promoting behavior only a few years later illustrates that in certain situations, the Paperclips had the upper hand. Here was Riedel at the saucer convention, stirring up UFO hysteria. He participated in the *Life* magazine article and was quoted saying that he was "completely convinced that [UFOs] have an out-of-world basis." If that did not engender what CIA director Bedell Smith called hysterical thinking, what would? Riedel was not just any old rocket scientist going on the record with America's most popular magazine. When asked about his profession, he told *Life* magazine that he was "engaged in secret work for the U.S."

What is publicly known about Dr. Riedel's American career is that he had begun at Fort Bliss, in Texas, as part of the V-2 rocket team, but after only a few years he was mysteriously traded by the government to work as an engineer for North American Aviation. There were rumors of "problems" with other Paperclip scientists at White Sands Missile Range. Once Riedel was in the private sector, he had a considerably longer leash, given that the government was not signing his paycheck anymore. Clearly he was valuable to North American Aviation: the company made him director of rocket-engine research. But from the moment he left government service, Riedel was a serious thorn in the CIA's side. A year after the UFO conference, the CIA was still keeping close tabs on Dr. Riedel. In early 1953, the Agency trailed Riedel to one of his lectures in Los Angeles. There, they were shocked to learn that the Paperclip scientist and his UFO-minded colleagues were "going to execute a planned 'hoax' over the Los Angeles area in order to test the reaction and reliability of the public in general to unusual aerial phenomena." Mention of a planned hoax went up the chain of command at the CIA and set off alarms in its upper echelons. In a secret memo dated February 9, 1953, declassified in 1993, the CIA's director of the Office of Scientific Intelligence expressed outrage over the company Riedel now kept. But because he was no longer a Paperclip, there was little the CIA could do except follow his moves and those of the men he associated with.

The CIA had also been trailing a colleague of Riedel named George P. Sutton, a fellow North American Aviation rocket scientist and ufologist. When Sutton gave a lecture entitled "Rockets Behind the Iron Curtain," the CIA was shocked to learn that the flying saucer group seemed to know more about UFO sightings inside the Soviet Union than the entire team of CIA agents who had been tasked with monitoring that same information.

Ever since Bedell Smith had taken office in 1950, he'd expressed frustration over how little information the CIA was able to get on UFO reports inside Russia. Joseph Stalin, it appeared, kept all information about UFOs out of the press. Between 1947 and 1952, CIA analysts monitoring the Soviet press found only one single mention of UFOs, in an editorial column that briefly referred to UFOs in the United States. So how did Riedel's group know more about Soviet UFO reports than the CIA knew?

Sufficiently concerned, the CIA instructed Riedel's Paperclip handlers to get him in line. His handler "suggested politely and perhaps indirectly to Dr. Riedel that he disassociate himself from official membership on CSI." But the obstinate scientist refused to cease and desist. What the consequences were for Riedel remains unclear. Whether or not Riedel and his fellow ufologist pulled off their hoax and how he and his colleagues were able to so freely gather information about Soviet UFOs and Soviet rockets behind the Iron Curtain is secreted away in Riedel's Project Paperclip file, most of which remains classified, even after more than fifty years.

By 1957, according to the CIA monograph "CIA's Role in the Study of UFOs," the U-2s accounted for more than half of all UFO sightings reported in the continental United States. Odarenko had been unsuccessful in his bid to be "relieved" of his UFO responsibilities and instead got to work creating CIA policy regarding UFOs. He sent a secret memo to the director of the Office of Scientific Intelligence outlining how he believed the Agency should handle reports of UFOs:

- Keep current files on UFOs: "maintain current knowledge of sightings of unidentified flying objects."
- Deny that the CIA kept current files about UFOs by stating that "the project [was] inactive."
- Divide the explainable UFOs, meaning the U-2 flights, from

the inexplicable UFOs: "segregate references to recognizable and explainable phenomena from those which come under the definition of 'unidentified flying objects.'"

The Agency's concerted effort to conceal from Congress and the public its interest in UFOs would, in coming decades, open up a Pandora's box and cause credibility issues for the CIA. "The concealment of CIA interest [in UFOs] contributed greatly to later charges of a CIA conspiracy and cover-up," wrote Gerald K. Haines, the historian for the National Reconnaissance Office and someone who is often introduced as the CIA's expert on the matter. But to get the UFO monkey off his back, Allen Dulles began a "psychological warfare" campaign of his own. When letters came in from concerned citizens about the sightings, the CIA's policy was to ignore them. When letters came in from UFO groups, the CIA's policy was to monitor the individuals in the group. When letters came in from congressmen or senators, such as the one from Ohio congressman Gordon Scherer in September of 1955, the CIA's policy was to have Director Dulles write a polite note explaining that UFOs were a law enforcement problem and the CIA was specifically barred from enforcing the law. The notes certainly portray Allen Dulles as an arrogant public servant, but they are prized by UFO collectors, who say they prove the CIA's sinister cover-up of extraterrestrial UFOs. Regardless of alleged CIA policy, the public's fascination with UFOs proved more formidable than the CIA had ever bargained for; average citizens simply could not get enough information about mysterious objects streaking across the skies. And the more information they were given, the more they wanted to know and the more questions they asked. It didn't take long for the public to become convinced that the CIA was covering *something* up, which, of course, it was.

CHAPTER FIVE

The Need-to-Know

Everything that happens at Area 51, when it is happening, is classified as TS/SCI, or top secret/sensitive compartmented information—an enigmatic security policy with protocols that are also top secret. "TS/SCI classification guides are also classified," says Cargill Hall, historian emeritus for the National Reconnaissance Office; this government espionage agency is so secret that even its name was classified top secret from the time it was founded, in 1958, to its declassification, in 1992. In 2011, most Americans still don't know what the NRO is or what it does, or that it is a partner organization routinely involved with Area 51, because that is classified information.

Information classified TS/SCI ensures that outsiders don't know what they don't know and insiders know only what they have a need-to-know. Winston Churchill famously said of Russia, "It is a riddle, wrapped in a mystery, inside an enigma." The same can be said about Area 51. In the lesser-known second part of Churchill's phrase, he said, "But perhaps there is a key. That key is Russian national interest." Facing a totalitarian government like the Soviet Union's, where secrets are easily kept, Area 51 had to mirror Soviet secrecy techniques in order to safeguard the U-2. It was in America's national interest to do so because human intelligence was failing. "We obtain little significant information from classical covert operations inside Russia," bemoaned the president's science advisers in a secret 1954 national security report in which they gunned for "science and technology to improve our intelligence take."

They got what they wanted at Area 51. By using Soviet-style secrecy protocols for its own operation, and putting these tactics in place out in the Nevada desert, the CIA felt it could give its archenemy a run for its money regarding the element of surprise. Even Air Force transport crews had no idea where they were going when they went to the base. A classified-missions pilot would fly to a set of coordinates over the Mojave Desert and contact a certain UHF frequency called Sage Control. There, a voice at the other end of the radio would deliver increasingly more specific coordinates, ending with a go-ahead to land at a spot nestled inside a circle of mountains where no airstrip was supposed to exist. Only when the aircraft was a few hundred feet off the ground would runway lights flash on.

CIA pilots were kept equally in the dark. Carefully culled from Strategic Air Command bases at Turner Air Force Base, in Georgia, and Bergstrom Air Force Base, in Texas, the men had no idea who they were going to be working for when they signed on. In retrospect it seems easy to recognize the hand of the CIA, but this was not the case in late 1955 when the Agency was just seven years old. "It was like something out of fiction," Hervey Stockman recalls. "I was given a date and told to be at Room 215 at the Austin Hotel and knock on that door at exactly 3:15. So I went down there at the appointed time and knocked on the door. An extremely good-looking guy in a beautiful tweed opened it and said, 'Come on in, Hervey...' That was my first introduction to the Agency."

Hervey Stockman was one of America's most accomplished pilots. He was as fearless as he was gentle, a man who fell in love with airplanes the first time he flew one for the Army Air Corps, shortly after leaving the comforts of Princeton University to fight the Nazis in the Second World War. By the time he arrived at Area 51 for training, part of the first group of seven U-2 fliers called Detachment A, he had already flown 168 combat missions in two wars, World War II and Korea.

Area 51 "was the boonies," Stockman says. "We lived in trailers, three to a trailer as I recall. We couldn't write or call home from out there at Groom Lake." When Stockman's group arrived in January of 1956, there were "probably fifty or so people on the site." The trailers were in walking distance from the hangars, and "there was a training building, which was also a trailer," right next door, which was where Stockman spent most of his time. He remembers the mess hall as being one of the only permanent structures besides the hangars on base. "It was just all desert out there," Stockman remembers. On occasion, wild horses roamed onto the lake bed looking for water or food. "To get to civilization you were pretty dependent on aircraft. There was some road traffic but it was very carefully watched. Security people everywhere."

The identities of the pilots were equally concealed. "We all had pseudonyms. Mine was Sampson...I hated the name Sampson so I asked, Can I use the name Sterritt? I said, 'Sterritt fits me better. I'm a little guy and Sterritt is more my speed.' They said, 'Feel free. If you want to be Sterritt, you're Sterritt.' But for their record keeping I was Sampson. The records are still there...in the basement. And they're under the name Sampson. The Agency was very smart about all of that." The pilots were watched during their time off, not so much to see what the men might be up to as to make sure KGB agents were not watching them. Detachment A pilots were given apartments in Hollywood, California, where they officially lived. During weekends they socialized at the Brown Derby Restaurant. "It was a gathering spot and the security people could keep an eye on us there," Stockman explains. Come Monday morning, when it was time to return to Area 51, the Derby was the rendezvous spot because "it was one of the few places that was always open at five a.m." The majority of the Derby clientele had been up all night; the six very physically fit, clear-eyed pilots with their Air Force haircuts, accompanied by two CIA handlers in sport jackets and bow ties, must have been a sight to behold. From there, the group drove the Cahuenga Pass through the Hollywood Hills to the Burbank airport, where they boarded a Lockheed airplane headed for the secret base. "At the time, we did not know of Lockheed's involvement in the program," Stockman explains. "Even that was concealed from us. We were called 'drivers.' There were a lot of reasons for it. At the time, I don't think any of us really understood why, but that's essentially what we were. We were just, by God, drivers. We were not glory boys." The drivers did not have a need-to-know about anything except how to fly the airplane. Stockman once asked his superiors what the policy would be if he were shot down and captured. "Effectively, we were told that if we were captured and we were pressed by our captors, we could tell them anything and everything. Because of our lowly position as 'drivers' we didn't know very much." He said that during training even the name "Groom Lake was not part of our lexicon."

Across the world, the Russians were busy working on their own form of espionage. If Area 51 had a Communist doppelgänger, it was a remote top secret facility forty miles northeast of Moscow called NII-88. There, a rocket scientist named Sergei Korolev—the Soviet Union's own Wernher Von Braun—was working on a project that would soon shame American military science and propel the arms and space race into a sprint. Fearing the CIA would assassinate Russia's key rocket scientist, Stalin declared Sergei Korolev's name a state secret, which it remained until his death, in 1966. Sergei Korolev was only referred to as Chief Designer, not unlike the way Richard Bissell was known to employees outside the CIA only as Mr. B. Just as insiders called Area 51 the Ranch, NII-88 was known to its scientists as the Bureau. Like Area 51, NII-88 did not exist on the map. Before the Communist Revolution, NII-88 had been a small village called Podlipki, same as the Groom Lake area had once been a little mining enclave called

Groom Mine. Both facilities began as outcroppings of tents and warehouses, accessible only to a short list of government elite. Both facilities would develop into multimillion-dollar establishments where multibillion-dollar espionage platforms would be built and tested, each having the singular purpose of outperforming what was being built on the other side.

In 1956, all the CIA knew of NII-88 was that it was the place where Russia kept dozens of its captured German scientists toiling away on secret science projects. These men were Russia's version of America's Paperclip scientists, and they included the four hundred German rocket scientists who'd been plied with alcohol and then seized in the middle of the night—just as former Messerschmitt pilot Fritz Wendel had said.

The CIA first learned about NII-88's existence in late 1955, when the Soviets decided they had milked their former Third Reich scientists for all they were worth and began sending them back home. When the CIA learned of Russia's repatriation program, the Agency leaped at the intelligence opportunity and initiated a program called Operation Dragon Return. CIA officers were dispatched to Germany to hunt down the scientists who had been working in Russia, and the information gleaned from the returnees was considerable. It included technical data on Russian advances in radio technology, electronics, and armaments design. But to the CIA's great frustration, when it came to NII-88, the repatriated German scientists claimed to have no clear idea about what was really going on there. It seemed that NII-88, like Area 51, worked with strict need-to-know protocols, and the German scientists hadn't been cleared with a need-to-know. All the Germans could tell the CIA agents debriefing them was that Moscow's top scientists and engineers were developing something there that was highly classified. Unlike in America, where German rocket scientists were put in charge of America's most classified missile program at White Sands Missile Range, German scientists in Russia had been relegated to the second tier. With no hard facts about the extraordinary technological enterprise that was under way at NII-88, the CIA was left guessing. The speculation was that the Russians were developing intercontinental ballistic missiles, or ICBMs, that could reach the United States by traveling over the top of the world.

The missile threat needed to be addressed, and fast. By 1956 Americans were constantly being reminded about this foreboding Red menace by the media. A January 1956 issue of *Time* magazine made Soviet missile technology its big story. The cover featured a drawing of an anthropomorphic rocket, complete with eyeballs and a brain, carrying a nuclear bomb and bearing down on a major U.S. city. The magazine's analysts declared that in a little more than five years, Russians would be winning the arms race. The editors went so far as to prophesize a nuclear strike on the Pacific Ocean that would send a "cloud of radioactive death drift[ing] downwind" over America. Making the threat seem worse was the fact that there was no end to the confidence and bravado projected by the Soviet premier. "We're making missiles like sausages," Nikita Khrushchev declared on TV. If Russia succeeded in making these ICBMs, as was feared, then Russia really could place a nuclear warhead in the missile's nose and strike anywhere in the United States. "I am quite sure that we shall have very soon a guided missile with a hydrogen-bomb warhead which would hit any point in the world," Khrushchev boasted shortly after the *Time* magazine article appeared.

While the Soviets were concentrating efforts on advancing missile technology, the powerful General LeMay had convinced the Joint Chiefs of Staff that long-range bombers were a far better way for America to go to war. LeMay was not shy about expressing his disdain for missiles; he brazenly opposed them. LeMay's top research-and-development commander, General Thomas S. Power, told Pentagon officials that missiles "cannot cope with contingencies" the way bomber pilots could. Another one of LeMay's generals, Clarence S. Irvine, stated, "I don't know how you show... teeth with a missile." While the Joint Chiefs were deciding whether it was better to build up America's arsenal with missiles or bombers, the nuclear warheads continued to roll off the production lines at Sandia, in New Mexico, with astonishing speed. Ten years earlier, in 1946, the U.S. nuclear stockpile had totaled two. In 1955, that stockpile had risen to 2,280 nuclear bombs. The reason for LeMay's opposition to the missile programs was obvious: if the Pentagon started pumping more money into missiles that could carry nuclear warheads, LeMay's bombers would lose importance. As it was, he was already losing money and men to the overhead reconnaissance nonsense being spearheaded by the CIA's Richard Bissell over at Area 51.

In early 1956, the Air Force retaliated against Khrushchev's war of words with the kind of response General Curtis LeMay knew best: threat, intimidation, and force. LeMay scrambled nearly a thousand B-47 bombers in a simulated attack on Russia using bomber planes that were capable of carrying nuclear bombs. Air Force pilots took off from air bases in Alaska and Greenland, charged over the Arctic, and flew to the very edge of Soviet borders before U-turning and racing home. This must have been a terrifying experience for the Soviets, who had no idea that LeMay's bombers were planning on turning around. Further provoking them, on March 21, 1956, LeMay's bomber pilots began flying top secret missions as part of Operation Home Run, classified until 2001. From Thule Air Force Base in Greenland, LeMay sent modified versions of America's fastest bomber, the B-47, over the Arctic Circle and into Russia's Siberian tundra to spy. The purpose was to probe for electronic intelligence, or ELINT, seeing how Soviet radar worked by forcing Soviet radars to turn on. Once the Soviets started tracking LeMay's bombers, technicians gathered the ELINT to decipher back home. Asked later about these dangerous provocations, LeMay remarked, "With a bit more luck, we could have started World War III."

Sam Pizzo worked as a navigator during the SAC espionage operation, planning flights over nuclear facilities, missile sites, naval installations, and radar sites. The 156 missions took place from March 21 to May 10, 1956, where the Russian landscape meets the Arctic Ocean, which made for total darkness twenty-four hours a day. The temperature outside varied between −35 degrees and −70 degrees Fahrenheit. Sam Pizzo recalls those Cold War missions: "Ambarchik, Tiksi, Novaya Zemlya, these were the territories we covered. This was the real deal. Our missions were not twelve miles off the coastline, to study electromagnetic wave propagation [as was reported]. We went in." An undetermined number of pilots were shot down. Several were believed to have survived their bailouts, only to be taken prisoner and thrown into the Russian gulags. Everyone knew that suffering a gulag imprisonment was a fate worse than death. The missions were so top secret, Pizzo explained, that very few people at Thule had any idea where the pilots were flying. As a navigator, Pizzo was among the elite group who charted the pilots' paths. Flying over the Arctic required a very specific expertise in navigation, a different skill set than was used anywhere else on the globe. At the top of the world, the magnetic field fluctuates radically, which means compasses simply do not work. Instead, navigators like Sam Pizzo used celestial shots of the North Star and drew maps accordingly. This was a skill that Pizzo would later use when he was recruited for work at Area 51.

As Operation Home Run continued, the CIA worried that General LeMay's aggressive missions were a national security threat. "Soviet leaders may have become convinced that the U.S. actually has intentions of military aggression in the near future," a nervous CIA panel warned the president in the winter of 1956. And President Eisenhower's science advisers told him that flying U-2s over Russia could not wait. The Agency's Russian nuclear weapons expert Herbert Miller, the man who accompanied Bissell on that first scouting trip to Area 51, explained that no other program "can so quickly bring so much vital information at so little risk and so little cost."

The CIA planned to have the first U-2 flights photograph the facilities where the Agency believed Russia was building its bombers, missiles, nuclear warheads, and surface-to-air missiles. And the U-2 pilots would seek out the location of the elusive facility called NII-88. Having completed pilot training at Area 51, four pilot detachments were ready to go, fully prepared to penetrate deep into denied Soviet territory. There, they would be able to photograph half of the Soviet Union's 6.5-million-square-mile landmass. But it had to happen fast.

President Eisenhower was gravely concerned. "I fear if one of these planes gets shot down [we run] the risk of starting a nuclear war," he wrote in his White House journal. Richard Bissell promised the president that there was no chance of shooting down the U-2 and very little chance of tracking it. Besides, if the U-2 did get shot down, Bissell said, it would most likely disintegrate on impact with the ground, killing the pilot and destroying the airplane.

The Moscow air show on June 24, 1956, foreshadowed the breaking of promises made to the president. In a show of ceremony, Soviet premier Nikita Khrushchev invited air force generals from twenty-eight foreign delegations, including General Nathan Twining, the U.S. Air Force chief of staff. For all the fanfare and bravado of the bombers and fighter jets sweeping across the skies, the more significant event occurred a few hours later, at a wooden picnic table in Gorky Park. There, General Twining and the leaders of the British and French delegations sat and listened to Khrushchev deliver a long-winded speech. Partway through, the Soviet premier raised his vodka glass and made a toast "in defense of peace." Years later, retired Russian colonel Alexander Orlov related what happened next: "In the midst of his toast [Khrushchev] turned to General Twining and said, 'Today we showed you our aircraft. But would you like a look at our missiles?'" Shocked by the offer, General Twining said, "Yes." Khrushchev shot back, "First show us your aircraft and stop sending intruders into our airspace." Khrushchev was referring to the bombers sent over the Arctic Circle by General LeMay. "We will shoot down uninvited guests. We will get all of your [airplanes]. They are flying coffins!"

It was a terribly awkward moment underscored by the mercurial Soviet leader's abrupt shift in tone, from applauding peace to talking about shooting down American airplanes. General Twining had been set up for a confrontation. Things got worse when

Khrushchev looked around the picnic table for reactions and saw a U.S. military attaché pouring his drink under a bush. "Here I am speaking about peace and friendship, but what does your military attaché do?" Khrushchev shouted at Ambassador Charles Bohlen, then demanded that the attaché drink a penalty toast. Once the man had swallowed his vodka, he got up and quickly left the picnic. If Khrushchev thought the Americans were trying to insult him in the park, he would be even more enraged two weeks later when he learned the CIA had sent a U-2 directly over the Kremlin to take photographs of the house in which Nikita Khrushchev slept.

Area 51 had a Washington, DC, complement for the U-2 program, an office on the fifth floor of an unmarked CIA facility at 1717 H Street. This served as the command center for Project Aquatone's first, secret missions over the Soviet Union. It was from this clandestine facility that, shortly before midnight on July 3, 1956, Richard Bissell made a historic telephone call over a secure line. He reached the U-2's secret base in Wiesbaden, West Germany, and gave the commander the authorization to proceed. There, in a nearby room, Hervey Stockman sat breathing pure oxygen from a ventilator as a flight surgeon monitored the levels of nitrogen in his blood. Outside the door, CIA men armed with machine guns stood guard. Given the time difference, where Stockman was sitting it was already the following morning, making it the anniversary of America's independence. The nation was 180 years old. If all went well, Stockman was about to become the first pilot to penetrate the Iron Curtain's airspace. He would fly all the way to Leningrad, around the coast, and back down, putting him forever in the record books as the first man to fly over the Soviet Union in a U-2.

Stockman and his U-2 took off from Wiesbaden a little after 6:00 a.m., the pilot and his airplane moving skyward in a dramatic incline. The U-2 rose at a remarkable fifteen thousand feet a minute, so steep a gradient that for airmen on the ground who were unfamiliar with the airplane, it must have looked like Stockman was about to pitch back and stall. Halfway to altitude, Stockman briefly let the fuselage even out, allowing his body fluids and the fluids in the fuel tanks to expand and adjust. Once, a U-2 pilot had ascended too quickly, and his fuel tanks exploded. The pilot was killed. After a few additional minutes of ascent, Stockman arrived at cruising altitude. The sky above him was black and he could see stars. Below him, the Earth curved. It would be an eight-and-a-half-hour journey without a sip of water or a bite of food. In the U-2's camera bay, Stockman transported a five-hundred-pound Hycon camera fitted with the most advanced photo lenses ever devised in America. To prove how accurate the camera was, Bissell had sent a U-2 from Groom Lake on a flight over President Eisenhower's Pennsylvania farm. From thirteen and a half miles up, the U-2's cameras were able to take clear photographs of Eisenhower's cows as they drank water from troughs.

After several hours, Stockman approached Russia's submarine city. "I was supposed to turn the cameras on when I reached Leningrad," Stockman recalls. "I was to fly along photographing the naval installations there as well as a couple of airfields that were all part of what we had been led to believe might hold long-range Soviet bombers." But there were no long-range bombers to be found. The famous bomber gap, it turned out, was false. What Stockman filmed on the first overflight into Russia provided the CIA with critical facts on an issue that had previously been the subject of contentious debate. Russian weapons expert Herbert Miller wrote a triumphant memo to Eisenhower after the film in Stockman's camera was interpreted, explaining just how many "new discoveries have come to light." Stockman's flight provided the Agency with four hundred thousand square miles of coverage. "Many new airfields previously unknown, industrial complexes of a size heretofore unsuspected were revealed...Fighter aircraft at the five most important bases covered were drawn up in orderly rows as if for formal inspection on parade." What astonished Miller was just how current the information was. "We know that the guns in the anti-aircraft batteries sighted were in a horizontal position rather than pointed upwards and 'on the ready.' We know that some harvests were being brought in, and that the small truck gardens were being worked." They denoted "real intentions, objectives and qualities of the Soviet Union." Hervey Stockman explains it this way: "What it portrayed was that as a people they were not all geared up to go to war. They were leading a normal Russian life, so that behind this 'Iron Curtain' there wasn't all this beating of drums and movement of tanks and everything that was envisioned. They were going about their way over there."

Stockman's photos made the CIA ecstatic and justified the entire U-2 program, as a flurry of top secret memos dated July 17, 1956, revealed. "For the first time we are really able to say that we have an understanding of what was going on in the Soviet Union, on July 4, 1956," Miller wrote. But as beneficial as Stockman's flight was for the CIA, the results proved disastrous for President Eisenhower's relationship with Nikita Khrushchev. Despite Bissell's assurances to the contrary, the U-2s were tracked by the Soviets' air-defense warning systems from the moment they hit the radar screens. Once the film from Stockman's flight was developed, CIA photo interpreters determined that the Soviets had attempted more than twenty interceptions of Stockman's mission. "MiG-17 and MiG-19 fighters were photographed desperately trying to reach the U-2, only to have to fall back to an altitude where the air was dense enough for them to restart their flamed-out, oxygen-starved engines," photo interpreter Dino Brugioni told *Air and Space* magazine after the U-2 program was declassified, in 1998.

When Khrushchev learned the Americans had betrayed him, he was furious. After the picnic at Gorky Park, Khrushchev had agreed to spend the Fourth of July at Spaso House, the official residence of Ambassador Charles Bohlen, located just down the street from the Kremlin. When Khrushchev learned that while he had been celebrating the American Independence Day with the country's ambassador, a U-2 had been soaring over Russia, he was humiliated. "The Americans [are] chortling over our impotence," Khrushchev told his son, Sergei, a twenty-one-year-old aspiring missile designer. But in addition to the personal affront they caused

Khrushchev, the U-2 overflights greatly embarrassed the Soviet Union's military machine. Soviet MiG fighter jets couldn't get a shot anywhere near Hervey Stockman's U-2, which flew miles above the MiG performance ceiling, just as Colonel Leghorn had predicted. In 1956, the land-based Soviet surface-to-air missiles could not get a shot up high enough to knock the airplane out of the sky. America's spy plane had flown over Russia with impunity. And if that fact became known, the Soviet Union would look weak.

Weighing the options—embarrass his own military, embarrass the American president, or say nothing—Khrushchev chose to remain silent, at least as far as the international press was concerned. As a result, the first U-2 overflights were kept secret between the two governments. But they seriously strained already tenuous relations. Eisenhower ordered the CIA to stop all overflights inside the Soviet Union until further notice. Even worse, the president told Richard Bissell that he had "lost enthusiasm" for the CIA's aerial espionage program.

Back at Area 51, Bissell had a lot to worry about. Concerned that his U-2 program was going to be canceled by the president, he hired a team to analyze the probability of a Soviet shoot-down of the U-2. The news was grim: the Soviets were advancing their surface-to-air missile technology so rapidly that in all likelihood, within eighteen months they would be able to get their SA-2 missile up to seventy thousand feet. Bissell decided that the only way to keep his program aloft was to hide the U-2 from Soviet radar by inventing some kind of radar-absorbing paint. Bissell shared his idea with Lockheed's Kelly Johnson, who told him that painting the U-2 was a bad idea. Paint was heavy, and the U-2 flew so high because of how light it was, Johnson explained. The weight that paint would add to the aircraft would result in a loss of fifteen hundred feet of altitude. Bissell didn't want to hear that. So he went to the president's scientific adviser James Killian and asked him to put together a group of scientists who could make the CIA some radar-absorbing paint. These scientists, who worked out of Harvard University and MIT's

Lincoln Laboratory and were called the Boston Group, told Bissell they could get him what he wanted. It was a radical idea that had never been tested before. The scientists and engineers at MIT prided themselves on meeting challenges that other scientists believed were impossible.

There was a second serious problem facing Richard Bissell in the summer of 1956 and that was General LeMay. Impressed with the spy plane's performance, LeMay was now angling for control of the airplane. Under a program called Project Dragon Lady, LeMay ordered a fleet of thirty-one U-2s specifically for the Air Force. To keep the program secret from Congress, the Air Force transferred money over to the CIA, which meant that while working to head off LeMay's usurpation, Bissell simultaneously had to act as the go-between between the Air Force and Lockheed for the slightly modified U-2s. With these new Air Force airplanes came a demand for more "drivers," which meant the arrival of two new groups of pilots at Area 51 — those picked for CIA missions and others chosen for Air Force ones. Among those selected for Air Force missions was Anthony "Tony" Bevacqua.

"I may have been the only U-2 pilot at Area 51 who never made a model airplane as a kid," Bevacqua recalls. Instead, he had spent all his time devouring books. His obsessive reading of paperbacks, usually those by Zane Grey or Erle Gardner, helped offset his fear that he be unable to read English, like his father. The son of Sicilian immigrants, Bevacqua was the youngest pilot to fly the U-2 at Groom Lake, which he did in the winter of 1957 at the age of twenty-four. But before the handsome, vibrant Bevacqua wound up at the CIA's secret base, he was the roommate of another dashing young pilot whose name would soon become known around the world.

Before the two fighter pilots arrived at Area 51 to fly the U-2, Bevacqua and Francis Gary Powers were a couple of type A pilots with the 508th Strategic Fighter Wing at Turner Air Force Base in Georgia. They lived in a rented four-bedroom house situated two miles from the main gate. Both had been flying F-84 fighter jets for almost two years when one day Powers, whom everybody called Frank, just up and disappeared. "There were rumors that Frank had gone off on some kind of secret program," Bevacqua says, "but this was just talk, not something you could really sink your teeth into." A few months later Bevacqua was approached by a squadron leader and asked if he wanted to volunteer for "an interesting flight program."

"About what?" Bevacqua asked. The recruiter said he could not say, only that it would involve flying and that Bevacqua would have to leave the Air Force but could later return. The program, he was told, needed "a volunteer." It was important, the recruiter said, a mysterious edge to his voice. Bevacqua signed on.

He was flown to the Berger Brothers Company, located in a nondescript building in New Haven, Connecticut, not far from Yale University, that was filled with seamstresses making girdles and bras. What was he doing in there? he wondered. He was led through the workstations and into a back room. The unlikely supplier had a perfect cover for CIA-contract work: making ladies' underwear. In reality, the company, later renamed the David Clark Company, had already proven itself thousands of times over. During World War II, it made parachutes for U.S. Army Air Forces and Navy pilots.

In a clandestine back room, behind the brassiere assembly lines, Tony Bevacqua was fitted for a high-altitude flight suit specifically tailored for his physique. For the duration of his contract, Bevacqua would be required to maintain his weight within ounces. An ill-fitting suit could mean death for a pilot and the inevitable loss of an airplane. Bevacqua understood the concept of need-to-know and was aware that it prohibited him from asking any questions about what the suit was for. But he knew enough about partial-pressure suits to realize that whatever aircraft he was going to be piloting was going to be flying very high indeed.

His next stop was Wright-Patterson Air Force Base for a battery of physical and psychological procedures. There, Bevacqua underwent a series of endurance tests. Some were familiar but others he found thought-provokingly strange. All U-2 pilots were put into the high-altitude chamber to simulate the experience of sitting in a cockpit in a flight suit that your life depended on. At 63,000 feet, blood boils because there is not enough pressure to sustain oxygen in the bloodstream. There was another test called the Furnace in which U-2 pilots were left in a room that was significantly hotter than a hot sauna. Bevacqua was spared that one but he did have liquids pumped into his every orifice, first water and then some kind of mineral oil. Many U-2 pilots were hooked up to odd machines and others were given electroshock. Bevacqua got what he called the dreaded corpse test instead. He recalled how he "was put in a small space, my arms crossed over my chest like I was in a casket at a morgue. It was absolutely impossible for me to move my extremities. I was told to hyperventilate for as long as I could."

Bevacqua surmised that he would be chosen for the prestigious, top secret assignment only if he was able to pass every test. He wanted the job badly and was entirely willing to push himself physically to the edge. "I came within a breath of passing out during the corpse test," he explains. "After they said I could breathe, the attendants then pulled at my arms and legs but there was no way they could move or bend my extremities. As I breathed oxygen back into my body my cheeks loosened and then the rest of my body gradually returned to normal." After a few minutes Bevacqua's vital signs stabilized. "Apparently, this test was to see if I would have a seizure," he explains.

The next test was a freezing experiment. "I was asked to put my arms in a bucket of ice for as long as I could stand it. I don't remember what happened exactly. Probably good that I don't. I remember that I felt like a guinea pig." Unknown to Bevacqua or the rest of America, the division of the aviation medicine school at Wright-Patterson that was responsible for testing the U-2 pilots was run by Project Paperclip doctors, doctors with controversial histories. The Air Force had been willing to turn a blind eye to the scientists' past work in order to get where it wanted to go in the future, which was the upper atmosphere and outer space. The work that these Paperclip doctors had done during the war would later become a shameful stain on the Air Force record.

In 1980, journalist Linda Hunt published an article in the *Bulletin of the Atomic Scientists* revealing publicly for the first time that several of the nation's leading German American aerospace doctors had previously worked at Nazi concentration camps. There, they had obtained aviation medicine data by conducting barbaric experiments on thousands of Jews, Poles, Gypsies, and other people considered disposable. Many newspaper articles and medical papers followed, documenting how Project Paperclip came to be and raising important questions about how much the government had known about the scientists' sordid pasts. The issues were well reported but often ignored by the public because of the heinous subject matter involved. The idea that the American military and its intelligence agents would overlook war crimes and crimes against humanity in the name of advancing American science was, and continues to be, an odious one. It is likely that this is the reason why the federal government has never fully declassified the Operation Paperclip files. In 1999, a government panel released 126,000 pages of previously classified documents on former German Paperclips, but the panel also revealed that there were over six hundred million still-classified pages waiting "for review." No significant release has occured since.

In March of 1957, Bevacqua finally passed his tests and arrived at Area 51, where the living conditions had improved. The canvas tents had been upgraded to Quonset huts. There were working showers. The mess hall had been expanded, and someone had built a makeshift bar. But the protocols for flying were as undeveloped as they'd been when Ray Goudey and others were first figuring out how to get the U-2 to fly high. The training that Tony Bevacqua experienced at Area 51 was unlike anything he had ever seen on an Air Force base. The CIA method to train pilots on the U-2 was as radical and as unorthodox as an Air Force pilot could imagine. At

Turner Air Force Base, Bevacqua had learned to fly F–84s the Air Force way. That meant first diligently studying the aircraft manuals, then practicing in a flight simulator, then practicing in a trainer, and finally going up in the airplane with an instructor. At Area 51, there was no manual for the U–2, no flight simulator, no trainer, and no instructor. "The original U–2s had only one seat and one engine, which meant the CIA instructor pilot gave you a lesson with your feet on the ground," Bevacqua explains. Flying this strange and secret spy plane came without a morsel of bureaucracy, never mind basic rules, making the overall experience profound. "You were basically given a talk by an instructor pilot. Then you were given a piece of cardboard with a checklist on the front side, and fuel and oxygen graphs on the back. Then it was time to fly. And that was that."

Coupled with the secrecy protocols, the experience for pilots at Area 51 verged on sublime. No one but his old roommate from Turner AFB, Francis Gary Powers, knew who Tony Bevacqua really was. At Area 51 he went by only a pilot number and his first name. His family members had no idea where he was, nor would they find out about his secret missions for decades to come. As for future assignments, very few people were told where Air Force pilots were headed in the U–2—including the pilots themselves. What everyone knew was that pilots who got shot down over enemy territory were almost always tortured for information. This meant that the less you knew as a pilot, the better it was for everyone involved.

Bevacqua couldn't wait for an assignment. For this small group of pilots—only 25 percent of candidates passed the physical tests— a U–2 mission carried with it a sacred sense of national pride. Tony Bevacqua was living the American dream and protecting it at the same time. He was not someone who ever forgot for a moment how lucky he was. "Always make the most of your opportunities," Bevacqua's Italian-speaking father had told him as a child. Tony Bevacqua had done just that. He couldn't have asked for a better opportunity. He was one of America's most important spy plane pilots. He was helping to save the free world.

By the winter of 1957, the Boston Group had completed what Richard Bissell wanted in radar-absorbing paint. Bissell received the paint and gave it to Lockheed engineers at Area 51. He asked them to coat the fuselage of several U-2s with it, which they did. Bissell understood that Kelly Johnson disapproved of the radar-absorbing-paint program, which he said made his U-2s "dirty birds." But Bissell was under too much presidential pressure to deal with the watchful eye of Kelly Johnson at this point. To measure how the dirty birds performed against radar, Bissell hired a different company to measure the radar returns, the defense contractor EG&G.

EG&G is an enigma in its own right. Beginning in 1947, EG&G was the most powerful defense contractor in the nation that no one had ever heard of. In many ways, this still remains the case in 2011. The early anonymity was intended. It was cultivated to help make secret-keeping easier. Originally called Edgerton, Germeshausen, and Grier, EG&G had once been a small engineering company run by three MIT professors. In 1927, Dr. Harold "Doc" Edgerton invented stop-motion photography, which utilized another of his patented inventions, the strobe light. Edgerton's famous stop-motion photographs include one of a bullet passing though an apple, a drop of water splashing on a countertop, and a hummingbird frozen in flight. Edgerton was fond of saying that his career began because he wanted to make time stand still. EG&G got its first known set of defense contracts during World War II, when Doc Edgerton's strobe lights and photographer's flashbulb were used to light up the ground during nighttime aerial reconnaissance missions, rendering the age-old flare obsolete. Thanks to Doc Edgerton, fliers like Colonel Richard Leghorn were able to photograph Normandy before D-day.

Kenneth J. Germeshausen worked in high-energy pulse theory

at MIT. He held more than fifty patents, including a number in radar. Together with the company's third partner, Herbert Grier, Germeshausen developed the firing system for the Hiroshima and Nagasaki nuclear bombs. The Manhattan Project contracts came to the three professors because of their affiliation with Vannevar Bush, the former dean of engineering at MIT and later the man in charge of the Manhattan Project.

In addition to the firing systems on the nuclear bombs, which were based on a simple signal-switching relay system called the DN-11 relay, EG&G handled the defense contract to take millions of stop-motion photographs of nuclear bomb explosions in the Pacific and at the Nevada Test Site. It was from these photographs, and from these photographs only, that EG&G scientists could determine for the Atomic Energy Commission and the Department of Defense the exact yield, or power, of an exploded nuclear bomb. For decades a great majority of the most highly classified engineering jobs related to nuclear weapons testing went to EG&G. In the 1960s, when special engineering teams were needed to clean up deadly radioactive waste that was the result of these nuclear tests, the contracts went to EG&G as well. They were trusted implicitly, and EG&G's operations were quintessential black. They also had other businesses, such as radar testing. In the early 1950s, EG&G ran a radar-testing facility approximately thirty miles south of Area 51, at Indian Springs. Very little information is known about that period or about what EG&G was working on, as the data remains classified in EG&G's unique Restricted Data files. At Bissell's behest, in 1957 EG&G agreed to set up a radar range on the outskirts of Area 51 to measure radar returns for the dirty-bird project. In a CIA monograph about the U-2, declassified in 1998, the EG&G tracking station just outside Groom Lake is alleged to be "little more than a series of radar sets and a trailer containing instrumentation" where engineers could record data and analyze results. And yet the exact location of this "small testing facility" has been redacted from the otherwise declassified U-2 record. Why? The key term is *EG&G*. Giving away too much information about EG&G could inadvertently open a can of worms. No one but an elite has a need-to-know where any exterior EG&G facilities are located at Area 51 — specifically, whether they are located outside the blueprint of the base.

And so, in April of 1957, with EG&G radar specialists tracking his aircraft's radar returns, Lockheed test pilot Robert Sieker took one of the newly painted U-2s to the skies over Groom Lake. His orders were to see how high he could get the dirty bird to climb. Sieker took off from Area 51 and flew for almost ninety miles without incident when suddenly, in a valley near Pioche, the Boston Group's paint caused the airplane to overheat, spin out of control, and crash. Sieker was able to eject but was killed when a piece of the spinning aircraft hit him in the head. Kelly Johnson was right. It was a bad idea to try to retrofit the U-2. CIA search teams took four days to locate Sieker's body and the wreckage of the plane. The crash had attracted the watchful eye of the press, and the U-2's cover story, that it was a weather research plane, wore thin. Halfway across the country, a headline at the *Chicago Daily Tribune* read "Secrecy Veils High-Altitude Research Jet; Lockheed U-2 Called Super Snooper."

A pilot was dead, and the camouflage paint had made the U-2 more dangerous, not more stealthy. Bissell knew he needed to act fast. He was losing control of the U-2 spy plane program and everything he had created at Area 51. His next idea, part genius and part hubris, was to petition the president for an entirely new spy plane. The CIA needed a better, faster, more technologically advanced aircraft that would break scientific barriers and trick Soviet radars into thinking it wasn't there. This new spy plane Bissell had in mind would fly higher than ninety thousand feet and have stealth features built in from pencil to plane. Bissell was taking a major gamble with his billion-dollar request. Bringing an entirely new black budget spy plane program to the president's attention at a time when the president was upset with the results of the previous work done at Area 51 was either madness or brilliance, depending on one's point of view. But just as Richard Bissell began presenting plans for his radical and ambitious new project to the president, a national security crisis overwhelmed the country. On October 4, 1957, the Soviets launched the world's first satellite, a 184-pound silver orb called Sputnik 1. This was the secret that Sergei Korolev had been working on at Area 51's Communist doppelgänger, NII-88.

At first, the White House tried to downplay the fact that the Soviets had beat the Americans into space. Eisenhower, at his country home in Pennsylvania for the weekend, didn't immediately comment on the event. But the following morning, the *New York Times* ran a headline of half-inch-high capital letters across all six columns, a spot historically reserved for the declarations of war.

SOVIET FIRES EARTH SATELLITE INTO SPACE; IT IS CIRCLING THE GLOBE AT 18,000 MPH; SPHERE TRACKED IN 4 CROSSINGS OVER U.S.

A satellite launch meant the Russians now had a rocket with enough propulsion and guidance to hit a target anywhere in the world. So much for the Paperclips Wernher Von Braun and Ernst Steinhoff being the most competent rocket scientists in the world. "As it beeped in the sky, Sputnik 1 created a crisis of confidence that swept the country like a windblown forest fire," Eisenhower's science adviser James Killian later recalled. British reporters at the *Guardian* warned, "We must be prepared to be told [by Russia] what the other side of the moon looks like." French journalists homed in on America's "disillusion and bitter[ness]" at the crushing space-race defeat. The French underscored America's scientific shame. "The Americans have little experience with humiliation in the technical domain," read the article in *Le Figaro*. Because members of the public had no idea about the CIA's U-2 spy plane program, they believed that with Sputnik, the Russians could now learn all of America's secrets, while America remained in the dark about theirs. For twenty-one days, Sputnik circled the Earth at a speed of 18,000 mph until its radio signal finally faded and died.

In deciding the best course of action, the president turned back to his science advisers. In the month following Sputnik, a new position was created for James Killian—special assistant to the president for science and technology—and for the next two years Killian would meet with the president almost every day. This became a defining moment for Richard Bissell. For as depressing as his Area 51 prospects had seemed only a month before, the news of Sputnik was, ironically for the CIA, a harbinger of good news. James Killian adored Richard Bissell; they'd been friends for over a decade. Immediately after the Russians launched Sputnik, Killian and Bissell found themselves working closely together again. Only this time, they weren't teaching economics to university students. The two men would work hand in glove to launch America's most formidable top secret billion-dollar spy plane, to be built and test-flown at Area 51. Advancing science and technology for military purposes was now at the very top of the president's list of priorities. With James Killian on his side, Bissell inadvertently found himself in the extraordinary position of getting almost whatever he wanted from the president of the United States. And as long as what Richard Bissell built at Area 51 could humiliate the Russians and show them who was boss, this included a bottomless budget, infinite manpower, total secrecy, and ultimate control.

CHAPTER SIX

Atomic Accidents

Richard Bissell once said that setting up Area 51 inside a nuclear testing facility kept the curiosity-seekers at bay. With Operation Plumbbob, a 1957 atomic test series that involved thirty consecutive nuclear explosions, he got more than he bargained for. With the arms race in full swing, the Department of Defense had decided it was just a matter of time before an airplane transporting an atomic bomb would crash on American soil, unleashing a radioactive disaster the likes of which the world had never seen. In the twenty-first century, this kind of weapon would be referred to as a dirty bomb.

The dirty bomb menace posed a growing threat to the internal security of the country, one the Pentagon wanted to make less severe by testing the nightmare scenario first. The organization needed to do this in a controlled environment, away from the urban masses, in total secrecy. No one outside the project, absolutely no one, could know. Officials from the Armed Forces Special Weapons Project decided that the perfect place to do this was Area 51, inside the Dreamland airspace, about four or five miles northwest of Groom Lake. If the dirty bomb was set off outside the legal perimeter of the Nevada Test Site, secrecy was all but guaranteed. As far as specifics were concerned, there was an apocalyptic prerequisite the likes of which no government had ever dealt with before. Weapons testers needed "a site that could be relinquished for 20,000 years."

Code-named the 57 Project, and later Project 57, the Atomic Energy Commission, the U.S. Air Force, and EG&G would work together to simulate an Air Force airplane crash involving an XW-25 nuclear warhead—a crash in which radioactive particles would "accidentally" be dispersed on the ground. The land around the mock crash site would be contaminated by plutonium, which, according to scientists, would take 24,100 years to decay by half. At the time, scientists had no idea what accidental plutonium dispersal in open air would do to beings and things in the element's path. The 57 Project was a test that would provide critical data to that end. There were further prerequisites, ones that had initially narrowed the possibilities of usable land to that within the Nevada Test Site. The place needed to contain "no preexisting contamination," to be reasonably flat, and to cover approximately fifty square miles. Ideally, it would be a dry lake valley, "preferably a site where mountain-valley drainage currents would induce large amount of shear," or flow. It had to be as far away as possible from prying eyes, but most important, it had to be a place where there was no possibility that the public could learn that officials were even considering such a catastrophic scenario, let alone preparing for one. It was decided that in press releases the 57 Project would only be referred to as "a safety test," nothing more. With a doctor named James Shreve Jr. in charge of things, the project had an almost wholesome ring to it.

One dry lake bed originally considered was Papoose Lake, located six miles due south of Groom Lake, also just outside the test site. But soil samples taken by weapons planners revealed the earth there already had trace amounts of plutonium, owing to previous nuclear explosions conducted inside the test site in 1951, 1952, and 1953, five miles to the west at another dry lake bed called Frenchman

Flat. Further complicating matters, Papoose Lake was the subject of contention between the Atomic Energy Commission and two local farmers, the Stewart brothers. The dispute was over eight dead cows that had been grazing at Papoose Lake in March of 1953 when a twenty-four-kiloton nuclear bomb called Nancy was detonated nearby. Nancy sent radioactive fallout on livestock across the region, including those grazing at Papoose Lake. Sixteen of the Stewart brothers' horses died from acute radiation poisoning, along with their cows. The commission had paid the Stewarts three hundred dollars for each dead horse but stubbornly refused to pay the men for the dead cows. Instead, a lieutenant colonel from the Army's Veterinary Corps, Bernard F. Trum, wrote a long, jargon-filled letter to the farmers stating there was "nothing to indicate that [the blast] was the actual cause of the [cows'] deaths." Instead, the commission insisted the cows' deaths were "text book cases... of vitamin-A deficiency."

Shamelessly, the commission had a second doctor, a bovine specialist with Los Alamos, to certify in writing that "Grass Tetany" or "general lack of good forage" had killed the cows, not the atomic explosion over the hill. To add insult to injury, the Atomic Energy Commission told the Stewart brothers that its Los Alamos scientists had subjected their own cows to atomic blasts in New Mexico during the original Trinity bomb test in 1945. Those cows, the commission stated, were "burnt by the radioactivity over their entire dorsum and yet have remained in excellent health for years." In essence, the commission was saying, Our nuked cows are alive; yours should be too.

The Stewart brothers remained unconvinced and requested a note of explanation they could understand. In 1957, as weapons planners were determining where to hold Project 57, the dispute remained unresolved. Fearing that any attention brought to Papoose Lake might ignite the unresolved Stewart brothers' controversy, officials crossed the Papoose Lake land parcel off the location list.

The focus narrowed to a large, flat expanse in the Groom Lake valley, the same valley where the CIA was running its U-2 program. There, to the northwest of Area 51, lay a perfect sixteen-square-mile flat parcel of land—relatively virgin territory that no one was using. A record search determined that all grazing rights to the area had been "extinguished," meaning that local farmers and ranchers were already prohibited from allowing their livestock to roam there. Then weapons-test planners made an aerial inspection of Groom Lake. Colonel E. A. Blue joined the project's director, Dr. Shreve, in an overhead scout. In a classified memo, the two men joked about how they spotted a herd of cows roaming around the chosen site, "60 to 80 cattle who hadn't gotten the word," and that "somehow information must be gotten to them and their masters." Gallows humor for cows.

A land-use deal between the Department of Defense, which controlled the area for the Air Force, and the Atomic Energy Commission, the civilian organization that controlled the test site, was struck. As it was with the rest of the loosely defined Area 51, this desired land parcel lay conveniently just outside the legal boundaries of the Nevada Test Site, to the northeast. This allowed the 57 Project to fall under the rubric of a military operation, which could assist in shielding it from official Atomic Energy Commission disclosures, the same way calling it a safety test did. Anyone with oversight regarding unsafe nuclear tests simply didn't know where to look. In the end, the land designation even allowed Project 57 to be excluded from official Nevada Test Site maps. As of 2011, it still is.

In March of 1957, workers cordoned off the area in preparation for Project 57. The nuclear warhead was flown from Sandia Laboratories in New Mexico to the Yucca Lake airstrip at the test site and transferred to Building 11, where it would remain in storage until explosion day. Since it needed its own name for record-keeping purposes, officials decided to designate it Area 13.

Richard Mingus was tired. The twenty-four-year-old Ohio native had been working double shifts at the Sands hotel for three years and four months, ever since he returned home from the front lines of the Korean War. Newly married, Mingus and his wife, Gloria, had their first baby on the way. The Sands was the most popular spot on the Las Vegas Strip. It was the place where high rollers and partygoers went for entertainment, where they could hear the Rat Packers sing in the Copa Room. The restaurant at the Sands was a first-class operation, with silver service delivered from over-the-shoulder trays. Richard Mingus was proud to work there. Once he even got to wait on Elizabeth Taylor and Eddie Fisher. But by the summer of 1956, the novelty of hearing celebrity singers like Frank Sinatra, Dean Martin, and Sammy Davis Jr. perform had taken a backseat to the financial uncertainty that comes with a waiter's life. When he'd learned Gloria, the light of his life, was pregnant, Mingus became elated. Then economic insecurity settled in. In addition to having a little one on the way, Mingus supported his widowed mother back east.

Looking back, Mingus reflects on that time in his life. "You can never guess what the future holds," he says. That summer, life dealt Richard and Gloria Mingus a cruel blow. Gloria delivered prematurely, and their baby died in the hospital. They were without health insurance, and the bills accompanying the tragedy left Richard Mingus overwhelmed. Gloria became despondent. "I needed a solid job. And one that came with hospital benefits," Mingus explains. "It was time for me to find a profession. So I asked one of the waiters at the Sands if he knew about anything." Mingus learned the federal government was hiring security guards. The following morning he drove over to Second Avenue and Bonanza Street to apply.

There, Mingus stood in a long line of about a hundred other applicants for what seemed like hours. The Nevada Test Site, which was a sixty-five-mile commute to the northwest, had jobs. Rumors were those jobs paid well. The atomic tests, which had begun five years earlier, in 1951, had brought tens of millions of dollars in business to the Las Vegas economy. For the most part, Las Vegas as a city had endorsed the tests because they were such an economic boon. And yet it had been more than a year since the last atomic test series, which was called Operation Teapot and which was made up of twelve nuclear bomb explosions, including one that was dropped from an airplane. Controversies about fallout, particularly debates involving strontium-90, the deadly by-product of uranium and plutonium fission, had made their way into the public domain. For a while, there was even talk among locals that the test site could get shut down. Standing in line, Mingus got the sense that closing down the test site was far from reality. And he was right—weapons planners were gearing up for the largest atomic bomb test series ever to take place in the continental United States.

Mingus stood in line for a long time. Finally, a sergeant took his fingerprints and asked him if he had any military background. When Mingus said he'd served in Korea, the sergeant nodded with approval and sent him into a separate room. Las Vegas in the 1950s was a town made up largely of gamblers, swindlers, and fortune seekers. The fact that Mingus was a former soldier with an honorable discharge made him an ideal candidate for what the government was after: good men who could qualify for a Q clearance, which was required for a job involving nuclear weapons. Mingus filled out paperwork and answered a battery of questions. In just a few hours, Mingus was, tentatively, offered a job. Exactly what the job entailed, the recruiter could not say, but it paid more than twice what the best local waiters made during a stellar night at the Sands. Most important to Mingus, the job came with health insurance— Gloria's dream. He could begin work as soon as his security clearance came in. That process could take as long as five months.

Richard Mingus had no idea that he was about to become one of the first Federal Services security guards assigned to Area 51. Or that the very first nuclear test he would be asked to stand guard over would be Project 57—America's first dirty bomb.

From the first atomic explosions of Operation Crossroads, in 1946, until the Nevada Test Site opened its doors, in 1951, America tested its nuclear weapons on atolls and islands in the Pacific Ocean. There, in a vast open area roughly twice the size of the state of Texas, the Pentagon enjoyed privacy. The Marshall Islands were a million miles away from the American psyche, which made secret-keeping easy. But the Pacific Proving Ground was a long haul for the Pentagon in terms of moving more than ten thousand people and millions of tons of equipment back and forth from the United States for each test series. Guarding these military assets en route to the Pacific required a near-war footing. The ship carrying the nuclear material also carried the lion's share of the nation's nuclear physicists, scientists, and weapons engineers. The precious cargo required constant air cover and an escort by destroyer battleships while it made its zigzag course across the ocean. When Dr. Edward Teller, the Hungarian émigré and father of the hydrogen bomb, began arguing for an atomic bombing range in America to make things easier on everyone, there was hardly a voice of dissent from Washington. Officials at the Pentagon, the Armed Forces Special Weapons Project, and the Atomic Energy Commission all agreed with Teller and began encouraging the president to authorize a continental test site.

Science requires trial and error, Dr. Teller explained. As nuclear bombs grew more powerful, as weapons went from kilotons to megatons, scientists at the Los Alamos National Laboratory were struggling with discrepancies between theoretical calculations— equations made on paper— and the actual results the weapons produced. If the Pacific Proving Ground was the Olympic stadium for nuclear bombs, the scientists needed a local gym, a place to keep in shape and try out new ideas. Nevada would be perfect, everyone agreed. It was only a two-hour plane ride away from Los Alamos in New Mexico, as compared to the weeklong journey it took to get people to the Pacific Proving Ground.

In 1950, a top secret feasibility study code-named Project Nutmeg determined for President Truman that a huge area in southern Nevada, one of the least populated areas in the nation not situated on a coastline, was the most ideal place in the continental United States to test nuclear weapons. The Nevada Test and Training Range quickly became 4,687 square miles of government-controlled land. "The optimum conditions as to meteorological, remote available land and logistics" can be found there, the study explained. Even more convenient, there was an airstrip located just seven miles from the entrance of the test site, at a government-owned airfield called Indian Springs.

Before the Nevada Test Site was a nuclear bombing range it had been an animal sanctuary. In the 1930s, the Department of the Interior made the region a wildlife reservation. Herds of antelope and wild horses roamed the high-desert landscape with mountain lions and bighorn sheep. Kit fox and sidewinder rattlesnakes were more prevalent there than anywhere else in the country. Centuries earlier, Native Americans lived in the caves in the mountains. They left behind magnificent paintings and ornate petroglyphs on the caves' rock walls. In the mid-1800s, settlers built silver- and copper-mining camps, giving the local geography colorful names such as Skull Mountain, Indian Springs, and Jackass Flats. But by 1942, America had entered World War II, and the entire region was withdrawn from public access for War Department use. The Army set up a conventional bombing range across what would later include the Nevada Test Site, Area 51, and the Nellis Air Force Base. It was an ideal place to train aerial gunners, far from people and resplendent with flat, dry lake beds, which were perfect for target practice and for landing airplanes. After the war ended, the bombing range was closed and its buildings were allowed to deteriorate. But the Army hung on to the land rights for possible future use. That future use became clear when 1,350 acres, or about one quarter of the restricted area, was parceled off and called the Nevada Test Site. On January 27, 1951, at 5:45 a.m., an Air Force B-50D bomber dropped the first atomic bomb on U.S. soil, onto a dry lake bed called Frenchman Flat, inside the Nevada Test Site.

Edward Teller loved the closeness of Nevada and referred to the bombs being set off there as "quickie" tests. Almost immediately, a second nuclear laboratory, called the Lawrence Radiation Laboratory at Livermore, was created by the Atomic Energy Commission with the goal of fostering competition with the Los Alamos nuclear lab. Shortly before the creation of Livermore, scientists at Los Alamos had started to challenge the military establishment regarding what the future of the nuclear bomb should or should not be. Uninterested in what the creators of the atomic bomb had to say, the Department of Defense pushed back by developing Livermore. Competition fosters productivity; the greater the rivalry, the more intense the competition will be. Indeed, it did not take long for a fierce competition to develop between the two outfits, with Los Alamos and Livermore fighting for weapons contracts and feasibility-study awards. Dreaming up prototypes for new weapons was how contracts were won. Dr. Teller argued for the need to experiment with certain "boosters," like the radioactive isotope of hydrogen tritium, which could further enhance yield. If a scientist or his lab could make a strong enough case for the necessity of testing such a thing, the Armed Forces Special Weapons Project and the Atomic Energy Commission could easily allocate money for it. The goal was singular: get the highest-yield bombs to fit inside the smallest packages, ideally ones that could be put into the nose cone of a missile designed by Wernher Von Braun.

In five short years, from January 1951 to January 1956, a total of forty-nine nuclear bombs were exploded at the Nevada Test Site, bringing the worldwide total for atmospheric nuclear explosions by the United States to eighty-five. Which is when Richard Mingus joined the security force at the Nevada Test Site and Area 51, just in time for Operation Plumbbob, the largest, most ambitious series of nuclear weapons tests in the United States so far. The first test scheduled in the thirty-test Plumbbob series was Project 57.

In the flat Nevada desert, Richard Mingus took to work in top secret nuclear security like a fish to water. He loved the formal protocols and the way everything was ordered. "I developed a reputation for being tough," Mingus recalls. From the checklists to the radio codes, everything at the Nevada Test Site and at Area 51 worked with a military precision that Mingus thrived on. What others may have found monotonous, spending long hours guarding nuclear weapons in a vast desert-landscape setting, Mingus found challenging. He passed the pistol training with flying colors. He studied the manuals with such intensity, he ended up scoring in the top 90 percent of all the trainees. His excellence earned Mingus a position as one of only five men chosen to guard the top secret base over the hill from Yucca Flat. For employees of Federal Services, Incorporated, the first thing learned was that the facility was to be referred to only as Delta site. The radio channel on which Mingus and his colleagues spoke could be heard by guards all over the test site. The code was important; it was Delta, nothing more. Mingus remembered how everything at Area 51 worked with top secret/sensitive compartmented information protocols. "Even my sergeant wasn't cleared to go over the hill to Delta. He was my superior but he didn't have a need-to-know what I was doing over there," Mingus explains. "So I was very curious the first time driving out there, looking out the window... wondering what's ahead. When we got there, it was not very fancy at all. Just an airstrip in the desert. Later, we were told the place was also called Watertown but never to use that word. Over the radio we always referred to our position at Delta, never anything else." That first day at Delta, aka Area 51, Richard Mingus and his four colleagues were met by a CIA security representative at the west-facing perimeter gate. "He drove us into the area. We went straight to the admin building, which was just a little wooden structure with a patch cord telephone system sitting there on a desk. The sergeant looked at me, pointed to a chair, and said, 'Dick, that's your post.'" A surge of intimidation swept over Mingus. "A country boy like me, I looked at the phone system and I thought, This is the hottest spot on the post, the place where all the communication from the CIA comes in. I had never used a switchboard before and I knew if I wanted to keep my job I'd have to learn real fast. As it turns out, there was plenty more time to learn. The phone almost never rang. 'Thirty-two thirty-two,' that's how I answered the telephone. There were not many calls. And when someone did call, they would almost always ask for the same person, a [generic] name like Joe Smith, the code name for the commander at the base."

At Area 51, Mingus and his colleagues rotated through four sentry posts: the administration building, the top of a seventy-five-foot water tower, and the east and west gates. The gate positions were used to control access to Area 51 by land. On more than one occasion, Mingus turned away what he calls "overly curious Air Force," individuals who "just because they had rank, they thought they should be able to come on in." Mingus denied access to anyone not badged for Area 51. "A few times things got real tense. We worked on strict orders and it was my job to keep people out." The water-tower post at the facility was used by guards to keep an eye on the sky. "We were on the lookout for a rogue helicopter or small aircraft, that type of thing," Mingus recalls. During this time, the security guards got to know many of the U-2 pilots. "They'd fly low enough over me so I could see their faces in the cockpit. They got a kick out of flying over our security posts. They'd buzz over us and after they landed they'd always make a joke about not wanting us sleeping on the job."

Richard Mingus had been guarding Area 51 for a little over a month when the Los Alamos scientists and the EG&G engineers began their final preparations for Project 57 at Area 13. A supervisor at the Nevada Test Site asked Mingus if he was willing to work some considerable overtime for the next few weeks. He had been requested to serve as the guard to keep both Area 51 and Area 13 secure. Considerable overtime meant double-time pay, and Mingus agreed. Finally, a shot date of April 3 was chosen. *Shot*, Mingus quickly learned, was commission-speak for "nuclear detonation." As was required by an agreement between the Atomic Energy Commission and the State of Nevada, the Department of Defense prepared a simple statement for the press. "A highly classified safety test [is] being conducted by Dr. James Shreve Jr., in April 1957," read the *Las Vegas Sun*. The public had no idea the Department of Defense and the Atomic Energy Commission would be simulating an airplane crash involving an XW-25 nuclear warhead by initiating a one-point detonation with high explosives at Area 13. Neither did any of the U-2 program participants living in Quonset huts just a few miles to the east. Scientists predicted the warhead would release radioactive plutonium particles, but because a test like Project 57 had never been conducted before, scientists really had no clear idea of what would happen.

Workers set up four thousand fallout collectors around a ten-by-sixteen-square-mile block of land. These galvanized steel pans, called sticky pans, had been sprayed with tacky resin and were meant to capture samples of plutonium particles released into the air. Sixty-eight air-sampler stations equipped with millipore filter paper were spread over seventy square miles. An accidental detonation of a nuclear weapon in an urban area would be far more catastrophic than one in a remote desert area such as Groom Lake, and the Department of Defense wanted to test how city surfaces would respond to plutonium contamination, so mock-ups of sidewalks, curbs, and pavement pieces were set out in the desert landscape. Some fourteen hundred blocks of highway asphalt and wood float finish concrete were fabricated and set around on the ground. To see how automobiles would contaminate when exposed to plutonium, cars and trucks were parked among the juniper bushes and Joshua trees. As zero day got closer, Mingus saw preparations pick up. Giant air-sampling balloons were tethered to the earth and floated over Area 13 at various elevations; some were five feet off the ground and others a thousand feet up, giving things a circus feel. Nine burros, 109 beagles, 10 sheep, and 31 albino rats were put in cages and set to face the dirty bomb. EG&G's rapatronic photographic equipment would record the radioactive cloud within the first few microseconds of detonation. A wooden decontamination building was erected just a few hundred yards down from Mingus's post. It was nothing fancy, just a wooden shack "stocked with radiation equipment and protective clothing, shower stalls… with a three-hundred-fifty-gallon hot-water supply and a dressing room with benches and hangers for clothes." Shortly before shot day, workers installed a "two-foot-wide wooden approach walk" and covered it with kraft paper.

Shot day came and went without the test. All nuclear detonations are subject to the weather; Mother Nature, not the Pentagon's Armed Forces Special Weapons Project officers, had final say regarding zero hour. Mother Nature's emissary at the test site was Harold "Hal" Mueller, a meteorologist from UCLA. In the case of Project 57, there was one weather problem after the next. It was April in the high desert, which meant heavy winds, too much rain, and thick clouds. For several days, snow threatened the skies. In the second week of April, the winds were so intense that a blimp moored twelve miles south, at Yucca Flat, crashed and deflated. On April 19, one of the Project 57 balloons broke loose, forcing General Starbird to issue a telegram notifying Washington, DC, of a potential public relations nightmare. The balloon had sailed away from Area 13 and was headed in the direction of downtown Las Vegas. "A twenty-three foot balloon towing two hundred feet one eighth inch steel aircraft cable escaped Area 13 at 2255 hours April 19 PD," read Starbird's terse memo. His "best estimate is that balloon will self-rupture and fall within boundaries of the Las Vegas bombing and gunnery range," and thereby go unnoticed. But General Starbird and everyone else involved knew if the balloon were to escape the test site's boundaries, the entire Plumbbob series was at risk of cancellation. Lucky for Starbird, the balloon crash-landed inside the Nevada Test and Training Range.

The concept of using balloons in nuclear tests was first used in this series. In thirteen of the thirty Plumbbob explosions scheduled to take place in spring and summer of 1957, a balloon would be carrying the nuclear device off the ground. Before balloons were used, expensive metal towers had been constructed to hold the bomb, towers that guards like Richard Mingus spent hours tossing paper airplanes from. "You needed something to keep your mind off the fact that the bomb you were standing next to was live and could flatten a city," Mingus says. To get weapons test engineers like Al O'Donnell up that high—the towers were usually three hundred, five hundred, or seven hundred feet tall—in order to wire the bomb, rudimentary elevators had to be built next to the bomb towers; these were also very expensive. A balloon shot was far more cost-effective and also produced a lot less radioactivity than vaporizing metal did. For the public, however, the safety and security of hanging nuclear bombs from balloons raised an obvious question: What if one of the balloons were to get away?

Finally, during the early-morning hours of April 24, the weather cleared and the go-ahead was given for Project 57. At 6:27 a.m., local time, the nuclear warhead in Area 13 was hand-fired by an employee from EG&G, simulating the plane crash without actually crashing a plane. Mingus remembers the day because "it was just a few days after Easter, as I recall. Finally a good weather day. I don't remember snow but I do remember I had to get muddy to get to my post. Area 13 was way out in the boondocks. Barely any people around because it was a military test, not AEC. There wasn't much traffic and from where I was parked in my truck, I could see a mile down the road. I remember it was cold and I had my winter coat on. No radiation-protection gear." The predicted pattern of fallout was to the north. When the dust from the small radioactive cloud settled, plutonium had spread out over 895 square acres adjacent to Groom Lake. Mingus says, "It wasn't spectacular. It didn't have a big fireball. But it involved an extreme amount of radiation, which made it nasty. I remember how dirty it was."

The bomb was indeed dirty. Plutonium, if inhaled, is one of the most deadly elements known to man. Unlike other radiation that the body can handle in low dosages, such as an X-ray, one-millionth of a gram of plutonium will kill a person if it gets in his or her lungs. According to a 1982 Defense Nuclear Agency request for an unclassified "extract" of the original report, most of which remains Secret/Restricted Data, Project 57 tests confirmed for the scientists that if a person inhales plutonium "it gets distributed principally in bone and remains there indefinitely as far as human life is concerned. One cannot outlive the influence because the alpha half-life of plutonium-239 is of the order of 20,000 years." These findings came as a result of many tests performed on the dead burros, beagles, sheep, and albino rats that had been exposed to the dirty bomb. So why wasn't Richard Mingus dead?

The same report revealed that "air samplers indicated high airborne concentrations of respirable plutonium remarkably far downwind." Plutonium is a poison of paradox. It can be touched without lethal effects. Because it emits alpha particles, the weakest form of radiation, plutonium can be blocked from entering the body by a layer of paper or a layer of skin. Equally incongruous is the fact that plutonium is not *necessarily* lethal if ingested. "Once in the stomach, its stay in the body is short, for [particles] are excreted as an inert material with virtually no body assimilation," read another report. In other words, plutonium is deadly for humans and animals only if particles reach the lower respiratory tract.

Mingus never breathed any particles into his lungs as he kept watch for ten to twelve hours at a time on a desolate stretch of land between Area 13 and Area 51, guarding two of the most classified projects in post–World War II American history: Projects 57 and Aquatone, the U-2. As the weeks wore on and Project 57's plutonium particles settled onto the desert floor, Mingus watched men from Sandia, Reynolds Electric and Engineering Company, and EG&G go in and out of the contamination site. They'd put on face masks and seal areas on their bodies where their clothing met their skin by using household tape. They passed by a small metal sign that read DO NOT ENTER, CONTAMINATED AREA so they could swap out trays, feed the animals that were still alive, and remove the dead and dying ones. They replaced spent millipore paper with fresh strips and then headed back down to the laboratory and the animal morgue inside the Nevada Test Site. Meanwhile, Mingus watched overhead as the U-2 pilots made their final test flights, putting in as many flight hours as they could before their missions became real. Soon these pilots would be dispatched overseas, where they would be stationed on secret bases and fly dangerous missions that technically did not exist and that the public would not learn about for decades.

Data obtained as a result of Project 57 confirmed for the Department of Defense what it already knew. "Plutonium has a 24,000 year half-life. It does not decay." Once plutonium embeds in soil, it tends not to move. "There are few instances of plutonium depletion with time. There is little tendency for the plutonium to change position (depth) in soil with time." Provided a person doesn't inhale plutonium particles, and provided the plutonium doesn't get into the bloodstream or the bones, a person can pass through an environment laden with plutonium and live into his eighties; Richard Mingus is a case in point.

Within a year of the detonation of the dirty bomb, the scientists were satisfied with their preliminary data, and Project 57 wound down. The acreage at Area 13 was fenced off with simple barbed wire. Stickers that read CONTAMINATED MATERIALS were attached to the bumpers and hoods of Atomic Energy Commission vehicles before they were buried deep underground. Clothing contaminated with "alpha-emitting material was sealed in plastic bags and buried in the contaminated waste area." And yet, by the summer of 1958, Project 57's director, Dr. James Shreve, authored a very troubling report—one that was marked Secret–Restricted Data—noting that the measurements research group had made a potentially deadly observation. "Charles Darwin studied an acre of garden in which he claimed 53,000 hard working earthworms moved 18 tons of soil," wrote Dr. Shreve. "Translocation of soil, earthworms' ingestion of plutonium, could turn out to be a significant influence, intentional or unintentional, in the rehabilitation of weapon-accident environment." In other words, plutonium-carrying earthworms that had passed through Area 13, or birds that ate those earthworms, could at some point in the future get to a garden down the road or trees in another field. "The idea of an entirely separate program on ecology in Area 13 had occurred to [names unclear] in the summer of 1957," wrote Shreve, "but the AEP/UCLA logical group to undertake the investigation was too committed on Operation Plumbbob to consider the responsibility." The twenty-nine nuclear bombs about to blow in the rest of the Plumbbob series would take precedent over any kind of effort to contain future harm done by the first test in the series, the Project 57 dirty bomb. Out in the desert, men with extraordinary power and punishing schedules worked without any effective oversight.

As one EG&G weapons engineer remarked, "Things at the test site rolled fast and loose." Not until as late as 1998 was the top layer of earth from Area 13 scraped up and removed. By then, earthworms in the area, and birds eating those earthworms, had been moving plutonium-laden soil who knows how far for more than forty years.

With the plutonium-contamination test out of the way, the Armed Forces Special Weapons Project began moving forward with the rest of the 1957 open-air nuclear-test series. It was a boon to the Las Vegas economy, supplying millions of dollars in resources and in jobs. Each test was reported to cost about three million dollars—approximately seventy-six million in 2011 dollars—although it is impossible to learn what that figure did or did not include.

Nearly seven thousand civilians were badged to work at the test site during Operation Plumbbob. Another fourteen to eighteen thousand employees of the Department of Defense also participated; official figures vary. But despite all the money being pumped into Las Vegas, the debate over fallout threatened to cancel the tests. Just two weeks before Project 57 contaminated 895 acres adjacent to Groom Lake with plutonium, Nobel Prize winner Linus Pauling made a statement that spooked the public and threatened the tests. Pauling said that as a result of nuclear tests, 1 percent of children born the following year would have serious birth defects. The Atomic Energy Commission responded by positioning their own doctors' opinions prominently in the news. Dr. C. W. Shilling, deputy director of biology and medicine for the Atomic Energy Commission, ridiculed Linus Pauling, saying that "excessively hot baths can be as damaging to the human sex glands as radioactive fallout in the amount received in the last five years from the testing of atomic weapons." In hindsight, this is astonishingly erroneous, but at the time it was what Americans were willing to believe.

Almost every newspaper in the country carried stories about the debate, often presenting diametrically opposed views on the subject in columns side by side. "Children are smaller on island sprinkled with nuclear fallout," read the *Santa Fe New Mexican;* "Study Finds Kids Born to Marshall Islanders Are Perfectly Normal," headlined another; "2000 Scientists Ask President to Ban Bomb Tests," the *Los Angeles Mirror* declared. Editorials, such as the one published on June 7 in the *Los Angeles Times,* suggested that a recent influx of seagull and pelican deaths along the California coast was proof that the biblical End of Times was at hand.

All across Europe there were protests. Japan tried to get the tests canceled. When it became clear that the tests would go forward, one hundred enraged Japanese students protested at the U.S. embassy in Tokyo. When things turned violent, heavy police reinforcements were called in. Prime minister of India Jawaharlal Nehru called the tests a "menace" and, in a personal appeal to President Eisenhower, proclaimed that unless all nuclear tests were stopped, the Earth would be hurled into a "pit of disaster." Soviet scientist Professor Federov publicly accused the United States of developing a weapon that was meant to cause worldwide drought and flood. To counter the campaign aimed at putting an end to nuclear testing, the Atomic Energy Commission kept the propaganda rolling out. Colorful characters such as Willard Frank Libby, one of the Agency's leading scientists and known as Wild Bill of the Atom Bomb, insisted that "science is like an art. You have to work at it or you will go stale. Testing is a small risk." In the end the weaponeers won. When it was finally announced that the Plumbbob series had received presidential approval, the press release described the twenty-four nuclear tests (the other six were called safety tests) as "low yield tests," promising none would be more than "30 kilotons." The six "safety tests" were generally excluded from mention. The magnitude of the megaton bombs set off in the Pacific had fundamentally warped the notion of atomic destruction. The Hiroshima bomb, which killed seventy thousand people instantly and another thirty to fifty thousand by radiation poisoning over the next few days, was less than half the size of what the U.S. government was now calling "low yield."

The tests were important, the president promised the public.

The government needed to build up its "encyclopedia of nuclear information." The Army needed its troops to practice "maneuvers" on a nuclear battlefield and to record how soldiers would perform in the event of a nuclear battle. The government had to know: At what distance could a military jeep drive through a nuclear shock wave? How did a blast wave affect a hill versus a dale? What effect would weapons have on helicopters, blimps, and airplanes when they flew close by a mushroom cloud? The Pentagon wondered and said it needed to find out. And so, in the sparsely populated desert of southern Nevada, the Plumbbob nuclear weapons tests went ahead as planned.

Following Project 57, the first nuclear explosion in the series to form a mushroom cloud was called Boltzmann, detonated on May 28, 1957. At twelve kilotons, it was approximately the same size as the Hiroshima bomb and caused Area 51 personnel located eleven miles over the hill to be temporarily evacuated from the base. The bomb was described in a press release simply as a "Los Alamos Scientific Laboratory device." On June 9, 1957, the *New York Times* printed the Atomic Energy Commission's "partial schedule" of the Operation Plumbbob atomic tests so that summer tourists wanting to see a mushroom cloud could plan their itineraries accordingly. "This is the best time in history for the non-ancient but none the less honorable pastime of atom-bomb watching," the *New York Times* said. According to Richard Mingus, it seemed that higher-ranking CIA officers at Area 51 did not agree with the Gray Lady's assessment. "After one blast really shook the place, a group of them jumped in someone's private aircraft and took off pretty fast." One report, declassified in 1993, noted the damage: "The blast buckled aircraft hangar doors, shattered windows in the mess hall and broke a ventilator panel on a dormitory." Area 51 employees were once again evacuated. Neither Richard Bissell nor his team was prepared for such drastic effects and certainly not as a matter of course. Whether the Agency protested or complied remains classified, but the U-2s were quickly flown to a remote area of the north base at Edwards Air Force Base in California and hidden in hangars there.

Nothing was going to stop the Atomic Energy Commission and its tests. Operation Plumbbob was in full swing.

Then came the Hood bomb.

It was the middle of the night on July 5, 1957. Richard Mingus was getting ready to head to the test site for work. Gloria was finally pregnant again, and it had been a celebratory Fourth of July. Now Mingus prepared himself for what he knew was going to be an exceedingly long day. The shot was going to be big; so big, the commission had already evacuated every last person from Area 51. Only the caretakers were left. Richard Mingus kissed Gloria good-bye and climbed into his new 1957 DeSoto. How Mingus loved his car, with its four doors and long fins, a luxury made affordable by long overtime hours at the test site. The morning of the Hood bomb, Mingus drove the sixty-five miles to the main gate at Camp Mercury, located at the southernmost end of the test site, off High-way 95. It was somewhere around 1:30 a.m. Hood was scheduled for detonation early that morning, in Area 9. On the seat beside him, Mingus carried his lunch, always lovingly packed by Gloria in a small, wooden lunch box. Inside there was a sandwich, a can opener, and a can of Mingus's favorite: Dinty Moore stew. Once inside the gates of the test site, Mingus parked his DeSoto and transferred his belongings into an Atomic Energy Commission truck. Then he drove the familiar route from Camp Mercury to the control point. First he made sure to stop by the ice house, where he could fill up a five-gallon can with water, making sure to put a big block of ice inside. "The size of the Hood bomb was classified but everyone knew it was going to be really big," Mingus explains.

Three miles to the north, at Area 9, the Army would be con-ducting hundreds of tests during and immediately after the explo-sion. Seventy Chester White pigs wearing military uniforms were enclosed in cages facing the bomb and placed a short distance from ground zero. The pigs had been anesthetized to counter the pain of the beta radiation burns they were certain to receive. Using the pigs, the Army wanted to determine which fabrics best withstood an atomic bomb blast. Farther back, lying in trenches, were one hundred soldiers, all of whom were participating in twenty-four scientific experiments. In classified papers obtained by the author, scientists called this the Indoctrination Project. A committee called the Committee on Human Resources was conducting these secret tests on soldiers to determine how they would react psychologically when nuclear bombs started going off. The Committee on Human Resources wanted to study the "psychology of panic" and thereby develop "emotional engineering programs" for soldiers for future use.

A second battalion of 2,100 troops was stationed farther back, in Area 4 and Area 7, troops whose job was to simulate a "mythical attack by an aggressor force against Las Vegas, conducted over four days." A mile to the south, twenty-five hundred Marines would be working on combined air-ground exercises during Hood, using an amphibian tractor called the LVTP5, the ship-to-shore vehicle that was used in the Pacific during World War II, an "armored monster capable of bringing Marines ashore with dry feet." Dozens of helicopters performed maneuvers as well. Medical divisions were present, tasked with studying "blast biology," to determine the primary and secondary effects of flying bricks, timber, and glass. Different types of wood houses had been built to see what could withstand a nuclear blast best: wood or wallboard; masonry or metal; asbestos-shingle or tar-paper roof. The Federal Civilian Defense Administration was testing different types of bomb shelters and underground domes. One structure was ninety feet by ninety feet across and had a reinforced door weighing a hundred tons that was mounted on a monorail. The Mosler Safe Company sponsored and paid for a $500,000 nuclear-bombproof steel vault, ideal for insurance companies and banks seeking ways to mitigate loss after a nuclear attack.

Richard Mingus was at the control point when the Hood bomb went off, all seventy-four kilotons of it. Almost immediately after the bomb detonated, a call came in from Mingus's boss, a man by the name of Sergeant May. There was a major security problem, May was told. The Atomic Energy Commission had forgotten to secure

Area 51. May needed to send Mingus over to the evacuated CIA facility immediately. "Once Sergeant May got off the phone he turned to me quick and said, 'Go to rad safe, check out a Geiger counter and get over to Building 23 fast.'" Mingus followed orders. He jumped into his Atomic Energy Commission truck and raced toward Building 23.

Not only the yield size of Hood was classified; so was the fact that despite the Atomic Energy Commission's assurance that it was not testing thermonuclear bombs, Hood was a thermonuclear bomb test. At seventy-four kilotons, it was six times bigger than the bomb dropped on Hiroshima and remains in 2011 the largest bomb ever exploded over the continental United States. The flash from the Hood bomb was visible from Canada to Mexico and from eight hundred miles out at sea. "So powerful was the blast that it was felt and seen over most of the Western United States as it lighted up the pre-dawn darkness," reported the United Press International. It took twenty-five minutes for the nuclear blast wave to reach Los Angeles, 350 miles to the west. "LA Awakened. Flash Seen, Shock Felt Here. Calls Flood Police Switch Board," headlined the *Los Angeles Times*. Right around the time the blast reached Los Angeles, Richard Mingus reached Building 23, a solid concrete bunker where radiation safety officers stayed during the explosions. In the distance, Mingus saw that a large swath of the desert was on fire.

"You know about Delta?" the security officer inside Building 23 asked Mingus.

"I've worked there many times," Mingus said.

"Grab another fella and get out there," the man said. "Find a place with the least amount of radiation and set up a roadblock between the test site and Delta." The Atomic Energy Commission may have moved Area 51 workers off the test site for the nuclear test, but entire buildings full of classified information remained behind. That the facility was not being physically secured by a guard had been an oversight. Now Richard Mingus was being asked to plug that security hole.

Mingus drove quickly up through the test site, heading north toward Area 51. "The whole of Bandit Mountain was on fire," Mingus explains, referring to the low hills between Papoose Lake and Yucca Flat. "You could see individual Joshua trees on fire." Mingus kept on driving, moving as fast as he could while avoiding an accident. But to get to where he needed to go, Mingus had to drive straight through ground zero. "There were huge rocks and boulders in the road sent there by the blast," Mingus explains. "I had my windows rolled up tight and I was driving like hell and my Geiger was screaming. I was worried if I drove too fast and had a wreck in that area, that wouldn't have been good. At guard post three eighty-five, my Geiger counter was chirping like hell. I remember distinctly it was reading eight point five Rs [never considered a safe amount]. We'd already deactivated that post because of the bomb and now it was way too hot to stay there so I drove on over the hill to Area 51."

When Mingus arrived at Groom Lake, his Geiger counter finally settled down. It had been approximately fifty minutes since the bomb had gone off. Having reached forty-eight thousand feet, the mushroom cloud would have already floated over Area 13 and Area 51 by that time. Most likely, it was somewhere over Utah now. "When I pulled into Area 51, it was like a ghost town," Mingus recalls. "I set up a west-facing post. I could see far. Pretty soon, the other guard arrived. He took up the post at the control tower and I stayed in the truck, parked there on the road facing west." Mingus was fewer than ten miles from ground zero, where the Hood bomb had exploded just an hour before. The blast wave had hit Area 51 with such force, it buckled the metal doors on several of the west-facing buildings, including a maintenance hangar and the supply warehouse. Radioactive ash floated down from the sky. And yet, despite the near-constant rain of nuclear fallout, the requirement for security took precedent. Mingus drank water from his five-gallon jug and waited for the smoke from the nuclear bomb to clear. He ate the sandwich that Gloria had made for him and watched the hills burn. After several hours, he took the can of Dinty Moore stew from his lunchbox and opened it with the can opener that Gloria always made sure to pack. Mingus got out of the AEC truck and opened the hood. He set the soup can on the control block and stirred it with a spoon. It didn't take long for the liquid to heat up. Mingus got back in the car and checked to see if his radio was working. "Delta is secure," Mingus said before kicking back to enjoy his stew. For the rest of the day and well into the night, every half hour a voice came over the radio from the control point asking if everything was "okay." Each time, Mingus let his boss know that Groom Lake was secure. He didn't see another soul out there in the desert for the rest of the day. By nightfall, all that was left of the fire were the Joshua trees smoldering on the hills. The land at the test site had been appropriately chosen; mostly it was just creosote bush and sand. The bushes had burned, and the sand, after being subjected to 5,400 degrees Fahrenheit, had fused into little pieces of glass. Between the fallout and the structural damage, Area 51 had become uninhabitable. After Hood, the once-bustling classified facility transformed into a ghost town overnight—not unlike the mining towns that had preceded it a century before. The future of the secret base was, almost literally, up in the air.

CHAPTER SEVEN

From Ghost Town to Boomtown

After the Plumbbob atomic tests rocked Area 51, the CIA base sat like a ghost town. Very little is known about what happened there from the summer of 1957 through the summer of 1959. According to Richard Mingus, a pair of caretakers lived at the Groom Lake facility, a man and his wife. No record of their names has been found. What is known is that after the Plumbbob series effectively shut down operations at Area 51, workers from the Atomic Energy Commission roamed the hills and valleys measuring fallout with Geiger counters in hand. As impossible as it is to imagine in the twenty-first century, in the early days of atomic testing there was no such thing as HAZMAT suits for workers performing tasks in environments laden with WMD. Instead, workers combed the desert floor dressed in white lab coats and work boots, looking for particles of nuclear fallout. According to Atomic Energy Commission documents made public in 1993, this radioactive debris varied in size, from pinhead particles to pencil-size pieces of steel.

Much to the surprise of the nuclear scientists, the atomic weapons tests revealed that sometimes, in the first milliseconds of destruction, the atomic energy actually jettisoned splintered pieces of the bomb tower away from the intense heat, intact, before vaporization could occur. These highly radioactive pieces were then carried aloft in the clouds and deposited down on places like Groom Lake, and Atomic Energy Commission workers could then locate them with magnets. But while workers measured fallout patterns, weapons planners moved ahead with preparations for the next atomic test series, which would take place the following fall. The Operation Hardtack II nuclear test series would prove even bigger than Plumbbob, in terms of the number of tests. From September 12 to October 30, 1958, an astonishing thirty-seven nuclear bombs were exploded—from tops of tall towers, in tunnels and shafts, on the surface of the earth, and hanging from balloons. Areas 3, 5, 7, 8, 9, 12, and 15 served as ground zero for the detonations, all within eighteen miles of Area 51.

All but abandoned by the CIA and left to the elements, the once-bustling Area 51 facility took on a spooky, postapocalyptic feel. Guards from the test site did occasional spot tests, but the classified material had all been moved. While the barren landscape weathered the fallout, the animals observed around Groom Lake suffered terribly. Wild horses, deer, and rabbits roamed around the abandoned hangars and vacant airfields covered with beta radiation burns—the skin lesions caused by radiation poisoning that had plagued so many people and animals in Hiroshima and Nagasaki after the war. It was also during this period that a rare breach of security over Area 51 airspace occurred. On July 28, 1957, a Douglas Aircraft Company employee named Edward K. Current made what he said was an emergency landing on the former U-2 airstrip at Groom Lake. Mr. Current told Atomic Energy Commission security officers who questioned him that he had been on a cross-country training flight when he became lost and ran low on fuel. He was held overnight and released. The following day, the Nevada Test Organization uncharacteristically issued a press release stating that a private pilot had mistakenly landed on the "Watertown landing strip." Mr. Current never made a public statement about his curious visit and remains the only civilian who ever landed at Area 51 uninvited in a private airplane, got out, and roamed around.

Meanwhile, in Washington, DC, Richard Bissell waited for presidential approval to plan more overflights using U-2s stationed at secret CIA facilities overseas. And on the West Coast, in Burbank, California, Lockheed's Kelly Johnson was busy drawing up plans for the secret new spy plane. If Johnson was able to secure the new CIA contract he was working on with Bissell, it would likely mean Lockheed would spend the next decade fulfilling contract work out at Area 51. But what Kelly Johnson needed at this point was a radar cross-section wizard.

It was September of 1957, and Edward Lovick was standing on Lockheed's antenna pattern range tinkering with echo returns when Kelly Johnson approached him for a chat. Lovick, then a thirty-eight-year-old physicist, was known among colleagues as Lockheed's radar man. Radar was still a relatively new science but Lovick knew more about the subject than anyone else at Lockheed at the time.

"Would you like to come work on an interesting project?" the boss asked Lovick. In his eight-and-a-half-year tenure at the company, Lovick had never seen Kelly Johnson before. But standing beside Johnson were William Martin and L. D. MacDonald, two scientists Lovick considered to be brilliant. Martin was Lovick's former boss, and the three men used to work together in the antenna lab. Martin and MacDonald had since disappeared to work on projects inside Building 82, a large, nondescript hangar at the north end of the facility where Lockheed's black operations went on. As for the project that Kelly Johnson was asking Lovick to join, Johnson said it might finish in six weeks. Instead, it lasted thirty-two years. Although Lovick had no idea at the time, he was being invited into Lockheed's classified group, officially called Advanced Development Projects but nicknamed the Skunk Works. In 1957, its primary customer was the CIA.

Lovick was granted his top secret security clearance and briefed on the U-2 aircraft. He learned about the death of test pilot Robert Sieker at Area 51, just four months before. "My first assignment at

Lockheed came as a direct result of this tragedy," Lovick recalls. Sieker's death had inadvertently played a role in the invention of the most significant military application of the twentieth century, and it led Ed Lovick to become known as the grandfather of stealth. What the Boston Group at MIT had attempted to do—add stealth features via paint to an existing airplane—had proved futile. But what Lovick and his team would soon discover was that stealth could be achieved if it was designed as a feature in the early drawing boards.

"The purpose of stealth, or antiradar technology," Lovick explains, "is to keep the enemy from sensing or detecting an aircraft, from tracking it, and therefore from shooting it down. The goal is to trick the enemy's air defenses though camouflage or concealment." Camouflage has been one of the most basic foundations of military strength since man first made spears. In ancient warfare, soldiers concealed themselves from the enemy using tree branches as disguise. Millennia later, American independence was gained partly because the British ignored this fundamental; their bright red coats made them easy targets for a band of revolutionaries in drab, ragtag dress. In the animal kingdom, all species depend on antipredator adaptation for survival, from the chameleon, which defines the idea, to the arctic fox, which turns from brown in summer months to white in winter. Lockheed's U-2s were being tracked over the Soviet Union because they had no camouflage or antiradar technologies, so the Soviets could not only detect the U-2s but also accurately track the spy planes' precise flight paths.

To stay ahead of the Russians, Richard Bissell envisioned a new spy plane that would outfox Soviet radar. The CIA wanted an airplane with a radar cross section so low it would be close to invisible, the theory being that the Russians couldn't object to what they didn't know was there.

The aircraft would be radically different, unlike anything the world had ever seen, or rather, not seen, before. It would beat Soviet advances in radar technology in three fields: height, speed, and stealth. The airplane needed to fly at ninety thousand feet and at a remarkably unprecedented speed of twenty-three hundred miles per hour, or Mach 3. In the late 1950s, for an aircraft to leave the tarmac on its own power and sustain even Mach 2 flight was unheard-of. Speed offered cover. In the event that a Mach 3 aircraft was tracked by radar, that kind of speed would make it extremely difficult to shoot down. By comparison, a U-2, which flew around five hundred miles per hour, would be seen by a Soviet SA-2 missile system approximately ten minutes before it was in shoot-down range, where it would remain for a full five minutes. An aircraft traveling at Mach 3 would be seen by Soviet radar for fewer than a hundred and twenty seconds before it could be fired upon, and it would remain in target range for fewer than twenty seconds. After that twenty-second window closed, the airplane would be too close for a Soviet missile to fire on it. The missile couldn't chase the airplane because, even though the top speed for a missile at the time was Mach 3.5, once a missile gets that far into the upper atmosphere, it loses precision and speed. Shooting down an airplane flying at three times the speed of sound at ninety thousand feet was equivalent to hitting a bullet whizzing by seventeen miles away with another bullet.

Lockheed was confident the speed element was possible, but it wasn't in charge of building the jet engines; the Pratt and Whitney corporation was. Height was achievable; Lockheed had mastered flying at seventy thousand feet with the U-2. Stealth was the feature that would be the most challenging, and it was also the single most important feature of the spy plane to the CIA. To create stealth, Lovick and his team had to master minutiae involving radar returns. Eventually, they'd need a wide-open space and a full-size airplane, which is how Ed Lovick and the Lockheed radar cross-section team became the first group of men after the atomic blast to set up shop at Area 51. But first, they did this inside a room within a hangar at Lockheed.

"Radar works analogous to a bat," Lovick explains. "The bat squeaks and the sound hits a bug. The squeak gets sent back to the bat and the bat measures time and distance to the bug through the echo it receives." So how does one get the bug to *absorb* the squeak? "The way in which to solve the radar problem for us at Lockheed was to create a surface that would redirect radar returns. We needed to send them off in a direction other than back at the Soviet radars. We could also do this by absorbing radar returns, like a diaper absorbs liquid. In theory it was simple. But it turned out to be quite a complicated problem to solve."

Lovick had been solving problems ever since he was a child growing up in Falls City, Nebraska, during the Depression—for instance, the time he wanted to learn to play the piano but did not want to disturb his family while he practiced. "I took the piano apart and reconfigured its parts to suppress the sound. Then I sent the vibrations from the strings electronically through a small amplifier to a headset I wore." This was hardly something most fourteen-year-old children were doing in 1933. Four years later, at the age of eighteen, Lovick published his first article on radar, for *Radio-Craft* magazine. Inspired to think he might have a career in radar technology, he wrote to Lockheed Corporation in faraway California asking for a job. Lockheed turned him down. So he took a minimum-wage job as a radio repairman at a local Montgomery Ward, something that, at the age of ninety-one, he still considers a serendipitous career move. "What I learned at Montgomery Ward, in an employment capacity that today some might perceive as a dead-end job, would later play an important role in my future spy plane career." Namely, that there is as much to learn from what doesn't work as from what does.

To learn how to outfox radar, Lovick returned to the trial-and-error principles he'd first cultivated as a child. He set about designing and overseeing the building of Lockheed's first anechoic chamber to test scale models of Skunk Works' proposed new spy plane. "An anechoic chamber is an enclosed space covered in energy-absorbing materials, the by-product of which is noiselessness," Lovick explains. It is so quiet inside the chamber that if a person stands alone inside its four walls, he can hear the blood flowing inside his body. "Particularly loud is the blood in one's head," Lovick notes. Only in such a strictly controlled environment could the physicist and his team accurately test how a one-twentieth-scale model would react to radar beams aimed at it. Lockheed's wood shop built tiny airplane models for the physicists, not unlike the models kids play with. Lovick and the team painstakingly applied radar-absorbing material to the models then strung them up in the anechoic chamber to test. Based on the radar echo results, the shape and design of the spy plane would change. So would its name. Over the next several months, the design numbers for the Archangel-1 went up incrementally, through eleven major changes. This is why the final and official Agency designation for the airplane was Archangel-12, or A-12 for short.

While imaging and then designing Lockheed's new spy plane, Edward Lovick accompanied Kelly Johnson on trips to Washington, DC. There, the men met with Richard Bissell and President Eisenhower's science advisers to deliver progress reports and attend briefings on the aircraft. President Eisenhower called it "the Big One." On these trips to DC, Bissell, whom Lovick knew only as Mr. B., would pepper Kelly Johnson with technical questions about stealth, or "low observables," which Lovick was responsible for answering. "We shared test data from the chamber work, which was going along fine," Lovick recalls. "But the Customer always wanted better. No matter how low we felt our observables were, the Customer always wanted them to be lower." This meant more work. In a final design stage, Skunk Works aerodynamicists and the radar team added downward slopes, called chines, on either side of the body of the aircraft, making the airplane look like a cobra with wings. With the plane's underbelly now flat, its radar cross section was reduced by an astonishing 90 percent. Still, Richard Bissell wanted a spy plane closer to invisible. Lovick needed a full-scale laboratory. Johnson got an idea: return to Area 51.

Johnson had met privately with an unnamed official to try to convince the CIA to allow a small cadre of Lockheed scientists and engineers to return to Area 51 for proof-of-concept tests. There and only there, Johnson argued, could his group do what needed to be done to meet the CIA's grueling radar-evasion demands. During this intense design phase, and despite the secrecy of the project, Lockheed was not the only contractor bidding on the job. Who exactly would land the CIA's contract to build the U-2's replacement airplane was still up in the air. The federal government liked to foster competition between defense contractors, which meant aerospace contractor Convair was also in play, hoping to secure the CIA's hundred-million-dollar contract for itself. Johnson knew reducing the aircraft's observables was his best shot at getting the contract. Permission was granted, and in the late summer of 1959, fifty Skunk Works employees returned to Area 51.

The days of measuring child-size airplane models in a tiny chamber in Burbank were over. The time had come to put a full-scale model of the world's first stealth airplane to the test. "On 31 March we started to build a full scale mockup and elevation device to raise the mockup 50 feet in the air for radar tests," Johnson wrote in documents declassified in July 2007. What Johnson was imagining in this "elevation device" would eventually become the legendary Area 51 pylon, or radar test pole.

Lockheed engineers brought with them a mock-up of the aircraft so detailed that it could easily be mistaken for the real thing. For accurate radar results, the model had to represent everything the real aircraft would be, from the size of the rivets to the slope on the chines. It had taken more than four months to build. When it was done, the wooden airplane, with its 102-foot-long fuselage and 55-foot-long wooden wings, was packed up in a wooden crate in preparation for its journey out to Area 51. Getting it there was a daunting task, and the road from Burbank to Area 51 needed to be prepared in advance. The transport crate had been disguised to look like a generic wide load, but the size made it considerably wider than wide. Crews were dispatched before the trip to remove obstructing road signs and to trim overhanging trees. In a few places along the highway, the road had to be made level.

What kind of cleanup went on at Area 51 before the arrival of Lockheed's radar cross-section crew remains unknown. Twelve months had passed since the last atomic bomb had been exploded next door; it was code-named Titania, like the mischievous queen of the fairies from Shakespeare's *A Midsummer Night's Dream.* If there was a formal decontamination of Area 51 or a summation of what the radiation levels were and whether it was safe to return, those details remain classified. As it was, the radar test system Lockheed set up was only temporary. The CIA did not yet have presidential approval to proceed with the A-12. "I had no more than 50 people on the project," Johnson wrote in a document called *History of the Oxcart by the Builder,* declassified in 2007. The small group of Skunk Workers bunked down in the Quonset huts where the U-2 pilots and engineers had once lived.

Beginning in the fall of 1959, a Lockheed C-47 shuttled engineers and mechanics from Burbank to Area 51 on Monday mornings and returned them home to their families late Friday afternoons. It was Ed Lovick's first experience working at what he'd been told was Paradise Ranch. Because of Lovick's key role in this phase of the project, he was transported in a Lockheed twin-engine Cessna, usually alone with the pilot. He disliked the commute because the fumes from the Cessna made him queasy. But once he arrived and deplaned he would lose himself in the intensity of the radar work going on. In Burbank, in the silence of the anechoic chamber, Lovick had been testing airplane models the size of his shoe. This full-size mock-up would reveal the results of two years' worth of chamber work. "The only way to get accurate information of how a full-size aircraft would perform in radar testing was to subject the full size mock-up of the A-12 to radar beams," Lovick explains.

At the edge of the dry lake bed, scientists mounted the airplane on the fifty-five-foot-high pole, centered in a concrete pad that would rise up and down from an underground chamber in the desert floor. "A control room was located underground to one side of the pad. An anemometer and a wind-direction weather vane were located near the edge of the pad, away from the line of sight," Lovick recalls. The radar antennas, manned and monitored by EG&G, were located a mile away from the pole. "The nose of the mock-up would be tipped down so the radar would see the air-plane's belly, the same way that Soviet radar would see it. It was an elaborate and time-consuming process," Lovick recalls. "The mock-up that was tested on the pole had to be housed in a hangar on the base at least a mile away. It was carried out and back on special carts."

In late 1959, the CIA did not know how far the Soviets had advanced their satellite technology—whether they were capable of taking photographs from space yet. The CIA's espionage concerns further complicated the radar work at Area 51. Each member of Lovick's crew carried in his pocket a small chart indicating Soviet satellite schedules. This often meant working odd hours, including at night. "It also made for a lot of technicians running around," Lovick explains. "Satellites passed overhead often. Getting an air-craft up on the radar test pole took eighteen minutes. It took another eighteen minutes to get it back down. That left only a set amount of time to shoot radar at it and take data recordings." As soon as technicians were done, they took the aircraft down and whisked it away into its hangar.

What Lovick remembered most about life on the Ranch during this period, besides the work going on around the pole, was how intense the weather was. At night, workers needed to bundle up in heavy coats and wool hats. But during the day, temperatures could reach 120 degrees. "Once, I saw a coyote chasing a rabbit and they were both walking," Lovick recalls.

In December of 1959, the president was briefed on the status of the A-12. Eager to move ahead, Eisenhower was also aware of the hundred-million-dollar check he would be writing to Lockheed from his discretionary funds for a fleet of twelve spy planes. Eisenhower told Bissell he had decided to request that Lockheed deliver results on a last proof-of-concept test, one that focused specifically on radar-evasion technology. Bissell had been informed that Lockheed's A-12 would appear on enemy radar as bigger than a bird but smaller than a man. But he had not yet been told about a problem in the aircraft's low observables that Lovick and the team had been unable to remedy while testing the mock-up out at Area 51. Lovick explains: "The exhaust ducts from the two huge jet engines that powered the aircraft were proving impossible to make stealthy. Obviously, we couldn't cover the openings with camouflage coating. During testing, the radar waves would go into the spaces where the engines would be, echo around, and come out like water being sprayed into a can. We'd tried screens and metallic grating. Nothing worked." Kelly Johnson believed the CIA would accept this design weakness. "Ike wants an airplane from Mandrake the magician," Johnson told the team and added that the president would settle for something less. Johnson was wrong.

With the president's final request on the table, settling for something less was no longer an option. On a final trip to Washington, DC, Kelly Johnson was going to have to explain to Bissell the exact nature of the design problem. "The meeting took place at an old ramshackle building in Washington, DC, inside a conference room with a mirrored wall," Lovick remembers. "Killian and [Edwin] Din Land were there, so was 'Mr. B.'" Kelly Johnson told the CIA about the problem with camouflaging the A-12's engine exhaust, how it was a weakness in the airplane's overall concept of stealth. "Bissell became furious. Throughout the process, I felt so comfortable working for Kelly, I don't think I realized how serious the situation was until that meeting. Bissell threatened to cancel the entire contract if someone didn't come up with a solution." It was a tense moment. "I knew that more than a hundred men had been lost trying to look over the fence. Shot down over Russia, killed, or listed as missing in training missions. I became aware there was a serious problem of information gathering. Before that, most of my concerns were as a scientist in a lab. [In that moment] I realized how poorly things were going in the world outside the lab. How important this airplane was, and that problem with the engine exhaust needed to be solved."

There in the conference room, Edward Lovick decided to speak up about an idea he had been considering for decades, "and that was how to ionize gas," he says, referring to the scientific process by which the electrical charge of an atom is fundamentally changed. "I suggested that by adding the chemical compound cesium to the fuel, the exhaust would be ionized, likely masking it from radar. I had suggested cesium would be the best source of free electrons because, in the gaseous state, it would be the easiest to ionize." If this complicated ionization worked—and Lovick believed it would—the results would be like putting a sponge in a can and running a hose into it. Instead of being bounced back, the radar return from the engines would be absorbed. "Bissell loved the idea," says Lovick, adding that the suggestion was endorsed heartily by several of the customer's consultants. An enthusiastic discussion ensued among the president's science advisers, whom Lovick sensed had very little understanding of what it was he was proposing. In the end, the results would be up to Lovick to determine; later, his theory indeed proved correct. Those results remain a key component of stealth and are still classified as of 2011.

Lockheed kept the contract. Lovick got a huge Christmas bonus, and the A-12 got a code name, Oxcart. It was ironic, an oxcart being one of the slowest vehicles on Earth and the Oxcart being the fastest. On January 26, 1960, Bissell notified Johnson that the CIA was authorizing the delivery of twelve airplanes. The specs were laid out: Mach, 3.2 (2,064 knots, or .57 miles per second); range, 4,120 nautical miles; altitude, 84,500–97,600 feet. The aircraft was going to be five times faster than the U-2 and would fly a full three miles higher than the U-2. Skunk Works would move into production, and a facility needed to be readied for flight tests. There was only one place equipped to handle a spy plane that needed to be hidden from the world, including members of Congress, and that was Area 51.

It was January of 1960, and for the first time since the atomic bombs had shuttered the place, in the summer of 1957, Area 51 was back in business. Only this time, the CIA and the Air Force were comanaging an aircraft that was bigger, faster, and budgeted at nearly five times the cost of the U-2. The program would involve more than ten times as many people, and, as it had with the U-2, the CIA hired work crews from next door at the Nevada Test Site, men with top secret security clearances already in place. There were two immediate requirements for the new airplane: a much longer runway and a 1.32-million-gallon fuel farm. The construction of a new runway and the fuel farm began first. Millions of gallons of cement had to be hauled in, along with enough building materials to construct a small city. Trucking this kind of volume through the test site would draw too much attention to the project, so a new road was built, allowing access to Groom Lake from the north. Contractors worked under cover of night, resurfacing eighteen miles of highway through the tiny town of Rachel, Nevada, so fuel trucks carrying five hundred thousand gallons of specially modified fuel each month would not crack the roadbed with their heavy loads.

The A-12 Oxcart was a flying fuel tank. It held eleven thousand gallons, which made the tanks the largest portion of the airplane. The fuel had requirements the likes of which were previously unknown. During the refueling process, which would happen in the air, at lower altitudes and lower airspeeds, the temperature of the fuel would drop to −90 degrees Fahrenheit. At Mach 3, it would heat up to 285 degrees Fahrenheit, a temperature at which conventional fuels boil and explode. To allow for this kind of fluctuation, JP-7 was designed to maintain such a low vapor pressure that a person could not light it with a match. This made for many practical jokes, with those in the know dropping lit matches into a barrel of JP-7 to make those not in the know duck and run for cover. It also required extreme precision of the man who was chosen to be in charge of the fuels team, Air Force sergeant Harry Martin.

This meant Martin was one of the first men to return to the nearly deserted secret base. "Winters were freezing on Groom Lake," Martin recalls, with temperatures dropping into the low teens. "I lived in a dilapidated trailer heated with kerosene. I've never worked so hard in my life as I did that first winter at Area 51." Martin had no idea what he was working on but gathered it was important when he was woken up in the middle of the night by a two-star general. "He said we had an important task. I thought to myself, 'If a general is up working at this hour, then I'm up too.' Working at Area 51 was the highlight of my career."

The A-12 was original in every way, meaning it had unforeseen needs that came up at every turn. The eighty-five-hundred-foot runway had to be created piece by piece because the standard Air Force runways would not work when it came to Oxcart. The longitudinal sections had to be made much larger, and the joints holding them together needed to run parallel to the aircraft's roll, not horizontal, as was standard with Air Force planes. Large, new aircraft hangars went into construction, ready to conceal what would become known as the CIA's "own little air force." Getting the Oxcart to fly would involve its own small fleet of aircraft: F-104 chase planes, proficiency-training airplanes, transport planes, and a helicopter for search and rescue.

Because the Oxcart would fly five times as fast as the U-2, the Agency needed a lot more restricted airspace at Area 51. Flying at speeds of 2,200 miles per hour, an Oxcart pilot would need a 186-mile swath just to make a U-turn. This meant an additional 38,400 acres of land around the base were withdrawn from public access, allowing the Federal Aviation Administration to extend the restricted airspace from a 50-square-mile box to 440 square miles. FAA employees were instructed not to ask questions about anything flying above forty thousand feet. The same was true at NORAD, the North American Aerospace Defense Command.

While the base was being readied for delivery of the twelve aircraft, pole testing continued on the lake bed at Area 51. All the while, the CIA feared the Russians were watching from space. Across the world, at NII-88, Sergei Korolev had designed a Soviet spy satellite called Object D, but the CIA did not know what exactly it was capable of. Also under way was a follow-on espionage platform called Zenit, a modified version of the Vostok spacecraft that had been equipped with cameras to photograph American military installations from space. The Russians took great delight in rubbing what they learned in the face of the State Department. Once, using diplomatic channels, they passed a simple sketch of the exact shape of Lockheed's top secret airplane to the CIA, whose employees were baffled as to how the enemy could have known such a thing, in view of the fact that operations personnel had been very careful to avoid the orbiting Soviet snoopers. Was there a double agent among them? The CIA, ever paranoid about KGB infiltration, worried in private that there could be a spy inside Area 51. Lovick finally figured it out: the Russians were using infrared satellites. In the desert heat, which could reach 125 degrees Fahrenheit in the summer, the mock-up of the aircraft left a heat signature as it sat on the tarmac while technicians were waiting to hoist it up on the test pole. The sketch reflected that.

While the Russians watched from space, the CIA continued to monitor and translate the Soviets' reaction to its aerial reconnaissance program. Memos from Soviet chief marshal of artillery S. Varentsov revealed the Russians' growing furor over the speed at which the United States was advancing its spy planes. Varentsov lamented that the Russians' own program had barely moved beyond technology from World War II. On the one hand, this was positive news for the CIA. In the world of overhead espionage, the Russians had been forced into a defensive posture. But it was also a double-edged sword. The Soviets couldn't advance their aerial reconnaissance program because so much of their efforts went into advancing surface-to-air missile technology. If the capitalist foes were going to continue to fly over Mother Russia, Nikita Khrushchev was hell-bent on shooting them down.

CHAPTER EIGHT

Cat and Mouse Becomes Downfall

Francis Gary Powers never slept well the night before a mission flight. When his 2:00 a.m. wake-up call came on May 1, 1960, Powers felt particularly anxious. His flight had already been postponed twice. It was sweltering hot in the ancient city of Peshawar, Pakistan, and Powers had spent the night on a cot in an aircraft hangar inside the CIA's secret facility there. Between the intense heat and the noise, sleep had been sporadic. The false starts had added a layer of uncertainty into the mix. Gary Powers got out of bed and took a shower. May was the hottest month in Pakistan. It was before 5:00 a.m. and yet the sun was already up, cooking the air. After only a few minutes, Powers would be drenched in sweat again. He dressed and ate his breakfast, all the while thinking about the radical mission that lay ahead. The Agency had never attempted to fly all the way across the Soviet Union before, from the southern border near Pakistan to the northern border near the Arctic Circle. From there, Powers would fly his U-2 to a secret CIA base in Norway and land. No Agency pilot had ever taken off and landed at two different bases in a U-2.

This overflight was particularly important to the CIA. Powers would gather valuable photographic information on two key sites. The first was the Tyuratam Cosmodrome, the Soviets' busiest missile launch base. Tyuratam was Russia's Cape Canaveral, the place from where Sputnik had been launched. For years the CIA was aware of only one launchpad at Tyuratam. Now there were rumored to be two, and a U-2 overflight in April revealed preparations for an upcoming launch—of what exactly, the CIA wanted to know. After Tyuratam, Powers would fly across Siberia and head up to a facility at Plesetsk, 186 miles south of the city of Archangelsk, in the Arctic Circle. Plesetsk was alleged to be the Soviet's newest missile-launch facility and was dangerously close to Alaska. Powers's flight would cover a record 3,800 miles, 2,900 of which would be inside the Soviet Union. He would spend nine nerve-racking hours over enemy territory. That would be a lot of time for the Soviets to try to shoot him down. The reverse would have been unthinkable. Imagine a Russian spy plane flying unmolested over the entire United States, from the East Coast to the West, snapping photographs that could provide details at two-and-a-half-foot increments from seventy thousand feet up.

After breakfast, Powers sat in the hangar waiting for a final weather check. He had already sweated through his long johns. Mother Nature always had the final say. For Powers, a slight wind change meant the schedule for his mission flight that morning was disrupted yet again. Not enough to cancel the mission, but enough so that his navigational maps had to be quickly corrected. The waiting was agonizing. It was also necessary. If his photographic targets were covered in clouds, images from the U-2's camera would be useless. The navigators needed to calculate when and if the weather would clear. As Powers sat waiting it out, his commanding officer, Colonel Shelton, crossed the cement floor and indicated he wanted to speak with him.

Colonel Shelton extended his hand and opened his palm. At the center was a large silver coin. "Do you want the silver dollar?" the colonel asked Powers. What Shelton was offering was no ordinary American coin. It was a CIA suicide gadget, designed to conceal a tiny poison pin hidden inside. The pin, which the pilot could find in his pocket by rubbing a finger gently around the coin's edge, was coated with a sticky brown substance called curare, the paralytic poison found in lethal Amazonian blowpipes. One prick of the poison pin and a pilot would be dead in seconds.

Gary Powers was one of the Agency's most accomplished U-2 pilots. He had flown a total of twenty-seven missions, including ones over China. He had once suffered a potentially fatal flameout over the Soviet Union and managed to survive. On many occasions he had been offered the suicide pill, and on each previous mission he had said no. But on May 1, 1960, Powers unexpectedly accepted the pin from Colonel Shelton, then slid it into the pocket of his flight suit. Later, Powers would wonder if he'd had a premonition of what was to come.

At 5:20 a.m., it was go time. The personnel equipment sergeant strapped Powers into the cockpit of the U-2. Two men held a shirt over Powers's head to protect him from the blaring sun and the heat while he went over radio codes with the Agency officer. Pilots knew never to use their radio while flying over denied territory, but they listened carefully for click codes being sent to them. A single click meant proceed. Three clicks meant turn around and head back to base. From under his heavy helmet, sweat poured down Powers's face, making him feel helpless. Finally Colonel Shelton came out for a briefing. Powers's overflight was now awaiting final approval by President Eisenhower himself. A last-minute delay like this had never happened before and Powers became convinced the flight would again be canceled for another day. Instead, at 6:20 a.m. a signal came from an intelligence officer. The two men who had been holding the shirt over Powers's head climbed down off the ladders; the personnel equipment sergeant closed the canopy, sealing him into the airplane; and Gary Powers was cleared for takeoff.

Up he went. After the U-2's extraordinarily steep and fast climb, Powers within minutes reached an altitude where it was 60 degrees below zero outside. No longer sweating, Powers switched on the U-2 autopilot mechanism so he could make notes in his flight log. Waiting was always a drag, offset immediately by the excitement of being up in the air. Using a pen, Powers wrote: "Aircraft #360, Sortie Number 4154, 0126 Greenwich Mean Time." He listened for the one-click signal over the radio, which would let him know he was good to proceed. The click came. Powers settled in for what was supposed to be a total of thirteen hours of flying time. His overflight would be the Agency's deepest penetration into the Soviet Union so far.

In Moscow, two thousand miles to the east, it was still dark outside when Soviet premier Nikita Khrushchev sat upright in bed, awakened by a ringing telephone. Defense minister Marshal Malinovsky was on the line. A high-flying aircraft had crossed the border over Afghanistan and was headed toward central Russia, Malinovsky said. Khrushchev became enraged. Today of all days. May 1 was Russia's national holiday. The streets were festooned with banners and ribbons for the May Day parade. This could mean only one thing, Khrushchev later told his son, Sergei. Eisenhower was ridiculing him again. The Soviet premier's Achilles' heel was his lack of formal education; he'd dropped out of school to work in the coal mines after the fourth grade. With his poor reading and writing skills, Khrushchev hated feeling that a more educated world leader was trying to make him appear the fool.

The Americans were especially duplicitous regarding holidays, Khrushchev believed. Four years earlier, on the Fourth of July, the Americans had double-crossed him with their first overflight of the U-2. If that overflight was a kick in the ribs, today's overflight was a sharp poke in the eye. "An uncomfortable situation was shaping up," Russian colonel Alexander Orlov explained in a historical review of the incident written for the CIA in 1998. Orlov, who spent most of his forty-six-year military career with Russia's air defense force, had been an eyewitness to the event; he was seated at the command post in Moscow when Gary Powers was shot down. "The May Day parade was scheduled to get underway at mid-morning and leaders of the party, the government and the Armed

Forces were to be present as usual," Orlov explained. "In other words, at a time when a major parade aimed at demonstrating Soviet military prowess was about to begin, a not-yet–identified foreign aircraft was flying over the heart of the country and Soviet air defenses appeared unable to shoot it down."

Not if Khrushchev had his way. "Shoot down the plane by whatever means," he shouted back at his defense minister. All across the country, the Soviet Air Force went on alert. Generals scrambled their fighter jets to go after Powers. In Siberia, officers from Soviet Air Defense Forces were summoned to their command posts with orders to shoot down the American spy. It was a matter of national pride. The orders came from Nikita Khrushchev himself.

Tucked snugly into the tiny cockpit of his U-2, Gary Powers sailed along. He was one and a half hours into his flight. The weather was proving to be worse than expected but clicks on the radio system indicated that he was to proceed. Over the majestic Hindu Kush mountain range, clouds rose all the way up to the top of the twenty-five-thousand-foot peaks, and the cloud cover made it difficult for Powers to determine exactly where he was on the map. Flying at seventy thousand feet meant the sky above him was pitch-black. Under normal circumstances he would have used the stars to determine where on the globe he was, but today his celestial navigation computations were unreliable—they'd been laid out for a 6:00 a.m. departure, not a 6:26 a.m. one. And so, with only a compass and sextant to keep him on track, Powers flew on. Spotting a break in the clouds, he determined his location to be just southeast of the Aral Sea, high above present-day Uzbekistan. Thirty miles to the north lay Powers's first target: the Tyuratam Cosmodrome.

Realizing he was slightly off course, Powers was correcting back when suddenly he spotted the condensation trail of a jet aircraft below him. "It was moving fast, at supersonic speed, paralleling my course, though in the opposite direction," Powers explained in his memoir *Operation Overflight*, published in 1970. Five minutes passed and now he knew at least one MiG was on his tail. Then he spotted another aircraft flying in the same direction as he was. "I was sure now they were tracking me on radar, vectoring in and relaying my headings to the aircraft" below him. But the MiG was so far below his U-2, it did not pose a real threat. Protected by height, Powers flew on. He felt confident he was out of harm's way. First he passed over the Ural Mountains, once considered the natural boundary between the East and the West. He headed on toward Sverdlovsk, which was situated thirteen hundred miles inside Russia. Before the Communists took over, Sverdlovsk was called Yekaterinburg. It was there in 1918 that Czar Nicholas II and his family were lined up against a kitchen wall and shot, setting off the Communist Revolution that had made the Cold War a reality. To the Communists, the city of Sverdlovsk played an important role in the Soviet military-industrial complex, a place where tanks and rockets were built. It was also home to the Soviets' secret bioweapons program, which on the date of Powers's flight was not yet known to the CIA.

Nearing Sverdlovsk, Powers made a ninety-degree turn. He headed toward what appeared to be an airfield not marked on his map. Suddenly, large thunderclouds appeared, obscuring his view. He switched his cameras on. Powers had no idea that he was about to photograph a secret facility called Kyshtym 40, which produced nuclear material and also assembled weapons. Kyshtym 40 was as valuable to Russia as Los Alamos and Sandia combined were to the Americans.

On the ground, a surface-to-air missile battalion tasked with guarding Kyshtym 40 had been tracking Powers's flight. At exactly 8:53 local time, the air defense battalion commander there gave the official word. "Destroy target," the commander said. A missile from an SA-2 fired into the air at Mach 3. Inside his airplane, Gary Powers was making notes for the official record—altitude, time, instrument readings—when he suddenly felt a dull thump. All around him, his plane became engulfed in a bright orange flash of light. "A violent movement shook the plane, flinging me all over the cockpit," Powers later wrote. "I assumed both wings had come off. What was left of the plane began spinning, only upside down, the nose pointing upward toward the sky." As the U-2 spun out of control, Powers's pressure suit inflated, wedging him into the nose of the airplane. The U-2 was crashing. He needed to get out. Thrown forward as he was, if he pushed the button to engage the ejection seat, both of his legs would be severed. Powers struggled, impossibly, against gravity. He needed to get out of the airplane and he needed to hit the button that would trigger an explosion to destroy the airplane once he was gone, but he was acutely aware that he couldn't get out of the airplane without cutting off his own legs. For a man who rarely felt fear, Gary Powers was on the edge of panic.

Suddenly, out of the chaos, three words came to him: *Stop and think.* An old pilot friend had once said that if he ever got in a jam, all he had to remember was to "stop and think." His thoughts traveled back to his old training days at Area 51, back when the U-2 didn't have an ejection seat. Back when escaping from the U-2 was the pilot's job, not a mechanical one. Reaching up, Powers unlocked the airplane canopy. It flew off and sailed into the darkness. Instantly, the centrifugal force of the spinning airplane sucked him out into the atmosphere. He was free at last; all he needed to do was deploy his parachute. Then, to his horror, he realized that he was still attached to the airplane by his oxygen hoses. Powers tried to think through his options, but the g-forces were too great. There was nothing he could do anymore. His fate was out of his hands. He blacked out.

Nearly two thousand miles away, at a National Security Agency listening post in Turkey, NSA operators eavesdropped on Soviet radar operators at Kyshtym 40 as operators there tried to shoot Gary Powers's U-2 out of the sky. The NSA had participated in many U-2 missions before. It was their job to equip CIA planes with listening systems, special recorders that gathered electronic intelligence, or ELINT. The NSA operators knew something was wrong the moment they heard a Soviet MiG pilot, the one who was chasing Powers from below, talking to the missile operators at Kyshtym 40. "He's turning left," the MiG pilot said, helping the missile operator to target Powers's exact location. Just a few moments later, NSA operators heard Kyshtym 40 say that Powers's U-2 had disappeared from their radar screens.

NSA immediately sent a message to the White House marked CRITIC. Meanwhile, in the Soviet command post in Moscow, Russian colonel Alexander Orlov received an urgent report from Siberia: the American spy plane had been shot down. A missile had been fired and the target had disappeared from radar screen. The news was phoned to Khrushchev, who demanded physical proof. The White House sent a message to the CIA that was received by Bissell's special assistant, Bob King. "Bill Bailey did not come home" was how Richard Bissell learned of the incident, in code.

Over Sverdlovsk, Francis Gary Powers was free-falling through the atmosphere. Somehow, he had detached from the spinning airplane. "My body [was] just falling perfectly free. It was a pleasant, exhilarating feeling," Powers would later recall. It felt "even better than floating in a swimming pool." His parachute deployed, and Powers floated into a wide, grassy field. His thoughts during the last ten thousand feet before the ground were sharp and clear. "Everything was cold, quiet, serene. There was no sensation of falling. It was as if I were hanging in the sky." A large section of the aircraft floated by, "twisting and fluttering like a leaf." Below him, the countryside looked beautiful. There were forests, lakes, roads, and small villages. The landscape reminded him of Virginia in the spring. As Powers floated down toward Earth, he noticed a small car driving down a dirt road alongside him, as if following his course. Finally, he made contact with the ground. The car stopped and men were helping him. One assisted with his chute. Another man helped him to his feet. A third man reached over to Powers's survival pack and took his pistol. A crowd of approximately fifty people had gathered around. The men motioned for Powers to follow them. They loaded him into the front seat of a truck and began driving.

The men seemed friendly. One of them offered Powers a cigarette. The emblem on the cigarette pack was that of a dog. Taking it, Powers realized the incredible irony of it all. The brand was Laika, and its emblem was the world's first space dog. Laika had flown inside Sputnik 2, the second Russian satellite to be launched from the Tyuratam Cosmodrome, the CIA target that Powers had photographed a little over an hour before. Gary Powers sat back and smoked the cigarette, noting how remarkably like an American cigarette it was.

With the U-2 spy plane and the SA-2 missile system, the Americans and the Soviets had been playing a game of cat and mouse: constant pursuit, near captures, and repeated escapes. Now that game was over. Powers, like the mouse, had been caught. But there was a second, even greater catastrophe in the works. When the White House staff learned Powers's U-2 had been shot down, they assumed he was dead. This was an assumption based on CIA "facts." Richard Bissell had personally assured the president that in the unlikely event that an SA-2 missile was able to reach a U-2 and shoot it down, the pilot would not survive. "We believed that if a U-2 was shot down over Soviet territory, all the Russians would have was the wreckage of an aircraft," Bissell later explained. And so, believing Gary Powers was dead, the White House denied that the airplane was on any kind of espionage mission, in opposition to Khrushchev's very public accusation. For five days, the White House claimed that Gary Powers had been gathering high-altitude weather data for the National Advisory Committee for Aeronautics, or NACA.

But Khrushchev had evidence, which he would soon make public. With great bravado, on May 5, he gathered all thirteen hundred members of the Soviet parliament inside the Great Kremlin Palace speaking hall and addressed them from the stage. The United States has been making a fool of Mother Russia, Khrushchev declared. The Americans had been sending spy planes over the Soviet Union for nearly four years. To underscore the significance of what had happened, Khrushchev gave a bold analogy. "Just imagine what would have happened had a Soviet aircraft appeared over New York, Chicago or Detroit? That would mean the outbreak of war!" Amid gasps of horror, Khrushchev explained how the Soviet Union had first used diplomatic channels to protest the spy flights. That he had called upon the U.N. Security Council to take action, but nothing was done. Just four days earlier, Khrushchev explained, on May 1, yet another illegal espionage mission had occurred. Only this time the Soviets had succeeded in shooting down the spy plane. The audience broke into wild cheers. Then came the heart of the matter in the form of a question. It was also Khrushchev's bait. "Who sent this aircraft across the Soviet frontier?" he asked. "Was it the American Commander-in-Chief who, as everyone knows, is the president? Or was this aggressive act performed by Pentagon militarists without the president's knowledge? If American military men can take such action on their own, the world should be greatly concerned." By now, Khrushchev's audience members were stomping their feet.

Halfway across the world, President Eisenhower continued to have no idea that Gary Powers was alive and had been talking to his captors. All the White House and the CIA knew was that the Soviets had a wrecked U-2 in their possession. Khrushchev had laid a dangerous trap, one in which President Eisenhower got caught. The White House sent its press officer Walter Bonney to the press room to greet journalists and to tell the nation a lie. Gary Powers's weather-sampling airplane was supposed to be flying over Turkey. Instead, it had gone astray. Two days later, on May 7, Khrushchev sprung his trap. "Comrades," he told the parliament, who'd been gathered for a second revelatory speech. "I must let you in on a secret." He smiled. "When I made my report two days ago I deliberately refrained from mentioning that we have the remains of the plane and we also have the pilot who is quite alive and kicking," Khrushchev said. For the United States, it was a diplomatic disaster of the worst order.

The president was trapped. Were he to deny knowing what his "militarists" were up to, he would appear uninformed by his own military. Were he to admit that he had in fact personally authorized Powers's flight, it would become clear he'd lied earlier when he claimed the downed airplane had been conducting weather research, not espionage. So despondent was the commander in chief about his untenable position that when he walked into the Oval Office two days later, he told his secretary Ann Whitman, "I would like to resign." Spying on Russia and defying Soviet airspace was one thing; lying about it after being caught red-handed made the president look like a liar in the eyes of the world. In 1960, American presidents were expected to be truth tellers; there was no public precedent for lying.

Khrushchev demanded an apology from his nemesis. Eisenhower wouldn't bow. Apologizing would only open Pandora's box. There were too many overflights to make them transparent. There had been at least twenty-four U-2 flights over Russia and hundreds more bomber overflights by General LeMay. To reveal the dangerous game of cat and mouse that had been going on in secret—at a time when thermonuclear weapons on both sides were ready to fly—would likely shock and frighten people more than having a president who lied. A national poll revealed that more than half of adult Americans believed they were more likely to die in a thermonuclear war with the Russians than of old age. So Eisenhower made the decision to keep the focus on Gary Powers's flight only and admit that he personally had authorized it. This was "the first time any nation had publicly admitted it was engaged in espionage," noted Eisenhower's lead U-2 photo interpreter at the time, Dino Brugioni.

Khrushchev could play the game too. And he did so by making a dangerous, offensive move. By the summer of 1960, he had authorized a Soviet military base to be set up in Cuba. The island, just ninety miles off the coast of Florida, was in America's backyard. Khrushchev's plan was to put nuclear warheads in striking distance of Washington, DC. In this way, Soviet missiles could be launched from Havana and obliterate the nation's capital in just twenty-five minutes' time. Khrushchev was showing Eisenhower that he could play cat and mouse too.

★   ★   ★

Immediately after Gary Powers had been shot down in his U-2 and picked up by the Soviets, he was flown from Sverdlovsk to Moscow, where he was put in a cell inside Lubyanka Prison, which doubled as headquarters for the KGB. There, his interrogation began. Powers had already decided on a tactic. He'd tell the Russians the truth, but "with definite limitation." The KGB wanted to know about Area 51. Where had he trained to fly the U-2? Powers was asked. According to Powers's memoir, he told the KGB that training took place at a base on the West Coast called Watertown. Powers wrote that the Soviets believed Watertown was located in Arizona and that they produced a map of the state, asking him to mark Watertown's exact location. Whether the Soviets were playing a game with Powers or whether he was telling his readers the truth but "with definite limitation" remains unclear. Either way, trial transcripts from August of 1960, declassified by the CIA in 1985, revealed that the Soviets knew exactly where Watertown was and that it was located inside the Nevada Test Site. During Powers's trial, Soviet procurator-general Rudenko asked his comrade judges if they were familiar with "the deposition of the accused Powers which he gave in the preliminary investigations and here in court on the preparations for flights in the U-2 aircraft at the Las Vegas firing range (poligon) in the Nevada desert," and then he fingered the base as being used by the CIA for "the training in the use of special reconnaissance aircraft." Not before the publication of this book has it been understood that the KGB clearly knew about Area 51 during the Powers trial.

Further, the trial revealed that the Soviets also had a much clearer picture of the inner workings of the American military-industrial complex and its defense-contracting system than the CIA had previously known. Rudenko was able to name "Lockheed company" as the manufacturer of the U-2. He argued that the existence of the "Las Vegas firing range," aka Area 51, and the Lockheed spy plane exemplified what he called a "criminal conspiracy" between "a major American capitalist company, an espionage and reconnaissance center, and the military of America." In his speech to the USSR International Affairs Committee, Rudenko had correctly identified the three players in the triangle of Area 51: defense contractors, the intelligence community, and the Pentagon.

After a three-day trial, the Soviets determined that Gary Powers, having been caught spying on Russia, exposed the United States for what it really was: "an enemy of the peace." Powers was sentenced to ten years in prison. President Eisenhower was judged to be a "follower of Hitler," the lowest insult in the Russian lexicon. Hitler had double-crossed Khrushchev's predecessor, Joseph Stalin, in 1941, and the result of that double cross was twenty million Russians dead. In comparing Eisenhower to Hitler, Khrushchev was sending a clear message: diplomacy was off the table. The upcoming east-west summit in Paris was canceled. How bad could things get?

The National Advisory Committee for Aeronautics issued a press release identifying Watertown as the U-2 training facility but stating falsely that it was no longer used as a training base. The Russians knew that statement was meant to mislead the American public and not Russia's intelligence service, the KGB—and the CIA knew the Soviets had first-person information about Area 51 in the form of Gary Powers, not just photographic images of the facility from the satellites they'd been sending overhead.

With the White House absorbing the fallout from the Gary Powers affair, the CIA and the Air Force were deeply involved in the Mach 3 replacement for the U-2 out at the Ranch. The 8,500-foot-long runway, designated 14/32 and believed to be the longest in the world, had been finished, complete with a two-mile semicircular extension called the Hook, which would allow an A-12 pilot extra room for maneuvering were he to overshoot the runway. Four new aircraft hangars were built, designated 4, 5, 6, and 7. The former U-2 hangars whose metal doors had buckled in the atomic blast were converted into maintenance facilities and machine shops. Navy housing units, 140 in all, were transported to the base and laid out in neat rows. The commissary was expanded, as was the movie house and fire station. Richard Bissell had a tennis court put in, and plans for an Olympic-size swimming pool were drawn. The airspace over the entire region was given its own designation, R-4808N, separate from what had previously been designated Prohibited Area P-275; it included the Nevada Test Site, Area 13, and Area 51. All the CIA was waiting for was Lockheed's delivery of the A-12 airplanes.

At Lockheed, each Mach 3 aircraft was literally being hand forged, part by part, one airplane at a time. The production of the aircraft, according to Richard Bissell, "spawned its own industrial base. Special tools had to be developed, along with new paints, chemicals, wires, oils, engines, fuel, even special titanium screws. By the time Lockheed finished building the A-12, they themselves had developed and manufactured thirteen million different parts." It was the titanium that first held everything up. Titanium was the only metal strong enough to handle the kind of heat the Mach 3 aircraft would have to endure: 500- to 600-degree temperatures on the fuselage's skin and nearly 1,000 degrees in places close to the engines. This meant the titanium alloy had to be pure; nearly 95 percent of what Lockheed initially received had to be rejected. Titanium was also critically sensitive to the chemical chlorine, a fact Lockheed engineers did not realize at first. During the summer, when chlorine levels in the Burbank water system were elevated to fight algae, inside the Skunk Works, airplane pieces started to mysteriously corrode. Eventually, the problem was discovered, and the entire Skunk Works crew had to switch over to distilled water. Next it was discovered that titanium was also sensitive to cadmium, which was what most of Lockheed's tools were plated with. Hundreds of toolboxes had to be reconfigured, thousands of tools tossed out. The next problem was power related. Wind-tunnel testing in Burbank was draining too much electricity off the local grid. If a reporter found out about the electricity drain, it could lead to unwanted questions. NASA offered Kelly Johnson an alternative wind-tunnel test facility up in Northern California, near the Mojave, which was where Lockheed engineers ended up—performing their tests late at night under cover of darkness. The complicated nature of all things Oxcart pushed the new spy plane further and further behind the schedule.

At Area 51, the concern continued to be stealth. The radar results from the pole tests were promising, but as the Oxcart advanced, so did Soviet countermeasures to shoot it down. Russia was spending billions of rubles on surface-to-air missile technology and the CIA soon learned that the Oxcart's new nemesis was a system called Tall King. Getting hard data on Tall King's exact capabilities before the Oxcart went anywhere near it was now a top priority for the CIA.

To understand countermeasures, the CIA initiated an esoteric research-and-development program called Project Palladium. The program would get its legs over Cuba and eventually move to Area 51. It would involve ELINT. In 1960, "there were many CIA officers who thought ELINT was a dirty word," recalls Gene Poteat, the engineer in charge of Project Palladium, which originated with the CIA's Office of Scientific Intelligence. Poteat was one of the early pioneers who helped change that perception inside the CIA. "We needed to know the sensitivity of Soviet radar receivers and the proficiency of its operators," Poteat explains. With Khrushchev using Cuba as a military base in the Western Hemisphere, the CIA saw an opportunity. "When the Soviets moved into Cuba with their missiles and associated radar, we were presented with a golden opportunity to measure the system sensitivity of the SA-2 aircraft missile radar," says Poteat. To do this, the CIA needed a brigade of missile wizards. This included men like T. D. Barnes.

Thornton "T.D." Barnes was a CIA asset at an age when most men hadn't graduated from college yet. Married at seventeen to his high-school sweetheart, Doris, Barnes became a self-taught electronics wizard, buying broken television sets, fixing them up, and reselling them for five times the amount. In doing so, he went from bitter poverty—raised on a Texas Panhandle ranch with no electricity or running water—to buying his new bride a dream home before he was old enough to vote. Barnes credited his mother for his becoming one of the CIA's most important radar countermeasure experts. "My mom saw an article on radar in *Life* magazine when I was no more than nine or ten. She said I should write a school report on the subject and so I did. That's when I got bit with the radar bug."

At age seventeen, Barnes lied about his age to join the National Guard so he could go fight in Korea. He dreamed of one day being an Army officer. Two years later he was deployed to the 38th Parallel to defend the region alongside a British and a Turkish infantry company. It was in Korea that Barnes began his intelligence career at the bottom of the chain of command. "I was the guy who sat on the top of the hill and looked for enemy soldiers. If I saw 'em coming, it was my job to radio the information back to base," Barnes recalls. He loved the Army. The things he learned there stayed with him all his life: "Never waste a moment. Shine your boots when you're sitting on the pot. Always go to funerals. Look out for your men." Once, in Korea, a wounded soldier was rushed onto the base. Barnes overheard that the man needed to be driven to the hospital, but because gas was scarce, all vehicles had to be signed out by a superior. With no superior around, Barnes worried the man might die if he didn't get help fast, so he signed his superior's name on the order. "I was willing to take the demerit," Barnes explains. His actions caught the attention of the highest-ranking officer on the base, Major General Carl Jark, and later earned him a meritorious award. When the war was over General Jark pointed Barnes in the direction of radar and electronics. "He suggested I go to Fort Bliss and get myself an education there," Barnes explains. So T.D. and Doris Barnes headed to Texas. There, Barnes's whole world would change. And it didn't take long for his exceptional talents to come to the attention of the CIA.

Barnes loved learning. At Fort Bliss, he attended classes for Nike Ajax and Nike Hercules missile school by day and classes at Texas Western University by night for the next fifty-four months. These were the missiles that had been developed a decade earlier by the Paperclip scientists, born originally of the German V-2 rocket. At Fort Bliss, Barnes read technical papers authored by former Nazi scientists. Sometimes the Paperclip scientists taught class. "No one really thought of them as former Nazis," says Barnes. "They were the experts. They worked for us now and we learned from them." By early 1960, Barnes was a bona fide missile expert. Sometimes, when a missile misfired over at the White Sands Missile Range, it was T.D. Barnes who was dispatched to disarm the missile sitting on the test stand. "I'd march up to the missile, take off the panel, and disconnect the wires from the igniter," Barnes recalls. "When you are young, it doesn't occur to you how dangerous something is." Between the academics and the hands-on experience, Barnes developed an unusual aptitude in an esoteric field that the CIA was just getting involved in: ELINT. Which was how at the age of twenty-three, T. D. Barnes was recruited by the CIA to participate in a top secret game of chicken with the Russians that was part of Project Palladium. Although Barnes didn't know it then, the work he was doing was for the electronic countermeasure systems that would later be installed on the A-12 Oxcart and on the ground at Area 51.

American military aviation began at the Fort Bliss airfield in 1916, when the First Aero Squadron used it as a staging base while hunting Pancho Villa in nearby Mexico. Now, almost half a century later, the airfield, called Biggs, was part of the Strategic Air Command and served as home base for heavy bombers like the B-52 Stratofortress. Beginning in 1960, the facility was also a staging area for secret CIA missions that were part of Project Palladium, and that same year, T. D. Barnes found himself standing on the tarmac at Biggs Airfield watching a group of airmen as they delicately loaded a Hawk missile into the cargo bay of an airplane. Weapons are supposed to go in the weapons bay, Barnes thought to himself. But the project Barnes was participating in was unusual, dangerous, and top secret. Barnes did not have a need-to-know what the big picture involved and he knew better than to ask. Instead, he climbed into the cargo bay and sat down beside the missile. "We had the nose cone off and part of the skin off too. The missile was loaded on a stand inside the plane. It was my job to watch the electronics respond," Barnes explains. The airplane and its crew took off from the airbase and headed for Cuba. The plan was for the airplane to fly right up to the edge of Cuban airspace but not into it. Moments before the airplane crossed into Cuban airspace, the pilot would quickly turn around and head home. By then, the Russian radar experts working the Cuban radar sites would have turned on their systems to track the U.S. airplane. Russian MiG fighter jets would be sent aloft to respond. The job of Project Palladium was to gather the electronic intelligence being sent out by the radar stations and the MiGs. That was the first step in figuring out how to create a jamming system for the A-12 at Area 51.

The Cubans and their Russian patrons could not have had any idea whether the Americans were playing another game of chicken or if this act meant war. "Soviet MiGs would scramble toward us," Barnes recalls. "At the time, ECM [electronic countermeasure] and ECCM [electronic counter-countermeasure] technology were still new to both the plane and the missile. We'd transmit a Doppler signal from a radar simulator which told their MiG pilots that a missile had locked on them. When the Soviet pilots engaged their ECM against us, my job was to sit there and watch how our missile's ECCM responded. If the Soviet signal jammed our missile and made it drift off target, I'd tweak my missile's ECCM electronics to determine what would override a Soviet ECM signal." Though primitive by today's standards, what Barnes and the NSA agents with him inside the aircraft did laid the early groundwork for electronic warfare today. "Inside the airplane, we'd record the frequencies to be replayed back at Fort Bliss for training and design. Once we got what we wanted we hauled ass out of the area to avoid actual contact with Soviet planes."

The info that Barnes and his colleagues were getting over Cuba was filling in gaps that had previously been unknown. Back at Fort Bliss, Barnes and the others would interpret what NSA had captured from the Soviet/Cuban ECM transmissions that they had recorded during the flight. In listening to the decrypted Soviet responses to the antagonistic moves, the CIA learned what the Soviets could and could not see on their radars. This technology became a major component in further developing stealth technology and electronic countermeasures and was why Barnes was later placed by the CIA to work at Area 51. For the U.S. Air Force, this marked the beginning of a new age of information warfare.

Even though the U.S. military airplane with a team of engineers, NSA agents, and a Hawk missile hidden inside would U-turn and fly away at the last moment, just before violating Cuban airspace, "there were repercussions," according to Barnes. "It scared the living daylights out of them and it escalated things." In January of 1961, Khrushchev gathered a group of Cuban diplomats at their embassy in Moscow. "Alarming news is coming from Cuba at present, news that the most aggressive American monopolists are preparing a direct attack on Cuba," Khrushchev told the group. Barnes believes Khrushchev "may have been referring to our messing with them with our Hawk missiles homing in on their planes." Were that the case, Khrushchev had a valid point. But the mercurial dictator had his own difficulties in sticking to the facts. Disinformation was a hallmark of the Soviet propaganda machine.

To a roomful of Cuban diplomats, many of whom knew otherwise, Khrushchev falsely claimed, "What is more, [the Americans] are trying to present the case as though rocket bases of the Soviet Union are being set up or are already established in Cuba. It is well known that this is foul slander. There is no Soviet military base in Cuba." Actually, this is exactly what the Soviets were doing. "Of course we knew better, and on January 3, 1961, severed all diplomatic ties with Cuba," Barnes explains.

Ten days later, the CIA convened its Special Group, a secret committee inside the National Security Council that had oversight regarding CIA covert activities. A formal decision was made that Castro's regime "must be overthrown." The man in charge of making sure this happened was Richard Bissell. In addition to being the highest-ranking CIA officer in the Special Operations

Group, Bissell was also the most trusted CIA officer in the eyes of John F. Kennedy, the dashing new president. Before taking office, a member of the White House transition team asked Kennedy who he trusted most in the intelligence community. "Richard Bissell," Kennedy said without missing a beat.

Bissell's official title was now deputy director of plans. As innocuous as it sounded, DDP was in fact a euphemism for chief of covert operations for the CIA. This meant Bissell was in charge of the Agency's clandestine service, its paramilitary operations. The office had previously been known as the Office of Policy Coordination, or OPC. As deputy director of plans, Richard Bissell would be doing a lot more than playing a gentleman's spy game from the air. The CIA's paramilitary operations spilled blood. During these covert anti-Communist operations, men were dying in droves from Hungary to Greece to Iran, and all of these operations had to be planned, staged, and approved by the deputy director of plans.

In such a position there was writing on the wall, script that Richard Bissell did not, or chose not to, see. The man he was replacing was Frank Wisner, his old friend and the man who first introduced Bissell to the CIA. It was Frank Wisner who'd knocked on Bissell's door unannounced and then spent a fireside evening in Bissell's Washington, DC, parlor eleven years before. It was Wisner who had originally asked Bissell to siphon off funds from the Marshall Plan and hand them over to the CIA, no questions asked. Wisner had served the Agency as deputy director of plans from August 1951 to January 1959, but by the end of the summer of 1958, the job proved too psychologically challenging for him— Frank Wisner had begun displaying the first signs of madness. The diagnosis was psychotic mania, according to author Tim Weiner. Doctors and drugs did not help. Next came the electroshock treatment: "For six months, his head was clamped into a vise and shot through with a current sufficient to fire a hundred-watt light bulb." Frank Wisner emerged from the insane asylum zombielike and went on to serve as the CIA's London station chief. A broken man, Wisner did not last long overseas. He shuffled in and out of madhouses for years until finally forced to retire in 1962: "He'd been raving about Adolf Hitler, seeing things, hearing voices. He knew he would never be well." Tragically, on October 29, 1965, Wisner was getting ready to go hunting with his old CIA friend Joe Bryan at his country estate when he took a shotgun out of his gun cabinet and put a bullet in his own head.

The pressure that came with being the deputy director of plans for the CIA was, for some, as treacherous as a loaded gun.

As workers toiled away at Area 51 getting ready for the arrival of the Oxcart spy plane, Richard Bissell focused on his orders to rid Cuba of Fidel Castro. By 1961, the Agency decided that Bahía de Cochinos, or the Bay of Pigs, was the perfect place to launch its "paramilitary plan." The little sliver of coastline on the south shore of the island was barely inhabited. A few summer cottages were scattered among little bays, used mostly for fishing and swimming, and there was a valuable asset nearby in "an airstrip not far from the beach."

Surely, the U-2 spy plane could help in gathering intel, Bissell decided. After Gary Powers was shot down, President Eisenhower had promised the world there would be no spy missions over Russia, but that promise did not include dangerous Soviet proxies like Cuba. In his new position as deputy director of plans, Bissell had used the U-2 to gather intelligence before. Its photographs had been helpful in planning paramilitary operations in Laos and the Dominican Republic. And in Cuba, overhead photographs taken by the Agency's U-2s revealed important details regarding the terrain just up the beach from the Bay of Pigs beach. Photo interpreters determined that the swampland in the area would be hard to run in unless the commandos familiarized themselves with preexisting trails. As for the water landing itself, from seventy thousand feet in the air, the beachhead at the Bay of Pigs looked flat and lovely. But because cameras could not photograph what lay underwater, Bissell had no idea that just beneath the surface of the sea there was a deadly coral reef that would later greatly impede the water landing by commandos.

Hundreds of pages, declassified after thirty years, reveal the hand of economics wizard Richard Bissell in the design of the paramilitary operation. Bissell painstakingly outlined: "Contingency Plans...Probabilities...Likelihood, chance of success...Plans for Operation 'T,'...Operation 'Z,'...Phase 1, Phase 2, and Phase 3... Pre-Day Day plans...D-Day plans...Post D-Day plans...Unattributable actions by the Navy...Post-Recognition Plans...Arguments for maximum sabotage...Arguments for simultaneous defection...Feasibility of declaration of war by certain Central American states...Disclosures...Non-Disclosures...Continuation of Psychological Warfare Plans...How to deal, and how not to deal with the press." For all the organization and preplanning, the operation might have been successful. But there are many reasons why it failed so tragically. When the Bay of Pigs operation was over, hundreds of CIA-trained, anti–Castro Cuban exiles were killed on approach or left to die on the beachhead at the Bay of Pigs. Those that lived to surrender were imprisoned and later ransomed back to the United States. When the story became public, so did brigade commander Pepe San Roman's last words before his capture: "Must have air support in the next few hours or we will be wiped out. Under heavy attacks by MiG jets and heavy tanks." Pepe San Roman begged Richard Bissell for help. "All groups demoralized...They consider themselves deceived." By the end of the day, Richard Bissell's world had begun to fall irreparably apart. The Bay of Pigs would be his downfall.

There was plenty of blame to go around but almost all of it fell at the feet of the CIA. In the years since, it has become clear that equal blame should be imputed to the Department of Defense, the Department of State, and President Kennedy. Shortly before he died, Richard Bissell blamed the mission's failure on his old rival General Curtis LeMay. Bissell lamented that if LeMay had provided adequate air cover as he had promised, the mission would most likely have been a success. The Pentagon has historically attributed LeMay's failure to send B-26 bombers to the Bay of Pigs to a "time zone confusion." Bissell saw the mix-up as personal, believing that LeMay had been motivated by revenge. That he'd harbored a grudge against Bissell for the U-2 and Area 51. Whatever the reason, more than three hundred people were dead and 1,189 anti-Castro guerrillas, left high and dry, had been imprisoned. The rivalry between Bissell and LeMay was over, and the Bay of Pigs would force Richard Bissell to leave government service in February of 1962. There were many government backlashes as a result of the fiasco. One has been kept secret until now, namely that President Kennedy sent the CIA's inspector general at the time, Lyman B. Kirkpatrick Jr., out to Area 51 to write up a report on the base. More specifically, the president wanted to assess what other Richard Bissell disasters in the making might be coming down the pipeline at Area 51.

Adding friction to an already charged situation was the fact that by some accounts, Kirkpatrick held a grudge. Before the Bay of Pigs, Richard Bissell was in line to succeed Allen Dulles as director of the CIA, and eight years earlier, Lyman Kirkpatrick had worn those coveted shoes. But like Bissell, Kirkpatrick was cut down in his prime. Kirkpatrick's loss came not by his own actions but by a tragic blow beyond his control. On an Agency mission to Asia in 1952, Lyman Kirkpatrick contracted polio and became paralyzed from the waist down. Confined to a wheelchair for the rest of his life, Kirkpatrick was relegated to the role of second-tier bureaucrat.

In a world of gentlemen spy craft and high-technology espionage, bureaucracy was considered glorified janitorial work. But when Kirkpatrick was dispatched to Area 51 by JFK, the fate and future of the secret base Richard Bissell had built in the Nevada desert lay in Lyman Kirkpatrick's hands.

CHAPTER NINE

The Base Builds Back Up

As the man in charge of property control at Area 51, Jim Freedman was a taskmaster. "It was my job to provide services for all the different groups at the area," Freedman explains. "This included the CIA, the Air Force, EG&G, REECo [Reynolds Electric and Engineering], and even Howard Hughes—an individual who very few people had any idea had his own hangar out at the Ranch." What exactly Hughes was doing at Area 51 remains classified as of 2011, but Freedman explains the dynamic that was at play. "The CIA liked to foster competition between groups. It was why we had Kodak and Polaroid, Lockheed and North American, EG&G and Hughes. They were all no-bid contracts for security reasons. But competition keeps people on their toes." Jim Freedman acted as the gofer among the groups from 1960 until 1974. If a scientist needed a widget, if an engineer needed an oscilloscope, or if a radar expert needed a piece of magnetic tape, it was Freedman's job to get it, fast. As a prerequisite for the job, Freedman knew how to keep secrets. He carried a top secret and a Q clearance and had worked for EG&G since 1953. "We worked under a code that said, 'What you learn here, leave here.' That was pretty simple to follow," says Freedman. "You couldn't afford to talk. You'd lose your job and you'd be blackballed. So instead, my wife and family thought I fixed TVs. 'How was your day, Dad?' my kids would ask when I got home. 'Great!' I'd say. 'I fixed twenty-four TVs.'"

As they had been with the Manhattan Project, the various jobs going on at Area 51 were compartmentalized for Oxcart, so that every person worked within very strict need-to-know protocols. The radar people had no idea about the ELINT people, who had no idea what any of the search-and-rescue teams were up to. Each group worked on its part of the puzzle. Each man was familiar with his single piece. Only a few individuals, officers working in managerial capacities, understood a corner of the puzzle—at most. But someone had to act as a go-between among these disparate groups, and in this way, Freedman became an individual who knew a lot more than most about the inner workings of Area 51.

He also knew the layout of the base. Most Area 51 workers were confined to the building, or buildings, they worked in, the building they slept in, and the mess hall, where everybody dined together. As the Area 51 runner, Freedman "went to places out there that I don't think other people even knew were out there." For example, Freedman says, there was "the faraway runway where people who were not supposed to be seen by others were brought into the base." Freedman tells a story of one such group, the exact date of which he can't recall but that was during the Vietnam War. "One day I was out there delivering something to someone, it was three in the morning, and I watched an airplane land. Then I watched forty-one Vietnamese men get off the plane. I never saw the men again, but a few days later I was sent on an errand. My supervisor said, 'Jim, can you go to Las Vegas and get me x number of pounds of a special kind of rice?' I'd say it was fairly obvious who that rice was being requested for." Freedman elaborates: "These [foreign nationals] were being trained to use state-of-the-art Agency equipment out at the Area, which they probably took with them when they left and went and put behind enemy lines."

Freedman's first job at the test site had been installing radios in EG&G vehicles used during weapons tests. Next, he was trained as an engineer in the art of wiring nuclear bombs. In the 1950s, Freedman participated in dozens of nuclear tests on the arming and firing party alongside Al O'Donnell at the test site and also at the Pacific Proving Ground. "I even managed to survive a helicopter crash in the Marshall Islands," Freedman adds. In 1957, EG&G learned that Freedman had studied photography after high school and assigned him to a team photographing nuclear explosions. But by 1960, the nuclear-test-ban treaty was in effect, testing had moved underground, and Freedman's life had taken what he called "a dull turn."

One afternoon, he was sitting inside an EG&G warehouse in Las Vegas, cleaning camera equipment. "I was thinking about how fast office work gets boring when my boss walked up to me and said, 'Hey, Jim, do you want to go work on a secret project?'" Freedman didn't hesitate. "I said yes, because it sounded interesting, and I wound up at Area 51. I'd never heard of the place before I went there. I never knew it existed just over the hill from the Nevada Test Site where I'd worked for so many years. Neither did anyone else who didn't have a need-to-know." When Freedman arrived at Area 51, it felt to him "like I was arriving on the far side of the moon. You know about the bright side of the moon; well, in relative terms, that was what the test site was like. Area 51 was the dark side." What began as a short-term contract in December of 1960 would last for Jim Freedman for the next fourteen years.

One day, in the late summer of 1961, just two months after the Bay of Pigs became public, Jim Freedman was walking around the base with a checklist of tasks. His priority job that week struck him as a very odd, very low-tech request. In a world of cutting-edge science and technological gadgets relating to espionage, the supervisor wanted Freeman to help Area 51 carpenters locate more plywood. "The workers were transforming a set of steps into a ramp," he explains. "This was happening all over the base. Lots of doorsills were becoming lots of ramps and I remember thinking, There's a lot of money going into getting something low and on wheels to be able to move around this base." Freedman knew not to ask questions. "But when a small airplane landed, and out came a man in the wheelchair, I watched my boss, Werner Weiss of the CIA, meet the man out on the tarmac. And I knew from watching their interaction just how important this man was to the CIA. He had white-silvery hair. A very memorable figure in a wheelchair. For years, I looked for him on TV." Freedman never saw the man on TV, but the man was Lyman Kirkpatrick, inspector general for the CIA. Working on presidential orders to assess Area 51, Kirkpatrick is the only CIA inspector general known to have visited the base. Despite being confined to a wheelchair, Kirkpatrick managed to meticulously cover the rugged high-desert terrain. After Kirkpatrick examined the various buildings he asked to be driven around the outer edges of the base. There, he found what he considered to be a security flaw. "The high and rugged northeast perimeter of the immediate operating area, which I visited in order to see for myself, is not under government ownership," Kirkpatrick wrote in his report, which was declassified in 2004 but has since been removed from the CIA library archives. "It is subject to a score or more of mineral claims, at least one of which is visited periodically by its owner," Kirkpatrick wrote, referring to the Black Metal and Groom mines. "Several claims are sites of unoccupied buildings or cellars which together with the terrain in general afford excellent opportunity for successful penetration by a skilled and determined opposition," Kirkpatrick warned. As inspector general for the CIA, Kirkpatrick was concerned that the base was not "rigorously protected against sabotage," most notably by "air violations." In the game of cat and mouse between the Soviet Union and the United States, tensions were at an all-time high. First there had been the Gary Powers incident, in May of 1960. Less than a year later came the CIA's failed commando operation at the Bay of Pigs. The president had been advised that the Soviets could be preparing their own operation as payback for either of those events. Former president Eisenhower told Kennedy that "the failure of the Bay of Pigs will embolden the Soviets to do something that they would otherwise not do," and Lyman Kirkpatrick warned that one type of sabotage operation the Soviets could be considering might involve hitting Area 51. It would be a strike between the eyes, meant to harm the office of the president in the view of the people. After Gary Powers, the White House had promised that the Watertown facility had been closed down. After the Bay of Pigs fiasco, the president promised to rein in covert activity by the CIA. Any public revelation that Area 51 existed would expose the fact that the CIA, the Air Force, and defense contractors were all working together on a black project to overfly Russia again—despite presidential assurances that they would do no such thing. If the nation were to discover the Mach 3 spy plane project moving forward at Area 51, what would they think about the president's promises? Area 51 was a target in exposure alone, the inspector general said.

Jim Freedman was one of the men assigned to photograph and assess the mines in the mountains—the terrain that Kirkpatrick had said would "afford excellent opportunity for successful penetration." Freedman's superior, Hank Meierdierck, decided to make a hunting trip out of the task. Meierdierck was a living legend at Area 51. In 1956 he had worked as the CIA's instructor pilot on base, teaching the Project Aquatone pilots how to fly the U-2. Now, during Oxcart, Hank Meierdierck had an office at the Pentagon but most of his time was spent out at Area 51. "One day Hank asked me if I liked to hunt," recalls Jim Freedman. "I said yes. Well, Hank smiled and said, 'Good. Bring your rifle out next time.'"

Weapons were not allowed on Lockheed transport planes flying in and out of Area 51 from McCarran Airport. But Freedman's level of clearance was such that security did not examine the things he carried with him. "The next trip to Area 51, I put my rifle in a box with an oscilloscope," Freedman explains, "and that's how I got my hunting rifle out there."

Meierdierck found a helicopter pilot to fly the men into the mountains north of Area 51 to photograph the old mines there. Then he dropped the two men and their hunting rifles off at a favored spot on Groom Mountain where Area 51 officials liked to surreptitiously hunt deer. Meierdierck told the helicopter pilot to return the next day.

From on top of Groom Mountain, the view down over Area 51 was spectacular. It was, as Kirkpatrick had speculated, a perfect place for a Soviet spy to disguise himself as a deer hunter and take notes. During the day, you could see the buildings down at Area 51 spread out in an H formation to the west of the runways. Jeeps and vans could be seen ferrying workers around. If you had binoculars, you could get a clear look at what was going on. At night, the whole place went dark; most of the buildings that had windows kept the curtains drawn. If an aircraft needed to land at night, the lights would quickly flash on, illuminating the runway. The airplane would land and the lights would quickly go off, bathing the valley in darkness once again.

For Freedman, the hunting trip dragged on a little long. "Hank was stubborn," Freedman explains. "He said he wasn't leaving until he got a deer. And he preferred to hunt on his own, so he suggested we split up and meet back at the campsite for dinner." Which is what they did. "There was very little for us to talk about," Freedman says. "We both knew we were on top secret projects. You couldn't afford to talk. Everyone had a wife and a family. No one could afford to lose their job." One subject the men could discuss was hunting. Only three years had passed since the last aboveground atomic tests had detonated across the valley down below. Freedman wondered if anyone who caught a deer up on Groom Mountain should even consider eating it because "the deer ate the foliage which was contaminated from alpha particles from all the tests." As it turned out, the men did not catch any deer anyway.

Come Monday, the helicopter pilot returned, and by the end of the next day, Freedman was sitting in his dining room in Las Vegas, eating dinner with his wife and kids. He was able to get his hunting rifle out of Area 51 the same way he got it in: "Inside the oscilloscope case."

Not long after Lyman Kirkpatrick filed his final inspector general's report on Area 51, Richard Bissell resigned. This was not before he had been offered a lesser job at CIA, as the director of the Office of Science and Technology. But in that new capacity Bissell's need-to-know would have been drastically reduced. In CIA parlance, having one's access curbed was an insult. Instead, he chose to leave the Agency.

Without Richard Bissell in charge of the secret CIA facility, what would become of Area 51? And who would run the Oxcart reconnaissance program? The decision about Bissell's replacement went up the chain of command to President Kennedy. He had been in office for less than a year and already he was up to his elbows in CIA backlash. President Kennedy's new secretary of defense was a man named Robert McNamara, an intellectually minded Harvard Business School graduate who had won the Legion of Merit during World War II for performing firebomb analysis from behind a desk. Now, as secretary of defense, after the Bay of Pigs, McNamara called for the Pentagon to assume control of all spy plane programs. McNamara was at the top of the chain of command of all the armed services and believed his Air Force should be in charge of all U.S. assets with wings. The public had lost confidence in the CIA, McNamara told the president.

But James Killian and his colleague Edwin Land, now both part of Kennedy's presidential foreign intelligence advisory board, told the president that the best move forward for national security was to keep the CIA in the spy plane business at Area 51. What happened with Bissell was unfortunate, they said, suggesting that Richard Bissell, and Richard Bissell alone, had gone rogue. They argued that the CIA was still the agency best equipped to deliver overhead intelligence to the president. If that wasn't possible, Killian and Land said, then the idea of who controls overhead reconnaissance should be restructured. One plan was that the CIA might work in better partnership with the Air Force. President Kennedy liked that. On September 6, 1961, he created a protocol that required the CIA deputy director and the undersecretary of the Air

Force to comanage all space reconnaissance and aerial espionage programs together as the National Reconnaissance Office, a classified agency within Robert McNamara's Department of Defense. A central headquarters for NRO was established in Washington, a small office with a limited staff but with a number of empire-size egos vying for power and control. The organization maintained a public face, an overt identity at the Pentagon called the Office of Space Systems, but no one outside a select few knew of NRO's existence until 1992.

Jim Freedman remembers the transition in the chain of command and how it affected his work at Area 51. "Because I was the person with a list of every employee at the area, it was my job to know not just who was who, but who was the boss of somebody's boss. An individual person didn't necessarily know much more about the person they worked for than their code name. And they almost certainly didn't know who was working on the other side of the wall or in the next trailer over. Wayne Pendleton was the head of the radar group for a while. He was my go-to person for a lot of different groups. One day, Pendleton suddenly says, 'I'm going to Washington, Jim.' So I said, 'What if I need you, what number should I call?' And Pendleton laughed. He said, 'You won't need me because where I'm going doesn't exist.' Decades later I would learn that the place where Wayne was going when he left the Ranch was to a little office in Washington called NRO."

After the Bay of Pigs and his resignation, Richard Bissell drifted away from Washington's power center like a man scorned. Quickly, his longtime, biggest supporters became his greatest detractors. Most notable among them was James Killian. The president's powerful science adviser, Killian had headhunted Bissell twice before, the first time in 1946 to work in the economics department at MIT, and then again in 1954 to manage the U-2 aerial espionage program for the CIA. For nearly twenty years, Killian had considered Richard Bissell not just a colleague but a friend. After the Bay of Pigs, Killian turned his back on his friend. In a clear case of the pot calling the kettle black, Killian told the CIA's historian Donald E.

Welzenbach that he was terribly upset when he learned of Bissell's role in covert CIA operations. In a *Studies in Intelligence* report for the CIA, Welzenbach wrote, "Killian looked upon science and technology almost as a religion, something sacred to be kept from contamination by those who would misuse it for unwholesome ends. Into this category fit the covert operations and 'dirty tricks' of Dick Bissell's Directorate of Plans."

It was hypocrisy of the highest order. James Killian had been up to his own dirty tricks, the true, perilous facts of which have remained buried until now. Unlike Richard Bissell, because of Killian's powerful role as President Eisenhower's chief science adviser, Killian did not get caught. But what Killian spearheaded in the name of so-called sacred science in retrospect hardly seems like science at all. In late 1958, Killian organized, oversaw, and then tried to cover up the facts regarding two of the most dangerous weapons tests in the history of the nuclear bomb. Two thermonuclear devices, called Teak and Orange, each an astonishingly powerful 3.8 megatons, were exploded in the Earth's upper atmosphere at Johnston Atoll, 750 miles west of Hawaii. Teak went off at 252,000 feet, or 50 miles, and Orange went off at 141,000 feet, 28 miles, which is exactly where the ozone layer lies. In hindsight, it was a ludicrous idea. "The impetus for these tests was derived from the uncertainty in U.S. capability to discern Soviet high-altitude nuclear detonation," read one classified report. Killian was in charge of the tests, and his rationale for authorizing them was that if sometime in the future the Soviets were to detonate a high-altitude nuclear bomb, our scientists would need to know what to look for.

Instead of being difficult to detect, a nuclear bomb exploding in the ozone layer was instantly obvious in horrific and catastrophic ways. The fireballs produced by both Teak and Orange burned the retinas of any living thing that had been looking up at the sky without goggles within a 225-mile radius of the blast, including hundreds of monkeys and rabbits that Killian authorized to be flown in airplanes nearby. The animals' heads had been locked in gadgets that forced them to witness the megaton blast. From Guam to Wake Island to Maui, the natural blue sky changed to a red, white, and gray, creating an aurora 2,100 miles along the geomagnetic meridian. Radio communication throughout a swath of the Pacific region went dead.

"We almost blew a hole in the ozone layer," explains Al O'Donnell, the EG&G weapons test engineer who in the twelve years since Crossroads had wired over one hundred nuclear bombs, including Teak and Orange. O'Donnell was standing on Johnston Island, 720 miles southwest of Honolulu, on August 1, 1958, when the Teak bomb went off. Due to a "program failure" on the Redstone missile system (which carried the warhead to its target), the rocket went straight up and detonated directly above where O'Donnell and the rest of the arming and firing party were working. The bomb was supposed to have detonated twenty-six miles to the south. In a sanitized film record of the event, men in flip-flops and shorts can be seen ducking for cover as a phenomenal fireball consumes the sky overhead. "It was scary," O'Donnell sighs, remembering the catastrophic event as an old man, half a century later. There is a hint of resignation in his voice when he says, "But we were all used to it by then. The bombs had become too big." In Teak's first ten milliseconds, its fireball grew ten miles wide—enough yield to obliterate Manhattan. At H + 1 second, the fireball was more than forty miles wide, which could have taken out all five boroughs of New York City. It was not as if Killian, who was in charge of the project, hadn't realized the potential for part of the ozone layer to be destroyed. "In late 1957 and early 1958, the question was raised as to whether or not the ultraviolet emissions from the Teak and Orange events would 'burn a hole' into the natural ozone layer," states a 1976 review of the event authored by Los Alamos National Laboratory. But "the pre-event discussions were inconclusive" and the tests barreled ahead anyway. Why? "It was argued that even in case of complete destruction of the ozone layer over an area with radius 50 km, the ozone loss would amount to only 2×10^{-5} of the global inventory. The 'hole' would be closed promptly by bomb-produced turbulence and ambient motions in the atmosphere." As astonishing and reckless as this was, the follow-up becomes even more unbelievable. "After the events, little attention was paid to this particular problem, evidently because no spectacular or unusual observations were made (because of lack of evidence one way or the other)." Apparently, no one thought to ask the dignitary on hand that day on Johnston Island, Wernher Von Braun.

In government archival film footage, Von Braun can be seen observing the Redstone rocket he had designed to get the nuclear weapon up to the ozone where it would explode. Wearing aviator sunglasses and a loose-fitting Hawaiian shirt and sporting an island tan, Von Braun appears more playboy than rocket scientist. But Von Braun was so spooked by the Teak blast that he left the island before the second test took place. Von Braun was not one to scare easily. When he worked for Adolf Hitler, he and his colleague Ernst Steinhoff were known to dash up to Hitler's lair, Wolfsschanze, in Steinhoff's personal airplane to brief the dictator on how the V-2 was coming along. But the power of the Teak bomb sent Von Braun running. Immediately after the deadened communications systems were restored, Von Braun fled. He never publicly said why.

Killian's high-altitude nuclear tests did not stop there. Two weeks later, another ultrasecret nuclear weapons project called Operation Argus commenced. Killian's nuclear bomb tests had now expanded to include outer space. "Argus was an unusual operation," a Defense Nuclear Agency summary from 1993 recalls. "It was completed in less than six months after Presidential approval, and it was completed in complete secrecy. Nuclear-tipped missiles were fired from ships for the first time." Oblique words used to conceal another one of the most radical, covert science experiments conducted by man. On August 27, August 30, and September 6, 1958, three nuclear warheads were launched from X-17 rockets from the deck of the USS *Norton Sound* as the warship floated off the coast of South Africa in the South Atlantic Ocean. Up went the missiles and the warheads until they exploded approximately three hundred miles into space. This "scientific experiment" was the brainchild of a Greek elevator operator turned physicist, Nicholas Christofilos. Christofilos convinced Killian that a nuclear explosion occurring above the Earth's atmosphere—but within the Earth's magnetic field—might produce an electronic pulse that could hypothetically damage the arming devices on Soviet ICBM warheads trying to make their way into the United States. While the phenomenon did occur in minutiae, meaning the arming devices registered "feeling" the pulse from the nuclear blast, Christofilos was wrong about the possibility that this would actually *stop* incoming enemy nuclear missiles in their tracks. In other words, the tests failed.

To cover his tracks as to the sheer waste and recklessness of the experiment, in the month following the nuclear detonation in space, Killian wrote a memo to President Eisenhower attempting to put a congratulatory spin on how quickly the project occurred and how terrific it was that secrecy was maintained. Dated November 3, 1958, Killian's letter began by describing Argus as "probably the most spectacular event ever conducted." More egregious self-congratulation came next: "The experiment was in itself an extraordinary accomplishment. Especially notable was the successful launching of a large, solid-fuel rocket carrying a nuclear payload from the heaving deck of a ship in the squally South Atlantic. Scarcely less so is the fact that the whole experiment was planned and carried out in less than five months...Impressive, too, is the fact that no leaks have occurred."

When the *New York Times*'s senior science writer Walter Sullivan hand-delivered a letter to Killian letting him know the *New York Times* was in possession of leaked information about these secret tests, the White House went into denial mode. "Neither confirm nor deny such leaks," the president's special assistant Karl G. Harr Jr. wrote in a secret memo to Killian. "If the *New York Times,* or anyone else, breaks a substantial part of the story," one possible response would be to say the White House had disclosed "all that we may safely say from a national security point of view." In regards to brazenly violating the White House policy of announcing every nuclear test, Killian's position was to be that "it was a scientific experiment utilizing a nuclear detonation to discharge electrons into the Earth's magnetic field." It was semantics that gave Killian the authority, or cover, to declare that a nuclear test was not a nuclear test. Adding one last ironic touch of deception, the president's special assistant told Killian that were the *New York Times* to make the Argus test public, a panel of scientists "should meet with the press in the Great Hall of the National Academy of Science in order to emphasize the scientific aspects of this experiment."

Were the president's top science advisers really making America safer? Or were they abusing their power with the president? Couple their power with the total lack of oversight they enjoyed, and it was the president's scientists who paved the road for the U.S. militarization of space. "It was agreed that I would be protected from congressional inquisition," Killian wrote in his memoirs, adding, "I think now this was the wrong decision. It would have been of help to Congress to have been more fully informed about the work of PSAC [President's Science Advisory Committee], and help me to have a better feeling for congressional opinion."

Beginning with Argus, the president's science advisers were using space as their laboratory, conducting tests that a Defense Nuclear Agency review board would later call "poorly instrumented and hastily executed." They did so with total disregard for potentially catastrophic effects on the planet, not to mention the effect it would have decades later on the arms race in space. According to the same report, Killian was aware of the risk and took a gamble. There had been discussions regarding the possibility that the Teak and Orange shots really could burn holes in the ozone. But those "pre-event discussions were inconclusive," the report said. And so the scientists went forward on the assumption that if a hole happened, it would later be closed.

In reality, Killian and others had no idea what would or would not happen when the megaton bomb exploded in the upper atmosphere. "And they didn't factor in to their equations what could have happened if they failed," recalls Al O'Donnell. "We were lucky. When the Teak bomb exploded right over our heads on Johnston Island, we thought we might be goners. It was an enormous bright white-light blast." The men did not have radio communications for eight hours. "All the birds on the island that had been pestering us during the setup, these big fearless birds we called Gooney birds, after the bomb went off, they just disappeared. Or maybe they died." When Admiral Parker of the Armed Forces Special Weapons Project finally reached O'Donnell and the rest of the EG&G crew by radio from his office in the Pentagon, his words were: "Are you still there?"

If American citizens were in the dark about the megaton thermonuclear weapons tests being conducted by the American military in space, the Russians certainly were not. They forged ahead with an unprecedented weapons test of their own. On October 30, 1961, the Soviet Union detonated the largest, most powerful nuclear weapon the world had ever known. Called the Tsar Bomba, the hydrogen bomb had an unbelievable yield of fifty megatons, roughly ten times the amount of all the explosives used in seven years of war during World War II, including both nuclear bombs dropped on Hiroshima and Nagasaki. Tsar Bomba, detonated over northern Russia, flattened entire villages in surrounding areas and broke windows a thousand miles away in Finland. Anyone within a four-hundred-mile radius who was staring at the blast would have gone blind. Soviet leader Nikita Khrushchev told the United Nations Assembly that the purpose of the test was to "show somebody Kuzka's mother"—to show somebody who's boss. The world was racing toward catastrophe. Would the A-12 spy planes heading to Area 51 really help, or would overhead espionage prove to be nothing more than a drop in the bucket?

CHAPTER TEN

Wizards of Science, Technology, and Diplomacy

Harry Martin stood on the tarmac mesmerized by the beauty of the Oxcart. With its long, shiny fuselage, the airplane resembled a cobra with wings. As the master fuels sergeant, Martin had been at Area 51 since the very first days of the Oxcart program, back when the tarmac he was standing on was being poured as cement. Now, something big was happening at Area 51. The Oxcart had arrived and it was getting ready to fly. For more than a week, Martin had watched dignitaries come and go, touching down and taking off in Air Force jets. The generals would inevitably show up in the hangar where Martin worked because it was the place where the airplane stayed. Martin's job was to prep the aircraft with fuel, which for weeks had been leaking as if through a sieve.

Martin had caught glimpses of General LeMay, shorter than he'd expected but chomping on his signature cigar like he did on the cover of magazines. Martin had also seen General Doolittle, of the harrowing World War II Doolittle Raid. Harry Martin never

Groom Lake, Nevada, in 1917. Once little more than a dry lake bed in the southern Nevada desert, what is now known as Area 51 has become the most secretive military facility in the world. *(Special Collections, University of Nevada–Reno)*

From up on top of the old Groom Mine in 1917, looking down. Not until the 1950s would the federal government take over the dry lake bed and adjacent land. *(Special Collections, University of Nevada–Reno)*

Vannevar Bush, age eighty, receives the Atomic Pioneer Award from President Nixon at a White House ceremony in 1970. Other recipients are (from left to right) Glenn T. Seaborg, the man who co-discovered plutonium; James B. Conant of the National Defense Research Committee; and General Leslie R. Groves, who was the commander of the Manhattan Project but took orders from Vannevar Bush. *(U.S. Department of Energy)*

Colonel Richard S. Leghorn during Operation Crossroads, at Bikini Atoll in the Marshall Islands, July 1946. Leghorn led the mission to photograph the nuclear explosions from the air, and he is credited with the concept of "overhead," which led to spy planes and satellites. *(Collection of Richard S. Leghorn / Army Air Forces)*

The Baker bomb at Operation Crossroads, July 25, 1946, was 21 kilotons, one and a half times more powerful than the bomb dropped on Hiroshima. Baker's underwater fireball produced a "chimney" of radioactive water 6,000 feet tall and 2,000 feet wide. Stalin had spies at the event. *(Library of Congress)*

The black device attached to this balloon in Area 9 of the Nevada Test Site is a 74-kiloton atomic bomb code-named Hood, the largest atmospheric nuclear weapon ever exploded in the United States. Standing on a ladder minutes before this photograph was taken on July 5, 1957, Al O'Donnell put the final touches on the bomb's firing system. Area 51 is over the hill to the right of the device. *(Collection of Alfred O'Donnell/National Nuclear Security Administration)*

A column of radioactive smoke rises from the Hood bomb. To the right of the mushroom stem the landscape can be seen on fire. Approximately one hour after the bomb went off, security guard Richard Mingus drove through ground zero to set up a guard post at the Area 51 guard gate, directly over the burning hills. *(National Nuclear Security Administration)*

In Area 12 of the Nevada Test Site, workmen enter an underground atomic bomb tunnel through its mouth, summer 1957. *(National Nuclear Security Administration)*

Operation Paperclip scientists at Fort Bliss, Texas, in 1946. Until 1945, these men worked for Adolf Hitler, but as soon as the war ended these "rare minds" began working for the American military and various intelligence organizations, the details of which remain largely classified. Rocket scientist Wernher von Braun is in the front row, seventh from the right with his hand in his pocket. *(National Aeronautics and Space Administration)*

Nazi Dr. Walther Riedel after his capture by the U.S. Army in 1945. Unsmiling in this never-before-published file photograph, Riedel is missing teeth, which had been knocked out by U.S. soldiers while questioning him about his role in Hitler's "bacteria bomb." *(National Archives)*

Alleged to be Stalin's secret UFO study team are (standing left to right) Sergei Korolev, chief missile designer and inventor of Sputnik; Igor Kurchatov, father of Russia's atomic bomb; and Mstislav Keldysh, mathematician, theoretician, and space pioneer. *(Collection of Museum of M. V. Keldysh, Russia)*

This photograph of the all-wing Horten V appeared in the Secret G-2 Combined Intelligence Objective Sub-Committee report "Horten Tailless Aircraft," dated May 1945. *(National Archives)*

The 1945 G-2 report on the Horten brothers airplanes included this photograph of the unusually shaped Parabola. Two years later, after the crash of a foreign disc-shaped aircraft in New Mexico, in July 1947, the Counter Intelligence Corps embarked on a manhunt across Western Europe to locate the Horten brothers and their so-called flying disc. *(National Archives)*

A German-designed V-2 rocket is hoisted up onto a U.S. Army test stand at the White Sands Proving Ground, in New Mexico, on January 1, 1947. Five months later one of the V-2s went off course. No one was killed, but the German Paperclip scientists in charge of the rocket launch were put under investigation. *(NASA/Marshall Space Flight Center)*

Part of a U–2 coming out of a transport airplane at Area 51 in 1955. The CIA's first spy plane was so secret that Air Force pilots transporting it to Area 51, in pieces inside larger airplanes, would fly to a set of coordinates over the Mojave Desert and contact a UHF frequency called Sage Control for orders. Only when the aircraft was a few hundred feet off the ground would runway lights flash on. *(Laughlin Heritage Foundation/CIA)*

Early U–2s on the flight line at Area 51 in 1956, a worker standing on a wing. *(Laughlin Heritage Foundation/CIA)*

Trailers at Area 51 where U-2 pilots like Hervey Stockman and Tony Bevacqua slept while learning how to fly the CIA's first spy plane. *(Laughlin Heritage Foundation/CIA)*

A rare perspective on Area 51 looking northeast in 1955. The triangular mountain peak (just right of center in the far distance) is Tikaboo Peak, the single remaining location from where the curious can catch a faraway glimpse of Area 51. *(Laughlin Heritage Foundation/CIA)*

Hervey Stockman left Princeton University to fly with the U.S. Army Air Corps during World War II. In 1956, he was the first man to fly over the Soviet Union in a U-2. He flew 310 combat missions in three wars. In June 1967 he was involved in a midair crash over North Vietnam and became a POW for nearly six years. *(Collection of Colonel Hervey S. Stockman)*

Headquarters Building At Watertown. Flag At Half Mast Following Seiker Crash.

After the tragic death of U-2 pilot Robert Sieker on April 4, 1957, the flag at Area 51 was flown at half-mast. *(Laughlin Heritage Foundation/CIA)*

The U-2 aloft, circa 1965. All indicators of ownership, including its former NACA designation, have been removed. *(Collection of Lockheed Martin)*

A rare look at Building 82, inside the fabled Lockheed Skunk Works, circa 1957. The world's first anechoic chamber can be seen at the far rear of the room. Shoe-sized models of the CIA's spy planes would be hung from the ceiling and tested. *(Collection of Lockheed Martin)*

Area 13 sits inside Area 51 and was contaminated with plutonium in a 1957 "dirty bomb" test. This photograph, part of a set never released publicly before, was taken during a 1960 Atomic Energy Commission investigation into theft of a "hot" item stored there. After the dirty bomb test, someone had cut the fence, ignored the "Warning Alpha Contamination" hazard signs, and stolen a 1952 model pickup truck that was contaminated with plutonium and scheduled for burial in a hazardous waste pit. *(National Nuclear Security Administration)*

President Kennedy touring the NERVA nuclear facility at Area 25. The plan was to build a nuclear-powered rocket ship to take men to Mars in the astonishingly short time frame of 124 days. *(Department of Energy)*

While working on the nuclear space ship program, T. D. Barnes walked to work each day through this 1,150-foot-long underground tunnel below Area 25. *(Department of Energy)*

The Nuclear Rocket Test Facility at Jackass Flats, located in Area 25, seen here from above sometime in the 1960s. Three test cells (ETS-1, E-MAD, and R-MAD) were connected by a remote-controlled railroad that transported the highly radioactive reactor between them. *(Department of Energy)*

The engine for the Mars rocket can be seen at the center of the Engine Test Stand-1, positioned upside down to prevent it from taking off during testing. Operating at 3680.6 degrees Fahrenheit meant the nuclear reactor inside the engine needed to be cooled down by liquid hydrogen, contained in white industrial dewars seen at right. *(Department of Energy)*

Moving the first A-12 to Area 51, over the Cajon Pass in California. The transport crate had been disguised to look like a generic wide load. *(CIA)*

A full-scale mock-up of the Oxcart being assembled at Area 51 in 1959, even before the CIA contract was officially secured. The facility had been deserted after nuclear fallout shuttered the place in the summer of 1957. These Lockheed Skunk Workers were among the earliest returnees. *(Collection of Roadrunners Internationale/CIA)*

Setting up the legendary Area 51 pylon, or radar test pole. The radar antennas, manned and monitored by EG&G, were located a mile away from the pole. *(Collection of Roadrunners Internationale/ CIA)*

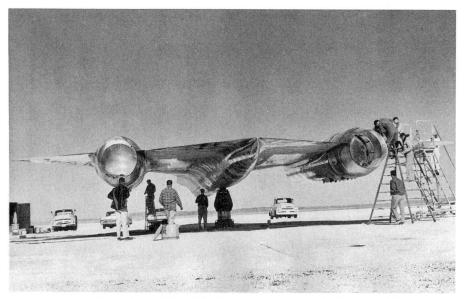

Less than eight feet of the fifty-five-foot-long pole is visible here. The rest of the pole is underground, below a concrete pad, and rises up from an underground chamber built inside the desert floor. *(Collection of Roadrunners Internationale/CIA)*

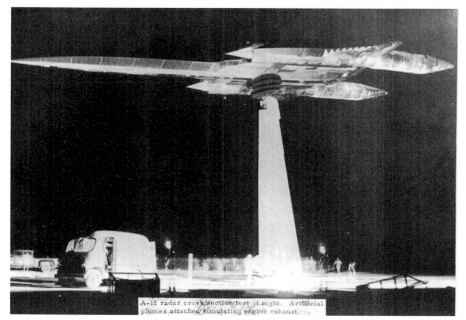

A-12 radar cross-section test at night. Artificial plumes attached simulating engine exhaust.

Working at night meant less of a chance of being surveilled by Soviet spy satellites. "Getting an aircraft up on the radar test pole took eighteen minutes. It took another eighteen minutes to get it back down," says Ed Lovick. "That left only a set amount of time to shoot radar at it and take data recordings." As soon as technicians were done, they took the aircraft down and whisked it away into its hangar. *(Collection of Roadrunners Internationale/CIA)* shook hands with any of the generals; they were busy and way above his pay grade. Besides, Martin's left hand was wrapped in a bandage, which made work slightly challenging, although he was most grateful to still have a thumb. Martin had been working with a saw and a pipe the week before when his tool slipped and nearly severed his most important finger. Fortunately, a flight surgeon was working with a project pilot in the hangar next door and Martin got his thumb sewn together fast.

It was April 25, 1962. Just a few buildings down from where Martin worked, Lockheed test pilot Louis Schalk sat in a recliner inside a Quonset hut taking a nap when a man from the Agency put a hand on his shoulder and said, "Lou, wake up!" The Oxcart was ready and it was time for Lou Schalk to fly. Two physiological support division officers helped Schalk into a flight suit, which looked like a coverall. There was no need for a pressure suit because today Schalk was only going to make a taxi test. Out on the tarmac, an engineer rolled up a metal set of stairs and Schalk climbed up into the strange-looking aircraft. There were no observers other than the crew. John Parangosky, who authored a secret interagency monograph called "The Oxcart History," declassified in 2007, noted that if anyone had been watching he would have been unable to process what he was looking at. "A casual observer would have been startled by the appearance of this vehicle; he would have perhaps noticed especially its extremely long, slim shape, its two enormous jet engines, its long, sharp projecting nose, and its swept-back wings which appeared far too short to support the fuselage in flight." It was a revolutionary airplane, Parangosky wrote, able to fly at three times the speed of sound for more than three thousand miles without refueling—all the way from Nevada to DC in less than an hour. "Toward the end of its flight, when fuel began to run low, it could cruise at over 90,000 feet."

But of course there were no casual observers present at Area 51. On that sunny day at Area 51 in April of 1962, this was the only A-12 Oxcart that Lockheed had completed for the CIA so far.

As for all the remarkable things the aircraft had been meticulously designed to do, it wasn't able to do any of them yet. Sitting on the tarmac, the aircraft was 160,000 pounds of titanium outfitted with millions of dollars' worth of expensive equipment that no one yet knew how to work, certainly not above seventy thousand feet. Like its predecessor the U-2, the Oxcart was an aircraft without a manual. Unlike the U-2, this aircraft was technologically forty years ahead of its time. Some of the records the Oxcart would soon set would hold all the way into the new millennium.

Lou Schalk fired up the engines and began rolling down the runway for the taxi test. To everyone's surprise, including Lou Schalk's, the aircraft unexpectedly got lift. Given the enormous engine power, the aircraft suddenly started flying—lifting up just twenty feet off the ground. Stunned and horrified, Kelly Johnson watched from the control tower. "The aircraft began wobbling," Johnson wrote in his notes, which "set up lateral oscillations which were horrible to see." Johnson feared the airplane might crash before its first official flight. Schalk was equally surprised and decided not to try to circle around. Instead he set the plane down as quickly as he could. This meant landing in the dry lake bed, nearly two miles beyond where the runway ended. When it hit the earth, the aircraft sent up a huge cloud of dust, obscuring it from view. Schalk turned the plane around and drove back toward the control towers, still engulfed in a cloud of dust and dirt. When he got back, the Lockheed engineers ran up to the airplane on the metal rack of stairs. Kelly Johnson had only four words for Schalk: "What in Hell, Lou?" For about fifteen very tense minutes, Johnson had thought Lou Schalk had wrecked the CIA's only Oxcart spy plane.

The following day, Schalk flew again, this time with Kelly Johnson's blessings but still not as an official first flight. Harry Martin was standing on the tarmac when the aircraft took off. "It was beautiful. Remarkable. Just watching it took your breath away," Martin recalls. "I remember thinking, This is cool. And then, all of a sudden, as Schalk rose up in the air, pieces of the airplane started to fall off!" The engineers standing next to Martin panicked. Harry Martin thought for sure the airplane was going to crash. But Lou Schalk kept flying. The pieces of the airplane were thin slices of the titanium fuselage, called fillets. Their sudden absence did not affect low-altitude flight. Schalk flew for forty minutes and returned to Area 51. It was mission accomplished for Schalk but not for the engineers. They spent the next four days roaming around Groom Lake attempting to locate and reattach the pieces of the plane. Still, it was a milestone for the CIA. Three years, ten months, and seven days had passed since Kelly Johnson first presented his plans for a Mach 3 spy plane to Richard Bissell, and here was the Oxcart, finally ready for its first official flight.

Agency officials were flown in from Washington to watch and to celebrate. Jim Freedman coordinated pickups and deliveries between McCarran Airport and the Ranch. It was a grand, congratulatory affair with lots of drinking in the newly constructed bar, called House-Six. Rare film footage of the historic event, shot by the CIA, shows men in suits milling around the tarmac slapping one another on the back over this incredible flying machine. They watch the aircraft take off and disappear from view. Schalk traveled up to thirty thousand feet, flew around in the restricted airspace for fifty-nine minutes, and came back down. His top speed was four hundred miles per hour. Watching from the tarmac was Richard Bissell, tall and gangly, wearing a dark suit and a porkpie hat. Bissell had been invited to attend the groundbreaking event as a guest of Kelly Johnson. It was a significant gesture; the two men had become friends, and Kelly Johnson was notably making a point. "Part of what made Kelly Johnson such a good man was that he was extremely loyal to the people he considered his friends," Ed Lovick explains. For Bissell, the visit to Area 51 had to have been bittersweet. It would be the last time he would ever set foot at the facility he had overseen for the CIA since it was nothing but a desert floor. Richard Bissell would never be invited back again.

And Area 51 would soon have a new mayor.

It was late at night in the summer of 1962 and Bud Wheelon sat in the library in the Washington, DC, home of Howard and Jane

Roman, two clandestine officers with CIA. It was only Wheelon's second month employed by the Agency, and because he was not a career spy, he had had a lot of catching up to do. Almost every night, he worked until ten, having just accepted the job that made him the Agency's first head of the Directorate of Science and Technology, or DS&T. Only thirty-three years old, Wheelon was a brilliant ballistic-missile scientist and signals intelligence analyst. He was also a graduate of MIT and had played rugby with James Killian when Killian was the president there. Now he had been hand-picked by President Kennedy's science advisers, including James Killian, to replace Richard Bissell on all overhead reconnaissance projects for the CIA. This included satellites, U-2 operations, and the Oxcart spy plane. It was the job Bissell had declined, but "in this way, I became the new 'Mayor of Area 51,'" Wheelon explains.

"I did not have much to do at night so I started reading clandestine reports, which I'd never seen before," Wheelon says. Although he found many uninteresting, one in particular caught his eye. "It made me concerned. At the time, there was a very serious National Intelligence Estimate under way for President Kennedy, one that would address the question: Will the Russians put nuclear missiles in Cuba? I had been briefed that the estimate was coming down on the side that the Russians would not do such a thing. The Pentagon had decided that putting missiles in Cuba was too reckless a move for the Russians and that they would not do such a reckless thing."

The Pentagon was dead wrong. As Wheelon read dozens of intelligence reports, one rose up like a red flag. "One thing you have to worry about with anyone informing against a person or a state is fabrication," Wheelon explains. "There were a lot of Cubans in Miami [at the time] whose sugar plantations had been taken away from them by Castro and they wanted action taken. But there was one report that caught my eye. The informant said that he'd seen very long trailers, big trucks, led by jeeps with Soviet security people inside. As these trucks made their way through certain villages, Cubans were directing traffic so the long trailers could get by. In South America, often on the street corners, you will find post-office boxes. They are not squat boxes with a level opening like you find in the States. Instead, they are more of a traditional letterbox attached at the top of a long pole. The informant witnessed one of these very long trailer trucks coming up to an intersection and not being able to make the curb. There was a letterbox blocking the way. Some of the Soviet security people got out of the truck. They grabbed an acetylene torch from the back and cut the letterbox right down. They didn't waste any time or give it a second thought. When I read that, I thought, Whoever reported this is no fabricator. This is not a detail you could make up. Whatever was in those trailers was too important to let a letterbox stand in the way."

Wheelon believed there were missiles inside the trailers. Missiles with nuclear warheads. Unknown to Wheelon at the time, his new boss, CIA director John McCone, also believed this was true. Except McCone wasn't around Washington, DC; he was in Paris, on his honeymoon. This left Wheelon in charge of more than was usual for a newcomer to the CIA. Concerned by the intelligence report, Wheelon asked to meet with the head of the board of the National Intelligence Council, Sherman Kent. "I went to him and I said, 'Sherm, I am new around here so you should discount a lot of what I say. I am not a professional intelligence person, but it looks to me like the evidence is overwhelming that they have missiles down there.'" Sherman Kent thanked Wheelon for his advice but explained that the board was going to present President Kennedy with the opposite conclusion—that there were no Soviet missiles in Cuba.

The Cuban missile crisis is a story of conflict between the United States and the Soviet Union, and the drama that culminated in a ten-day standoff between two superpowers on the brink of thermonuclear war. But it is also the story of two powerful rivals within the American services, the CIA and the U.S. Air Force, and how they set aside historical differences to work together to save the world from near nuclear annihilation. Like so many international crises of the Cold War, the Cuban missile crisis had its link to Area 51—through the U-2.

During the crisis, the CIA and the Air Force worked together to conduct the U-2 spy mission that caused the Soviet Union to back down. How this was accomplished not only involved two key Area 51 players but also set a precedent for the power-sharing arrangement at Area 51 that worked well for a while, until it didn't work anymore. The diplomatic efforts of one Army Air Force old-timer and one CIA newcomer helped set the stage for success. The old-timer was General Jack Ledford, and the newcomer was Bud Wheelon.

On the afternoon of August 29, 1962, a U-2 spy plane flying over Cuba spotted eight surface-to-air missile sites in the western part of Cuba, the same SA-2 missile systems that had shot down Gary Powers two years before. The following week, three more missile sites were discovered on the island, as well as a Soviet MiG-21 parked on the Santa Clara airfield nearby. For two months, the Agency had been analyzing reports that said between 4,000 and 6,000 individuals from the Soviet bloc had arrived in Cuba, including 1,700 Soviet military technicians. Cuban citizens were being kept from entering port areas where the Soviet-bloc ships were unloading unusually large crates, ones big enough to "contain airplane fuselage or missile components." The implications were threefold: that Russia was building up the Cuban armed forces, that they were establishing multiple missile sites, and that they were establishing electronic jamming facilities against Cape Canaveral in Florida as well as other important U.S. installations. The director of the CIA, John McCone, had already told the president's military advisers that he believed the Soviets were laying a deadly trap involving nuclear missiles. But there was no hard evidence of the missiles themselves, the military argued, and their position on that fact was firm. (The Pentagon did not doubt that the Soviets wanted to put nuclear missiles on Cuba; officials just didn't think they'd accomplished that yet.) McCone left for his honeymoon in Paris.

In the following month, September, bad weather got in the way of good photographic intelligence. Day after day it rained over

Cuba or the island was shrouded in heavy cloud cover. Finally, on September 29, a CIA U-2 mission over the Isle of Pines and the Bay of Pigs revealed yet another previously unknown missile site. President Kennedy's top advisers were convened. The CIA warned the advisers of more unknown dangers in Cuba and pushed for additional overflights so as to gain better intelligence on military installations there. Secretary of Defense Robert McNamara and Secretary of State Dean Rusk were opposed to the idea. Not another Gary Powers incident, they said. But on October 5 and 7, the CIA got presidential approval to run two additional missions of its own. The resultant news was hard to ignore: there were now a total of nineteen surface-to-air missile sites on the island of Cuba, meaning there was something very important that the Soviets were intent on defending there. The Pentagon held firm. There was still no hard data revealing actual missiles, McNamara and Rusk said. Making matters even more complicated, JFK's Air Force chief of staff, General Curtis LeMay, was pushing for preemptive strikes against Cuba. It was a volatile and incredibly dangerous situation. If the CIA was correct and there already were nuclear missiles in Cuba, then LeMay's so-called preemptive strikes would actually initiate a nuclear war, not prevent one.

What the Agency needed desperately was a wizard of diplomacy, someone who could help the rival agencies see eye to eye so they could all work together to get the Soviets to back down. The Agency and the Air Force had decidedly different ideas on imminent missions; the CIA wanted to gather more intelligence with the U-2; the Air Force wanted to prepare for war. An individual who could wear both hats with relative objectivity was needed, someone who could see both sides of the debate. In a rare moment of accord, both sides agreed that the man for the job was Brigadier General Jack Ledford. Just a few weeks earlier, Ledford had been asked by McCone to serve as the director of the Office of Special Activities at the Pentagon, meaning he would be the Pentagon liaison to the CIA at Area 51. Ledford had just graduated from the Industrial College of the Armed Forces and was looking forward to moving out west when his old World War II commander General LeMay encouraged him to take the new CIA liaison job.

LeMay had known Ledford since the war in the Pacific when Ledford flew under his command. A former Olympic diver, Ledford was tall, charismatic, and handsome. According to Wheelon, "He was someone whose charisma was contagious. Ledford was impossible not to like to be around." There was, of course, the legendary story of Ledford's plane crash, involving heroics in the Pacific theater during World War II. As a captain in the Air Force, Ledford was making a bombing run over Kyushu Island, Japan, when he was attacked by Japanese fighter jets, his airplane and his own body hit with fire. Ledford's flight engineer, Master Sergeant Harry C. Miller, was hit in the head. The medic on board treated Miller and tried to treat Ledford with opiates, who declined so he could keep his head clear. With the aircraft crashing, Ledford and the medic opened a parachute, cut the shroud lines, and attached the chute to the unconscious flight engineer. They dropped the man through the nose of the wheel well; Captain Ledford followed, delaying opening his own parachute so he could be next to Sergeant Miller when he landed. Miller would be unconscious when he hit the earth, and without Ledford's help he would likely have broken his back. The medic, not far behind, later recounted how amazing it was that Ledford's daring and dangerous plan had actually worked.

Now, two decades later, at the Cuban missile crisis round table, Ledford showed the same foresight in preempting a potentially deadly situation. The first thing General Ledford did was present the CIA and the Air Force with a shoot-down analysis, detailing the odds for losing a U-2 on another overflight. The chances were one in six, Ledford said. He pushed for the U-2 mission, arguing that it was better to know now if there really were nuclear missiles in Cuba than to wish you knew later on, when it could be too late. Once these cold hard facts were on the table, the heart of the debate became clear. The point of contention was not whether or not to fly the mission. Rather, it was *who* would fly the mission — the Air Force or the CIA. As it turned out, each organization wanted the job. President Kennedy felt the mission needed to involve a pilot wearing a blue U.S. Air Force pilot suit. Kennedy felt that if a CIA spy plane were to get shot down over Cuba, there would be too much baggage attached to the event, that it would rekindle hostilities over the Gary Powers shoot-down. But General Ledford knew what the president did not: that the CIA had higher-quality U-2 airplanes, ones far less likely to end up getting shot down. Agency U-2s flew five thousand feet higher than their heavier Air Force U-2 counterparts, which were weighed down by additional reconnaissance gear. The CIA airplanes also had better electronic countermeasure packages, meaning they had more sophisticated means of jamming SA-2 missiles coming at them. So Ledford performed diplomatic wizardry by convincing the CIA to actually loan the Air Force its prized U-2 airplanes. With the fate of the free world at stake, the CIA and the Air Force agreed to work together to solve the crisis.

On October 14, an Air Force pilot flying a CIA U-2 brought home film footage of Cuba that the White House needed to see. Photographs showing nuclear missiles supplied by the Soviet Union and set up on missile stands in Cuba. Those eight canisters of film brought back by the CIA's U-2 set in motion the Cuban missile crisis, bringing the world closer than it had ever come to all-out nuclear war. They would also give the work going on at Area 51 a shot in the arm. The Pentagon told the CIA they wanted the Oxcart operations ready immediately so the aircraft could be used to overfly Cuba. A CIA review of Oxcart, declassified in 2007, said it flatly: "The Oxcart program suddenly assumed greater significance than ever, and its achievement of operational status became one of the highest national priorities."

CHAPTER ELEVEN

What Airplane?

Gardening helped CIA pilot Kenneth Collins relax. He had over a hundred rosebushes in his garden, which he and his wife, Jane, pruned together on weekends after Collins returned home from a long, mysterious week at the Ranch. At Area 51, where he worked as a project pilot, Collins went by the code name Ken Colmar. "Same first name because you will instantly respond to it when called," Collins explains. "Colmar for the *C*, in case you had something monogrammed." His call sign was Dutch 21 but most men on base called him the Iceman. The pressure-suit officers came up with the nickname. "I was known to show no emotion or irritation even after a particularly dangerous flight," Collins recalls. The pressure-suit officers could gauge how tough a flight was by how sweaty a pilot's underwear was when they helped pilots undress. Collins's underwear was always remarkably dry.

Flying Oxcart was, to an Air Force pilot, the single most elite job in the nation at the time. Ken Collins "commuted" to Area 51 each week, flying in from sunny Southern California, where he and other pilots who now worked for the CIA pretended to live normal lives with their pretty wives and, ideally, a few children. Having a stable marriage and family had become a CIA-pilot mandate during Oxcart, something that was not in place during the U-2. It was Gary Powers's alcoholic wife who'd triggered the change. Some in the Agency believed she put the secrecy of the entire U-2 program at risk with behavior that even they could not control. Once, Barbara Powers got it into her head to visit her husband at his clandestine post in Turkey. She made it as far as Athens before the officer assigned to watch her notified Powers that he would be out of a job if he couldn't keep his impetuous wife in line. Ken Collins was told this story during his first interview at the Pentagon. Loose lips didn't just sink ships, he was reminded; loose lips could trigger nuclear war. Collins also learned that his wife, Jane, would be subject to psychological screening were he to be accepted into a top secret program rumored to involve "space travel."

Collins and his family were moved from their home in South Carolina to a Los Angeles suburb called Northridge and into a four-bedroom raised ranch with a two-car garage and an avocado tree out front. He was thirty-six years old. Jane attended church and collected antique china. All four of Jane and Ken Collins's children, two boys and two girls, maintained good grades in school. The neighbors were told Mr. Collins worked for Hughes Aircraft Company. Collins was told to report nosy neighbors to the CIA, and if any foreign-borns tried to befriend the Collinses, they were to notify the Agency, who would look into the matter.

Each Monday morning, Collins left his home and drove to Burbank Airport, nine miles to the southwest. There, he and the other Oxcart pilots climbed aboard Constellation propeller planes and headed to Area 51, never with more than two pilots per airplane—a guideline put into place after the Mount Charleston crash eight years earlier. The deaths of those top Agency and Air Force managers and scientists had set progress on the U-2 program back several months. Now, in 1963, Oxcart was already more than a year behind schedule. The Agency could not afford to lose any pilots. The vetting process alone took eighteen months and getting familiar with the aircraft took another year.

After leaving Burbank, Collins and his fellow pilots were flown, two by two, up over the Mojave Desert to the northeast, past China Lake, and into the Tikaboo Valley. Flying into the restricted airspace above the Nevada Test Site, Collins would look out the window and make a mental note of the ever-growing landscape of giant craters. The appearance of a new, moonlike subsidence crater was often a weekly occurrence now that nuclear testing had moved underground. When seen from above, the landscape at the Nevada Test Site looked like a battlefield after the apocalypse. For Collins, the destruction was a solid visual reminder of what scorched earth would look like after a nuclear war.

The Agency couldn't have chosen a more dedicated pilot. Collecting intelligence on dangerous reconnaissance flights was Ken Collins's life mission; it was what he did best. He seemed to be propelled by a natural talent and kept alive by an unknown force Collins called fate. "Fate is a hunter," Collins believes. "When it comes for you, it comes," and for whatever reason it was not time for death to come to him yet. This was a notion Collins formulated during the Korean War while flying reconnaissance missions and watching so many talented and brave fellow pilots die. How else but by fate did he survive all 113 combat missions he had flown? On those classified missions, the young Collins was armed with only a camera in the nose of his airplane as he flew deep into North Korea, sometimes all the way over the Yalu River, being fired at by MiG fighter jets. During the war, he was awarded a Distinguished Flying Cross and also the coveted Silver Star for valor, the third-highest military decoration a member of the armed services can receive. Both medals were pinned on Collins's chest before he turned twenty-four.

But now, as an Oxcart pilot, Collins kept his medals tucked away in a drawer, never mentioning that he had received them. As with many servicemen, glory was a difficult distinction to contemplate when so many of your fellows had died. Accepting fate as the hunter made things easier for Collins, which is how he dealt with the memory of his closest friend and former wingman from the Fifteenth Tactical Reconnaissance Squadron, Charles R. "Chuck" Parkerson. The two men had flown on many missions together, but there was one from which Parkerson never came home. "We had flown into North Korea and back out side by side," Collins recalls. "We were almost home when Parkerson radioed me. He said the engine on his RF-80 had flamed out and he was unable to restart it. I saw he was losing altitude quickly and he knew that soon he would crash." Parachuting into enemy territory meant certain death. "Over the radio, Parkerson asked me, 'What should I do?'" Collins explains. "I said, 'Fly out over the Yellow Sea and I'll fly with you.' I told him to bail out in the water and I'd send his coordinates back to base for a rescue team." It seemed like a good idea, and Collins flew alongside his wingman as they headed toward the Yellow Sea. Parkerson prepared for a bailout. "But there was a problem," Collins recalls. "The canopy on Parkerson's RF-80 was stuck. Jammed. It wouldn't open, which meant he was trapped inside the airplane. There was nothing I could do for my friend except to fly alongside him all the way until the end." Collins watched Parkerson land his airplane on the sea. With Parkerson unable to get out of the sinking aircraft, Collins waited, watching from the air as his friend drowned. "When your time is up, it is up," Collins recalls.

Ten years later, it was 1963, the Korean War was history, and there was an airplane to get ready at Area 51. After the twin-prop passed over the last set of hills on the Nevada Test Site's eastern edge, the airstrip at Groom Lake came into view, and Collins thought about how no one but his fellow CIA pilots had any idea who he really was. During training missions, the papers in Collins's flight pouch identified him only as a NASA weather pilot. His space-age-looking aircraft was registered to an airfield called Watertown Strip, Nevada. He was never to carry any personal effects with him in the airplane. When the Lockheed Constellation landed on the tarmac at Area 51, security guards took his ID and papers and locked them away in a metal box. Each Friday, before the afternoon flight home, Collins's identity was returned to him.

His mission flight that day, May 24, 1963, should have been like any other flight. By now, there were a total of five Oxcarts being flight-tested at Area 51, and Collins breezed through his pre-briefing with the Lockheed engineers, making mental notes about the different tasks he was to perform during the flight. The engineers wanted to know how certain engine controls worked during acceleration and slow cruise. Today's test would be subsonic with the high-performance aircraft traveling somewhere around 450 miles per hour, like a racehorse out for a trot. It was to be a short mission up over Utah, into Wyoming, and back to Area 51. Air Force chase pilot Captain Donald Donohue would start out following Collins in an F-101 Voodoo. Later, Jack Weeks, also an Oxcart project pilot, would pick up the task.

For a little over an hour, everything appeared to be normal. Heading into Wendover, Utah, Collins made note of a large cumulus cloud that lay ahead. As Collins slowed down, Jack Weeks signaled that he was going to head back to Area 51. The F-101 could not handle flying as slow as Collins needed to fly that day. Besides, from Weeks's perspective, everything on the Oxcart looked fine. Collins gave Weeks the okay signal with one hand in the cockpit window and headed into the cloud.

"Suddenly, the altimeter was rapidly unwinding, indicating a rapid loss of speed," Collins recalls. In heavy clouds, Collins had no visual references to determine where he was. "I advanced the throttles to counter the loss of airspeed. But instead of responding, and without any warning, the aircraft pitched up and flipped over with me trapped underneath. Then it went into an inverted flat spin." The Agency's million-dollar A-12 Oxcart was unrecoverable and crashing. Collins needed to bail out.

Collins had no idea how close he was to the Earth's surface because he was in the middle of a cloud and couldn't see out of it. He also did not know if he was over a mountain range, which would mean he had even less time to eject. Collins closed his visor and grabbed the ejection ring that was positioned between his legs. He pushed his head firmly against the headrest and pulled. This kind of radical ejection from a prized top secret aircraft is not easy to forget, and Collins recalls dramatic details. "The canopy of the aircraft flew off and disappeared but I was still upside down, with the aircraft on top of me," he explains. "Having pulled the D-ring, my boot stirrups snapped back. The explosive system in the seat rocket engaged, shooting me downward and away from the aircraft." First Collins separated from the Oxcart. Next he separated from his seat. After that, he was a body falling through the air until a small parachute called a drogue snapped open, slowing his body down. In his long history of flying airplanes, this was the first time Collins had ever had to bail out. Falling to Earth, he tried to get a sense of what state he might be over. Was he in Nevada or Utah? The ground below him appeared to be high-desert terrain, low hills but no mountains that he could see. He was still too high up to discern if there were roads. As he floated down, in the distance he spotted the heavy black aircraft tumbling through the air until it disappeared from sight. "I remember seeing a large, black column of smoke rise up from the desert floor and thinking, That's my airplane." Only now there was nothing left of it but an incinerated hunk of titanium smoldering on the ground. Fate was a hunter, all right.

Suddenly, Collins felt his parachute break away and he began to free-fall once again. Had his luck run out? he wondered. Was today the day he was going to die? But then, as suddenly as the one parachute had broken away, he felt another tug at his shoulders, and a second parachute blossomed above him. This one was more than twice the size of the drogue. He began to float gently toward Earth. Collins hadn't been told that the A-12 Oxcart ejection system had two separate parachutes. The first parachute, or drogue, was small enough to slow the pilot down and get him to an altitude of fifteen thousand feet. Then the drogue chute would jettison away in advance of the main parachute deploying. This large, thirty-five-foot-diameter landing aid was the one most pilots were familiar with.

With the ground below him quickly getting closer, Collins could see roads and sagebrush. He wondered how long it might take for anyone to locate him. When fellow pilot Jack Weeks had left him, just minutes before the crash, everything on Collins's aircraft had seemed fine, but because of secrecy protocols, Collins had not made radio contact with the command post before he bailed out. He could see that he was most likely somewhere north of the Salt Lake salt flats. Collins tucked his legs up and assumed the landing position. When he hit the ground, he rolled. His mind went through the checklist of what to do next.

Collins unclipped himself from the parachute and began collecting everything around him. Flight-protocol pages and film-strips of navigational maps fluttered across the desert. As he hurried to collect the top secret papers, he was surprised to hear a car motor in the distance. Looking up, he saw a pickup truck bouncing toward him along a dirt desert road. "As it got closer, I could see there were three men in the front cab," Collins recalls. "The truck pulled alongside me and came to a stop. I could see they had my aircraft canopy in the back of their pickup."

The men, who appeared to be local ranchers, sized up Collins. Because the flight had been subsonic, Collins was wearing a standard flight suit and not a high-altitude pressure suit, which would have made him look like an astronaut or an alien and likely prompted a lot more questions. Instead, the ranchers asked Collins if he wanted a ride. They said they knew exactly where his airplane had crashed, and if he hopped in, they'd give him a ride back to his plane. Until that moment, no civilian without a top secret security clearance had ever laid eyes on the Oxcart, and Collins had strict orders to keep it that way. He'd been briefed on what to do in a security breach such as this one, given a cover story by the Agency that fit perfectly with the proximity to the Nevada Test Site—and with the times. Collins told the ranchers that his aircraft was an F-105 fighter jet and that it had a nuclear weapon on board. The men's expressions changed from helpful to fearful. "They got very nervous and said if I wanted a ride, I better jump in quick because they were not staying around Wendover for long," Collins recalls.

The ranchers drove Collins to the nearest highway patrol office. There, he jumped out, took his airplane canopy from the back of the truck, and watched the men speed off. Collins reached into the pocket of his flight suit. Inside, he found the note that read *call this number,* followed by a telephone number. Also in his pocket was a dime. Inside the highway patrol office, Collins asked the officer on duty where he could find the nearest pay phone. The man pointed around to the side of the building, and using the Agency's dime, Collins made the phone call that no Agency pilot ever wants to make. A little less than an hour later, Kelly Johnson's private airplane landed in Wendover, Utah, along with several men from the CIA. After a brief exchange of words so Kelly Johnson could confirm that Collins was physically okay, Collins boarded the airplane. During the two-hour flight to the Lovelace Clinic in New Mexico, no one said a word. "There would be plenty of talking to do during the debriefing," Collins says, "and with the Agency's tape recorders taking everything down." A crash of a CIA spy plane meant someone had some explaining to do.

Back in the control room at Groom Lake, navigator Sam Pizzo had a monumental amount of work on his hands. News of Collins's crash had just hit the command post, and it was up to Colonel Holbury, the air commander of Detachment 1 of the 1129th U.S. Air Force Special Activities Squadron, to put together a search team for the crash site. "Maintenance guys, security guys, navigators, we all took off in trucks and airplanes and headed to Utah," Pizzo explains. With Collins confirmed alive, the goal now was to locate every single piece of the wrecked airplane, "every nut, bolt, and sliver of fuselage." The efforts would be staged from an old, abandoned airfield northwest of the dry lakes. These were the same facilities where World War II bombers had practiced for the Hiroshima and Nagasaki atomic bomb runs. The quarters there, long since deserted, were rudimentary. There was no running water or heat. This meant the men from Groom Lake brought their own cooks, cots, and gear as part of their crash-recovery team.

Once they found the site, the work crew had a lot of digging to do. The aircraft, Article #123, hadn't broken apart in flight, but given the speed at which it had hit the earth, huge sections of the airplane had become buried. Critically important was locating every loose piece of the titanium fuselage. The metal was rare and expensive, and the fact that the Agency's spy plane was hand-forged from titanium was a closely held secret. If a news reporter or a local got a hold of even the smallest piece of the aircraft, its unusual composition would raise questions that might threaten the cover of the entire Oxcart program. Equally critical to national security was making sure the radar-absorbing materials, known as composite and that covered the entire airplane, remained in government control. If a piece of the plane got into the wrong hands, the results could be disastrous: the Russians could learn the secret of stealth.

Along with a crew of more than one hundred men, the Agency brought its own horses to the crash site. Men from Groom Lake took to the desert terrain on horseback and began their search. For two days they scoured the ground, looking for stray pieces of airplane as well as for flight papers and maps that had been in the cockpit with Collins. "By the time we were done, we'd combed over every single square inch of ground," Pizzo recalls. A massive C-124 transport plane hauled the pieces of the airplane back to Area 51. In a heavily guarded hangar there, what was left of the airplane was spread out, piece by piece, in an effort to re-create its shape.

Richard Bissell's departure from Area 51 a year earlier had left a huge power vacuum at the base. There was a general feeling among the men working there now that the vacuum was being filled by Air Force brass. This made perfect sense. Whereas the U-2 was, in essence, a motorized glider, the A-12 Oxcart was the highest, fastest, most state-of-the-art piloted aircraft in the world. For men who prided themselves on airpower—as did everyone involved in the U.S. Air Force—the supersonic Oxcart was the top dog. The Area 51 facility was now one of the Air Force's most prestigious billets, a place where officers got to be in charge of their "own little air force," as Major General Paul Bacalis had once said. What this meant was that Pentagon favorites, usually World War II heroes who had survived dangerous, death-defying missions, were rewarded with key positions at Area 51. Men like Colonel Robert Holbury.

At Area 51, Holbury's official title was air commander of the U.S. Air Force Special Activities Squadron at Las Vegas, the non-classified reference name for Oxcart. A former fighter pilot during World War II, Holbury had been given a commendation by General Patton for a dangerous low-flying reconnaissance mission over the Saar River, in western Germany, which he survived despite coming under heavy enemy fire. This meant Holbury was the official wing commander at the base when Ken Collins crashed the first Oxcart spy plane. In Air Force culture, when an airplane crashes, someone has to take the blame. Collins explains: "In the SAC [Strategic Air Command] mind-set, if there's an accident, the wing commander suffers the consequences." Instead, Collins believes, Holbury tried to get Collins to be the fall guy. "Holbury didn't want blame; he wanted a star. He wanted to become a general, so he tried to put the blame on me. After the crash, even before the investigation, he requested that I be fired."

Collins was unwilling to accept that. Fortunately for Collins's career, Kelly Johnson, the builder of the aircraft, didn't care about blame as much as he wanted to find out what had gone wrong with his airplane. Listening to Collins describe what had happened during the debriefing, Johnson couldn't figure out what caused the aircraft to crash. He wondered if there was something Collins had forgotten, or was maybe leaving out. "I was clear in my mind that the crash was a mechanical error and not a pilot error," Collins explains. "So when Kelly Johnson asked would I try unconventional methods like hypnosis and truth serum, I said yes. I was willing to do anything I could to get to the truth." While the Pentagon's accident board conducted a traditional investigation, Collins submitted to a far less conventional way of seeking out the truth of the cause of the crash.

Inside the flight surgeon's office at Lockheed, Collins sat with a CIA-contracted hypnotist from Boston, "a small, rotund man dressed in a fancy suit," as Collins recalls. "He tried very hard to put me in a trance, only it didn't work. I don't think he realized that hypnotizing a fighter pilot was not as easy as he thought it might be." Next, Collins was injected with sodium thiopental, also known as truth serum. Collins remembers the day well. "I told my wife, Jane, I was going to work for a few hours, which was unusual to begin with because it was a Sunday. The point of the treatment was to see if I could remember details other than those I relayed in the original debrief with the CIA. But yes, even with the sodium pentothal in my system, everything I said was exactly the same. The treatment takes a lot out of you and after it was over, I was very unsteady on my feet. Three CIA agents brought me home late that Sunday evening. One drove my car, the other two carried me inside and laid me down on the couch. I was still loopy from the drugs. They handed Jane the car keys and left without saying a word."

When Collins woke up the next morning, he figured the only conclusion his wife could have drawn was that her husband had gone out on a Sunday and gotten drunk. Feeling bad, he confided in her that he'd been given truth serum and could not say anything more. Jane told her husband a story of her own. She said that he didn't have to explain further because she had a pretty good idea what had happened to him on the job. Earlier in the week, Jane explained, immediately after Collins's crash, family friend and fellow Oxcart pilot Walt Ray had broken protocol and called Jane from Area 51 to tell her that Ken had bailed out of an airplane but that he was all right. "Where is he?" Jane had asked. Walt Ray said he didn't know. Jane then asked, "How can you know if Ken is okay if you don't even know where he is?" At the time Walt Ray didn't have an answer for that. So now, hangover or no hangover, Jane Collins was happy to have her husband home alive. After a lengthy investigation it was determined that a tiny, pencil-size part called a pitot tube had in fact caused the crash. The pitot tube measured the air coming into the aircraft and thereby controlled the airspeed indicator. Unlike in a car, where the driver can feel relative speed, in a plane, without a proper reading from an airspeed indicator, a pilot has no awareness of how fast he is going, and without correct airspeed information a pilot cannot land. When Collins flew into the cloud, the pitot tube reacted adversely to the moisture inside and froze. The false airspeed indicator caused the aircraft to stall. As a result of the stall, the Oxcart flipped upside down and crashed.

Ken Collins's crash in Utah caused the CIA to redouble its secrecy efforts regarding operations at Area 51. The press was told an F-105 crashed, and as of 2011, the Air Force still has it listed that way. Worried its cover was about to be blown, the Agency decided to shore up an accounting of who knew what about Oxcart. An analyst was assigned the task of combing through all the files the CIA had been keeping on journalists, civilians, and even retired Air Force personnel—anyone who showed a curiosity about what might be going on at Area 51. Beginning in the spring of 1963, the noted instances of what the CIA called "Project Oxcart Awareness Outside Cleared Community" drastically increased. Declassified in 2007 and never before made public, the CIA had been monitoring phone conversations of journalists who seemed interested in the Oxcart program. "Mr. Marvin Miles, Aviation Editor, Los Angeles Times, telephonically contacted Westinghouse Corp., Pittsburgh, attempting to confirm if employees of that firm were traveling covertly to 'the desert' each week in connection with top secret Project which he suspects may have 'CIA' association," read one memo. Another stated that "Mr. Robert Hotz, Editor Aviation Week, indicated his awareness of developments at Burbank." Of particular concern to the Agency was an article in the *Hartford Courant* that referred to the "secret development" of the J-58 engine. Another article in the Fontana, California, paper the *Herald News* speculated about the existence of Area 51, calling it a "super secret Project site." An increasingly suspicious CIA worked overtime to monitor journalists, and they also monitored regular citizens, including a Los Angeles–based taxi driver who was described in a memo marked "classified" as once having asked a Pratt and Whitney employee if he was "en route to Nevada."

With the Air Force steadily gaining a foothold in day-to-day operations at Area 51, it was the Air Force that the CIA should have been watching more closely in terms of the future of the spy plane program as a whole. It was not as if there weren't writing on the wall. In the year before Collins's crash, the Air Force had decided it wanted a Mach 3 Oxcart-type program of its own. Just as it had with the U-2, the Pentagon moved in on the CIA's spy plane territory. Only with the Oxcart, the Air Force ordered not one but three Air Force variants for its stable. One version, the YF-12A, would be used as an attack aircraft, its camera bay retrofitted to hold two 250-kiloton nuclear bombs. The second Oxcart variant the Air Force ordered could carry a drone on its back. The third was a two-seater version of the CIA's stealth spy plane, only instead of being designed to conduct high-speed, high-altitude reconnaissance missions over enemy territory during peacetime, the Air Force supersonic spy plane was meant to go in and take pictures of enemy territory immediately after a nuclear strike by U.S. bomber planes—to see if any strategic targets had been missed. Designated the RS-71 Blackbird, this now-famous aircraft had its letter designation accidentally inverted by President Lyndon B. Johnson in a public speech. Since the president is rarely ever "corrected," the Air Force changed its letter designation, which is how the SR-71 Blackbird got its name. (Originally, the letters stood for "Reconnaissance/Strike.")

There was no end to the irony in all of this. The Air Force's Mach 3 airplanes were a far cry from President Eisenhower's original idea to let the CIA create a spy plane with which to conduct espionage missions designed to prevent nuclear war. This new Air Force direction underscored the difference in the two services: the CIA was in the business of spying, and the Air Force was in the business of war.

There were other motives in play, including the ego of General Curtis LeMay. The Air Force had already spent eight hundred million dollars developing the B-70 bomber airplane—a massive, triangle-shaped, Mach 3, eight-engined bomber that had been General LeMay's passion project since its inception in 1959. When a fleet of eighty-five of these giant supersonic bombers was first proposed to Congress, LeMay, then head of the Strategic Air Command, had his proposition met with cheers. But the Gary Powers shoot-down in May of 1960 had exposed the vulnerability of LeMay's B-70 bombers, which would fly at the same height as the U-2. In 1963 LeMay was no longer head of the Strategic Air Command—instead, he was President Kennedy's Air Force chief of staff. Despite evidence showing the B-70 bomber was not a practical airplane, LeMay was not about to give up his beloved bomber without a fight.

When the CIA first briefed President Kennedy on how high and how fast the A-12 Oxcart would fly, the president was astonished. His first question, according to CIA officer Norman Nelson, was "Could it be converted into a long-range bomber to replace the B-70?" LeMay was in the room when Kennedy asked the question. The thought of losing his pet program to the Agency drove General LeMay wild. He lobbied the Pentagon to move forward with the B-70, and he stepped up his public relations campaign, personally promoting the B-70 bomber program in magazine interviews from *Aviation Week* to *Reader's Digest*. He was committed to appealing to as many Americans as possible, from aviation buffs to housewives. But by 1963, Kennedy was leaning toward canceling the B-70. In a budget message, he called it "unnecessary and economically unjustifiable." Congress cut back its B-70 order even further. The original order for eighty-five had already been cut down to ten, and now Congress cut that to four.

LeMay was furious. He flew from Washington, DC, to Burbank, California, to see Kelly Johnson at the Skunk Works. Longtime rivals, Kelly Johnson greeted LeMay with skepticism when LeMay asked for a briefing about the A-12. After Johnson was finished, LeMay gave Johnson a quid pro quo. "Johnson, I want a promise out of you that you won't lobby anymore against the B-70,"

LeMay said. Provided Kelly Johnson complied, LeMay promised to send Lockheed an Air Force purchase order for an interceptor version of Lockheed's A-12 Oxcart, in addition to the preexisting order. For Lockheed, this would mean a big new invoice to send to the Air Force. At first, Kelly Johnson was suspicious of LeMay's sincerity. That changed just a few weeks later when Secretary of Defense Robert McNamara showed up at the Skunk Works with the secretary of the Air Force and the assistant secretary of defense in tow. Now McNamara asked for a briefing on the A-12, during which he took "copious notes." Within a matter of months, the Pentagon ordered twenty-five more A-12 variants. The Pentagon already had a catchy name for its versions of the Oxcart. They would call them Blackbirds. *Black* because they had been developed in the dark by the CIA, and *birds* because they could fly. The meeting touched off the long-running battle between the two agencies over control of Area 51 and control of any U.S. government asset with wings. But this is exactly what had happened with the U-2. The CIA did all of the heavy lifting to get the aircraft aloft, only to have the program eventually taken over by the Pentagon for the Air Force.

At the Ranch, it was business as usual. No one but the generals had any idea that the CIA's spy plane program now officially had in the Pentagon a formidable rival that threatened its very existence. Instead, pilots, engineers, operators, scientists, and Air Force enlisted men worked triple shifts, around the clock, to get the A-12 Oxcart mission ready. These were the men who made up and supported the 1129th Special Activities Squadron at Groom Lake.

The J-58 jet engines built by Pratt and Whitney had taken forever to finish but now they were ready to fly. In January of 1963 they were finally delivered to the Ranch. A host of new problems occurred when the engines were first powered up. In one instance, engineers suspected a foreign object was stuck in an engine's heart, called the power plant, and was damaging internal parts. An X-ray showed the outline of a pen that had fallen into the engine's cover, called a nacelle, during final assembly in Burbank. From then on, Lockheed workers got coveralls without breast pockets. There were other problems. The engines worked like giant vacuums. Once powered up on the tarmac, they sucked in every loose object lying around, including rocks and metal screws. As a solution, Area 51 workers took to sweeping and then vacuuming the runway before each flight. It was a tedious but necessary job.

The next goal was to get the airplane to cruise at Mach 3. Nearly five times as fast as any commercial airplane, this was an aerodynamic feat that had never been accomplished before. Pushing through the lower Mach numbers was a laborious and dangerous task. Performance margins were met gradually, with a new set of challenges cropping up each day. As the airplane reached higher speeds, the 500-plus-degree temperatures began melting electrical components, many of which had to be redesigned and rewired. Chuck Yeager is credited with breaking the sound barrier in 1947, but every time a new aircraft moves through the speed of sound, which is 768 miles per hour, complications can arise. In the case of the Oxcart, the sonic shock unexpectedly caused the fuselage to flex in such a way that many structural parts became dangerously compromised. These parts had to be redesigned and replaced.

Some performance benchmarks came surprisingly quickly. In July of 1963, Lou Schalk flew briefly at Mach 3, much to the Agency's delight. But sustaining flight for ten minutes at Mach 3 took another seven months to achieve. Every flight was like an operational mission, with navigators plotting a course and making maps days before as they worked to test the Oxcart's internal navigation system, or INS. "When you're flying at that altitude and that speed, you need big checkpoints to validate information from the INS," recalls navigator Sam Pizzo. "Any old geographical landmark, like a mountain or a river, would not do. The Oxcart traveled too fast. Pilots would have to look for landmarks on the scale of the Grand Canyon or the Great Lakes," says the veteran navigator. "You can't imagine what new territory this was for a navigator. No amount of experience can prepare you when you work on an airplane that goes two or three times as fast as anything you navigated for before."

The essence of Area 51 was that everything that happened there happened big. Because all efforts were being made on orders of the president, and given the colossal scale of secrecy surrounding the project, there was a deeply patriotic sense that the free world depended on the work being performed at Area 51. The men worked tirelessly and with phenomenal ingenuity to overcome challenges that would have stymied countless others. And yet the strange paradox underlying all efforts at the Ranch was that Project Oxcart was also subject to unforeseeable world events. It could be given the ax at a moment's notice—which is what almost happened on November 22, 1963.

It was late in the day after a rainstorm and Captain Donald Donohue was working with a crew out on the dry lake bed. An F-101 chase plane had run off the airstrip and sunk into a layer of gypsum that was several inches deep. Working with a group of engineers and mechanics, Donohue led the efforts to lay down several long planks of steel that could then be used to tow the airplane out of where it had become stuck in the soggy lake bed.

"Pizzo came out," Donohue remembers. "He looked kinda pale. Then he said, 'Clean up and go home.' Well, something was not right. Sam Pizzo was a lot more talkative than that. Then he said something to the effect of 'We'll call you if we need you to come back.'"

"What the hell is going on?" Donohue remembers asking.

"President Kennedy has just been assassinated, in Dallas," Pizzo said solemnly.

It was a terrible shock, Donohue remembers. "Our commander in chief. Dead? I recall it like it was yesterday. Pizzo was right. We had to go home and wait this thing out. When [Lyndon] Johnson was vice president, he was entirely unaware about the existence of the A-12 program. And he didn't have a clue about Area 51." The future of Oxcart was contingent on the new president's call.

With President Kennedy dead, Lyndon Johnson would be briefed on the CIA's secret domestic base by CIA director John McCone on his eighth day as commander in chief. Until then, what Johnson would decide about the CIA's supersonic spy plane program was anybody's guess. The relationship between a new president and the CIA is always tenuous starting out. What happened to President Kennedy with the CIA and the Bay of Pigs raised the bar in terms of jeopardy for all future presidents of the United States. Only time would tell if Lyndon Johnson would authorize the completion of the Agency's Mach 3 spy plane out at Area 51.

CHAPTER TWELVE

Covering Up the Cover-Up

Jim Freedman remembers the first time he brought up the subject of UFOs with his EG&G supervisor at Area 51. It was sometime in the middle of the 1960s and "UFOs were a pretty big thing," Freedman explains. Flying saucer sightings had made their way into the news with a fervor not seen since the late 1940s. "I heard through the rumor mill that one of the UFOs had gone to Wright-Pat and was then brought to a remote area of the test site," Freedman says. "I heard it was in Area 22. I was driving with my supervisor through the test site one day and I told him what I had heard and I asked him what he thought about that. Well, he just kept looking at the road. And then he turned to me and he said, 'Jim, I don't want to hear you mention anything like that, ever again, if you want to keep your job.' " Freedman made sure never to bring the subject of UFOs up again when he was at work.

In the mid-1960s, sightings of unidentified flying objects around Area 51 reached unprecedented heights as the A-12 Oxcart flying from Groom Lake was repeatedly mistaken for a UFO. Not since the U-2 had been flying from there were so many UFO reports being dumped on CIA analysts' desks. The first instance happened only four days after Oxcart's first official flight, on April 30, 1962. It was a little before 10:00 a.m., and a NASA X-15 rocket plane was making a test flight in the air corridor that ran from Dryden Flight Research Center, in California, to Ely, Nevada, during the same period of time when an A-12 was making a test flight in the vicinity at a different altitude. From inside the X-15 rocket plane, test pilot Joe Walker snapped photographs, a task that was part of his mission flight. The X-15 was not a classified program and NASA often released publicity photographs taken during flights, as they did with Walker's photographs that day. But NASA had not scrutinized the photos closely before their public release, and officials missed the fact that a tiny "UFO" appeared in the corner of one of Walker's pictures. In reality, it was the Oxcart, but the press identified it as a UFO. A popular theory among ufologists about why aliens would want to visit Earth in the first place has to do with Earthlings' sudden advance of technologies beginning with the atomic bomb. For this group, it follows that the X-15—the first manned vehicle to get to the edge of space (the highest X-15 flight was 354,200 feet—almost 67 miles above sea level) would be particularly interesting to beings from outer space.

Two weeks after the incident, the CIA's new director, John McCone, received a secret, priority Teletype on the matter stating that "on 30 April, A-12 was in air at altitude of 30,000 feet from 0948-106 local with concurrent X-15 Test" and that "publicity releases mention unidentified objects on film taken on X-15 flight." This message, which was not declassified until 2007, illustrates the kind of UFO-related reports that inundated the CIA at this time. In total, 2,850 Oxcart flights would be flown out of Area 51 over a period of six years. Exactly how many of these flights generated UFO reports is not known, but the ones that prompted UFO sightings created the same kinds of problems for the CIA as they had in the previous decade with the U-2, only with elements that were seemingly more inexplicable. With Oxcart, commercial airline pilots flying over Nevada or California would look up and see the shiny, reflective bottom of the Oxcart whizzing by high overhead at triple-sonic speeds and think, UFO. How could they not? When the Oxcart flew at 2,300 miles per hour, it was going approximately five times faster than a commercial airplane—aircraft speeds that were unheard-of in those days. Most Oxcart sightings came right after sunset, when the lower atmosphere was shadowed in dusk. Seventeen miles higher up, the sun was still shining brightly on the Oxcart. The spy plane's broad titanium wings coupled with its triangle-shaped rear fuselage—reflecting the sun's rays higher in the sky than aircraft were known to fly—could understandably cause alarm.

The way the CIA dealt with this new crop of sightings was similar to how it handled the U-2s'. Colonel Hugh "Slip" Slater, Area 51's base commander during this time, explains "commercial pilots would report sightings to the FAA. The flights would be met in California, or wherever they landed, by FBI agents who would make passengers sign inadvertent disclosure forms." End of story, or so the CIA hoped. Instead, interest in UFOs only continued to grow. The public again put pressure on Congress to find out if the federal government was involved in covering up UFOs. When individual congressmen asked the CIA if it was involved in UFOs, the Agency would always say no.

On May 10, 1966, the most trusted man in America, Walter Cronkite, hosted a CBS news special report called *UFO: Friend, Foe or Fantasy?* To an audience of millions of Americans, Cronkite announced that the CIA was part of a government cover-up regarding UFOs. The CIA had been actively analyzing UFO data despite repeatedly denying to Congress that it was doing so, Cronkite said. He was absolutely correct. The Agency had been tracking UFO sightings around the world since the 1950s and actively lying about its interest in them. The CIA could not reveal the classified details of the U-2 program—the existence of which had been outed by the Gary Powers shoot-down but the greater extent of which would remain classified until 1998—nor could it reveal anything related to the Oxcart program and those sightings. That remained top secret until 2007. In Cronkite's exposé, the CIA looked like liars.

It got worse for the Agency. The Cronkite program also reopened a twelve-year-old can of UFO worms known as the Robertson Panel report of 1953. Dr. Robertson appeared on a *CBS Reports* program and disclosed that the UFO inquiry bearing his name had in fact been sponsored by the CIA beginning in 1952, despite repeated denials by officials. The House Armed Services Committee held hearings on UFOs in July of 1966, which resulted in the Air Force laying blame for the cover-up on the CIA. "The Air Force...approached the Agency for declassification," testified secretary of the Air Force Harold Brown. Brown stated that while there was no evidence that "strangers from outer space" had been visiting Earth, it was time for the CIA to come clean on its secret studies regarding UFOs.

According to CIA historian Gerald Haines, "The Agency again refused to budge. Karl H. Weber, Deputy Director of OSI [Office of Scientific Intelligence], wrote the Air Force that 'we are most anxious that further publicity not be given to the information that the panel was sponsored by the CIA.'" Weber's words, said Haines, were "shortsighted and ill considered" because the Air Force in turn gave that information to a journalist named John Lear, the science editor of the *Saturday Review*. Lear's September 1966 article "The Disputed CIA Document on UFO's" put yet another spotlight on the CIA's ongoing cover-up of UFOs. Lear, unsympathetic to the idea of extraterrestrials, demanded the release of the report. The CIA held firm that its information was classified, and the full, unsanitized facts regarding the Agency's role in unidentified flying objects remains classified as of 2011.

The public was outraged by the layers of obfuscation. The year 1966 was the height of the Vietnam War, and the federal government's ability to tell the truth was under fire. Pressure on Congress to make more information known did not let up. And so once again, as it had been in the late 1940s, the Air Force was officially "put in charge" of investigating individual UFO claims. The point of having the Air Force in charge, said Congress, was to oversee the untrustworthy CIA. One of the great ironies at work in this was that only a handful of Air Force generals were cleared for knowledge about Oxcart flights blazing in and out of Area 51, which meant that to most Air Force investigators, Oxcart sightings were in fact unidentified flying objects. Further feeding public discord, several key Air Force officials who had previously been involved in investigating UFOs now believed the Air Force was also engaged in covering up UFOs. Several of these men left government service to write books about UFOs and help the public persuade Congress to do more.

For more than two hundred years, since the invention of the hot-air balloon, people all over the world have been terrified of unidentified flying objects because their very existence makes man feel vulnerable from an attack from above. The *War of the Worlds* radio-broadcast phenomenon was far from the first such incident. The first pictorially recorded panic over a UFO event occurred in August of 1783, shortly after two French brothers named Joseph and Etienne Montgolfier secured patronage from the king of France to design and fly a hot-air balloon — the eighteenth-century version of a modern-day defense contract. During one of the Montgolfiers' early flight tests, a balloon got caught in a thunderstorm and crashed in a small French village called Gonesse. The peasants that inhabited the town thought the balloon was a monster attacking them from the sky. A pen-and-ink drawing from that time shows men with pitchforks and scythes ripping the crashed balloon to shreds. Townsfolk in the background can be seen running away, flailing their arms above their heads in fear. From this story, it is easy to see that with any new form of flight comes the archetypal fear of an attack from above. In the more than two hundred years since, these fears have taken dramatic twists and turns.

Twenty years into the American jet age, in the mid-1960s, fears of unidentified flying objects continued to shape cultural thinking and spawn industries. By then, millions of Americans correctly believed that various factions inside the U.S. government were actively engaged in a cover-up regarding UFOs. Many citizens believed the government was trying to cover up the existence of extraterrestrial beings; people did not consider the fact that by overfocusing on Martians, they would pay less attention to other UFO realities, namely, that these were sightings of radical aircraft made by men. By the late 1960s, the two government agencies at the forefront of citizens' wrath—the CIA and the Air Force—had been using cover and deception as tools to keep classified programs out of the public eye. Cover conceals the truth, and deception conveys false information. From cover stories about airplane crashes to deception campaigns about covert UFO study programs, both organizations had created complex webs of lies. How exactly a deception campaign works on ordinary people is best exemplified by this factual, dawn-of-the-jet-age U.S. Army Air Corps tale.

In 1942, when the jet engine was first being developed, the Army Air Corps desired to keep the radical new form of flight a secret until the military was ready to unveil the technology on its own terms. Before the jet engine, airplanes flew by propellers, and before 1942, for most people it was a totally foreign concept for an airplane to fly without the blades of a propeller spinning around. With the jet engine, in order to maintain silence on this technological breakthrough, the Army Air Corps entered into a rather benign strategic deception campaign involving a group of its pilots. Every time a test pilot took a Bell XP-59A jet aircraft out on a flight test over the Muroc dry lake bed in California's Mojave Desert, the crew attached a dummy propeller to the airplane's nose first. The Bell pilots had a swath of airspace in which to perform flight tests but every now and then a pilot training on a P-38 Lightning would cruise into the adjacent vicinity to try to get a look at the airplane. The airplane was seen trailing smoke, and eventually, rumors started to circulate at local pilot bars. Pilots wanted to know what was being hidden from them.

According to Edwards Air Force Base historian Dr. James Young, the chief XP-59A Bell test pilot, a man by the name of Jack

Woolams, got an idea. He ordered a gorilla mask from a Holly-wood prop house. On his next flight, Woolams removed the mock-up propeller from the nose of his jet airplane and put on the gorilla mask. When a P–38 Lightning came flying nearby for a look, Woolams maneuvered his airplane close enough so that the P–38 pilot could look inside the cockpit of the jet plane. The Lightning pilot was astonished. Instead of seeing Woolams, the pilot saw a gorilla flying an airplane—an airplane that had no propeller. The stunned pilot landed and went straight to the local bar, where he sat down and ordered a stiff drink. There, he began telling other pilots what he had definitely seen with his own eyes. His colleagues told him he was drunk, that what he was saying was an embarrassment, and that he should go home. Meanwhile, the concept of the gorilla mask caught on among other Bell XP-59A test pilots and soon Woolams's colleagues joined the act. Over the course of the next few months, other P–38 Lightning pilots spotted the gorilla flying the propellerless airplane. Some versions of the historical record have the psychiatrist for the U.S. Army Air Corps getting involved, helping the Lightning pilots to understand how a clear-thinking fighter pilot could become disoriented at altitude and believe he had seen something that clearly was not really there. Everyone knows that a gorilla can't fly an airplane. Whether or not the psychiatrist really did get involved—and if he did, whether he was aware of the gorilla masks—remains ambiguous to Dr. Craig Luther, a contemporary historian at Edwards Air Force Base. But for the purposes of a strategic deception campaign, the point is clear: no one wants to be mistaken for a fool.

Ockham's razor is an idea attributed to a fourteenth-century English friar named William of Ockham. It asks when trying to explain a phenomenon, does the alternative story explain more evidence than the principal story, or is it just a more complicated and there-fore a less useful explanation of the same evidence? In other words, according to Ockham, when man is presented with a riddle, the answer to the riddle should be simpler, not more complicated, than the riddle itself. Ockham's razor is often applied to the phenomenon of unidentified flying objects, or UFOs. In the case of the flying-gorilla story, the true explanation—that the gorilla was actually a pilot with a gorilla mask on—offered the simplest answer to what appeared to be an inexplicable phenomenon. The same can be said about the truth regarding the Roswell crash. But it would take decades for more to be revealed.

One of the more enigmatic figures involved in the Roswell mystery was Rear Admiral Roscoe H. Hillenkoetter, the first man to run the CIA. Hillenkoetter was the director of Central Intelligence from May 1, 1947, until October 7, 1950. After his retirement from the CIA, Hillenkoetter returned to a career in the navy. Curiously, after he retired from the Navy, in the late 1950s, he served on the board of governors of a group of UFO researchers called the National Investigations Committee on Aerial Phenomena. Hillenkoetter's placement on the board was a paradox. He was there, in part, to learn what the UFO researchers knew about unidentified flying crafts. But he also empathized with their work. While Hillenkoetter did not believe UFOs were from outer space, he knew unidentified flying objects were a serious national security concern. In his position as CIA director Hillenkoetter knew that the flying disc at Roswell had been sent by Joseph Stalin. And he knew of the Joint Chiefs of Staff's fear that what had been achieved once could happen again. Which makes it peculiar that, in February of 1960, in a rare reveal by a former cabinet-level official, Hillenkoetter testified to Congress that he was dismayed at how the Air Force was handling UFOs. To the Senate Science and Astronautics Committee he stated that "behind the scenes, high-ranking Air Force officers are soberly concerned about UFOs. But through official secrecy and ridicule, many citizens are led to believe the unknown flying objects are nonsense." He also claimed that "to hide the facts, the Air Force has silenced its personnel."

Hillenkoetter remained a ranking member of the National Investigations Committee on Aerial Phenomena until 1962, when he mysteriously resigned. Equally puzzling was that the man who later replaced Hillenkoetter and became the head of the board of the National Investigations Committee on Aerial Phenomena in 1969 was Joseph Bryan III—the CIA's first chief of political and psychological warfare. Not much is known about Bryan's true role with the ufologists because his work at the CIA remains classified as of 2011. If his name sounds familiar, it is because Joe Bryan was the man scheduled for a hunting trip with Frank Wisner, Richard Bissell's friend and predecessor at the CIA. But before Bryan arrived that day, on October 29, 1965, Wisner shot himself in the head.

At the CIA, during the mid-1960s, the thinking regarding UFOs began to move in a different direction. Since the birth of the modern UFO phenomenon, in June of 1947, the CIA had maintained three lines of thought on UFOs. They were (a) experimental aircraft, (b) the delusions of a paranoid person's mind, or (c) part of a psychological warfare campaign by the Soviet Union to create panic among the people and sow seeds of governmental mistrust. But by 1966, a faction within the CIA added a fourth line of thought to its concerns: maybe UFOs were real. This new postulation came from the Agency's monitoring of circumstances in the Soviet Union, which was also in the midst of a UFO sea change.

In the 1940s and until Stalin's death in 1953, CIA analysts of Soviet publications had found only one known mention of UFOs, in an editorial published in a Moscow newspaper in 1951. Khrushchev appeared to have continued the policy. The analysts at CIA assigned to monitor the Soviet press during his tenure found no stories about UFOs. But curiously, in 1964, after Khrushchev's colleagues removed him from power and installed Leonid Brezhnev in his place, articles on UFOs began to emerge. In 1966, a series of articles about UFOs were published by Novosti, Moscow's official news agency. Two leading scientists from the Moscow Aviation Institute not only were writing about UFOs but were split on their opinions about them, which was highly unusual for Soviet state-funded scientists. One of the scientists, Villen Lyustiberg, promoted the idea that UFOs were the creation of the American government and that "the U.S. publicizes them to divert people from its failures and aggressions." A second leading scientist, Dr. Felix Zigel, had come to believe that UFOs were in fact real.

Declassified CIA memos written during this time reveal a concern that if the leading scientists and astronomers in the Soviet Union believed UFOs were real, maybe UFOs truly were real after all. In 1968, the CIA learned that a Soviet air force general named Porfiri Stolyarov had been named the chairman of a new "UFO Section of the All-Union Cosmonautics Committee" in Moscow. After learning that Russia had an official UFO committee, the CIA went scrambling for its own science on UFOs. For the first time in its history, America's spy agency internally allowed for the fact that UFOs might in fact be coming from outer space. "The hypothesis that UFOs originate in other worlds, that they are flying craft from other planets other than Earth, merits the most serious examination," read one secret memo that was circulated among CIA analysts.

Had the original UFO cover-up—the crash of the Horten brothers' flying disc at Roswell—created this Hydra-like monster? Had maintaining secrecy around the follow-up program, which had been clandestinely set up in the Nevada desert just outside Area 51, resulted in such endemic paranoia among analysts at the CIA that these individuals sensed they were being lied to? That the dark secret the government was hiding was that UFOs really *were* from outer space? Or was an elite group with a need-to-know allowing—perhaps even fostering—exactly this kind of conjecture among analysts because it was better to have insiders on a wild-goose chase than to have them on the trail leading to the original enigma of Area 51?

CHAPTER THIRTEEN

Dull, Dirty, and Dangerous Requires Drones

Starting in 1963, preparing for Oxcart missions involved punishing survival-training operations for the pilots, many of which occurred in the barren outer reaches of Area 51. For Ken Collins, a mock nighttime escape from an aircraft downed over the desert was meant to simulate hell. Collins knew the kind of challenge he would be up against as he stood on the tarmac at Groom Lake watching the sun disappear behind the mountains to the west. Soon, it would be dark and very cold. Collins climbed into a C-47 aircraft and noticed that the windows were blacked out. Neither he nor any of the other Oxcart pilots he was with had any idea where they were headed. "We got inside and flew for a little while," Collins recalls, "until we landed in another desert airfield, somewhere remote." The men were unloaded from the aircraft and put into a van, also with the windows blacked out. They were driven for miles, Collins thought going in circles, until the doors of the van opened into what appeared to be thick, rough, high-desert terrain. "We were told that we were in Chinese enemy territory. To escape and survive the best that you can. There were electronic alarms, trip wires, and explosive charges on the ground."

Collins ran and took cover under a bush. In the darkness, he lay on his belly and gathered his thoughts. He had been through a series of survival trials during Oxcart training already. Once, he and another pilot were taken to the Superstition Mountains in Arizona for a mountain-survival trial. "On that exercise we had minimal food, sleeping bags, and a very small tent. We walked and camped in the mountains for five days. The first three days were comfortable; the third night a weather front moved in with cold rain," making things a little more challenging. A second exercise took place in Kings Canyon, in the Sierra Mountains. During that trip, Collins and another pilot had to live in snow for three days. They dug a snow cave and made beds of pine boughs. A third trip, to Florida, simulated jungle survival. "I was taken out to a swamp, given a knife, and told to survive on my own for four days." What Collins remembers vividly was the food. "I caught some turtles to eat, but found them difficult to open, so my staple became the heart of palm. I'd cut the new palm buds out from the center. It was thin fare, but sustainable," Collins says. But the high-desert survival training at Area 51 felt different. Unlike the other sessions, this one would involve psychological warfare by the mock enemy Chinese.

Collins crawled along the desert floor through the darkness, feeling for the trip wires and considering his next move. He pulled his small compass from his survival pack so he could chart a path. "I crawled slowly through the brambles, bugs, and mud for about thirty minutes when, suddenly, I hit a trip wire and alarms went off. A glaring spotlight came on and ten Chinese men in uniform grabbed me and dragged me to one of their jeeps." Collins was handcuffed, driven for a while, put into a second vehicle, and taken to so-called Chinese interrogation headquarters. There, he was stripped naked and searched. "A doctor proceeded to examine every orifice the human body has, from top to bottom—literally," which, Collins believes, "was more to humiliate and break down my moral defenses than anything else." Naked, he was led down a dimly lit hallway and pushed into a concrete cell furnished with a short, thin bed made of wood planks. "I had no blanket, I was naked, and it was very cold. They gave me a bucket to be used only when I was told."

For days, Collins went through simulated torture that included sleep deprivation, humiliation, extreme temperature fluctuation, and hunger, all the while naked, cold, and under surveillance by his captors. "The cell had one thick wooded door with a hole for viewing. This opening had a metal window that would clank open and shut. A single bright light was on and when I was about to doze off, the light would flash off, which would immediately snap me out of sleep." For food, he was given watery soup, two thin pepper pods, and two bits of mysterious meat. "I had no water to drink and I was always watched. I didn't know day from night so there was no sense of time. The temperature varied from hot to very cold. The voice through the viewing window shouted demands."

Soon Collins began to hallucinate. Now it was interrogation time. Naked, he was led to a small room by two armed guards. He stood in front of his Chinese interrogators, who sat behind a small desk. They grilled him about his name, rank, and why he was spying on China. The torturous routine continued for what Collins guessed was several more days. Then one day, instead of being taken to his interrogators, he was told that he was free to go.

But halfway across the world, on November 1, 1963, Ken Collins's experience was being mirrored for real. A CIA pilot named Yeh Changti had been flying a U-2 spy mission over a nuclear facility in China when he was shot down, captured by the Chinese Communist government, and tortured. Yeh Changti was a member of the Thirty-Fifth Black Cat U-2 Squadron, a group of Taiwanese Chinese Nationalist pilots (as opposed to the Communist Chinese, who inhabited the mainland) who worked covert espionage missions for the CIA. In the 1960s, the Black Cats flew what would prove to be the deadliest missions in the U-2's fifty-five-year history, all of which were flown out of a secret base called Taoyuan on the island of Taiwan. When the CIA declassified most of the U-2 program, in 1998, "no information was released about Yeh Changti or the Black Cats," says former Black Cat pilot Hsichun Hua. The program, in entirety, remains classified as of 2011.

Colonel Hugh "Slip" Slater, the man who would later become the commander of Area 51, remembers Yeh Changti before he got shot down. "His code name was Terry Lee and he and I played tennis on the base at Taoyuan all the time. He was a great guy and an amazing acrobat, which helped him on the court. Sometimes we drank scotch while we played. Both the sport and the scotch helped morale." Slater says that the reason morale was low was that "the U-2 had become so vulnerable to the SA-2 missiles that nobody wanted to fly." One Black Cat pilot had already been shot down. But that didn't stop the dangerous missions from going forward for the CIA.

Unlike what had happened with the Gary Powers shoot-down, the American press remained in the dark about these missions. For the CIA, getting hard intelligence on China's nuclear facilities was a top national security priority. On the day Yeh Changti was shot down, he was returning home from a nine-hour mission over the mainland when a surface-to-air missile guidance system locked on to his U-2. Colonel Slater was on the radio with Yeh Changti when it happened. "I was talking to him when I heard him say, 'System 12 on!' We never heard another word." The missile hit Yeh Changti's aircraft and tore off the right wing. Yeh Changti ejected from the airplane, his body riddled in fifty-nine places with missile fragments. He landed safely with his parachute and passed out. When he woke up, he was in a military facility run by Mao Tse-tung.

This was no training exercise. Yeh Changti was tortured and held prisoner for nineteen years until he was quietly released by his captors, in 1982. He has been living outside Houston, Texas, ever since. The CIA did not know that Yeh Changti had survived his bailout and apparently did not make any kind of effort to locate him. A second Black Cat pilot named Major Jack Chang would also get shot down in a U-2, in 1965, and was imprisoned alongside Yeh Changti. After their release, the two pilots shared their arduous stories with fellow Black Cat pilot, Hsichun Hua, who had become a general in the Taiwanese air force while the men were in captivity. Neither Yeh Changti nor Major Jack Chang was ever given a medal by the CIA. The shoot-down of the Black Cat U-2 pilots, however, had a major impact on what the CIA and the Air Force would do next at Area 51. Suddenly, the development of drones had become a national security priority, drones being pilotless aircraft that could be flown by remote control.

Drones could accomplish what the U-2 could in terms of bringing home photographic intelligence, but a drone could do it without getting pilots captured or killed. Ideally, drones could perform missions that fell into three distinct categories: dull, dirty, and dangerous. *Dull* meant long flights during which pilots faced fatigue flying to remote areas of the globe. *Dirty* included situations where nuclear weapons or biological weapons might be involved. *Dangerous* meant missions over denied territories such as the Soviet Union, North Korea, and China, where shoot-downs were a political risk. Lockheed secured a contract to develop such an unmanned vehicle in late 1962. After Yeh Changti's shoot-down, the program got a big boost. Flight-testing of the drone code-named Tagboard would take place at Area 51 and, ironically, getting the Lockheed drone to fly properly was among the first duties assigned to Colonel Slater after he left Taoyuan and was given a new assignment at Area 51.

"Lockheed's D-21 wasn't just any old drone, it was the world's first Mach 3 stealth drone," says Lockheed physicist Ed Lovick, who worked on the program. "The idea of this drone was a radical one because it would fly at least as fast, if not faster, than the A-12. It had a ram jet engine, which meant it was powered by forced air. The drone could only be launched off an aircraft that was already moving faster than the speed of sound." The A-12 mother ship was designated M-21, *M* as in *mother,* and was modified to include a second seat for the drone launch operator, a flight engineer. The D-21 was the name for the drone, the *D* standing for *daughter.* But launching one aircraft from the back of another aircraft at speeds of more than 2,300 mph had its own set of challenges, beginning with how not to have the two aircraft crash into each other during launch. The recovery process of the drone also needed to be fine-tuned. Lovick explains, "The drone, designed to overfly China, would travel on its own flight path taking reconnaissance photographs and then head back out to sea." The idea was to have the drone drop its photo package, which included the camera, the film, and the radio sensors, by parachute so it could be retrieved by a second aircraft nearby. Once the pallet was secure, the drone would crash into the sea and sink to the ocean floor.

Practicing this process at Area 51 translated into a lot of lost drones. Colonel Slater directed the test missions, which took place in what was called the special operating area, or Yuletide, just north of Groom Lake airspace. Colonel Slater and Frank Murray would follow the M-21/D-21 in chase planes and oversee the subsonic launches of the drone. "They'd launch, and then disappear," Colonel Slater recalls. Helicopter pilot Charlie Trapp was sent to find them, along with a crew of search-and-rescue parajumpers, called PJs. "First, we'd locate the lost drones. Then I'd lower my parajumpers down on ropes. They'd hook the lost pods to a cargo hook and we'd pull the drones off the mountain that way," Trapp explains. "Sometimes it got tricky, especially if the drone crash-landed on the top of a mountain ridge. We had some tense times with PJs nearly falling off cliffs." When Colonel Slater felt the Oxcart and its drone were ready for a Mach 3 test, it was time to add ocean-survival training to the mix. For public safety reasons, the plan was to launch the triplesonic drone off the coast of California in March of 1966 for the first test, and to prepare his pilots, Colonel Slater had them swim laps each day in the Area 51 pool, first in bathing suits and then with their pressure suits on. "We'd hoist the guys up over the water in a pulley and then drop them in the pool. As soon as they hit the water the first time, the pressure suit inflated, so we had to have that fixed," Slater recalls. When it came time to practice an actual landing in a large body of water, the Agency's highest-ranking officer on base, Werner Weiss, got the Coast Guard to seal off a large section of Lake Mead, the largest reservoir of water in the United States, located just east of Las Vegas.

Slater remembers the pilot training well. "We were out there in this little Boston Whaler and the plan was to get the project pilots hoisted up into a parasail and then let them drop down in the water in their full pressure suits. First [Agency pilot Mele] Vojvodich went. His test went fine. By the time we got [Agency pilot Jack] Layton up, the wind had picked up. When Layton went down in the water, the Whaler started dragging him, and the water in his parachute started pulling him underneath. I called it off. 'Stop!' I said. 'We're gonna lose somebody out here!'"

They were prescient words. On the night of July 30, 1966, the 1129th Special Activities Squadron at Groom Lake prepared to make the first official nighttime drone launch off the coast of California. From the tarmac at Area 51, Lockheed's chief flight test pilot, Bill Park, was about to close the canopy on the M-21 Oxcart when Colonel Slater approached him with some final words. "I said, 'Bill, it's a dangerous mission,'" Slater remembers. "There were only a few feet between the drone and the tail of the A-12. Park knew that. We all did. In back was the flight engineer, Ray Torick; he knew that too. The canopy closed and I got into another Mach 3 aircraft we had flying alongside during the test." Both aircraft flew west until they were a hundred and fifty miles off the coast of California. There, the M-21, piloted by Bill Park, prepared for the D-21 launch. A camera in Slater's airplane would capture the launch on 16-millimeter film. Down below, on the dark ocean surface, a rescue boat waited. Park hit Ignite, and the drone launched up and off the M-21. But during separation, the drone pitched down instead of up and instantly split the mother aircraft in half. Miraculously, the drone hit neither Park nor Torick, who were both trapped inside.

The crippled aircraft began to tumble through the sky, falling for nearly ten thousand feet. Somehow, both men managed to eject. Alive and now outside the crashing, burning airplane, both men were safely tethered to their parachutes. Remarkably, neither of the men was hit by the burning debris falling through the air. Both men made successful water landings. But, as Slater recalls, an unforeseen tragedy occurred. "Our rescue boat located Bill Park, who was fine. But by the time the boat got to Ray Torick, he was tied up in his lanyard and had drowned."

Kelly Johnson was devastated. "He impulsively and emotionally decided to cancel the entire program and give back the development funding to the Air Force and the Agency," Johnson's deputy Ben Rich recalled in his 1994 memoir about the Lockheed Skunk Works. Rich asked Johnson why. "I will not risk any more test pilots or Blackbirds. I don't have either to spare," Johnson said. But the Air Force did not let the Mach 3 drone program go away so quickly. They created a new program to launch the drone from underneath a B-52 bomber, which was part of Strategic Air Command. President Johnson's deputy secretary of defense, Cyrus Vance, told Kelly Johnson, "We need this program to work because our government will never again allow a Francis Gary Powers situation develop. All our overflights over denied territory will either be with satellites or drones."

Three years later, in 1969, the D-21 drone finally made its first reconnaissance mission, over China, launched off a B-52. The drone flew into China and over the Lop Nur nuclear facility but had then somehow strayed off course into Soviet Siberia, run out of fuel, and crashed. The suggestion was that the drone's guidance system had failed on the way home, and it was never seen or heard from again. At least, not for more than twenty years. In the early 1990s, a CIA officer showed up in Ben Rich's office at Skunk Works with a mysterious present for him. "Ben, do you recognize this?" the man asked Rich as he handed him a hunk of titanium. "Sure I do," Rich said. What Ben Rich was holding in his hand was a piece of composite material loaded with the radar-absorbing coating that Lovick and his team had first developed for Lockheed four decades before. Asked where he got it, the CIA officer explained that it had been a gift to the CIA from a KGB agent in Moscow. The agent had gotten it from a shepherd in Siberia, who'd found it in the Siberian tundra while herding his sheep. According to Rich, "The Russians mistakenly believed that this generation-old panel signified our current stealth technology. It was, in a way, a very nice tribute to our work on Tagboard."

The use of drones in warfare has its origins in World War II. Joseph Kennedy Jr., President Kennedy's older brother, died in a secret U.S. Navy drone operation against the Germans. The covert mission, dubbed Operation Aphrodite, targeted a highly fortified Nazi missile site inside Germany. The plan was for the older Kennedy to pilot a modified B-24 bomber from England and over the English Channel while his crew armed 22,000 pounds of explosives piled high in the cargo hold. Once the explosives were wired, the crew and pilot needed to quickly bail out. Flying not far away, a mother ship would begin remotely controlling the unmanned aircraft as soon as the crew bailed out. Inside the bomber's nose cone were two cameras that would help guide the drone into its Nazi target.

The explosive being used was called Torpex, a relatively new and extremely volatile chemical compound. Just moments before Joseph Kennedy Jr. and his crew bailed out, the Torpex caught fire, and the aircraft exploded midair, killing everyone on board. The Navy ended its drone program, but the idea of a pilotless aircraft caught the eye of general of the Army Henry "Hap" Arnold. On Victory over Japan Day, General Arnold made a bold assertion. "The next war may be fought by airplanes with no men in them at all," he said. He was off by four wars, but otherwise he was right.

The idea behind using remotely piloted vehicles in warfare is a simple one — keep the human out of harm's way — but the drone's first application was for pleasure. Nikola Tesla mastered wireless communication in 1893, years before any of his fellow scientists were even considering such a thing. At the Electrical Exhibition in Madison Square Garden in 1898, Tesla gave a demonstration in which he directed a four-foot-long steel boat using radio remote control. Audiences were flabbergasted. Tesla's pilotless boat seemed to many to be more a magic act than the scientific breakthrough it was. Ever a visionary, Tesla also foresaw a military application for his invention. "I called an official in Washington with a view of offering him the information to the government and he burst out laughing upon telling him what I had accomplished," Tesla wrote. This made unfortunate sense—the military was still using horses for transport at the time. Tesla's friend writer Mark Twain also envisioned a military future in remote control and offered to act as Tesla's agent in peddling the "destructive terror which you have been inventing." Twain suggested the Germans might be good clients, considering that, at the time, they were the most scientifically advanced country in the world. In the end, no government bought Tesla's invention or paid for his patents. The great inventor died penniless in a New York hotel room in 1943, and by then, the Germans had developed remote control on their own and were wreaking havoc on ground forces across Europe. The Germans' first war robot was a remote-controlled minitank called Goliath, and it was about the size of a bobsled. Goliath carried 132 pounds of explosives, which the Nazis drove into enemy bunkers and tanks using remote control. Eight thousand Goliaths were built and used in battle by the Germans, mostly on the Eastern Front, where Russian soldiers outnumbered German soldiers nearly three to one. With no soldiers to spare, the Germans needed to keep the ones they had out of harm's way.

In America, the Army Air Forces developed its first official drone wing after the war, for use during Operation Crossroads at Bikini Atoll in 1946. There, drones were sent through the mushroom cloud, their operators flying them by remote control from an airborne mother ship called Marmalade flying nearby. To collect radioactive samples, the drones had been equipped with air-collection bags and boxlike filter-paper holders. Controlling the drones in such conditions was difficult. Inside the mushroom cloud, one drone, codenamed Fox, was blasted "sixty feet higher than its flight path," according to declassified memos about the drone wing's performance there. Fox's "bomb doors warped, all the cushions inside the aircraft burst and its inspection plates and escape hatch blew off." Remarkably, the drone pilot maintained control from several miles away. Had he witnessed such a thing, Nikola Tesla might have smiled.

During the second set of atomic tests, called Operation Sandstone, in April of 1948, the drones were again used in a job deemed too dangerous for airmen. During an eighteen-kiloton atomic blast called Zebra, however, a manned aircraft accidentally flew through a mushroom cloud, and after this, the Air Force made the decision that because the pilot and crew inside the aircraft had "suffered no ill effects," pilots should be flying atomic-sampling missions, not drones. Whether or not pilots were exposed to lethal amounts of radiation during the Zebra bomb or hundreds of other atomic tests has never been accurately determined. The majority of the records regarding how much radiation pilots were exposed to in these early years and who died of radiation-related diseases have allegedly been destroyed or lost. But when the Air Force pilot accidentally flew through the Zebra bomb's mushroom cloud, the incident "commenced a chain of events that resulted in manned samplers."

"Manned samplers were simply more efficient," wrote officer Colonel Paul H. Fackler in a 1963 classified historical review of atomic cloud sampling made for the Air Force systems command, declassified in 1986. As the official radiation safety officer assigned to Operation Sandstone, Fackler held sway. Fackler's colleague Colonel Cody also argued in favor of man over drone. Cody said the drone samples were obtained haphazardly by "potluck." A human pilot would be able to maneuver around a cloud during penetration so that the "most likely parts of the cloud could be sampled." It was a case of dangerous semantics; *most likely* was a euphemism for "most radioactive." For future tests, Air Force officials decided to pursue both manned and unmanned atomic-sampling wings.

Both kinds of aircraft would be needed for an ultrasecret test that was pending in the Pacific in 1951. Operation Greenhouse would involve a new kind of nuclear weapon that was being hailed as the "Super bomb." It was a thermonuclear weapon, or hydrogen bomb, the core of which would explode with the same energy found at the center of the sun. Los Alamos scientists explained to weapons planners that the destructive power of this new kind of science, called nuclear fusion, was entirely unknown. Fusion involves exploding a nuclear bomb inside a nuclear bomb, and privately the scientists expressed fear that the entire world's atmosphere could catch on fire during this process. Scientists became deeply divided over the issue and whether or not to go forward. The push to create the Super was spearheaded by the indomitable Dr. Edward Teller and cosigned by weapons planners with the Department of Defense. The opposition to the Super was spearheaded by Robert Oppenheimer, the father of the atomic bomb and now Teller's rival. Oppenheimer, who felt that developing a weapon capable of ending civilization was immoral, would lose his security clearance over his opposition to the Super bomb. According to Al O'Donnell, the EG&G weapons test engineer who wired many of Dr. Teller's Super bombs in the Marshall Islands, what happened to Oppenheimer sent a strong message to everyone involved: "If you want to keep your job, don't oppose decisions" on moral grounds. In the end, the weapons planners won, and the world's first thermonuclear bomb moved forward as planned.

Drones were needed to take blast and gust measurements inside the thermonuclear clouds, and to take samples of radioactive debris inside. During the Greenhouse test series, which did not wind up setting the world on fire, the first drone in went out of control and crashed into the sea before it ever reached the stem of the mushroom cloud. Two other drone missions were aborted after not responding to controls, and a fourth sustained such heavy damage in the shock wave, it lost control and crash-landed on a deserted island called Bogallua, where it caught fire and exploded. When the test series was over, the Air Force ultimately concluded that the unmanned samplers were unreliable. "Following Operation Greenhouse, the Air Force and the Atomic Energy Commission looked more favorably upon manned samplers," wrote a Defense Nuclear Agency historian in 1963. "Greenhouse became the last atomic test series during which drone aircraft were used for this purpose." So when it came time to detonate the world's first full-scale thermonuclear device—an unimaginably monstrous 10.4 megaton bomb code-named Mike—in the next test series, called Operation Ivy in the fall of 1952, it was decided that six human pilots, all volunteers, would fly straight into the center of the radioactive stem and mushroom cloud. Another group of pilots was assigned to fly along the outer edges of the predicted fallout zones. That group included Hervey Stockman, who, four years later, would become the first CIA pilot to fly over the Soviet Union in a U-2.

In anticipation of the Mike bomb's manned sampling mission, the pilots practiced at the airfield at Indian Springs, thirty miles due south of Area 51. These pilots, including Stockman, then flew sampling missions through the kiloton-size atomic bombs being exploded at the Nevada Test Site as part of a spring 1952 test series called Operation Tumbler-Snapper. "Up to this time," Stockman explains, "the scientists had put monkeys in the cockpits of remotely controlled drone aircraft [at the test site]. They would fly these things through the [atomic] clouds. Then they began to be interested in the effects of radiation on humanoids. They realized that with care and cunning they could put people in there."

The Air Force worked hard to change the pilots' perception of themselves as guinea pigs, at least for the historical record. According to a history of the atomic cloud sampling program, declassified in 1985, by the time Stockman and his fellow pilots left Indian Springs for the Marshall Islands to fly missions through megaton-size thermonuclear bomb clouds, the men accepted that they "were doing something useful... not serving as guinea pigs as they seriously believed when first called upon to do the sampling."

Stockman offers another perspective. "In those days, I didn't think much about the moral questions. I was young. The visual picture when these things go off is absolutely stunning. I was very much in awe of it," Stockman recalls. "The [atomic bombs] that were going on in the proving grounds in Nevada were minute in comparison to these [thermonuclear bomb] monsters out there in the Pacific. Those were big brutes. When they went off they would punch right through the Earth's atmosphere and head out into space."

After finally arriving in the Pacific, pilots flew "familiarization flights and rehearsals" in the days leading up to the Mike bomb.

But nothing could prepare an airman for the actual test. Stockman's colleague Air Force pilot Jimmy P. Robinson was one of the six pilots who "volunteered" to fly through the Ivy Mike mushroom cloud. Because the physical bomb was the size of a large airplane hangar, it couldn't be called a weapon per se. The bomb was so large that it was built from the ground up, on an island on the north side of the atoll called Elugelab. Given the extraordinary magnitude of the thermonuclear bomb, it is utterly remarkable to consider that shortly after Robinson flew his F–84G straight through its mushroom stem, he was able to radio back clear thoughts to his commanding officer, who was located twenty-five miles to the south, on Eniwetok. "The glow was red, like the inside of a red hot furnace," the record states Robinson said. He then described how his radio instrument meters were spinning around in circles, "like the sweep second hand on a watch." After going inside the cloud a second time, Robinson reported that his "airplane stalled out and gone [sic] into a spin." His autopilot disengaged and his radio cut out, but the courageous pilot flew on as instructed. He flew around in circles and finally he flew back into and out of the mushroom stem and the lower part of its cloud—for nearly four more hours. Only when it was time for Robinson to refuel did he realize that the electromagnetic pulse from the thermonuclear bomb had ruined his control beacon. This meant that it was impossible for him to locate the fuel tanker.

Robinson radioed the control tower on Eniwetok for help. He was told to head back to the island immediately. "Approximately ninety-six miles north of the island, [Robinson] reported that he'd picked up a signal on Eniwetok," according to the official record, declassified in 1986 but with Robinson's name redacted. At that point, he was down to six hundred pounds of fuel. Bad weather kicked in; "rain squalls obstructed his views." Robinson's fuel gauge registered empty and then his engine flamed out. "When he was at 10,000 feet, Eniwetok tower thought he would make the runway, he had the island in sight," wrote an Air Force investigator assigned to the case. But he couldn't glide in because his aircraft was lined with lead to shield him from radiation. At five thousand feet and falling fast, Robinson reported he wasn't going to make it and that he would have to bail out. Now Robinson faced the ultimate challenge. Atomic-sampling pilots wore lead-lined vests. How to land safely and get out fast? Fewer than three and a half miles from the tarmac at Eniwetok, at an altitude of between five hundred and eight hundred feet, Robinson's aircraft flipped over and crashed into the sea. "Approximately one minute later [a] helicopter was over the spot," the Air Force investigator wrote. But it was too late. All the helicopter pilot could find was "an oil slick, one glove, and several maps." Robinson's body and his airplane sank to the bottom of the sea like a stone. His body was never recovered, and his family would learn of his fate only in 2008, after repeated Freedom of Information Act requests were finally granted by the Air Force.

Back on Elugelab Island, the dust was settling after the airplane-hangar-size Mike bomb had exploded with an unfathomable yield of 10.4 megatons—nearly twice that of its predicted size. Elugelab was not an island anymore. The thermonuclear bomb had vaporized the entire landmass, sending eighty million tons of pulverized coral into the upper atmosphere to float around and rain down. One man observing the bomb with high-density goggles was EG&G weapons test engineer Al O'Donnell. He'd wired, armed, and fired the Ivy bomb from the control room on the USS *Estes,* which was parked forty miles out at sea. O'Donnell says that watching the Mike bomb explode was a terrifying experience. "It was one of the ones that was too big," says the man who colleagues called the Triggerman for having wired 186 nuclear bombs. The nuclear fireball of the Ivy Mike bomb was three miles wide. In contrast, the bomb dropped on Hiroshima had a fireball that was a tenth of a mile wide. When the manned airplanes flew over ground zero after the Ivy Mike bomb went off, they were horrified to see the island was gone. Satellite photographs in 2011 show a black crater filled with lagoon water where the island of Elugelab once existed.

CHAPTER FOURTEEN

Drama in the Desert

Before he became president of the United States, Lyndon Baines Johnson liked to ride through rural Texas in his convertible Lincoln Continental with the top down. According to his biographer Randall B. Woods, Johnson also liked to keep a loaded shotgun in the seat next to him, which allowed him to pull over and shoot deer easily. On the night of October 4, 1957, the then senator was entertaining a group of fellow hunting enthusiasts at his rural retreat, in the dining room of his forty-foot-tall, glass-enclosed, air-conditioned hunting blind that Johnson called his "deer tower." All around the edge of the lair were powerful spot-lights that could be turned on with the flip of a switch, blinding unsuspecting deer that had come to graze and making it easier to kill them.

It was an important night for Johnson, one that would set the rest of his life on a certain path. October 4, 1957, was the night the Russians launched Sputnik, and the senator began an exuberant anti-Communist crusade. That very night, once the guests had gone home and the staff of black waiters had cleaned up, Johnson retired to his bedroom with newfound conviction. "I'll be dammed if I sleep by the light of a Red Moon," he told his wife, Lady Bird.

At the time, Lyndon Johnson was not just any senator. He was the Democratic majority leader, which made him the most powerful legislator in the United States. Within hours of Sputnik's launch, Johnson seized on the Red Moon moment for political gain. The Russians were a threat to America's existence, he declared: "Soon they will be dropping bombs on us from space like kids dropping rocks onto cars from Freeway overpasses."

For many Americans, Johnson's reaction was easier to comprehend than President Eisenhower's seemingly muted response. Before he was president, Eisenhower had spent his career as a soldier. He was a five-star general. As former commander of the Allied Forces in Europe during World War II, Eisenhower had faced many a deadly threat. He had led the invasion at Normandy and commanded the Allied Forces in the last great German offensive, the Battle of the Bulge, which meant he and his men shot at a lot more than blinded deer. In October of 1957, he believed that the 184-pound Russian satellite called Sputnik was not a cause for panic or alarm.

The nation felt quite different. The public consensus was that Sputnik gave reason for serious concern. The orb was seen as ominous and foreboding, a visual portent of more bad things to come from the skies, with 4 percent of Americans claiming to have seen Sputnik with their own eyes. In reality, explained historian Matthew Brzezinski, "What most actually saw was the one-hundred-foot-long R-7 rocket casing that [Sputnik's designer Sergei] Korolev had craftily outfitted with reflective prisms. It trailed some 600 miles behind the twenty-two-inch satellite," which in reality could only be seen by a person using a high-powered optical device. Motivated by the public's alarm, Senator Lyndon Johnson provided a foil to Eisenhower's nonconfrontation, demanding a "full and exhaustive inquiry" from Congress to learn how the Russians had beaten the Americans into space. In doing so, Johnson cemented his persona as being tough on Communists. In turn, this made him an inadvertent advocate for missile defense and the military-industrial complex. Ultimately, it forced him to be a proponent for the Vietnam War.

Now, six years and one month after Sputnik, Lyndon Johnson was president. Seven days after Kennedy was shot dead, Johnson sat in the Oval Office with CIA director John McCone being briefed on Oxcart and Area 51. Johnson loved the idea of the Agency's secret spy plane, but not for the reasons anyone expected. Johnson seized on one detail in particular: the aircraft's speed. At the time, the world was under the impression that the Russians held the record for airspeed, which was 1,665 miles per hour. When Johnson learned the men at Area 51 had repeatedly beaten that record, he wanted to make that fact publicly known. What better way to begin a presidency than by one-upping the Russians?

In reality, outing the most expensive secret spy plane program ever undertaken in order to win a competition with the Russians did not make the best national security sense. Surfacing Oxcart would compromise the Agency's technological pole position in the overhead espionage field. Oxcart was singularly capable of flying "any place in the world," McCone explained. It was almost "invisible" to Soviet radar, with a "radar cross section in the order of 1/1000 of [a] normal aircraft." If McCone had had a crystal ball, he could have told the president that the Oxcart was so far ahead of its time, it would hold aviation records for sustained height and speed through the end of the century. Also in the room were Secretary of Defense Robert McNamara, Secretary of State Dean Rusk, and national security adviser McGeorge Bundy, the administration's most powerful trio. Conveniently for the Pentagon, all three men agreed with President Johnson that outing the Oxcart was a terrific idea.

The reason for the trio's desire for transparency was that the Air Force had clear designs on cutting the CIA loose from the business of spy planes once and for all. Outing a program made the need for cover obsolete. Before Kennedy's assassination, the Air Force high command had been writing secret proposals arguing for ways in which they could take over Oxcart. Four months earlier, Air Force commander General Schriever wrote a memo to Eugene Zuckert, secretary of the Air Force, suggesting that "an incident during the flight test program could force a disclosure." The CIA had gotten lucky with Ken Collins's Oxcart crash, General Schriever said, but if another one of the Agency's secret spy planes were to crash "it would be extremely difficult to avoid some public release." The subtext being that maybe there was a way that the Air Force could help facilitate this public disclosure. There was a final option, one that involved getting "the President on board." A few weeks before Kennedy's death, the Air Force had gone to him with a proposal to make Oxcart public; Kennedy had said to sit tight. Now it appeared that President Johnson was going to be much easier to manipulate.

To counter Air Force demands McCone tried a different approach, one that involved money. He told the president that more than half of Oxcart's budget had already been spent producing fifteen airplanes. To expose Oxcart now was a terrible idea, McCone said, not just in terms of national security but because it would be a colossal waste of money. Johnson agreed. But the president still wanted to one-up the Russians, so he settled on a slightly different plan. Through a veil of half-truths, he would out the Air Force's attack version of the Oxcart, the YF-12, as the speed-breaker. The YF-12 would be given a false cover, the fictitious name A-11. Respecting McCone's national security concerns, the actual A-12 Oxcart program—its true speed, operational ceiling, and near invisibility to radar—would remain classified top secret until the CIA declassified the Oxcart program, in 2007.

Three months later, on February 29, 1964, Johnson held a press conference in the International Treaty Room at the State Department. "The world record for aircraft speed, currently held by the Soviets, has been repeatedly broken in secrecy by the... A-11," President Johnson declared from the podium, thrilled to give the Russians a poke in the ribs. At Area 51, caught off guard by the requirement to do a presidential dog-and-pony show, the 1129th Special Activities Squadron scrambled to get an airplane to Edwards Air Force Base in California for a press junket, which was called for immediately after the president's grand announcement. Two YF–12s belonging to the Air Force but being tested at Area 51 were quickly flown in from Groom Lake and driven into a special hangar at Edwards. The airplanes' titanium surfaces were so hot they set off the hangar's sprinkler system, which mistook the high-temperature metal for a fire. When the press junket began, the aircraft were still dripping wet. Never mind; no one noticed. Like the president, the reporters were enamored by the notion of Mach 3 speed. Of much more significance was what the event meant to the CIA. The rivalry between the Agency and the Air Force for control over Oxcart was hotter than ever.

With the two departments' gloves off, the fate of Oxcart now hung precariously in the balance. Secretary of Defense Robert McNamara snidely told CIA director John McCone that he doubted the Oxcart would ever be used. If it was used, McNamara said, it would "probably have to be done without the specific knowledge of the President," alluding to the Gary Powers shoot-down. Never again could a president be linked to a CIA aerial espionage mission. John McCone shot back that he had "every intention of using Oxcart and had so advised the President." McNamara may have won the battle by getting President Johnson to surface part of the Oxcart program, but McCone was letting him know on behalf of the Agency that the Pentagon hadn't yet won the war.

A second Air Force–Agency debate that involved the fate of the Oxcart, which in turn involved the fate of Area 51, centered on improvements in satellite and drone technology. McNamara told McCone that these two platforms would eventually eliminate the need for the Agency's expensive, cumbersome Oxcart program. And yet both men knew that for the time being, Oxcart could deliver what satellites could not, and on two separate but equally important counts. In the six years since Sputnik, satellites had advanced to the degree that their spy images were good, though not great. But satellites had an inherent limitation in the world of espionage: they worked on fixed schedules. This would forever negate any element of surprise. The average satellite took ninety minutes to circle the world, and overflight schedules were easily determined by analysts at NORAD. The ironically named Oxcart was an attack espionage vehicle: quick and versatile, nimble and shrewd, with overpasses that would be totally unpredictable to any enemy. But most of all, in terms of clear photographic intelligence, nothing could compete with what Oxcart was about to be able to deliver to the president: two-and-a-half-foot blocks of detail made clear by film frames shot from seventeen miles up.

While McNamara and McCone fought, a presidential election loomed for Johnson. Nikita Khrushchev, ever the antagonist, decided to make things difficult for the saber-rattling Texan. During the campaign summer of 1964, the increasingly bellicose Khrushchev declared that any U-2s flying over Cuba would be shot down. The CIA saw the threat by the Soviet dictator as an opportunity to let Oxcart show its stuff, and McCone pushed President Johnson for an official mission. Finally, the president approved the Oxcart for Operation Skylark, a plan to fly missions over Cuba if Khrushchev showed signs of putting missiles in Cuba again. Skylark provided a terrific opportunity for the CIA to flex its overhead muscle and gain an edge on the Air Force. The only problem was that out at Area 51, the Oxcart wasn't quite ready.

Kenneth Collins sat in the cockpit of the world's fastest aircraft as it climbed through sixty thousand feet. On this particular flight, navigators had him flying north to the border of Canada, where he was to turn around and head back. Flight-testing the Oxcart was the best job in the world, according to Ken Collins. Most jobs came with a daily routine, and for Collins each day of work at Area 51 meant another performance field to tackle—anything but routine.

For months, the pilots had been testing the hydraulics, navigation system, and flight controls on the aircraft. After each flight, the data from flight recorders was analyzed by a team of Lockheed engineers. Changes were made daily at Groom Lake. The wiring continued to be problematic until replacement materials that could withstand 800 degrees were finally located. Another problem that took forever to solve involved the buildup of the liquid chemical triethylborane (TEB) that had been preventing the engine after-burners from starting. Finally, that too was solved. But one danger-ous problem remained, and that was the dreaded un-starts.

Moving through seventy-five thousand feet now, Collins watched the gauges in front of him. It was −70 degrees Fahrenheit outside with exhaust gas coming out of both engines at 3,400 degrees Fahrenheit. Each one of a pair of specially designed J-58 turbojet engines behind him generated as much power as all four of the tur-bines on the 81,000-ton ocean liner the *Queen Mary*. It was those insanely powerful engines that enabled the aircraft to fly so high and so fast. But the *Queen Mary* carried more than three thousand people; the Oxcart just one. Collins counted on those engines. If anything went wrong with either of them it could mean catastro-phe. Carefully, he moved the aircraft through the dangerous win-dow between Mach 2.5 and Mach 2.8, which translates to something around 2,000 mph—as fast as a rifle bullet goes. Getting up to and through that speed asked more of the aircraft than anything else. It was also the place where an un-start was most likely to occur, and why Collins was counting on the aircraft engines to perform.

To the pilots, there was nothing scarier than an engine un-start. To the engineers, there was nothing to explain the cause of it. Fly-ing at a certain pitch, one of the two J-58 engines could inexplica-bly experience an airflow cutoff and go dead. At that speed, the inlets were swallowing ten thousand cubic feet of air each second. One engineer likened this to the equivalent of two million people inhaling at once; an un-start was like all those people suddenly cut short of air. During the ten seconds it took to correct the airflow problem—one engine dead, the other generating enough power to propel an ocean liner—a violent yawing would occur as the air-craft twisted on a vertical axis. This caused a pilot to get slammed across the cockpit while desperately trying to restart the dead engine. The fear was that the pilot could get knocked unconscious, which would mean the end of the pilot, and the end of the airplane.

As Collins moved through Mach 2.7, the Earth below him hurtled by at an astonishing rate of more than half a mile each second. The aircraft's preset flight path kept it away from urban centers, bridges, and dams for safety reasons, and from Indian burial grounds for political reasons. Once, a pilot flying over semirural West Virginia had to restart an engine at thirty thousand feet. The resulting sonic boom shattered a chimney inside a factory on the ground, and two men working there were crushed to death. And if a pilot had to bail out, as Collins had in 1963, the aircraft needed significant amounts of remote land on which to crash. At 123,000 pounds, this airplane had about as much glide in it as a tire iron falling from the sky.

Collins pushed the aircraft through Mach 2.8. In another forty-five seconds he would be out of the danger zone. Nearing eighty-five thousand feet, the inevitable tiny black dots began to appear on the aircraft windshield, sporadic at first, like the first drops of summer rain. Only a few months earlier, scientists at Area 51 had been baffled by those black dots. They worried it was some kind of high-atmosphere corrosion until the mystery was solved in the lab. It turned out the black spots were dead bugs that were cycling around in the upper atmosphere, blasted into the jet stream by the world's two superpowers' rally of thermonuclear bombs. The bugs were killed in the bombs' blasts and sent aloft to ninety thousand feet in the ensuing mushroom clouds where they gained orbit.

Collins was just seconds away from Mach 3, which meant cruising altitude at last. If there was a brief moment where he might allow himself to relax, maybe even glance outside at the round Earth below and enjoy the cruise, that moment would come soon. But then the un-start happened. In a critical instant, the airplane banged and yawed so dramatically it was as if the airplane's tail were trying to catch its nose. Collins's body was flung forward in his harness. His plastic flight helmet crashed against the cockpit glass, denting the helmet and nearly knocking him unconscious. As the airplane slid across the atmosphere, Collins steeled himself and restarted the engine. The aircraft's second engine kicked back into motion almost as quickly as it had stopped.

Things in the cockpit returned to normal. Inside his pressure suit, Collins felt his heart beating like a jackhammer in his chest. Fate really is a hunter, he thought. It lurks behind you in constant pursuit. When it will catch up to you and take you is anybody's guess.

Death didn't get him this time, and for that he was grateful. But somebody needed to fix this un-start problem, fast. With his feet firmly planted on the earth again, Collins discussed the issue of the un-starts with Bill Park during his debrief. Park was Lockheed's chief flight-test pilot and he always sat patiently with the project pilots after their flights, listening intently about what went on during the flight and what needed work. No detail was too small. Park agreed with Collins; the un-start problem was major and had to be fixed before somebody died. Park was the liaison between the project pilots and Kelly Johnson, and Park was directed to Lockheed's thermodynamicist Ben Rich to get the un-start problem solved. Park had experienced his own share of un-starts, and giving Ben Rich an ultimatum was not something he had any problem with.

Rich's office was sparely decorated with a few trophies and some plaques on the walls. There were papers everywhere, and pencils with the erasers gone. A hand-cranked calculator and a metal slide rule sat on Rich's desk. Park set his flight helmet down—it had its own crack, similar to Collins's—and pointed to it. "Fix it," Park said. "And I mean the un-start problem, not my helmet. Time to suit up, Ben. Time for you to see how it feels." The pilots figured that the only way to get Ben Rich to understand just how unacceptable this un-start business was would be to have Rich experience the nightmare scenario himself, and there just happened to be a two-seater version of the Oxcart on base. The Air Force was currently testing its drone-carrying version of the Oxcart, the M-21/D-21, in the skies over Groom Lake, and the pilots had seen the two-seater going in and out of the hangar all week. Park told Ben Rich the time had come for him to take a Mach 3 ride.

In a burst of what he would later describe as "a crazy moment of weakness," Ben Rich agreed. Rich was a self-described Jewish nerd. Totally unathletic, he was a kid who never made the high school baseball team. Before joining Skunk Works, Ben Rich had only one claim to fame: being awarded a patent for designing a nickel-chromium heating system that prevented a pilot's penis from freezing to his urine elimination pipe. He was a design wizard, not an airplane cowboy. He'd never come close to flying supersonic before, and he had absolutely no desire to go that fast. But he was chief engineer for Skunk Works, so fixing the un-start problem was his job. "I'll do it," Ben Rich said.

Before Ben Rich could get into the world's fastest aircraft, he had to go through a battery of physical tests. You can't just climb into an aircraft that gets up to ninety thousand feet without being checked out in a pressure suit in an altitude chamber first. The flight surgeons on base prepped Rich for tests, the way they usually did pilots. Rich passed the physical and a few early stress tests but when he got to the pressure-chamber test—the one that simulated ejection at fifty thousand feet—things did not go as the engineer had planned. The moment the chamber door closed behind Ben Rich, he panicked. "I was sucking oxygen like a marathon runner and screaming, 'Get me out of here!'" Rich later recalled. Without ever getting close to simulating what it was like to fly at Mach 3, let alone experiencing an un-start at that speed, Ben Rich admitted in his memoir that he had still nearly dropped dead from fright.

But the point was made. Rich dedicated all his efforts to fixing the un-start problem. Like so many engineering challenges facing the scientists at Area 51, fixing it involved great ingenuity. In this case, Rich and his team didn't exactly fix the problem. Instead, they created a go-around that made things not so life-threatening for the pilots. Rich invented an electronic control that made sure that when one engine experienced an un-start, the second engine dropped its power as well. The control switch would then restart both engines at the same time. After the new fix, pilots were notified of the un-start by a loud buzzing noise in the cockpit. And as far as nearly getting knocked unconscious at 2,000 miles per hour, Oxcart pilots could cross that off their lists of concerns.

In addition to the problems the pilots were having getting the

airplane up to speed, there were problems with the electronic countermeasures, or ECMs. The reports being analyzed back at Langley
said if Operation Skylark was to happen over Cuba, cruise speed
would have to be at a minimum Mach 2.8, because there was a real
chance that the Soviet radar systems in Cuba would be able to detect
Oxcart flights and possibly even shoot them down. While Project
Palladium officers continue to work on jamming methods, the
Office of Special Activities at the Pentagon decided that the solution lay in working to enhance stealth. The phenomenally low
radar cross section on the Oxcart had to be lowered even further.
This meant that Lockheed physicist Edward Lovick and the radar
cross-section team were summoned back to Area 51.

In a hangar not far from the radar range, Edward Lovick got to
work on a one-eighth-scale model of the Oxcart. In what became
known as Project Kempster-Lacroix, Lovick designed a system
straight out of Star Trek or James Bond. "Two giant electron guns
were to be mounted on either side of the aircraft," Lovick recalls.
Remarkably, the purpose of the guns would be "to shoot out a
twenty-five-foot-wide ion cloud of highly charged particles in
front of the plane as it flew over denied territory." That gaseous
cloud, Lovick determined, would further absorb radar waves coming up from radar tracking stations on the ground.

Using the small-scale model, the scientists were able to prove
the scheme worked, which meant it was time to build a full-scale
mock-up of Kempster-Lacroix. Testing the system out on a full-
size aircraft, the scientists discovered that the radiation emitted by
the electron guns would be too dangerous for the pilots. So a separate team of engineers designed an X-ray shield that the pilots
could wear over their pressure suits while flying an Oxcart outfitted with Kempster-Lacroix. When one of the pilots made a test
run, he determined that the thickness of the shield was far too
cumbersome to wear while trying to fly an airplane at Mach 3.
Then, while Lovick was working on a solution, the Air Force
changed its mind. The Oxcart's low observables were low enough,
the Pentagon said. Project Kempster-Lacroix was abandoned.

It was ironic, to say the least. Not the flip-flopping by the Air Force but the concerns about radiation. By 1964, the government had exploded 286 nuclear bombs within shouting distance of Area 51. One year earlier, the United States and the Soviet Union had signed the Limited Test Ban Treaty prohibiting nuclear testing in the air, space, or sea. The initiative had been in the works for years but negotiations had repeatedly failed. Now that it was finally signed, testing had moved underground. Neither superpower trusted the other to honor the commitment for very long, and the number of tests per month actually accelerated after the treaty; the idea was to stay weapons-ready in the event one side broke the treaty. Between September 1961 and December 1964, a record-breaking 162 bombs were exploded at the Nevada Test Site inside underground tunnels and shafts. Nearly half of these explosions resulted in the "accidental release of radioactivity" into the atmosphere.

In addition to weapons tests, the nuclear laboratories were racing to find ways to use nuclear bombs for "peaceful applications." This included ideas like widening the Panama Canal or blowing up America's natural geography to make room for future highways and homes. These proposed earthmoving projects fell under the rubric of Project Plowshares, a name chosen from a verse in the Old Testament, Micah 4:3:

> And they shall beat their swords into plowshares and their spears into pruning hooks: nations shall not lift up sword against nation, neither shall they learn war anymore.

But that was just semantics. Test ban treaty or not, the Department of Defense had no intention of putting down its swords. The men were fully committed to the long haul that was the Cold War.

Finally satisfied with the radar cross section, the CIA decided to set up its own electronic countermeasures office at Area 51. In 1963, the first group consisted of two men from Sylvania, a company better known for making lightbulbs than for its top secret work for the

CIA. "The first jamming system was called Red Dog; later it became Blue Dog," explains Ken Swanson, the first official ECM officer at Area 51. The Red Dog system was designed to detect Russian surface-to-air missiles coming after Oxcart and then jam those missiles with an electronic pulse. The work was exciting when the airplanes were flying and there was actual data to collect, but if the Red Dog system failed and needed fixing, it meant a lot of waiting around.

These were the early days of electronic warfare, and there were not a lot of Red Dog spare parts lying around. As a result, Ken Swanson worked many long weekends at Area 51. Swanson says that sometimes he and his Sylvania colleague felt like they were the only ones on the base. One weekend the men took the Area 51 motor pool's four-wheel-drive vehicle up to Bald Mountain, the tallest peak on the Groom Range, to have a look around. "We found a bunch of old Model Ts and had no idea what they were doing there," Swanson recalls. Another time he went solo to investigate the old mines. "I was wearing tennis shoes and Bermuda shorts and I bumped into a bunch of rattlers sunning themselves. Next time I went back, I wore snake boots," he says. During winter weekends, there were even fewer people at Area 51, and for entertainment, after a long day performing high-tech electronic-countermeasures work, Swanson would go joyriding around the dry lake bed. He'd borrow an Econoline van from the motor pool, take it out on the frozen tarmac, and do spins. "But I stopped after I had the van on two wheels once," Swanson says.

With Red Dog, the CIA wanted to see how the Oxcart would show up on Soviet radar, and so, at the southern tip of Groom Lake, on EG&G Road, Sylvania built two ECM systems, one to simulate Russian SA-2 radar and a second to simulate the Fan Song surface-to-air missile system that was showing up in North Vietnam. The goal was to see what Oxcart looked like, or hopefully did not look like, on these radars. An equally important part of the radar testing system was the radar pole that had to be installed on the top of Bald Mountain. For that, the CIA recruited one of the best rescue helicopter pilots in the country, Charlie Trapp.

"I was minding my own business in South Carolina," Trapp recalls, "when these guys from the Air Force called me up and asked if I want to come fly a two-airplane helo unit in Nevada, one hundred miles from the nearest town. They said it was important and that I'd have to be able to hover and land at nine thousand feet." Trapp thought it sounded interesting as well as challenging and he signed on. "We flew in from Nellis in the H-43 [helicopter] and before we even landed at Area 51, they said, 'Let's go see how you land on top of the mountain first,' that's how important the mountain project was to the beginning of my Area 51 assignment." For months, Trapp hauled cement in thousand-pound buckets from the Area 51 operations center up to the top of Bald Mountain. "I'd hover over the top and lower the equipment down," Trapp explains. "There were high winds and serious dust storms." Finally, Trapp helicoptered in the one-hundred-foot-long radar pole, which a team of workers cemented into place. Mission accomplished. "We did such a good job, the CIA gave us air medals," Trapp says. On his way back down to Area 51 in the helicopter, Trapp would fly around the different mountain peaks. "Once, I came across an old graveyard. In a helicopter you can hover and look. The graves were made of piles of rocks. I remember two of them were really small. They must have been kids' graves." The mountain had a psychological pull with many of the men at Area 51 during the Oxcart years. It was also the only place the men were allowed to go that was technically "off base."

Down on the tarmac, every time an A-12 Oxcart took off, it was Trapp's job to hang out airborne, two hundred feet above the runway and off to one side, "in case the aircraft crashed," Trapp explains. "My helicopter contained firefighting equipment, and I always had two PJs with me, para-rescue jumpers, [who perform] like a Navy SEAL. It was a lot of work having us airborne and I told the boss, Colonel Holbury, that I could be airborne in less than two minutes' time. So the policy changed." Instead, Trapp was on standby in the event of an accident, "which meant I got to drive the only golf cart around the Area 51 base." The golf cart came in handy at night. "We played a lot of poker in the House-Six bar," Trapp explains. "The loser had to do the late-night cheeseburger run over to the mess hall. With the golf cart, you could get there and back in five minutes."

For all the technology that was around at Area 51, entertainment was decidedly old-school. "We did a lot of arm wrestling," Trapp says. "Some guys played racquetball and other guys played three-hole golf." When Trapp gained ten pounds eating so many late-night cheeseburgers, he was ordered to lose the weight or risk losing his job. To assist in the effort, Colonel Holbury challenged Trapp to weekly rounds of squash. Once, someone brought a sailboard out to Area 51, and the pilots pulled rank and got the men in the machine shop to affix wheels to the bottom of the board. "We took the thing out to Groom Lake when the wind was blowing really hard," Trapp recalls. "It didn't go that fast but we didn't care."

Of all the pastimes, the unanimous favorite was flying model airplanes using remote control. "We had two areas for flying model planes," Trapp recalls. "Out on the grass by the golf course, and on the tarmac out on the dry lake. Sometimes the airplanes would go so far and so high they'd get lost. A guy would come up to me and say, 'Hey, Charlie, when you're out in the helicopter, can you keep your eye out for my model plane? It's got a five-foot wing span and yellow wings.' We found ways to entertain ourselves at Area 51. We had to; there weren't any girls."

The man who took the model airplane flying most seriously was Frank Murray. He was also the chase pilot with the most flying time during Project Oxcart. "You could always find Frank sitting in his room gluing model airplanes together," Colonel Slater recalls. "That was his idea of fun. Or maybe he was the only guy at 51 who wasn't half-drunk at eleven o'clock at night." Which is how Murray accumulated the most flying time. "If somebody's kid got hurt in the middle of the night, which happened more than you think, and I need a pilot to get someone off base fast, I'd round up Frank," Colonel Slater explains. When master fuels sergeant Harry Martin's grandfather died, it was Frank Murray who flew him back east so he could get to the funeral in time. "Frank was always willing to do the job," Colonel Slater explains. "Most people require time off from flying. Not Frank."

Murray flew model airplanes to keep his head clear for flying real airplanes. "Everyone had their different thing," Colonel Slater says. "Bud Wheelon from CIA used to want to play tennis at midnight when he was on base. Some liked to go hunting up in the mountains by the old Sheehan mine. Holbury used to like to make the guard dogs run. Some guys threw rocks at rattlesnakes. I liked to drive around in the jeep and find petrified wood."

As an Oxcart chase pilot, Murray spent his days and nights chasing the Mach 3 airplane in the F-101. The Voodoo was a two-seat, supersonic jet fighter the Air Force used to accompany the Oxcart on takeoffs and landings. "We flew it with Oxcart up through the special operating area, or Yuletide, which was the airspace just north of the base," Murray explains. "The Agency had us fly alongside the Oxcart in the Voodoo until we couldn't keep up with the Oxcart anymore." Flying chase meant Murray got assigned most of the grunt work and enjoyed little of the glamour. "I was a little jealous of the Oxcart pilots," he admits. "How can a pilot not be? But I was happy as a pig in the Voodoo. For a farm boy from San Diego, flying chase for the 1129th was a good time."

Murray flew the F-101 doing just about everything that needed to be done in support of Oxcart operations. This included flying against the Red Dog simulators, observing tanker refuels, overseeing takeoffs and landings, and flying Lockheed photographers around on CIA photo shoots. But Murray's path in life took a significant redirection when General Ledford, the head of the Office of Special Activities at the Pentagon, decided he wanted to learn how to fly the F-101 while he was overseeing activities at Area 51. Murray recalls: "The general had been a bomber pilot in World War Two but he hadn't ever flown anything as fast as the Voodoo could go, which was around twelve hundred or thirteen hundred miles per hour. So he decided that he wanted to learn how to fly it and when it came to choosing an IP, an instructor pilot, the general chose me."

Murray now had to teach a legendary war hero, someone who also happened to be the highest-ranking military officer on the Oxcart program, how to fly supersonic. It might have been a daunting task. Except that it was not in Frank Murray's character to be apprehensive. To Murray, it sounded like fun. "Out at the Ranch we had eight 101s that ran chase and one of them was a two-holer, with two cockpits and two sticks. 'Come on, Frankie,' the general said. He got in the back and up we went."

General Ledford began to spend more and more time at the Ranch, where, in addition to the serious work being done, operations had taken on a boys' club atmosphere. After a day of intense flying, nights were spent eating, socializing, and having drinks. "Sometimes, on the late side of things after dinner, Ledford would get a hair in his hat that he wanted to get back to Washington to see his wife, Polly," Murray says. "He'd slap me on the back. That was my cue to take him home." Home, in Washington, DC, was 2,500 miles away, and with supersonic aircraft at one's disposal, this could actually happen this late at night. "Ledford was my student but he was also the general so on these trips home, I started letting him sit in the front of the plane; I'd sit in back. Well, all those hours flying back and forth from Area 51 to Washington, that cemented it. He was my boss but he also became my friend." Ledford had other friends as well, several in high places at the Air Force, which made getting back to the East Coast from Nevada in the middle of the night a relatively easier trip. "Ledford had a buddy who was still in SAC, an air division commander at Blytheville Air Force Base in northeast Arkansas, just about halfway between 51 and Washington. Ledford would radio him when we were up in the air approaching the next state over and he'd say, 'Have you got a tanker in the area?' If he did or didn't you could bet your fifty there'd be a tanker lining up next to you somewhere over Arkansas," Murray says. What this meant was that when Murray and the general were traveling from Area 51 to the East Coast late at night, they never even had to stop for gas.

After a little more than two hours in the air, the men would land at Andrews Air Force Base and taxi up to the generals' quarters—similar to a luxury hotel suite on the base—and enjoy a postflight scotch. "Ledford had a fancy setup on base quarters that had a fully equipped bar," Murray explains. "We'd have a pop and chat a little before his wife, Polly, arrived to pick him up and take him home. I'd spend the night in the generals' quarters. Get some sleep and in the morning head home to 51."

It was an exciting time for Frank Murray. He couldn't have imagined living this life. Only a few years earlier, he'd been flying Voodoos at Otis Air Force Base as part of the Air Defense Command when he had seen an interesting sign tacked on a bulletin board that read *NASA is looking for F-101 chase pilots.* He thought working for NASA sounded like fun. He had no idea that was just a cover story and that the Air Force, not NASA, was really looking for chase pilots for the Oxcart program at Area 51. Murray applied and got in. He moved the family to Nevada and swore an oath not to tell anyone what he did, not even Stella, his wife. But he knew his family would be super proud of him. For a farm boy from San Diego, he was at the top of his game.

While Project Oxcart worked to get mission-ready, back in Washington the widening of the conflict in Vietnam by the Communists in the north was becoming a nightmare for President Johnson. He had won the favor of the people back in 1957 by declaring Communism to be the world's greatest threat. In comparison to the thermonuclear-armed Soviet Union, Vietnam was to Johnson a sideshow. But it was also a piece in the widely held domino theory: if Vietnam fell to Communism, the whole region would ultimately fall. President Johnson had inherited Vietnam from President Kennedy when it was a political crisis and not yet a war. That changed in the second summer Johnson held office, in August of 1964, with the Gulf of Tonkin. The Pentagon declared that the U.S. Navy had suffered an unprovoked attack by North Vietnam against the USS *Maddox,* and the National Security Agency had evidence, McNamara said. This event allowed Johnson to push the Gulf of Tonkin resolution through Congress, which authorized war. (In 2005 NSA released a detailed confession admitting that its intelligence had been "deliberately skewed to support the notion that there had been an attack.") To avenge the USS *Maddox* attack, Johnson ordered air attacks against the North Vietnamese, sending Navy pilots on bombing missions over North Vietnam. When a number of U.S. pilots were shot down, the North Vietnamese took them as prisoners of war.

The war's escalation led Secretary of Defense Robert McNamara to perform an about-face regarding Oxcart. The Agency's spy plane could be vitally useful after all, McNamara now said, certainly when it came to gathering intelligence in North Vietnam. The Agency knew the Russians had begun supplying surface-to-air missile systems to the Communists in North Vietnam, and now they were shooting down American boys. Both the Air Force and the Agency sent U-2s on reconnaissance missions, and these overflights revealed that missile sites were being set up around Hanoi. But the Pentagon needed far more specific target information. In June, McNamara sat down with the CIA and began drawing up plans to get the Oxcart ready for its first mission at last.

CHAPTER FIFTEEN

The Ultimate Boys' Club

At Groom Lake throughout the 1960s, at least once a month and always before dawn, base personnel would be shaken from their beds by a violent explosion. When the rumbling first started happening, Ken Collins would leap from bed as a sensation that felt like a massive earthquake rolled by. A nuclear bomb was being exploded next door, underground, just a few miles west of Oxcart pilots' quarters. Next, the blast wave would hit Collins's Quonset hut and then roll on, heading across the Emigrant Mountain Range with a surreal and unnatural force that made the coyotes wail.

In the years that Collins had been test-flying the Oxcart at Area 51, the Department of Defense had been testing nuclear bombs with bravado. After a while, being awoken before dawn meant little to Collins, and he'd roll over and go back to sleep. But on this one particular morning something felt different. It was a banging he was hearing, not a boom. Collins opened his eyes. Someone was indeed banging on his Quonset hut door. Next came a loud voice that sounded a lot like Colonel Slater's. Collins leaped out of bed and opened his door. Colonel Slater had an unusual look of concern, and without explanation, he ordered Collins to get into his flight suit as fast as he could. This was a highly unusual request, Collins thought. It was definitely before dawn. Behind where Slater stood on the Quonset hut stoop, Collins could see it was still dark outside. For a brief moment, he feared the worst. Had America gone to war with the Soviets? What could possibly force an unplanned Oxcart mission flight? Rushing to put on his clothes, Collins heard Colonel Slater waking up the flight surgeon who lived in the apartment quarters next door.

Collins followed Slater in a run toward the hangar where the Oxcart lived. There he was quickly briefed on the situation: the Pentagon had called to say that a Russian reconnaissance balloon was flying across the United States, floating with the prevailing winds in a westerly direction. Collins was to find the Soviet balloon—fast. Normally, the flight surgeon would have spent two hours just getting Collins into his pressure suit. That morning Collins was suited up and sitting in the cockpit of the Oxcart in a little over thirty minutes. Up he went, blasting off the tarmac, north then east, on direct orders by the Pentagon to "hunt and find" the Soviet weather balloon visually and using radar.

Up in the air it dawned on Collins what a wild-goose chase he was on. What would a Russian reconnaissance balloon look like? What were the chances of making visual contact with such a thing? At speeds of more than 2,200 mph, he was traveling more than half a mile each second. Even if he saw the balloon, in just a fraction of a second it would be behind him. Even worse, what if he actually did get that close to the flying object? If the Oxcart hit anything while moving at Mach 3, the plane would break apart instantly and he'd be toast.

Flying somewhere over the middle of the continent, Collins briefly identified an object on radar about 350 miles away. As instructed, he flew around the object in the tightest circle he could perform at Mach 3, which meant his circle had a radius of about 400 miles. He never saw the balloon with his own eyes.

After Collins returned to base, engineers scrambled to read the information on the data recorder. The incident has never been declassified. Admitting that the Soviets invaded U.S. airspace—whether in a craft or by balloon—is not something any U.S. official has ever done. Collins never asked any follow-up questions. That's how it was to be a pilot: the less you knew, the better. He knew too many fellow pilots from Korea who had come home from POW camps missing fingernails—if they came home at all. Now, ten years later, pilots shot down over North Vietnam were experiencing the same kinds of torture, maybe worse. The less you knew, the better. That was the pilots' creed.

As deputy director of the CIA, Richard Helms was a huge fan of Oxcart. He worked closely on the program with Bud Wheelon, whose efforts earned him the title of first director of science and technology for the CIA. Now that Richard Bissell was gone, there were few men in the Agency as devoted to the Area 51 spy plane program as Wheelon and Helms. Whereas Wheelon saw his position at the CIA as a temporary one—he signed on for a four-year contract, fulfilled it, and left the CIA—Helms was a career Agency man. He'd worked closely with Bissell on the U-2 from its inception and he knew what important intelligence could come from overhead photographs. The United States learned more about the Soviets' weapons capabilities from its first U-2 overflight than it had in the previous ten years from its spies on the ground. Off McNamara's inquiry about possibly using the Oxcart on spy missions over North Vietnam, Helms made a personal trip out to Area 51 to sign off on Oxcart design specifications himself. Helms was also acutely aware of the Air Force's plans to push Oxcart out of the way in favor of their own reconnaissance spy plane, the SR-71 Blackbird. If Helms could get a mission for Oxcart, the chances of the CIA maintaining its supersonic espionage program greatly increased.

Almost everyone who visited Area 51 became enamored with the desert facility, and Helms was no exception. It was impossible not to be fascinated by the power and prestige the secret facility embodied. It was the quintessential boys' club, both exotic and elite. Most of all, it gave visitors the sense of being a million miles away from the hustle and bustle of Washington, DC. There were no cars to drive—instead, Agency shuttles moved men around the base. No radio, almost no TV. As a visitor to Area 51, Helms was particularly careful not to step on any powerful Air Force toes. The base was, operations-wise, Air Force turf now. The CIA was in charge of missions, but there were no missions, which only underscored a growing sense of Agency impotence. The Air Force controlled most of the day-to-day operations on the base, including proficiency flights and air-to-air refuelings, which were practiced regularly so everyone in the 1129th Special Activities Squadron stayed in shape.

During his visit, Helms kept a relatively low profile, making sure to spend more of his time in the field—on the airstrip with the pilots and in the aircraft hangars with the engineers—than drinking White Horse Scotch with Air Force brass in the House-Six bar. During test flights, Helms liked to roll up his sleeves and stand on the tarmac when the Oxcart took off. He likened the experience to standing on the epicenter of an 8.0 earthquake and described the great orange fireballs that spewed out of the Oxcart's engines as "hammers from hell." Helms, an upper-middle-class intellectual from Philadelphia, loved colorful language. He'd once told a room of military men that the Vietnam War was "like an incubus," a nightmarish male demon that creeps up on sleeping women and has intercourse with them. Helms's grandiose language, most likely intentional, separated him from straight-talking military men.

Despite playing a key role in planning and executing covert operations in Vietnam, Richard Helms did not believe the United States could win the war there. This posture kept him out of step with Pentagon brass. Helms believed Vietnam was fracturing consensus about America's need to win the Cold War, which he saw as the more important battle at hand. He was an advocate of using technology to beat the Russians by way of overhead reconnaissance from satellites and spy planes, which was why he liked Oxcart so much. And unlike Pentagon and State Department officials, who, for the most part, cautioned the president against ever sending spy planes over the Soviet Union again, Helms, like McCone, felt the president should do just that. "The only sin in espionage is getting caught," Helms once said. He believed the best intelligence was "objective intelligence." Photographs didn't have an opinion and couldn't lie. Helms attributed his respect for objectivity to his working as a journalist for the wire service United Press International. In 1936, a then twenty-four-year-old Richard Helms got his first big scoop: covering the Berlin Olympics as a reporter, he was invited to interview Adolf Hitler. Six years later, Helms would be recruited by the Office of Strategic Services, the precursor organization to the CIA, to spy on Hitler's men.

With Richard Helms at Area 51 in December of 1965, the Oxcart was finally declared operational. Celebrations were in order. One of the pilots offered to fly a C-130 Hercules on a seafood run to Westover Air Force Base in Massachusetts, where Werner Weiss had coolers full of lobsters, oysters, and crab legs ready to be taken to Area 51. Big-budget black operations had stomach-size perks too. After such feasts, the kitchen staff buried the shells in compost piles along the base perimeter, and the joke among Air Force support staff was that future archaeologists digging in the area would think Groom Lake had been an ocean as late as the 1960s.

As secret and compartmentalized as the base was, the mess hall was the one place where the men gathered together to break bread. Technical assistants would rub elbows with three- and four-star generals visiting there. Ernie Williams, who had helped find Area 51's first well in 1955 and now helped coordinate meals, loved it when Werner Weiss invited him into the mess hall to eat steaks with generals who wore stars on their chests. And after the meal was over, the men would again go their separate ways. The Special Projects program managers and the engineering nerds usually retired to their quarters to play poker and drink bottled beer. The scientists were known to return to their respective hangars, where they'd stay up until all hours of the night engrossed in various problems they needed to solve. The Air Force guys went to the House-Six bar to roll dice, have a drink, and share war stories.

When on base, Richard Helms was known to stop in for a drink. He was a great conversationalist but almost always refrained from telling stories about himself. And as far as World War II was concerned, Helms rarely discussed the subject. In 1945, as a young OSS officer, Helms had worked in postwar Berlin. He was one of the key players in Operation Paperclip; Helms had been tasked with finding a group of Hitler's former scientists and offering them positions on classified programs back in the United States. Jobs involving biological weapons, rockets, and stealth. Years later, Helms justified his recruitment of former Nazis by saying that if the scientists hadn't come to work for us, they'd have gone to work for "them." Helms knew things other men did not know. At the Agency he was the man who kept the secrets.

In 1975, Helms would unwittingly become an internationally recognized figure famous for destroying CIA documents to avoid having their secrets revealed. After allegations surfaced that the CIA had been running a human-research program called MKULTRA—which involved mind-control experiments using drugs such as LSD—Helms as director of the CIA was asked to take the stand. While testifying to Congress, Helms stated that he had ordered all the MKULTRA files destroyed two years earlier, in 1973.

In the labyrinthine organizational chart that kept men at Area 51 in their respective places, no one was more important to the spy plane project's overall progress than the commander of the base, a position granted to an Air Force officer whose salary came from the CIA. In 1965, the position was filled by Colonel Slater. Slater was the ideal commander. He was astute, practical, and an excellent listener, which put him in direct contrast to the more elitist Colonel Holbury, who'd held the position before. What the pilots appreciated most about Slater was that he was funny. Not sarcastic funny, but the kind of funny that reminded pilots not to take their jobs so seriously all the time. One of the first things Colonel Slater did after taking command of the base was to hang a sign over the House-Six bar that listed Slip Slater's Basic Rules of Flying at Groom Lake. There were only three rules.

- Try to stay in the middle of the air.
- Do not go near the edges of it.
- The edges of the air can be recognized by the appearance of ground, buildings, sea, trees and interstellar space. It is much more difficult to fly there.

Like all the pilots at Area 51, Slater flew every chance he got. Now, as commander of the base, he began each day by making the first run. Around five thirty each morning, coffee mug in hand, Slater was driven by one of the enlisted men to the end of a runway, where he'd jump in an F-101 and fly around the Box on what he called "the weather run." Because Area 51 had a large box of restricted airspace, Slater could fly in a manner not seen at other Air Force bases. Colonel Roger Andersen, who had been recruited to Area 51 to work in the command post, remembers the first time he flew with Slater in a two-seater T-33 to Groom Lake. "We were doing proficiency flying. I'd been getting teased by the other pilots because my background was flying tankers for the Air Force, not jets," Andersen explains. "Up in the air, Slater says to me, 'You need to loosen up, Andersen, Let's rack it around.' At which point Slater does a loop, a roll, and a spin... in a row. You could do that kind of thing up at Area 51."

Everyone knew stories about Slater's flying career: flying against the Germans in World War II, flying as the detachment commander for the Black Cats, and of course the remarkable story of his flying an airplane with a dead engine for a hundred miles on a glide—through a hurricane—in 1946. As a young hero just back from the war, Slater had been chosen by the Army Air Forces to fly a brand-new P-80 Shooting Star on a training mission from March Air Force Base to Jamaica. The P-80 was the first jet fighter used by the Army Air Forces at a time when jets in America were relatively new. As Slater remembers it, he was "one hundred miles out at sea off of Key West when the engine quit. I was just north of Cuba, which was under hurricane. There was turbine failure and a flameout so I turned around and glided back to the Keys." Jet airplanes do not normally glide without engine thrust, at least not without a skilled pilot at the controls. When a jet engine loses all power, it usually crashes. Slater rode the jet stream for a hundred miles over the Atlantic Ocean until he found an abandoned airstrip at Marathon Key, in Florida, on which to land. The amazing story made its way to the pages of the *New York Times*.

Richard Helms was a fan of Slater, and before leaving Area 51 to get back to Washington, Helms made sure to congratulate Colonel Slater on all the fine work that had been achieved to get Oxcart operational. Now Slater had to be prepared to fly himself to Washington on a moment's notice on Oxcart's behalf. Over the next several months, Slater and General Ledford would be asked to participate in the top secret covert-action review board the 303 Committee, which would be assigning Oxcart its mission. (The 303 Committee was a successor to the Special Operations Group, which Bissell had been in charge of during his tenure at the CIA.)

Slater flew himself to Washington in an F–101 more times than he could count. There, however eloquently the Agency advocated on the Oxcart squadron's behalf, the Pentagon put up roadblocks. Slater's input had little effect on the naysayers. He was looked upon as the man in charge of a billion-dollar black operations program, a golden goose that the Air Force desperately wanted to wrest from the CIA. Every time the Agency proposed a mission, the review board denied the CIA's request.

That the groundbreaking spy plane was trapped in a stalemate between the CIA and the Air Force was, at first, unbelievable to Colonel Slater. Throughout his career, Slater had moved effortlessly between different armed services and intelligence worlds, applying his talents wherever they were needed most. As a twenty-two-year-old fighter pilot, Slater flew eighty-four missions over France and Germany in a P–47 Thunderbolt. When the Army desperately needed support from airmen during the Battle of the Bulge, Slater fought side by side with soldiers on the ground at the bloody Siege of Bastogne. Later, as commander of the Black Cat Squadron flying dangerous missions over mainland China, Slater wore both CIA and Air Force hats with ease. The common goal was gathering intelligence. Colonel Slater saw no rivalry among the men.

During that winter of 1966, flying back and forth between Area 51 and the Pentagon, Slater had a front-row seat for the power struggle between the Air Force and the CIA. Secretary of Defense Robert McNamara had changed his mind again on the usefulness of Oxcart in Vietnam. He decided to wait until the Air Force SR-71 program came online. Bud Wheelon believes that "McNamara was delaying finding a mission for the Oxcart on purpose. He was an empire builder. Oxcart did not fit into his empire because it was never his." With each month that passed, the Air Force's SR-71 Blackbird was that much closer to being operations-ready, and the men in charge of Blackbird were in McNamara's chain of command. As soon as the Air Force's spy plane was ready, the CIA's almost identical spy plane would be out of a job.

In June of 1966, Richard Helms was made director of the CIA. Now one of the most powerful men in Washington, Helms lobbied hard on Oxcart's behalf, and in July, the Joint Chiefs of Staff voted in favor of sending Oxcart over North Vietnam to gather intelligence on missile sites there. McNamara and Secretary of State Dean Rusk dug in their heels and again offered dissent. Both men argued that putting CIA planes on the ground at the U.S. Air Force base in Okinawa, Japan, posed too great a political risk. McNamara was playing the same card he had played with John McCone when McCone was running the CIA, namely, that if a CIA spy plane were to get shot down on an espionage mission, the president would face the same backlash that Eisenhower had after the Gary Powers incident.

In August, a vote for or against Oxcart deployment was tallied in the presence of President Johnson. The majority voted against deployment, and the president upheld that decision. The ice around the Oxcart program was getting thin. Colonel Slater responded as best he knew how: when the going gets tough, the tough keep flying. Back at Area 51, he was determined to keep his men mission-ready. There was no point in letting his men know that the program was on the verge of collapse. Who could have imagined that the seminal Oxcart was in danger of being mothballed before it ever got a job? Instead, Slater gave his men a new goal. He wanted them to shave six days off the time it took the squadron to go from mission notification to deployment overseas. It had been a twenty-one-day response time; Slater now wanted it reduced by nearly 30 percent.

Area 51 became like a Boy Scout camp on steroids, a stomping ground for the world's fastest and now most expensive airplane. The six aircraft that would be used for deployment were put through a whole new battery of flight-simulation tests. Commander Slater kept pilot morale high and Pentagon dissent at bay. A bowling alley was built. The pilots kept in shape playing water sports in the Olympic-size swimming pool. They kept their minds clear flying model airplanes and hitting golf balls off the dry lake bed up into the hills. Even the contractors were encouraged to pick up the pace. Slater challenged a lazy work crew to dig a lake. Five decades later, Groom Lake's artificial body of water would still be referred to as Slater Lake. With the aircraft now flying at full speed and maximum height, it was time to break performance records. In December of 1966, one of the pilots set a speed record that would last into the twenty-first century. Bill Park flew 10,195 miles in a little over six hours at an average speed of 1,660 miles per hour. Park had flown over all four corners of America and back to the base in less time than most men spend at the office on any given day. To the project pilots itching for missions, it seemed like they could be deployed any day. And then, in January of 1967, tragedy struck.

Project pilot Walt Ray was, by all accounts, a terrific pilot. He and his new wife, Diane, also made for good company with Ken Collins and his wife, Jane. Diane and Jane did not have to keep up any pretenses; they both accepted that they had no idea what their husbands really did besides fly airplanes. The Rays and the Collinses lived close to each other in the San Fernando Valley, and they would often go on holidays together. "Once we took a small prop plane and flew down to Cabo San Lucas, Mexico, and spent a couple days down there playing tennis, swimming, and flying around," Collins recalls. "There were so few runways in Mexico in the early sixties, mostly we landed in big fields. The goats would see us coming, or hear us coming; they'd run away, and we'd land. Walt Ray loved to fly as much as I did. We'd take turns flying the airplane." Quiet and unassuming, Walt Ray also liked to hunt. "Right after New Year, Walt took me with him on a RON [remain overnight] in Montana. We did some hunting, spent the night in a motel, and flew home," Roger Andersen remembers. The following day, on the afternoon of January 5, 1967, Walt Ray was flying an Oxcart on a short test flight. At the Ranch, it had been snowing. Walt Ray was passing over the tiny town of Farmington, New Mexico, at exactly 3:22 p.m. when he looked down and saw the black line on his fuel gauge move suddenly, dramatically, and dangerously to the left.

"I have a loss of fuel and I do not know where it is going," Walt Ray told Colonel Slater though his headset, breaking radio silence to communicate on a radio frequency reserved for emergencies. The transcript would remain classified until 2007. "I think I can make it," Walt Ray said. He was 130 miles from the tarmac at Area 51, flying subsonic to conserve fuel. But twenty minutes later, over Hanksville, Utah, Ray declared an emergency. He'd gotten the aircraft down to thirty thousand feet when one of its engines flamed out. The sixty-seven-million-dollar spy plane had run out of fuel.

"I'm ejecting" was the last thing Walt Ray said to Colonel Slater.

When Walt Ray ejected, the seat he was strapped into was propelled away from the airplane by a small rocket. The strings of his parachute became tangled in his seat's headrest, which meant he was unable to separate from his seat. Walt Ray fell thirty thousand feet without a parachute and crashed into the side of a mountain near Leith, Nevada. Within seconds of the pilot's last transmission, Commander Slater gave the order to dispatch three aircraft from Area 51 to go find Walt Ray and whatever was left of his airplane. No one had any idea that the thirty-year-old pilot was already dead. In addition to the fleet of search-and-rescue that took off from Groom Lake, the Air Force dispatched four aircraft and two helicopters from Nellis Air Force Base. The crash site needed to be secured quickly before any civilians arrived on the scene.

Twenty-three hours passed. No pilot, no airplane. A U-2 was sent aloft to photograph the general area where Walt Ray was believed to have gone down. While the U-2 pilots flew high, Roger Andersen flew in low, in a T-33. The terrain was challenging, and it was difficult to see the ground. "There was cactus and vegetation everywhere; we had to conserve fuel and fly as low as we could," Andersen explains. Helicopter pilot Charlie Trapp found the aircraft first. "I saw these large film pieces rolling across the top of a ridge," Trapp recalls. "I landed where I could and let my parajumpers jump out. They ran over to the Oxcart, what was left of it, and when they came back they said, 'Walt's not in there and neither is his ejection seat.'" The Oxcart had crashed in the remote high desert on a mountain slope dotted with chaparral. Trapp and his crew went back to Area 51 and, with the navigators' help, mapped out on the board in the command post all the places where Walt Ray might have landed after ejection. Then they went back out and continued the search.

Charlie Trapp found Walt Ray uphill from the crash site, three miles away. "I caught a glimpse of light reflecting from his helmet," Trapp recalls. "He was still in his seat, under a large cedar tree." A perimeter was set up and the dirt roads leading up to the crash site were barricaded and secured by armed guards. Herds of wild horses watched as trucks rolled in and workers carted up the jet wreckage to take back to Groom Lake. The entire process took nine days. After an investigation, officials determined that a faulty fuel gauge was all that was wrong with the triple-sonic spy plane.

At first, the gauge had erroneously indicated to Walt Ray he had enough fuel to get back to the Ranch. Minutes later the gauge told him he was about to run out of fuel.

One man's tragedy can become another man's opportunity, which is what happened to Frank Murray after Walt Ray was killed. After the accident, General Ledford came out to the area to participate in the ensuing investigation. When Ledford was ready to return to Washington, he asked Frank Murray to fly him home. "Up in the air," Murray recalls, "Ledford said to me over the radio, 'How'd you like to fly the plane?' I said, 'Throw me in that puddle, boss' and that was about the extent of the pilot-selection process for me." Murray was given Walt Ray's call sign of Dutch 20. No longer a chase pilot, Murray was now part of the CIA's elite team of overhead espionage pilots.

Defense Department officials used the tragic death of Walt Ray and the loss of another CIA aircraft to their advantage. The Office of the Budget and the Office of the Secretary of Defense met alone, in secret, without representation from the CIA. There, they highlighted the fact that the CIA's several-hundred-million-dollar black budget operation had produced fifteen airplanes, five of which had already crashed. They presented their findings to President Johnson with the recommendation that the Oxcart program be "phased out."

Richard Helms was furious. In an eight-page letter to the president, he told Johnson that to mothball the Oxcart would be a scandalous waste of an asset. The CIA had successfully and meticulously managed 435 spy plane overflights by the U-2 in thirty hostile countries, and only one, the Gary Powers crash, had produced an international incident, Helms said. But the Gary Powers incident had actually strengthened the argument as to why the CIA, not the Air Force, should run the spy plane program, Helms explained. It was because Powers was an intelligence officer, and not a military man, that the Soviets hadn't taken retaliatory action against the United States. Ultimately Powers had been released in a Soviet spy exchange. Helms further strengthened his argument by stating that, unlike the military, the CIA "controls no nuclear weapons, which rules out any propaganda suggestion that an irrational act by some subordinate commander might precipitate a nuclear war." Helms had a point. But would the president see things his way?

The following month, in February of 1967, Colonel Slater was again summoned to Washington. It was his fifth trip in six months. In a roomful of 303 Committee members, Slater was told the Oxcart would be terminated effective January 1, 1968. There was no room for debate. The Oxcart's fate had been decided. The case was closed. Slater was instructed to return to Area 51 and keep his squadron operations ready while the Air Force's SR-71 Blackbird passed its final flight tests. Even though Colonel Slater was Air Force to his core he was very much for the CIA's Oxcart program. Slater was the program's commander, and at that moment, the Oxcart was undeniably the most remarkable aircraft in the world.

Colonel Slater had flown himself to Washington in an F-101 and now he had to fly himself home. He was uncharacteristically disheartened by it all. Stopping at Wright-Patterson Air Force Base to refuel, Slater showed his identification documents, which pushed him to the front of the refueling line, ahead of a two-star general who had been waiting there. With everyone staring at him and wondering who this officer was, Slater considered the irony of it all. In justifying why Oxcart was being terminated, the 303 Committee claimed that the Oxcart exemplified CIA black budget excess. From Slater's perspective, save for a few line-cutting perks, the Oxcart was worth every Agency dime. The scientific barriers broken by the Oxcart program would likely impress scientists and engineers in another thirty years. It was the incredible sense of achievement shared by everyone involved that Slater would miss most. But so it goes, thought Slater. Oxcart would never get a mission, and the American public would probably never know what the CIA had been able to accomplish, in total secrecy, at Groom Lake—at least not for a long time.

Colonel Slater waited for his airplane to be refueled and thought about the journey home, likely his last from DC to Area 51. It was a mistake to cancel Oxcart, Slater thought. But he also knew that his opinion didn't matter. His skills as a commander were what he was counted on for. He would return to Area 51 and, like all good military men, follow orders.

Three months later, on a balmy spring day in May of 1967, Colonel Slater decided he was going to take the Oxcart for a last ride. Some of the pilots had four hundred hours in the air in the Oxcart. Walt Ray had had 358 when he died. Colonel Slater had only ten. Why not take the world's most scientifically advanced aircraft out for a ride while he still had the chance? Soon, the Oxcart would disappear into the experimental-test-plane graveyard. There, it would collect dust in some secret military hangar way out in Palmdale, California, where no one would ever fly it again. Slater went to visit Werner Weiss to see if Weiss could arrange for Slater to take one last Mach 3 ride.

"Consider it done," Werner Weiss said to Colonel Slater's request.

Up in the air, Slater quickly took the Oxcart to seventy thousand feet. Slater had forgotten how light the Oxcart was. It had an airframe like a butterfly, which allowed pilots to get it up so high. Flying at Mach 2.5 made things hot inside the cockpit. It was like an oven set on warm. If Slater were to take off his glove and touch the window, he'd get a second-degree burn. He moved up to Mach 3 cruising speed at ninety thousand feet, traveling the seven hundred miles to Billings, Montana, in about twenty-three minutes.

The fallacy was that at this height and speed, a pilot could look out the window and take in the view. You couldn't. Even when you reached cruising height, you had to keep your eyes on every gauge, oscillator, and scope in front of you. There were too many things to pay attention to. Too many things that could go wrong.

Colonel Slater headed toward the Canadian border, where he took a left turn and flew along the U.S. perimeter until he reached Washington State. There, he took another left turn and flew down over Oregon and into California. Finally, he took the aircraft down to twenty-five thousand feet and prepared for a scheduled refuel. Minutes later, Slater met up with the KC-135 that had been dispatched from the Air Force's 903rd Air Refueling Squadron out of Beale Air Force Base in Yuba County, California.

The process of taking on fuel was one of the more dangerous things an Oxcart pilot could do. In order to connect its fuel line to the tanker, the aircraft had to slow down to between 350 and 450 mph, so slow it could barely keep its grip on the sky. The issue of speed was equally taxing on the flying fuel tank. The KC-135 tanker had to travel at its top speed just to keep up with the slowed-down triple-sonic airplane. This was always a slightly nerve-racking process, complicated for Colonel Slater by the fact that a call came in over the emergency radio at exactly that time. Whatever was going on back at Area 51 that merited this emergency call was most likely not a welcome event.

Slater answered. It was Colonel Paul Bacalis, the man who'd taken over Ledford's job as director of the Office of Special Activities for the CIA. Bacalis told Slater that an urgent call had come in for him from the Pentagon and he should get back to Area 51 immediately.

"I'm refueling," Colonel Slater said.

"Finish and dump it," Bacalis said.

"Can't it wait?" Colonel Slater asked.

"No," Bacalis said. "Where are you?"

"I'm over California," Colonel Slater said.

"Head out to sea, dump the fuel, and come home" was Colonel Bacalis's command.

Slater let loose forty thousand pounds of fuel and watched it evaporate into the atmosphere. It was critical that he save ten thousand gallons of fuel to get home, not much more and definitely not less. Too little fuel and you wound up like Walt Ray. Too much fuel meant the aircraft could blow out its brakes on landing and overshoot the runway. Now, Slater needed to make a quick U-turn to head home. When traveling three times the speed of sound, the Oxcart needed 186 miles of space just to make the hook. This meant Slater's U-turn took him from off the coast of Big Sur to high above Santa Barbara on a tight curve.

When Slater got back to base, Werner Weiss and Colonel Bacalis were waiting in his office. Both men wore grins. Colonel Bacalis dialed the Pentagon and handed Slater the telephone. As the phone rang, Bacalis told Slater what was happening so as to prepare him for the call.

Colonel Slater couldn't believe his ears.

" 'The president has given Oxcart a go,' " Slater recalls Bacalis saying, and that "orders are en route." Then came the ultimate challenge — one for which he was prepared. Bacalis asked Slater if he could deploy his men for Oxcart missions starting in fifteen days.

CHAPTER SIXTEEN

Operation Black Shield and the Secret History of the USS Pueblo

The new director of the CIA, Richard M. Helms, had to work hard to become a member of President Johnson's inner coterie. The president had once told his CIA director that he "never found much use for intelligence." But eventually Helms managed to acquire a coveted seat at the president's Tuesday lunch table. There, President Johnson and his closest advisers discussed foreign policy each week. Outsiders called the luncheons Target Tuesdays because so much of what was discussed involved which North Vietnamese city to bomb. In 1967, air battles were raging in the skies over Hanoi and Haiphong with so many more American pilots getting shot down than enemy pilots that the ratio became nine to one. The Pentagon had been unable to locate the surface-to-air missile sites in North Vietnam responsible for so many of the shoot-downs although they'd been looking for them all year. Thirty-seven U-2 missions had been flown since January, as had hundreds of low-flying Air Force drones. Still, the Pentagon had no clear sense of where exactly the Communist missile sites were located. There were other fears. The Russians were rumored to be supplying the North Vietnamese with surface-to-surface missiles, ones with enough range to reach American troops stationed in the south.

Which is how the Oxcart, already scheduled for cancellation, serendipitously got its mission—during a Target Tuesday lunch. On May 16, 1967, Helms made one last play on behalf of the CIA's beloved spy plane, nine years in the making but just a few days away from being mothballed for good. Helms told the president that by deploying the Oxcart on missions over North Vietnam, war planners could get those high-resolution photographs of the missile sites they had been looking for. "Sharp point photographs, not smudged circles," Helms promised the president. Secretary of Defense Robert McNamara, angling hard for Air Force control of aerial reconnaissance, had promised the president that the SR-71 Blackbird, the Air Force version of the Oxcart, was almost operations-ready. But the mission had to happen now, CIA director Helms told the president. It was already May. Come June, Southeast Asia would be inundated with monsoons. Weather was critical for good photographs, Helms said. Cameras can't photograph through clouds. President Johnson was convinced. Before the dessert arrived, Johnson authorized the CIA's Oxcart to deploy to Kadena Air Base on Okinawa, Japan.

It was a coup for the CIA. By the following morning, the airlift to Kadena from Area 51 had begun. The 1129th Special Activities Squadron was being deployed for Operation Black Shield. A million pounds of matériel, 260 support crew, six pilots, and three airplanes were en route to the East China Sea. Nine years after Kelly Johnson presented physicist Edward Lovick with his drawing of the first Oxcart, Johnson would write in his log notes: "the bird should leave the nest."

Kadena Air Base was located on the island of Okinawa just north of the Tropic of Cancer in the East China Sea. It was an island scarred by a violent backstory, haunted by hundreds of thousands of war dead. Okinawa had been home to the single largest land-sea-air battle in the history of the world. This was the same plot of land where, twenty-two years earlier, the Allied Forces fought the Japanese. Okinawa was the last island before mainland Japan. Over the course of eighty-two days in the spring of 1945, the battle for the Pacific reached its zenith. At Okinawa, American casualties would total 38,000 wounded and 12,000 killed or missing. Japan's losses were inconceivable in today's wars: 107,000 soldiers dead and as many as 100,000 civilians killed. When Lieutenant General Ushijima Mitsuru finally capitulated, giving the island over to U.S. forces on June 21, 1945, he did so with so much shame in his heart that he committed suicide the following day. Thousands of Okinawans felt the same way and leaped off the island's high coral walls. After the smoke settled and the blood soaked into the earth, Okinawa belonged to the U.S. military. Two decades later, it still did.

By the time Ken Collins stepped foot on Okinawa, the Kadena Air Base occupied more than 10 percent of the island and accounted for nearly 40 percent of all islanders' income. The 1129th Special Activities Squadron was stationed at a secluded part of the base, the place from where Operation Black Shield would launch. No one was supposed to know the squadron was there. The project pilots were to keep an extremely low profile, living in a simple arrangement of Quonset huts almost identical to those at Area 51. Instead of on the sand-and-sagebrush landscape at Area 51, the facilities on Kadena sat in fields of green grass. Leafy ficus trees grew along little pathways. It was spring when the pilots arrived, which meant tropical flowers were in full bloom. The pilots' residence was called Morgan Manor. An American cook kept the pilots fed, serving up high-protein diets on request. On days off the pilots drank bottled beer. Sometimes the men ventured out to have a drink or eat a meal at the officers' club, where a full Filipino orchestra always played American dance tunes.

The Oxcart mission was covert and classified, and there would be "no plausible cover story" as to why an oddly shaped, triple-sonic aircraft would be flying in and out of the air base with regularity for the next year. For this reason, the Joint Chiefs of Staff suggested that Commander Slater "focus on security, not cover." One idea was to "create the illusion of some sort of environmental or technical testing involved." But no one believed that cover story would hold. Within a week of the first Oxcart landing on the tarmac at Kadena, an ominous-looking Russian trawler sailed into port and anchored within viewing distance of the extralong runway. "The Russians knew we were there and we knew they knew we were there," Colonel Slater recalls.

Impossible as it seemed, the first Oxcart mission over the demilitarized zone in North Vietnam occurred as promised, just fifteen days after Helms made history for the CIA at that Target Tuesday lunch in May. CIA pilot Mele Vojvodich was assigned the first mission. He took off at 11:00 a.m. local time in a torrential downpour — the Oxcart's first real ride in the rain. In the little more than nine minutes Vojvodich spent over North Vietnam, at a speed of Mach 3.1 and an altitude of 80,000 feet, the Oxcart photographed 70 of the 190 suspected surface-to-air missile sites. The mission went totally undetected by the Chinese and the North Vietnamese.

After the first mission was completed, the film was sent to a special processing center inside the Eastman Kodak plant in Rochester, New York. But by the time the photographic intelligence got back to field commanders in Vietnam, the intelligence was already several days old. The North Vietnamese were moving missile sites and mock-ups of missile sites around faster than anyone could keep track of them. The CIA realized it needed a dramatically faster turn-around time, which resulted in a photo center being quickly set up on the mainland in Japan. Soon, field commanders had intel in their hands just twenty-four hours from the completion of an Oxcart mission over North Vietnam.

Still, that did not stop the North Vietnamese from moving their missiles around and avoiding bombing raids. They had help from the Soviet Union. "That was the reason for the Russian trawler parked at the end of the Kadena runway. Someone was watching and taking notes every time we flew," recalls Roger Andersen, who was stationed in the command post on Kadena, which he'd been in charge of setting up. "It was almost identical to the command post at Area 51, except it was smaller," Andersen says.

On Kadena, the operations officers tried to trick the Russian spies in the trawler by flying at night, and yet of the first seven Black Shield missions flown, four were "detected and tracked." The North Vietnamese were able to predict Oxcart's overhead pass based on the time the aircraft left the base. With this information relayed by the Russians, the Communists' Fan Song guidance radar was able to lock on the A-12's beacon. The first attempted shoot-down happened during Operation Black Shield's sixteenth mission. In photographs taken by the Oxcart, contrails of surface-to-air missiles can be seen below. Fortunately for the pilots, the missiles could not get up as high as the Oxcart. In this newest round of cat and mouse, Oxcart was resulting in a draw. Oxcart was fast, high, and stealthy. The aircraft could not be shot down. But the enemy knew the plane was there, meaning it was a long way from being invisible as Richard Bissell and President Eisenhower had originally planned.

For American pilots flying over North Vietnam, the real danger remained down low, halfway between Oxcart and the earth, at around forty-five thousand feet. That was where the surface-to-air missiles and the MiG fighter jets were shooting down U.S. pilots at the horrifying nine-to-one rate. Ken Collins recalled what this felt like at the time: "During Black Shield, we, as pilots, were relatively safe at eighty-five thousand feet. It was the pilots who were flying lower than us who were really the ones in harm's way. These were guys most of us had been in the Air Force with, before we got sheep-dipped and began flying for the CIA."

Extraordinary pilots like Hervey Stockman. Stockman had been the first man to fly over the Soviet Union in a U-2, on July 4, 1956. Eleven years later, on June 11, 1967, Stockman was flying over North Vietnam, searching for information about North Vietnam weapons depots, when he was involved in a midair crash. A pilot of exceptional skill and remarkable courage, Stockman was on his 310th mission in a career that had covered three wars when his F-4 C Phantom fighter jet collided with another airplane in his wing. He and Ronald Webb both survived the bailout. Upon landing, they were captured by North Vietnamese soldiers, beaten, and taken prisoner. Stockman would spend the next five years and 268 days as a prisoner of war in a seven-by-seven-foot cell. First he was housed in the notoriously brutal Hanoi Hilton. Later, he was moved to other, equally grim prisons over the course of his incarceration. During Black Shield, the CIA tasked Oxcart pilots with search missions to find U.S. airmen who'd gone down over North Vietnam. The cameras on the Oxcarts took miles of photographs, seeking information on the prison complexes where American heroes like Hervey Stockman and hundreds of other POWs were being held, but to no avail. The North Vietnamese moved captured POWs around almost as often as they moved missile sites around.

The captured pilots became a purposeful part of Communist propaganda campaigns against the West. The POWs were beaten, tortured, chained, and dragged out in front of cameras, often forced to denounce the United States. If the Communists wanted to create unrest at home, which they did, they succeeded by using captured pilots for their own propaganda gains. All across America, opposition to the war was on the rise. The White House and the Pentagon fought back with propaganda and erroneous facts. "We are beginning to win this struggle," Vice President Hubert Humphrey boasted on NBC's *Today* show in November of 1967. While closed-door hearings for the Senate Armed Services Committee revealed that U.S. bombing campaigns were having little to no effect on winning the war, Humphrey told America that more Communists were laying down arms than picking them up. That our anti-Communist "purification" programs in Vietnam were going well. Later that same month, America's top commander, General Westmoreland, dug his own grave. He told the National Press Club that the Communists were "unable to mount a major offensive." That America might have been losing the war in 1965, but now America was winning in Vietnam. In an interview with *Time* magazine, Westmoreland taunted the Communists by calling them weak. "I hope they try something because we are looking for a fight," he declared. Which is exactly what he got. At the end of January, the Communists pretended to agree to a three-day cease-fire to celebrate the new year, which in Vietnamese is called Tet Nguyen Dan. Instead, it was a double-cross. On January 31, 1968, the Communists launched a surprise attack on the U.S. military and the forces of South Vietnam. The notorious Tet Offensive stunned the Pentagon. It also resulted in violent antiwar protests. The Tet Offensive was a major turning point in America's losing the Vietnam War.

It was at this same time that another major crisis occurred, one in which Oxcart played a secret role, the precise details of which were only made public in 2007. On the foggy morning of January 23, 1968, approximately two thousand miles to the northeast of Vietnam, the U.S. Navy ship USS *Pueblo* sailed into icy waters off the coast of North Korea and dropped anchor. The *Pueblo*'s cover story was that it was conducting scientific research; really, it was on an espionage mission, a joint NSA-Navy operation with the goal of gathering signals intelligence, or SIGINT. In addition to the regular crew, there were twenty-eight signals intelligence specialists working behind locked doors in a separate and restricted part of the vessel. Parked 15.8 miles off North Korea's Ung-do Island, technically the *Pueblo* was floating in international waters.

North Korea's Communist regime did not see it that way. The ship was close enough to be eavesdropping on Wonson harbor, which made it an open target for the North Korean People's Army, the KPA. After one of the *Pueblo*'s crew members picked up on radar that a KPA ship was approaching fast, *Pueblo*'s captain, Lloyd M. Bucher, went up to the bridge to have a look around. Through his binoculars, Bucher saw not just a military ship but one with its rocket launchers aimed directly at the *Pueblo*. Bucher ordered certain flags to be raised, ones that indicated the USS *Pueblo* was on a surveying mission, something the North Koreans obviously already did not buy. Within minutes, Chief Warrant Officer Gene Lacy spotted several small vessels on the horizon: torpedo boats coming from Wonson. Next, two MiG-21 fighter jets appeared on the scene.

Captain Bucher now had a national security nightmare on his hands. His boat was filled with thousands of classified papers, cryptographic manuals, and encryption machines. Most significantly, the *Pueblo* carried a KW-7 cipher machine, which was the veritable Rosetta stone of naval encryption. The captain considered sinking his ship, which would take forty-seven minutes, but later explained that he knew if he had done so a gun battle was certain to ensue. Most of the *Pueblo*'s life rafts would be shot at and destroyed. Without life rafts, the men would die in the icy waters in a matter of minutes, Bucher was certain. He made the decision to flee.

The North Korean ship raised a flag that signaled "Heave to or I will open fire on you." Captain Bucher raised a signal flag in response: "Thank you for your consideration. I am departing the area." But the North Koreans opened fire. Bucher himself was hit, taking shrapnel in his foot and backside. As the *Pueblo* took off, the North Koreans continued to fire, killing a U.S. sailor named Duane Hodges. Meanwhile, behind the secret door, SIGINT specialists smashed cipher equipment with axes and shoved documents into a small incinerator there. Despite the speed at which the analysts worked to burn the secret papers, 90 percent of the documents survived. Sixty-one minutes after being shot, Captain Bucher was no longer in control of his ship. The North Korean People's Army stormed the *Pueblo* and took the captain and his eighty-two crew members hostage. For the first time in 160 years, an American vessel had been seized by a foreign nation. The timing could not have been worse. America was already losing one war.

President Johnson was outraged. Within hours of the *Pueblo*'s capture, the Pentagon began secretly preparing for war against North Korea. The following day, McNamara summoned the war council to lay out plans for a ground attack. "Our primary objective is to get the men of the *Pueblo* back," McNamara said, emphasizing just how secret his plan was to remain: "No word of the discussion in this meeting should go beyond this room." A stunning air attack over North Korea was laid out. An estimated fifteen thousand tons of bombs would be dropped from the air to complement the ground assault. Given the huge numbers of soldiers and airmen fighting in Vietnam, the war with North Korea would require a call-up of the reserves. A massive U.S. strategic airlift was set in motion, designated Operation Combat Fox. That the North Vietnamese were just six days from launching the sneak attack called the Tet Offensive was not yet known. A war with North Korea over the USS *Pueblo* would have been a war America could ill afford.

Richard Helms suggested an Oxcart be dispatched from nearby Kadena to photograph North Korea's coast and try to locate the USS *Pueblo* before anyone even considered making a next move. As it stood, immediately after the *Pueblo*'s capture, there was no intelligence indicating exactly where the sailors were or where the ship was being held. Richard Helms counseled the president that if the goal was to get the eighty-two American sailors back, a ground attack or air attack couldn't possibly achieve that end if no one knew where the USS *Pueblo* was. A reconnaissance mission would also enable the Pentagon to see if Pyongyang was mobilizing its troops for war over the event. Most important of all, it would give the crisis a necessary diplomatic pause.

Three days after the *Pueblo*'s capture, on January 26, Oxcart pilot Jack Weeks was dispatched on a sortie from Kadena to locate the missing ship. From the photographs Weeks took on that overflight, the United States pinpointed the *Pueblo*'s exact location as it floated in the dark-watered harbor in Changjahwan Bay. Before completing his mission but after taking the necessary photographs, Jack Weeks experienced aircraft problems. When he got back to base, he told his fellow pilots about the problems he'd had on the flight but not about his photographic success; detailed information regarding the USS *Pueblo* was so highly classified, very few individuals had any idea that Weeks's mission had delivered photographs that had prevented war with North Korea.

"The [Oxcart] quickly located the captured *Pueblo* at anchor in Wonson harbor," President Johnson's national security adviser Walt Rostow revealed in 1994. "So we had to abandon any plans to hit them with airpower. All that would accomplish would be to kill a lot of people including our own. But the [Oxcart's] photo take provided proof that our ship and our men were being held. The Koreans couldn't lie about that." The Pentagon's secret war plan against North Korea was called off. Instead, negotiations for the sailors' return began. But the ever-suspicious administration, now deeply embroiled in political fallout from the Tet Offensive, worried the *Pueblo* incident could very well be another Communist double cross. What if North Korea was secretly mobilizing its troops for war? Three and a half weeks later, on February 19, 1968, Frank Murray was assigned to fly Oxcart's second mission over North Korea. Murray's photographs indicated that North Korea's army was still not mobilizing for battle. But by then, the *Pueblo* was on its way to Pyongyang, where it remains today—the only American naval vessel held in captivity by a foreign power. Captain Bucher and his men were prisoners of North Korea for eleven months, tortured, put through mock executions, and made to confess espionage before finally being released. In 2008, a U.S. federal judge determined that North Korea should pay sixty-five million dollars in damages to several of the *Pueblo*'s crew, but North Korea has yet to respond.

A year had passed since Black Shield began. It was springtime on Kadena again. On days off Ken Collins and fellow pilot Jack Weeks would slip into their canvas shoes and swimming trunks and head out to the beach. The drive into the countryside was beautiful and relaxing, with its tropical bamboo forests and small ponds. Camellias and Japanese apricot trees were in bloom. There were beautiful sunsets to watch over the East China Sea. "We had a different rapport, Jack and I, than the other pilots, I think. We did more than just get along. Jack Weeks and I became friends," Collins says.

When the two pilots weren't at the beach, Collins and Weeks

would take the 1129th Special Activities Squadron staff car, "an old clunker of a station wagon," and head into Kozu, a sprawling little city of cement-block high-rises and crooked telephone poles. "Jack and I had kids who were about the same age. We'd head into Kozu and buy these little plastic airplanes and remote-control tank models which we intended to bring home to our kids. But sometimes we'd get bored back in Morgan Manor and open up the toy packages and end up making the little tank models for ourselves," Collins recalls. "We had a lot of fun doing that." Life's simple pleasures during the Vietnam War.

The Agency's six Oxcart pilots—Mele Vojvodich Jr., Jack W. Weeks, J. "Frank" Murray, Ronald J. "Jack" Layton, Dennis B. Sullivan, and Kenneth B. Collins—had collectively flown twenty-nine missions: twenty-four over North Vietnam, three over North Korea, and two over Cambodia and Laos. Countless surface-to-air missile sites had been located and destroyed as a result. Despite Pentagon fears, the photographs never located a single surface-to-surface missile able to reach American forces on the ground. "We also flew overhead during Air Force bombing raids, using our jamming systems on the bird to mess with the Communists' antiaircraft systems," Murray recalls. But for all the success of the CIA's Oxcart program, the reality was that the Air Force's Blackbird, the SR-71, was finally ready to deploy. The CIA could no longer compete with the Pentagon for Mach 3 missions, and the Oxcart program reached its inevitable end. "Even if you didn't have a 'need-to-know,' it was obvious when the SR-71 Blackbirds started showing up," Collins recalls. The Blackbirds were arriving on Kadena to take Oxcart's place. The Air Force version of the Oxcart, with its two seats and reconnaissance/strike modifications, had officially won the battle between the CIA and the Air Force over anything with wings.

Back in Washington, behind closed doors, Secretary of Defense Robert McNamara told President Johnson he no longer believed the war in Vietnam could be won. This did not sit well with the president, and in February of 1968, Robert McNamara stepped down. In his place came a new secretary of defense named Clark

Clifford who "reaffirmed the original decision to end the A-12 program and mothball the aircraft." The men from the 1129th began packing up to head home to Area 51. The missions were over. The drawdown phase had begun.

Jack Weeks and Denny Sullivan were each given the assignment of flying an A-12 Oxcart back to Area 51; Collins was scheduled to do final engine tests from Kadena. But during the last weeks of the program, Jack Weeks became ill, so Collins stepped in, completing back-to-back rotations in Weeks's place. With the schedule change, it would now be Collins and Sullivan who would fly the A-12s home, with Weeks doing the final engine check, on June 4, 1968, and not Collins, as originally planned.

Collins and Sullivan returned to Area 51 to keep up on proficiency flying in preparation for their final transcontinental flights. When it was time to return to Kadena, they flew from Groom Lake to Burbank in a Lockheed propeller plane and then took a commercial flight from the West Coast all the way to Tokyo. "That night, we had dinner in the Tokyo Hilton," Collins remembers. "We finished up dinner and were heading back up to the rooms when we heard on the radio that Bobby Kennedy had been assassinated in Los Angeles." Stunned, Collins went downstairs to buy a newspaper, the English-language version of the *Tokyo Times*. "There, in the lower right-hand corner of the paper, a small article caught my eye. The headline read something like 'High-Altitude Crash of a U.S. Air Force Airplane.' Well, that was enough to get my attention. I had a terrible feeling I knew what 'high-altitude' meant."

The following day, Collins and Sullivan flew to the island of Kadena. An Agency driver picked them up at the airport. As soon as the door shut and the men were alone, the driver turned around and said solemnly, "We lost an airplane."

"We lost a pilot," Collins said.

It was former U-2 pilot Tony Bevacqua who was assigned to fly the search mission for Jack Weeks and his missing airplane. After Bevacqua had left Groom Lake, in 1957, he'd spent the next eight years flying dangerous U-2 reconnaissance missions and atomic sampling missions all over the world, from Alaska to Argentina. During the Vietnam War, Bevacqua flew SR-71 reconnaissance missions over Hanoi. (On one mission, on July 26, 1968, the photographs taken from the camera on his Blackbird show two SA-2 missiles being fired up at him.) But no single mission would stay with him into old age like the mission he was asked to fly on June 5, 1968, looking for Jack Weeks.

Bevacqua had arrived on Kadena the month before, having been selected to fly the Air Force version of the Oxcart, the SR-71. "All I had been told that day was that someone was missing," Bevacqua remembers. "I didn't have a need to know more. But I think I knew that the pilot was CIA." The downed pilot, he learned, might be floating somewhere in the South China Sea, approximately 520 miles east of the Philippines and 625 miles south of Okinawa. "As I set out, my heart was pumped up and I was thinking, Maybe I will find this guy. I remember anticipation. Hopeful anticipation of maybe seeing a little yellow life raft floating somewhere in that giant sea." Instead, Bevacqua saw nothing but hundreds of miles of open water. "It was like looking for a drop of water in the ocean," Bevacqua remembers. The day after the mission, Bevacqua went to the photo interpreters to ask if they'd found anything on the film. "They said, 'No, sorry. Not a thing.' And that was the end of that," Bevacqua explains.

Jack Weeks was gone. Vanished into the sea. Neither his body nor any part of the airplane was ever recovered. "Fate is a hunter," Collins muses, recalling the destiny of his friend Jack Weeks. "I was supposed to be flying that aircraft that day but Jack got sick and we switched in the rotation. Jack Weeks went down. I'm still here."

The 1129th Special Activities Squadron had reached its end. The CIA held a special secret ceremony at Area 51 for the remaining Oxcart pilots and their wives. Some of the pilots had their pictures taken with the aircraft but did not receive copies for their scrapbooks or walls. "The pictures went into a vault," says Colonel Slater.

"We were told we could have copies of them when, or if, the project got declassified." Roger Andersen recalls how quickly the operation rolled up. "By that time, in 1968, there were a lot of other operations going on at Area 51, none of which I had a need-to-know." Andersen had the distinction of flying the last Project Oxcart support plane, a T-33, back to Edwards Air Force Base. "Flying out of Area 51, I knew I'd miss it up there," Andersen says. "Even after all these years, and having lived all over the world, I can say that Area 51 is unlike anywhere else in the world." For certain, there would be no more barrel rolls with Colonel Slater over Groom Lake.

The men moved on. If you are career Air Force or CIA, you go where you are assigned. Ken Collins was recruited by the Air Force into the SR-71 program. Because the A-12 program was classified, no one in the SR-71 program had any idea Collins had already put in hundreds of hours flying in the Mach 3 airplane. "It left many in the SR-71 program confused. It surprised many people when it appeared I already knew how to fly the aircraft that was supposedly just built. They didn't have a need-to-know what I had spent the last six years of my life doing. They didn't learn for decades," not until the Oxcart program was declassified, in 2007.

Frank Murray volunteered to fight on the ground, or at least low to the ground, in Vietnam. "During Black Shield, no one had any idea where I'd been. Quite a few people thought maybe I'd dodged the war. I decided to go back in and fly airplanes in combat in Vietnam." In November of 1970, Murray was sent to the Nakhon Phanom Air Base on the Mekong River across from Laos, where he volunteered to fly the A-1 Skyraider—a propeller-driven, single-seat airplane that was an anachronism in the jet age. "It flew about a hundred and sixty-five miles per hour at cruise," says Murray. "I went from flying the fastest airplane in the world to the slowest one. The Oxcart taxied faster than the A-1 flew." Because the Skyraider flew so slow, it was one of the easiest targets for the Vietcong. One in four Skyraiders sent on rescue missions was shot down. "We got shot at often but the Skyraider had armaments and

I shot back." In his one-year tour of duty, Murray, the squadron commander, flew sixty-four combat missions. The Skyraider's most famous role was as the escort for the helicopters sent in to rescue wounded soldiers from the battlefield. "Our mission was to support the Jolly Green Giants. We pulled quite a few wounded Green Berets out of the battlefield that year."

Colonel Slater was assigned to the position of vice commander of the Twentieth Tactical Fighter Wing at the Wethersfield Air Force Base in England. By all accounts, he was well on the way to becoming a general in the U.S. Air Force. Then tragedy struck. Colonel Slater's eldest daughter, Stacy, was in Sun Valley, Idaho, on her honeymoon when the private plane she was flying in with her husband struck a mountain peak and crashed. Stranded on the side of a frozen mountain for twenty-four hours, Stacy Slater Bernhardt was paralyzed from the waist down. The recovery process was going to be long and painful, and the outcome was entirely unknown. "My wife, Barbara, and I needed to be with our daughter, with our family, so I requested to be transferred back to the United States," Colonel Slater says. For Slater, a career military man, the decision was simple. "Love of country, love of family."

Back in America, and after many months, his daughter recovered with near-miraculous results (she learned to walk with crutches). Colonel Slater was assigned to Edwards Air Force Base, where he began flying the Air Force's attack version of the Oxcart, the YF-12, which comes equipped to carry two 250-kiloton nuclear bombs. "I loved it," Slater says, always the optimist. "I enjoyed working for the CIA, but no matter how old I get, I will always be a fighter pilot at heart."

CHAPTER SEVENTEEN

The MiGs of Area 51

To engineer something is to apply scientific and technical know-how to create an entity from parts. To reverse engineer something is to take another manufacturer's or scientist's product apart with the specific purpose of learning how it was constructed or composed. The concept of reverse engineering is uniquely woven into Area 51 legend and lore, with conspiracy theorists claiming Area 51 engineers are reverse engineering alien spacecraft inside the secret base. Historically, reverse engineering has played an important role at Area 51, as exemplified in formerly classified programs, including one from the late 1960s and 1970s, to reverse engineer Russian MiGs.

It began one scorching-hot morning in August of 1966 when an Iraqi Air Force colonel named Munir Redfa climbed into his MiG-21 fighter jet at an air base in southern Iraq and headed toward Baghdad. Redfa then made a sudden turn to the west and began racing toward Jordan. Iraqi ground control notified Redfa that he was off course.

"Turn back immediately," he was told. Instead, Redfa began

flying in a zigzag pattern. Recognizing this as an evasive maneuver, an Iraqi air force commander told Colonel Redfa if he didn't turn back at once he would be shot down. Defying orders, Redfa switched off his radio and began flying low to the ground. To avoid radar lock, in some places he flew as low as seven hundred and fifty feet. Once he was at altitude, Redfa flew over Turkey, then toward the Mediterranean. But his final destination was the enemy state of Israel. There, one million U.S. dollars was waiting for him in a bank account in Tel Aviv.

Six hundred miles to the west, the head of the Israeli air force, Major General Mordechai Hod, waited anxiously for Munir Redfa's MiG to appear as a blip on his own radar screen. When it finally appeared, General Hod scrambled a group of delta-wing Mirage fighters to escort Redfa to a secret base in the Negev Desert. It was a groundbreaking event. Israel was now the first democratic nation to have in its possession a Russian-made MiG-21, the top gun fighter not just in Russia and its Communist proxies but throughout the Arab world.

The plan had been years in the making. Four years, to be exact, dating back to 1963, when Meir Amit first became head of the Mossad. Amit sat down with the Israeli air force and asked them what they would consider the single greatest foreign-intelligence contribution to national security. The answer was short, simple, and unanimous: bring us an MiG. The enemy air forces of Syria, Egypt, Jordan, and Iraq all flew Russian MiGs. Before Redfa's defection, the Mossad had tried twice, unsuccessfully, to acquire the airplane. In one case, an Egyptian-born Armenian intelligence agent known as John Thomas was caught in the act of espionage. His punishment was death; he and several coconspirators were hanged in an Egyptian public square.

For years, Mossad searched for a possible candidate for defection. Finally, in early 1966, they found a man who fit the profile in Munir Redfa, a Syrian Christian who had previously expressed feelings of persecution as a religious minority in a squadron of Muslims. Mossad dispatched a beautiful female intelligence agent to

Baghdad on a mission. The agent worked the romance angle first, luring Redfa to Paris with the promise of sex. There, she told Redfa the truth about what she was after. In return for an Iraqi air force MiG, Redfa would be paid a million dollars and given a new identity and a safe haven for himself and his family. Redfa agreed.

With an MiG now in their possession, the Israelis set to work understanding the strengths and weaknesses of the aircraft in flight. If it ever came to war, the Israelis would be uniquely prepared for air combat. Which is exactly what happened in June of 1967. What Israel learned from Munir Redfa's MiG ultimately allowed them to overpower the combined air forces of Syria, Egypt, and Jordan during the Six-Day War.

Back in Washington, CIA chief Richard Helms was briefed on Redfa's story by James Jesus Angleton, the man running the CIA station in Tel Aviv. Angleton was a Harvard- and Yale-educated intelligence officer who had been in the espionage business for twenty-five years. Angleton, who died in 1987, remains one of the Agency's most enigmatic and bellicose spies. He is famous within the Agency for many things, among them his idea that the Soviet propaganda machine worked 24-7 to create an ever-widening "wilderness of mirrors." This wilderness, Angleton said, was the product of a myriad of KGB deceptions and stratagems that would one day ensnare, confuse, and overpower the West. Angleton believed that the Soviets could manipulate the CIA into believing false information was true and true information was false. The CIA's inability to discern the truth inside a forest of Soviet disinformation would be America's downfall, Angleton said.

James Jesus Angleton allegedly had as many enemies inside the Agency as inside the KGB, but Richard Helms trusted him. Helms and Angleton had known each other since World War II, when they worked in the OSS counterintelligence unit, X-2. In the 1960s, in addition to acting as the liaison between the CIA and the FBI, Angleton controlled the Israeli "account," which meant he provided Helms with almost everything Helms knew about Israel.

During the course of negotiating the deal to get the MiG, the details of which remain classified, Angleton acquired additional information regarding Israel that he provided to Helms, and that Helms provided to the president. This included seemingly prophetic information about the Six-Day War before the Six-Day War began. The Israelis had been telling the State Department that they were in great danger from their Middle East neighbors when really, Helms explained to the president, Israel had the tactical advantage. Israel was playing the weak card in the hope of winning American military support. Helms also said that he'd recently met with a senior Israeli official whose visit he saw as "a clear portent that war might come at any time." Coupled with Angleton's assessment, Helms said this meant most likely in a matter of days. When Israel launched an attack three days later, Helms's status with President Johnson went through the roof. "The subsequent accuracy of this prediction established Helms's reputation in the Johnson White House," wrote a CIA historian.

The story of Redfa's defection made international headlines when it happened, in 1966. But what didn't make the news was what happened once Israel finished with the MiG: the Soviet-made fighter was shipped to Area 51. Colonel Slater, who was commander of Area 51 at the time, remembers how "it arrived in the middle of the night, hidden inside a C-130 [cargo plane], hand-delivered by Israeli intelligence agents." What had been a major coup for Israel was now an equally huge break for the United States. To the Israelis, the MiG was the most dangerous fighter in the Arab world. To the Americans, this was the deadly little aircraft that had been shooting down so many American fighter pilots over Vietnam. The Russians had been supplying the North Vietnamese with MiG-21 aircraft and MiG pilot training as well. Now, with an MiG at Area 51, Agency engineers once again had high-value foreign technology in their hands. "We could finally learn how to beat the MiG in air-to-air combat," Colonel Slater explains.

The path to Area 51 is different for everyone. For T. D. Barnes it began in 1962 when the CIA wanted him to go to Vietnam to be an "adviser" there. Barnes was just back from Bamburg, Germany, where he'd been deployed during the Berlin Wall crisis, tasked with running Hawk missile sites along the border with Czechoslovakia. It had been two years since he'd worked on the CIA's Project Palladium out of Fort Bliss.

"I said I'd go work for the Agency. But I had this dream of becoming an Army officer, which meant going through officer training school first. The Agency and the Army agreed and sent me to officer school." There, during survival training Barnes ripped open his knees and got a rare blood disease. "It just about nearly killed me. I was never going to do combat. I'm lucky I didn't die," says Barnes. He recovered but because of the blood disability, he couldn't go to Vietnam for the CIA. This also meant that after ten years of service, his military career was over. Barnes and his wife, Doris, moved home to Oklahoma and bought a house there with a yard for their two little girls, and one day when Doris was reading the classified section of the local newspaper, she found an advertisement of interest. "A contractor called Unitech was looking for telemetry and radar specialists that could work on a project involving space," Barnes recalls.

Barnes figured Unitech was harvesting résumés. "Getting a list of people who might be qualified to work on a highly specialized kind of a project if a contract were to materialize with, say, NASA down the road." Barnes told Doris it wasn't worth the phone call. Doris said to call anyway. "Within two days our house was on the market, we were packed up, and we were traveling to this little one-horse town in the Mojave Desert called Beatty." Beatty, Nevada. Population somewhere around 426, depending on who wants to know.

In 1964, Beatty, Nevada, was one strange town. Situated 120 miles northwest of Las Vegas, it lay on a strip of land between Death Valley and Nevada's atomic bomb range. Beatty had one sheriff—he was eighty years old, was a great shot with a rifle, and was missing most of his teeth. Beatty also had nine gas stations, eleven churches, an airstrip, and a whorehouse called the Vicky Star Ranch. Behind the facade, Beatty housed a collection of three- and four-letter federal agencies, many of which were working different angles on various overt and covert operations there. "Nobody knew what anybody else in Beatty was really doing there and since you didn't have a need-to-know you didn't ask," recalls Barnes. Forty-five years later he still hadn't "figured out what the service stations or the churches were a cover for."

How Beatty worked and who was running whom left much to the imagination. "When Doris and I drove into town that first day," Barnes recalls, "we pulled up to the service station to get some gas. One of the town characters, a semi-homeless person everyone called Panamint Annie, walked up to us and leaned against our car. She looked at me—it was summer—and she said, 'Well, it's hotter than Hell's hubs, now isn't it, Barnes?' I thought, How the hell does she know my last name?" Technically, Barnes had been recruited by Unitech. It turned out they had a contract with the National Aeronautics and Space Administration, or NASA, after all. "But there were lots of other agencies in Beatty who were working in the dark," Barnes says. "Unitech was the sign on the door."

America's space agency set up shop in Beatty in the mid-1960s in order to develop programs that would help get man to the moon. But before NASA landed on Earth's nearest celestial body, they had to conquer space, and to do so, they needed help from the U.S. Air Force. And before NASA conquered space, they had to get to the edge of space, which was why Barnes was in Beatty. He was hired to work on NASA's X-15 rocket plane, a prototype research vehicle that looked and acted more like a missile with wings than an airplane. Each day, Barnes got picked up for work by a NASA employee named Bill Houck, who drove a federal van around town and made a total of ten stops to retrieve all the members of the secret team. They would drive out to the edge of town and begin the short trek to the top of a chaparral-covered mountain where one hangar that was roughly the size of a tennis court, three trailers, and a number of radar dishes made up the NASA high-range tracking station at Beatty. Day after day, the ten-man crew of electronics and radar wizards manned state-of-the-art electronic systems, tracking the X-15 as it raced across the skies above the Mojave, from the Dryden Flight Research Center in California up toward the edge of space. Once, the airplane was forced to make an emergency landing on a dry lake bed not far from Beatty. There was a rule prohibiting transport trucks to haul cargo through Death Valley after dark on weekends, which meant the X-15 rocket had to spend the night in Barnes's driveway. His daughters, ages five and eight, spent the weekend running circles around the James Bond–looking rocket ship parked out front cheering "Daddy's spaceship!" No one else in Beatty said a thing.

To get into the air, the X-15 was jettisoned off a B-52 mother ship, after which its rocket engine would launch it into the atmosphere like a missile until it reached the edge of space. Touching the tip of space, the X-15 would then turn around and "fly" home, getting up to speeds of Mach 6. That kind of speed made for an incredibly bumpy ride. In a matter of months, Barnes became a hypersonic-flight-support expert. He monitored many things, including telemetry, and was always amazed watching how each of the pilots responded differently to physical stress. "We knew more about what was going on with the pilots' bodies than the pilots knew themselves. From Beatty, we monitored everything. Their heart rates, their pulse, and also everything going on with the pilot and the plane." In case of an accident, NASA had emergency crews set up across California, Nevada, and Utah on various dry lake beds where the X-15 could land if need be. One of those lake beds was Groom Lake. Barnes says, "From watching my radars, I knew something was going on over there at Groom. I could see things on my radar I wasn't supposed to see. One of those 'things' went really, really fast. Later, when I was briefed on Oxcart, I figured out what I had been watching. But at the time, I didn't have a need-to-know so I didn't say anything about what I saw at Groom Lake and nobody asked."

The X-15 was an exciting and fast-paced project to work on,

with groundbreaking missions happening twice a week. As it was with so many of the early projects involving high-speed and high-altitude flight, many different agencies were involved in the program, not just NASA. The Air Force funded a large part of the program. The CIA didn't care about space travel but they were very interested in the ram-jet technology on the X-15, something they had wanted to use on their own D-21 drone. "Everyone monitored each other, technology-wise," Barnes says. To keep the various parties in the loop, there was a designated radio network set up for everyone involved in the project. "There were people from Vandenberg Air Force Base, White Sands Missile Range, Dryden, and CIA monitoring what was going on all day long."

Even though he was only twenty-seven years old, Barnes was the most senior radar specialist in Beatty. And almost immediately he noticed there seemed to be a major problem with the radar. "We tracked the X-15 with radar stations at Edwards, in California, and at Ely, in Nevada. My radar in Beatty was fine but I noticed there was a problem at Edwards and Ely. When the X-15 was parked on the tarmac at either place, the radars there read that it was at an altitude of two thousand feet instead of being on the ground."

Barnes got on the radio channel and told mission control at the Dryden Flight Research Center about the problem. Dryden blamed it on the radar at Beatty, even though Barnes's radar agreed with the airplane's. Over the radio network, Barnes argued his point. The site manager in Beatty was horrified that Barnes dared to challenge his superiors and shot Barnes a dirty look. *Back down,* he mouthed silently. Barnes complied. But just a few weeks later, when he learned that the X-15 was going through a fitting and there weren't going to be any flights for three weeks, Barnes seized the moment. "Now would be a good time to fix your radar problem," Barnes said into the radio network. There were dozens of senior officials listening in. "There was silence on the channel," Barnes remembers. "My site manager whirled around on his chair and glared at me. 'You're on your own, Barnes,' he said. Another one of the other guys, Bill Houck, leaned over to my station, gave me a big old grin and a thumbs-up. But Dryden still wouldn't listen to me. They said the problem was inherent to the radar. That it couldn't be fixed."

By now, Barnes had gotten friendly with the X-15 pilots. Even though they had never met in person, a great rapport had developed between them; understandable, given how much time they spent communicating on headset during flights. Barnes cared about the pilots' safety more than he cared about what his site manager perceived to be insubordination on his part. So Barnes told Dryden exactly what he believed was true. "I've been in radar long enough to know there's no such thing as an inherent problem in radar," Barnes said. "I agree with the airplane. If you don't fix your radar, you're gonna kill one of the pilots one of these days."

There was a deathly silence on the network. Back at Dryden, the communication had been overheard by the pilots who were in the pilots' lounge. X-15 pilot "Joe Walker got on a headset and said, 'Effective immediately, there will be no X-15 flights until the radar problem is fixed.'" Now Dryden had no choice but to get on it. First, they flew up to the Beatty tracking station in a T-33, where they flew calibration flights to compare radar data with the airplane's altimeter. At Ely, they did the same thing. Barnes was right. The radar at Beatty was correct. Though both agreed with their data, the Dryden Flight Research Center and the Ely tracking station were off by two thousand feet. The radars were torn down and reassembled, to no avail. It was finally discovered that they were vintage radars, left over from World War II, and they had never been retrofitted with the field modification the way the radar at Beatty had. Unitech got a huge Christmas bonus, and no one got killed.

Of major significance for Barnes was that somewhere off in the black operations ether a man named John Grace had been listening as the whole scenario went down. John Grace worked for the CIA, and Barnes's name rang a bell. Grace asked his staff to look into this Barnes character, the man whose unique confidence in radar had wound up saving the day. Grace wanted to get Barnes hired for a project that would be coming to Groom Lake—something that even Barnes had been in the dark on back then.

Working at Beatty meant running multiple jobs, and there was a second aircraft Barnes was in charge of tracking—the XB-70. This experimental program was all that remained of General LeMay's once-beloved B-70 bomber now that it had been canceled by Congress, despite four billion dollars invested. The X in front of B-70 indicated that the bomber was now an experimental test bed for supersonic transport. It was a behemoth of an airplane, the fastest-flying six-engined aircraft in the world. On June 8, 1966, the mission for the day was a photo op with the XB-70 as the centerpiece. An F-4, an F-5, a T-38, and an F-104 would fly in formation alongside. Barnes was in charge of monitoring telemetry, radar, and communications from the Beatty tracking station. "General Electrics had built the engines on all six airplanes flying that day," Barnes says. "They wanted a photograph of all their aircraft flying in a tight formation for the cover of their shareholders' meeting manual that year."

It was a clear day, with very little natural turbulence in the air. The six aircraft took off from Dryden and headed west. About thirty minutes later, the pilots began getting into formation over the Mojave Desert. Barnes was monitoring data and listening on headphones. Using his personal Fischer recording system, Barnes was also taping the pilot transmissions. For this particular photo op, the X-15 pilot, Joe Walker, whom Barnes had gotten to know well, was flying in the F-104. Walker was on the right wing of the aircraft and was trying to hold his position when turbulence by the XB-70's six engines made him uncomfortable. "Walker came on the radio and spoke very clearly," Barnes recalls. "He said, 'I'm opposing this mission. It is too turbulent and it has no scientific value.'"

Only a few seconds later, a catastrophic midair collision occurred. "We heard the pilots screaming, 'Midair! Midair! And I realized at first the XB-70 didn't know it had been hit," Barnes remembers. Joe Walker's F-104 had slammed into the much larger airplane, caught fire, and exploded. On the XB-70, both vertical stabilizers had been shorn off, and the airplane began to crash. Continuing to pick up speed, the XB-70 whirled uncontrollably into a flat spin. As it headed toward the ground, parts of the aircraft tore loose. One of the XB-70 pilots, Al White, ejected. The other, Major Carl Cross, was trapped inside the airplane as it slammed into the desert floor. There, just a few miles from Barstow, California, it exploded into flames.

"It was so damn senseless," Barnes says. "A damn photograph." The worst was yet to come. "A lot of people blamed Joe Walker. Easy, because he was dead. There was, of course, the tape of him saying he was opposing the mission. That the vortex on the damn XB-70 was sucking him in. Bill Houck, the NASA monitor at our station, asked me to give him the tape recording to send to Dryden. Once NASA got a hold of it," Barnes says, "someone there quietly disposed of it."

The XB-70 tragedy more or less closed down the program, and the X-15 rocket plane program was finishing up as well. For Barnes, life in Beatty was nearing an end, but one afternoon, Barnes received a phone call. A man identifying himself as John Grace wanted to know if he'd like to come work on an "interesting project" not far away. "Grace said it would be a commute from Las Vegas," Barnes says. Grace told Barnes he would have to get a top secret clearance first. Whatever it was, it sounded exciting. Barnes told Grace, "Sign me up." T. D. Barnes was officially on his way to Groom Lake.

In March of 1968, his top secret clearance finally in place, Barnes learned his new employer was going to be EG&G. He was instructed by a "handler" to arrive at a remote, unmarked hangar at McCarran Airport for his first day at work. There, Barnes was met by a man who shook his hand and escorted him into a small Constellation airplane. "They didn't say anything to me about where we were going and I knew enough about black operations not to ask. It was a nice, quiet ride in the airplane. Just before we landed at Area 51, I heard the pilot say to the copilot, 'They've got the doughnut out.' Then the pilots quickly closed all the curtains on the airplane so when we landed I couldn't see a thing. I wondered what the doughnut was. I didn't ask. I was taken to the EG&G Special Projects building and introduced to our group. The boss said, 'What's your first name?' I said, 'T.D.' He said, 'Not anymore. You're Thunder out here.'" Later that first day, Barnes was taken inside one of the hangars at Area 51. "They opened the door. There sat a Russian MiG. They said, 'This here's the doughnut.' I got a chuckle about that. The pilots who'd brought me to the area had no idea that the whole reason I'd been brought in was because of the doughnut."

Munir Redfa's MiG had been nicknamed the doughnut because the jet fighter's nose had a round opening in it, like a doughnut's. It was the first advanced Soviet fighter jet ever to set its wheels down on U.S. soil. Colonel Slater, overseeing Black Shield in Kadena at the time, remembers getting a call in the middle of the night from one of his staff, Jim Simon. "Simon called me up all excited and said, 'Slater, you are not going to believe this!' He told me about the MiG. How it landed at [Area] 51 in the middle of the night, hidden inside a cargo plane. How it was accompanied by someone from a foreign government. Simon couldn't get over it and I couldn't wait to see it," Slater remembers. Oxcart pilot Frank Murray remembers the excitement of seeing it as well. During Operation Black Shield Murray was on rotation between Area 51 and Kadena when he was taken into the secret hangar to have a look at the MiG. "It was a tiny little sucker, considering how deadly it was," Murray says. "We couldn't believe we had a captured one up there at the Ranch."

T. D. Barnes and the EG&G Special Projects Group at Area 51 got to work reverse engineering Colonel Redfa's MiG—taking it apart and putting it back together again. All the engineers knew that this was the best way to really understand how something had been built. The EG&G Special Projects Group appeared to have advance expertise in this technical process of reverse engineering aircraft. At the time, no one knew why, and Barnes, new to the EG&G engineering team, knew better than to ask. He was excited to get to work. "We broke the MiG down into each of its individual pieces. Pieces of the cockpit, the gyros, oscillograph, fuel flow meter, radio…everything. Then we put it back together. The MiG didn't have computers or fancy navigation equipment." Still, Barnes and his crew were stumped. How was it that this Soviet plane was beating the supposedly more capable U.S. fighters in air-to-air engagements? No one could explain why. So a second program was conceived, the MiG's Have Doughnut tactical phase. During the Have Doughnut, the MiG would begin flying tactical missions against U.S. airplanes in the skies over Groom Lake. The Air Force said it wasn't interested but the Navy leaped at the chance.

"Breaking it down was the first step in understanding the aircraft. But it was by sending the MiG flying that we really figured out how it maneuvered so damn fast," Barnes says. Test pilots flew a total of 102 MiG missions over Groom Lake. Mock air battles between the MiG and American fighter jets were a daily event for a period of six weeks during the spring of 1968. The program (not including its Area 51 locale) was declassified by the U.S. Air Force Foreign Technology Division in October of 1997 and by the Defense Intelligence Agency in March of 2000. "We learned that you had to sneak right up on it and shoot it down before it had a chance to maneuver. That was the key. Get it on the first chance you get. There were no second chances with a MiG," Barnes explains. Constant flying takes a toll on any aircraft, but with a captured enemy airplane this proved especially challenging. "Since no spare parts were available, ground crews had to reverse engineer the components and make new ones from raw materials," Barnes says. "But when both phases were over, the technical and the tactical ones, we'd unlocked the secrets of the MiG."

There were repercussions from the Soviets. "The fact that we had a MiG at Area 51 infuriated the Russians," explains Barnes. "They retaliated by sending more spy satellites overhead at Area 51, sometimes as often as every forty-five minutes." Up to this point, the Soviets had gotten used to monitoring the routine activity at the base, which consisted primarily of takeoffs and landings of the

Oxcart and a few drones. But once the MiG showed up, the U.S. Air Force Foreign Technology Division appeared on the scene too, and with them came various models of Soviet-built radar systems captured in the Middle East. And once the Soviets discovered engineers at Groom Lake were testing these foreign radar systems, they again decided to monitor the situation more closely from overhead.

The newly acquired Soviet radar systems started cropping up around the western edges of the Groom dry lake bed and also around Slater Lake, which was about a mile northwest of the main hangars. Technical evaluation of the radar was quickly assigned to Barnes. He requested a Nike missile system and was surprised at just how quickly his request was filled. "I think the CIA went and got a Nike missile system at my old stomping ground, Fort Bliss, just about the very next day," Barnes says. With radars scattered all over the range, including acquisition radar that rotated and searched for incoming targets, a geek like Barnes had a field day. "We used the Nike to track the MiGs and other airplanes to evaluate their ECM against X-band radar." What Barnes did not know was that these radar systems were being acquired for the upcoming radar cross-section analysis of an Air Force plane in the works. The Russians had no idea what the Air Force was dreaming up either, but they were duly angry about the captured radars that were now sitting in the hills overlooking Groom Lake.

"We were pinned down," says Barnes. For weeks on end, the Special Projects Group couldn't turn on a single radar system; the Russians were monitoring the area that intensely. Barnes and his group passed the time by playing mind games with the Soviets. They painted strange shapes on the tarmac, "funny-looking impossible aircraft," which they then heated up with portable heaters to confuse the Soviets who were shooting infrared satellite pictures of the work going on there. "We got a kick out of imagining what the Russians thought of our new airplanes," Barnes says. With all the time on their hands, Barnes and his group of twenty-three electronics specialists began dreaming up other ways to entertain themselves. They made up riddles. They placed bets. They played with mixed chemicals that made their tennis sneakers glow in the dark. They rewired the Special Projects motor pool car so it would give the first guy to drive it a series of low-voltage shocks. They rigged up a tall TV antenna on top of their living quarters, hoping to draw reception from Las Vegas. Instead, they tapped into an international channel broadcast out of Spain. "For many months, all we watched were bullfights in Madrid," Barnes recalls.

This was a group of highly trained specialists gathered to pioneer radar technology, so when they finally ran out of practical jokes and bullfights, their attention turned back to problem solving. They started to occupy themselves by examining minutiae on printouts from radar returns. In a serendipitous way, this led to a technological breakthrough at Groom Lake. The EG&G Special Projects Group figured out they could identify specific types of aircraft by the tiniest nuances in the patterns their radar signatures left on various radar systems. This was made possible by the group's unusual advantage of having two things at their disposal: several bands of radar, which allowed them to compare results, and an entire fleet of military aircraft, which were to be used in the tactical phase of the exploitation of the MiG.

What would normally have been a technical endeavor to determine electronic countermeasures against enemy aircraft became a major breakthrough in the further development of stealth technology. From studying the minutiae, Barnes and his fellow radar experts identified what the enemy could and could not see on their radars back home. This information would eventually be shared with Lockheed during radar testing at Area 51, as Lockheed further developed stealth. Technology was doing for humans what humans had forever been trying to do for themselves; to spy on the enemy means to learn as much about him as he knows about himself. That was the technical breakthrough. There was a tactical breakthrough as well. The ultrasecret MiG program at Area 51 gave birth to the Top Gun fighter-pilot school, a fact that would remain secret for decades. Officially called the United States Navy Fighter Weapons School, the program was established a year after the first MiG arrived, in March of 1969, and based out of Miramar, California. Instructor pilots who had fought mock air battles over Groom Lake against Munir Redfa's MiG began training Navy pilots for sorties against Russian MiGs over Vietnam. When these Top Gun–trained Navy pilots resumed flying in Southeast Asia, the results were radically different than the deadly nine-to-one ratio from before. The scales had tipped. Now, American pilots would begin shooting down North Vietnamese pilots at a ratio of thirteen to one. The captured Soviet-made MiG-21 Fishbed proved to be an aerial warfare coup for the United States. And what followed was a quid pro quo. To thank the Israelis for supplying the United States with the most prized and unknowable aircraft in the arsenal of its archnemesis, America began to supply Israel with jet fighters to assist Israel in keeping its rivals at bay.

CHAPTER EIGHTEEN

Meltdown

The idea behind a facility like Area 51 is that dangerous top secret tests can be conducted there without much scrutiny or oversight. To this end, there is no shortage of death woven into the uncensored history of Area 51. One of the most dangerous tests ever performed there was Project 57, the dirty bomb test that took place five miles northwest of Groom Lake, in a subparcel called Area 13. And yet what might have been the one defensible, positive outcome in this otherwise shockingly outrageous test—namely, lessons gleaned from its cleanup—was ignored until it was too late.

Unlike the spy plane projects at Groom Lake, where operations tend to have clear-cut beginnings and ceremonious endings, Project 57 was abandoned midstream. If the point of setting off a dirty bomb in secret was to see what would happen if an airplane carrying a nuclear bomb crashed into the earth near where people lived, it follows that serious efforts would then be undertaken by the Atomic Energy Commission to learn how to clean up such a nightmare scenario after the catastrophe occurs. No such efforts were initially made.

Instead, about a year after setting off the dirty bomb, the Atomic Energy Commission put a barbed-wire fence around the Area 51 subparcel, marked it with HAZARD/DO NOT ENTER/NUCLEAR MATERIAL signs, and moved on to the next weapons test. The bustling CIA facility five miles downwind would be relatively safe, the nuclear scientists and the weapons planners surmised. Alpha particles are heavy and would rest on the topsoil after the original dust cloud settled down. Furthermore, almost no one knew about the supersecret project, certainly not the public, so who would protest? The closest inhabitants were the rank and file at the CIA's Groom Lake facility next door, and they also knew nothing of Project 57. The men there followed strict need-to-know protocols, and as far as the commission was concerned, all anyone at Area 51 needed to know was to not venture near the barbed-wire fence marking off Area 13.

And yet the information gleaned from a cleanup effort would have been terribly useful, as was revealed eight years and eight months after Project 57 unfurled. On the morning of January 17, 1966, a real-life dirty bomb crisis occurred over Palomares, Spain. A Strategic Air Command bomber flying with four armed hydrogen bombs — with yields between 70 kilotons and 1.45 megatons — collided midair with a refueling tanker over the Spanish countryside.

On the morning of the accident, an Air Force pilot and his six-man crew were participating in an exercise that was part of Operation Chrome Dome, something that had begun in the late 1950s as part of Strategic Air Command. In a show of force inherent to the military doctrine of the day — something called mutual assured destruction, or MAD — airplanes regularly circled Earth carrying thermonuclear bombs. The idea behind MAD was that if the Soviet Union were to make a sneak attack on America, SAC bombers would already be airborne to strike back at Moscow with nuclear weapons of their own, thereby assuring the mutual destruction of both sides.

That morning, the bomber lined up with the tanker and had just begun refueling when, in the words of pilot Larry Messinger, "all of a sudden, all hell seemed to break loose" and the two aircraft collided. There was a massive explosion and the men in the fuel tanker were instantly incinerated. Somehow Messinger, his copilot, the instructor pilot, and the navigator managed to eject from the airplane carrying the bombs. Their parachutes deployed, and the men floated down, landing in the sea. The four nuclear bombs— individually powerful enough to destroy Manhattan—also had parachutes, two of which did not deploy. One parachuted bomb landed gently in a dry riverbed and was later recovered relatively intact. But when the two bombs without parachutes hit the earth, their explosive charges detonated, breaking open the nuclear cores. Nuclear material was released at Palomares in the form of aerosolized plutonium, which then spread out across 650 acres of Spanish farmland—consistent with dispersal patterns from the Project 57 dirty bomb test. The fourth bomb landed in the sea and became lost. Palomares was then a small fishing village and farming community located on the Mediterranean Sea. As fortune would have it, January 17 was the Festival of Saint Anthony, the patron saint of Palomares, which meant most people in the village were at church that day and not out working in the fields.

Five thousand miles away, in Washington, DC, President Johnson learned of the disaster over breakfast. He'd been sitting in his bedroom sipping tea and eating melon and chipped beef when a staffer from the White House Situation Room knocked, entered, and set down a copy of his daily security briefing. On the first page, the president read about the war in Vietnam. On the second page he learned about the Palomares incident. The daily brief said nothing about widespread plutonium dispersal or about the lost thermonuclear bomb. Only that the "16th Nuclear Disaster Team" had been dispatched to the area." The "16th Nuclear Disaster Team" sounded official enough, but if fifteen nuclear disaster teams had preceded this one or existed concurrently, no record of any of them exists in the searchable Department of Energy archives. In reality, the group was ad hoc, meaning it was put together for the specific purpose of dealing with the Palomares incident. An official nuclear disaster response team did not exist in 1966 and would not be created for another nine years, until 1975, when retired Brigadier General Mahlon E. Gates, then the manager of the Nevada Test Site, put together the Nuclear Emergency Search Team, or NEST.

In 1966, the conditions in Palomares, Spain, were strikingly similar to the conditions at the Nevada Test Site in terms of geology. Both were dry, hilly landscapes with soil, sand, and wind shear as significant factors to deal with. But considering, with inconceivable lack of foresight, the Atomic Energy Commission had never attempted to clean up the dirty bomb that it had set off at Area 13 nine years before, the 16th Nuclear Disaster Team was, essentially, working in the dark.

Eight hundred individuals with no hands-on expertise were sent to Palomares to assist in the cleanup efforts there. The teams improvised. One group secured the contaminated area and prepared the land to remove contaminated soil. A second group worked to locate the lost thermonuclear bomb, called a broken arrow in Defense Department terms. The group cleaning up the dispersed plutonium included "specialists and scientists" from the Los Alamos Laboratory, the Lawrence Radiation Laboratory, Sandia Laboratories, Raytheon, and EG&G. It was terribly ironic. The very same companies who had engineered the nuclear weapons and whose employees had wired, armed, and fired them were now the companies being paid to clean up the deadly mess. This was the military-industrial complex in full swing.

For the next three months, workers labored around the clock to decontaminate the site of deadly plutonium. By the time the cleanup was over, more than fourteen hundred tons of radioactive soil and plant life were excavated and shipped to the Savannah River plant in South Carolina for disposal. The majority of the plutonium dispersed on the ground was accounted for, but the Defense Nuclear Agency eventually conceded that the extent of the plutonium particles scattered by wind, carried as dust, and ingested by earthworms and excreted somewhere else "will never be known." As for the missing hydrogen bomb, for forty-four days the Pentagon refused to admit it was lost despite the fact that it was widely reported as being missing. "I don't know of any missing bomb," one Pentagon official told the Associated Press. Only after the bomb was recovered from the ocean floor did the Pentagon admit that it had in fact been lost.

The nuclear accidents did not stop there. Two years and four days later there was another airplane crash involving a Strategic Air Command bomber and four nuclear bombs. On January 21, 1968, an uncontrollable fire started on board a B–52G bomber during a secret mission over Greenland. Six of the seven crew members bailed out of the burning airplane, which crested over the rooftops of the American air base at Thule and slammed into the frozen surface of North Star Bay. The impact detonated the high explosives in at least three of the four thermonuclear bombs—similar to exploding multiple dirty bombs—spreading radioactive plutonium, uranium, and tritium over a large swath of ice. A second fire started at the crash site, consuming bomb debris, wreckage from the airplane, and fuel. After the inferno burned for twenty minutes the ice began to melt. One of the bombs fell into the bay and disappeared beneath the frozen sea. In November of 2008, a BBC News investigation found that the Pentagon ultimately abandoned that fourth nuclear weapon after it became lost.

Once again, an ad hoc emergency group was put together; there was still no permanent disaster cleanup group. This time five hundred people were involved. The conditions were almost as dangerous as the nuclear material. Temperatures fell to −70 degrees Fahrenheit, and winds blew at ninety miles per hour. Equipment froze. In a secret SAC document, made public by a Freedom of Information Act request in 1989, the Air Force declared their efforts would be nominal, "a cleanup undertaken as good housekeeping measures," with officials anticipating the removal of radioactive debris "to equal not less than 50%" of the total of what was there. For eight months, a crew calling themselves the Dr. Freezelove Team worked around the clock. When they were done, 10,500 tons of radioactive ice, snow, and crash debris was airlifted out of Greenland and flown to South Carolina for disposal.

Back at the Nevada Test Site, a new industry had been born in nuclear accident cleanup. But before anything can get cleaned up, an assessment must be made regarding how much lethal radiation is present, where exactly, and in what form. All across the desert floor, new proof-of-concept, or prototypes, of radiation-detection instruments appeared. Before the nuclear bomb accidents in Spain and Greenland, individual radiation-detection machines were limited to handheld devices like Geiger counters, used to examine workers' hands and feet and to search for radiation in limited local areas. Finally, gadgets and gizmos flooded the Nevada Test Site for field-testing in a post–nuclear accident world. After the Nuclear Test Ban Treaty of 1963, testing had moved underground, but often these underground tests "vented," releasing huge plumes of radiation from fissures in the earth. The test site was the perfect place to test equipment because there was an abundance of plutonium, americium, cesium, cobalt, europium, strontium, and tritium in the topsoil, and no shortage of radiation in the air.

First came new handheld devices, like a briefcase called the Neutron Detector Suitcase, a prototype designed by EG&G, which was followed by more advanced means of detecting radiation, including ground vehicles. The Sky Scanner, developed by the Lawrence Radiation Laboratory at Livermore, roamed down the test site's dirt roads measuring radioactivity escaping from atomic vents. The Sky Scanner looked like a news van with a satellite dish, but inside it was full of equipment that could determine how much fallout was in the air. Next came fixed-wing aircraft that could patrol the air over an accident site. Used to detect fallout since Operation Crossroads, they were now equipped with state-of-the-art, still-classified radiation-detection devices. This marked the birth of a burgeoning new military technology that would become one of the most important and most secret businesses of the twenty-first century. Called remote sensing, it is the ability to recognize levels of radioactivity from a distance using ultraviolet radiation, infrared, and other means of detection.

Within a decade of the disastrous nuclear accidents at Palomares and Thule, EG&G would so dominate the radiation-detection market that the laboratory built at the Nevada Test Site for this purpose was initially called the EG&G Remote Sensing Laboratory. After 9/11, the sister laboratory, at Nellis Air Force Base in Las Vegas, was called the Remote Sensing Laboratory and included sensing-detection mechanisms for all types of WMD. This facility would become absolutely critical to national security, so much so that by 2011, T. D. Barnes says that "only two people at Nellis are cleared with a need-to-know regarding classified briefings about the Remote Sensing Lab." Barnes is a member of the Nellis/Creech Air Force Base support team and its civilian military council. But in the 1960s, three nuclear facilities— Los Alamos, Lawrence Livermore, and Sandia—and one private corporation—EG&G—were the organizations uniquely positioned to see the writing on the wall. If nuclear accidents were going to continue to happen, then these four entities were going to secure the government contracts to clean things up.

EG&G had been taking radiation measurements and tracking radioactive clouds for the Atomic Energy Commission since 1946. For decades, EG&G Energy Measurements has maintained control of the vast majority of radiation measurements records going back to the first postwar test at Bikini Atoll in 1946. Because much of this information was originally created under the strict Atomic Energy classification Secret/Restricted Data—i.e., it was "born classified"—it has largely remained classified ever since. It cannot be transferred to another steward. For decades, this meant there was no one to compete with EG&G for the remote sensing job. How involved EG&G is in remote sensing today, their corporate headquarters won't say.

So secret are the record groups in EG&G's archives, even the president of the United States can be denied access to them, as President Clinton was in 1994. One year earlier, a reporter named Eileen Welsome had written a forty-five-page newspaper story for the *Albuquerque Tribune* revealing that the Atomic Energy Commission had secretly injected human test subjects with plutonium starting in the 1940s without those individuals' knowledge or consent. When President Clinton learned about this, he created an advisory committee on human radiation experiments to look into secrets kept by the Atomic Energy Commission and to make them public. In several areas, the president's committee succeeded in revealing disturbing truths, but in other areas it failed. In at least one case, regarding a secret project at Area 51, the committee was denied access to records kept by EG&G and the Atomic Energy Commission on the grounds that the president did not have a need-to-know about them. In another case, regarding the nuclear rocket program at Area 25 in Jackass Flats, the president's committee also failed to inform the public of the truth. Whether this is because the record group in EG&G's archive was kept from the committee or because the committee had access to it but chose not to report the facts in earnest remains unknown. Instead, what happened at Jackass Flats, well after atmospheric testing had been outlawed around the world, gets a one-line reference in the Advisory Committee's 937-page Final Report, grouped in with dozens of other tests involving "intentional releases" near human populations. "At AEC sites in Nevada and Idaho, radioactive materials were released in tests of the safety of bombs, nuclear reactors, and proposed nuclear rockets and airplanes," the report innocuously reads.

If Area 51 had a doppelgänger next door at the test site, it would certainly be Area 25, which encompasses 223 square miles. The flat, sandy desert expanse got its name during the gold rush when miners used to tie their donkeys to trees in the flat area while searching the surrounding mountains for gold. Like Area 51, Jackass Flats is surrounded by mountain ranges on three of its four sides, making them both hidden sites within federally restricted land. Unlike Area 51, which technically does not exist, Jackass Flats in the 1950s and 1960s maintained a polished public face. When President Kennedy visited the Nevada Test Site in 1962, he went to Jackass Flats to promote the space travel programs that were going on there. Richard Mingus was one of the security guards assigned to assist the president's Secret Service detail that day. Photographs that appeared in the newspapers showed the handsome president, wearing his signature sunglasses and dark suit, flanked by aides while admiring strange-looking contraptions rising up from the desert floor; Mingus stands at attention nearby. Next to the president is Glenn Seaborg, then head of the Atomic Energy Commission and the man who co-discovered plutonium. But as with most nuclear projects of the day, the public was only told a fraction of the story. There was a lot more going on at Jackass Flats behind the scenes—and in underground facilities there—about which the public had no idea.

Area 25 began as the perfect place for America to launch a nuclear-powered spaceship that would get man to Mars and back in the astonishingly short time of 124 days. The spaceship was going to be enormous, sixteen stories tall and piloted by one hundred and fifty men. Project Orion seemed like a space vehicle from a science fiction novel, except it was real. It was the brainchild of a former Los Alamos weapons designer named Theodore Taylor, a man who saw space as the last "new frontier."

For years, beginning in the early 1950s, Taylor designed nuclear bombs for the Pentagon until he began to doubt the motives of the Defense Department. He left government service, at least officially, and joined General Atomics in San Diego, the nuclear division of defense contractor General Electric. There, he began designing nuclear-powered spaceships. But to build a spaceship that could get to Mars required federal funding, and in 1958 General Atomics presented the idea to President Eisenhower's new science and technology research group, the Advanced Research Projects Agency, or ARPA. The agency had been created as a result of the Sputnik crisis, its purpose being to never let the Russians one-up American scientists again. Today, the agency is known as DARPA. The D stands for defense.

At the time, developing cutting-edge space-flight technology meant hiring scientists like Wernher Von Braun to design chemical-based rockets that could conceivably get man to the moon in a capsule the size of a car. Along came Ted Taylor with a proposal to build a Mars-bound spaceship the size of an office building, thanks to nuclear energy. For ARPA chief Roy Johnson, Ted Taylor's conception was love at first sight. "Everyone seems to be making plans to pile fuel on fuel on fuel to put a pea into orbit, but you seem to mean business," the ARPA chief told Taylor in 1958.

General Atomics was given a one-million-dollar advance, a classified project with a code name of Orion, and a maximum-security test facility in Area 25 of the Nevada Test Site at Jackass Flats. The reason Taylor's spaceship needed an ultrasecret hiding place and could not be launched from Cape Canaveral, as other rockets and spaceships in the works could be, was that the Orion spacecraft would be powered by two thousand "small-sized" nuclear bombs. Taylor's original idea was to dispense these bombs from the rear of the spaceship, the same as a Coke machine dispenses sodas. The bombs would fall out behind the spaceship, literally exploding and pushing the spaceship along. The Coca-Cola Company was even hired to do a classified early design.

At Area 25, far away from public view, Taylor's giant spaceship would launch from eight 250-foot-tall towers. Blastoff would mean Orion would rise out of a column of nuclear energy released by exploding atomic bombs. "It would have been the most sensational thing anyone ever saw," Taylor told his biographer John McPhee. But when the Air Force took over the project, they had an entirely different vision in mind. ARPA and the Air Force reconfigured Orion into a space-based battleship. From high above Earth, a USS *Orion* could be used to launch attacks against enemy targets using nuclear missiles. Thanks to *Orion*'s nuclear-propulsion technology, the spaceship could make extremely fast defensive maneuvers, avoiding any Russian nuclear missiles that might come its way. It would be able to withstand the blast from a one-megaton bomb from only five hundred feet away.

For a period of time in the early 1960s the Air Force believed Orion was going to be invincible. "Whoever builds Orion will control the Earth!" declared General Thomas S. Power of the Strategic Air Command. But no one built Orion. After atmospheric nuclear tests were banned in 1963, the project was indefinitely suspended. Still wanting to get men to Mars, NASA and the Air Force turned their attention to nuclear-powered rockets. From now on, there would be no nuclear explosions in the atmosphere at Jackass Flats—at least not officially. Instead, the nuclear energy required for the Mars spaceship would be contained in a flying reactor, with fuel rods producing nuclear energy behind barriers that were lightweight enough for space travel but not so thin as to cook the astronauts inside. The project was now called NERVA, which stood for Nuclear Engine Rocket Vehicle Application. The facility had a public name, even though no one from the public could go there. It was called the Nuclear Rocket Test Facility at Jackass Flats. A joint NASA/Atomic Energy Commission office was created to manage the program, called the Space Nuclear Propulsion Office, or SNPO.

For T. D. Barnes, working on the NERVA nuclear reactor was a bit of a stretch—his area of expertise was missile and radar technologies. But when things got slow over at Area 51 in the late 1960s, Barnes, a member of EG&G Special Projects team, would be dispatched over to Area 25 to work on the NERVA program. Even though NERVA had been sold to Congress as a public program, all its data was classified, as were the day-to-day goings-on in Area 25. Barnes's workstation could not have been more hidden from the public. It was underground, built into the side of a mountain that rose up from the flat desert landscape. Each morning Barnes and his fellow Q-cleared coworkers who lived in and around Las Vegas parked in employee parking lots down at the entrance to the Nevada Test Site, at Camp Mercury, and were then shuttled out to Jackass Flats in Atomic Energy Commission motor pool vans. "Some of the people working on NERVA lived in Beatty and Amargosa Valley and drove to the tunnel themselves," Barnes adds.

All NERVA employees entered work through a small portal in the side of the mountain, "shaped like the entrance to an old mining shaft, but spiffed up a bit," Barnes recalls, remembering "large steel doors and huge air pipes curving down from the mesas and entering the tunnel." Inside, the concrete tunnel was long and straight and ran into the earth "as far as the eye could see." Atomic Energy Commission records indicate the underground tunnel was

1,150 feet long. Barnes remembered it being brightly lit and sparkling clean. "There were exposed air duct pipes running the length of the tunnel as well as several layers of metal cable trays, which were used to transport heavy items into and out of the tunnel," he says. "The ceiling was about eight feet tall, and men walked through it no more than two abreast." There was also a tarantula problem at Jackass Flats, which meant every now and then, Barnes and his colleagues would spot a large hairy spider running down the tunnel floors or scampering along its walls.

Deep in the tunnel Barnes would come up against a last set of closed doors. When they opened, they revealed a succession of brightly lit rooms filled with desks. Barnes explains, "Moving closer to ground zero where the tunnel ended, we entered a large subterranean room stacked floor to ceiling with rows of electronic amplifiers, discriminator circuits, and multiplexing components and banks of high-tech equipment lining the walls." Standing in front of the row of electronics was an engineer "usually with a cart full of electronic test equipment calibrating and repairing electronic circuits," Barnes explains. These workers were all preparing for what was actually going on aboveground, and that was full-power, full-scale nuclear reactor engine tests. In order for NASA and the Atomic Energy Commission to be able to verify that NERVA could actually propel a spaceship filled with astronauts the 34 million to 249 million miles to Mars (the distance depends on the positions of the two planets in their orbits), those federal agencies had to witness NERVA running full power for long periods of time here on Earth first. To test that kind of thrust without having the engine launch itself into space, it was caged inside a test stand and positioned upside down.

For each engine test, a remote-controlled locomotive would bring the nuclear reactor over to the test stand from where it was housed three miles away in its own cement-block-and-lead-lined bunker, called E-MAD. "We used to joke that the locomotive at Jackass Flats was the slowest in the world," Barnes explains. "The only thing keeping the reactor from melting down as it traveled down the railroad back and forth between E-MAD and the test stand was the liquid hydrogen [LH$_2$] bath it sat in." The train never moved at speeds more than five miles per hour. "One spark and the whole thing could blow," Barnes explains. At −320 degrees Fahrenheit, liquid hydrogen is one of the most combustible and dangerous explosives in the world. James A. Dewar, author of *To the End of the Solar System: The Story of the Nuclear Rocket,* gets even more specific. "One hundredth of what one might receive from shuffling along a rug and then touching a wall can ignite hydrogen," Dewar wrote in 2004. To help visualize what the facilities aboveground at Jackass Flats looked like, Barnes likens them to Cape Kennedy. "Imagine a one-hundred-twenty-foot-tall aluminum tower rising up from a plateau of cement surrounded by a deep, concrete aqueduct. Add some huge, spherical thermos-like dewars sitting around, each containing something like two hundred and sixty thousand gallons of liquid hydrogen, and you can visualize the space-launch appearance of things," Barnes explains. In Atomic Energy photographs from the 1960s, a single set of train tracks can be seen running along the bottom of the cement aqueduct and disappearing into an opening underneath the tall metal tower. "The railroad car carried the nuclear reactor up to the test stand and lifted it into place using remotely controlled hydraulic hands," Barnes explains. "Meanwhile, we were all underground looking at the reactor through special leaded-glass windows, taking measurements and recording data as the engine ran." The reason the facility was buried inside the mountain was not only to hide it from the Soviet satellites spying on the U.S. nuclear rocket program from overhead, but to shield Barnes and his fellow workers from radiation poisoning from the NERVA reactor. "Six feet of earth shields a man from radiation poisoning pretty good," says Barnes.

When running at full power, the nuclear engine operated at a temperature of 2,300 Kelvin, or 3,680.6 degrees Fahrenheit, which meant it also had to be kept cooled down by the liquid hydrogen on a permanent basis. "While the engine was running the canyon was like an inferno as the hot hydrogen simultaneously ignited upon contact with the air," says Barnes. These nuclear rocket engine tests remained secret until the early 1990s, when a reporter named Lee Davidson, the Washington bureau chief for Utah's *Deseret News,* provided the public with the first descriptive details. "The Pentagon released information after I filed a Freedom of Information Act," Davidson says. In turn, Davidson provided the public with previously unknown facts: "bolted down, the engine roared...sending skyward a plume of invisible hydrogen exhaust that had just been thrust through a superheated uranium fission reactor," Davidson revealed. Researching the story, he also learned that back in the 1960s, after locals in Caliente, Nevada, complained that iodine 131—a major radioactive hazard found in nuclear fission products—had been discovered in their town's water supply, Atomic Energy officials denied any nuclear testing had been going on at the time. Instead, officials blamed the Chinese, stating, "Fresh fission products probably came from an open-air nuclear bomb test in China." In fact, a NERVA engine test had gone on at Area 25 just three days before the town conducted its water supply test.

Had the public known about the NERVA tests when they were going on, the tests would have been perceived as a nuclear catastrophe in the making. Which is exactly what did happen. "Los Alamos wanted a run-away reactor," wrote Dewar, who in addition to being an author is a longtime Atomic Energy Commission employee, "a power surge until [the reactor] exploded." Dewar explained why. "If Los Alamos had data on the most devastating accident possible, it could calculate other accident scenarios with confidence and take preventative measures accordingly." And so, on January 12, 1965, the nuclear rocket engine code-named Kiwi was allowed to overheat. High-speed cameras recorded the event. The temperature rose to "over 4000°C until it burst, sending fuel hurtling skyward and glowing every color of the rainbow," Dewar wrote. Deadly radioactive fuel chunks as large as 148 pounds shot up into the sky. One ninety-eight-pound piece of radioactive fuel landed more than a quarter of a mile away.

Once the explosion subsided, a radioactive cloud rose up from the desert floor and "stabilized at 2,600 feet" where it was met by an EG&G aircraft "equipped with samplers mounted on its wings." The cloud hung in the sky and began to drift east then west. "It blew over Los Angeles and out to sea," Dewar explained. The full data on the EG&G radiation measurements remains classified.

The test, made public as a "safety test," caused an international incident. The Soviet Union said it violated the Limited Test Ban Treaty of 1963, which of course it did. But the Atomic Energy Commission had what it wanted, "accurate data from which to base calculations," Dewar explained, adding that "the test ended many concerns about a catastrophic incident." In particular, the Atomic Energy Commission and NASA both now knew that "in the event of such a launch pad accident [the explosion] proved death would come quickly to anyone standing 100 feet from ground zero, serious sickness and possible death at 400 feet, and an unhealthy dose at 1000 feet."

Because it is difficult to believe that the agencies involved did not already know this, the question remains: What data was Atomic Energy Commission really after? The man in charge of the project during this time, Space Nuclear Propulsion Office director Harold B. Finger, was reached for comment in 2010. "I don't recall that exact test," Finger says. "It was a long time ago."

Five months later, in June of 1965, disaster struck, this time officially unplanned. That is when another incarnation of the nuclear rocket engine, code-named Phoebus, had been running at full power for ten minutes when "suddenly it ran out of LH_2 [liquid hydrogen and] overheated in the blink of an eye," wrote Dewar. As with the planned "explosion" five months earlier, the nuclear rocket reactor first ejected large chunks of its radioactive fuel out into the open air. Then "the remainder fused together, as if hit by a giant welder," Dewar explained. Laymen would call this a meltdown. The cause of the accident was a faulty gauge on one of the liquid hydrogen tanks. One gauge read a quarter full when in reality there was nothing left inside the tank.

So radiated was the land at Jackass Flats after the Phoebus accident, even HAZMAT cleanup crews in full protective gear could not
enter the area for six weeks. No information is available on how the
underground employees got out. Originally, Los Alamos tried to send
robots into Jackass Flats to conduct the decontamination, but according to Dewar the robots were "slow and inefficient." Eventually
humans were sent in, driving truck-mounted vacuum cleaners to
suck up deadly contaminants. Declassified Atomic Energy Commission photographs show workers in protective gear and gas masks picking up radioactive chunks with long metal tongs. Like many Atomic
Energy Commission officials, Dewar saw the accident as "achiev-
ing some objectives." That "while certainly unfortunate, unplanned,
unwanted and unforeseen," he believed that "calling the accident
'catastrophic' mocks the meaning of the word." The cleanup process
took four hundred people two months to complete.

So what happened to NERVA in the end? When Barnes
worked on NERVA in 1968, the project was well advanced. But
space travel was on the wane. By 1970, the public's infatuation with
getting a man to Mars had made an abrupt about-face. Funding
dried up, and NASA projects began shutting down. "We did develop
the rocket," Barnes says. "We do have the technology to send man
to Mars this way. But environmentally, we could never use a
nuclear-powered rocket on Earth in case it blew up on takeoff. So
the NERVA was put to bed." That depends how one defines *put to
bed*. President Nixon canceled the program, and it officially ended
on January 5, 1973. Several employees who worked at the NERVA
facility at Jackass Flats say the nuclear rocket program came to a dramatic, cataclysmic end, one that has never before been made public.
"We know the government likes to test accidents in advance," Barnes
says. Darwin Morgan, spokesman for the National Nuclear Security
Administration, Nevada Site Office, says no such final test ever happened. "Something like that would have been too huge of an event
to have happened to 'cover up,'" Morgan says. "I've talked to people
in our classified repository. They don't have anything."

The record suggests otherwise. In studying Area 25 to determine how former Atomic Energy Commission workers and contractors with cancer may have been exposed to potentially lethal doses of radiation there, investigators for the National Institute for Occupational Safety and Health determined that "two nuclear reactors" were in fact destroyed there. "Due to the destruction of two nuclear reactors and transport of radioactive material, the area was extensively contaminated with enriched uranium, niobium, cobalt, and cesium," the authors of the report concluded in 2008.

The full data relating to the last tests conducted on the NERVA nuclear rocket remain classified as Restricted Data and the Department of Energy has repeatedly declined to release the documents. Atomic Energy Commission records are "well organized and complete but unfortunately, most are classified or kept in secure areas that limit public access," Dewar wrote. As for the records from the Space Nuclear Propulsion Office, Dewar said that "many SNPO veterans believe its records were destroyed after the office was abolished in 1973" and that "in particular, the chronology file of Harold Finger, Milton Klein and David Gabriel, SNPO's directors, would [be] invaluable" in determining the complete story on NERVA. When reached for comment, Harold Finger clarified that he left the program as director in 1968. "I have no knowledge of any meltdown," Finger said, suggesting that his former deputy Milton Klein might know more. "I left the program as director in 1971," Klein said, "and do not have any information about what happened to NERVA in the end."

In January of 2002, as part of the Nevada Environmental Restoration Project, the National Nuclear Security Administration conducted a study regarding proposed cleanup of the contaminated land at Area 25. The report revealed that the following radioactive elements were still present at that time: "cobalt-60 (Co-60); strontium-90 (Sr-90); yttrium-90 (Y-90); niobium-94 (Nb-94); cesium-137 (Cs-137); barium-137m (Ba-137m); europium-152, -154, and -155 (Eu-152, Eu-154, and Eu-155); uranium-234, -235, -238 (U-234, U-235, U-238); plutonium-239/240 (Pu-239/240); and americium-241 (Am-241)," and that these radioactive contaminants "may have percolated into underlying soil."

Twenty-eight years after NERVA's questionable end at Jackass Flats, shortly after the terrorist attacks of 2001, the radiated land at Area 25 started to serve a new purpose when the Department of Homeland Security and the military began training exercises there—including how to deal with cleaning up after a terrorist attack involving a nuclear weapon. T. D. Barnes served as a consultant on several of these endeavors.

NNSA spokesman Darwin Morgan discussed the WMD training that goes on at the test site in a government film that plays at the Atomic Testing Museum in Las Vegas. "It's a PhD experience for first responders," Morgan said of the test site, "because the site offers real radiation they can't get anywhere else." Still, the National Nuclear Security Administration declined to elaborate on how, exactly, this "real radiation" that contaminated Area 25 occurred.

Perhaps in the early 1970s, the thinking at the Atomic Energy Commission was that one day a nuclear facility could very well melt down in an American city. Were this to happen, the commission could have argued, it would be a good thing to know what to expect. By 1972, the nuclear energy industry had experienced five "boom year(s)," according to Atomic Energy Commission archives. Without any kind of regulatory arm in place, the commission had been promoting and developing nuclear reactor "units," which are the fuel cores that provide energy for nuclear power plants. By the end of 1967, the commission had placed thirty units around the country. The following year, that number jumped to ninety-one, and by 1972 there were one hundred and sixty nuclear reactor units that the Atomic Energy Commission was in charge of overseeing at power plants around the nation.

Six years after the end of the NERVA program at Jackass Flats, the nuclear facility at Three Mile Island nearly melted down, on March 28, 1979. The nuclear reactor there experienced a partial core meltdown because of a loss of coolant. Officials were apparently stunned. "The people seemed dazed by a situation that wasn't covered in the manuals, torn between logic and standard operating procedures, indecisive in the absence of a strong executive power," read a 1980 report on the disaster prepared for the public by the newly formed Nuclear Regulatory Commission's Special Inquiry Group. Even though similar accident scenarios had been conducted at Area 25, the "executive power," which was the Atomic Energy Commission, apparently did not share the information with its partners at the power plants.

At the same time the Three Mile Island accident happened, a movie called *The China Syndrome* was opening in theaters across the country. The movie was about a government plot to conceal an imminent nuclear meltdown disaster, with Jane Fonda playing a reporter determined to expose the plot. Although it was clear to moviegoers that the film was fictional, it had been made with great attention to technical detail. The Nuclear Regulatory Commission's Special Inquiry Group determined that the combination of the two events—the real and the fictional—resulted in a media firestorm. The fact that the near nuclear meltdown happened in the media glare, wrote the commissioner, "may be the best insurance that it will not reoccur." The public's so-called mass hysteria, feared for decades by government elite, really did work in the public's interest after all. At Three Mile Island, the media firestorm and the public's response to it proved to act as a democratic "checks and balances" where the federal government had failed.

For as many nuclear accidents of its own making as the Atomic Energy Commission could foresee, they could not have predicted what happened on January 24, 1978, when a nuclear-powered Russian spy satellite crashed on North American soil, in Canada. NORAD analysts had been tracking Cosmos 954 since it launched, on September 18, 1977, but after three months, the movements of the spy satellite were causing NORAD ever-increasing alarm. The Russian satellite had been designed to track U.S. submarines running deep beneath the surface of the sea, and what NORAD knew about the satellite was that it was forty-six feet long and weighed 4.4 tons. To get that much payload into orbit required phenomenal power, most likely nuclear.

In December of 1977, analysts determined that the Russian satellite was slipping out of orbit, dropping closer and closer to Earth on each ninety-minute rotation of the globe. Calculations indicated that unless the Russians could get control of their satellite, Cosmos would, in all probability, reenter the atmosphere and crash somewhere in North America within a month. President Carter's national security adviser Zbigniew Brzezinski pressed Moscow for information about what exactly was on board the crashing satellite. The Russians told Brzezinski that Cosmos 954 carried 110 pounds of highly enriched uranium 235.

Richard Mingus worked at the Department of Energy's emergency command center, located in Las Vegas, during the crisis. The center was in charge of controlling public information about the looming nuclear disaster, following directions from the CIA. According to a secret CIA report declassified in 1997, a decision was made not to inform the public. Trying to predict the public's reaction to a nuclear satellite crash was like "playing night baseball with the lights out," wrote CIA analyst Gus Weiss, because "the outcome of [Cosmos] 954 would be akin to determining the winner of a train wreck." The CIA knew exactly what would happen, and that was that "the satellite was coming down carrying a live reactor." The CIA also believed that "a sensationalized leak would disturb the public in unforeseeable ways." This information has never been made public before.

"It was extremely tense," recalls Richard Mingus, who spent several days fielding calls at the emergency command center. By 1978, NEST—Nuclear Emergency Search Team—was finally trained to handle nuclear disasters. The man in charge was Brigadier General Mahlon E. Gates, also the manager of the Nevada Test Site. According to Gates, "the nucleus for NEST-related activity was established within EG&G, which had responsibility for overall logistics" to the nuclear lab workers and those assigned to NEST by the federal government. The team waited on standby at McCarran Airport, "ready to go the minute the thing crash-landed," Mingus says. "Our job at the emergency command center was to keep people across America from panicking." All that Brzezinski had said publicly was that America was experiencing a "space age difficulty." Mingus believes this was the right move. "The satellite was still pretty high up, there was no radioactive danger until it actually hit the ground. But imagine the panic if people, or say a mayor of a city, started calling for cities to evacuate based on where they thought the satellite was going to crash down on the next ninety-minute rotation?" Mingus says the feeling at the command center was that if that were to happen, it would be panic like in *The War of the Worlds*.

When Cosmos 954 finally crashed, it hit the earth across a large swath of ice in the middle of the frozen Canadian tundra, one thousand miles north of Montana on Great Slave Lake. At McCarran Airport a fleet of unmarked NEST vans—meant to look like bakery vans but really loaded with banks of gamma- and neutron-detection equipment inside—drove into the belly of a giant C-130 transport plane and prepared to head north. NEST personnel included the usual players in the nuclear military-industrial complex: scientists and engineers from Los Alamos, Livermore, Sandia, and EG&G. Troy Wade was the lead federal official dispatched to the crash site. Looking back, he explains, "It was the radioactive fuel we were most concerned about. If a piece comes down that weighs a ton, you can't predict how far and wide the debris, including all that fuel, will go."

For this reason, the first order of business was detecting radiation levels from the air. Wade and the EG&G remote-sensing team loaded small aircraft and helicopters into the belly of the C-130, alongside the unmarked bread vans, and headed for the Canadian tundra. As part of Operation Morning Light, NEST members scoured a fifty-by-eight-hundred-mile corridor searching for radioactive debris. "This was long before the advent of GPS. There were no mountains to navigate by," Wade says. "The pilots had no reference points. Just a lot of snow and ice out there. Temperatures of nearly fifty degrees below zero." Helping out from high above was an Air Force U-2 spy plane.

After several long months, 90 percent of the debris from Cosmos 954 had been recovered. In the postaccident analysis, officials at NORAD determined that if the satellite had made one last orbit before crashing, its trajectory would have put it down somewhere on America's East Coast.

CHAPTER NINETEEN

The Lunar-Landing Conspiracy
and Other Legends of Area 51

Two hundred and fifty thousand miles from the Nevada Test Site, on July 20, 1969, with less than ninety-four seconds of fuel remaining, Neil Armstrong and copilot Buzz Aldrin were facing almost certain death as they approached the Sea of Tranquillity on the moon. The autotargeting on their lunar landing module, famously called the *Eagle,* was taking them down onto a football-field-size crater laden with jagged boulders. To have crash-landed there would have meant death. The autotargeting was burning precious fuel with each passing second; the quick-thinking Neil Armstrong turned it off, took manual control of the *Eagle,* and, as he would tell NASA officials at Mission Control in Houston, Texas, only moments later, began "flying manually over the rock field to find a reasonably good area" to land. When Armstrong finally set the *Eagle* down safely on the moon, there was a mere twenty seconds' worth of fuel left in the descent tanks.

Practice makes perfect, and no doubt Armstrong's hundreds of hours flying experimental aircraft like the X-15 rocket ship—in dangerous and often death-defying scenarios—helped prepare him for piloting a safe landing on the moon. As with most seminal U.S. government accomplishments, particularly those involving science, it took thousands of men working hundreds of thousands of hours inside scores of research centers and test facilities—not to mention a number of chemical rockets designed by Wernher Von Braun—to get the Apollo 11 astronauts and five additional crews (Apollos 12, 14, 15, 16, and 17) to the moon and back home. A little-known fact is that to prepare for what it would actually be like to walk around on the geology of the moon, the astronauts visited the Nevada Test Site. There, they hiked inside several atomic craters, learning what kind of geology they might have to deal with on the lunar surface's inhospitable terrain. The Atomic Energy Commission's Ernie Williams was their guide.

"I spent three days with the astronauts in Areas 7, 9, and 10 during astronaut training, several years before they went to the moon," Williams recalls. In the 1960s, astronauts had rock-star status, and Williams remembered the event like it was yesterday. "The astronauts had coveralls and wore field packs, mock-ups of the real thing, strapped on their backs. They had cameras mounted on their hats and they took turns walking up and down the subsidence craters. It was steep, rocky terrain," he explains. Williams originally worked for the Atomic Energy Commission in feeding and housing, making sure the "feed wagon" got to remote areas of the atomic bombing range. "We'd get mashed potatoes and gravy to the faraway places inside the test site," Williams says, "hot food being a key to morale." But the multitalented Williams quickly became the test site's jack-of-all-trades, including astronaut guide. His other jobs included being in charge of the motor pool and helping CIA engineers drill for Area 51's first water well. But for Williams, the highlight of his career was escorting the first men on the moon inside the atomic craters.

"I was with them in 1965, and again five years later when they came back," Williams recalls. This time the astronauts arrived with a lunar roving vehicle to test what it might be like driving on the moon. The astronauts were taken out to the Schooner crater, located on the Pahute Mesa in Area 20. "We picked them up at the Pahute airstrip and took them and the vehicle into the crater where there was pretty rough terrain," Williams explains. "Some boulders out there were ten feet tall. One of the astronauts said, 'If we encounter this kind of thing on the moon, we're not going to get very far.'" Williams recalls the astronauts learning how to fix a flat tire on the moon. "They took off a steel tire and put on a rubber one" out in the field.

The lunar roving vehicle was not a fast-moving vehicle, and the astronauts took turns driving it. "NASA had built it and had driven it in a lot of flat places," Williams explains. "But before it came to the test site and drove on the craters, the vehicle had no real experience on inhospitable terrain. The astronauts also did a lot of walking out there," Williams adds. One of the requirements of the Apollo astronauts who would be driving during moon missions was that they had to be able to walk back to the lunar module if the rover failed.

The craters Williams was talking about are subsidence craters—geologic by-products of underground bomb tests. When a nuclear bomb is placed in a deep vertical shaft, as hundreds were at the test site (not to be confused with tunnel tests), the explosion vaporizes the surrounding earth and liquefies the rock. Once that molten rock cools, it solidifies at the bottom of the cavity, and the earth above it collapses, creating the crater. The glass-coated rock, giant boulders, and loose rubble that remain resemble the craters found on the moon. So similar in geology were the atomic craters to moon craters that in voice transcripts sent back during the Apollo 16 and Apollo 17 missions, astronauts twice referred to the craters at the Nevada Test Site. During Apollo 16, John W. Young got specific. A quarter of a million miles away from Earth, while marveling at a lunar crater laden with rocks, Young asked fellow astronaut Charles M. Duke Jr., "Remember how it was up at that crater? At Schooner." He was referring to the atomic crater Ernie Williams took the astronauts to in Area 20. During Apollo 17, while looking at the Haemus Mountains, Harrison H. Schmitt can be heard talking about the Buckboard Mesa craters in Area 19. For Ernie Williams, hearing this comparison was a beautiful moment. For lunar-landing conspiracy theorists, of which there are millions worldwide, the feeling was one of suspicion. For these naysayers, Schmitt's telemetry tapes, the moon photographs, the moon rocks — everything having to do with the Apollo moon missions would become grist for a number of ever-growing conspiracies that have been tied to man's journey to the moon.

Just two months after Armstrong and Aldrin returned home, a UFO-on-the-moon conspiracy was born. On September 29, 1969, in New York City, the newest installment of *National Bulletin* magazine rolled off the printing press with a shocking headline: "Phony Transmission Failure Hides Apollo 11 Discovery. Moon Is a UFO Base," it read. The author of the article, Sam Pepper, said he'd been leaked a transcript of what NASA had allegedly edited out of the live broadcast back from the moon, namely, that there were UFOs there. Various UFO groups pressed their congressmen to take action, several of whom wrote to NASA requesting a response. "The incident... did not take place," NASA's assistant administrator for legal affairs shot back in a memo from January 1970.

As time passed the ufologists continued to write stories about the moon being a base for aliens and UFOs. For the most part, NASA ignored them. But then, in the midseventies, a newly famous film director named Steven Spielberg decided to make a film about aliens coming down to visit Earth. He sent NASA officials his script for *Close Encounters of the Third Kind,* expecting their endorsement. Instead, NASA sent Spielberg an angry twenty-page letter opposing his film. "I had wanted co-operation from them," Spielberg said in a 1978 interview, "but when they read the script they got very angry and felt that it was a film that would be dangerous. I think they mainly wrote the letter because *Jaws* convinced so many people around the world that there were sharks in toilets and bathtubs, not just in the oceans and rivers. They were afraid the same kind of epidemic would happen with UFOs." Fringe ufologists were one thing as far as NASA was concerned. Steven Spielberg had millions of movie fans. He was a modern-day version of Orson Welles.

Right around the same time, another moon conspiracy theorist let his idea loose on the American public, a theory that did not involve UFOs. In 1974, a man named William Kaysing self-published a book called *We Never Went to the Moon: America's Thirty-Billion-Dollar Swindle.* With these three questions, Kaysing became known as the father of the lunar-landing conspiracy:

How can the American flag flutter when there is no wind on the moon?
Why can't the stars be seen in the moon photographs?
Why is there no blast crater where Apollo's landing vehicle landed?

Kaysing, who died in 2005, often said his skepticism began when he was an analyst and engineer at Rocketdyne, the company that designed the Saturn rockets that allowed man to get to the moon. While watching the lunar landing live on television, he said he experienced "an intuitive feeling that what was being shown was not real." Later, he began scrutinizing the moon-landing photographs for evidence of a hoax. Kaysing's original three questions have since planted seeds in millions upon millions of people who continue to insist that NASA did not put men on the moon. The lunar-landing conspiracy ebbs and flows in popularity, but as of 2011, it shows no signs of going away.

In August 2001 Kaysing was interviewed by Katie Couric on the *Today* show. By then, Kaysing's theory had morphed to involve Area 51. He was often quoted as saying that the Apollo landings were filmed at a movie studio there. "Area 51 is one of the most heavily guarded facilities in the United States," Kaysing said, and anyone who tried to go there "could be shot and killed without any warning. With good reason . . . because the moon sets are still there."

In the twenty-first century, a new generation of moon hoaxers walk in Kaysing's footsteps to expose what they say is NASA's fraud. Like the game of Whac-A-Mole, as soon as one element of the conspiracy appears to be disproven another allegation surfaces— from missing telemetry tapes to outright murder. So aggravated has America's formidable space agency become over the moon hoaxers that in 2002, NASA hired aerospace historian Jim Oberg to write a book meant to challenge conspiracy theorists' questions and claims— now numbering hundreds—in a point-by-point rebuttal. When news of the project was leaked to the media, NASA got such bad press over it they canceled the book.

The idea that the moon landing was faked was born at a time of high government mistrust. In 1974, for the first time in history, a U.S. president resigned. In 1975, the CIA admitted it had been running mind-control programs, a number of which involved human experiments with dangerous, illegal drugs. Then, in April, Saigon fell. The general antigovernment feeling was heightened by the fact that while government proved capable of many nefarious deeds it had been unable to win the war in Vietnam; 58,193 Americans were killed trying.

Kaysing was also tapping into a tradition. There had been one successful Great Moon Hoax already, over 130 years earlier, in 1835. Beginning on August 25 of that year, the *New York Sun* published a series of six articles claiming falsely that life and civilization had been discovered on the moon. According to the newspaper story, winged humans, beavers the size of people, and unicorns were seen through a powerful telescope belonging to Sir John Herschel, the most famous astronomer at the time. Editions of the newspapers sold out, were reprinted, and sold out again. Circulation soared, and the *New York Sun* made tremendous profits over the story, which readers believed to be true. On the subject of the public's gullibility, Edgar Allan Poe, who also wrote for the paper, said, "The story's impact reflects on the period's infatuation with progress." But the original Great Moon Hoax came and went without a conspiratorial bent because there was no government entity to blame. It was a publicity stunt to sell papers, not perceived as a nefarious plan by a government elite to manipulate and control the common man.

Shortly after Kaysing's book was published (it is still in print as of 2011), a 1978 Hollywood film followed along the same lines. Peter Hyams's *Capricorn One* told the story of a faked NASA landing on Mars. Even James Bond entered the act, referencing a lunar-landing conspiracy in the film *Diamonds Are Forever.* From there, the moon-hoax theory remained a quiet staple among conspiracy theorists for decades, but with the rise of the Internet in the late 1990s, the moon-hoax concept resurfaced and eventually made its way into the mainstream press. In February of 2001, Fox TV aired a documentary-style hourlong segment called *Conspiracy Theory: Did We Land on the Moon?* and the debate was rekindled around the world. This gave way to an unusual twenty-first-century moon-hoax twist.

In September of 2002, Buzz Aldrin, the second man on the moon, agreed to be interviewed by Far Eastern TV. This was because "they seemed like legitimate journalists," Aldrin explains. Buzz Aldrin has the highest profile of the twelve Apollo astronauts who walked on the moon, and he regularly gives interviews. A former fighter pilot, Aldrin flew sixty-six combat missions and shot down two MiG-15s in the Korean War. He is also an MIT-trained physicist, which affords him extra fluency when discussing outer space. Sitting in a suite in the Luxe Hotel in Beverly Hills in the fall of 2002, it did not take long for Aldrin to realize something was awry when the TV interviewer began asking him questions involving conspiracy theories. "I tried redirecting the discussion back to a legitimate discussion about space," Aldrin says. Instead the interviewer played a clip from the Fox documentary about moon hoaxes. Aldrin believes "conspiracy theories are a waste of everybody's time and energy," and he got up and left the interview. "I'm someone who has dealt with the exact science of space rendezvous and orbital mechanics, so to have someone approach me and seriously suggest that Neil, Mike, and I never actually went to the moon, but that the entire trip had been staged in a sound studio someplace, has to rank with one of the most ludicrous ideas I've ever heard," says Aldrin.

Then, down in the hotel lobby, a large man in his midthirties approached Buzz Aldrin and tried to spark a conversation. The man, whose name was Bart Sibrel, had a film crew with him. "Hey, Buzz, how are you?" Sibrel asked, the cameras rolling. Aldrin said hello and headed out toward the street. Sibrel hurried along beside him, asking more questions. Then he pulled out a very large Bible and began shaking it in the former astronaut's face. "Will you swear on the Bible that you really walked on the moon?" Aldrin, who was seventy-two at the time, said, "You conspiracy people don't know what you're talking about" and turned to walk in the other direction. The man began hurling personal insults and accusations at Aldrin. "Your life is a complete lie!" the man shouted. "And here you are making money by giving interviews about things you never did!" The conspiracy theorist ran in front of Aldrin, blocking his way across the road. Aldrin, who had his stepdaughter with him, walked back to the hotel and asked the bellman to call the police. "You're a coward, Buzz Aldrin!" shouted the conspiracy theorist. "You're a liar; you're a thief!" Aldrin said he'd had enough: "Maybe it was the West Point cadet in me, or perhaps it was the Air Force fighter pilot. Or maybe I'd just had enough of his belligerent character assassination...I popped him." The second man on the moon punched the lunar-landing conspiracy theorist squarely in the jaw, cameras catching it all on tape.

In no time, the video footage was airing on the news, on CNN, on Jay Leno and David Letterman. CNN political commentator Paul Begala gave Aldrin the thumbs-up for pushing back against conspiracy theorists. But elsewhere, all across America, many millions of people agreed with the conspiracy theorists who believed that the lunar landing was a hoax. By the fortieth anniversary of the historic Apollo 11 mission, in 2009, polls conducted in America, England, and Russia revealed that approximately 25 percent of the people interviewed believed the moon landing never happened. Many said they believed that it was faked and filmed at Area 51.

★   ★   ★

As of 2011, the lunar-landing conspiracy is one of three primary conspiracies said to have been orchestrated at Area 51. The other two that dominate conspiracy thinking involve captured aliens and UFOs, and an underground tunnel and bunker system that supposedly exists below Area 51 and connects it to other military facilities and nuclear laboratories around the country. Each conspiracy theory contains elements of fact, and each is perceived differently by the three government agencies they target: NASA, the CIA, and the Department of Defense. In each conspiracy theory lies an important clue about the real truth behind Area 51.

Michael Schratt, who writes books and travels around the country giving lectures about government cover-ups at Area 51, says that the secret facility is "directly connected to Edwards [Air Force Base] North Base Complex and Air Force Plant 42 at Palmdale by an underground tube-shuttle tunnel system developed by the Rand Corporation and others [circa] 1960." Schratt also says that Area 51 is "very likely connected to Wright-Patterson Air Force Base in Ohio" this same way. "The tunnels were dug by a nuclear-powered drill that can dig three miles of tunnel a day," Schratt says. "These tunnels also connect, by underground train, to other military facilities where leaders of government will go and live after a nuclear event" such as World War III.

In fact, underground tunnels, called N-tunnels, P-tunnels, and T-tunnels, have been drilled next door to Area 51, at the Nevada Test Site, for decades. The 1,150-foot-long tunnel at Jackass Flats, drilled into the Calico Mountains, through which NERVA scientists and engineers like T. D. Barnes accessed their underground workstations is but one example of an underground tunnel at the Nevada Test Site. The NERVA complex in Area 25 has since been dismantled and "deactivated," according to the Department of Energy, but elsewhere at the test site dozens of tunnel complexes exist. In the 1960s, one tunnel dug into the granite mountain of Rainer Mesa, in Area 12, reached down as far as 4,500 feet, nearly a mile underground. There are many such government tunnels and bunkers around America, but it was the revelation of the Greenbrier bunker by *Washington Post* reporter Ted Gup in 1992 that set off a firestorm of conspiracy theories related to postapocalypse hideouts for the U.S. government elite—and since 1992, these secret bunkers have been woven into conspiracy theories about things that go on at Area 51.

The Greenbrier bunker is located in the Allegheny Mountains, 250 miles southwest of the nation's capital. Beginning in 1959, the Department of Defense spearheaded the construction of a 112,544-square-foot facility eight hundred feet below the West Virginia wing of the fashionable five-star Greenbrier resort. This secret bunker, completed in 1962, was to be the place where the president and certain members of Congress would live after a nuclear attack. The Greenbrier bunker had dormitories, a mess hall, decontamination chambers, and a hospital staffed with thirty-five doctors. "Secrecy, denying knowledge of the existence of the shelter from our potential enemies, was paramount to all matters of operation," Paul Bugas, the former onsite superintendent at the Greenbrier bunker, told PBS when asked why the facility was kept secret from the public. Many citizens agree with the premise. Conspiracy theorists disagree. They don't believe that the government keeps secrets to protect the people. Conspiracy theorists believe the leaders of government are only looking to protect themselves.

The underground tunnels and bunkers at the Nevada Test Site may be the most elaborate underground chambers ever constructed by the federal government in the continental United States. The great majority of them are in Area 12, which is located approximately sixteen miles due west of Area 51 in a mountain range called Rainier Mesa. Beginning in 1957, massive tunnel complexes were drilled into the volcanic rock and granite by hard-rock miners working twenty-four hours a day, seven days a week. To complete a single tunnel took, on average, twelve months. Most tunnels ran approximately 1,300 feet below the surface of the earth, but some reached a mile underground. Inside these giant cavities, which averaged one hundred feet wide, the Atomic Energy Commission and the Department of Defense have exploded at least sixty-seven nuclear bombs. There, the military has tested nuclear blast and radiation effects on everything from missile nose cones to military satellites. A series called the Piledriver experiments studied survivability of hardened underground bunkers in a nuclear attack. The Hardtack tests sought to learn how "to destroy enemy targets [such as] missile silos and command centers" using megaton bombs. Inside the T-tunnels, scientists created vacuum chambers to simulate outer space, expanding on those dangerous late-1950s upper atmospheric tests code-named Teak and Orange. And the Department of Defense even tested how a stockpile of nuclear weapons inside an underground bunker would hold up to a nuclear blast.

Richard Mingus has spent many years inside these underground tunnel complexes, guarding many of the nuclear bombs used in the tests before they were detonated. In Mingus's five decades working at the test site, these were his least favorite assignments. "The tunnels were dirty, filthy, you had to wear heavy shoes because there was so much walking on all kinds of rock rubble," Mingus explains. "The air was bad and everything was stuffy. There were so many people working so many different jobs. Carpenters, welders... There were forty-eight-inch cutting machines covering the ground." Most of the equipment was hauled in on railroad tracks, which is at least partially responsible for inspiring conspiracy theories that include trains underneath Area 51 — though the conspiracy theorists believe they're able to ferry government elite back and forth between Nevada and the East Coast. In reality, according to Atomic Energy Commission records, the Defense Department built the train system in the tunnels to transport heavy military equipment in and out. If employees wanted to, men like Richard Mingus could ride the train cars down into the underground tunnel complexes, but Mingus preferred to walk.

Unlike atmospheric weapons tests or the atomic tests in vertical shafts that made the moonlike craters, for the T-tunnel nuclear tests, the bomb was one of the first items to arrive on scene. "The bomb was cemented in the back of the tunnel, in a room called the zero room," Mingus says. "That was about three-quarters of a mile distance." Sometimes, Mingus would stand guard with the nuclear bomb at the end of the tunnel for eight- or ten-hour shifts, so he chose to walk in each morning "for the exercise." Mingus also disliked the assignments inside the underground tunnels because they reminded him of a part of his early life he would rather have forgotten. "When I was a kid working the coal mines," Mingus explains. But as anxious as a man standing guard over live nuclear bombs might have been, Mingus remained calm. He says the coal mines of his youth were far more dangerous. "There were no electric drills back then so my brother and I drilled by hand. We'd get down on our knees in those little tunnels—three and a half feet wide, not tall enough to stand up in. We'd use black powder as an explosive, not dynamite. We'd set the powder in the hole, tap it with a rod, use a fuse that was like toilet paper, light it, run out, and then wait for the smoke to clear. Some things you never forget even if you want to," Mingus says.

Before the Limited Test Ban Treaty of 1963, the Pentagon maintained a policy of announcing nuclear weapons tests to the public, usually one or two hours before shot time, which meant somewhere around 3:30 a.m. the day of the blast. After the test ban, the Pentagon reversed its policy. Information about underground tests— when they were to take place and how big they would be—was now classified secret. Only if a scientist predicted that an earthquake-like tremor might be felt in Las Vegas, sixty-five miles to the south, was a public announcement made in advance of the nuclear test. And so, from 1963 until the last test in 1992, approximately eight hundred tests were conducted underground. By the late 1990s, decades after the first drills bored into the rock at the Nevada Test Site, the nuclear bombs, the hard-rock miners, and Area 51 had merged into one entity. As it is with many urban legends regarding Area 51, the underground-tunnels idea has been spun from facts.

As creative as conspiracy theorists can be when it comes to Area 51, it is surprising how they have missed the one underlying element that connects the three primary conspiracy theories about the secret facility to the truth. For conspiracy theorists, in the captured-aliens-and-UFOs narrative, the federal agency orchestrating the plot is the CIA. In the lunar-landing conspiracy the agency committing the fraud is NASA. In the underground tunnels and bunker plot, the evil operating force is the Department of Defense. And yet the one agency that plays an actual role in the underlying facts regarding all three of these conspiracy theories is the Atomic Energy Commission.

Why have conspiracy theorists missed this connection? Why has the Atomic Energy Commission escaped the scrutiny it deserves? The truth is hidden out in the desert at the Nevada Test Site. To borrow the metaphor of CIA spymaster James Angleton, that is where a "wilderness of mirrors" can be found. Angleton believed the Soviets spun lies from lies and in doing so were able to keep America's intelligence agents lost in an illusory forest. In this same manner, throughout the Cold War the Atomic Energy Commission created its own wilderness of mirrors out in the Nevada desert, built from illusory half-truths and outright lies. The commission was able to send the public further and further away from the truth, not with "mirrors" but by rubber-stamping documents with Restricted Data, Secret, and Confidential, to keep them out of the public eye. The Area 51 conspiracy theories that were born of the Cold War—the ones peopled by aliens, piloted by UFOs, set in underground cities and on movie sets of the moon—these conspiracies all stand to aid and assist the Atomic Energy Commission in keeping the public away from secret truths.

It is no coincidence that the agency behind some of the most secret and dangerous acts out in the desert—at the Nevada Test and Training Range, the Nevada Test Site, and Area 51—has changed its name four times. First it was called the Manhattan Project, during World War II. Then, in 1947, it changed its name to the Atomic Energy Commission, or AEC. In 1975 the agency was renamed the Energy Research and Development Administration, or ERDA. In 1977 it was renamed again, this time the

Department of Energy, "the government department whose mission is to advance technology and promote related innovation in the United States," which conveniently makes it sound more like Apple Corporation than the federal agency that produced seventy thousand nuclear bombs. Finally, in 2000, the nuclear weapons side of the agency got a new name for the fourth time: the National Nuclear Security Administration, or NNSA, a department nestled away inside the Department of Energy, or DOE. In August 2010, even the Nevada Test Site changed its name. It is now called the Nevada National Security Site, or NNSS.

Since the National Security Act of 1947 reorganized government after the war, the Department of Defense, the CIA, the Army, the Navy, and the Air Force have all maintained their original names. The cabinet-level Departments of State, Labor, Transportation, Justice, and Education are all called today what they were when they were born. The Federal Bureau of Investigation has changed its name once since its formal beginning in 1908. Originally it was called the Bureau of Investigation, or BOI. By changing the name of the nation's nuclear weapons agency four times since its creation in 1942, does the federal government hope the nefarious secrets of the Atomic Energy Commission will simply disappear? Certainly, many of its records have.

James Angleton spent his career trying to prove Soviet deception. Angleton argued that totalitarian governments had the capacity to confuse and manipulate the West to such a degree that the downfall of democracy was inevitable unless the Soviet deceivers could be stopped. Angleton's belief system made him paranoid and extreme. For three years, he imprisoned a Soviet double agent and former KGB officer named Yuri Ivanovich Nosenko in a secret CIA prison in the United States—subjecting Nosenko to varying degrees of torture in an effort to break him and get him to tell the "truth." (After passing multiple polygraph tests, Nosenko was eventually released and resettled under an assumed identity. His true allegiance remains the subject of debate.) The Nosenko affair brought about Angleton's personal downfall. He was fired and he left the Agency disgraced. Deception may be a game between governments but the consequences of engaging in it are, for some, very real.

During the Cold War, the Soviet Union did not have the monopoly on deception. In 1995, after President Clinton ordered his Advisory Committee on Human Radiation Experiments to look into Cold War secret-keeping at the Atomic Energy Commission, disturbing documentation was found. In a memorandum dated May 1, 1995, the subject line chosen by Clinton's committee to sum up early AEC secret-keeping protocol read: "Official Classification Policy to Cover Up Embarrassment." One of the more damaging documents unearthed by Clinton's staff was a September 1947 memo by the Atomic Energy Commission's general manager John Derry. In a document Clinton's staff called the Derry Memo the Atomic Energy Commission ruled: "All documents and correspondence relating to matters of policy and procedures, the given knowledge of which might compromise or cause embarrassment to the Atomic Energy Commission and/or its contractors," should be classified secret or confidential.

Clinton's staff also discovered a document that read: "...there are a large number of papers which do not violate security, but do cause considerable concern to the Atomic Energy Commission Insurance Branch." In other words, the commission classified many documents because it did not want to get sued. A particular problem arose, the memo continued, "in the declassification of medical papers on human administration experiments done to date." To find a way around the problem the commission consulted with its "Atomic Energy Commission Insurance Branch." The conclusion was that if anything was going to be declassified it should first be "reworded or deleted" so as not to result in a legal claim.

The Internet is where conspiracy theorists share ideas, the great majority of which involve government plots. It is ironic that the Internet, originally called the DARPA Internet Program, was launched by the Defense Advanced Research Projects Agency (originally called ARPA) in 1969 as a means for the military to communicate digitally during the Vietnam War. In 2011 there are an estimated 1.96 billion Internet users worldwide—almost one-third of the people on the planet—and the most popular conspiracy Web site based in America is AboveTopSecret.com. According to CEO Bill Irvine, the site sees five million visitors each month. Above-TopSecret.com has approximately 2.4 million pages of content, including 10.6 million individual posts. The Web site's motto is Deny Ignorance, and its members say they are people who "rage against the mindless status-quo."

Of 25,000 AboveTopSecret.com users polled in 2011, the second most popular discussion thread involves extraterrestrials and UFO cover-ups at Area 51. But the single most popular discussion thread at AboveTop Secret.com is something called the New World Order. According to Bill Irvine, this idea has gained momentum at an "astonishing rate" over the past two years. Irvine says it serves as a nexus conspiracy for many others, including those based at Area 51.

The premise of the New World Order conspiracy theory is that a powerful, secretive cabal of men are aspiring to take over the planet through a totalitarian, one-world government. Some believers of the New World Order call it the Fourth Reich because, they say, it will be similar to Germany's Third Reich, including Nazi eugenics, militarism, and Orwellian monitoring of citizens' private lives. As outlandish as this New World Order conspiracy may seem to non–conspiracy thinkers, it touches upon the original secret at Area 51—the real reason why the U.S. government cannot admit that Area 51 exists.

CHAPTER TWENTY

From Camera Bays to Weapons Bays,
the Air Force Takes Control

W hat happened at Area 51 during the 1980s? Most of the work remains classified and very little else is known. One of the most sensational near catastrophes to happen at Area 51 during this time has never before been revealed—notably not even hinted at in Area 51 legend or lore. It involved a mock helicopter attack at the guard station that separates the Nevada Test Site from Area 51. So serious was the situation, which included semiautomatic weapons and a nuclear bomb, that both the Pentagon and the White House stepped in.

One of the greatest potential threats to Area 51 in terms of an enemy attack would be from low-flying aircraft or helicopter. "A helicopter would be the aerial vehicle of choice," says Barnes. "Whereas an airplane would be seen airborne long before it reached its target, a helicopter could be trucked in and then launched only a short distance from the restricted area. In that case, the helicopter would breach the security protection before defending aircraft from Area 51 could become airborne." Which is why, to prepare against such threats, security guards like Richard Mingus would often participate in counterattack tests using large low-flying helium balloons as targets. "The balloons simulated helicopters," Mingus explains. The tests used aging V-100 Commando armored personnel carriers, complete with mounted machine guns, left over from the Vietnam War. With four-wheel drive, high clearance, and excellent mobility, the retired amphibious armored car would ferry Mingus and his team of heavily armed sensitive assignment specialists as far as they could get up the mountain range, until the terrain became too steep.

"We'd park the V-100, run the rest of the way up the mountain with machine guns, set up on top of the mountain, and fire at these forty-inch weather balloons. There'd always be a driver, a supervisor, and a loader on the SAS team. We each had an assignment. One guy kept score." Scores were important because the stakes were so high. The Nevada Test Site was the single most prolific atomic bombing facility in the world. It had a three-decade-long history of impeccable security, as did Area 51. Which is what made the breach that Mingus witnessed so radical.

It was a scorching-hot day during the Ronald Reagan presidency, the kind of day at the test site when people knew not to touch metal surfaces outside or they'd wind up getting burned. Mingus believes it was 1982 but can't say for sure, as the event was specifically kept off of his Department of Energy logbook. No longer a security guard, Mingus had been promoted to security operations coordinator for Lawrence Livermore Laboratory. At the time the near catastrophe occurred, the rank-and-file security entourage was escorting a nuclear device down Rainier Mesa Road. The bomb, one of eighteen exploded underground at the Nevada Test Site in 1982, was going to be exploded in an underground shaft. As the five-man security response team trailed behind the bomb transport vehicle (in an armored vehicle of its own), they made sure to keep a short distance behind the nuclear device, as was protocol. "There was a driver, a supervisor, a gunner operating the turret, a loader making sure the ammo feeds into the machine guns and doesn't jam, and two riflemen," Richard Mingus explains. There is always distance between the security team and the bomb: "One of the riflemen handles the tear gas and the other works the grenade launcher. You can shoot both weapons from either the shoulder or the hip. They'll hit a target fifty or seventy-five yards away because if you find yourself under attack and having to shoot, you want distance. You don't want the tear gas coming back and getting you in the nose."

After the security response team and the nuclear bomb arrived at that day's ground zero, a team of engineers and crane operators began the process of getting the weapon safely and securely inside an approximately eight-hundred-foot-deep hole that had been drilled into the desert floor and would house the bomb. Inserting a live nuclear weapon into a narrow, five-foot-diameter shaft required extraordinary precision by a single engineer operating a heavy metal crane. There was no room for error. The crane worked in hundred-foot increments, which in test site–speak were called picks. Only after the second pick was reached, meaning the bomb was two hundred feet down, was the security eased up. Then and only then would two of the men from the response team be released. Until that moment, the bomb was considered unsecured.

Richard Mingus had been part of dozens of ground zero teams over the past quarter of a century but on this particular morning circa 1982 Mingus was coordinating security operations for Livermore from inside a building called the control point, which was located in Area 6, ten miles from the bomb. The nuclear bomb was just about to reach the second pick when chaos entered the scene.

"I was sitting at my desk at the control point when I got the call," Mingus says. "Dick Stock, the device systems engineer supervising the shot at ground zero, says over the phone, 'We're under attack over at the device assembly building!'" In the 1980s, the device assembly building was the place where the bomb components were married with the nuclear material. Because there were several nuclear weapons tests scheduled for that same week, Mingus knew there were likely additional nuclear weapons in the process of being put together at the device assembly building, in Area 27, which Mingus had good reason to believe was now under attack. "Dick Stock said he heard the information coming over the radios that the guys on the security response team were carrying" on their belts. Now it was up to Mingus to make the call about what to do next.

In the twenty-six years he had been employed at the test site, Richard Mingus had worked his way up from security guard to Livermore's operations coordinator. He was an American success story. After his father died in 1941, Mingus dropped out of high school to work the coal mines. Eventually he went back to school, got a diploma, and joined the Air Force to serve in the Korean War. At the test site, Mingus had paid his dues. For years he stood guard over classified projects in the desert, through scorching-hot summers and cold winters, all the while guarding nuclear bombs and lethal plutonium-dispersal tests. By the mid-1960s, Mingus had saved enough overtime pay to buy a home for his family, which now included the young son he and Gloria had always dreamed about. By the mid-1970s, Mingus had enough money to purchase a second home, a hunting cabin in the woods. By the early 1980s, he had been promoted so many times, he qualified for GS-12, which in federal service hierarchy is only three rungs below the top grade, GS-15. "I attended the school for nuclear weapons orientation at Kirtland Air Force Base and had passed a series of advanced courses," Mingus says. "But nothing, and I mean nothing, prepares you for the experience of thinking the nuclear material you are guarding is under attack."

During that chaotic morning, Mingus knew all he could afford to focus on was the bomb in the hole. "I thought to myself, Dick Stock said the bomb is almost two picks down the hole. We're under attack here. What's best? I asked myself. If someone put a gun to the head of the crane operator and said, 'Get it out' they'd have a live nuclear bomb in their possession. I knew I had to make a decision. Was it safer to pull the bomb up or keep sending it

Area 51 as seen from the air, circa 1964. This rare photograph has never been published before. *(Collection of Roadrunners Internationale)*

Yucca Flat, which spans several Areas at the Nevada Test Site, is one of the most bombed-out places on earth. In this photo taken during the winter months from a helicopter above Area 10, the Sedan Crater can be seen in the forefront. A 104-kiloton bomb was buried at a depth of 635 feet, and its detonation produced a crater 1,280 feet wide and 320 feet deep, moving 12 million tons of radioactive dirt in an instant and creating a hole that can be seen from space. *(National Nuclear Security Administration)*

Ed Lovick, at Skunk Works in the mid-1960s, with the waveguide, as he works to reduce the radar cross section for the A-12 to meet the CIA's demands. *(Collection of Edward Lovick/Lockheed Martin)*

A-12 ejection-seat test on Groom Lake's dry lake bed. *(Collection of Roadrunners Internationale/CIA)*

The A-12 Oxcart hidden behind a barrier at Area 51. It took 2,400 Lockheed Skunk Works machinists and mechanics to get a fleet of fifteen ready for the CIA. Visible on either side of the aircraft are the uniquely adjustable inlet cones that regulated airflow and allowed the CIA spy plane to cruise in afterburner and reach peak speeds of Mach 3.29 by May 1965. *(Lockheed Martin)*

Richard Bissell, known best for his role in the Bay of Pigs fiasco, was the CIA officer who built Area 51 from the ground up. In this rare photograph, he shakes hands with CIA pilot Louis Schalk after the first flight of the A-12 Oxcart in April 1962. Bissell had already resigned. *(Lockheed Martin)*

The A–12 Oxcart lands on the runway at Area 51, April 1962. *(Collection of Roadrunners Internationale/CIA)*

Charlie Trapp was chief of Rescue and Survival at Area 51 from 1962 to 1967. It was in this H-43B helicopter that Trapp found the body of Oxcart pilot Walt Ray and his airplane after a fatal crash. Trapp received the Air Medal for the twenty-five-day operation. *(Collection of Charles E. Trapp)*

CIA pilot Ken Collins, in full flight gear, hanging above the Area 51 swimming pool during ocean-survival training circa 1965. Charlie Trapp sits on the diving board with a technician, name unknown. *(Collection of Charles E. Trapp Jr.)*

Radar station at the top of Bald Mountain. *(Collection of Charles E. Trapp Jr.)*

The A–12 trainer during a test flight. Note the two canopies, one for the instructor pilot and another for the trainee. The A–12 trainer aircraft could not reach the upper Mach numbers; CIA pilots experienced that remarkable feat on their own. *(CIA)*

This CIA project, code-named Tagboard, was an Oxcart with a Mach 3 drone on its back, circa 1965. To avoid confusion with the A-12, the mother ship was designated M-21 (as in "mother") and the drone was designated D-21 (as in "daughter"). *(Collection of Lockheed Martin)*

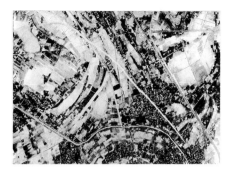

Former U-2 spy plane pilot Tony Bevacqua flies over Hanoi in the fabled SR-71 Blackbird, the Air Force variant of the A-12 Oxcart. This reconnaissance photograph shows an SA-2 missile being fired at Bevacqua from a ground station below. It was the first time an SR-71 was ever fired upon. July 26, 1968. *(Collection of Tony Bevacqua/U.S. Air Force)*

Colonel Hugh "Slip" Slater served as commander of Area 51 during the Oxcart program. Before he was put in charge of Project Oxcart, he served as commander for the CIA's Black Cat U-2 Squadron, which flew covert espionage missions over China. Here he is with the YF-12, the attack version of the A-12 Oxcart, circa 1971. *(Collection of Colonel Hugh Slater/U.S. Air Force)*

Area 51 as seen from above in 1968. *(U.S. Geological Survey/Federation of American Scientists)*

Frank Murray started out flying chase on Project Oxcart in the F–101 Voodoo. After CIA pilot Walt Ray was killed outside Area 51 during testing, General Ledford asked Murray to take Ray's place. Here Murray is on Kadena, Okinawa, before a Black Shield mission over North Vietnam. *(Collection of Frank Murray)*

Jack Weeks and Ken Collins preparing for a Black Shield mission over North Vietnam, inside the command center on Kadena in 1968. A few months later Weeks would be preseumed dead; no trace of the A-12 airplane or his body was ever found. *(Collection of Ken Collins)*

Area 51 radars, circa 1968. T. D. Barnes and his fellow EG&G Special Project engineers worked in the building at left. To pass the time when the Soviets pinned them down with spy satellites, they pulled pranks, like painting odd-shaped aircraft on the tarmac and heating the images up with hair dryers to add a heat signature. *(Collection of Thornton D. Barnes / Roadrunners Internationale)*

Radar antennae on the outskirts of Area 51, 1968. *(Collection of Thornton D. Barnes/Roadrunners Internationale)*

T. D. Barnes, age nineteen, serving in Korea in 1956. A photo of his new bride, Doris, sits on his desk in this photograph, as it still does in 2011. Barnes, a radar expert, started working for the CIA in 1958. *(Collection of Thornton D. Barnes)*

The Beatty High Range, where radar expert T. D. Barnes worked for joint NASA/CIA projects prior to his transfer to Area 51. From Beatty, Barnes could track airplanes over at Groom Lake, sixty miles as the crow flies. *(NASA)*

A Russian MiG 21 inside a hangar at Area 51. The CIA borrowed one from the Mossad, reverse engineered it, and then flew it in mock air battles over the Nevada desert. This secret program, which took place in the winter of 1968, was called Operation Have Doughnut and gave birth to the Navy's fabled Top Gun program. *(Collection of Roadrunners Internationale/U.S. Air Force)*

Apollo astronauts trained on the subsidence craters at the Nevada Test Site before they went to the moon. Ernest "Ernie" Williams was their tour guide; he helped CIA engineers locate the original water spring at Area 51. *(Department of Energy)*

Astronauts study the geology on the atomic craters while carrying mock-ups of space backpacks and other gear. *(Department of Energy)*

Richard Mingus worked security at Area 51 and the Nevada Test Site for decades. He is seen here during weapons training in 1979. *(Collection of Richard Mingus/National Nuclear Security Administration)*

A Predator drone on the tarmac at Creech Air Force Base, Nevada, June 2008. Located just thirty miles south of Area 51, the airstrip here was formerly called Indian Springs. It is where atomic sampling pilots once trained to fly through mushroom clouds; where Dr. Edward Teller, "father of the H-bomb," used to land before atomic bomb tests; and where Bob Lazar says he was taken and interrogated after getting caught trespassing on Groom Lake Road. *(U.S. Air Force/Steve Huckvale)*

From Creech Air Force Base, Nevada, U.S. Air Force pilots fly drones over Iraq and Afghanistan using remote control. *(U.S. Air Force/author collection)*

Site of former EG&G offices on the edge of downtown Las Vegas as it looked in 2009. *(Author collection)*

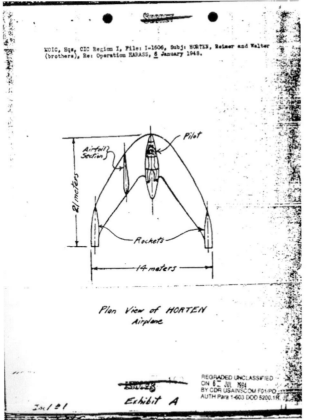

Operation Harass and the search for the Horten brothers netted this sketch of a possible advanced Horten aircraft design. *(Department of Defense)*

Walter Horten holding a scale model of the Horten 10B in Baden–Baden, Germany, in 1987. *(Collection of David Myhra)*

Reimar Horten in Argentina, 1985. *(Collection of David Myhra)*

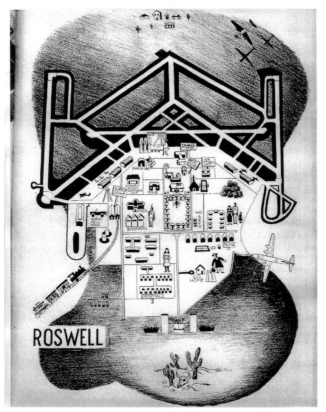

The Operation Crossroads 1946 commemorative yearbook depicts the Roswell Army Air Base as the military facility from which the opening shot in the Cold War was fired. *(Collection of Richard S. Leghorn/Army Air Forces)*

down? I decided it was better to have a big problem at ground zero than somewhere else so I gave the order. I said, 'Keep the device going down.'"

Mingus had a quick conversation with Joe Behne, the test director, about what was going on. The men agreed Mingus should call the head of security for the Department of Energy, a woman by the name of Pat Williams. "She said, 'Yes, we hear the same thing and we have to assume the same thing. We are under attack as far as I know,'" Mingus recalls.

Next Mingus called Larry Ferderber, the resident manager of the Nevada Test Site for the Lawrence Livermore National Laboratory. "Two minutes later Ferderber confirms the same thing, he says, 'I hear we're under attack.'" Mingus and Behne went through the protocol checklist. "Joe and I discussed going down to the basement and destroying the crypto which was in my building. Then we decided that it was too early for that. When you look out and you see guns firing, like on the USS *Pueblo,* then it's time to start destroying things. But not before."

Instead, Mingus called Bill Baker, the man who ran the device assembly building. With an attack now confirmed by the spokesperson for the Department of Energy and the test site manager, Mingus had to work fast. "I asked Bill Baker what was going on," Mingus recalls. "He said, real calm, 'We're fine over here. I'm looking out the window. I can see Captain Williams standing outside.'" Mingus got off the telephone and had another discussion with Joe Behne. "I told Joe, I said, 'We can't buy his word. He could be under duress. He could have a knife at his neck or a gun at his head.'"

Meanwhile, just a few miles to the east, hovering several hundred feet over the guard post between the test site and Area 51, a group of men were leaning out of a helicopter firing semiautomatic weapons at the guards on the ground. But the bullets in their weapons were blanks, not real ammunition, and the men in the helicopter were security guards from Wackenhut Security, not enemies of the state. Wackenhut Security had decided to conduct a mock attack of an access point to Area 51 to test the system for weaknesses.

With astounding lack of foresight, Wackenhut Security had not bothered to inform the Department of Energy of their mock-attack plans.

Back at the control point, in Area 6, Richard Mingus's telephone rang. It was Pat Williams, the woman in charge of security for the Department of Energy. "She was real brief," Mingus says. "She said, 'It was a test and we didn't know about it.' Then she just hung up." Mingus was astonished. "Looking back, in all my years, I have to say it was one of the scariest things I'd ever run into. It was like kids were running the test site that day." Mingus didn't write up any paperwork on the incident. "I don't believe I made a note in my record book," he says. Instead, Mingus kept working. "We had a nuclear bomb to get down into its hole and explode." Test director Joe Behne believes paperwork exists. "I know it's in the record. It was not a minor incident," he says. "For those of us that were there that day it was almost unbelievable, except we believed [briefly] it was real—that Ground Zero was being attacked from a warlike enemy. The incident is bound to be in the logbooks. All kinds of people got calls."

Far from the test site, things did not return to calm so quickly. The Department of Energy notified the FBI, who notified the Pentagon and the White House that Area 51 was under attack. The Navy's nuclear-armed submarines were put on alert, which meant that Tomahawk cruise missiles were now targeting the Nevada Test Site and Area 51. Crisis was averted before things elevated further, but it was a close call. Troy Wade was at the Pentagon at the time and told Mingus he "remembers hearing about how high up it went." Guards from Wackenhut Security lost their jobs, but like most everything at Area 51, there were no leaks to the press. Only with the publication of this book has the incident come to light.

The nuclear bomb Mingus was in charge of overseeing was live and not secured, meaning an actual attack on the test site at that moment would have raised the possibility of a nuclear weapon being hijacked by an enemy of the nation. But there was another reason that the nuclear submarines were put on alert that day: the extremely sensitive nature of a black project the Air Force was running at Area 51. The top secret aircraft being tested there was the single most important invention in U.S. airpower since the Army started its aeronautical division in 1907. Parked on the tarmac at Area 51 was the F-117 Nighthawk, the nation's first stealth bomber.

The F-117 would radically change the way America fought wars. As a Lockheed official explained at a banquet honoring the F-117 in April of 2008, "Before the advent of stealth, war planners had to determine how many sorties were necessary to take out a single target. After the invention of the F-117 stealth bomber, that changed. It became, How many targets can we take out on a single sortie?"

Lockheed physicist Edward Lovick worked on each rendition of the stealth bomber, which began in the early 1970s with Harvey, a prototype aircraft named after the Jimmy Stewart film about an invisible rabbit. Harvey's stealth qualities were initially engineered using slide rules and calculators, the same way Lockheed had developed the A-12 Oxcart. Only with the emergence of the mainframe computer, in 1974, did those tools become obsolete. "Two Lockheed engineers, named Denys Overholser and Dick Scherrer, realized that it might be possible to design a stealth aircraft that would take advantage of some of the results of a computer's calculations," Lovick says. "In 1974 computers were relatively new and most of them were the size of a car. Our computer at Lockheed ran on punch cards and had less than 60 K worth of memory." Still, the computer could do what humans could not do, and that was endless calculations.

"The concept behind the computer program involved mirrors reflecting mirrors," Lovick explains. Mathematician Bill Schroeder set to work writing Lockheed's original computer code, called Echo. If the CIA's James Jesus Angleton was correct and the Soviet security forces really were using black propaganda to create a "wilderness of mirrors" to ensnare the West, the Air Force was going to create its own set of reflective surfaces to beat the Russians back with the F-117 stealth bomber. "We designed flat, faceted panels and had them act like mirrors to scatter radar waves away from the plane," Lovick says. "It was a radical idea and it worked."

The next, on-paper incarnation of the F-117 Nighthawk began in 1974 and was called the Hopeless Diamond, so named because it resembled the Hope Diamond and because Lockheed engineers didn't have much hope it would actually fly. After the Hopeless Diamond concept went through a series of redesigns it became a full-scale mock-up of an aircraft and was renamed Have Blue. T. D. Barnes was the man in charge of radar testing Lockheed's proof-of-concept stealth bomber at Area 51. "Lockheed handed it over to us and we put it up on the pole," Barnes says. "It was a very weird, very crude-looking thing that actually looked a lot like the ship from *Twenty Thousand Leagues Under the Sea*. Our job was to look at it from every angle using radar to see how it showed up on radar." Radars had advanced considerably since the early days of the Cold War. "Initially, it was as visible as a big old barn," says Barnes. So the Have Blue mock-up was sent back to the Skunk Works for more fine-tuning. Several months later, a new version of the mock-up arrived at Area 51. "Lockheed had changed the shape of the aircraft and a lot of the angles of the panels. Once we put the new mock-up on the pole it appeared to us as something around the size of a crow." There was a final round of redesigns, then the airplane came back to Area 51 again. "We put it up on the pole and all we saw was the pole." Now it was time for Lockheed to present the final rendition of the Have Blue to the Air Force, in hopes of landing the contract to build the nation's first stealth bomber.

The director of science and engineering at Skunk Works, a man named Ed Martin, went to Lovick for some advice. "Ed Martin asked me how I thought the aircraft might appear on enemy radar. I explained that if the Oxcart showed up as being roughly equivalent to the size of a man, the Have Blue would appear to a radar like a seven-sixteenth-inch metal sphere—roughly the size of a ball bearing." Ed Martin loved Lovick's analogy. A ball bearing. That was something a person could relate to. Before Martin left for Washington, DC, Lovick went to the Lockheed tool shop and borrowed a bag of ball bearings. He wanted Ed Martin to have a visual reference to share with the Air Force officials there. "Later, I learned the ball-bearing illustration was so effective that the customers began rolling the little silvery spheres across the conference table. The analogy has become legendary, often still used to make an important visual point about the stealthy F-117 Nighthawk with its high-frequency radar signature that is as tiny as a ball bearing." In 1976, Lockheed won the contract. Immediately, they began manufacturing two Have Blue aircraft in the legendary Skunk Works Building 82. The man in charge of engineering, fabrication, and assembly of the pair of stealth bombers was Bob Murphy, the same person who twenty-one years earlier had begun his career in a pair of overalls at Area 51, working for Kelly Johnson as chief mechanic on the U-2.

Testing a bomber plane would be a radically different process from testing a spy plane, and the F-117 was the first bomber to be flight-tested at Area 51. Most notably, the new bomber would require testing for accuracy in dropping bombs on targets. For nearly twenty-five years, the CIA and the Air Force had been flying spy planes and drones in the Box. But there was simply not enough flat square footage at Groom Lake to drop bombs. There was also the issue of sound. With multiple projects going on at Area 51, not everyone was cleared for the F-117.

A second site was needed, and for this, the Air Force turned to the Department of Energy, formerly the Atomic Energy Commission. A land-use deal was struck allowing the Air Force to use a preexisting, little-known bombing range that the Atomic Energy Commission had quietly been using for decades. It was deep in the desert, within the Connecticut-size Nevada Test and Training Range. Located seventy miles northwest of Area 51, the Tonopah Test Range was almost in Death Valley and had been in use as a bombing range and missile-launch facility for Sandia Laboratories since 1957. The Department of Energy had no trouble carving a top secret partition out of the 624-square-mile range for the Air Force's new bomber project. To be kept entirely off the books, the secondary black site was named Area 52. Like Area 51, Area 52 has never been officially acknowledged.

The sparsely populated, high-desert outpost of Tonopah, Nevada, was once the nation's most important producer of gold and silver ore. In 1903, eighty-six million dollars in metals came out of the area's mines, nearly two billion in 2011 dollars, and at the turn of the century, thirty thousand people rushed to the mile-high desert city seeking treasure there. Tonopah's nearest neighbor, the town of Beatty, where T. D. Barnes lived in the 1960s, became known in 1907 as the Chicago of the West. For several years the Las Vegas & Tonopah Railroad maintained a rail line between the two cities, which at one point was the West's busiest rail line. And then, almost overnight and like so many towns ensnared in the gold rush, Tonopah went bust. Within ten years, it was just a few families too many to be called a ghost town. Even the railroad company ripped up its steel tracks and carted them away for better use. Packs of wild horses and antelope came back down from the mountains and began to graze as they had before the boom, pulling weeds and scrub from the parched desert landscape between the Cactus and the Kawich mountain ranges. When a group of weaponeers from Sandia descended upon the area four decades later, in 1956, they were thrilled with what they found. Tonopah was a perfect place for "secret testing [that] could be conducted safely and securely." Years later, boasting to their corporate shareholders, the Sandians, as they called themselves, would quote Saint Paul of Tarsus to sum up their mission at Tonopah Test Range: "test all things; hold fast that which is good."

Between 1957 and 1964, Sandia dropped 680 bombs and launched 555 rockets from what was now officially but quietly called the Sandia National Laboratories' Outpost at Tonopah. In 1963, Sandia conducted a series of top secret plutonium-dispersal tests, similar to the Project 57 test that had been conducted at Groom Lake just a few years earlier. Called Operation Roller Coaster, three dirty bomb tests were performed to collect biological data on three hundred animals placed downwind from aerosolized plutonium clouds generated from three Sandia nuclear weapons. With seven hundred Sandians hard at work in the desert flats for Operation Roller Coaster, a report called it Sandia's "highlight of 1963." Tonopah was so far removed from the already far removed and restricted sites at Area 51 and the Nevada Test Site that no one outside a need-to-know had ever even heard of it.

In October of 1979, construction for an F-117 Nighthawk support facility at Tonopah began inside Area 52. The facility at Area 51 served as a model for the facility being built at Area 52. Similarly styled runways and taxiways were built, as well as a maintenance hangar, using crews already cleared for work on Nevada Test Site contracts. Sixteen mobile homes were carted in, and several permanent support buildings were constructed. Sandia didn't want to draw attention to the project, so the Air Force officers assigned to the base were ordered to grow their hair long and to grow beards. Sporting a hippie look, as opposed to a military look, was less likely to draw unwanted attention to a highly classified project cropping up in the outer reaches of the Nevada Test Site. That way, the men could do necessary business in the town of Tonopah.

The two facilities, Area 51 and Area 52, worked in tandem to get the F-117 battle-ready. When the mock attack at the guard gate at Area 51 occurred, in 1982, test flights of the F-117 — which only ever happened at night — were already in full swing. For some weeks, a debate raged as to how an act of idiocy by a small group of Wackenhut Security guards nearly outed a billion-dollar aircraft as well as two top secret military test facilities that had remained secret for thirty years. An estimated ten thousand personnel had managed to keep the F-117 program in the dark. There was a collective mopping of the brow and succinct orders to move on, and then, two years later, the program was nearly outed again when an Air Force general broke protocol and decided to take a ride in one of Area 51's prized MiG fighter jets.

The death of Lieutenant General Robert M. Bond on April 26, 1984, in Area 25 of the Nevada Test Site was an avoidable tragedy. With 267 combat missions under his belt, 44 in Korea and 213 in

Vietnam, Robert M. Bond was a highly decorated Air Force pilot revered by many. At the time of his accident, he was vice commander of Air Force Systems Command at Andrews Air Force Base, in Maryland, which made him a VIP when it came to the F-117 program going on at Area 51. In March of 1984, General Bond arrived at the secret facility to see how things were progressing. The general's visit should have been no different than those made by the scores of generals whose footsteps Bond was following in, visits that began back in 1955 with men like General James "Jimmy" Doolittle and General Curtis LeMay. The dignitaries were always treated in high style; they would eat, drink, and bear witness to top secret history being made. Following in this tradition, General Bond's first visit went without incident. But in addition to being impressed by the F-117 Nighthawk, General Bond was equally fascinated by the MiG program, which was still going on at Area 51. In the fifteen years since the CIA had gotten its hands on Munir Redfa's MiG-21, the Agency and the Air Force had acquired a fleet of Soviet-made aircraft including an MiG-15, an MiG-17, and, most recently, the supersonic MiG-23. Barnes says, "We called it the Flogger. It was a very fast plane, almost Mach 3. But it was squirrelly. Hard to fly. It could kill you if you weren't well trained."

On a visit to Area 51 the following month, General Bond requested to fly the MiG-23. "There was some debate about whether the general should be allowed to fly," Barnes explains. "Every hour in a Soviet airplane was precious. We did not have spare parts. We could not afford unnecessary wear and tear. Usually a pilot would train for at least two weeks before flying a MiG. Instead, General Bond got a briefing while sitting inside the plane with an instructor pilot saying, 'Do this, do that.'" In other words, instead of undergoing two weeks of training, General Bond pulled rank.

Just a few hours later, General Bond was seated in the cockpit of the MiG, flying high over Groom Lake. All appeared to be going well, but just as he crossed over into the Nevada Test Site, Bond radioed the tower on an emergency channel. "I'm out of control," General Bond said in distress. The MiG was going approximately Mach 2.5. "I've got to get out, I'm out of control" were the general's last words. The MiG had gone into a spin and was on its way down. Bond ejected from the airplane but was apparently killed when his helmet strap broke his neck. The general and the airplane crashed into Area 25 at Jackass Flats, where the land was still highly contaminated from the secret NERVA tests that had gone on there.

General Bond's death opened the possible exposure of five secret programs and facilities, including the MiG program, the F-117 program, Area 51, Area 52, and the nuclear reactor explosions at Jackass Flats. Unlike the deaths of CIA pilots flying out of Area 51, which could be concealed as generic training accidents, the death of a general required detailed explanation. If the press asked too many questions, it could trigger a federal investigation. One program had to come out of the dark to keep the others hidden. The Pentagon made the decision to out the MiG. Quietly, Fred Hoffman, a military writer with the Associated Press, was "leaked" information that Bond had in fact died at the controls of a Soviet MiG-23. The emphasis was put on how the Pentagon was able to obtain Soviet-bloc aircraft and weaponry from allies in Eastern Europe, the Middle East, and Asia. "The government has always been reluctant to discuss such acquisitions for fear of embarrassing the friendly donors, but the spotlight was turned anew on the subject after a three-star Air Force general was killed April 26 in a Nevada plane crash that was quickly cloaked in secrecy," Hoffman wrote, adding "sources who spoke on condition they remain anonymous have indicated the MiG-23, the most advanced Soviet warplane ever to fall permanently into U.S. hands, was supplied to this country by Egypt."

With this partial cover, the secrets of Area 51, Area 52, Area 25, and the F-117 were safe. It would be another four years before the public had any idea the F-117 Nighthawk existed. In November of 1988, a grainy image of the arrowhead-shaped, futuristic-looking craft was released to an awestruck public despite the fact that variations of the F-117 had been flying at Area 51 and Area 52 for eleven years.

*   *   *

By 1974, the Agency had ceded control of Area 51. Some insiders say the transition occurred in 1979, but since Area 51 does not officially exist, the Air Force won't officially say when this handover occurred. Certainly this had to have happened by the time the stealth bomber program was up and running; the F–117 program was the holy grail of Pentagon black projects—and, during that time period, the Air Force dominated Area 51. Having no business in bombs, the CIA maintained a much smaller presence there than historically it had before. During the 1970s, the Agency's work concentrated largely on pilotless aircraft, or drones. Hank Meierdierck, the man who wrote the manual for the U–2 at Area 51, was in charge of one such CIA drone project, which began in late 1969. Code-named Aquiline, the six-foot-long pilotless aircraft was disguised to look like an eagle or buzzard in flight. It carried a small television camera in its nose and photo equipment and air-sampling sensors under its wings. Some insiders say it had been designed to test for radiation in the air as well as to gather electronic intelligence, or ELINT. But Gene Poteat, the first CIA officer ever assigned to the National Reconnaissance Office, offers a different version of events. "Spy satellites flying over the Caspian Sea delivered us images of an oddly shaped, giant, multi-engined watercraft moving around down there on the surface. No one had any idea what this thing was for, but you can be sure the Agency wanted to find out. That is what the original purpose of Aquiline was for," Poteat reveals. "To take close-up pictures of the vehicle so we could discern what it was and what the Soviets might be thinking of using it for. Since we had no idea what it was, we made up a name for it. We called it the Caspian Sea Monster," Poteat explains. Project Aquiline remains a classified project, but in September of 2008, *BBC News* magazine produced a story about a Cold War Soviet hydrofoil named Ekranopian, which is exactly what the CIA's Aquiline drone was designed to spy on.

At Area 51, Hank Meierdierck selected his former hunting partner Jim Freedman to assist him on the Aquiline drone program. "It flew low and was meant to follow along communication lines in foreign countries and intercept messages," Freedman says. "I believe the plan was to launch it from a submarine while it was waiting in port." The Aquiline team consisted of three pilots trained to remotely control the bird, with Freedman offering operational support. "Hank got the thing to fly," Freedman recalls. Progress was slow and "it crash-landed a lot." The program ended when the defense contractor, McDonnell Douglas, gave a bid for the job that Meierdierck felt was ninety-nine million dollars over budget. McDonnell Douglas would not budge on their bid so Hank recommended that the CIA cancel Project Aquiline, which he said they did. After the program was over, Hank Meierdierck managed to take a mock-up of the Aquiline drone home with him from the area. "He had it sitting on his bar at his house down in Las Vegas," Freedman recalls.

Project Aquiline was not the CIA's first attempt to gather intelligence using cover from the animal kingdom. Project Ornithopter involved a birdlike drone designed to blend in with nature by flapping its wings. And a third, even smaller drone was designed to look like a crow and land on windowsills in order to photograph what was going on inside CIA-targeted rooms. The tiniest drone program, orchestrated in the early 1970s, was Project Insectothopter, an insect-size aerial vehicle that looked like a dragonfly in flight. Insectothopter had an emerald green minifuselage and, like Ornithopter, flapped its wings, which were powered by a miniature engine that ran on a tiny amount of gas. Through its Office of Research and Development, or ORD, the CIA had also tried turning live birds and cats into spies. In one such program, CIA-trained pigeons flew around Washington, DC, with bird-size cameras strapped to their necks. The project failed after the extra weight tired out the pigeons and they hobbled back to headquarters on foot instead of in flight. Another CIA endeavor, Acoustic Kitty, involved putting electronic listening devices in house cats. But that project also backfired after too many cats strayed from their missions in search of food. One acoustic kitty got run over by a car. The Agency's pilotless-vehicle projects were forever growing in ambition and in size. One robotic drone from the early 1970s, a project financed with DARPA, was disguised to look like an elephant—ready to do battle in the jungles of Vietnam.

Several projects, like Aquiline, involved only a handful of special-access personnel. But a few other projects took place on a considerably larger scale. In July of 1974, the CIA's Special Activities Division filed a memorandum of agreement with the Air Force to set up a classified project at Area 51 that was extensive enough that it required five hangars of its own. Aerospace historian Peter Merlin, who wrote monographs for NASA, explains: "The top-secret project, with a classified code-name, was expected to last about one year. Six permanent personnel were assigned to the test site, with up to 20 personnel on site during peak periods of short duration activity." The Air Force designated Hangar 13 through Hangar 17, located at the south end of the facility, as CIA-only. What mysterious project the CIA was working on there, those without a need-to-know have no idea. The work remains classified; rumor is that it was a Mach 5 or Mach 6 drone.

Some operations at Groom Lake in the 1970s involved the Agency's desire to detect facilities for weapons of mass destruction, or WMD, including bioweapons and chemical weapons, before those weapons facilities were in full-production mode. This work, the CIA felt, could ideally be performed by laying sensors on the ground that were capable of "sniffing" the air. Since the 1950s, the Agency had been advancing its use of sensor drones to detect WMD signatures by monitoring changes in the air, the soil, and an area's energy consumption. Early efforts had been made using U-2 pilots, who had to leave the safety of high-altitude flight and get down dangerously low in order to shoot javelinlike sensors into the earth. But those operations, part of Operation Tobasco, risked exposure. Several U-2 pilots had already been shot down. Because these delicate sensors needed to be accurately placed very close in to the WMD-producing facilities, it was an ideal job for a stealthy, low-flying drone.

Decades before anyone had rekindled an interest in drones, the

CIA saw endless possibilities in them. But to advance drone technology required money, and in 1975, a Senate committee investigating illegal activity inside the CIA, chaired by Senator Frank Church and known as the Church Committee, did considerable damage to the Agency's reputation as far as the general public was concerned. Budgets were thinned. During Jimmy Carter's presidency, which began in 1977, CIA discretionary budgets were at an all-time low, and the CIA didn't get very far with its drones—until late 1979, when the Agency learned about a lethal anthrax accident at a "probable biological warfare research, production and storage installation" in Sverdlovsk, Russia—the same location where Gary Powers had been taking spy photographs when his U-2 was shot down nineteen years before. As a result of the Sverdlovsk bioweapons accident, the CIA determined that as many as a hundred people had died from inhaling anthrax spores. The incident gave the CIA's drone program some legs. But without interest from the Air Force, drones were perceived largely as the Agency's playthings.

For twenty-five years, from 1974 to 1999, the CIA and the Air Force rarely worked together on drone projects at Area 51. This lack of cooperation was evident, and succinctly summed up in an interview Secretary of Defense Robert Gates gave *Time* magazine in April of 2008. Gates said that when he was running the CIA, in 1992, he discovered that "the Air Force would not co-fund with CIA a vehicle without a pilot." That changed in the winter of 2000, when the two organizations came together to work on a new drone project at Area 51, one that would forever change the face of warfare and take both agencies toward General Henry "Hap" Arnold's Victory Over Japan Day prediction that one day in the future, wars would be fought by aircraft without pilots sitting inside. In the year 2000, that future was now.

The project involved retrofitting a CIA reconnaissance drone, called Predator, with antitank missiles called Hellfire missiles, supplied by the army. The target would be a shadowy and obscure terrorist the CIA was considering for assassination. He lived in Afghanistan, and his name was Osama bin Laden.

CHAPTER TWENTY-ONE

Revelation

It was January of 2001, nine months before the terrorist attacks of 9/11, and the director of the CIA's Counterterrorism Center, Cofer Black, had a serious problem. The CIA had been considering assassinating Osama bin Laden with the Predator, but until that point, the unmanned aerial vehicle had been used for reconnaissance only, not targeted assassination. Because two technologies needed to be merged—the flying drone and the laser-guided precision missile—engineers and aerodynamicists had concerns. Specifically, they worried that the propulsion from the missile might send the drone astray or the missile off course. And the CIA needed a highly precise weapon with little possibility of collateral damage. The public would perceive killing a terrorist one way, but they would likely perceive killing that terrorist's neighbors in an altogether different light. This new weaponized drone technology was tested at Area 51; the development program remains classified. After getting decent results, both the CIA and the Air Force were confident that the missiles unleashed from the drone could reach their targets.

Along came another hurdle to overcome, one that was unfolding not in the desert but in Washington, DC. The newly elected administration of President George W. Bush realized that it had no policy when it came to taking out terrorists with drones. Osama bin Laden was known to be the architect of the 1998 U.S. embassy suicide bombings in East Africa, which killed more than 225 people, including Americans. He masterminded the suicide bombing of the USS *Cole* and had officially declared war against the United States. But targeted assassination by a U.S. intelligence agency was illegal, per President Ronald Reagan's Executive Order 12333, and since the situation required serious examination, State Department lawyers got involved.

There was one avenue to consider in support of the targeted-killing operation, and that was the fact that the FBI had a bounty on the man's head. By February of 2001, the State Department gave the go-ahead for the assassination. Then State Department lawyers warned the CIA of another problem, the same one that had originally sent the Predator drone to Area 51 for field tests; namely, potential collateral damage. The State Department needed to know how many bin Laden family members and guests staying on the compound the CIA was targeting could be killed in a drone attack. Bin Laden's compound was called Tarnak Farm, and a number of high-profile Middle Eastern royal family members were known to visit there.

To determine collateral damage, the CIA and the Air Force teamed up for an unusual building project on the outer reaches of Area 51. They engineered a full-scale mock-up of Osama bin Laden's compound in Afghanistan on which to test the results of a drone strike. But while engineers were at work, CIA director George Tenet decided that taking out Osama bin Laden with a Hellfire missile–equipped Predator drone would be a mistake. This was a decision the CIA would come to regret.

Immediately after the terrorist attacks of September 11, 2001, the Pentagon knew that it needed drones to help fight the war on terror, which meant it needed help from the CIA. For decades, the Air Force had been thumbing its nose at drones. The pride of the Air Force had always been pilots, not robots. But the CIA had been researching, developing, and advancing drone technology at Area 51 for decades. The CIA had sent drones on more than six hundred reconnaissance missions in the Bosnian conflict, beginning in 1995. CIA drones had provided intelligence for NATO forces in the 1999 Kosovo air campaign, collecting intelligence, searching for targets, and keeping an eye on Kosovar-Albanian refuge camps. The CIA Predator had helped war planners interpret the chaos of the battlefield there. Now, the Air Force needed the CIA's help going into Afghanistan with drones.

The first reconnaissance drone mission in the war on terror was flown over Kabul, Afghanistan, just one week after 9/11, on September 18, 2001. Three weeks later, the first Hellfire-equipped Predator drone was flown over Kandahar. The rules of aerial warfare had changed overnight. America's stealth bombers were never going to locate Osama bin Laden and his top commanders hiding out in mountain compounds. Now pilotless drones would be required to seek out and assassinate the most wanted men in the world.

Although drones had been developed and tested at Area 51, Area 52, and Indian Springs for nearly fifty years, the world at large would come to learn about them only in November of 2002, when a drone strike in Yemen made headlines around the world. Qaed Salim Sinan al-Harethi was a wanted man. A citizen of Yemen and a senior al-Qaeda operative, al-Harethi had also been behind the planning and bombing of the USS *Cole* two years before. On the morning of November 2, 2002, al-Harethi and five colleagues drove through the vast desert expanse of Yemen's northwest province Marib oblivious to the fact that they were being watched by eyes in the skies in the form of a Predator drone flying several miles above them.

The Predator launched its missile at the target and landed a direct hit. The al-Qaeda operatives and the vehicle were instantly reduced to a black heap of burning metal. It was an assassination plot straight out of a Tom Clancy novel, except that it was so real and so dramatic—the first visual proof that al-Qaeda leaders could be targeted and killed—that Assistant Secretary of Defense Paul

Wolfowitz began bragging about the Hellfire strike to CNN. The drone attack in Yemen was "a very successful tactical operation," Wolfowitz said. Except it was supposed to be a quiet, unconfirmed assassination. Wolfowitz's bravado made Yemen upset. Brigadier General Yahya M. Al Mutawakel, the deputy secretary general for the People's Congress Party in Yemen, gave an exclusive interview to the *Christian Science Monitor* explaining that the Pentagon had broken a secrecy agreement between the two nations. "This is why it is so difficult to make deals with the United States," Al Mutawakel explained. "They don't consider the internal circumstances in Yemen. In security matters, you don't want to alert the enemy."

Yemen pushed back against the United States by outing the secret inner workings of the operation. It was the U.S. ambassador to Yemen, Edmund Hull, an employee of the State Department, who had masterminded the plot, officials in Yemen explained. Hull had spearheaded the intelligence-gathering efforts, a job more traditionally reserved for the CIA. Hull spoke Arabic. He had roots in the country and knew people who knew local tribesmen in the desert region of Marib. The State Department, Yemen claimed, was the agency that had bribed local tribesmen into handing over information on al-Harethi, which allowed the CIA to know exactly where the terrorist would be driving and when. Revealing Ambassador Hull to be the central organizing player in the drone strike exposed the Department of State as having a hand in not just the espionage game but targeted assassination as well. Surprisingly, little fuss was made about any of this, despite the fact that diplomats are supposed to avoid assassination plots.

In political circles, Ambassador Hull was greatly embarrassed. He refused to comment on his role in what signaled a sea change in U.S. military assets with wings. The 2002 drone strike in Yemen was the first of its kind in the war on terror, but little did the public know that hundreds more drone strikes would soon follow. The next one went down the very next week, when a Predator targeted and killed al-Qaeda's number-three, Mohammed Atef, in Jalabad, Afghanistan. As the war on terror progressed, some drone strikes would be official while others would go unmentioned. But never again would the CIA or the State Department admit to having a hand in any of them. When Mohammed Atef was killed, initial reports said a traditional bomber aircraft had targeted and destroyed Atef's home. Only later was the strike revealed as being the work of a Predator drone and a targeted assassination spearheaded by the CIA.

Almost everything that has happened at Area 51 since 1968 remains classified but it is generally understood among men who formerly worked there that once the war on terror began, flight-testing new drones at Area 51 and Area 52 moved full speed ahead. This new way of conducting air strikes, from an aircraft without a pilot inside, represented a fundamental reconfiguration of the U.S. Air Force fighting force and would continue to remain paramount to Air Force operations going forward. This meant that a major element of the drone program, i.e., the CIA's role in overhead, needed to return quietly and quickly into the "black." The Air Force has a clear-cut role in wartime. But the operations of the CIA, a clandestine organization at its core, can never be overtly defined in real time. Remarkably, after nearly fifty years, the CIA and the Air Force were back in the business of overhead, and they would model their partnership on the early spy plane projects at Area 51. As the war on terror expanded, budgets for drone programs went from thin to virtually limitless almost overnight. As far as developing weapons using cutting-edge science and technology was concerned, it was 1957 post-Sputnik all over again.

No longer used only for espionage, the Predator got a new designation. Previously it had been the RQ-1 Predator: *R* for *reconnaissance* and *Q* indicating unmanned. Immediately after the Yemen strike, the Predator became the MQ-1 Predator, with the *M* now indicating its *multirole* use. The company that built the Predator was General Atomics, the same group that was going to launch Ted Taylor's ambitious spaceship to Mars, called *Orion,* from Jackass Flats back in 1958.

A second Predator, originally called the Predator B, was also coming online. Described by Air Force officials as "the Predator's younger, yet larger and stronger brother," it too needed a new name. The Reaper fit perfectly: the personification of death. "One of the big differences between the Reaper and the Predator is the Predator can only carry about 200 pounds [of weapons]. The Reaper, however, can carry one and a half tons, and on top of carrying Hellfire missiles, can carry multiple GBU-12 laser-guided bombs," said Captain Michael Lewis of the Forty-second Wing at Creech Air Force Base. The General Atomics drones were single-handedly changing the relationship between the CIA and the Air Force. The war on terror had the two services working together again, exactly as had happened with the advent of the U-2. This was not simply a coincidence or a recurring moment in time. Rather it was the symbiotic reality of war. If the CIA and the Air Force are rivals in peacetime—fighting over money, power, and control—in war, they work together like a bow and arrow. Each organization has something critical the other service does not have. The CIA's drones could now give Air Force battlefield commanders visual images from which they could target individuals in real time. Now, intelligence capabilities and military could work seamlessly together as one. Which is exactly what happened next, as the war on terror widened to include Iraq.

On the night of March 29, 2004, an MQ-1 Predator drone surveilling the area outside the U.S. Balad Air Base in northern Iraq caught sight of three men digging a ditch in the road with pickaxes. Brigadier General Frank Gorenc was remotely viewing the events in real time from an undisclosed location somewhere in the Middle East. He watched the men as they placed an improvised explosive device, or IED, in the hole. Gorenc was able to identify that the men were burying an IED in the road because the resolution of the images relayed back from the Predator's reconnaissance camera was so precise, Gorenc could see wires. Gorenc and other commanders in Iraq knew what the Predator was capable of. Gorenc described this technology as allowing him to "put a weapon on a target within minutes," and he authorized a strike. The Predator operator, seated at a console next to Gorenc, launched a Hellfire missile from the Predator's weapons bay, killing all three of the men in a single strike. "This strike," explained Gorenc, "should send a message to our enemies that we're watching you, and we will take action against you any time, day or night, if you continue to stand in the way of progress in Iraq." Eyes in the sky, dreamed up in the 1940s, had become swords in the sky in the new millennium. Reconnaissance and retaliation had merged into one.

Simultaneous with the early drone strikes in Iraq, the CIA and the Air Force had begun comanaging a covert program to kill al-Qaeda and Taliban commanders in the tribal areas in the northwest of Pakistan, on Afghanistan's border, using drones. To get the program up and running required effort, just as the U-2 and the Oxcart had. A drone wing, like a U-2 detachment or a squadron of Oxcarts, involved building more Predators and Reapers, training drone pilots, creating an Air Force wing, building secret bases in the Middle East, hooking up satellites, and resolving other support-related issues. From 2003 to 2007 the number of drone strikes rose incrementally, little by little, each year. Only in 2008 did the drones really come online. During that year, which included the last three weeks of the Bush administration, there were thirty-six drone strikes in Pakistan, which the Air Force said killed 268 al-Qaeda and Taliban. By 2009 the number of drone strikes would rise to fifty-three. Since the Air Force does not release numbers, and the CIA does not comment on being involved, those numbers are approximate best guesses, put together by journalists and researchers based on local reports. Since journalists are not allowed in many parts of the tribal areas in Pakistan, the actual number of drone strikes is unknown.

As much publicity as drones are getting today, there is a lot more going on in the skies than the average citizen comprehends. According to T. D. Barnes, "There are at least fifteen satellites and an untold number of Air Force aircraft 'parked' over Iraq and Afghanistan, providing twenty-four-hour-a-day coverage for airmen and soldiers on the ground. The Air Force is currently flying surveillance with the U-2, Predator, MQ-9 Reaper, and Global Hawk. These are just the assets we know about. Having been in the business, I would expect we have surveillance capability being used that we won't know about for years." The majority of these platforms, all classified, are "in all probability" being built and tested at Area 51, says Barnes.

In April of 2009, reporters with a French aviation newspaper published drawings of a reconnaissance drone seen flying over Afghanistan. With its long wings, lack of tail, and two wheels under its belly in a line, like on a bicycle, what became known as the Beast of Kandahar looks reminiscent of the Horten brothers' flying wing of 1944. What was this new drone built for? It seemed not to have a weapons bay. Eight months later, in December of 2009, the Defense Department confirmed the existence of the drone, which the Air Force calls the RQ-170 Sentinel. Built by Lockheed Skunk Works and tested at Area 51 and Area 52, the newest drone appears to be for reconnaissance purposes only. As such, it follows in the footsteps of the U-2 and the A-12 Oxcart, comanaged by the Air Force and the CIA at Area 51. Save for its name, all details remain classified. It is likely flying over denied territory, including Iran, North Korea, China, and Russia. Fifty-five years after Richard Bissell set Area 51 as a secret place to test-fly the nation's first peacetime spy planes, new aircraft continue to be built with singular design and similar intention. Despite the incredible advances in science and technology, the archetypal need for reconnaissance remains.

Quick and adaptable, twenty-first-century surveillance require-ments means the future of overhead lies in unmanned aerial vehi-cles, or drones. The overhead intelligence take once provided by CIA spy pilots like Gary Powers, Ken Collins, Frank Murray, and others now belongs to remotely piloted drones. The old film cam-eras, which relied on clear skies, have been replaced by state-of-the-art imaging systems developed by Sandia and Raytheon, called synthetic aperture radar, or SAR. These "cameras" relay real-time images shot through smoke, dust, and even clouds, during the day or in the dark of night. But as omnipotent and all-seeing as the drones may appear, there is one key element generally overlooked by the public—but certainly not by the Pentagon or the CIA—when considering the vulnerability of the Air Force's most valuable asset with wings. Drones require satellite links.

To operate a drone requires ownership in space. All unmanned aerial vehicles require satellites to relay information to and from the pilots who operate the drones via remote control. As the Predator flies over the war theater in the Middle East, it is being operated by a pilot sitting in a chair thirty miles south of Area 51, at Indian Springs. The pilot is seated in front of a computer screen that provides a visual representation of what the Predator is looking at on the ground in the battlefield halfway across the world. Two sensor operators sit beside the pilot, each working like a copilot might have in another age. The pilot and the sensor operators rely on a team of fifty-five airmen for operational support. The Predator Primary Satellite Link is the name of the system that allows communication between the drone and the team. The drone needs only to be in line of sight with its ground-control station when it lands. Everything else the drone can do, from capture images to fire missiles, it does thanks to its satellite link.

Indian Springs is the old airstrip where Dr. Edward Teller, father of the H-bomb, and all the other nuclear physicists used to land when they would come to witness their atomic bomb creations being set off as tests from 1951 to 1992. Indian Springs is where the atomic-sampling pilots trained to fly through mushroom clouds. It is where EG&G set up the first radar-testing facility on the Nevada Test and Training Range in 1954. Indian Springs is where Bob Lazar said he was taken and debriefed after getting caught trespassing on Groom Lake Road. And in 2011, Indian Springs, which has been renamed Creech Air Force Base, is the place where Air Force pilots sit in war rooms operating drones.

For the Department of Defense, the vulnerability of space satellites to sabotage has created a new and unprecedented threat.

According to a 2008 study on "Wicked Problems" prepared by the Defense Science Board, in a chapter significantly entitled "Surprise in Space," the board outlines the vulnerability of space satellites in today's world. By the Pentagon's definition, "Wicked problems are highly complex, wide-ranging problems that have no definitive formulation...and have no set solution." By their very nature, wicked problems are "substantially without precedent," meaning the outcome of them cannot be known because a wicked problem is one that has never before been solved. Worst of all, warned the Pentagon, efforts to solve wicked problems generally give way to an entirely new set of problems. The individual tasked with keeping abreast of the wicked problem is called a wicked engineer, someone who must be prepared to be surprised and be able to deal with unintended consequences because "playing the game changes the game."

By relying on satellites to fight the war on terror as well as many of the foreseeable conflicts in the immediate future, the single greatest wicked problem facing the Pentagon in the twenty-first century is the looming threat of the militarization of space. To weaponize space, historical thinking in the Pentagon goes, would be to safeguard space in a preemptive manner. A war in space over satellite control is not a war the United States necessarily wants to fight, but it is a war the United States is most assuredly unwilling to lose.

"Over eighty percent of the satellite communications used in U.S. Central Command's area of responsibility is provided by commercial vendors," reads the Pentagon's "Surprise in Space" report. And when, in 2007, the Chinese—unannounced and unexpectedly—shot down one of their own satellites with one of their own weapons, the incident opened the Pentagon's eyes to a whole host of potential wicked-problem scenarios in space.

Around 5:00 p.m. eastern standard time on July 11, 2007, a small, six-foot-long Chinese satellite was circling the Earth 539 miles up when it was targeted and destroyed by a Chinese ballistic missile launched from a mobile launcher at the Songlin test facility in Szechuan Province, running on solid fuel and topped with a "kinetic kill vehicle," or explosive device. The satellite was traveling at speeds of around sixteen thousand miles per hour, and the ballistic missile was traveling approximately eighteen thousand miles per hour. The hit was dead-on. As radical and impressive as it sounds, the technology was not what raised flags and eyebrows at the Pentagon. The significance of the event came from the fact that with China's satellite kill, the world moved one dangerous step closer to the very wicked problem of weaponizing space. To enter into that game means entering into the kind of mutual-assured-destruction military industrial–complex madness that has not been engaged in since the height of the Cold War.

Actions of this magnitude, certainly by those of a superpower like China, are almost always met by the U.S. military with a response, either overt or veiled, and the Chinese satellite kill was no exception. Seven months later, in February of 2008, an SM-3 Raytheon missile was launched off the deck of the USS *Lake Erie* in the North Pacific. It traveled approximately 153 miles up into space where it hit a five-thousand-pound U.S. satellite described as being about the size of a school bus and belonging to the National Reconnaissance Office. The official Pentagon story was that the satellite had gone awry and the United States didn't want the satellite's hazardous fuel source, stated to be the toxin hydrazine, to crash on foreign soil. "Our objective was to intercept the satellite, reduce the mass that might survive re-entry [and] vector that mass into unpopulated areas ideally the ocean," General James Cartwright, the vice chairman of the Joint Chiefs of Staff, told the press. International leaders cried foul, saying the test was designed to show the world that the United States has the technology to take out other nations' satellites. "China is continuously following closely the possible harm caused by the U.S. action to outer space security and relevant countries," declared Liu Jianchao, China's foreign ministry spokesman—certainly an example of the pot calling the kettle black.

In the 1950s, the United States and the Soviet Union actually considered using space as a launching pad for war. President Eisenhower's science adviser James Killian—a man with so much power that he was not required to tell the truth to Congress—fielded regular suggestions from the Pentagon to develop, in his own words, "satellite bombers, military bases on the moon, and so on." Killian was the man who spearheaded the first nuclear weapon explosions in space, first in the upper atmosphere (Orange), then near the ozone layer (Teak), and finally in outer space (Argus). But Killian shied away from the idea of weaponizing space not because he saw putting weapons in space as an inherently reckless or existentially bad idea but because Killian believed nuclear weapons would not work well from space.

"A satellite cannot simply drop a bomb," Killian declared in a public service announcement released from the White House on March 26, 1958, a report written for "nontechnical" people at the behest of the president. "An object released from a satellite doesn't fall. So there is no special advantage in being over the target," Killian declared. Here was James Killian, who, by his own admission, was not a scientist, explaining to Americans why dropping bombs from space wouldn't work. "Indeed the only way to 'drop' a bomb directly down from a satellite is to carry out aboard the satellite a rocket launching of the magnitude required for an intercontinental missile." In other words, Killian was saying that to get an ICBM up to a launchpad in space was simply too cumbersome a process. Killian believed that the better way to put a missile on a target was to launch it from the ground. That the extra effort to get missiles in space wasn't worth the task. This may have been true in the 1950s, but decades later James Killian would be proven wrong.

Flash forward to 2011. Analysts with the United States Space Surveillance Network, which is located in an Area 51–like facility on the island of Diego Garcia in the Indian Ocean, spend all day, every day, 365 days a year, tracking more than eight thousand man-made objects orbiting the Earth. The USSS Network is responsible for detecting, tracking, cataloging, and identifying artificial objects orbiting Earth, including active and inactive satellites, spent rocket bodies, and space debris. After the Chinese shot down their own satellite in 2007, the network's job got considerably more complicated. The Chinese satellite kill produced an estimated thirty-five thousand pieces of one-centimeter-wide debris and another fifteen hundred pieces that were ten centimeters or more. "A one-centimeter object is very hard to track but can do considerable damage if it collides with any spacecraft at a high rate of speed," said Laura Grego, a scientist with the Global Security Program at the Union of Concerned Scientists. The United States said the NRO satellite it shot down did not create space debris because, being close to Earth when it was shot down, its pieces burned up as they reentered Earth's atmosphere.

These scenarios create another wicked problem for the U.S. military. Every modern nation relies on satellites to function. The synchronized encryption systems used by banks around the world rely on satellites. Weather forecasts are derived from satellite information, as is the ability of air traffic controllers to keep airplanes safely aloft. The U.S. global positioning system, or GPS, works on satellites, as will the European version of GPS, the Galileo positioning system, which will come online in 2012. The U.S. military relies on satellites not just for its drone programs but for almost all of its military communications worldwide. Were anyone to take down the satellite system, or even just a part of it, the world would see chaos and panic that would make *The War of the Worlds* seem tame. When considering the actions of the United States and the Soviet Union during the atomic buildup of the 1940s, '50s, and '60s—the nuclear hubris, the fiscal waste, and the imprudent public policy—it is nothing short of miraculous that the space-based nuclear tests of the late 1950s and early 1960s did not propel the two superpowers to fight for military control of space. Instead, in the last decades of the Cold War, the United States and the USSR worked with a tacit understanding that space was off-limits for warfare. Neither nation tried to put missiles on the moon. And neither nation shot down another nation's spy satellites. According to Colonel Leghorn, this is because "spy satellites launched into space were accepted as eyes in the skies that governments had to live with." The governments Leghorn is referring to are Russia and the United States. But today, allegiances and battle lines have been considerably redrawn. At least one enemy army, that of al-Qaeda, would rather die than live according to the superpowers' rules.

In spite of, or perhaps because of, his ninety-one years, Leghorn speaks with great authority. In addition to being considered the father of aerial reconnaissance, Leghorn founded the Itek Corporation in 1960, which developed the high-resolution photographic system for America's first reconnaissance satellite, Corona. The Corona program was highly successful and, most notably, was originally designed and run by Richard Bissell for the CIA at the same time he was in charge of operations at Area 51. After leaving the Air Force, Leghorn spent decades in the commercial-satellite business. From the satellite images produced by Itek satellites, the CIA learned that in order to escape scrutiny by America's eyes in the sky, many foreign governments moved their most secret military facilities underground.

Out in the Nevada desert, while the CIA redoubled its efforts at Area 51 to develop ground sensor technology and infrared tracking techniques to learn more about underground facilities (which also requires the use of drones), the Department of Defense and the Air Force got to work on a different approach. In the 1980s, the military worked to develop the bunker buster, a nuclear weapon designed to fire deep into Earth's surface, hit underground targets, and detonate belowground. Weapons designer Sandia was brought on board. It was called the W61 Earth Penetrator, and testing took place at Area 52 in 1988. The idea was to launch the earth-penetrator weapon from forty thousand feet above but after many tests (minus the nuclear warhead), it became clear that a nuclear bomb would have little or no impact on granite, which is the rock of choice in which to build sensitive sites underground. After President Clinton ended all U.S. nuclear testing in 1993 (the Comprehensive Nuclear-Test-Ban Treaty was adopted by the United Nations General Assembly in 1996 and signed by five of the then seven or eight nuclear-capable countries), the idea of developing an earth-penetrating nuclear weapon lost its steam. But the building of underground facilities by foreign governments continued to plague war planners, so along came a nonnuclear space-based weapons project called Rods from God. That weapons project involved slender metal rods, thirty feet long and one foot in diameter, that could be launched from a satellite in space and hit a precise target on Earth at ten thousand miles per second. T. D. Barnes says "that's enough force to take out Iran's nuclear facility, or anything like it, in one or two strikes." The Federation of American Scientists reported that a number of similar "long-rod penetration" programs are believed to currently exist.

After the Gulf War, DARPA hired a secretive group called the JASON scholars (a favored target in conspiracy-theorist circles) and its parent company, MITRE Corporation, to report on the status of underground facilities, which in government nomenclature are referred to as UGFs. The unclassified version of the April 1999 report begins, "Underground facilities are being used to conceal and protect critical activities that pose a threat to the United States." These threats, said JASON, "include the development and storage of weapons of mass destruction, principally nuclear, chemical, and biological weapons," and also that "the proliferation of such facilities is a legacy of the Gulf War." What this means is that the F-117 stealth bomber showed foreign governments "that almost any above ground facility is vulnerable to attack and destruction by precision guided weapons." For DARPA, this meant it was time to develop a new nuclear bunker buster—Comprehensive Nuclear-Test-Ban-Treaty or not.

In January of 2001, the Federation of American Scientists reported their concern over the disclosure that the nuclear weapons laboratories were working on low-yield nukes, or "mini-nukes," to target underground facilities despite the congressional ban against "research and development which could lead to the production by the United States of a new, low-yield nuclear weapon." Los Alamos fired back, claiming they could develop a mini-nuke conceptually. "One could design and deploy a new set of nuclear weapons that do not require nuclear testing to be certified," stated Los Alamos associate director for nuclear weapons Stephen M. Younger, asserting that "such simple devices would be based on a very limited nuclear test database." The Federation of American Scientists saw Younger's assertion as improbable: "It seems unlikely that a warhead capable of performing such an extraordinary mission as destroying a deeply buried and hardened bunker could be deployed without full-scale [nuclear] testing" first. On July 1, 2006, Stephen Younger became president of National Security Technologies, or NSTec, the company in charge of operations at the Nevada Test Site, through 2012.

In 2002, with America again at war, the administration of George W. Bush revived the development of the nuclear bunker-buster weapon, now calling it the Robust Nuclear Earth Penetrator. In April of the same year, the Department of Defense entered into discussions with the Lawrence Livermore National Laboratory to begin preliminary design work on the new nuclear weapon. By fiscal year 2003, the Stockpile Services Robust Nuclear Earth Penetrator line item received $14.5 million; in 2004 another $7.5 million; and in 2005 yet another $27.5 million. In 2006, the Senate dropped the line item. Either the program was canceled or it got a new name and entered into the black world—perhaps at Area 51 and Area 52.

Or perhaps next door at the Nevada Test Site, underground. For as far-fetched and ironic as this sounds—developing a bunker-busting nuclear bomb at an underground nuclear testing facility in Nevada—this is exactly what DOE officials proposed in an unclassified report released quietly in 2005. In this report, officials with the agency formerly known as the Atomic Energy Commission proposed to revive the NERVA program—the Area 25 nuclear-powered rocket program designed to send man to Mars—and to do it, of all places, underground.

Unlike the NERVA program of the 1960s, argued Michael Williams, the author of the report, "DOE Ground Test facilities for space exploration enabling nuclear technologies can no longer be vented to the open atmosphere," meaning a facility like the one that previously existed out at Jackass Flats was out of the question. But for the new NERVA project, Williams proposed, the Department of Energy could easily conduct its nuclear tests inside "the existing [underground] tunnels or new tunnels at the Nevada Test site for this purpose."

Former Los Alamos associate director of nuclear weapons Stephen Younger, who currently serves as the president of operations at the Nevada Test Site, categorically denies that any underground nuclear weapons tests are in the works at the test site. But he does confirm that "subcritical" nuclear tests currently take place there, inside an underground tunnel complex located beneath Area 1. To access that facility, Younger says, employees use an elevator that travels a thousand feet underground. What goes on there are "scientific experiments with plutonium and high explosives," Younger says, "not weapons tests." Younger insists the "same cannot be said about the Russians." He says that inside their underground facility at Novaya Zemlya—the location where the Soviet Union detonated their fifty-megaton thermonuclear bomb, called Tsar Bomba, in 1961—"the Russians are developing new nuclear weapons around the clock. Mr. [Vladimir] Putin has said that repeatedly. He keeps saying that because they want us to know."

There is no way to know precisely what is happening today at the Nevada Test and Training Range—aboveground at Area 51 or Area 52, or in the underground tunnels beneath the test site, because most of what is currently happening out in the Nevada desert is classified and the federal agencies involved believe the people do not have a need-to-know. The question is, does the public have a right to know? Does Congress? Many secret projects that have gone on at Area 51 have delivered results that have kept America safe. The first flight over the Soviet Union, by Hervey Stockman in a U-2 spy plane in 1956, provided the CIA with critical intelligence, namely, that the Russians were not lining up their military machine for a sneak attack. The intelligence provided by an A-12 Oxcart spy plane mission kept the Johnson administration from declaring war on North Korea during the Vietnam War. The F-117 stealth bomber crippled Saddam Hussein's WMD programs. But there are other kinds of secret actions that have gone on at Area 51, at least one of which should never have been authorized and should not be kept as a national secret anymore.

★ ★ ★

After World War II, the American government's hiring and protection of Nazi scientists was based on the premise that these scientists were the world's best and their information was needed in order to advance science—and win the next war. In doing so, America made a deal with the devil. This deal became a wicked problem for the agencies involved, and playing the game with former Nazis gave way to an entirely new set of problems, one of which has been the federal government's ongoing complicity in covering up many of these scientists' original crimes. Approximately six hundred million pages of information about the government's postwar use of Nazi criminals' expertise remains classified as of 2011. Many documents about Area 51 exist in that pile.

The reason why the federal government will not officially admit that Area 51 exists is not the secret spy planes, the stealth bombers, or the drones that were, and still are, flight-tested there. The reason is something else. It is a program undertaken by five EG&G engineers at Area 51. This program involved the Roswell crash remains and predated the development of the original CIA facility, currently called Area 51, which was built by Richard Bissell beginning in 1955. Area 51 is named as such not because it was a randomly chosen quadrant, as has often been presumed, but because the 1947 crash remains from Roswell, New Mexico, were sent from Wright-Patterson Air Force Base out to a secret spot in the Nevada desert—in 1951.

The gypsies have a saying: You're not really dead until the last person who knows you dies. For investigative journalists it goes something like this: As long as there is an eyewitness willing to tell the truth, the truth can be known.

The flying craft that crashed in New Mexico, the myth of which has come to be known as the Roswell Incident, happened in 1947, sixty-four years before the publication of this book. Everyone directly involved in that incident—who acted on behalf of the government—is apparently dead. Like it does about Area 51, the U.S. government refuses to admit the Roswell crash ever happened, but it did—according to the seminal testimony of one man interviewed over the course of eighteen months for this book. He participated in the engineering project that came about as a result of the Roswell Incident. He was one of the elite engineers from EG&G who were tasked with the original Area 51 wicked engineering problem.

In July of 1947, Army intelligence spearheaded the efforts to retrieve the remains of the flying disc that crashed at Roswell. And as with other stories that have become the legends of Area 51, part of the conspiracy theory about Roswell has its origins in truth. The crash did reveal a disc, not a weather balloon, as has subsequently been alleged by the Air Force. And responders from the Roswell Army Air Field found not only a crashed craft, but also two crash sites, and they found bodies alongside the crashed craft. These were not aliens. Nor were they consenting airmen. They were human guinea pigs. Unusually petite for pilots, they appeared to be children. Each was under five feet tall. Physically, the bodies of the aviators revealed anatomical conundrums. They were grotesquely deformed, but each in the same manner as the others. They had unusually large heads and abnormally shaped oversize eyes. One fact was clear: these children, if that's what they were, were not healthy humans. A second fact was shocking. Two of the child-size aviators were comatose but still alive.

Everything related to the crash site was sent to Wright Field, later called Wright-Patterson Air Force Base, in Ohio, where it all remained until 1951. That is when the evidence was packed up and transported to the Nevada Test Site. It was received, physically, by the elite group of EG&G engineers. The Atomic Energy Commission, not the Air Force and not the Central Intelligence Agency, was put in charge of the Roswell crash remains. According to its unusual charter, the Atomic Energy Commission was the organization best equipped to handle a secret that could never be declassified. The Atomic Energy Commission needed engineers they could trust to handle the work that was about to begin. For this, they looked to the most powerful defense contractor in the nation that no one had ever heard of—EG&G.

The engineers with EG&G were chosen to receive the crash

remains and to set up a secret facility just outside the boundary of the Nevada Test Site, sixteen miles to the northwest of Groom Lake, approximately five and a half miles north of the northernmost point where Area 12 and Area 15 meet. A facility this remote would never be visited by anyone outside a small group with a strict need-to-know and would never have to be accounted for or appear on any official Nevada Test Site map. These five men were told there was more engineering work to be done, and that they would be the only five individuals with a set of keys to the facility. The project, the men were told, was the most clandestine, most important engineering program since the Manhattan Project, which was why the man who had been in charge of that one would function as the director of this project as well.

Vannevar Bush had been President Roosevelt's most trusted science adviser during World War II. He held engineering doctorates from both Harvard University and MIT, in addition to being the former vice president and former dean of engineering at MIT. The decisions Vannevar Bush made were ostensibly for the good of the nation; they were sound. The men from EG&G were told that the project they were about to work on was so important that it would remain black forever, meaning it would never see the light of day. The men knew that a secrecy classification inside the Atomic Energy Commission charter made this possible, because they all worked on classified engineering projects that were hidden from the rest of the world. They understood *born classified* meant that no one would ever have a need-to-know what Vannevar Bush was going to ask them to do. The operation would have no name, only a letter-number designation: S-4, or Sigma-Four.

The problem that the EG&G engineers would face would be highly complex, wide-ranging, without a definite formulation and with no set solution. This wicked problem was wholly without precedent. Solving it would undoubtedly have unintended consequences, because playing the engineering game would change the game. But there were two puzzles to solve, not just one. Two engineering mysteries for the elite group of EG&G engineers to unlock.

There was the crashed craft that had been sent by Stalin—with its Russian writing stamped, or embossed, in a ring around the inside of the craft. So far, the EG&G engineers were told, no one working on the project when it had been headquartered at Wright-Patterson Air Force Base had been able to discern what made Stalin's craft hover and fly. Not even the German Paperclip scientists who had been assigned to assist. So the crashed craft was job number one. Reverse engineer it, Vannevar Bush said. Take it apart and put it back together again. Figure out what made it fly.

But there was the second engineering problem to solve, the one involving the child-size aviators. To understand this, the men were briefed on what it was they were dealing with. They had to be. They were told that they, and they alone, had a need-to-know about what had happened to these humans before they were put in the craft and sent aloft. They were told that seeing the bodies would be a shocking and disturbing experience. Because two of the aviators were comatose but still alive, the men would have to transfer them into a Jell-O-like substance and stand them upright in two tubular tanks, attached to a life-support system. Sometimes, their mouths opened, and this gave the appearance of their trying to speak. Remember, the engineers were told, these humans are in a comatose state. They are unconscious; their bodies would never spark back to life.

Once, the children had been healthy humans. Not anymore. They were about thirteen years old. Questions abounded. What made their heads so big? Had their bodies been surgically manipulated to appear inhuman, or did the children have genetic deformities? And what about their haunting, oversize eyes? The engineers were told that the children were rumored to have been kidnapped by Dr. Josef Mengele, the Nazi madman who, at Auschwitz and elsewhere, was known to have performed unspeakable experimental surgical procedures mostly on children, dwarfs, and twins. The engineers learned that just before the war ended, Josef Mengele made a deal with Stalin. Stalin offered Mengele an opportunity to continue his work in eugenics—the science of improving a human population by controlled breeding to increase desirable, heritable characteristics—

in secret, in the Soviet Union after the war. The engineers were told that this deal likely occurred just before the war's end, in the winter of 1945, when it was clear to many members of the Nazi Party, including Mengele, that Nazi Germany would lose the war and that its top commanders and doctors would be tried and hanged for war crimes.

In Josef Mengele's efforts to create a pure, Aryan race for Hitler, at Auschwitz and elsewhere, he conducted experiments on people he considered subhuman so as to breed certain features out. Mengele's victims included Jewish children, Gypsy children, and people with severe physical deformities. He removed parts of children's craniums and replaced them with bones from larger, adult skulls. He removed and transplanted eyeballs, and injected people with chemicals that caused them to lose their hair. On Mengele's instruction, an Auschwitz inmate, a painter named Dina Babbitt, made comparative drawings of the shapes of heads, noses, mouths, and ears of people before and after the grotesque surgeries Mengele performed. Another inmate doctor forced to work for Mengele, named Dr. Martina Puzyna, recounted how Mengele had her keep detailed measurements of the shapes and sizes of children's body parts, casting those of crippled children—particularly their hands and heads—in plaster molds. When Mengele left Auschwitz, on January 17, 1945, he took the documentation of his medical experiments with him. According to his only son, Rolf, Mengele was still in possession of his medical research documents after the war.

The EG&G engineers were told that part of Joseph Stalin's offer to Josef Mengele stated that if he could create a crew of grotesque, child-size aviators for Stalin, he would be given a laboratory in which to continue his work. According to what the engineers were told, Mengele held up his side of the Faustian bargain and provided Stalin with the child-size crew. Joseph Stalin did not. Mengele never took up residence in the Soviet Union. Instead, he lived for four years in Germany under an assumed name and then escaped to South America, where he lived, first in Argentina and then in Paraguay, until his death in 1979.

When Joseph Stalin sent the biologically and/or surgically

reengineered children in the craft over New Mexico hoping it would land there, the engineers were told, Stalin's plan was for the children to climb out and be mistaken for visitors from Mars. Panic would ensue, just like it did after the radio broadcast of *The War of the Worlds*. America's early-warning radar system would be overwhelmed with sightings of other "UFOs." Truman would see how easily a totalitarian dictator could control the masses using black propaganda. Stalin may have been behind the United States in atomic bomb technology, but when it came to manipulating the people's perception, Stalin was the leader with the upper hand. This, says the engineer, is what he and the others in the group were told.

For months I asked the engineer why President Truman didn't use the remains from the Roswell crash to show the world what an evil, abhorrent man Joseph Stalin was. I guessed that maybe Truman didn't want to admit the breach of U.S. borders. For a long time, I never got an answer, just a shaking of the head. Here was the engineer who had the answer to the riddle inside the riddle that is Area 51, but he was unwilling to say more. He is the only one of the original elite group of EG&G engineers who is still alive. He said he wouldn't tell me more, no matter how many times I asked. One day, I asked again. "Why didn't President Truman reveal the truth in 1947?" This time he answered.

"Because we were doing the same thing," he said. "They wanted to push science. They wanted to see how far they could go."

Then he said, "We did things I wish I had not done."

Then, "We performed medical experiments on handicapped children and prisoners."

"But you are not a doctor," I said.

"They wanted engineers."

"On whose authority did you act?"

"The Atomic Energy Commission was in charge. And Vannevar Bush," he said. "People were killed. In this great United States."

"Why did we do that?"

"You do what you do because you love your country, and you

are told what you are doing is for the good of the country," the engineer said. Meaning out at the original Area 51, starting in 1951, the EG&G engineers worked in secret on a nefarious Nazi-inspired black project that would remain entirely hidden from the public because Vannevar Bush told them it was the correct thing to do.

"It was a long, long time ago," the engineer said. "I have tried to forget."

"When did it end?" I asked.

No answer.

"In 1952?" I asked. Still no answer. "In 1953...1954...?"

"At least through the 1980s it was still going on," he said.

"I believe you should tell me the whole story," I said. "Otherwise, once you are gone, you will take the truth with you."

"You don't want to know," he said.

"I do."

"You don't have a need-to-know," he said.

For many months, I tried to learn more. I got pieces. Slivers of pieces. One-word details. "This" confirmed and "that" reconfirmed, regarding what he had previously said. One day, when we were eating lunch in a restaurant, I recounted back to the engineer everything I knew. I asked for his permission to put it all in this book. He did not say yes. He did not say no. We interviewed for more than one year. Then one day, I asked him how much of the story I now knew.

"You don't know half of it," he said sadly.

I took a crouton, left over from my lunch, and set it down in the middle of the restaurant's white china plate. "If what I know equals this crouton," I said, pointing at the little brown piece of bread, "then is what I don't know as big as this plate?"

"Oh, my dear," he said, shaking his head. "The whole truth is bigger than this table we are eating on, including the chairs."

He wouldn't say more. He said he was hurting. That soon he would die. That, really, it was best that I did not learn any more because I didn't have a need-to-know. But it is not just me who needs to know. We need to be able to keep secrets, but this kind of secret-keeping—of this kind of secret—is the work of totalitarian states, like the one we fought against for five decades during the Cold War. Fighting totalitarianism was America's rationale for building seventy thousand nuclear weapons in sixty-five styles. In a free and open democratic society, conducting projects in the name of science is one thing. Keeping forty-year-old secrets from a president even after he tries to find them out is an entirely different problem for a democratic nation. It sets a precedent. It makes it easier for a group of powerful men to set up a program that defies the Constitution and defiles morality in the name of science and national security, all under the deceptive cover that no one has a need-to-know. I believe that even though the engineer didn't tell me everything, that is why he told me what he did.

According to my source, the Atomic Energy Commission conducted experiments on humans in a classified government facility in the Nevada desert beginning in 1951. Although this was done in direct violation of the Nuremberg Code of 1947, it is far from the first time the Commission had acted in violation of the most basic moral principle involving voluntary human consent. In 1993, reporter Eileen Welsome wrote a newspaper story stating that the Atomic Energy Commission had conducted plutonium experiments on human beings, most notably retarded children and orphan boys from the Fernald State School, outside Boston, without the children's or their guardians' knowledge or consent. After this horrible revelation came to light, President Clinton opened an investigation to look into what the Atomic Energy Commission had done and the secrets it had been able to safeguard inside its terrifying and unprecedented system of secret-keeping. I asked the engineer why President Clinton hadn't learned about the S-4 facility at Area 51 — or had he?

"I think he might have come very close," the engineer said about President Clinton. "But they kept it from him."

"Who are *they?*" I asked. The engineer told me that his elite group had been given the keys to the original facility at Area 51. "Who inherited those keys from you five engineers?" I wanted to know.

"You don't have a need-to-know" is all he would say.

EPILOGUE

I n the summer of 2010 a book arrived in the mail from Colonel
Leghorn, the father of overhead reconnaissance, age ninety-one.
The pages were musty and smelled like an attic. What he had
sent was his 1946 Army Air Forces commemorative yearbook from
the Operation Crossroads atomic bomb tests. What is most striking
is how the story of America's first postwar nuclear test begins as a
"mysterious Army-Navy assignment" in a "sand-swept town—
Roswell."

"Roswell . . . Roswell . . . Roswell . . . Roswell . . . Roswell . . .
Roswell."

The word repeats six times in the first few pages of the
government-issued yearbook, making it clear that it was from the
Roswell Army Air Field in New Mexico that the first shot in what
would be a forty-three-year-old Cold War was fired. And what a
colossal opening shot Operation Crossroads was, an unprecedented
show of force aimed at letting Joseph Stalin know that America
was not done with the nuclear bomb. Forty-two thousand people
were present in the Pacific for the two nuclear bomb tests, including

Stalin's spies. The U.S. government spent nearly two billion dollars (adjusted for inflation) to show the world the nuclear power it now possessed.

"Stalin learned from Hitler," the EG&G engineer says, "revenge... and other things." And that to consider Stalin's perspective one should think about two key moments in history, one right before World War II began and another right before it ended. On August 23, 1939, one week before war in Europe officially began, Hitler and Stalin agreed to be allies and signed the Molotov-Ribbentrop Pact, meaning each country promised not to attack the other when war in Europe broke out. And yet almost immediately after shaking hands, Hitler began plotting to double-cross Stalin. Twenty-two months later, Hitler's sneak attack against Russia resulted in millions of deaths. And then, just a few weeks before World War II ended, Stalin, Truman, and Churchill met in Potsdam, Germany—from July 17, 1945, to August 2, 1945—and agreed to be postwar allies. Just one day before that conference began, America had secretly tested the world's first and only atomic bomb, inside the White Sands Proving Ground in the New Mexico desert. Truman's closest advisers had suggested that Truman share the details of the atomic test with Stalin at Potsdam, but Truman did not. It didn't matter. Nuclear weapons historians believe that Joseph Stalin was already well aware of what the Manhattan Project engineers had accomplished. Stalin had spies inside the Los Alamos nuclear laboratory who had been providing him with bomb blueprints and other information since 1941. By the time the Potsdam conference rolled around, Stalin was already well at work on his own atomic bomb. Despite Stalin and Truman pretending to be allies, neither side trusted the other side, neither man trusted the other man. Each side was instead making plans to build up its own atomic arsenal for future use. When Operation Crossroads commenced just twelve months after the handshakes at Potsdam, the Cold War battle lines were already indelibly drawn.

It follows that Stalin's black propaganda hoax—the flying disc peopled with alien look-alikes that wound up crashing near Roswell,

New Mexico—could have been the Soviet dictator's revenge for Truman's betrayal at Crossroads. His double cross had to have been in the planning stages during the handshaking at Potsdam, metaphorically mirroring what Hitler had done during the signing of the Molotov-Ribbentrop Pact. By July of 1947, Stalin was still two years away from being able to successfully test his own nuclear bomb. The flying disc at Roswell, says the EG&G engineer, was "a warning shot across Truman's bow." Stalin may not have had the atomic bomb just yet, but he had seminal hover and fly technology, pilfered from the Germans, *and* he had stealth. Together, these technologies made the American military gravely concerned. Perplexed by the flying disc's movements, and its radical ability to confuse radar, the Army Air Forces was left wondering what else Stalin had in his arsenal of unconventional weapons, usurped from the Nazis after the war.

"Hitler invented stealth," says Gene Poteat, the first CIA officer in the Agency's history to be assigned to the National Reconnaissance Office, or NRO. Gene Poteat's job was to assess Soviet radar threats, and to do this, he observed many spy plane tests at Area 51. "Hitler's stealth bomber was called the Horten Ho 229," Poteat says, "which is also called the Horten flying wing. It was covered with radar-absorbing paint, carbon embedded in glue. The high graphic content produced a result called 'ghosting,' which made it difficult for radar to see."

The Horten Ho 229 to which Poteat refers was the brainchild of two young aircraft designers who worked for Hitler's Luftwaffe, Walter and Reimar Horten. These are the same two brothers who, in the fall of 1947, became the subject of the U.S. Army Intelligence's massive European manhunt called "Operation Harass"— the search for a flying-saucer-type aircraft that could allegedly hover and fly.

Whatever happened to the Horten brothers? Unlike so many Nazi scientists and engineers who were recruited under Operation Paperclip, Walter and Reimar Horten were originally overlooked. After being captured by the U.S. Ninth Army on April 7, 1945, at their workshop in Göttingen, they were set up in a guarded London high-rise near Hyde Park. There, they were interrogated by the famous American physicist and rocket scientist Theodore Von Kármán, who decided the Horten brothers did not have much to offer the U.S. Army Air Forces by way of aircraft technology—at least not with their flying wing. After being returned to Germany, Reimar escaped to Argentina, where he was set up in a beautiful house on the shores of Villa Carlos Paz Lake, thanks to Argentinean president and ardent Nazi supporter Juan Perón. Walter lived out his life in Baden-Baden, Germany, hiding in plain sight.

The information about the Horten brothers comes from the aircraft historian David Myhra, who, in his search to understand all-wing aircraft, industriously tracked down both Horten brothers, visited them in their respective countries in the 1980s, and recorded hundreds of hours of interviews with them on audiotape. These tapes can be found in the archives of the Smithsonian Air and Space Museum.

"Reimar had me agree to two restrictions before I went to South America to interview him," Myhra explains. "One was that I couldn't ask questions about Hitler or the Third Reich." And the second was that "he said he didn't want to talk about the CIA. Reimar said there was this crazy idea that he'd designed some kind of a flying saucer and that the CIA had [supposedly] been looking for him." Myhra says Reimar Horten was adamant in his refusal to discuss anything related to the CIA. "The subject was off-limits for him," Myhra says. The conversation with Reimar Horten that Myhra refers to took place in the decade before Army Intelligence released to the public its three-hundred-page file on Operation Harass. This is the file that discusses the U.S. manhunt for the Horten brothers and their so-called flying disc. The Operation Harass file makes clear that someone from an American intelligence organization made contact with Reimar in the late 1940s to interrogate him about the flying disc. More than forty years later, Reimar Horten still refused to talk about what was said. A 2010 Freedom of Information Act request to the Department of the

Army, Office of the General Counsel, Army Pentagon, issued a "no records response." A secondary appeal was also "denied."

If Stalin really did get the Horten brothers' flying disc, either from the brothers themselves or from blueprints they had drawn, how did Stalin get their flying disc to hover and fly on like that? What became of the craft's hover technology, powered by some mysterious power plant, which was also so fervently sought by Counter Intelligence Corps agents during Operation Harass? The EG&G engineer says that while he does not know what research was conducted on the "equipment" when it was at Wright-Patterson, beginning in 1947, he does know about the research conducted on the "power plant" after he received the "equipment," in Nevada in 1951.

"There was another [important] EG&G engineer," he explains. That engineer was assigned the task of learning about Stalin's hover technology, "which was called electromagnetic frequency, or EMF." This engineer "spent an entire year in a windowless room" inside an EG&G building in downtown Las Vegas trying to understand how EMF worked. "We figured it out," the EG&G engineer says. "We've had hover and fly technology all this time."

I asked the EG&G engineer to take me to the place where hover and fly technology was allegedly solved, and he did. Archival photographs and Atomic Energy Commission video footage confirm that the site once contained several buildings that were operated by EG&G. Not anymore. Instead, the facility inside of which an EG&G engineer unlocked one of Area 51's original secrets in the early 1950s is now nothing but an empty lot of asphalt and weeds ringed by a chain-link fence. Is this what will become of Area 51 in sixty years? Will it too be moved? Will it go underground? Has it already?

What about flying saucers from a physicist's point of view? Edward Lovick, the grandfather of America's stealth technology, says that in the late 1950s, Kelly Johnson had him spend many months in Lockheed's anechoic chamber radar testing small-scale models of flying saucers. "Little wooden discs built in the Skunk

Works wood shop," Lovick recalls. According to Lovick, Kelly Johnson eventually decided that round-shaped aircraft—flying discs without wings—were aerodynamically unstable and therefore too dangerous for pilots to fly. This was before the widespread use of pilotless aircraft, or drones.

What about the child-size pilots inside the flying disc? Shortly after the Roswell crash in July 1947, a press officer from the Roswell Army Air Field, a man named Walter Haut, was dispatched to the radio station KGFL in Roswell with a press release saying the Roswell Army Air Force was in possession of a flying disc. Haut was the emissary of the original Roswell Statement, which, in addition to being broadcast over the airwaves, was famously printed in the *San Francisco Chronicle* the following day. It was Walter Haut who, three hours later, was sent back to KGFL by the commander of the Army Air Field with a second press release, one that said that the first press release was actually incorrect.

Walter Haut died in December 2005 and left a sworn affidavit to be opened only after his death. In the text, Haut said the second press release was fraudulent, meant to cover up the first statement, which was true. Haut also said that in addition to recovering a flying craft, the military recovered bodies from a second crash site— small, child-size bodies with disproportionately large heads. "I am convinced that what I personally observed was some kind of craft and its crew from outer space," Haut wrote.

The EG&G engineer's explanation about the child pilots inside the flying disc answers the riddle of the so-called Roswell aliens, certainly in a manner that would satisfy the fourteenth-century English friar and philosopher William of Ockham. It is an answer that is not more complicated than the riddle itself. According to the EG&G engineer, the aviators were not aliens but were created to look like them, by Josef Mengele, "shortly before or immediately after the end of the war." Children would have had great difficulty piloting an aircraft. The engineer says he was told the flying disc was piloted remotely, but offered almost no information about what would have had to have been the larger aircraft from which this early "drone" was launched. "It came down over Alaska," he says.

What about Bob Lazar? In the course of interviewing thirty-two individuals who lived and worked at Area 51, I asked the majority what they thought of Lazar's 1989 revelation about Area 51. Most made highly skeptical comments about Bob Lazar; none claimed ever to have met him. While it appears that Lazar lied about his education, his statements about S-4 should not be summarily dismissed as fraud.

The EG&G engineer says that the S-4 facility that housed the original Roswell "equipment" continued on for decades, which fits with Bob Lazar's time line. Lazar says he worked at Area 51 from 1988 to 1989. Lazar told newsman George Knapp that at S-4, he saw something through a window, inside an unmarked room, that could have been an alien. Was what happened to Lazar just like what happened to the P-38 Lightning pilot who, flying over the California desert during the dawn of the jet age, thought he saw a gorilla flying an airplane when really he saw Bell Aircraft chief test pilot Jack Woolams wearing a gorilla mask? Perhaps Lazar drew the only conclusion he could have drawn based on the information he had. And perhaps the Atomic Energy Commission had taken a page out of the CIA's playbook on deception campaigns: it needed to produce the belief that something false was something true. Perhaps scientists and engineers who were brought to S-4 in the later years were told that they were working on alien beings and alien spacecraft. Try going public with that story and you will wind up disgraced like Bob Lazar. As it was with the P-38 Lightning pilots in 1942, it remains today. No one likes being mistaken for a fool.

"It's difficult to be taken seriously in the scientific community when you're known as 'the UFO guy,'" Bob Lazar stated on the record in 2010 for this book.

For decades, hundreds of serious people—civilians, lawmakers, and military personnel—have made considerable efforts to locate the records for the Roswell crash remains. And yet no such record group has ever been located, despite formal investigations by senators, congressmen, the governor of New Mexico, and the federal government's Government Accountability Office. This is because no one has known where to look. Until now, the world has been knocking on the wrong door. The information has been protected from declassification by draconian Atomic Energy Commission classification rules, hidden inside secret Restricted Data files that were originally created for the Atomic Energy Commission by EG&G.

So now it is known.

How did Vannevar Bush get so much power? He was once the most important scientist in America. President Truman awarded him the Medal for Merit in a White House ceremony, President Johnson presented him with the National Medal of Science, and the queen of England dubbed him a knight. The statements made by the EG&G engineer about what Vannevar Bush authorized engineers and scientists to do at Area 51's S-4 facility are truly shocking and almost unbelievable. Except a clear historical precedent exists for Vannevar Bush having exactly this kind of power, secrecy, and control.

Vannevar Bush lorded over the mother of all black operations—the engineering of the world's first nuclear bomb. And as director of the Office of Scientific Research and Development, which controlled the Manhattan Project, Vannevar Bush was also in charge of human experiments to study the effects of the bioweapons lewisite and mustard gas on man. Some of those human guinea pigs were soldiers and others were conscientious objectors to the war, but a 1993 study of these programs by the National Academy of Sciences made clear that the test subjects were not consenting adults. "Although the human subjects were called 'volunteers,' it was clear from the official reports that recruitment of the World War II human subjects, as well as those in the later experiments, was accomplished through lies and half-truths," wrote the Institute of Medicine.

The "later experiments" to which the committee refers were

conducted by a group also under Vannevar Bush's direction, this one called the Committee on Medical Research. As discovered by President Clinton's advisory committee on human experiments, this so-called medical research involved using as guinea pigs individuals living at the Dixon Institution for the Retarded, in Illinois, and at the New Jersey State Colony for the Feeble-Minded. The doctors were testing vaccines for malaria, influenza, and sexually transmitted diseases. Some programs continued until 1973.

Even more troubling is this: buried in Atomic Energy Commission archives is the fact that the first incarnation of the Manhattan Project had a letter-number designation of S-1. Were there two other programs that transpired between S-1 and S-4? And if so, what were they? What else might have been done to push science in a way that the ends could justify the means?

In this book, many pieces of the Area 51 puzzle are put into place, but many questions remain. What goes on at Area 51 now? We don't know. We won't know for decades. Airplanes have gotten faster and stealthier. Remote-controlled spy planes fire missiles. Classified delivery systems drop bombs. The players are mostly the same: CIA, Air Force, Department of Energy, Lockheed, North American, General Atomics, and Hughes. These are but a few.

The biggest players tend to remain, as always, behind the veil. Almost a century ago, in 1922, Vannevar Bush cofounded a company that contracted first with the military and later with the Atomic Energy Commission. He called his company Raytheon because it meant "light from the gods." Raytheon has always maintained a considerable presence at the Nevada Test Site, the Nevada Test and Training Range, and Area 51. Currently, it is the fifth-biggest defense contractor in the world. It is the world's largest producer of guided missiles and the leader in developing radar technology for America's early-warning defense system. This is the same system that, in the 1950s, CIA director General Walter Bedell Smith feared the Soviets might overrun with a UFO hoax, leaving the nation vulnerable to an air attack.

As for EG&G, they were eventually acquired by the powerful

Carlyle Group at the end of the twentieth century but later resold, in 2002, to another corporate giant called URS. Currently, EG&G remains partnered with Raytheon in a joint venture at the Nevada Test and Training Range and at Area 51. The program, called JT3—Joint Test, Tactics, and Training, LLC—provides "engineering and technical support for the Nevada Test and Training Range," according to corporate brochures. When asked what exactly that means, EG&G's parent company, URS, declined to comment. This is corporate America's way of saying, "You don't have a need-to-know."

The veil has been lifted. The curtain has been pulled back on Area 51. But what has been revealed in this book is like a single bread crumb in a trail. There is so much more that remains unknown. Where does the trail lead? How far does it go? Will it ever end?

ACKNOWLEDGMENTS

Many have asked me how this book came to be. In 2007, I was at a Christmas Eve dinner when my husband's uncle's wife's sister's husband—a spry physicist named Edward Lovick, who was eighty-eight years old at the time—leaned over to me and said, "Have I got a good story for you." As a national security reporter, I hear this line frequently—my work depends on it—but what Lovick told me ranked among the most surprising and tantalizing things I'd heard in a long time. Until then, I was under the impression that Lovick had spent his life designing airplane parts. Over dinner I learned that he was actually a physicist and that he'd played a major role in the development of aerial espionage for the CIA. The reason Lovick could suddenly divulge information that had been kept secret for fifty years was because the CIA had just declassified it. When I learned that much of Lovick's clandestine work took place at that mysterious and mythic location Area 51, also called Groom Lake, I smiled. So, the place was real after all. Immediately, I wrote to the Office of the Assistant Secretary of Defense requesting an official tour of the Groom

Lake Area—Lovick also told me that the CIA had given up control of the place decades earlier. My request was formally denied, on Department of Defense letterhead, but oddly with the words "the Groom Lake Area" separated out in quotes attributed to me, so as to make clear the Pentagon's official position regarding their Nevada base: *That locale may be part of your lexicon,* they seemed to be saying, *but it is most definitely not officially part of ours.* As an investigative journalist I sought to know why.

Since then, more individuals than I could have ever imagined have generously shared their Area 51 stories with me. I am indebted to each and every one of them. The list I thank includes everyone in this book: the legendary soldiers, spies, scientists, and engineers—professionals who, for the most part, are not known for sharing their inner lives. That so many individuals opened up with me—relaying their triumphs and tragedies, their sorrows and joys—so that others may make sense of it all has been an experience of a lifetime. Why I was given access to information that countless others have been denied remains a great mystery to me. A reporter is dependent on primary sources. From their stories, and using keywords such as operational cover names, I was then able to locate corroborating documents, often found deeply buried in U.S. government archives. I wouldn't have had a clue where to look without their aid. Specific examples are sourced in the Notes section.

T. D. Barnes is one of the most generous people I have met. He introduced me to many people, who in turn introduced me to their colleagues and friends. Barnes took me to Creech Air Force Base, at Indian Springs, Nevada, as part of a very private tour. There I was allowed to watch U.S. Air Force pilots fly drones halfway across the world, in Afghanistan and Iraq. Barnes also arranged for my tours of Nellis Air Force Base in Las Vegas, where I sat inside a Russian MiG fighter jet and examined the Hawk missile system and the F-117 Nighthawk up close. And it was Barnes who, in the fall of 2010, advocated tirelessly on my behalf to allow me to join a group of pilots and engineers at CIA headquarters in Langley, Virginia, and at the Defense Intelligence Agency Headquarters in Washington, DC, as part of a week-long symposium on overhead espionage. I met many people during this trip who were extraordinarily helpful to me, on background, and I thank them all.

Ken Collins lives in the same city as I do, which meant that for a year and a half I got to interview him regularly over lunch. He is a remarkable pilot and an even more extraordinary person. Thank you, Colonel Slater, Frank Murray, Roger Andersen, Tony Bevacqua, and Ray Goudey, for sharing so many unique flying stories with me. Thank you, Buzz Aldrin, for explaining to me what it feels like up there on the moon.

Al O'Donnell arranged for my temporary security clearance so that I could accompany him to the federally restricted land that is the Nevada Test Site. Looking into the Sedan nuclear crater—so vast it is visible from outer space—is not something I will ever forget. While Area 51, Area 25, and Area 13 were off-limits to us on that visit, that I was able even to get within a stone's throw of these three hidden places is thanks to O'Donnell. And a special thanks to Ruth, Al's very capable wife. From Jim Freedman I learned things that could be contained in their own book. Freedman has the unusual ability to share deeply personal experiences with stunning clarity, objectivity, and conviction. Once, he explained why: "I tell you all this, Annie, because you give a damn."

Dr. Bud Wheelon, the CIA's first deputy director of science and technology, has given only a few interviews in his life. I am grateful to have joined those ranks. During one of our interviews he stopped mid-story to thoroughly explain missile technology to me. From that moment on I understood what was at stake during the Cuban missile crisis. How close we came to nuclear war.

Lieutenant Colonel Hervey Stockman and Colonel Richard Leghorn are legends among legendary men. Colonel Leghorn generously shared with me artifacts he had stored away in his attic, shipping original photographs, long-lost articles, and out-of-print books across the country for my review. Thanks to his assistant, Barbara Austin, for her help. Hervey Stockman was not so easy to locate at first, but when I finally did reach him, on the telephone, it was a magical moment. Thank you, Peter Stockman, for sending me a copy of Hervey's oral history, which was an invaluable source of information.

For all the investigating that goes on in writing a book like this, sometimes the most sought-after information comes in the most whimsical of ways. In the summer of 2009, I went to the Nuclear Testing Archive library in Las Vegas to locate declassified documents on the Project 57 "dirty bomb" test, ones that were mysteriously missing from the Department of Energy's online repository. Even in person, the staff was unable to fulfill my records request. Hindered and frustrated, I took a walk around the adjacent atomic-testing museum to cool down. Reporter's notebook in hand, I was staring at a photograph of a mushroom cloud hanging on the wall when the museum's security guard walked up and said hello. It was Richard Mingus. We'd met briefly before, on an earlier visit. I told Mingus that I felt records on Project 57 were being withheld from me over at the library. In his characteristic matter-of-fact style Mingus said, "Well, I worked on that test. What is it you'd like to know?" Mingus, I quickly learned, was also one of the CIA's original Area 51 security guards. Thanks to Mingus, the "missing" Project 57 documents became easier to locate.

At the National Archives and Records Administration, thank you to Timothy Nenninger, chief of the Textual Records Reference Staff, Martha Murphy, chief of Special Access and FOIA Staff, and Tom Mills, who specializes in World War II records; thank you, Rita Cann, at the National Personnel Records Center in St. Louis, Missouri; Martha DeMarre of the Nuclear Testing Archive in Las Vegas; Troy Wade of the Nevada Test Site Historical Foundation; Tech Sergeant Jennifer Lindsey of the U.S. Air Force; Staff Sergeant Alice Moore, Creech Air Force Base; Dr. David R. Williams, NASA; Dr. David Robarge, chief historian, Central Intelligence Agency; Tony Hiley, curator and director of the CIA Museum; Cheryl Moore, EEA CIA; Jim Long, Laughlin Heritage Foundation Museum; R. Cargill Hall, historian emeritus, National

Reconnaissance Office; Dr. Craig Luther, chief historian, Edwards Air Force Base; S. Eugene Poteat, president of the Association of Former Intelligence Officers; Melissa Dalton, Lockheed Martin Aeronautics; Dr. Jeffrey Richelson, National Security Archives; David Myhra, author and aviation historian; Fred Burton, former special agent with the U.S. Diplomatic Security Service; Sherre Lovick, former Lockheed Skunk Works engineer; Colonel Adelbert W. "Buz" Carpenter, former SR-71 pilot; Charles "Chuck" Wilson, former U-2 pilot; Arthur Beidler, 67th Reconnaissance Tactical Squadron, Japan; Dennis Nordquist, Pratt & Whitney mechanical engineer; Tony Landis, NASA photographer; Michael Schmitz, Roadrunners Internationale photographer; Joerg Arnu, Norio Hayakawa, and Peter Merlin of Dreamlandresort.com. A special thank you to Doris Barnes, Barbara Slater, Stacy Slater Bernhardt, Stella Murray, Mary Martin, and Mary Jane Murphy. Thank you, Jeff King, for making me such an excellent map, and Ploy Siripant, for a phenomenal job on the jacket. Thank you Tommy Harron, Jerry Maybrook, and Jeremy Wesley for the great work on the audio book.

Once I completed a draft of this manuscript, my editor, John Parsley, helped me to refine it into the book that it is. What I learned from John about storytelling is immeasurable. Thank you also to Nicole Dewey, Geoff Shandler, and Michael Pietsch.

I owe a debt of gratitude to Jim Hornfischer, the perfect agent for someone like me, and to my confidant Frank Morse. Thank you for the wise counsel, Steve Younger, David Willingham, Aron Ketchel, Eric Rayman, and Karen Andrews.

It takes a village to make a writer. I'm one of the lucky ones who has always known writing is what I was meant to do. I arrived at St. Paul's School in Concord, New Hampshire, at the age of fifteen, typewriter in hand, and wrote for nearly twenty years straight without earning as much as one cent. Only at the age of thirty-four did things shift for me, and I've earned my living as a writer ever since. I say that for all of the writers following in my footsteps. Don't give up. My village fire keepers—those to whom I am deeply indebted for their individually imperative roles—include Alice and Tom Soininen, Julie Elkins, John Soininen; my writing teacher at St. Paul's School, Michael Burns, and at Princeton University, Paul Auster, Joyce Carol Oates, and P. Adams Sitney; my storytelling hero in Greece, John Zervos; those who supported me in Big Sur: Lisa Firestone, Thanis Iliadis, Alex Timken, Robert Jolliffe, Harriet and Jeremy Polturak, James Young, Nate Downey, Emmy Starr and Stephen Vehslage, Samantha Muldoon, Erin Gafill and Tom Birmingham; my mentors in Los Angeles: Rachel Resnick, Keith Rogers, Kathleen Silver, Rio Morse, and my friend and editor in chief at the *Los Angeles Times Magazine,* Nancie Clare, who commissioned my original two-part series on Area 51 for the magazine; my fellow writers from group: Kirston Mann, Sabrina Weill, Michelle Fiordaliso, Nicole Lucas Haimes, Annette Murphy, Terry Rossio, Jolly Stamat, Moira McMahon, Lisa Gold; fellow storyteller Lucy Firestone; my mother-in-law, Marion Wroldsen, not only for her deep love of reading but for lending me her son.

Nothing in this world is so joyful as being the wife of Kevin Jacobsen and the mother of our two boys. While writing this book, it was Kevin who made endless sandwiches for me, brewed pots of coffee, and let me travel to wherever it was that I needed to go. Kevin hears out every first draft, usually standing in our kitchen or yard. Everything gets better after I listen to what he has to say.

NOTES

Prologue: The Secret City

xi Nevada Test and Training Range: Map reference number NTTR01, NGA stock no. 84413.

xi Nevada Test Site: Map based on NTS Boundary Coordinates: FFACO, appendix 1, January 1998, revision 2, 6. On Aug 23, 2010, the Nevada Test Site changed its name to the Nevada National Security Site. Throughout the book, I refer to it as the Nevada Test Site, as that is the name it went by for nearly sixty years.

xii 105 nuclear bombs: Department of Energy, "United States Nuclear Tests," xii–xv. Total atmospheric for Nevada Test Site (NTS) is officially listed as 100 and total Nellis Air Force Range (NAFR) is listed as 5. Underground is 804 by U.S. plus 24 by U.S./UK for a total of 933.

xii weapons-grade plutonium and uranium: Darwin Morgan, spokesman for the National Nuclear Security Administration, Nevada Site Office, clarified: "The [Nevada Test Site] has never been a repository for weapons grade plutonium or uranium. Of course there is the 'expended' material from 828 underground nuclear weapons tests that is contained within the cavities where the tests were conducted." E-mail, September 21, 2010.

xii two known exceptions: Memo, Top Secret Oxcart, Oxcart Reconnaissance Operation Plan, BYE 2369-67, 15; second example from interview with Peter Merlin.

xiii bomb's price tag: Brookings Institute, "50 Facts about U.S. Nuclear Weapons," fact no. 1 (1996 dollars: $20,000,000,000; 2011 dollars: $28,000,000,000).

[xiii] was relayed to him by two men: Wiesner, *Vannevar Bush,* 98. This fact is hardly known; credit is usually given to General Leslie R. Groves and War Secretary Henry L. Stimson. Wiesner, Vannevar Bush's biographer at the National Academy of Sciences (he was also a science adviser to President Eisenhower), wrote: "Bush...had the duty, after the death of President Roosevelt, of giving President Truman his first detailed account of the bomb."

[xiii] no one knew the Manhattan Project was there: Wills, *Bomb Power,* 10–13. Wills elaborated on how Truman had some suspicions when he was vice president and approached War Secretary Henry L. Stimson, who told him to back off, which Truman did.

[xiii] who would control its "unimaginable destructive power": Smyth, *Atomic Energy for Military Purposes,* 13.7. Also known as *The Smyth Report,* it was released by the government six days after Hiroshima, on August 12, 1945. Here, Smyth chronicled the administrative and technical history of the Manhattan Project, also called the Manhattan Engineering District (MED). The purpose of the report was allegedly to give citizens enough information about nuclear energy for them to participate in a public debate about what to do next. The report also encouraged the idea that handing the bomb over to civilian control, as opposed to military control, would be a more democratic scenario. Instead, the controls imposed by the Atomic Energy Commission would ultimately prove to be even more impenetrable than military controls; Hewlett and Anderson, *New World.*

[xiv] the concept "born classified" came to be: Quist, *Security Classification,* 1. Here Quist writes: "The Atomic Energy Act of 1946 was the first and, other than its successor, the Atomic Energy Act of 1954, to date the only U.S. statute to establish a program to restrict the dissemination of information. This Act transferred control of all aspects of atomic (nuclear) energy from the Army, which had managed the government's World War II Manhattan Project to produce atomic bombs, to a five-member civilian Atomic Energy Commission (AEC). These new types of bombs, of awesome power, had been developed under stringent secrecy and security conditions. Congress, in enacting the 1946 Atomic Energy Act, continued the Manhattan Project's comprehensive, rigid controls on U.S. information about atomic bombs and other aspects of atomic energy. The Atomic Energy Act designated the atomic energy information to be protected as 'Restricted Data' and defined that data."

[xiv] seventy thousand nuclear bombs: Brookings Institute, "50 Facts about U.S. Nuclear Weapons," fact no. 6.

^{xiv} Atomic Energy was the first entity to control Area 51: This is one of the central organizing premises of my book and will no doubt be contested by the Atomic Energy Commission until they are forced to declassify the project to which I refer.

^{xiv} when President Clinton: The Advisory Committee on Human Radiation Experiments (ACHRE) was created by President Clinton on January 15, 1994, to investigate and make public the use of human beings as subjects of federally funded research. Created by executive order and subject to the Federal Advisory Committee Act (FACA), the advisory committee was obligated to provide public access to its activities, processes, and papers, some of which can be viewed at http://www.gwu.edu/~nsarchiv/radiation/.

^{xiv} he did not have a need-to-know: Author interview with EG&G engineer.

^{xiv} "give[s] the professional classificationist unanswerable authority": Quist, *Security Classification,* 24; Schwartz, *Atomic Audit,* 442–51.

^{xv} largest facility is, and always has been, the Nevada Test Site: Written correspondence with Darwin Morgan, September 21, 2010, U.S. Department of Energy, Nevada Operations Office, Office of Public Affairs and Information.

^{xv} not controlled by the Department of Defense: It cannot yet be determined for certain if the Department of Defense (DOD) was involved in running the very first program at Area 51. Research at NARA (National Archives and Records Administration) reveals that DOD had a lot more to do with Paperclips than previously known publicly. For example, documents obtained by me through a FOIA request reveal "in the early 1950s the Defense Department [Office of Defense Research and Engineering (ORE)] and the JIOA took up overall direction of PAPERCLIP, which ran under the acronym of DEFSIP, or Defense Scientist Immigration Program." JIOA stands for Joint Intelligence Objectives Agency and was run by the Joint Chiefs of Staff. These multiple agencies and multiple chains of command serve to hide information.

Chapter One: The Riddle of Area 51

Interviews: Joerg Arnu, George Knapp, Thornton "T.D." Barnes, Colonel Hugh Slater, Richard Mingus, Ernest "Ernie" Williams, Dr. Albert "Bud" Wheelon, Colonel Kenneth Collins, Colonel Sam Pizzo, Norio Hayakawa, Stanton Friedman

[4] Nighttime is the best time: Interview with Joerg Arnu.

[5] Robert Scott Lazar appeared on *Eyewitness News:* Interview with George Knapp; George Knapp, "Bob Lazar: The Man Behind Area 51," Eyewitness News Investigates, http://area51.eyewitnessnews8.com/.

[5] veiled threats of incarceration: A common note among most Area 51 employees interviewed, certainly among the Air Force enlisted men, was the "threat of Leavenworth," meaning incarceration at the largest federal security prison in the United States at Fort Leavenworth, Kansas.

[6] Dr. Edward Teller: Teller, who died in 2003 at the age of ninety-five, never confirmed or denied that he referred Lazar to EG&G for work at Area 51.

contaminated with plutonium: Interviews with Richard Mingus; see notes for chapter 6.

[6] for a lecture Teller was giving: The subject of Teller's lecture was the nuclear freeze movement under way in a post–Three Mile Island world.

[6] a page–1 story featuring Bob Lazar: *Los Alamos Monitor,* June 27, 1982, identifies Lazar as "a physicist at the Los Alamos Meson Physics Facility."

[6] Lazar's life had reached an unexpected low: The most comprehensive information on Lazar is available at the Area 51 research Web site Dreamland-resort.com, created by Joerg H. Arnu in 1999. In "The Bob Lazar Corner" one can find a time line of Lazar's story as well as a compilation of public records, letters, and commentary about Lazar by his critics and his friends, as researched by Tom Mahood, whom I interviewed.

[6] Tracy Murk: According to the wedding certificate researched by Tom Mahood. Also according to Mahood's research, Tracy Ann Murk and Lazar married for a second time, on October 12, 1986 (the first wedding was April 19, 1986), with Murk inexplicably using the name Jackie Diane Evans.

[6] committed suicide by inhaling carbon monoxide: Ibid. Death certificate #001423-86, Clark County Health District, Las Vegas, NV; cause of death: "inhalation of motor vehicle exhaust." Sourced by Tom Mahood.

[7] Fly to Area 51: Descriptions based on multiple eyewitness interviews; see Primary Interviews.

[8] designed by Raytheon to detect incoming missile signals: Interview with T. D. Barnes.

⁹ The miner kept the secrecy oath: Interview with Colonel Slater.

⁹ access point Gate 385: Interview with Richard Mingus.

⁹ trucks from the Atomic Energy Commission motor pool: Interview with Ernie Williams. A farm boy from Nebraska, Williams's father was a "water witch," and Williams inherited some water-locating charm. In this manner, he is the man credited by many Roadrunners as having officially found Area 51's first water well.

¹⁰ men dressed in HAZMAT suits: R. Kinnison and R. Gilbert, "Estimates of Soil Removal for Cleanup of Transuranics at NAEG Offsite Safety Shot Sites," FY 1981, 1984, 1986–91.

¹⁰ would have gone through security there: Interview with anonymous EG&G employee who worked for the airline.

¹⁰ tennis matches: Interview with Dr. Wheelon.

¹⁰ jumping into the pool: Interview with Ken Collins.

¹⁰ Area 51 bar, called Sam's Place: Interview with Colonel Pizzo.

¹¹ According to Lazar: Lazar's original interviews with George Knapp are available on YouTube in six parts.

¹² He glanced sideways, through a small nine-by-nine-inch window: Lazar's interview with George Knapp, part two of six, minutes 4:10–5:05. Knapp: "In an earlier interview, you had mentioned you saw what you thought may be an alien. Was it an alien? What did you see?" Lazar: "What I had said and all that occurred was that I was walking by a door, ah, a door that had a small, nine-by-nine window in it, little wires running through it. And glanced in there, and there were two . . . ah, either technicians, scientists, or whoever they were, looking down at something. And what that something was caught my eye and I never really did see what it was. A lot of people have asserted, well, there was an alien, they're aliens working around there and so on and so forth, I mean, I don't think that was the case. But, ah, who knows. I was. You know. You're seeing all these fantastic things and your mind gets going and you know you catch something out of the corner of your eye, who knows what your mind is going to come up with so I certainly wouldn't stand on that as fact by any means." See http://www.youtube.com/watch?v=XAfVZcAsTxk.

¹² what was maybe an alien: Lazar's interview with George Knapp, part two of six, minutes 2:33–3:30. Lazar says he was told the UFO he was assigned to

work on originated from another planet. He says he was shown autopsy photographs of the craft's alien pilots, which he described to Knapp in their interview: "One or two autopsy photographs I saw ah, dealt with just a small photograph, a bust shot essentially, just head, shoulders, and chest of an alien where the ah, ah, chest was cut open in a 'T' fashion and one single organ was removed. The organ itself in the other picture was cut and vivisectioned essentially the, ah, showing the different chambers in there. This was totally unrelated to anything I was doing but from that photograph it looked like what you see in UFO lore as the typical 'gray' [slang for *alien*] so how tall it was from what I could see, I couldn't tell, 'cause I only saw a portion of the photograph but if everything else you see is correct, I would imagine it was three and a half or four feet tall. But ah, there again, you know all I had to see was a photograph. And you know, I didn't have much to go on." See http://www.youtube.com/watch?v=XAfVZcAsTxk&feature=related.

[12] The group made a trip: Tom Mahood, "The Robert Lazar Timeline, as assembled from Public Records and Statements," July 1994, updated July 1997, from dreamlandresort.com. In this time line Lazar and various friends made a total of three trips into the mountains behind Groom Lake. It was on the third trip that his group was stopped by guards.

[13] transcripts of his wife's telephone conversations: Ibid.

[13] Norio Hayakawa: Interview with Norio Hayakawa.

[14] He had bodyguards: In the interview with Knapp, Lazar said he was shot at while driving on the freeway (YouTube interview five of six, minute 6:00) and that during his debrief at Indian Springs a gun was pointed at him (ibid., minute 8:00).

[15] Lie detector tests: WSVN-7 News reporter Dan Hausle's interview with former policeman Terry Cavernetti, accessed on December 21, 2010, YouTube, "Bob Lazar Passes the Lie Detector on UFOs."

[15] Stanton Friedman: Interview with Stanton Friedman. Friedman was employed for fourteen years as a nuclear physicist and worked on many advanced nuclear and space travel systems for companies like General Motors, General Electric, and Westinghouse. He has published eighty UFO papers, written six books, and appears in many UFO documentaries.

[15] Stanton Friedman's exposé on the Roswell incident: *Recollections of Roswell, Testimony from 27 Witnesses Connected with Recovery of 2 Crashed Flying Saucers in New Mexico in July 1947*, DVD, 105 minutes.

[17] a book based on Friedman and Moore's research was published: Berlitz and Moore, *Roswell Incident*. Friedman said it was a group decision to give Berlitz author credit instead of him, as Berlitz was from the Berlitz Language School family and had the credibility necessary to sell the publisher on the book's controversial subject matter. Charles Berlitz spoke twenty-five languages and is often listed as one of the most important linguists of the twentieth century. His 1974 book, *The Bermuda Triangle,* sold an estimated ten million copies.

Chapter Two: Imagine a War of the Worlds

Interviews: Colonel Richard S. Leghorn, Ralph "Jim" Freedman, Alfred "Al" O'Donnell, Lieutenant Colonel Hervey Stockman, Colonel Slater, David Myhra

[19] became convinced that Martians were attacking Earth: *Trenton Evening Times,* October 31, 1938. Many documents relating to *The War of the Worlds* radio play are available at http://www.war-ofthe-worlds.co.uk/documents.htm.

[20] Switchboards jammed: Ibid., "Log from Jersey Police, Port Norris Station."

[21] the FCC's role: Associated Press, "Mars Monsters Broadcast Will Not Be Repeated. Perpetrators of the Innovation Regret Causing of Public Alarm," November 1, 1938.

[22] Adolf Hitler took note as well: Hand, *Terror on the Air!* 7.

[22] Joseph Stalin had also been: Author interview with EG&G engineer.

[22] Vannevar Bush, observed the effects: Correspondence between Vannevar Bush and W. C. Forbes, June 8, 1939; Vannevar Bush, A Register of His Papers in the Library of Congress, Manuscript Division, Library of Congress, Washington, DC.

[22] "Science Discovers Real Frankenstein": Winthrop, "Science Discovers."

[22] *War of the Worlds* radio broadcast as an example: Zachary, *Endless Frontier,* 190.

[22] President Roosevelt had appointed: "Vannevar Bush, A Collection of His Papers in the Library of Congress," Manuscript Division, Library of Congress, Washington DC.

[23] his next move: Zachary, *Endless Frontier,* 285. Zachary wrote, "Bush's role in the A-bomb's birth actually burnished his reputation. Like Truman, most Americans were thrilled by Japan's surrender and the end of the war... Rather

than interrogate the leaders of the Manhattan Project, the public embraced them. Bush's reputation as a scientific seer grew; his image as an unmatched organizer of expertise solidified. For Bush, the atomic bomb capped off his five-year rise to celebrity from relative obscurity."

[23] As Americans celebrated peace: "Majority Supports Use of Atomic Bomb on Japan in WWII": David Moore, Gallup News Service, August 5, 2005.

[24] Operation Crossroads was in full swing: Author interview with Colonel Leghorn, who was the commanding officer of Task Force 1.5.2 for the operation. I am indebted to Colonel Leghorn not only for generously sharing with me recollections of his historic role at Crossroads, beginning with his departure by airplane from the Roswell Army Air Field, but for lending me original photographs taken from his airplane during the 1946 nuclear tests. He also loaned me two original yearbook-type books where I learned the operation involved more than ten thousand instruments and nearly half the world's supply of film. The Air Force alone took nine million photographs.

[24] There were barracuda everywhere: Interview with Ralph "Jim" Freedman. Freedman's first visit to Bikini was for the nuclear test Castle Bravo, six years after Crossroads, but the barracuda problem was the same.

[24] led by a king named Juda: Bradley, *No Place to Hide,* 158.

[24] The U.S. Navy had evacuated the natives to Rongerik Atoll: The documentary *Radio Bikini* (1987), directed by Robert Stone, includes remarkable outtakes of AEC footage showing military personnel rehearsing how to best pitch propaganda to the natives.

[24] three-bomb atomic test series: Schwartz, *Atomic Audit,* 102. Operation Crossroads cost an astonishing $1.3 billion in 1946 eleven months after the war's end, more than any subsequent test series. Crossroads involved 95 ships and 42,000 military and civilian personnel. It was a show of force.

[24] a young man named Alfred O'Donnell: Interview with Alfred "Al" O'Donnell.

[26] "In the face of intense fire": Air Force Historical Research Agency, 30 Reconnaissance Squadron (ACC), Lineage, Assignments, Stations, and Honors, Major Richard S. Leghorn, http://www.afhra.af.mil/factsheets/factsheet .asp?id=10193.

[27] Curtis LeMay rarely smiled: Kozak, *LeMay,* iv.

[27] five cents per bird: Ibid., 9.

[27] "Caveman in a Jet Bomber": I. F. Stone, *The Best of I. F. Stone,* 326–28.

[27] LeMay was at Bikini to determine: Rhodes, *Dark Sun,* 261–62.

[27] Operation Crossroads was a huge event: The *New York Times* described it as the largest and "most stupendous single set of experiments in history." Senator Huffman called the test a "Roman holiday in the Pacific" and promised that the "only important impression these tests are going to give the world is that the United States is not done with war." Members of the Southern Dairy Goat Owners and Breeders Association recommended that the sheep being used during the test be substituted with U.S. congressmen, on the grounds that good goats were harder to find than congressmen were. In the days leading up to the event, protesters picketed the White House with signs that read, BIKINI: REHEARSAL FOR WORLD WAR THREE.

[27] one million tons of battle-weary steel: Fact sheet, Operation Crossroads, Defense Nuclear Agency, Public Affairs Office, Washington, DC, April 5, 1984.

[28] Alfred O'Donnell stood below deck: Interview with O'Donnell.

[28] the DN-11 relay system: Interview with O'Donnell; copy of a handwritten letter by Herbert Grier from O'Donnell's collection.

[29] What Leghorn witnessed horrified him: Interviews with Colonel Leghorn.

[29–30] tossed up into the air like bathtub toys: United States Atomic Energy Commission Memorandum for the Board, August 23, 1973, #718922, Naval Vessels Sunk During Operation Crossroads; AEC film footage of the explosion, Atomic Testing Museum library, Las Vegas, NV.

[30] west of the Volga River: Pedlow and Welzenbach, *Central Intelligence Agency,* 22.

Leghorn believed: Interview with Colonel Leghorn.

[30] what shipyards or missile-launch facilities: Ibid.; interview with Hervey Stockman, who was the first man to fly over the Soviet Union in a U-2 spy plane.

[32] Halfway across the world: Rhodes, *Dark Sun,* 261.

[33] chain-reacting atomic pile would go critical: O'Keefe, *Nuclear Hostages,* 134.

[33] Joseph Stalin was developing another secret weapon: Author interview with EG&G engineer.

[33] secret weapon, called Hermes: Interview with Lisa Blevins, U.S. Army public affairs officer, White Sands Missile Range, New Mexico; "Report on Hermes Missile Project," Washington National Records Center, Record Group 156.

[33] belonged to Adolf Hitler: Hunt, *Secret Agenda,* 27.

[33] secret project called Operation Paperclip: Paperclip was a postwar operation carried out by the Joint Intelligence Objectives Agency, a special intelligence office that reported to the director of intelligence in the War Department. Today, this would be the equivalent of reporting to the intelligence chief for the Joint Chiefs of Staff. Most details about Project Paperclip remain classified despite the government's insistence otherwise. Paperclip began before the war ended, and it was originally called Project Overcast and/or Project Pajamas. It had two primary goals: to exploit the minds of German scientists for American Cold War research projects and to keep the Russians from getting the German scientists, no matter how heinous their war crimes might have been. It is believed that at least sixteen hundred scientists were recruited by various U.S. intelligence groups and brought, with their dependents, to the United States. Paperclip had a number of secret, successor projects that remain classified as of 2011.

[33] Wernher Von Braun: G-2 Paperclip "Top Secret" files, WNRC Record Group 330. Also from FBI dossier "Wernher Magnus Maximilian Von Braun, aka Freiherr Von Braun," file 116-13038, 297 pages; also see Neufeld, *Von Braun.*

[34] Dr. Ernst Steinhoff: G-2 Paperclip "Top Secret" files, WNRC, Record Group 319.

[34] inside the two-million-square-acre: Schwartz, *Atomic Audit,* 169. Now called the White Sands Missile Range, the facility is the largest military installation in the country—the size of Delaware and Rhode Island combined. The first atomic bomb, Trinity, was exploded near the north boundary of the range.

[34] Dr. Steinhoff said nothing: Hunt, *Secret Agenda,* 27; Neufeld, *Von Braun,* 239.

[34] terrifying citizens: "V-2 Rocket, Off Course, Falls Near Juárez," *El Paso Times,* May 30, 1947.

[35] Allegations of sabotage: Army Intelligence, G-2 Paperclip, Memorandum for the AC of S G-2, Intelligence Summary, Captain Paul R. Lutjens, June 6, 1947, RG 319, Washington National Records Center (WNRC), Suitland, Maryland. Hunt, *Secret Agenda,* chapter 3; Major Lyman G. White, "Paperclip Project, Ft. Bliss, Texas and Adjacent Areas," MID 918.3, November 26, 1947.

[35] "beating a dead Nazi horse": In a March 1948 letter to the State Department regarding "German scientists [who] were members of either the Nazi Party or one or more of its affiliates," Bosquet Wev, director of the Joint Intelligence Objectives Agency, wrote, "[R]esponsible officials...have expressed opinions to the effect that, in so far as German scientists are concerned, Nazism no longer should be a serious consideration from a viewpoint of national security when the far greater threat of Communism is now jeopardizing the entire world. I strongly concur in this opinion and consider it a most sound and practical view, which must certainly be taken if we are to face the situation confronting us with even an iota of realism. To continue to treat Nazi affiliations as significant considerations has been aptly phrased as 'beating a dead Nazi horse.'"

[36] What made the aircraft extraordinary: Interview with EG&G engineer.

[36] fighter jet: Interviews with Colonel Slater, Area 51 base commander (1963–68), Chandler's personal friend. Chandler relayed this story to Slater decades after it happened.

[36] The recovered craft looked nothing like a conventional aircraft: Interview with EG&G engineer, who was an eyewitness.

[37] Cyrillic alphabet had been stamped: Interview with EG&G engineer.

[37] near the Alaskan border: Interview with EG&G engineer.

[38] What if atomic energy propelled the Russian craft: Interview with EG&G engineer.

[38] Amerika Bomber: Myhra, *The Horten Brothers and Their All-Wing Aircraft,* 217–20; interview with David Myhra, who interviewed both Horten brothers, Walter in Germany and Reimar in Argentina, for hundreds of hours in the 1980s.

[38-39] Paperclip scientists...called on for their expertise: This is my defensible speculation based on interviews with the EG&G engineer. The Paperclip group attached to the project, I learned through sources with secondhand information, allegedly included Von Braun, Ernst Steinhoff, and also Dr. Hubertus Strughold, a former Nazi and, in 1947, a research doctor at the Aeromedical Laboratory at Randolph Field in San Antonio, Texas. While employed by the Third Reich, Strughold was the leading expert on how the human body handles high altitude during flight. During World War II, Strughold had been chief of staff of aviation medicine for the German air force, or Luftwaffe. For more on Strughold, see Bower, *Paperclip Conspiracy,* 214–323.

[39] secreted away in a manner so clandestine: Interview with EG&G engineer.

[39] top secret project called Operation Harass: Jacobsen, U.S. Army Intelligence and Security Command (INSCOM) FOIA request, "Horten Brothers and Operation Harass." The file was declassified by INSCOM beginning on July 6, 1994, CDR USAINSCOM FO1/PO Auth para 1-603 DOD 5200.1R, 358 pages. Notes for pages 38 through 62 refer to this record group.

[39] testimony of America's Paperclip scientists: Headquarters, Counter Intelligence Corps Region I, 970th Counter Intelligence Corps, Detachment European Command, APO-154, January 6, 1948, 92. "Scientists who have better than average knowledge of the HORTEN brothers' work are: (2) Lippisch, Prof., fnu, Wright Field, Ohio, U.S.A." Dr. Lippisch was transferred to Wright Field, along with his senior staff Ernst Sielaff and Dr. Ringleb, from Luftfahrt-forshungsandstalt Wien—a German aeronautical research institute for the development of high-speed aircraft.

[39] The manhunt was on: The earliest dated Operation Harass memo in the file is from November 10, 1947, APO 189, Subject: Flying Saucers, 139. It reads, "Considerable material has been gathered by the Air Materiel Command WRIGHT FIELD, Ohio, concerning the appearance, description and functioning of the object popularly known as the 'Flying Saucer.' A copy of the request of the report from the Air Materiel Command is on file at this Headquarters, 2. The opinion was expressed that some sort of object, such as the flying saucer, did exist. At the present time, construction models are being built for wind tunnel tests." This, however, is clearly not the first memo. On page 106 of the FOIA file, in memo APO 134, January 2, 1948, a reference is made to an earlier letter, "RE: HORTEN Brothers, SUBJECT: Flying Saucers, dated 28, October 1947."

[39] Walter and Reimar Horten . . . had somehow been overlooked: Interview with David Myhra.

[39] been a later-model Horten in the works: "HORTEN, Walter-" LKL: A.V.V. Gottingen (14-5-46) "Expert on 'flying-wing' aircraft, including HO VIII IX & X," 155 (note there are two separate pages numbered 155).

[40] Timothy Cooper filed a request for documents: Because the Flying Saucer memos reveal that immediately after the crash at Roswell, the Army was seeking information on aircraft made by German scientists and not by extra-terrestrials, the memos have been discounted by many ufologists as being Army intelligence propaganda. In fact, they reveal an important clue in under-

standing the EG&G engineer's truth about the Roswell mystery, namely, that the Joint Chiefs of Staff and perhaps the highest rank at Air Materiel Command knew the flying disc was in fact a Russian vehicle of German design.

[40] "Extreme maneuverability and apparent ability to almost hover": Air Intelligence [illegible] for alleged "Flying Saucer Type Air Craft," 152–56.

[41] American Paperclip scientists living at Wright Field: Headquarters Sub Region Frankfurt, Counter Intelligence Corps Region III, APO 757, 4 February 1948, 71–72. "Leiber also stated that a Dr. Alexander LIPPISCH, who is at present working at WRIGHT Field, Ohio, USA, is also familiar with the work of the HORTON brothers."

[41] Messerschmitt test pilot named Fritz Wendel: Headquarters Counter Intelligence Corps Region IV, 970th Counter Intelligence Corps Detachment APO 407-A, US ARMY, IV-2574. Subj: WENDEL, Fritz, 1 March 1948, 6 pages. Includes Sheets I, II, III, and IV—Sketches made by WENDEL re HORTEN aircraft; No. 179332, WENDEL, Fritz, "Ex-Luftwaffe Squadron leader. Presently working for Graf Von Ledebur, French Intell [sic] officer in Vienna Austria," 56–63.

[41] "very much like a round cake with a large sector cut out": Memo, Secret, Headquarters Berlin Command, Office of Military Government for Germany (US), S-2 Branch, Subject "Flying Saucers," 3 December 1947, 126; Drawing, Directrix, Secret, 128.

[41] Could it hover?: Ibid., 57.

[42] if groups could fly tightly together: Ibid., 58.

[42] "high speed escapement methods": Ibid., 59.

[42] Could the flying disc be remotely controlled?: Ibid., 58.

[42] Did Wendel have any idea about the tactical purposes: Ibid.

[42] a rocket engineer named Walter Ziegler: Memo, Secret, Headquarters Counter Intelligence Corps Region IV, 970th Counter Intelligence Corps APO 407-A Subj: ZIEGLER, Walter Erich, 1 March 1948, 52–55.

[42] four hundred men from his former rocket group: Ibid., 53. Ziegler called the town "Kubischew," and said it was located "east of Moscow . . . where they are presently constructing rockets under Russian supervision."

[43] The Horten brothers had been found: Headquarters 970th Counter

Intelligence Corps Detachment European Command, APO 757, D-198239, Subject Flying Saucers, dated 12 March 1948, 44.

[43] "The Horten 13": This is a transcription of a "report" originally written in German cursive writing and translated by SFC Dale R. Blohm. It is missing a cover page. The text suggests that the USG is making plans to hire "6 to 30" German scientists to create for them the "Horten-Parabel." It reads, "The Discussions concerning the Project 'Horten-Parabel' are finalized. The results can be summed up in the following manner. 1). The Russians are in possession of the relevant planes and will be supported by German specialists. The construction series of the so called Horten 13 (Model with 2-TL (SIC) Power Unit) should not be developed beyond the initial stages by the Russians." At the end of the memo, the writer concluded, "to begin work, we ask for exact orders for the U.S. Army, for example timber work style, how many power units, operating radius, additional load, crew size, weapons layout, etc.," 196–97, 202–4.

[43] "Walter Horten has admitted his contacts with the Russians": Memo from European Command Message Control Secret Priority, Ref S-3773, To: United States Forces in Austria, for Director of Intelligence, 20 May 1948, 231; extracts from Horten, Walter, From D-154654, "Walter HORTEN points out that the possibility of the glider of parabolic design flown by a Russian pilot in 1925-1926 at the Rhaen competitive race may have been developed into a flying saucer. In the event the Russians further developed this glider, or, after the war, installed into it jet units of the Junkers or BMW type, the result may be the flying saucer," 232–33.

[44] stay at Wright-Patterson for approximately four years: Interview with EG&G engineer.

Chapter Three: The Secret Base

Interviews: Colonel Leghorn, T. D. Barnes, Lieutenant Colonel Roger Andersen, Millie Meierdierck, Bob Murphy, Ray Goudey, Edward Lovick

[45] was sitting in his parlor: Bissell, *Reflections of a Cold Warrior,* 68.

[45] paramour of Princess Caradja: Thomas, *The Very Best Men,* 103.

[46] As for the mysterious office called OPC: CIA History Staff, "Office of Policy Coordination 1948–1952," 57 pages. Approved for release March 1997.

[46] "funds generated by the Marshall Plan": Bissell, *Reflections of a Cold Warrior,* 68.

[47] Leghorn went back to Washington: Interview with Colonel Leghorn.

[48] as part of Operation Lusty: Samuel, *American Raiders*. Operation Lusty (Luftwaffe Secret Technology) was the U.S. Army Air Forces' effort to capture and evaluate German aeronautical technology beginning at the end of World War II.

[48] Putt listened: Pedlow and Welzenbach, *Central Intelligence Agency*, 35.

[48] Whereas Putt was uninterested: P. Taubman, *Secret Empire*, 105.

[49] Killian and Land reasoned: Pedlow and Welzenbach, *Central Intelligence Agency*, 27–37.

[49] "impression of World War I as a cataclysm": Bissell, *Reflections of a Cold Warrior*, 4.

[50] James Killian, who recruited Richard Bissell: Pedlow and Welzenbach, *Central Intelligence Agency*, 16. Bissell joined the Agency in late January 1954; however, his first association with the Agency came in 1953 when he worked as a contractor. On July 26, 1954, Eisenhower authorized Killian to recruit a panel of experts to study what a U-2-type aircraft might accomplish. The group was called the Technological Capabilities Panel. In August, the idea was formally presented to Bissell. Ibid., 30.

[50] a secret CIA test facility: There are several accounts of who went to Groom Lake with Bissell on that historic first trip. I compile mine from Bissell's memoir and my interviews with Lockheed test pilot Ray Goudey.

[51] Goudey had shuttled atomic scientists: Interview with Ray Goudey.

[51] "I recommended to Eisenhower": Bissell, *Reflections of a Cold Warrior*, 102–3.

[52] the tents would blow away: Interview with Ray Goudey.

[52] to defend against rattlesnakes: Interview with Edward Lovick.

[53] The same variable occurred: Interview with Tony Bevacqua.

[54] a lot of time in a recliner: Interview with Ray Goudey.

[55] Bob Murphy's job: Interviews with Bob Murphy. The U-2 engine was a P-37 specially designed by Connecticut engine maker Pratt and Whitney.

[55] Mr. B., as he was known to the men: Interview with Edward Lovick.

[56] Hank Meierdierck: The stories of Hank Meierdierck, the man who

trained the U-2 pilots at Area 51, were relayed to me by his friends from the old days at the Ranch as well as from his personal papers, which were made available to me by his wife, Millie Meierdierck.

56 "unconventional way": Killian, *Sputnik, Scientists and Eisenhower,* 82. Killian wrote, "Eisenhower approved the development of the U-2 system, but he stipulated that it should be handled in an unconditional way so that it would not become entangled in the bureaucracy of the Defense Department or troubled by rivalries among the services." Also see Bissell, *Reflections of a Cold Warrior,* 95.

56 hidden from Congress: Top Secret Memorandum of Conference with the President 0810, 24 November 1954. "Authorization was sought from the President to go ahead on a program to produce thirty, special high performance aircraft at a cost of about $35 million. The President approved this action. Mr. Allen Dulles indicated that his organization could not finance this whole sum without drawing attention to it, and it was agreed that Defense would seek to carry a substantial part of the financing." From the Eisenhower Archives, DDE's Papers as President, Ann Whitman Diary Series, Box 3, ACW Diary, November 1954.

57 stand-alone organization: Bissell, *Reflections of a Cold Warrior,* 105. Bissell wrote, "To preserve the secrecy and expeditiousness that Eisenhower and Allen Dulles insisted on, I argued for removing the U-2 project from the agency's organizational chart and setting it up as a stand-alone organization. As a result, the entire project became the most compartmented and self-contained activity within the agency."

57 five-page brief: Eisenhower was uniquely invested in Area 51 because the success of the U-2 program, which came to be during his administration, was critical to the nation's security.

57 The Air Force was almost entirely left out: As recalled by General Leo Geary, Bissell's Air Force deputy, in an interview with Jonathan Lewis, tape recording, Chevy Chase, MD, 11 February 1994; Bissell, *Reflections of a Cold Warrior,* 100.

58 LeMay was, understandably, enraged: "Eventually President Eisenhower settled the dispute." Pedlow and Welzenbach, *Central Intelligence Agency,* 60; Bissell, *Reflections of a Cold Warrior,* 109.

58 the president's decision: "I want this whole thing to be a civilian operation," the president wrote. "If uniformed personnel of the armed services of the United States fly over Russia, it is an act of war—legally—and I don't

want any part of it.' " From Pedlow and Welzenbach, *Central Intelligence Agency,* 60.

[59] Bob Murphy would often chat with George Pappas: Interview with Bob Murphy.

[60] Had Pappas been just thirty feet higher: From Hank Meierdierck's personal papers; Meierdierck located the crash remains from a U-2 he took out on a search mission.

[62] the CIA acknowledged the plane crash in 2002: As part of a tribute given by the U.S. Forest Service. The CIA did not, however, acknowledge that the aircraft was traveling to Area 51; also see Kyril Plaskon, *Silent Heroes.*

[62] security systems for Air Force One: EG&G, a Division of URS, Albuquerque Operations Web site. "EG&G has provided security systems for U.S. Government facilities: Department of Energy Headquarters, U.S. Bureau of Engraving, Presidential AF-1 Hangar Complex, Rocky Flats [nuclear weapons production facility in Colorado], Tooele [Utah, Army Depot for WMD]."

Chapter Four: The Seeds of a Conspiracy

Interviews: Lieutenant Colonel Tony Bevacqua, Edward Lovick, Ray Goudey, Al O'Donnell, Jim Freedman, Wayne Pendleton, T. D. Barnes

[63] Area 51, reports of UFO sightings: Haines, "CIA's Role," 73.

[63] U-2 look like a fiery flying cross: Interview with Tony Bevacqua; the wingspan is 103 feet and the fuselage is 63 feet.

[64] the crash at Roswell occurred: Hereafter, when I refer to the "crash at Roswell," I am referring to an aircraft, not a balloon, as has also been written. While there was a balloon-borne radar-reflector project going on at White Sands in the summer of 1947, this is not what crashed at Roswell. To learn about that project and the balloon theory put forth by one of its participants, Charles B. Moore, see Saler, Ziegler, and Moore, *UFO Crash at Roswell.*

[64] Project Sign: U.S. Air Force Air Materiel Command, "Unidentified Aerial Objects; Project SIGN"; Haines, "CIA's Role," 68.

[64] Project Grudge: U.S. Air Force, Project Grudge and Blue Book, Reports 1–12. Since the declassification of Projects Saucer, Sign, Grudge, Twinkle, and

Blue Book, which began incrementally in the 1970s, the collection is housed in the National Archives; see http://www.archives.gov/foia/ufos.html.

[65] disliked technology in general: Pedlow and Welzenbach, *Central Intelligence Agency*, 17, "High altitude reconnaissance of the Soviet Union did not fit well into Allen Dulles's perception of the proper role of an intelligence agency. He tended to favor the classical form of espionage, which relied on agents rather than technology." Allen Dulles's predilection to work with former Nazis has become more obvious and more troubling as time goes by and Paperclip files are slowly declassified. The last line in Dulles's three-page CIA biography, "Secret Security Information: Subject Allen W. Dulles 7/2-127," reads: "At any rate, the American policy in the postwar period as regards [to] Germany has been directly and deeply influenced by MR. DULLES. He has a greater trust in the Germans than he has, for instance, in the French and the Italians."

[65] The UFO division was placed: Office Memorandum, United States Government, To: Acting Assistant Director for Scientific Intelligence, From: Todos Odarenko, Chief, Physics and Electronics Division, SI, Subject, Current Status of Unidentified Flying Objects (UFOB) Projects, 17 December 1953.

[65] Walter Bedell Smith: Weiner, *Legacy of Ashes,* 4, 87, 122, 131.

[65] included the flying disc retrieved at Roswell: This is my defensible speculation based on interviews with the EG&G engineer and my understanding of Bedell Smith's role, particularly with James Forrestal, secretary of the Navy during the war and the nation's first secretary of defense, who committed suicide on May 22, 1949.

[65] Bedell Smith was the ambassador to the Soviet Union: CIA Center for the Study of Intelligence, Directors and Deputy Directors of Central Intelligence, Walter Smith, General, U.S. Army.

[65] Governors Island, New York: National Archives Records Administration, RG 338, Box 27, G-2 Section, Headquarters First Army, Governors Island, New York, 4, New York, Case Files.

[66] summarily rejected the idea that UFOs: There are several CIA documents, declassified starting in 1996, that I base my interpretation of General Bedell Smith's attitude toward UFOs on during his tenure at CIA. All quotes come from these documents: Central Intelligence Agency, Washington 25, D.C. Office of the Director, ER-3-2809, Memorandum to Director, Psychology Strategy Board, Subject Flying Saucers, 2 pages, signed Walter B. Smith Director, undated; Memorandum for file OSI, Meeting of OSI Advisory Group on

UFO, January 14 through 17, 1953, 3 pages; Scientific Advisory Panel on Unidentified Flying Objects 14–17 January 1953, Evidence Presented, 2 pages; CIA Scientific Advisory Panel on Unidentified Flying Objects, Comments and Suggestions of UFO Panel, 19 pages; Minutes of Branch Chief's Meeting of 11 August 1952, 3 pages; Memorandum for Director of Central Intelligence, From Deputy Director, Intelligence, Subject Flying Saucers, Dated September 7, 1952, 5 pages.

[67] flying discs appeared in many different forms of art: http://www.crystalinks .com/ufohistory.html.

[67] like the boy who cried wolf: Memo, CIA Scientific Advisory Panel on Unidentified Flying Objects, Comments and Suggestions of UFO Panel, 10. "Potential related dangers. c. Subjectivity of public to mass hysteria and greater vulnerability to possible enemy psychological warfare."

[68] "hysterical mass behavior": Haines, "CIA's Role," 72.

[68] the publishers of *Life* magazine: H. B. Darrach and Robert Ginna, "Have We Visitors from Space?" *Life* magazine, April 7, 1952.

[69] originally called Project Saucer: Haines, "CIA's Role," 67–68.

[70] Green Fireballs: Project Twinkle, Final Report, November 27, 1951.

[70] curious members of Congress: Interview with Stanton Friedman.

[71] Air Force concluded for the National Security Council: U.S. Air Force Air Materiel Command, "Unidentified Aerial Objects; Project SIGN."

[73] UFO convention in Los Angeles: "Minutes of the Meeting of Civilian Saucer Investigations."

[73] Dr. Riedel had been working on Hitler's bacteria bomb: Neufeld, *Von Braun,* 206.

[74] There were rumors of "problems": Ibid., 216–22.

[74] "going to execute a planned 'hoax'": CIA Office Memorandum to Assistant for Operations, OSI, From Chief Contact Division, CO, Date: 9 February 1953, Subject California Committee for Saucer Investigations.

[74] set off alarms in its upper echelons: Special National Intelligence Estimate 100-2-57, No. 19, "Soviet Capabilities for Deception," Submitted by the Director of Central Intelligence, 16 pages. Based on recommendations made

by the Technical Capabilities Panel, chaired by Dr. Killian, the recommendation read: "We need to examine intelligence data more broadly, or to invent some new technique, for the discovery of hoaxes."

[74] trailing a colleague of Riedel named George Sutton: Curiously, the CIA document referenced above names George Sutton as a Riedel colleague and ufologist. Was he a plant? Was he turned? Did he reform on his own? According-ing to the Smithsonian Papers, National Air and Space Museum, Archives Division, MRC 322, Washington, DC, 20560, in the G. Paul Sutton collec-tion: "George Paul Sutton (1920–) was an aerospace engineer and manager. He received degrees from Los Angeles City College (AA, 1940) and the California Institute of Technology (BS, 1942; MS [ME], 1943) before going to work as a development engineer for the Rocketdyne Division of North American Aviation. He remained at Rocketdyne into the late 1960s, while also sitting as Hunsaker Professor of Aeronautical Engineering at MIT (1958-59) and serving as Chief Scientist, Advanced Research Projects Agency [ARPA] and Division Director, Institute of Defense Analysis for the Depart-ment of Defense (1959-60). Following his work at Rocketdyne he joined the technical staff at the Lawrence Livermore National Laboratory."

[75] Agency should handle reports of UFOs: Odarenko, Office Memoran-dum, August 8, 1955.

[76] Allen Dulles as an arrogant public servant: Letter from Director of Cen-tral Intelligence Allen Dulles to Congressman Gordon Scherer, October 4, 1955, ER-7-4372A.

Chapter Five: The Need-to-Know

Interviews: Colonel Slater, Hervey Stockman, Ken Collins, Frank Murray, Tony Bevacqua, Colonel Pizzo, Edward Lovick, Ray Goudey

[77] protocols that are also top secret: Correspondence with Cargill Hall. The Federation of American Scientists provides a nonclassified Central Intelligence Directive from 1995 at http://www.fas.org/irp/offdocs/dcid1–19.

[78] bemoaned the president's science advisers: Welzenbach, "Science and Technology," 16.

[78] Sage Control: Interview with Colonel Slater.

[78] "It was like something out of fiction": Interview with Hervey Stockman. Also sourced in this section with Stockman are passages from his compelling

oral history, a project that was spearheaded by his son Peter Stockman and the results of which are "Conversations with Colonel Hervey S. Stockman," edited by Ann Paden and Earl Haney (not published).

[79] The identities of the pilots were equally concealed: Interviews with Ken Collins, Frank Murray, Tony Bevacqua, and Hervey Stockman.

[80] NII-88: Brzezinski, *Red Moon Rising,* 22–23, 26–30, 39–44, 98, 102; Harford, *Korolev,* 77–80, 93, 95, 117. Also called Scientific Research Institute-88, which included the former NII-1, per Stalin on May 13, 1946.

[80] Stalin declared Sergei Korolev's name a state secret: Harford, *Korolev,* 1.

[81] multibillion-dollar espionage platforms: Ibid., 93. Harford quotes Gyorgi Vetrov, Korolev's Russian biographer, as saying about NII-88's radical transformation: "Hardly anyone suspected that the plant was destined to become a production base for such complicated and demanding technologies as rockets and space vehicles for traveling to other plants."

[81] Russia's version of America's Paperclip scientists: Ibid., 75. In addition to the Army intelligence CIC memos that I cited earlier regarding Fritz Wendel, Harford wrote "perhaps as many as 5,000 skilled Germans...were literally kidnapped and shipped with their families, by trains, freight cars and trucks to workplaces outside of Moscow."

[81] Operation Dragon Return: Goodman, *Spying on the Nuclear Bear,* 177.

[82] "cannot cope with contingencies": Brzezinski, *Red Moon Rising,* 81.

[83] LeMay scrambled nearly a thousand B-47 bombers: Ibid., 25. The entirety of these Arctic overflights is still classified. Missions are written about in Burrows, *By Any Means Necessary,* 208–15, and in Bamford, *Body of Secrets,* 35–36. The National Security Agency cosponsored many of the ELINT missions. In *Secret Empire,* Philip Taubman wrote, "At least 252 air crewmen were shot down on spy flights between 1950 and 1970, most directed against the Soviet Union. It is certain that 90 of these men survived, for they were either rescued by American forces or their capture but the Soviet Union or another country was confirmed. But the fate of 138 men is unknown," 47.

[83] top secret missions as part of Operation Home Run: Interview with Colonel Sam Pizzo.

[84] "Soviet leaders may have become convinced": CIA Staff, "Analysis of the Soviet Union 1947–1999," 27.

[85] President Eisenhower was gravely concerned: Top Secret Memorandum of Conference with the President, July 8, 1959. With Dulles and Bissell present at the meeting, USAF Brigadier General A. J. Goodpaster observed, "There remains in the President's mind the question of whether we were getting to the point where we must decide if we are trying to prepare to fight a war, or trying to prevent one." Office of the Staff Secretary, Subject Series, Alphabetical Subseries, Box 15, Intelligence Matters.

[85] Richard Bissell promised the president: Oral history interview with Richard M. Bissell Jr. by Theodore A. Wilson and Richard D. McKinzie, East Hartford, Connecticut, July 9, 1971.

[85] Alexander Orlov related: Orlov, "The U-2 Program," 5–14.

[85] "We will shoot down uninvited guests": Ibid., 7.

[86] he would be even more enraged: Ibid.; Brzezinski, *Red Moon Rising,* 124–35.

[86] CIA men armed with machine guns: Interview with Hervey Stockman.

[87] Eisenhower's cows: P. Taubman, *Secret Empire,* 167.

[87] Stockman approached Russia's submarine city: Stockman also recalled in our interview, "This was good solid proof that what so many had thought to be over there, that there was this huge, dominant, strategic bomber force for the Soviet Union, [proved] not to be there."

[87] Herbert Miller wrote a triumphant memo: Declassified in 2000, the memo is called Top Secret Memorandum for: Project Director, Subject: Suggestions re the Intelligence Value of Aquatone, July 17, 1956. Three more U-2 flights followed Hervey Stockman's. On July 10, 1956, the Soviet Union filed a note of protest. Later that same day, Eisenhower ordered Bissell to stop all overflights until further notice. Miller's memo summarizes the intelligence value of the U-2 flights for the president and argues that the danger of stopping them was far greater than of continuing them.

[88] Khrushchev told his son, Sergei: W. Taubman, *Khrushchev,* 443.

[89] "lost enthusiasm" for the CIA's aerial espionage program: Pedlow and Welzenbach, *Central Intelligence Agency,* 110. Further, the president noted that if Russia were to make these kinds of incursions over U.S. airspace, "The reaction would be drastic." Also from Andrew J. Goodpaster, memorandum on the

record, July 19, 1956. The president expressed concern that if the public found out about the overflights, they would be shocked. "Soviet protests would be one thing, any loss of confidence by our own people would be quite another."

[89] he hired a team to analyze: Interview with Edward Lovick.

[89] painting the U-2 was a bad idea: Ibid.

[90] Air Force transferred money over to the CIA: Pedlow and Welzenbach, *Central Intelligence Agency,* 77.

[90] Among those selected: Interview with Tony Bevacqua.

[92] The next test was a freezing experiment: Interview with Bevacqua. Cold experiments were presented in the Nuremberg doctors' trials as "The Effect of Freezing on Human Beings," the purpose of which was for Nazi doctors to determine at what temperature a human subject dies from heart failure when being frozen.

[92] aviation medicine school at Wright-Patterson: Hunt, *Secret Agenda,* 10, 16, 19, 21. Hunt wrote that during the war, Lieutenant General Donald "Putt gathered the Germans together and, without approval from higher authorities in the War Department, promised them jobs at Wright Field," sourcing her interview with Lieutenant General Putt; "Report on Events and Conditions Which Occurred During Procurement of Foreign Technical Men for Work in the U.S.A.," September 25, 1945, Department of the Air Force, History of the AAF Participation in Project Paperclip, Appendix, May 1945–March 1947.

[93] previously worked at Nazi concentration camps: Bower, *Paperclip Conspiracy,* 214–323. Colonel Harry Armstrong, a surgeon with the U.S. Eighth Air Force, petitioned for the Nazi doctors to come to America after the war and "at the end of his distinguished career, in 1976, he would boast that the thirty-four German aviation doctors he brought to America had saved 'a great many millions of dollars.'" Armstrong had obtained approval from Eisenhower for an operation to "exploit certain uncompleted German aviation medicine research projects." Also see Staff Memo to Members of the Advisory Committee on Human Radiation Experiments, "Post-World War II Recruitment of German Scientists—Project Paperclip," April 5, 1995 (as per President Clinton). The committee obliquely concludes: "Follow-up Research. The staff believes this trail should be followed with more research before conclusions can be

drawn about the Paperclip scientists...It is possible that still-classified intelligence documents could shed further light on these connections."

[93] conducting barbaric experiments: In Linda Hunt's *Secret Agenda,* chapter 5, "Experiments in Death," she chronicles several Nazi scientists who became Paperclips. Siegfried Ruff and Hermann Becker-Freyseng conducted death experiments on prisoners at Dachau, placing them in a pressure chamber that simulated high altitudes of up to 39,260 feet. "The U.S. military still viewed Ruff and Becker-Freyseng as valuable assets, despite their connection to these crimes. They were even employed under Paperclip [at the AAF Aero Medical Center in Heidelberg, Germany] to continue the same type of research that had resulted in the murder of Dachau prisoners," Hunt wrote. Ruff and Becker-Freyseng never got permanent U.S. Paperclip jobs; both were eventually arrested and tried at Nuremberg. Ruff was acquitted, Becker-Freyseng was convicted and given a twenty-year prison sentence. Another notable case was that of Konrad Schaefer. In an effort to study if Luftwaffe pilots could survive on seawater, Schaefer forced prisoners to drink seawater until they went mad from thirst. He then punctured their livers in order to sample fluid and blood. Schaefer was tried at Nuremberg and acquitted, at which point the United States hired him as a Paperclip. "When he arrived at San Antonio in 1950," wrote Hunt, "he was touted as 'the leading German authority on thirst and desalinization of seawater.'"

[93] six hundred million still classified: Pauline Jelinek, "U.S. Releases Nazi Papers," Associated Press, November 2, 1999. But in reality, this number is just a guess, since documents can be hidden inside agencies that are still classified (as the National Reconnaissance Office, NRO, was from 1961–1992); *Nazi War Crimes and Japanese Imperial Government Records,* April 2007. In 1998, President Clinton signed into law the Nazi War Crimes Disclosure Act, which "required the U.S. Government to locate, declassify, and release in their entirety, with few exceptions, remaining classified records about war crimes committed by Nazi Germany and its allies." An interagency working group was created to oversee this work. Steven Garfinkel, acting chair of this five-year effort, wrote: "the IWG has ensured that the public finally has access to the entirety of the operational files of the Office of Strategic Services (OSS), totaling 1.2 million pages; over 114,200 pages of CIA materials; over 435,000 pages from FBI files; 20,000 pages from Army Counterintelligence Corps files; and over 7 million additional pages of records." Garfinkel makes no mention of any Atomic Energy Commission files or the files of private contractors inside the Atomic Energy Commission, such as EG&G, who control documents classified as Restricted Data (RD).

[93] U-2 was as radical and as unorthodox: Interview with Tony Bevacqua.

[95] Edgerton's famous stop-motion photographs: Available for viewing at the Edgerton Center at MIT, 77 Massachusetts Avenue, Room 4-405, in Cambridge, Massachusetts, as well as online at Edgerton.org; Grundberg, "H.E. Edgerton, 86, Dies, Invented Electronic Flash," *New York Times,* January 5, 1990.

[95] Kenneth J. Germeshausen: Joan Cook, "Kenneth Germeshausen, 83, Dies; Was Nuclear and Radar Pioneer," *New York Times,* August 21, 1990. Information on Germeshausen also comes from the Kenneth J. Germeshausen Center for the Law of Innovation and Entrepreneurship at the Franklin Pierce Law Center; MIT archives; author interviews with Al O'Donnell, Jim Freedman.

[96] the most highly classified engineering jobs: Interviews with former EG&G employees Al O'Donnell, Jim Freedman, Wayne Pendleton, T. D. Barnes, and others.

[96] EG&G agreed to set up a radar range: Pedlow and Welzenbach, *Central Intelligence Agency,* 130. It is also interesting to note that in the footnotes in this CIA monograph, the source for information regarding the location of EG&G's radar range is redacted, only that they are from Office of Special Activity (OSA) records. Written requests to the CIA were denied.

[97] Lockheed test pilot Robert Sieker: Among pilots living at Area 51, a debate ensued about the cause of Sieker's crash. U-2 pilots Tony Bevacqua and Ray Goudey told me they believe pilot error caused Sieker's crash. According to them, he was known to open up his faceplate and take bites of candy bars during flight. Bevacqua himself flew a U-2 dirty bird and lived to tell the tale. Many of these mission flights were made over Asia. Lovick maintains it was the Boston Group's paint that caused the aircraft to overheat.

[98] "As it beeped in the sky": Killian, *Sputnik, Scientists and Eisenhower,* 7.

[99] Killian and Bissell found themselves: Welzenbach, "Science and Technology," 18. "Killian had confidence in Bissell. A special relationship existed between Killian and Bissell going back to 1942."

[99] formidable top secret billion-dollar spy plane: Top Secret Memorandum of Conference with the President, July 20, 1959. "It will have a radar cross section so low that the probability of hostile detection and successful tracking would be very low. It would have a 4000-mile range at mach 4, with 90,000 feet altitude." Office of the Staff Secretary, Subject Series, Alphabetical Subseries, Box 15, Intelligence Matters.

[99] Advancing science and technology for military purposes: The Advanced Research Projects Agency was Eisenhower's response to Sputnik, "a high-level defense organization to formulate and execute R&D projects that would expand the frontiers of technology beyond the immediate and specific requirements of the Military Services and their laboratories." In 1972, ARPA became DARPA. The *D* denotes *Defense*.

Chapter Six: Atomic Accidents

Interviews with Richard Mingus, Al O'Donnell, Jim Freedman, Dr. Wheelon, Troy Wade, Darwin Morgan, Stephen M. Younger

[100] involved thirty consecutive nuclear explosions: Defense Threat Reduction Agency, fact sheet, Operation Plumbbob: "Operation Plumbbob, the sixth series of atmospheric nuclear tests conducted within the continental United States, consisted of 24 nuclear detonations and six safety tests. The Plumbbob series lasted from April 24 to Oct. 7, 1957, and involved about 14,000 Department of Defense (DoD) personnel."

[100] airplane transporting an atomic bomb would crash: Atomic Energy Commission, Summary of Project 57, the First Safety Test of Operation Plumbbob, report to the General Manager by the Director, Division of Military Application, 24.

[100] the perfect place to do this was Area 51: Ref. Sym 5112-(127), Appendix A, Administrative Committee Report, J. D. Shreve Jr., Sandia Corporation (seven pages, no date). "B. Area Chosen (clockwise perimeter) (Groom Mine Map) Start at intersection of 89 with north NTS boundary; follow 89 north to 51 (off map); 90 east on 51 to 04, south on 04 to Watertown (north) boundary, thence west to 95, south to NTS line, and finally west along NTS line to 89. More simply, it is the rectangle of land (1) bounded north and south by grids 51 and an extension of the north NTS edge respectively, (2) bounded east and west by grids 04 and 89 respectively, (3) excluding all area assigned to Watertown," 5.

[101] "relinquished for 20,000 years": Operation Plumbbob, Summary Report, Test Group 57, Nevada Test Site, Extracted Version, May–October 1957, ITR-1515 (Extracted Version), 17.

[101] "no preexisting contamination": Minutes, First General Meeting, the 57 Project, January 18, 1957, at Sandia Corporation, Red. Sym 5112-(127), declassified 8/9/83.

[101] "a safety test": Memo dated April 2, 1957, LAV-57-33 Atomic Energy Commission, Las Vegas Branch, Office of the Branch Chief; also see Safety Experiments, November 1955–March 1958, Defense Nuclear Agency, United States Atmospheric Nuclear Weapons Tests, Nuclear Test Personnel Review, Report Number DNA 6030.

[102] dispute was over eight dead cows: The University of Tennessee Agricultural Experiment Station, Knoxville, November 30, 1953, #404942, Stewart Brothers, Las Vegas, Nevada. Through courtesy of Joe Sanders of AEC, 1–5.

[102] The commission had paid the Stewarts: Memo to Dr. W. S. Johnson, Section Leader, Test Operations Section, University of California, Los Alamos Scientific Laboratory, Los Alamos, New Mexico, October 20, 1953, #4049641.

[103] aerial inspection of Groom Lake: Col. E. A. Blue, DMA/AEC; J. D. Shreve Jr., SC, W. Allaire (ALO), M. Cowan (SC) all inspected the area from the air on a special flight prior to January 18.

[103] "60 to 80 cattle who hadn't gotten the word": Minutes, First General Meeting, the 57 Project, January 18, 1957, at Sandia Corporation, Red. Sym 5112-(127), 3.

[103] excluded from official Nevada Test Site maps: Ref. Sym 5112-(127) Appendix A, Administrative Committee Report, J. D. Shreve Jr., Sandia Corporation (seven pages, no date). "It remains undecided whether Area 13 is considered on-site or off-site so far as NTS is concerned... This is very important to rule on soon." Ultimately, it was decided to *exclude* Area 13 from all maps and it remains this way on declassified maps today because Area 13 lies inside Area 51. Denoting it on a map would lead to questions that the Atomic Energy Commission does not want asked.

[103] nuclear warhead was flown: Ibid., 6. "It will be requested that weapon be flown to Yucca Lake air strip March 15, transferred to Building 11 for storage awaiting ready date for the shot. Checkout would be done in Building 10 and the unit moved from there to Area 13 (requested designation for site) for firing."

[103] Richard Mingus was tired: Interviews with Richard Mingus.

[105] America's first dirty bomb: Operation Plumbbob, Summary Report, Test Group 57, Nevada Test Site, Extracted Version, May–October 1957, ITR-1515 (Extracted Version), 85 pages.

[106] Pacific Proving Ground: General information comes from Buck, *History of the Atomic Energy Commission;* O'Keefe, *Nuclear Hostages;* Fehner and Gosling, *Battlefield of the Cold War.*

[106] made its zigzag course: Fehner and Gosling, *Origins of the Nevada Test Site,* 39.

[106] arguing for an atomic bombing range: Ibid., 46–47.

[106] Armed Forces Special Weapons Project: "History of the Air Force Special Weapons Center 1 January–30 June 1957." Department of Defense, DNA 1. 950210.019, declassified with deletions 2/2/95.

[106] code-named Project Nutmeg: Bugher, *Review of Project Nutmeg,* #404131.

[106] "The optimum conditions": Fehner and Gosling, *Battlefield of the Cold War,* 37.

[107] the goal of fostering competition: Interview with Dr. Bud Wheelon; also see Nevada Test Organization, Background Information on Nevada Nuclear Tests, Office of Test Information, July 15, 1957, #403243, 25.

[108] most ambitious series: Plumbbob Series 1957, Technical Report, Defense Nuclear Agency 6005F, DARE Tracking 48584, 60–75.

[109] Delta, nothing more: Interview with Richard Mingus.

[111] scientists really had no clear idea: Safety Experiments, November 1955–March 1958, Defense Nuclear Agency, United States Atmospheric Nuclear Weapons Tests, Nuclear Test Personnel Review, Report Number DNA 6030.

[111] Workers set up: Ref. Sym 5112-(127) Appendix B, Particle Physics Committee Report, M. Cowan, Sandia Corporation Presiding (nine pages, no date). This document refers to various objectives of the particle physics program, an "experimental approach" to fallout collection, "balloon born precipitators," air samplers on the ground, collection of fallout trays. It described how "some small plywood shacks with open windows and doors will be constructed in the fallout array. Air and surface contamination levels will be measured within the structures and compared to readings on the outside."

[111] "stocked with radiation equipment and protective clothing": Plumbbob Series 1957, Technical Report, Defense Nuclear Agency 6005F, DARE Tracking 48584, 60-75, 316.

[112] Mother Nature's emissary: Interviews with Richard Mingus and Al O'Donnell, who introduced me to Mueller's widow.

[112] 57 Project balloons broke loose: Telex TWX 01A 2008242, From Reeves Attention Gen AD Starbird, 1957 Apr 20 AM 3:39; also see "Feasibility of Weapon Delivery By Free Balloons," OSTI ID: 10150708; Legacy ID: DE98056381, 34 pages.

[113] hand-fired by an employee from EG&G: Operation Plumbbob, Summary Report, Test Group 57, Nevada Test Site, Extracted Version, May–October 1957, ITR–1515 (EX). Sandia Corporation, Albuquerque, NM, October 10, 1958. "At 0350 PST. April 24, a surface charge of 110 pounds of stick dynamite was fired 1,000 feet east of Zone C (as position 42-61) to verify predictions of cloud height. Timing and firing circuits were the ultimate in simplicity; the weapon was hand fired by EG&G at the Test Group Director's instruction."

[113] fallout was to the north: Ibid., 55 (6.1., Weather Observations). The weather was meticulously recorded, which is ironic given how "fast and loose" everything else was running out at the test site, as stated by an EG&G employee who also worked as a liaison to the Pentagon. "April 10, 1957. Hodographs during the period 2100 to 2330 PST showed that satisfactory conditions existed at 2100 PST, but a recommendation for cancellation was made after the wind shifted to northwest on the 2300 PST soundings. April 1F, [sic] 1957. Satisfactory wind conditions existed at 0441 PST, but the morning inversion broke more quickly than expected. By 0530 PST, winds were too strong and the shear had disappeared, forcing cancellation. April 20, 1957, Intermittent light showers began at 2330 PST on the 19th and continued through the remainder of the night and following morning. Hodographs indicated that satisfactory winds existed during this period, but moisture on the instrumentation forced cancellation. April 24, 1957. Scattered middle clouds were observed and a moderate dew formed during the night. The sequence of wind changes from 0415 to 0756 is shown by the hodographs. The shot was fired at 0627 PST."

[113] The bomb was indeed dirty: In June of 1982, Sandia Corporation produced an extracted 102-page report on the results of its dirty bomb or plutonium-contamination effects study on Project 57 for the director of the Defense Nuclear Agency, in lieu of a proposed cleanup of Area 13 (see chapter 18). Information in this chapter comes from portions of that extracted study. The stated objectives of the project "were to estimate the immediate and long-term distribution of plutonium and gain an understanding of how this distribution comes about, to conduct a biomedical evaluation of plutonium-laden environments, to investigate relevant methods of decontamination, and to

evaluate alpha field survey instruments and monitoring procedures." And yet Area 13 soil decontamination was not even considered for twenty-five years.

[113] "extract" of the original report: The full, still-classified document, originally prepared by Sandia Corporation in Albuquerque, New Mexico, in October of 1958, is called ITR-1515.

[113] "the alpha half life of plutonium-239": Ibid., 17 ("Motivation and Mission, 1.1 Historical Resume"). The text reads: "once in the stomach, their stay in the body is short, for they are excreted as an inert material with virtually no body assimilation. Inhalation is a different mechanism entirely and one which presents a considerable threat. Any particle small enough to reach the lower respiratory tract apparently has an excellent chance of clinging to alveolar surfaces and staying to do radiation damage . . . One cannot outlive the influence, because the alpha half life of plutonium-239 is of the order of 20,000 years."

[114] "respirable plutonium remarkably far downwind": Ibid., 7 ("Foreword, Abstract").

[115] "earthworms moved 18 tons of soil": Ibid., 101 (8.6, "A New Program"). "Finally, Dr. Kermit Larson agreed to exploit an idea which grew out of discussions among participants in the anniversary measurements—earthworms. Compton's Encyclopedia reports that the renowned Charles Darwin studied an acre of garden in which he claimed 53,000 hard-working earthworms moved 18 tons of soil. Translocation of soil, the possibility that earthworm body chemistry may vary plutonium form, etc., could turn out to be significant influences, intentional or unintentional, in the rehabilitation of a weapon-accident environment."

[116] Pauling said: The quotes in this two-page section, and also the newspaper quotes on pages 119–121, are from the extensive newspaper archive collection located in the Atomic Testing Museum library reading room in Las Vegas, Nevada.

[118] The Pentagon wondered: Fehner and Gosling, *Battlefield of the Cold War,* 159–82.

[118] caused Area 51 personnel: Interview with Richard Mingus.

[120] "the Indoctrination Project: DNA 6005F, Plumbbob Series 1957, United States Atmospheric Nuclear Weapons Tests, Nuclear Test Personnel Review, Chapter 4, Exercise Desert Rock VII and VIII Programs, 81, 96.

[120] Committee on Human Resources: Memorandum, Members of the

Advisory Committee on Human Radiation Experiments, September 8, 1994, "Human Experiments in Connection with the Atomic Bomb Tests," attachment 5, item 10.

[120] "mythical attack by an aggressor force": During the Hood nuclear bomb, the Marine Corps conducted coordinated air-ground assault maneuvers that included helicopter airlifts and tactical air support; "Exercise Desert Rock VII-VIII, Operation Plumbbob," Defense Nuclear Agency 4747F.

[121] Mingus saw that a large swath of the desert was on fire: Interview with Mingus.

[123] Area 51 had become uninhabitable: Interview with Richard Mingus; also Office Memorandum, United States Government, Observed Damage at Watertown, Nevada, following the Sixth Nuclear shot of Plumbbob, July 9, 1957. R. A. Gilmore, Off-Site Rad-Safe, NTO, #0150371.

Chapter Seven: From Ghost Town to Boomtown

Interviews: T. D. Barnes, Peter Merlin, Al O'Donnell, Richard Mingus, Jim Freedman, Ed Lovick, Tony Bevacqua, Ray Goudey, Ernie Williams, Harry Martin, Colonel Slater, Frank Murray

[124] measuring fallout with Geiger counters in hand: Interview with T. D. Barnes; Operation Plumbbob Projects and Reports: Program 2, Project 2.2., Neutron Induced Activities in Soil Elements WT-1411; Project 2.5 Initial Gamma Radiation Intensity and Neutron-Induced Gamma Radiation of NTS Soil WT-1414.

[124] dressed in white lab coats and work boots: Photographs viewed at the Atomic Testing Museum library, Las Vegas.

[124] from pinhead particles to pencil-size pieces of steel: DNA 6005F, Plumbbob Series 1957, United States Atmospheric Nuclear Weapons Tests, Nuclear Test Personnel Review, Chapter 4, Exercise Desert Rock VII and VIII Programs, Civil Effects Test Group, Fallout Studies, 204-247; AEC Research and Development Report BNWL-481-1, 113 pages.

[124] surprise of the nuclear scientists: McPhee, *Curve of Binding Energy,* 166–67.

[125] could locate them with magnets: Roadrunners Internationale newsletter, August 1, 2009, 34th edition. From the personal diary of Dan Sheahan, owner

and operator of the Groom Mine, provided to the Roadrunners Internationale by his great-granddaughter Lisa Heawood.

[125] weapons planners moved ahead: Interviews with Al O'Donnell, Richard Mingus, and Jim Freedman. There was a nuclear test ban moratorium on the horizon, which meant that all weapons tests were scheduled to end on October 31, 1958. At the test site, weapons engineers worked at a frenzied pace to finish as many nuclear tests as they could before the deadline.

[125] the animals observed: An anonymous eyewitness related to me the horror of watching a dying horse seek water at Area 51. The AEC has never declassified its animal observations, which I understand are extensive. In an AEC document released to the public on July 15, 1957, entitled "Responsibility for U.S. Nuclear Weapons Programs," in a section called "Operating Controls," it is stated that "cattle and horses grazing within a few miles of the detonation suffered skin deep beta radiation burns on their hides (1952 and 1953 series) with no effect on their breeding value and no effect on the cattle's beef quality. Radiation fallout more than a few miles from detonation has been quite harmless to humans, animals or crops." In *The Day We Bombed Utah*, John G. Fuller presents the opposite argument.

[125] emergency landing on the former U-2 airstrip: Interview with Peter Merlin.

[126] Edward Lovick was standing on: Interview with Edward Lovick.

[127] grandfather of stealth: Before working on the A-12, Lovick's first job at Skunk Works was to try to reduce the radar reflections being bounced back from the U-2 to the Soviet radar systems. With Area 51 still shuttered from atomic fallout, the physicist's first efforts took place at a remote hangar in the north corner of Edwards Air Force Base in California. There, Lovick and colleagues spent hours coming up with all kinds of antiradar schemes: "It was our job to invent something that would neither compromise the aircraft's height, nor allow its hydraulic system to overheat as had happened with Sieker. Kelly Johnson had a rule: one pound of extra weight applied to the aircraft would reduce its altitude by one foot. This meant our camouflage coating couldn't exceed a quarter of an inch and had to weigh as little as possible."

[127] aircraft would be radically different: Interviews with Ed Lovick, Dr. Wheelon, T. D. Barnes. Other federal agencies were also secretly experimenting with supersonic flight, but not sustained flight at Mach 3. The Air Force, NASA, and the Navy were involved in the experimental X-15, a hypersonic airplane that would lay the groundwork for travel into space. But the X-15 was

boosted off the back of a mother ship, whereas the Agency's new plane would leave the tarmac on its own power and return to the base the same way.

[128] twenty-second window: Peebles, *Dark Eagles*, 51.

[128] it loses precision and speed: Interview with Dr. Wheelon.

[128] minutiae involving radar returns: Jones, *The Wizard War*. Lovick spent hours describing for me the fundamental concepts of radar, which is an acronym for radio detection and ranging, which first came into being in 1904 when a German engineer named Christian Hulsmeyer figured out that electromagnetic waves could be used to identify, or "see," a metal ship floating in dense fog. It didn't take long for the military to realize the inherent value of radar as a way to detect large, moving metal objects otherwise invisible to the naked eye. This was especially true for ships and airplanes, two key means of transport in twentieth-century warfare.

[129] fourteen-year-old children were doing in 1933: Interview with Lovick. By high school, Lovick had created a radio receiver from scrap metal, vacuum tubes, and discarded radio parts which enabled him "to detect signals a hundred miles away, which gave me the intense feeling of discovering something that I did not previously have evidence as being there."

[130] the Archangel-1: Robarge, *Archangel*, 4–5. *Archangel* is a term meaning "an angel of high rank" and it is also a port city in northwestern Russia, home to many Soviet radar stations that would one day be trying to track the A-12.

[131] fifty Skunk Works employees returned to Area 51: Ibid., 6.

[131] "build a full scale mockup": Johnson, *History of the Oxcart Program*, 5.

[132] code-named Titania: United States Nuclear Tests July 1945 through September 1992 DOE/NV–209–REV 15, 144. The bomb was named after a satellite of the planet Uranus.

[133] Each member of Lovick's crew: Interview with Lovick.

[134] "Ike wants an airplane from Mandrake the magician": Rich, *Skunk Works*, 198.

[135] "by adding the chemical compound cesium": Johnson, *History of the Oxcart Program*, 4. Johnson wrote: "we proposed the use of cesium additive to the fuel. This was first brought up by Mr. Ed Lovick of ADP, its final development was passed over to P&W." Lovick recalls traveling to Pratt and Whitney's research center in Florida where the aircraft engines were being tested. "I

realized that I had utilized theory that applied to thermal ionization of gases and would need to use parameters appropriate to electron emission from hot solid surfaces. Our results indicated that we were dealing with mixtures of the two states but we did not know how to determine how much of each kind of material, gas or solid, was involved in the production of the ionization that we measured. The results were encouraging, but we needed to know more. So we were moved to much better facilities at the P. & W. Willgoos Turbine Laboratory in East Hartford, Connecticut." It was there that the problem was solved.

[135] Oxcart being the fastest: CIA Document EO 12958 3.3(b) Oxcart Facts: A-12 Specifications; A-12 Experience Record (as of July 10, 1967). Note that in November of 1961, the X-15 rocket plane flew Mach 6, or 4,092 mph. At the time of this meeting, the CIA thought they were building the fastest airplane in the world, which technically it was, because the X-15 didn't take off on its own power. As per interviews with T. D. Barnes, who worked on both projects.

[135] Area 51 was back in business: Parangosky, *The Oxcart Story,* 3 (per Dr. Wheelon, Parangosky was the true author of this seminal work on Oxcart; any other name was a pseudonym). The contract was officially signed on February 11, 1960.

[136] the CIA hired work crews from next door: Interview with Ernie Williams.

[136] The construction of a new runway and the fuel farm: Interview with Harry Martin; Pedlow and Welzenbach, *Central Intelligence Agency,* 25–26.

[136] The A-12 Oxcart was a flying fuel tank: Interview with Harry Martin.

[137] CIA's "own little air force": Interview with Colonel Slater.

[137] Getting the Oxcart to fly: Interview with Frank Murray.

[137] 186-mile swath just to make a U-turn: Interview with Colonel Slater.

[137] same was true at NORAD: Interviews with Dr. Wheelon, Colonel Slater.

[138] they passed a simple sketch: Interview with Ed Lovick.

[138] S. Varentsov: CIA Memo, S. Varenstov, Chief Marshal, USSR, The Problem of Combat with the Nuclear Means of the Enemy and Its Solution, August 1961.

[138] advancing surface-to-air-missile technology: Interviews with Dr. Wheelon, Ed Lovick, T. D. Barnes.

Chapter Eight: Cat and Mouse Becomes Downfall

Interviews: Gary Powers Jr., T. D. Barnes, Dr. Wheelon, Jim Freedman, Gene Poteat, Helen Kleyla (Richard Bissell's longtime secretary, via written correspondence)

[139] drenched in sweat: Powers, *Operation Overflight,* 75.

[140] Tyuratam was Russia's Cape Canaveral: CIA report on U-2 Vulnerability Tests, April 1960, Eisenhower Archives, Office of the Staff Secretary, Subject Series, Alphabetical Subseries, Box 15, Intelligence Matters. Memo: ICBM Targets — The Urals and Tyura Tam, "Sverdlovsk in the Urals is the best bet on the location of a major ICBM factory." Notable color U-2 flight maps are in this file.

[140] head up to a facility at Plesetsk: Harford, *Korolev,* 112. "R-7s and R-7As were deployed at only two launch pads at Baikonur and, eventually, four at Plesetsk, a launch center readied by 1959 . . . Plesetsk soon became the busiest of the USSR's three launch facilities, having responsibility for placing in orbit reconnaissance and other military satellites."

[140] two-and-a-half-foot increments: Brugioni, *Eyeball to Eyeball,* 185.

[140] indicated he wanted to speak with him: Powers, *Operation Overflight,* 69.

[141] had a premonition: Ibid.

[142] awakened by a ringing telephone: W. Taubman, *Khrushchev,* 443.

[142] a sharp poke in the eye: Khrushchev, *Khrushchev Remembers,* 444. "Sverdlovsk, was an especially deep penetration into our territory and therefore an especially arrogant violation . . . They were making these flights to show up our impotence. Well, we weren't impotent any longer."

[142] "An uncomfortable situation was shaping up": Orlov, "The U-2 Program," 10.

[144] Soviets' secret bioweapons program: Hoffman, *The Dead Hand,* 119.

[144] Kyshtym 40 was as valuable: Brugioni, *Eyeball to Eyeball,* 43.

[144] "Destroy target": Orlov, "The U-2 Program," 11.

[145] *Stop and think:* Powers, *Operation Overflight,* 83.

[145] "He's turning left": Jack Anderson, "US Heard Russians Chasing U-2," *Washington Post,* May 12, 1960.

[146] NSA operators heard: Bamford, *Body of Secrets,* 49.

[146] "Bill Bailey did not come home": Richelson, *Wizards of Langley,* 18.

[147] The brand was Laika: Powers, *Operation Overflight,* 91.

[147] "We believed that if a U-2 was shot": Bissell, *Reflections of a Cold Warrior,* 121–22. But Bissell also admitted that the Agency agreed "unanimously" that the "big rolls of film aboard the plane would not be destroyed... Their non-flammable base would prevent them from burning, and they could be dropped from a height of ten miles and survive. We always knew that in the event of a crash there was going to be a couple rolls of film lying around, and there was not much we could do about it."

[147] the White House claimed: Department of State, for the Press, No. 249, May 6, 1960; Department of State, for the Press, No. 254, May 9, 1960.

[147] But Khrushchev had evidence: Incoming telegram, Department of State, Control 6700, May 10, 1969.

[147] With great bravado: W. Taubman, *Khrushchev,* 455–58.

[149] "I would like to resign": P. Taubman, *Secret Empire,* 396.

[149] Eisenhower wouldn't bow: Bamford, *Body of Secrets,* 53–54. "For Eisenhower, the whole process was quickly turning into Chinese water torture. Every day he was being forced to dribble out more and more of the story."

[149] "the first time any nation had publicly admitted": Brugioni, *Eyeball to Eyeball,* 49.

[149] authorized a Soviet military base: Ibid., 55.

[149] twenty-five minutes' time: Havana, Cuba, to Washington, DC, is 1,130 miles. In 1960, a Russian missile traveled at approximately Mach 3.5.

[150] During Powers's trial: "Report on Conclusion of Powers Trial, USSR International Affairs," August 22, 1960, approved for release September 1985, 39 pages.

[150] "Las Vegas firing range (poligon) in the Nevada desert": Ibid., RB-6.

[150] "criminal conspiracy": Ibid.

[151] "follower of Hitler": Ibid., RB-20.

[151] Watertown as the U-2 training facility: Powers, *Operation Overflight*, 114.

[151] out at the Ranch: Parangosky, *The Oxcart Story*, 6–7.

[152] Richard Bissell had a tennis court put in: Interview with Dr. Wheelon.

[152] Prohibited Area P-275: Interview with Peter Merlin.

[152] "thirteen million different parts": Bissell, *Reflections of a Cold Warrior*, 133.

[152] the titanium that first held everything up: Pedlow and Welzenbach, *Central Intelligence Agency*, 21–22.

[152] nearly 95 percent of what Lockheed initially received: Robarge, *Archangel*, 11.

[153] Russia was spending billions of rubles: Interview with Ed Lovick.

[153] "who thought ELINT was a dirty word": Poteat, "Engineering and the CIA," 24.

[155] Barnes was recruited by the CIA: Interview with Barnes; CIA Personal Resume, 1966, Barnes, Thornton Duard.

[157] Castro's regime "must be overthrown": Bissell, *Reflections of a Cold Warrior*, 153.

[158] "Richard Bissell," Kennedy said: Thomas, "Wayward Spy," 36.

[159] put a bullet in his own head: Weiner, *Legacy of Ashes*, 303.

[159] Bahía de Cochinos, or the Bay of Pigs: Kirkpatrick, *The Real CIA*, chapter 8; Pfeiffer, *CIA's Official History of the Bay of Pigs;* Warner, "CIA's Internal Probe."

[159] could help in gathering intel: Oral history interview with Richard M. Bissell Jr. by Theodore A. Wilson and Richard D. McKinzie, East Hartford, Connecticut, July 9, 1971.

[160] Bissell blamed the mission's failure on his old rival General Curtis LeMay: Bissell, *Reflections of a Cold Warrior*, 176. In discussing the decision of the Joint Chiefs, which included LeMay sitting in for the commandant of the Marines, "to cancel the air strikes so readily," Bissell stated, "one could make a case that their view reflected rivalry between the air force and the CIA. The agency's earlier success with the overhead reconnaissance programs had disturbed certain high-ranking members of the air force." Certainly he is referring to LeMay. "Friends of mine in the military spoke frankly to me about this," Bissell added. "There was no denying that the sentiment existed among

military that all the air activities undertaken by the CIA in the U-2, SR-71 [note: Oxcart had not been declassified yet] and spy satellite programs should have come under jurisdiction of the air force. Robert Amory recalled in a 1966 interview that, after I was put in charge of the U-2 program, 'essentially the air force's eye was wiped in you-know-what and they resented that from the beginning.'" For Bissell, "the resentment never died."

[160] if LeMay had provided adequate air cover: Ibid., 175. "Curtis LeMay (who was sitting in for the absent commandant of the Marines) and several of the chiefs admitted their doubt about the absolute essentiality of air cover...I was shocked. We all knew only too well that without air support, the project would fail."

[160] "time zone confusion": Ibid., 189. Bissell wrote, "When the B-26s lumbered into the air the next day, however, no navy cover appeared. It seemed that a misunderstanding about the correct time standard had prevented the air support from being at the target area when expected. As a result, the B-26s were either forced from the field of battle or shot down, the final tragic blow." From the National Security Archive: "The unmarked jets failed to rendezvous with the bombers, however, because the CIA and the Pentagon were unaware of a time zone difference between Nicaragua and Cuba."

[161] Lyman B. Kirkpatrick Jr.: Interviews with Jim Freedman.

[161] Lyman Kirkpatrick contracted polio: Biography of Lyman B. Kirkpatrick, Princeton University Library, Department of Rare Books and Special Collections, Seeley G. Mudd Manuscript Library, Public Policy Papers. Lyman B. Kirkpatrick Papers, circa 1933–2000, Call Number MC209.

[161] relegated to the role of second-tier bureaucrat: In his memoir, Bissell does not mince words. He calls Kirkpatrick "an ambitious man who, in spite of paralysis from polio, aspired to position of director of central intelligence. His illness necessitated a move from the exciting and challenging directorate of plans to the more mundane, bureaucratic position of inspector general, a shift he always resented." Bissell, *Reflections of a Cold Warrior,* 193.

Chapter Nine: The Base Builds Back Up

Interviews with Harry Martin, Jim Freedman, T. D. Barnes, Al O'Donnell, Peter Merlin, Millie Meierdierck

[162] the man in charge of property control at Area 51: Interviews with Jim Freedman, T. D. Barnes, Al O'Donnell.

[165] "The high and rugged northeast perimeter": Interview with Peter Merlin, who obtained copies (largely redacted) of Kirkpatrick's visit to Area 51 from the CIA's online reading room (CIA.gov). These documents appear to have since been removed.

[166] "Bay of Pigs will embolden the Soviets": Absher, *Mind-Sets and Missiles,* 10.

[166] Area 51 was a target: Interviews with Peter Merlin, Jim Freedman.

[166] decided to make a hunting trip: Interview with Jim Freedman; Hank Meierdierck's personal papers.

[168] Richard Bissell resigned: Oral history interview with Richard M. Bissell Jr. by Theodore A. Wilson and Richard D. McKinzie, East Hartford, Connecticut, July 9, 1971 (Harry S. Truman Library and Museum), http://www.trumanlibrary .org/oralhist/bissellr.htm.

[168] keep the CIA in the spy plane business: Welzenbach, "Science and Technology," 23.

[168] Richard Bissell alone, had gone rogue: Ibid., 22.

[168] CIA might work in better partnership: Richelson, *Wizards of Langley,* 58–60.

[169] "Wayne Pendleton was the head of the radar group": Interview with Wayne Pendleton.

[170] "and 'dirty tricks' of Dick Bissell's": Welzenbach, "Science and Technology," 22. The full passage reads: "However, a note of discord crept into Bissell's relations with Land and Killian . . . both Land and Killian looked upon science and technology almost as a religion, something sacred to be kept from contamination by those who would misuse it for unwholesome ends. Into this category fit the covert operations and dirty tricks of Dick Bissell's Directorate of Plans."

[170] called Teak and Orange: Film footage viewed at the Atomic Testing Museum, Las Vegas.

[170] which is exactly where the ozone layer lies: Hoerlin, "United States High-Altitude Test," 43.

[170] "The impetus for these tests": Ibid., 47.

[170] his rationale: Ground stations were supposed to measure acoustic waves that would happen as a result of the blast but Teak detonated seven miles laterally off course to the south and the communication systems were knocked out. Orange detonated four miles higher than it was supposed to and "the deviations affected data acquisitions."

[170] The animals' heads had been locked in gadgets: Oral history interview with Air Force colonel John Pickering, 52. Film footage viewed at the Atomic Testing Museum, Las Vegas.

[171] "Teak and Orange events would 'burn a hole' into the natural ozone layer": Hoerlin, "United States High-Altitude Test," 43.

[172] Von Braun can be seen examining the Redstone rocket: Teak shot film footage viewed at the Atomic Testing Museum library, Las Vegas.

[172] left the island before the second test: Interview with Al O'Donnell; Neufeld, *Von Braun,* 332.

[172] to dash up to Hitler's lair: Neufeld, *Von Braun,* 127.

[172] project called Operation Argus commenced: Final Review of Argus Fact Sheet, 16 Apr. 82. "The tests were conducted in complete secrecy and were not announced until the following year."

[173] Christofilos convinced Killian: Killian, *Sputnik, Scientists and Eisenhower,* 187.

[173] "probably the most spectacular event ever conducted": The White House Memorandum for the President, From J.R. Killian Jr., Subject: Preliminary Results of the ARGUS experiment, dated November 3, 1958, declassified 5/20/77.

[173] Walter Sullivan hand-delivered a letter to Killian: The letter is marked "By Hand" and dated February 2, 1959, written on *New York Times* letterhead, and addressed to Dr. James R. Killian Jr. at the White House.

[173] "Neither confirm nor deny such leaks": Memorandum to Dr. James R. Killian, Jr. Subject: Release of Information on ARGUS. Dated January 20, 1959, signed Karl G. Harr, Jr. Special Assistant to the President. Among other things, it is interesting to note here that on White House stationery, Killian is referred to as "Dr. Killian." He was not a doctor; he never received a PhD but rather a bachelor's degree in management. This fact was confirmed for me by MIT library staffer Jennifer Hirsch. "Mr. Killian always went out of his way to remind people he was not a doctor," I was told—apparently not so with the White House.

[174] "I would be protected from congressional inquisition": Killian, *Sputnik, Scientists and Eisenhower*, 25.

[175] "Are you still there?": Admiral Parker of the Armed Forces Special Weapons Project; Defense Technical Information Center Staff, *Defense's Nuclear Agency 1947–1997*, 140; Defense Threat Reduction Agency, 2002.

Chapter Ten: Wizards of Science, Technology, and Diplomacy

Interviews: Harry Martin, Louise Schalk, Dr. Wheelon, Colonel Slater, Frank Murray, Roger Andersen, Ken Collins

[176] Martin had been at Area 51 since the very first days: Interviews with Harry Martin.

[176] The generals would inevitably show up: Classified Message, Secret 2135Z 14 May 62, To Director, Prity [sic] OXCART. "1. General Power, General Compton, Col Montoya and Col Geary [redacted], A-12...During the flight the visitors were shown [redacted]...Kelly Johnson flew back to Las Vegas with the group...General Power seemed very impressed with the aircraft." Declassified by CIA, August 2007.

[177] "Lou, wake up!": Interview with Louise Schalk.

[178] "The aircraft began wobbling": Johnson, *History of the Oxcart Program*, 12.

[178] "What in Hell, Lou?": Rich, *Skunk Works*, 219.

[178–179] Martin thought for sure the airplane was going to crash: Interview with Harry Martin.

[179] Rare film footage of the historic event: CIA footage, T. D. Barnes's personal collection.

[179] Bud Wheelon: Central Intelligence Agency, "Biographic Profile, Albert Dewell Wheelon," May 10, 1966, NARA, MRB, RG 263.

[179–180] Howard and Jane Roman: Helms, *A Look Over My Shoulder*, 275. "When the CIA Counterintelligence Staff was established, Jim Angleton assumed responsibility for operational liaison with the FBI. Jane Roman, a veteran OSS X-2 officer, handled the daily meetings..."; interview with Dr. Wheelon.

[180] hand-picked by President Kennedy's science advisers: Central

Intelligence Agency, R. V. Jones Intelligence Award Ceremony Honoring Dr. Albert Wheelon, December 13, 1994.

[180] "in this way, I became the new 'Mayor of Area 51' ": Interview with Dr. Wheelon.

[182] Agency had been analyzing reports: McAuliffe, *CIA Documents on the Cuban Missile Crisis 1962,* 1–31.

[182] including 1,700 Soviet military technicians: Ibid., 37.

[182] jamming facilities against Cape Canaveral: Ibid.

[182] McCone left for his honeymoon in Paris: Interview with Dr. Wheelon.

[183] Not another Gary Powers incident: This was a common theme among military planners all through the 1960s.

[183] the CIA got presidential approval: Office of Special Activities DD/S&T Chronological History, 30 August 1966, Top Secret, Approved for release Jul 2001, 5. "5 October 1962, Last CIA Flight over Cuba (50 flown in all)."

[183] pushing for preemptive strikes: Brugioni, *Eyeball to Eyeball,* 265.

[183] Ledford had been asked by McCone: Interview with Dr. Wheelon.

[184] General LeMay encouraged him to take the CIA liaison job: Richelson, *Wizards of Langley,* 53.

[184] Ledford's plane crash, involving heroics: Official Website of U.S. Air Force, biography of Brigadier General Jack C. Ledford, retired Oct. 1, 1970; died Nov. 16, 2007.

[184] tried to treat Ledford with opiates: This story was legendary among the men who worked under Ledford at Area 51 and is sourced from multiple interviews including with Colonel Slater and Frank Murray. A version of it can be read at the Arlington National Cemetery Web site. Ledford's back-seater, Sergeant Harry C. Miller, died of his original wounds several hours after Ledford and the medic helped him out of the plane.

[184] The chances were one in six, Ledford said: Richelson, *Wizards of Langley,* 53.

[185] Kennedy felt that if a CIA spy plane: Interview with Dr. Wheelon.

[185] Air Force pilot flying an Agency U-2: Richelson, *Wizards of Langley,* 54.

[185] Photographs showing nuclear missiles: Brugioni, *Eyeball to Eyeball,* photographic inserts.

Chapter Eleven: What Airplane?

Interviews: Ken Collins, Don Donohue, Sam Pizzo, Frank Murray, Roger Andersen, Florence DeLuna, Frank Micalizzi, Harry Martin

[186] Collins went by the code name Ken Colmar: Interviews with Ken Collins, who had never revealed his code name before.

[187] She made it as far as Athens: Powers, *Overflight,* 59.

[188] he flew deep into North Korea: Citation, First Lieutenant Kenneth S. Collins, SO. No. 221 Hq FEAP, APO925, 6 May 53, by Command of General Weyland.

[188] fired at by MiG fighter jets: Ibid.

[188] Distinguished Flying Cross: Citation to Accompany the Award of the Distinguished Flying Cross (First Oak Leaf Cluster) to Kenneth S. Collins. AO 2222924, United States Air Force.

[188] coveted Silver Star for valor: Citation for Silver Star, First Lieutenant Kenneth S. Collins, by direction of the president.

[190] a total of five Oxcarts being flight-tested at Area 51: Robarge, *Archangel,* 17.

[190] Captain Donald Donohue would start out following Collins: Interview with Don Donohue.

[190] Later, Jack Weeks: Interview with Ken Collins.

[190] "Suddenly, the altimeter was rapidly unwinding": Interview with Ken Collins.

[193] Sam Pizzo had a monumental amount of work: Interview with Sam Pizzo.

[194] took to the desert terrain on horseback: Interview with Ken Collins.

[194] filled by Air Force brass: Interview with Colonel Slater.

[195] Holbury had been given a commendation by General Patton: General Robert J. Holbury biography, Air Commander, Detachment 1 of the 1129th U.S. Air Force Special Activities Squadron at Groom Lake, Nevada; Roadrunners Internationale official Web site.

[196] a pitot tube had in fact caused the crash: Interview with Collins; Parangosky, *The Oxcart Story,* 11.

[197] monitoring phone conversations: Briefing Note for the Deputy Director of Central Intelligence, 10 March 1964. Attachment 1 to BYE-2015-64, "Project Oxcart Awareness Outside Cleared Community." The Agency also had a system in place to monitor air traffic chatter during Oxcart test flights to see if any commercial or military pilots spotted the plane.

[197] increasingly suspicious CIA: Col. Redmond White, Diary Notes, September 27, 1963, Secret. White was the CIA's deputy director/support and his notes include a second reference to the disclosure to *Aviation Week* as well as a notation that CIA director John McCone said, "OXCART is going to blow sooner or later."

[198] the Air Force ordered not one but three variants: Pedlow and Welzenbach, *Central Intelligence Agency,* 33.

[198] letters stood for "Reconnaissance/Strike": Memorandum, Secretary of the Air Force Eugene Zuckert to General Bernard Schriever, April 8, 1963, w/att: Procurement and Security Provisions for the R-12 Program, Top Secret.

[198–199] eight hundred million dollars developing the B-70 bomber airplane: Marcelle Size Knaack, *Encyclopedia of U.S. Air Force Aircraft and Missile Systems, Post-World War II Bombers,* 559. The XB-70A had its genesis in Boeing Aircraft Corporation's Project MX-2145. Also see Ball, *Politics and Force Levels,* 216–18.

[199] the President was astonished: Rich, *Skunk Works,* 228.

[199] "unnecessary and economically unjustifiable": President Kennedy, Special Message to the Congress of Urgent National Needs, delivered in person before a joint session of Congress, May 25, 1961.

[199] Congress cut back its B-70 order even further: House Armed Services Committee, Authorizing Appropriations for Aircraft, Missiles and Naval Vessels for the Armed Forces (1961), 569, see FY 1962, 1564–65, 1577.

[199] "Johnson, I want a promise out of you": Rich, *Skunk Works,* 231.

[200] LeMay promised to send Lockheed: Robarge, *Archangel,* 52. The Air Force initially envisioned a fleet of as many as a hundred YF-12s, designed to intercept a Soviet supersonic bomber rumored to be in the works.

[200] At the Ranch, it was business as usual: Interview with Colonel Slater.

[200] finally delivered to the Ranch: Robarge, *Archangel,* 17. The J–57 engine could reach a maximum speed of Mach 1.6 and a maximum height of 40,000 feet; interview with John Evans of Pratt and Whitney.

[200–201] An X-ray showed the outline of a pen: Interview with Ed Lovick.

[201] new set of challenges: Pedlow and Welzenbach, *Central Intelligence Agency,* 38.

[202] F–101 chase plane had run off the airstrip: Interview with Don Donohue.

[202] Lyndon Johnson would be briefed: CIA Memo, Meeting with the President, Secretary Rusk, Secretary McNamara, Mr. Bundy and DCI. Re: Surfacing the OXCART, 29 November, 1963, 1.

Chapter Twelve: Covering Up the Cover-Up

Interviews: Jim Freedman, Colonel Slater, T. D. Barnes, Stanton Friedman

[204] "I heard it was in Area 22": Interview with Jim Freedman. In contemporary maps of the test site, Area 22 is located down by Camp Mercury. In the 1950s and 1960s, many of the quadrants were numbered differently.

[205] "on 30 April, A-12 was in air": Priority Secret Classified Message to Director from———2219Z Classified Message Secret 15 May 62, ZE19C "Oxcart Secure Ops."

[205] 354,200 feet—almost 67 miles up: Jenkins, *Hypersonics Before the Shuttle,* 119. The Kármán line, commonly used to define the boundary between the Earth's atmosphere and outer space, is at an altitude of approximately 328,000, or 62 miles above sea level. The U–2 flew at 70,000 feet, or approximately 13 miles; the A–12 flew at 90,000 feet, or approximately 17.5 miles.

[206] "commercial pilots would report sightings": Interview with Colonel Slater; Annie Jacobsen, "The Road to Area 51," *Los Angeles Times Magazine,* April 5, 2009, 26–28, 77.

[206] Walter Cronkite hosted a CBS news special report: The report can be viewed online, "From the Vault," *CBS Reports.*

[207] Dr. Robertson appeared on a *CBS Reports:* Haines, "CIA's Role," 74.

[207] House Armed Services Committee held hearings on UFOs: "Congress Reassured on Space Visits," *New York Times,* April 6, 1966.

[207] Pitting the Air Force against the CIA: Walter L. Mackey, executive officer, memorandum for DCI, "Air Force Request to Declassify CIA Material on Unidentified Flying Objects (UFO)," September 1, 1966.

[207] According to CIA historian Gerald Haines: Haines, "CIA's Role."

[207] journalist named John Lear: Lear, "The Disputed CIA Document on UFO's," *Saturday Review,* September 3, 1966.

[211] One of the more enigmatic figures: Hillenkoetter took over amid negotiations on May 1, 1947, of what would be the National Security Act of 1947, so when the CIA came into being on September 18, 1947, he was already DCI, per the Central Intelligence Agency Library, Roscoe Henry Hillenkoetter, Rear Admiral, US Navy, CIA.gov.

[211] served on the board of governors: Haines, "CIA's Role," 74.

[211] Hillenkoetter testified to Congress: "Air Force Order on 'Saucers' Cited; Pamphlet by the Inspector General Called Objects a 'Serious Business,'" *New York Times,* February 28, 1960.

[211] he mysteriously resigned: NICAP Web site, "The Who Was Series," Hillenkoetter, Vice-Admiral Roscoe, http://www.nicap.org/photobio.htm; in my interview with Stan Friedman, Friedman said there was nothing mysterious about Hillenkoetter's resigning, "he just resigned." Nor does Friedman believe that Hillenkoetter was planted at NICAP to gather information.

[212] Bryan's true role with the ufologists: Ibid. In the official NICAP bio for Hillenkoetter, it is written, "He resigned from NICAP in Feb 1962 and was replaced on the NICAP Board by a former covert CIA high official, Joseph Bryan III, the CIA's first Chief of Political & Psychological Warfare (Bryan never disclosed his CIA background to NICAP or Keyhoe)."

[212] the CIA had maintained three lines of thought on UFOs: Memorandum for file OSI, Meeting of OSI Advisory Group on UFO, January 14 through 17, 1953, 3 pages; Scientific Advisory Panel on Unidentified Flying Objects, 14–17 January 1953, Evidence Presented, 2 pages; CIA Scientific Advisory Panel on Unidentified Flying Objects, Comments and Suggestions of UFO Panel, 19 pages. The CIA party line on UFOs had been firmly established by General Bedell Smith during his tenure and was maintained until sometime around 1966, when this new thinking emerged.

[212] This new postulation came from the Agency's monitoring: CIA Memo, Translation, Vitolniyek, R. (Director) Flying phenomena, *Sovetsknya Latviya,*

no. 287, 10 Dec. 67; CIA Memo, 10 Aug. 67, "Report on Conversations with Soviet Scientists on Subject of Unidentified Flying Objects in the USSR"; CIA Memo, Translation of Memo from *Konsomol'skaya pravda,* no. 13, 20 January 68, author Zigel, 3.

[212] Villen Lyustiberg: CIA Memo, Translation, Lyustiberg V. (Science commentator for [illegible]), "Are Flying Saucers a Myth?" *Pravda, Ukrainy,* no. 40, 17 Feb. 68.

[212] "the U.S. publicizes them to divert people from its failures and aggressions": CIA Memo, Translation, "Nothing But the Facts on UFOs or Which Novosti Writer Do You Read?" 9 April 1968, 12 pages.

[213] Zigel, had come to believe: The CIA followed Zigel closely. In the Agency's author biography on him, it states: "Zigel, F. Yu., Dr of Technical Science, writes under auspices of Moscow Aviation Institute, Associate Professor there as of 1969." CIA analysts discovered that Zigel's interest in UFOs began with his interest in astronomy and mathematics in 1936, after he participated in an expedition to Kazakhstan to observe a solar eclipse. Zigel had also visited the Tunguska crater in Siberia, where a comet likely exploded, in 1908. The blast knocked over approximately 80 million trees and flattened 830 square miles of Siberian forest. In the early 1960s Zigel stunned his colleagues by suggesting that the Tunguska crater could have been created by an outer space vehicle that crashed there.

[213] "UFO Section of the All-Union Cosmonautics Committee": Title: Unidentified flying objects, Source: *Soviet Life,* no. 2 1968, 27–29, 1.

[213] "The hypothesis that UFOs originate in other worlds": Ibid.

Chapter Thirteen: Dull, Dirty, and Dangerous Requires Drones

Interviews: Ken Collins, Charlie Trapp, Colonel Slater, General Hsichun "Mike" Hua, Edward Lovick, Changti "Robin" Yeh (via written correspondence), Hervey Stockman

[214] Collins knew the kind: Interview with Ken Collins.

[215] simulated jungle survival: Interviews with Ken Collins, Charlie Trapp.

[216] CIA pilot named Yeh Changti: Hua, *Lost Black Cats,* ix.

[216] the Black Cats flew: Ibid., viii–x.

[217] "no information was released about Yeh Changti": Interview with General Hua.

[217] "His code name was Terry Lee": Interview with Colonel Slater. Yeh Changti's American name is Robin Yeh (the Chinese put family names first).

[217] getting hard intelligence on China's nuclear facilities: National Photographic Interpretation Center, Mission [GRC-169], 23 August 1963, 30 pages. The designation for these missions was Operation Church Door. Images of targets photographed by the Black Cats include the Lop Nur nuclear facility, missile launch sites, airfields, ports, and industrial complexes.

[217] Yeh Changti was tortured and held prisoner: Interview with General Hua; in Lost Black Cats, Hua, a former CIA Black Cat U-2 pilot, tells the tragic and amazing story of the nineteen years Changti and Chang spent as captives of Communist China, based on personal interviews. The sacrifices made by Changti and Chang have never been acknowledged by the CIA. On September 17, 1998, the CIA held a symposium called "U-2: A Revolution in Intelligence" to honor the declassification of many CIA-controlled U-2 operations and to celebrate its success. But the symposium omitted any mention of the Black Cat U-2 pilots according to my interview with General Hua.

[218] second Black Cat pilot named Major Jack Chang: Ibid., ix. To clarify, General Hua also refers to Major Jack Chang as Chang Liyi—Jack being the pilot's American nickname and Liyi being his "first name" in Chinese, which is his family name, the reverse of Western usage.

[218] dull, dirty, and dangerous: Interview with T. D. Barnes.

[219] "and then head back out to sea": Interview with Lovick. "A colleague named Mike Ash and I designed an electrical circuit into the drone's pallet to select an antenna to be used to radiate the recovery beacon signal. If the sensor package was not recovered by an aircraft and it fell into the water, an antenna was deployed to allow radio signals to enable recovery." If the sensor package landed upside down, Lovick and Ash had created a system which allowed the seawater to act like a switch and activate a second antenna.

[219] Yuletide: Interviews with Colonel Slater, Frank Murray.

[219] "with PJs nearly falling off cliffs": Interview with Charlie Trapp.

[220] flight engineer, Ray Torick: There are many different ideas about why and how Torick died. I adhere to Colonel Slater's view of the events. The drone's first official test launch was on March 5, 1966, and during that flight, the drone launched successfully off the back of the mother ship while traveling at a speed of Mach 3.2. It then flew approximately 120 miles before it ran out

of fuel and crashed into the sea, as was planned. A month later, a second launch sent a drone flying for 1,900 miles, at Mach 3.3, until it fell into the sea. It was on the third test launch that disaster struck and Torick died.

221 "he impulsively and emotionally decided": Rich, *Skunk Works,* 267.

221 "never again allow a Francis Gary Powers situation": Ibid.

221 "Ben, do you recognize this?" Ibid., 270.

222 dubbed Operation Aphrodite: Singer, *Wired for War,* 48.

222 Tesla's pilotless boat: Tesla, "Inside the Lab–Remote Control," PBS, http://www.pbs.org/tesla/ins/lab_remotec.html.

223 Goliath carried 132 pounds of explosives: "Rise of the Machines," ArmyTechnology.com, May 21, 2008, http://www.army-technology.com/features/feature1951/.

223 mother ship called Marmalade: AFSC History Staff, *History of Air Force Atomic Cloud Sampling,* 9.

223 Fox, was blasted "sixty feet higher": Ibid., 11.

224 Operation Sandstone: For the Air Force, maintaining a drone wing was expensive. It was also a security risk. In early 1947, that more atomic tests were being planned was a closely guarded national secret because the public was being led to believe that the United States was genuinely considering outlawing the bomb—or at least putting the United Nations in control of atomic energy. In reality, it was during this period of alleged international debate that the drone unit was again called back into action for the next test series in the Pacific. Operation Crossroads was supposed to have been a singular event, and so talk surfaced among the drone pilots. Being reactivated could only mean one thing: more nuclear tests in the pipeline. This security leak made its way up the chain of command.

224 accidentally flew through the Zebra bomb's mushroom cloud: AFSC History Staff, *History of Air Force Atomic Cloud Sampling,* 21.

224 "Now pilots, not drones, would be sent": Ibid., 23–24.

225 fear that the entire world's atmosphere could catch on fire: Interviews with Al O'Donnell and Jim Freedman.

225 what happened to Oppenheimer sent a strong message: Interview with Al O'Donnell.

[225] measurements inside the thermonuclear clouds: Now called Task Group 3.4 and operating out of Eglin Air Force Base in Florida, these new drones were modified T–33 aircraft, as opposed to the old TF–80s used in earlier tests. The wing fell under the command of Colonel Thomas Gent, who was also in command of the 550th Guided Missile Wing of the Air Proving Ground.

[225] crash-landed on a deserted island called Bogallua: AFSC History Staff, *History of Air Force Atomic Cloud Sampling,* 37.

[226] That group included Hervey Stockman: Ibid., 82. Hervey's name is misspelled as "Harvey."

[226] Hervey Stockman, then flew sampling missions: Ibid., 80–85. Interview with Hervey Stockman.

[226] "scientists put monkeys in the cockpits": "Conversations with Colonel Hervey S. Stockman," edited by Ann Paden and Earl Haney (not published), from a section called "Nuclear testing program."

[226] "not serving as guinea pigs": AFSC History Staff, *History of Air Force Atomic Cloud Sampling,* 66.

[226] "In those days": "Conversations with Colonel Hervey S. Stockman," edited by Ann Paden and Earl Haney (not published), from a section called "Pacific testing ground."

[227] Jimmy P. Robinson was one of the six pilots: The details of Robinson's story, including where I quote him, can be found in AFSC History Staff, *History of Air Force Atomic Cloud Sampling,* 69–75. Robinson's name is redacted from the monograph, the words "privacy act material removed" stamped in their place. In 2009, Mark Wolverton wrote "Into the Mushroom Cloud" for *Air and Space* magazine and revealed the pilot's name publicly for the first time. Robinson was posthumously awarded the Distinguished Flying Cross about a year after his death, but his family had no idea how he actually had died. Wolverton wrote that Robinson's daughter Rebecca, "a baby when her father died, spent years petitioning the government for more information about his last mission, with only limited access." Rebecca Robinson says most of the information about her father's death is "still classified."

[228] Atomic sampling pilots wore lead-lined vests: AFSC History Staff, *History of Air Force Atomic Cloud Sampling,* 101.

[228] "It was one of the ones that was too big": Interview with Al O'Donnell.

[228] In contrast, the bomb dropped on Hiroshima: Rhodes, *Dark Sun,* photograph #76, "Mike over Manhattan." Here, the Ivy Mike fireball is shown in comparison with a Nagasaki-scale atomic bomb. Mike's stem was 20 miles in diameter and its mushroom cap only began at 50,000 feet, approximately twice as high as commercial airplanes fly. The top of the mushroom cloud extended into the troposphere and was approximately 200 miles wide.

Chapter Fourteen: Drama in the Desert

Interviews: Colonel Slater, Dr. Wheelon, Ken Collins, Kenneth Swanson, Frank Murray, Charlie Trapp, Frank Murray, Tony Bevacqua, Dr. Robert B. Abernethy

[229] air-conditioned hunting blind: Woods, *LBJ,* 313.

[230] "I'll be dammed": Brzezinski, *Red Moon Rising,* 175.

[230] "Soon they will be dropping": Dickson, *Sputnik,* 117.

[230] not a cause for panic: Korda, *Ike,* 700.

[230] "What most actually saw": Brzezinski, *Red Moon Rising,* 176.

[231] Johnson sat in the Oval Office with CIA director: CIA Memo, Meeting with the President, Secretary Rusk, Secretary McNamara, Mr. Bundy and DCI. Re: Surfacing the OXCART, 29 November, 1963, 1.

[231] it would hold aviation records: T. D. Barnes explained, "Officially, the SR-71 Blackbird still holds the world speed record for sustained flight in an oxygen-breathing plane in horizontal flight but it is common knowledge throughout the Blackbird community that the A-12 flew higher and faster because of the sacrifices the SR-71 made to accommodate a second passenger. The reason the SR-71 holds the 'records' is because those of the A-12 were not certified. The A-12 Oxcart didn't exist when the Air Force was setting records."

[231] outing the Oxcart was a terrific idea: If the public knew about Oxcart, there would no longer be a reason to have the Agency in charge of a program that needed secrecy as a cover. The Air Force knew the CIA had done all the work getting Oxcart up and running; now was the time to push the Agency

aside. This echoes what happened with Curtis LeMay's early summation of the U-2 program in 1955: "We'll let [the CIA] develop it and then we'll take it from them," from Brugioni, *Eyeball to Eyeball,* 24.

[231] they could take over Oxcart: Letter, General Bernard Schriever to Eugene M. Zuckert, July 11, 1963, Top Secret.

[232] McCone tried a different approach: CIA Memo, Meeting with the President, Re: Surfacing the OXCART, 29 November, 1963, 1. "The development of the CIA and Air Force reconnaissance planes (15 in number) would cost about $700 million, of which about $400 million have now been spent." This figure does not include the aircraft's "extraordinary engines," made by Pratt and Whitney. Regarding those costs, Lockheed Skunk Works chief (from 1975–1991) Ben Rich wrote, "The CIA unhappily swallowed the enormous development costs of $600 million."

[232] the fictitious name A-11: Parangosky, *The Oxcart Story,* 4: "The President's reference to the 'A-11' was of course deliberate. 'A-11' had been the original design designation for the all-metal aircraft first proposed by Lockheed; subsequently it became the design designation for the Air Force YF-12A interceptor which differed from its parent mainly in that it carried a second man for launching air-to-air missiles. To preserve the distinction between the A-11 and the A-12 Security had briefed practically all participating personnel in government and industry on the impending announcement. OXCART secrecy continued in effect. There was considerable speculation about an Agency role in the A-11 development, but it was never acknowledged by the government."

[232] "The world record for aircraft speed": Public Papers of Presidents of the United States, Lyndon B. Johnson, 1963–1964, 1:322–23.

[233] the aircraft were still dripping wet: Interview with Colonel Slater.

[233] "without the specific knowledge of the President": Summary of Meeting with Secretary McNamara and Secretary Gilpatric, General Carter and Mr. McCone on 5 July 1962. DCI Records dated 6 July 1962.

[234] approved the Oxcart for Operation Skylark: Carter Memorandum to Wheelon, "SKYLARK," 22 Aug. 1964.

[234] according to Ken Collins: Interview with Ken Collins.

[235] specially designed J-58 turbojet engines: Interview with Dr. Robert Abernethy. Robarge, *Archangel,* 12–13.

[236] two men working there were crushed to death: Rich, *Skunk Works,* 221.

[236] tiny black dots began to appear: Ibid., 223, from a story told by Norm Nelson, the CIA-Lockheed Skunk Works liaison during Oxcart.

[236] nearly knocking him unconscious: Interview with Ken Collins.

[237] he always sat patiently with the project pilots: Ibid.

[237] "Fix it," Park said: Rich, *Skunk Works,* 221. This story was also clarified for me by Ken Collins, who provided additional details.

[238] " 'Get me out of here!' " Rich later recalled: Rich, *Skunk Works,* 227.

[239] Project Kempster-Lacroix: Interview with Ed Lovick; Pedlow and Welzenbach, *Central Intelligence Agency,* 42.

[240] the government had exploded 286 nuclear bombs: Through Operation Hardtack there were 119 aboveground tests. Testing resumed on September 15, 1961. From then through the end of 1964, there were 167 underground tests at NTS, including 4 at Nellis Air Force Range.

[241] "The first jamming system was called Red Dog": Interview with Kenneth Swanson.

[242] Trapp thought it sounded interesting: Interview with Charlie Trapp.

[244] General Ledford, the head of the Office of Special Activities: My portrait of General Ledford is based on my interviews with men who knew him well, including Dr. Wheelon, Colonel Slater, and Frank Murray, in addition to his U.S. Air Force biographical information.

[245] it was not in Frank Murray's character: Interview with Colonel Slater.

[247] In 2005 NSA admitted: Weiner, *Legacy of Ashes,* 276–80.

[247] Robert McNamara performing an about-face regarding Oxcart: Robarge, *Archangel,* 31.

[247] supplying surface-to-air-missile systems: Helms Memorandum to the 303 Committee, OXCART Reconnaissance of North Vietnam, with Attachment, 15 May 1967.

[247] set up around Hanoi: Interview with Tony Bevacqua; photographs from Bevacqua's personal collection.

Chapter Fifteen: The Ultimate Boys' Club

Interviews: Ken Collins, Colonel Slater, Frank Murray, Fred White, Charlie Trapp, William "Bill" Weaver, Brigadier General Raymond L. Haupt

[248] shaken from their beds: Interview with Ken Collins. A moratorium on testing meant that the Titania bomb, exploded on October 30, 1958, was the last nuclear bomb fired at the Nevada Test Site for a period of nearly three years. In August of 1961, the Russians announced they were resuming testing and conducted thirty-one nuclear tests over the next three months, including the fifty-eight-megaton Tsar Bomba, the largest bomb ever exploded. In response, Kennedy had the AEC resume testing at the Nevada Test Site; interview with Al O'Donnell.

[250] The incident has never been declassified: Interview with Collins.

[250] the less you knew, the better: A sentiment unanimously shared by all CIA and USAF pilots interviewed.

[251] No radio, almost no TV: Interviews with Slater, Murray, Collins.

[251] "like an incubus": Helms, *A Look Over My Shoulder,* 309.

[252] "The only sin in espionage is getting caught": David Robarge, "Richard Helms."

[252] Helms would be recruited by the Office of Strategic Services: Helms, *A Look Over My Shoulder,* 31.

[252] a seafood run to Westover Air Force Base: Interview with Colonel Slater.

[253] MKULTRA files destroyed: The authority on this subject is John Marks, a former State Department analyst and staff assistant to the intelligence director. In June of 1977, Marks obtained access to part of seven boxes of MKULTRA, the only ones allegedly not lost and consisting mostly of financial records. In his book *The Search for the Manchurian Candidate,* Marks wrote that shortly before leaving the CIA, "Helms presided over a wholesale destruction of documents and tapes—presumably to minimize information that might later be used against him," 219.

[255] front page of the *New York Times:* According to Colonel Slater.

[255] Slater and General Ledford would be asked: No. 303 National Security Action Memorandum, June 2, 1964; Top Secret, From the Director of Central Intelligence, Memorandum for the 303 Committee, 22 March 1966.

[256] "McNamara was delaying finding a mission": Interview with Dr. Wheelon.

[256] if a CIA spy plane were to get shot down: CIA Memorandum, "Reactions to a possible US Course of Action," 17 March 1966; "OXCART Development Summary and Progress," 1 October 1966–31 December 1966.

[256] The majority voted against deployment: Robarge, *Archangel,* 33.

[257] Slater now wanted it reduced by nearly 30 percent: Interview with Colonel Slater.

[257] Park had flown over all four corners of America: John Parangosky, deputy for technology, OSA, wrote in summation of Park's flight: "An impressive demonstration of the OXCART capability occurred on 21 December 1966 when Lockheed test pilot Bill Park flew 10,198 statute miles in six hours. The aircraft left the test area in Nevada and flew northward over Yellowstone National Park, thence eastward to Bismarck, North Dakota, and on to Duluth, Minnesota. It then turned south and passed Atlanta en route to Tampa, Florida, then northwest to Portland, Oregon, then southwest to Nevada. Again the flight turned eastward, passing Denver and St. Louis. Turning around at Knoxville, Tennessee, it passed Memphis in the home stretch back to Nevada. This flight established a record unapproachable by any other aircraft; it began at about the same time a typical government employee starts his work day and ended two hours before his quitting time." Full text at Roadrunners Internationale official Web site.

[257] Walt Ray was, by all accounts, a terrific pilot: Interviews with Colonel Slater, Walt Murray, Ken Collins, Roger Andersen, Charlie Trapp.

[258] "flew down to Cabo San Lucas": Interview with Ken Collins.

[258] fuel gauge move suddenly: Briefing Memorandum for Acting Deputy Director for Science and Technology, Subject Loss of Oxcart A-12 Aircraft, 6 January 1967.

[258] Walt Ray told Colonel Slater through his headset: Interview with Colonel Slater.

[258] "I'm ejecting": Interview with Colonel Slater. Immediately after the crash Air Force channels reported that an SR-71 flying on a routine flight out of Edwards Air Force Base had gone missing and was presumed down in Nevada.

[258] unable to separate from his seat: Memorandum for Acting Deputy Director for Science and Technology, Subject Loss of Article 125 (Oxcart Aircraft), 25 January 1967, 2.

[259] Roger Andersen flew in low, in a T-33: Interview with Roger Andersen.

[259] Charlie Trapp found the aircraft first: Interview with Charlie Trapp.

[260] " 'How'd you like to fly the plane?' ": Interview with Frank Murray.

[260] eight-page letter to the president: Top Secret Idealist/Oxcart, Central Intelligence Agency Office of the Director, BYE-2915-66 Alternative A, 14 December 1966.

[260] a scandalous waste of an asset: DRAFT, Director of Special Activities, Comments to W.R. Thomas III Memorandum to the Director, BOB, 27 July 1966, 11.

[260] Gary Powers incident had actually strengthened: Ibid., 3.

[261] the CIA "controls no nuclear weapons": Top Secret Idealist/Oxcart, Central Intelligence Agency Office of the Director, BYE-2915-66 Alternative A, 14 December 1966, 4.

[261] But would the president see things his way: Memorandum for the President, Subject: Advanced Reconnaissance Aircraft, December 26, 1966, Top Secret. Participants included Cyrus Vance (deputy secretary of defense), Donald Hornig (the president's science adviser), C.W. Fischer (bureau of the budget), and Helms. All except Helms recommended mothballing Oxcart. On December 28, the president approved this memo recommendation and ordered the phaseout of the A-12 fleet by January 1968.

[261] Slater was instructed to return to Area 51: Interview with Colonel Slater.

[261] ahead of a two-star general: Ibid.

[262] Slater went to visit Werner Weiss: Ibid.

Chapter Sixteen: Operation Black Shield and the Secret History of the USS Pueblo

Interviews: Colonel Slater, Ken Collins, Roger Andersen, Hervey Stockman, Peter Stockman, Frank Murray, Ronald L. "Jack" Layton, Eunice Layton, Charlie Trapp

[265] "never found have much use for intelligence": Hathaway and Smith, *Richard Helms,* 2. The most telling comment comes from Helms (ibid., 7): "With President Johnson...I finally came to the conclusion that what I had to say I should get into the first 60, or at least 120 seconds, that I had on my feet. Because after that he was pushing buttons for coffee or Fresca, or talking to

Rusk, or talking to McNamara, or whispering here or whispering there. I had lost my principal audience."

[265] Target Tuesday lunch: Barrett, "Doing 'Tuesday Lunch,'" 676–77.

[266] Helms told the president: John Parangosky, Deputy for Technology, OSA, wrote in summation, "Director of Central Intelligence, Richard Helms, submitted to the 303 Committee another formal proposal to deploy the OXCART. In addition, he raised the matter at President Johnson's 'Tuesday Lunch' on 16 May, and received the Presidents approval to 'go.' Walt Rostow later in the day formally conveyed the President's decision, and the BLACK SHIELD deployment plan was forthwith put into effect."

[266] A million pounds of matériel, 260 support crew: Johnson, *History of the Oxcart Program,* 1. The three A-12s that were deployed to Kadena flew nonstop from Groom Lake across the Pacific. They refueled twice en route and got to Kadena in a little less than six hours; interview with Colonel Slater, Ken Collins, Frank Murray, Roger Andersen.

[266] "the bird should leave the nest": CIA Director of Special Activities to CIA Director of Reconnaissance, "Operation readiness of the OXCART System," 12 November 1965.

[267] nearly 40 percent of all islanders' income: CIA NLE MR Case No. 2000-69, Ryukyu Islands (Okinawa) June 1960, 2. "The military economy employs 13% of the working population and generates 36% of the national income."

[267] to keep an extremely low profile: Interview with Ken Collins.

[267] "no plausible cover story": Interview with Colonel Slater.

[268] the first Oxcart mission: Photographic Interpretation Report: Black Shield Mission X-001, 31 May 1967. NPIC/R-112/67, June 1967.

[268] by the time the photographic intelligence got back: John Parangosky, Deputy for Technology, OSA, wrote: "Film from earlier missions was developed at the Eastman Kodak plant in Rochester, New York. By late summer an Air Force Center in Japan carried out the processing in order to place the photointelligence in the hands of American commanders in Vietnam within 24 hours of completion of a BLACK SHIELD mission."

[269] four were "detected and tracked": CHESS RUFF TRINE OXCART, BYE–44232/67, Black Shield Reconnaissance Missions 31 May–15 August 1967, 22 Sept. 1967, Central Intelligence Agency, 1. Declassified in August 2007.

[269] first attempted shoot-down: Robarge, *Archangel,* 36.

[269] when he was involved in a midair crash: interview with Hervey Stockman; also from *Conversations with Hervey Stockman* (not numbered) in a section called "Mid-air collision."

[270] to find U.S. airmen who'd gone down: Interview with Frank Murray.

[271] "I hope they try something because we are looking for a fight": Karnow, *Vietnam,* 514.

[271] it was on an espionage mission: CIA Top Secret [Redacted], 24 January 1968, Memorandum: Chronology of Events Concerning the Seizure of the USS *Pueblo,* 8 pages.

[272] two MiG-21 fighter jets appeared on the scene: Ibid., 3.

[272] The captain considered sinking his ship: Bamford, *Body of Secrets,* 259.

[272] 90 percent of the documents survived: Ibid., 305.

[272] Pentagon began secretly preparing for war: Department of Defense, Top Secret Memorandum for the Secretary of Defense, January 25, 1968.

[273] pinpointed the *Pueblo*'s exact location: TOP SECRET TRINE OXCART, BYE–1330/68 Figure 9; a map of Weeks's flight is noted as Mission BX-6847, 26 January 1968, figure 5.

[273] he told his fellow pilots about the problems: Interviews with Frank Murray, Ken Collins.

[273] very few individuals had any idea: In fact, for forty years, Frank Murray believed he had located the USS *Pueblo* because, in a bizarre twist, the CIA told him he did. Only in 2007, when the CIA declassified the official documents on the Oxcart program, was Jack Weeks's true role in the crisis finally revealed. Murray's other mission remains classified.

[274] "So we had to abandon any plans to hit them with airpower": Rich, *Skunk Works,* 44. This is in a section of Rich's book written by Walt W. Rostow, President Johnson's national security adviser from 1966 to 1968.

[274] Murray was assigned to fly Oxcart's second mission over North Korea: TOP SECRET TRINE OXCART, BYE–1330/68 figure 7. Mission BX-6853, 19 February 1968.

[274] a U.S. federal judge determined: Wilber, "Hell Hath a Jury."

[274] There were beautiful sunsets to watch: Interview with Ken Collins.

[275] collectively flown twenty-nine missions: Robarge, *Archangel,* 35. The pilots were put on alert to fly a total of fifty-eight. Of the twenty-nine, twenty-four were over North Vietnam, two were over Cambodia, Laos, and the DMZ, and three were over North Korea.

[275] "using our jamming systems on the bird": Interview with Frank Murray. The Pentagon was also using Oxcart photographs to identify potential targets for U.S. Air Force air strikes. TOP SECRET CHESS RUFF TRINE Oxcart BYE–44232/67.

[275] The Blackbirds were arriving on Kadena to take Oxcart's place: Interviews with Ken Collins and Tony Bevacqua. The SR-71 began arriving in March of 1968.

[276] "reaffirmed the original decision to end the A-12 program": Helms Memorandum to Paul Nitze (DOD) and Horning, "Considerations Affecting OXCART Program Phase Out," 18 April 1968.

[276] Jack Weeks became ill: Interview with Ken Collins.

[276] After Bevacqua had left Groom Lake: Interview with Tony Bevacqua.

[277] mission on July 26, 1968: This was the first time an SR-71 was fired upon by an SA-2. With Bevacqua, in the backseat, was reconnaissance systems officer Jerry Crew. www.blackbirds.net/sr71/sr-crew-photos/(accessed December 29, 2010).

[277] The 1129th Special Activities Squadron had reached its end: The Oxcart program lasted just over ten years, from its inception as a drawing on a piece of paper called A-1, in 1957, to termination in June of 1968. Lockheed produced fifteen A-12 Oxcarts, three YF-12As, and thirty-one SR-71 Blackbirds. The CIA's John Parangosky wrote in summation, "The 49 supersonic aircraft had completed more than 7,300 flights, with 17,000 hours in the air. Over 2,400 hours had been above Mach 3. Five OXCART were lost in accidents; two pilots were killed, and two had narrow escapes. In addition, two F-101 chase planes were lost with their Air Force pilots during OXCART testing phase."

[277] The CIA held a special secret ceremony at Area 51: Interviews with Ken Collins, Frank Murray, Colonel Slater, and Jack Layton. Vice Admiral Rufus L. Taylor, deputy director of Central Intelligence, presented the CIA Intelligence Star for Valor to Kenneth S. Collins, Ronald L. Layton, Francis J. Murray, Dennis B. Sullivan, and Mele Vojvodich. Jack W. Weeks's award was accepted by his widow, Sharlene Weeks. The United States Air Force Legion

of Merit was presented to Colonel Hugh Slater and his deputy, Colonel
Maynard N. Amundson.

[278] The men moved on: Interviews with Ken Collins, Colonel Slater, Frank
Murray, Charlie Trapp, Roger Andersen.

Chapter Seventeen: The MiGs of Area 51

Interviews: T. D. Barnes, Doris Barnes, Tony Landis, Peter Merlin, Colonel
Slater, Frank Murray, Roger Andersen, Grace Weismann (Joe Walker's
widow)

[280] Iraqi air force colonel named Munir Redfa: Uzi Mahnaimi, "Stolen Iraqi
Jet Helped Israel Win Six-Day War," *Sunday Times of London,* June 3, 2007.

[280] "Turn back immediately": Geller, *Inside the Israeli Secret Service.* I use
information from chapter 3, "Stealing a Soviet MiG."

[281] Redfa flew over Turkey: Obituary, "Major-General Meir Amit,"
Telegraph, July 22, 2009.

[281] Amit sat down with the Israeli air force: Ibid.

[282] James Jesus Angleton: Helms, *A Look Over My Shoulder,* 275. "Jim's
interest in Israel was of exceptional value... To my knowledge, only Israel has
ever dedicated a monument to a foreign intelligence officer." Angleton worked
as "the Agency's liaison with the FBI... The best of Angleton's operational
work is still classified and in my view should remain so."

[282] Agency's most enigmatic and bellicose spies: Author visit to CIA spy
museum, CIA Headquarters, Langley, Virginia.

[282] "wilderness of mirrors": Helms, *A Look Over My Shoulder,* 277. The phrase
has become synonymous with Angleton's thinking and most notably included
Angleton's belief that the split between the Soviet Union and China was not real.
According to Helms, Angleton's "conviction that the Sino–Soviet split was
mirage created by Soviet deception experts [was] interesting but simply not true."

[282] when they worked in the OSS counterintelligence unit, X-2: Ibid.,
chapter 28, "Beyond X-2."

[283] Helms's status with President Johnson: Weiner, *Legacy of Ashes,* 319.

[283] But what didn't make the news: Interviews with Colonel Slater, Frank
Murray, T. D. Barnes.

[284] Doris was reading the classified: Interview with Doris Barnes.

[284] Beatty, Nevada, was one strange town: Details about Beatty in the 1960s come from interviews with Doris Barnes and T. D. Barnes.

[286] "Daddy's spaceship!": Interviews with the Barnes's two daughters, who wish to remain anonymous.

[286] where the X-15 could land if need be: Interview with Peter Merlin; Barnes, "NASA X-15 Program," 1.

[287] Barnes got on the radio channel: The dates and data regarding X-15 mission flights can be found in Jenkins, *Hypersonics Before the Shuttle.* This story of the missing audiotape comes from Barnes.

[289] a catastrophic midair collision occurred: I tell the story as Barnes related it to me. Another account appears in Donald Mallick's *The Smell of Kerosene,* 132–35. Mallick was assigned the helicopter mission to locate Walker's crash site.

[291] reverse engineering Colonel Redfa's MiG: Interview with Barnes.

[292] Test pilots flew a total of 102 MiG missions: Barnes, "Exploitation of MiGs at Area 51, Project Have Doughnut," http://area51specialprojects.com/migs_area51.html; Tolip, "Black Ops: American Pilots Flying Russian Aircraft During the Cold War," MilitaryHeat.com, October 4, 2007.

[294] gave birth to the Top Gun fighter-pilot school: Interview with Barnes.

[295] The scales had tipped: Wilcox, *Scream of Eagles,* 76–77.

Chapter Eighteen: Meltdown

Interviews: Richard Mingus, T. D. Barnes, Troy Wade, Darwin Morgan, Milton M. Klein, Harold B. Finger

[296] to see what would happen: Atomic Energy Commission, Summary of Project 57, the first safety test of Operation Plumbbob, report to the General Manager by the Director, Division of Military Application, Objective, 24.

[297] bomber flying with four armed hydrogen bombs: "Palomares Summary Report," Kirtland Air Force Base, New Mexico: Field Command Defense Nuclear Agency Technology and Analysis Directorate, January 15, 1975.

[297] SAC bombers would already be airborne: When LeMay left SAC in 1957 to become the Air Force vice chief of staff, he left behind a fighting force of

1,665 bomber aircraft, 68 bases around the world, and 224,014 men. The man who took over was Thomas S. Powers.

[297] "all of a sudden, all hell": Ron Hayes, "H–bomb Incident Crippled Pilot's Career," *Palm Beach Post,* January 17, 2007.

[298] aerosolized plutonium: Gordon Dunning, "Protective and Remedial Measures Taken Following Three Incidents of Fallout," United States Atomic Energy Commission, 1968. This was originally given as a speech called "Radiation Protection of the Public in Large Scale Nuclear Disaster," for an international agency symposium in Interlaken, Switzerland, in May 1968.

[298] President Johnson learned: Moran, *Day We Lost the H-Bomb,* 36.

[298] official nuclear disaster response team: Memo, Secret, United States Atomic Energy Commission, No. 234505, "Responsibility for Search and Rescue Operations," to M. E. Gates, Manager, Nevada Operations, November 19, 1974.

[299] to assist in the cleanup efforts: Nuclear Weapon Accident Response Procedures (NARP) Manual, Assistant to the Secretary of Defense (Atomic Energy), September 1990, xii.

[299] "will never be known": Schwartz, *Atomic Audit,* 408.

[299] "I don't know of any missing bomb": Anthony Lake, "Lying Around Washington," *Foreign Policy,* no. 2 (Spring 1971): 93. Thirty-eight U.S. Navy ships participated in the search for the bomb, which was eventually located five miles offshore in 2,850 feet of water by a submersible called Alvin.

[300] during a secret mission over Greenland: SAC History Staff, *Project Crested Ice,* SECRET/RESTRICTED DATA, SPECIAL HANDLING REQUIRED, AFR 127-4: FOIA 89-107 OAS-) 1793. This source document provided many facts for this section.

[300] A second fire started at the crash site: The cloud formed by the explosion measured "850 m high, 800 m in length, and 800 m in depth, and undoubtedly carried some plutonium downwind," according to the Los Alamos National Laboratory.

[300] One of the bombs fell into the bay: Gordon Corea, "Mystery of Lost US Nuclear Bomb," *BBC News,* November 10, 2008.

[300] "a cleanup undertaken as good housekeeping measures": SAC History Staff, *Project Crested Ice*, 28.

[301] "abundance of plutonium, americium, cesium": Rollins, "Nevada Test Site—Site Description," Table 2-4.

[301] Called remote sensing: Department of Energy Fact Sheet DOE/NV #1140. The Remote Sensing Laboratory was established in the 1950s, an offshoot of atomic cloud sampling projects. Today, it is a secret industry about which very little is known publicly; http://www.nv.doe.gov/library/factsheets/DOENV_1140.pdf.

[302] initially called the EG&G Remote Sensing Laboratory: EG&G Energy Measurements Division (EG&G/EM) of EG&G, Inc., managed and operated the research facility under DOE Contract DE–ACO3–93NV11265. On January 1, 1996, Bechtel Nevada Corporation operated the research and production facilities under DOE M&O Contract DE–ACO8–96NV11718.

[302] to secure the government contracts to clean things up: And what a massive market it would become. In addition to future nuclear accidents, there would be a colossal amount of radiation detection work to be done in, on, and around the Pacific Proving Ground. Between 1946 and 1958, the Atomic Energy Commission had exploded forty nuclear bombs, including the largest thermonuclear bomb ever exploded by the United States, the fifteen-megaton Castle Bravo bomb—a thousand times as powerful as the weapon dropped on Hiroshima. In June of 1971, an EG&G crew was dispatched to Eniwetok Atoll by the Atomic Energy Commission "for the purposes of pre-cleanup surveying." EG&G had armed, wired, and fired all the bombs in the Pacific. Now, using radiation detection equipment, the company determined that the island was still uninhabitable by all life forms in the water and the air—even after thirteen years. But clean-up efforts could begin. These efforts would take decades, cost untold dollars, and involve several different contractors. EG&G would lead the way.

[302] EG&G had been taking radiation measurements: Interviews with Al O'Donnell, Jim Freedman; Eniwetok Precleanup Survey Soil and Terrestrial, Radiation Survey (Lynch, Gudiksen and Jones) No. 44878; draft revised 5/14/73.

[302] corporate headquarters won't say: Interview with Meagan Stafford, EG&G/URS public relations, Sard Verbinnen & Co., July 16, 2010.

[302] President Clinton was in 1994: Interview with EG&G engineer. DOE Openness Initiative, Human Radiation Experiments, EG&G Energy Measurements, Las Vegas, Nevada, Finding Aids, Radioactive Fallout: "EG&G/ EM played an important role in monitoring airborne radiation from weapons testing, and it retained many records relating to monitoring air-borne radiation including reports on the Nevada Aerial Tracking Systems for the 1960s. The company has developed a computerized inventory of the collection which includes some 24,000 classified documents, films, view-graphs, and other materials. Currently the company is attempting to reorganize its archives into a usable collection designed to accommodate future research efforts. The dismantling process that was begun in 1986 has been halted. The CIC will retain fallout records from the aboveground testing program. All other original research documentation, film, note-books, and other records relating to EG&G/EM's important role in monitoring airborne radiation and weapons testing, including reports and maps of cloud tracking still housed at EM, will be retained by EM. Classified Material Control (CMC) contains numerous reports on later testing programs and Aerial Tracking Systems reports for the 1960s. The company also holds original survey data for the period before 1971, but this has not been inventoried. There is an effort under way to obtain the funding to inventory and create a computerized database for these records."

[303] the president did not have a need-to-know: Interview with EG&G engineer.

[303] one-line reference: *Advisory Committee on Human Radiation Experiments Final Report,* 506–507.

[303] If Area 51 had a doppelgänger: At Groom Lake, for a thirteen-year period beginning in 1955, the CIA and the U.S. Air Force comanaged spy plane programs using science and technology to advance the art of aerial espionage. Forty miles to the southwest, at Jackass Flats, beginning around 1955 and for a period of seventeen years, the Atomic Energy Commission, NASA, and the Department of Defense comanaged nuclear rocket programs using science and technology to try to get man to Mars. There is an interesting paradox. At Area 51, the spy plane programs were funded by black budgets, meaning their existence was hidden from Congress and the public. Not until they were declassified by the CIA—the U-2 program in 1998 and the A-12 Oxcart program in 2007—were their existences confirmed. The term *Area 51* has remained redacted, or blacked out, from declassified documents. When Air Force and CIA officials are asked to comment on Area 51, they have no comment, because technically the facility does not exist. At Area 25, the nuclear rocket

ship programs have been funded with public awareness. No one at the Air Force, the Atomic Energy Commission, or NASA will deny that nuclear rocket development went on there. But what was really going on behind the facade at Jackass Flats has always been labeled Restricted Data, which is classified.

[304] piloted by one hundred and fifty men: McPhee, *The Curve of Binding Energy*, 168.

[304] Taylor designed nuclear bombs for the Pentagon: According to Taylor's colleague the legendary Freeman Dyson, Ted Taylor made "the smallest, the most elegant and the most efficient bombs...freehand without elaborate calculation. When they were built and tested they worked." Dyson left Princeton University's Institute for Advanced Study to work on the Mars spaceship with Taylor.

[305] "Everyone seems to be making plans": McPhee, *The Curve of Binding Energy*, 170.

[305] same as a Coke machine: Ibid., 174.

[305] "It would have been the most sensational thing anyone ever saw": Ibid.

[305] "Whoever builds Orion will control the Earth": Ibid., 184.

[306] Space Nuclear Propulsion Office, or SNPO: Dewar, *To the End of the Solar System*, xix.

[306] built into the side of a mountain: Interview with Barnes; see photographs. On Nevada Test Site official maps, these mountains, in Area 25, are called Calico Hills.

[306-307] the underground tunnel was 1,150 feet long: "Corrective Investigation Plan For Corrective Action Unit 165: Areas 25 and 26 Dry Well and Washdown Areas, Nevada Test Site, Nevada." DOE/NV-788, Environmental Restoration Division, National Nuclear Security Administration, January 2002, 12.

[307] 34 million to 249 million miles to Mars: According to NASA, "the distance between Earth and Mars depends on the positions of the two planets in their orbits. It can be as small as about 33,900,000 miles (54,500,000 kilometers) or as large as about 249,000,000 miles (401,300,000 kilometers)."

[307] a remote-controlled locomotive: DOE/NV #1150, "Last Stop for the Jackass & Western."

[308] "One hundredth of what one might receive": Ibid., 287.

[308] Soviet satellites spying: Dewar, *To the End of the Solar System,* appendix F, "The Russian Nuclear Rocket Program." Dewar wrote, "The Soviets built a test complex vaguely similar to Jackass Flats."

[308] 2,300 degrees: Finger and Robbins, "An Historical Perspective," 7.

[309] "The Pentagon released information after I filed a Freedom of Information Act": Interview with Lee Davidson. Davidson's original 1990s story is from the *Deseret News,* where he was the Washington bureau reporter for twenty-eight years. During this time, Davidson reported on a number of secret AEC radiation tests in Utah, at Dugway Proving Grounds. "They had a lot of money to play with," Davidson says of the AEC. "Here in Utah, they were trying to figure out what a meltdown would look like from a number of different angles. The AEC released more radiation in Utah than was released during the partial meltdown at Three Mile Island."

[309] "Los Alamos wanted a run-away reactor": Dewar, *To the End of the Solar System,* 280.

[309] "data on the most devastating accident possible": Ibid. Notably, Dewar lays blame for the original idea of exploding the reactor on Los Alamos. The nuclear laboratory may have come up with the idea but Los Alamos takes marching orders from the Atomic Energy Commission, and in the end, the two entities agreed to go ahead and explode the nuclear reactor on the grounds that it was a safety test. "It was critical to know the total energy release in the explosion and the amount and pattern of radioactive distribution," Dewar wrote.

[309] "over 4000°C until it burst": Ibid., 281.

[309] chunks as large as 148 pounds: Ibid., 282.

[310] "equipped with samplers mounted on its wings": Ibid., 281.

[310] "blew over Los Angeles": Ibid., 280.

[310] "accurate data from which to base calculations": Ibid., 285.

[310] "I don't recall that exact test": Interview with Harold Finger.

[310] code-named Phoebus: Barth, Delbert, Final Report of the Off-Site Surveillance for the Phoebus 1-A Experiment, SWRHL-19r, January 17, 1966. "The data collected indicate that radioactivity levels did not exceed the safety criteria established by the Atomic Energy Commission for the off-site population."

[310] "suddenly it ran out of LH_2": Dewar, *To the End of the Solar System,* 129.

[311] cleanup crews in full protective gear could not enter the area for six weeks: "Decontamination of Test Cell 'C' at the Nuclear Rocket Development Station After a Reactor Accident," January 18, 1967, LA-3633; Dewar, *To the End of the Solar System,* 129–31.

[311] long metal tongs: The workers dropped the radioactive chunks into one-gallon paint cans, which were driven out of Area 25 on a lead dolly.

[311] officially ended on January 5, 1973: Dewar, *To the End of the Solar System,* 203.

[311] no such final test: Interview with Darwin Morgan.

[312] records are "well organized and complete": Ibid., 323.

[312] "Due to the destruction of two nuclear reactors": Rollins, "Nevada Test Site — Site Description," 25 of 99.

[312] Milton Klein might know: Interview with Harold Finger; interview with Milton Klein. Klein also says he "takes issue with the use of the word *meltdown* because that's not exactly what happens to a reactor when it's deprived of coolant."

[312] radioactive elements were still present: Table 3-2, "Corrective Investigation Plan For Corrective Action Unit 165: Areas 25 and 26 Dry Well and Washdown Areas, Nevada Test Site, Nevada," 32.

[312] "may have percolated into underlying soil." Ibid. Certainly, Barnes's eye-witness testimony suggests as much. "When we would run the reactor, we had to clear out forty miles of the canyon around Calico Hills, it would emit that much radiation," Barnes explained. "And every time we ran the reactor, giant dewars of water would flood the whole area, which would help cool everything down. Enough water to make a temporary pond of water several feet deep."

[313] Area 25 began serving a new purpose: Interview with T. D. Barnes.

[313] "It's a PhD experience for first responders": Film shown on a loop at the Atomic Energy Museum in Las Vegas. Also in this section of the museum was a photograph of Area 25, which depicted desert terrain interrupted by a bright blue sign on a post that read: "EG&G Training 295-6820" — an indication that the federal partner in WMD training at Area 25 was EG&G. Morgan denies this partnership existed and insists EG&G stopped working as an "official contractor" at the test site in the 1990s. The photograph at the Atomic

Testing Museum has since been taken down, but as of December 30, 2010, the telephone number remained in service (using the local area code) with a voice mail stating: "You have reached [name redacted] in the training department. Please leave a message and I will return your call as soon as possible."

[313] one day a nuclear facility could very well melt down: For an understanding of nuclear reactor physics, how a power reactor differs from a nuclear rocket reactor, and how both differ from a nuclear bomb, see Dewar, *To the End of the Solar System*, xvii.

[313] five "boom year(s)": Rogovin, *Three Mile Island Report*, 182–83.

[313] nuclear reactor "units": Ibid., 182.

[314] dispatched an EG&G remote sensing aircraft: EG&G, Inc., Las Vegas Operations, "An Aerial Radiological Survey of the Three Mile Island Station Nuclear Power Plant," U.S. Department of Energy, 1977. The cover page of the president's commission on the accident at Three Mile Island features a thermal photo accredited to EG&G.

[314] "may be the best insurance that it will not reoccur": Rogovin, *Three Mile Island Report*, 5.

[314] nuclear-powered Russian spy satellite crashed: Gates, Mahlon, *Operation Morning Light, Northwest Territories, Canada 1978, A Non-Technical Summary of U.S. Participation;* "The Soviet Space Nuclear Power Program," Directorate of Intelligence, CIA.

[315] a decision was made not to inform the public: Weiss, "The Life and Death of Cosmos 954." Marked Secret, Not to be Released to Foreign Nationals, 7 pages, no date. Declassified 10/24/97.

[315] "playing night baseball with the lights out": Ibid., 2.

[315] "It was extremely tense": Interview with Richard Mingus.

[315] NEST: Secret, United States Atomic Energy Commission, No. 234505, Responsibility for Search and Rescue Operations, to M.E. Gates, Manager, Nevada Operations. November 19, 1974; see also Gates, "Nuclear Emergency Search Team," 2, www.nci.org.

[315] "established within EG&G": Gates, "Nuclear Emergency Search Team," 2.

[315] "space age difficulty": "Cosmos 954: An Ugly Death," *Time* magazine, February 6, 1978.

[316] would be panic like in *The War of the Worlds:* Interview with Richard Mingus.

[316] meant to look like bakery vans: Interview with Troy Wade.

[316] Troy Wade was the lead federal official: Note that Mahlon Gates, who authored *Operation Morning Light* and put together NEST, was the senior U.S. government representative on the project and also the head of DOE Nevada Operations but did not have an active role in the boots-on-the-ground operation.

[316] high above was an Air Force U-2: Weiss, "The Life and Death of Cosmos 954," 3.

[316] somewhere on America's East Coast: *Time* magazine reported, "The craft crashed into the atmosphere over a remote Canadian wilderness area last week, apparently emitting strong radiation. American space scientists admitted that if the satellite had failed one pass later in its decaying orbit, it would have plunged toward Earth near New York City—at the height of the morning rush hour."

Chapter Nineteen: The Lunar–Landing Conspiracy and Other Legends of Area 51

Interviews: Buzz Aldrin, Colonel Slater, Ernie Williams, Richard Mingus, Michael Schratt, Bill Irvine, James Oberg

[317] July 20, 1969: For details regarding Apollo 11, "Humankind's first steps on the lunar surface," http://nasa.gov; for transcripts of the first lunar landing, visit "Apollo 11 Lunar Surface Journal," by Eric M. Jones, http://history.nasa .gov/alsj/a11/a11.landing.html.

[317-318] Armstrong's hundreds of hours flying: Jenkins, *Hypersonics before the Shuttle,* appendix 9.

[318] astronauts visited the Nevada Test Site: NASA, Appendix E. Geology Field Exercises: Early Training, Field Training Schedule for the first 3 Groups of Astronauts (29), 3, Feb 17–18 & 24–25, 1965 & March 3–4, 1965. "The trip provided an opportunity to examine in detail the craters and ejecta formed by detonation of subsurface nuclear devices in lavas and unconsolidated sediments"; USGS Open-File Report 2005-1190, Table 1, "Geologic field-training of NASA Astronauts between January 1963 and November 1972."

[318] Ernie Williams was their guide: Interview with Ernie Williams.

[318] first water well: Interviews with T. D. Barnes, Colonel Slater, Ernie Williams.

[318-319] astronauts arrived with a lunar rover vehicle: Gerald G. Schaber, "A Chronology of Activities from Conception through the End of Project Apollo (1960-1973)," U.S. Geological Survey, Branch of Astrogeology.

[319] by-products of underground bomb tests: "The Containment of Underground Nuclear Explosions," #69043 Congress of the United States, Office of Technology Assessment, 32.

[319] astronauts twice referred to: DOE/NV 772 REV 1, "Apollo Astronauts Train at the Nevada Test Site," 2. The mission commentary voice transmissions can be downloaded at http://www.jsc.nasa.gov/history/mission_trans/apollo17.htm.

[320] hearing this comparison was a beautiful moment: Interview with Ernie Williams.

[320] Just two months after Armstrong and Aldrin returned: Author interview with James Oberg, and from a chapter in his book *UFOs and Outer Space Mysteries*. In addition to being an aerospace historian and leading debunker of lunar-landing and UFO-on-the-moon conspiracies, Oberg spent his career as a rocket scientist working for NASA contractors, including at Mission Control in Houston, Texas.

[320] moon being a base for aliens and UFOs: Interview with James Oberg.

[320] Spielberg said in a 1978 interview: Matthew Alford, "Steven Spielberg," *Cinema Papers*, 1978.

[321] With these three questions: The answers, presented by a popular Web site dedicated to debunking the moon-hoax theory, are: Q: How can the American flag flutter when there is no wind on the moon? A: The movement comes from the twisting motion of the pole. Q: Why can't the stars be seen in the moon photographs? A: There are plenty of Apollo photos released by NASA in which you can see stars. Q: Why is there no blast crater where Apollo's landing vehicle landed? A: The moon's surface is covered by a rocky material called lunar regolith, which responds to blast pressure similar to solid rock; http://www.braeunig.us/space/hoax.htm.

[321] he experienced "an intuitive feeling": Fox Television broadcast, "Conspiracy Theory: Did We Land on the Moon?" February 15, 2001.

[321] the *Today* show: A transcript of Kaysing's interview with Katie Couric, cohost of the *Today* show, which aired on NBC, August 8, 2001, can be read online at Global Security.

[322] canceled the book: Dr. David Whitehouse, "NASA Pulls Moon Hoax Book," BBC News, November 8, 2002.

[322] CIA admitted it had been running mind-control programs: Marks, *The Search for the "Manchurian Candidate,"* 211. During the 1977 Senate hearings, CIA director Stansfield Turner summed up some of MKULTRA's eleven-year legacy: "The program contracted out work to 80 institutions, which included 44 colleges of universities, 15 research facilities or private companies, 12 hospitals or clinics, and 3 penal institutions."

[322] 58,193 Americans were killed trying: The National Archives, Statistical information about casualties of the Vietnam War, ARC ID: 306742.

[322] Great Moon Hoax: Goodman, *The Sun and the Moon,* 12.

[323] Buzz Aldrin, the second man on the moon: This section is based on my interview with Buzz Aldrin, and also from chapter 20 in his book *Magnificent Desolation,* which addresses the event and is called "A Blow Heard Around the World," 332–46 (galley copy).

[324] 25 percent of the people interviewed: Brandon Griggs, "Could Moon Landings Have Been Faked? Some Still Think So," CNN, July 17, 2009. Griggs noted that a "Google search this week for 'Apollo moon landing hoax' yielded more than 1.5 billion results."

[325] involve captured aliens and UFOs: AboveTopSecret.com.

[325] "The tunnels were dug by a nuclear-powered drill": Interview with Michael Schratt.

[325] N-tunnels, P-tunnels, and T-tunnels: U.S. Congress, Office of Technology Assessment, *The Containment of Underground Nuclear Explosions.*

[325] "deactivated," according to the Department of Energy: Michael R. Williams, "Ground Test Facility for Propulsion and Power Modes of Nuclear Engine Operation," 4.

[326] the revelation of the Greenbrier bunker: Ted Gup, "The Ultimate Congressional Hideaway," *Washington Post,* May 31, 1992.

[326] "Secrecy, denying knowledge of the existence": KCET American Experience, "Race for the Superbomb," interview with Paul Fritz Bugas, former on-site superintendent, the Greenbrier bunker.

[326] on average, twelve months: U.S. Congress, Office of Technology Assessment, *The Containment of Underground Nuclear Explosions,* 18.

[327] at least sixty-seven nuclear bombs: U.S. Department of Energy, *United States Nuclear Tests, July 1945 through September 1992,* 15.

[327] Piledriver experiments studied survivability: Cherry and Rabb, "Piledriver Drilling," UCRL-ID-126150, August 9, 1967.

[327] "to destroy enemy targets [such as] missile silos": Operation Hardtack II, Defense Nuclear Agency, 3 December 1982; interview with DOE officials during my tour of the Nevada Test Site, October 7, 2009.

[327] guarding many of the nuclear bombs: Interview with Richard Mingus.

[328] After the test ban, the Pentagon reversed its policy: U.S. Congress, Office of Technology Assessment, *The Containment of Underground Nuclear Explosions,* 21.

[329] has changed its name four times: See NNSA Timeline, http://www.nnsa .energy.gov/aboutus/ourhistory/timeline. Notably, there is another agency that has changed its name four times, the Armed Forces Special Weapons Project (AFSWP), which, like the Atomic Energy Commission, also began as the Manhattan Project. On May 6, 1959, it changed its name to the Defense Atomic Support Agency (DASA); on July 1, 1971, it changed its name to the Defense Nuclear Agency; on June 26, 1996, it changed its name to the Defense Special Weapons Agency. Schwartz, *Atomic Audit,* 61.

[330] "mission is to advance technology and promote related innovation": Google DOE.gov and this statement is the subhead. Or go to http://www.energy.gov/.

[330] formal beginning in 1908: Federal Bureau of Investigation Official Web site, Timeline of FBI History, 1900–1909.

[330] Yuri Ivanovich Nosenko in a secret CIA prison: Edward Jay Epstein and Susana Duncan, "The War of the Moles," *New York,* 28–37.

[330] His true allegiance remains the subject of debate: Walter Pincus, "Yuri I. Nosenko, KGB Agent Who Defected to the U.S.," *Washington Post,* August 27,

2008. In CIA documents released decades later, Nosenko is quoted as forgiving the CIA for the harsh treatment, stating "while I regret my three years of incarceration, I have no bitterness and now understand how it could happen." Shortly before he died, CIA officials gave Nosenko a ceremonial U.S. flag from CIA director Michael Hayden.

[331] memorandum dated May 1, 1995: Memorandum to Members of the Advisory Committee on Human Radiation Experiments, from Advisory Committee Staff, May 1, 1995, "Official Classification Policy to Cover Up Embarrassment." Clinton Staff Memo is marked "Draft, For Discusssion Purposes Only," and cites 1947 memo listed below.

[331] "All documents and correspondence": "Report of Meeting of Classification Board During Week of September 8, 1947," Atomic Energy Commission.

[331] "cause considerable concern to the Atomic Energy Commission insurance Branch": September 28, 1947, memorandum from J.C. Franklin, manager Oak Ridge Operations to Carroll L. Wilson, General Manager Re: Medical Policy, 2–3; located circa 1995 by Clinton staff.

[331] "medical papers on human administration experiments done to date": Ibid.

[331] "reworded or deleted": October 8, 1947, Memorandum to Advisory Board on Medical and Biology Re: Medical Policy, 8; located circa 1995 by Clinton staff.

[331-332] In 2011 there are an estimated 1.8 billion Internet users: According to Miniwatts Marketing Group.

[332] Deny Ignorance: Interview with AboveTopSecret CEO Bill Irvine.

[332] the New World Order conspiracy theory: Wikipedia has an interesting overview of New World conspiracy theories, with bibliography.

Chapter Twenty: From Camera Bays to Weapons Bays, the Air Force Takes Control

Interviews: Richard Mingus, Ed Lovick, Bob Murphy, T. D. Barnes, Gene Poteat, Peter Merlin, Harry Martin, Millie Meierdierck, Dr. Wheelon, Joe Behne

[333] most sensational near catastrophes: Interview with Richard Mingus. Interview with Joe Behne.

[333] a mock helicopter attack: The details of the mock helicopter attack remain classified. Darwin Morgan, spokesman for the NNSA, Nevada Site Office, would neither confirm nor deny the event. Both Mingus and Behne were able to discuss this event with me because the details of the helicopter attack were only ever relayed to them secondhand. Their jobs had to do with the nuclear bomb going down the hole. In other words, while both men were privy to the security scare, neither man was ever officially briefed on the mock attack.

[334] The bomb, one of eighteen: U.S. Department of Energy, *United States Nuclear Tests, July 1945 through September 1992,* 14.

[334] five-man security response team: Interview with Mingus. This is one of the rare security stories from the secret base. Mingus tells it because the procedure is now obsolete.

[337] Quick conversation with Joe Behne: Interview with Joe Behne.

[338] With astounding lack of foresight, Wackenhut Security: Interview with Richard Mingus. Interview with Joe Behne.

[339] using slide rules and calculators: Interview with Ed Lovick.

[340] "roughly the size of a ball bearing": Interview with Lovick and specifically "based on 15GhHz radar, .08 wavelength."

[341] The man in charge of engineering, fabrication, and assembly: Interviews with Bob Murphy.

[341] at Groom Lake to drop bombs: Barnes points out that some bombs were dropped close in to the dry lake bed at Area 51.

[341] to use a preexisting, little-known bombing range: Johnson, "Tonopah Test Range Outpost of Sandia National Laboratories," Sandia Report SAND96-0375 UC-700 March 1996, U.S. DOE Contract DE-AC04-94AL85000.

[342] the Chicago of the West: State Historic Preservation Office, Beatty, Center of the Gold Railroads, "Chicago of the West," Nevada Historical Marker 173.

[342] "secret testing [that] could be conducted safely and securely": Johnson, "Tonopah Test Range Outpost of Sandia National Laboratories," 8.

[342] would quote Saint Paul of Tarsus: Ibid., 9.

[342] Operation Roller Coaster, three dirty bomb tests: Ibid., 47; Operation

Roller Coaster Sites, TTR SAFER Plan, Section 2.0. Map page 7; NVO-171 Environmental Plutonium on the Nevada Test Site and Environs, June 1977, 35.

[343] construction for an F-117 Nighthawk support facility: Interview with Peter Merlin.

[343] grow their hair long and to grow beards: Interview with Richard Mingus, who lived there.

[343] test flights of the F-117: Crickmore, *Lockheed F-117 Nighthawk,* 4. Major Al Whitley became the first operational pilot to fly the Nighthawk in October of that year.

[343] Lieutenant General Robert M. Bond: U.S. Air Force official Web site, biography.

[344] men like General James "Jimmy" Doolittle: Interview with Harry Martin.

[344] "There was some debate about whether the general": Barnes had left Area 51 by this time; this is a secondhand story. Having been involved in the MiG program since its inception, Barnes was privy to information about Bond but was never formally briefed.

[345] were the general's last words: Transcript reads: 10:17:50 a.m., Bond: "How far to the turn?" 10:17:53 a.m. Ground control: "Turn now, right 20." Bond responds with two clicks. At 10:18:02 a.m. Bond: "I'm out of control. I'm out of..." At 10:18:23 a.m. Bond: "I've got to get out, I'm out of control."

[345] Fred Hoffman, a military writer: Hoffman, "Allies Help Pentagon Obtain Soviet Arms," Associated Press, May 7, 1984.

[345] at Area 51 and Area 52 for eleven years: Johnson, "Tonopah Test Range Outpost of Sandia National Laboratories," 79. The first flight of Have Blue was December 1, 1977, by Bill Park at 7:00 p.m. as noted in Crickmore, *Lockheed F-117 Nighthawk.*

[346] Code-named Aquiline: Hank Meierdierck's personal papers; interview with Jim Freedman; interview with Millie Meierdierck, who had the only known mock-up of the drone sitting on the bar in her home.

[346] original purpose of Aquiline: Interview with Gene Poteat.

[346] Cold War Soviet hydrofoil named Ekranopian: James May, "Riding the Caspian Sea Monster," *BBC News* magazine, September 27, 2008.

[346] Jim Freedman to assist him on the Aquiline drone: Interview with Jim Freedman.

[347] ninety-nine million dollars over budget: Hank Meierdierck's personal papers.

[347] Project Ornithopter: Richelson, *Wizards of Langley,* 148.

[347] Project Insectothopter: Seen by the author at the CIA museum, located inside CIA headquarters in Langley, Virginia.

[347] "Acoustic Kitty": Richelson, *Wizards of Langley,* 147.

[348] sensor drones to detect WMD signatures: Interview with Dr. Wheelon.

[348] Early efforts had been made using U-2 pilots: Interview with Tony Bevacqua, who flew "sniffer" missions in U-2s for the U.S. Air Force. The Black Cat pilots flew some of these dangerous missions, per my interview with Colonel Slater.

[348] Operation Tobasco, risked exposure: Richelson, *Wizards of Langley,* 93–94.

[349] did considerable damage to the Agency's reputation: Marks, *Search for the "Manchurian Candidate,"* 220. Marks's entire chapter 12, "The Search for Truth," is a particularly searing portrait of how the CIA was perceived during this time.

[349] "probable biological warfare research": CIA Top Secret, Biological Warfare, USSR: Additional Rumors of an Accident at the Biological Warfare Institute in Sverdlovsk. Dated October 15, 1979. Declassified 6/10/96.

[349] Hellfire missiles: Lockheed makes the Hellfire, which is an acronym for its original design: helicopter-launched, fire-and-forget.

[349] his name was Osama bin Laden: Coll, *Ghost Wars,* 533: "While hovering over Tarnak Farm outside Kandahar, the Predator photographed a man who appeared to be bin Laden."

Chapter Twenty-one: Revelation

Interviews: T. D. Barnes, Colonel Leghorn, Hervey Stockman, Gerald Posner, Stephen Younger, John Pike, Gene Poteat, EG&G engineer, David Myhra

[350] engineers and aerodynamicists had concerns: Interview with Barnes.

This is educated speculation; Barnes did not work on the drone project. Coll also writes about this.

[351] targeted assassination by a U.S. intelligence agency was illegal: December 4, 1981, President Ronald Reagan Executive Order 12333.

[351] State Department gave the go-ahead: Coll, *Ghost Wars,* 539.

[351] CIA and the Air Force teamed up for an unusual building project: Ibid., 534. "The Air Force ought to pay for the Afghan operation, CIA officers believed, in part because the Pentagon was learning more about the drone's capabilities in a month than they could in a half a year of sterile testing in Nevada... Having seen the images of bin Laden walking toward the mosque at Tarnak, Black was now a vocal advocate of affixing missiles to the drone."

[351] on the outer reaches of Area 51: In *Ghost Wars,* Steve Coll places the mock-up "in Nevada" (549). One source interviewed by me placed the mock-up at Area 51; a second source interviewed by me placed the mock-up inside the Nevada Test and Training Range (speculating Area 52). The exact location where this took place remains classified.

[351] CIA director George Tenet decided: Coll, *Ghost Wars,* 535. "There was a child's swing. Families lived at Tarnak. The CIA estimated that the compound contained about one hundred women and children—bin Laden's family and family members of some top aides." Tenet would have made the final call.

[352] CIA drones provided intelligence for NATO forces: Jim Garamone, "Predator Demonstrates Worth Over Kosovo," American Forces Press Service, September 21, 1999.

[352] The first reconnaissance drone mission in the war on terror: *9/11 Commission Report,* 213–214.

[353] "a very successful tactical operation": Wolfowitz's interview with CNN anchor Maria Ressa appeared in print as "U.S. Missile Strike Kills al Qaeda Chief," CNN, November 5, 2002. Wolfowitz added, "one hopes each time you get a success like that, not only to have gotten rid of somebody dangerous, but to have imposed changes in their tactics and operations and procedures."

[353] exclusive interview to the *Christian Science Monitor:* Philip Smucker, "The Intrigue Behind the Drone Strikes: Yemeni Official Says US Lacks Discretion as Antiterror Partner," *Christian Science Monitor,* November 12, 2002.

[353] Hull spoke Arabic: Ibid.; Seymour Hersh, "Manhunt: The Bush

Administration's New Strategy in the War Against Terrorism," *New Yorker,* December 23, 2002.

[353] Mohammed Atef, in Jalalabad, Afghanistan: Peter Bergen and Katherine Tiedemann, "The Drone War: Are Predators Our Best Weapon or Worst Enemy," *New Republic,* June 3, 2009.

[354] targeted assassination spearheaded by the CIA: Mark Hosenball and Evan Thomas, "The Opening Shot," *Newsweek,* November 18, 2002.

[354] Predator got a new designation: MQ-1B Predator, official Web site of U.S. Air Force, fact sheet.

[354] company that built the Predator: General Atomics Aeronautical, http://www.ga-asi.com/accessed December 30, 2010.

[355] "big differences between the Reaper and the Predator": Travis Edwards, "First MQ-9 Reaper Makes Its Home on Nevada Flightline," *U.S. Air Force Public Affairs,* March 14, 2007.

[355] Brigadier General Frank Gorenc was remotely viewing: Major John Hutcheson, "Balad Predator Strikes Insurgents Placing Roadside Bomb Near Balad," *Red Tail Flyer,* 332nd Air Expeditionary Wing, Public Affairs, Balad Air Base, Iraq, March 31, 2006, 5.

[356] "put a weapon on a target within minutes": Ibid.

[356] By 2009 the number of drone strikes would rise to fifty-three: http://www.longwarjournal.org/pakistan-strikes.php; these numbers vary. Peter Bergen and Katherine Tiedemann are considered the authorities on the subject of drone strikes. The pair keep track of numbers and provide analysis for organizations including New America Foundation and the *New Republic* magazine.

[357] "These are just the assets we know about": This is because when missiles are fired it is often the work of the CIA, and CIA drone strikes are not made public. As per my interview with Pentagon officials, "That we can't confirm or deny." State Department officials also refuse to comment on CIA drone attacks and deflect attempts to get confirmation on the CIA's role in drone operations. While visiting Pakistan in December of 2009, Secretary of State Hillary Clinton told a group of journalists who were inquiring specifically about drone strikes, "I'm not going to comment on any particular tactic or technology." In reality, the strategic partnership between the CIA and the Air Force that began with Bissell's CIA and LeMay's Air Force in 1955 is back together again.

[357] the Beast of Kandahar: Originally reported by *Air & Cosmos* magazine, http://www.air-cosmos.com/site/, the story was quickly picked up in the U.S. press. David Hambling, "Mysteries Surround Afghanistan's Stealth Drone," *Wired* magazine, Danger Room Blog, December 4, 2009; interview with unnamed Lockheed official.

[357] Defense Department confirmed: Interview with secretary of the Air Force, Public Affairs Engagements Office.

[357] synthetic aperture radar, or SAR: Sandia National Laboratories: Synthetic Aperture Radar: What is Synthetic Aperture Radar? Sandia Synthetic Aperture Radar Programs (Unclassified programs and participants); http://www.sandia.gov/.

[358] thirty miles south of Area 51, at Indian Springs: Physical tour of Creech Air Force Base, Indian Springs, Nevada, October 9, 2009.

[359] "Wicked Problems": "Report of the Defense Science Board, 2008 Summer Study on Capability Surprise, Volume II: Supporting Papers, January 2010. Office of the Under Secretary of Defense For Acquisition, Technology, and Logistics, Washington, DC, 20301-3140, chapter 2, Appendix 2-A, Wicked Problems, 127–31.

[359] "playing the game changes the game": Ibid., 127.

[359] shot down one of their own: Carl Hoffman, "China's Space Threat: How Missiles Could Target U.S. Satellites," *Popular Mechanics,* July 2007.

[360] The official Pentagon story: Jim Garamone, "Navy to Shoot Down Malfunctioning Satellite," American Forces Press Service, February 14, 2008; "Navy Says Missile Smashed Wayward Satellite," MSNBC.com News Services, February 21, 2008; "U.S. Missile Shoots Down Satellite—But Why?" *Christian Science Monitor,* February 22, 2008.

[360] not required to tell the truth to Congress: Killian, *Sputnik, Scientists and Eisenhower,* 25.

[361] "A satellite cannot simply drop a bomb": Ibid., 287. Killian originally wrote this as "a study of space science and technology made at the request of the President for the non technical reader," which was released from the White House on March 26, 1958. "Much has been written about space as a future war theatre, raising such questions as satellite bombers, military bases on the moon and so on...most of these schemes, nevertheless, appear to be clumsy and ineffective ways of doing a job. Take one example, the satellite as a bomb carrier. A satellite simply cannot drop a bomb."

[361] by his own admission, was not a scientist: James Killian had only an undergraduate degree in management, as per my interview with MIT's archivist who researched the question for me in March of 2010.

[361] United States Space Surveillance Network: NASA Orbital Debris Program Office, Frequently Asked Questions, July 2009, http://orbitaldebris.jsc.nasa.gov/faqs.html.

[362] "A one-centimeter object is very hard to track": Carl Hoffman, "China's Space Threat: How Missiles Could Target U.S. Satellites," *Popular Mechanics,* July 2007.

[362] "spy satellites launched into space": Interview with Colonel Leghorn.

[362] Leghorn founded the Itek Corporation: Itek, which stood for Information (*I*) Technology (*tek*), was founded in 1957 with seed money from venture capitalist Laurance Rockefeller. Itek built Corona cameras from the beginning of the program until Corona ended in 1972. The CIA/NRO follow-on systems were contracted out to Perkin-Elmer; interviews with Colonel Leghorn, Dr. Wheelon. In his memoir, Helms wrote, "Corona flew 145 secret missions, with equally rewarding results," 267.

[363] Leghorn spent decades in the commercial-satellite business: U.S. Air Force official Web site, Biography of Colonel Richard Sully Leghorn, Retired, Air Force Space Command, http://www.afspc.af.mil/library/biographies/bio.asp?id=9942.

[363] W61 Earth Penetrator: Leland Johnson, "Sandia Report: Tonopah Test Range Outpost of Sandia National Laboratories, SAND96-0375, UC-700," March 1996, 80.

[363] launch the earth-penetrator weapon: Nelson, "Low-Yield Earth-Penetrating Nuclear Weapons," 3, figure 3.

[363] and signed by five of the then seven or eight nuclear-capable countries: Comprehensive Nuclear-Test-Ban Treaty Organization (http://www.ctbto.org/). The Comprehensive Nuclear-Test-Ban Treaty was signed by the United States, China, France, the United Kingdom, and Russia on September 26, 1996, in New York. The nuclear-armed states who did not sign (and as of 2011 have not signed) are India, Israel, and Pakistan. According to CTBTO, Israel has not reported testing but is generally assumed to be a nuclear-armed state. In 2006, Korea announced that it had conducted a nuclear test. Notably, the 1963 Partial Test Ban Treaty, to which I also refer, prohibits nuclear explosions

in the atmosphere, outer space, and underwater but allowed for underground nuclear tests. The Comprehensive Nuclear-Test-Ban Treaty of 1996 prohibits *all* nuclear explosions, including those conducted underground.

[364] Rods from God: Eric Adams, "Rods from God," *Popular Science,* June 1, 2004.

[364] "that's enough force": Interview with Barnes.

[364] "long-rod penetration": Nelson, "Low-Yield Earth-Penetrating Nuclear Weapons," 4.

[364] April 1999 report: JSR-97-155, "Characterization of Underground Facilities." JASON, MITRE Corporation, McLean, Virginia.

[364] Los Alamos fired back: Interview with Stephen Younger.

[365] operations at the Nevada Test Site: "NSTec Contracted to Operate NNSA Test Site," *United Press International,* December 22, 2008. Interview with Stephen Younger.

[365] In 2006, the Senate dropped the line item: CRS Report for Congress, "Bunker Busters": Robust Nuclear Earth Penetrator Issues, FY2005-FY2007; Domenici: RNEP Funds Dropped from Appropriations Bill," press release, Senator Pete Domenici, October 25, 2005, FY2006 hearings. From the transcript: Representative Terry Everett: "Could you please tell me directly if there's a military need for this, for robust earth—nuclear earth penetrator?" Secretary of Defense Donald Rumsfeld: "It is a question that's difficult to answer, because sometimes they say 'military requirement.' And that's a formal process. There was no military requirement for unmanned aerial vehicles until they came along."

[365] proposed to revive the NERVA program: Michael R. Williams, "Ground Test Facility for Propulsion and Power Modes of Nuclear Engine Operation,"SavannahRiverNationalLaboratory,DepartmentofEnergy,WSRC-MS-2004-00842.

[367] six hundred million pages of information: Pauline Jelinek, "U.S. Releases Nazi Papers," Associated Press, November 2, 1999.

[367] Many documents about Area 51 exist in that pile: Interviews with EG&G engineer.

[367] the Roswell crash remains: which certainly explains why the CIA and the Air Force have not been able to locate Roswell crash remains in their archives.

[368] the most powerful defense contractor in the nation: In 1999, EG&G was acquired by the Carlyle Group. In 2002 it was acquired by URS. In 2000, EG&G formed a joint venture with Raytheon to create JT3 (Joint Test, Tactics, and Training) LLC, which provides "engineering and technical support for the Nevada Test and Training Range, the Air Force Flight Test Center, the Utah Test and Training Range, and the Electronic Combat Range." Interview with Meagan Stafford, EG&G/URS Public Relations, Sard Verbinnen & Co., July 16, 2010.

[369] former dean of engineering at MIT: Vannevar Bush papers located at National Security Archives, Truman Library, the Roosevelt Library, and MIT Archives; Zachary, *Endless Frontier,* Library of Congress, "Vannevar Bush, a Collection of His Papers in the Library of Congress," Manuscript Division, Library of Congress, Washington, DC.

[370] kidnapped by Dr. Josef Mengele: Interview with Gerald Posner; Posner and Ware, *Mengele: The Complete Story,* 83.

[370] performed unspeakable experimental surgical procedures: Spitz, *Doctors From Hell: The Horrific Account of Nazi Experiments on Humans.* Spitz worked as a typist during the Nuremberg trials. *Forgiving Dr. Mengele,* a film by Bob Hercules and Cheri Pugh (2006); CANDLES Holocaust Museum, Biography of Eva Mozes Kor. The Japanese also performed grotesque experiments on humans during the war. "U.S. War Department, War Crimes Office, Judge Advocate General's Office, #770475." Japan's version of Josef Mengele, General Ishii, was pardoned by the U.S. War Crimes Office on the grounds that information regarding the grotesque medical experiments he performed would somehow benefit the United States. Although it is science fiction, *The Island of Dr. Moreau,* written in 1896 by H. G. Wells, tells a twisted tale of human experimentation on a remote island.

[370] children, dwarfs, and twins: Koren and Negev, *In Our Hearts We Were Giants,* 85–197.

[371] Josef Mengele's efforts to create a pure, Aryan race: Erik Kirschbaum, "Cloning Wakes German Memories of Nazi Master Race," Reuters, February 27, 1997. America is not exempt from eugenic theology; see Edwin Black, "Eugenics and the Nazis: The California Connection," *San Francisco Chronicle,* November 9, 2003.

[371] painter named Dina Babbitt: Ibid., 103–31 and photographic inserts. Bruce Weber, "Dina Babbitt, Artist at Auschwitz, Is Dead at 86," *New York*

Times, August 1, 2009. Babbitt's maiden name (used at Auschwitz) was Gottlieb.

[371] Dr. Martina Puzyna: Koren and Negev, *In Our Hearts We Were Giants,* 109.

[371] According to his only son, Rolf: Interview with Gerald Posner. Posner interviewed Rolf Mengele and was given access to 5,000 pages of Mengele's written correspondence as well as his personal journals written after the war.

[371] Mengele held up his side of the Faustian bargain: Interview with EG&G engineer.

[371] Mengele never took up residence in the Soviet Union: Interview with Posner.

[374] Eileen Welsome wrote a newspaper story: Eileen Welsome, "The Plutonium Files: America's Secret Medical Experiments in the Cold War," *Albuquerque Tribune,* November 1993.

[374] direct violation of the Nuremberg Code: Trials of War Criminals before the Nuremberg Military Tribunals under Control Council Law No. 10, Vol. 2, Washington, DC: U.S. Government Printing Office, 1949. Nuremberg Code: (1). The voluntary consent of the human subject is absolutely essential. (2). The experiment should be such as to yield fruitful results for the good of society, unprocurable by other methods or means of study, and not random and unnecessary in nature. Full text available at http://ohsr.od.nih.gov/guidelines/nuremberg.html.

[374] President Clinton opened an investigation. The advisory committee was made of fourteen members who reported to the president through a cabinet-level group called the Human Radiation Interagency Working Group, and it included the secretaries of defense and energy (formerly the Atomic Energy Commission) as well as the attorney general and the director of the CIA. The committee was dissolved in October of 1995 after publishing its findings. Today, the Office of Health, Safety and Security (HSS), a Department of Energy office, maintains a Web site. Of its efforts, DOE says, "We have undertaken an intensive effort to identify and catalogue relevant historical documents from DOE's 3.2 million cubic feet of records scattered across the country." Given that there are approximately 2,000 pages of documents in a single cubic foot, it is telling that a record search for "EG&G" at the HSS/DOE database delivers a paltry 500 documents.

Epilogue

Interviews: Colonel Leghorn, Ed Lovick, EG&G engineer, David Myhra

[375] Army Air Forces commemorative yearbook: This is the government-issued "Official Report, Task Force 1.52" and is meant to look like a high school yearbook.

[376] The U.S. government spent nearly two billion dollars: *Atomic Audit,* 102. "Operation Crossroads was an astonishing $1.3 billion [circa 1996 dollars], far more than any of the subsequent thermonuclear tests conducted during the 1950s."

[376] Truman's closest advisers: "Potsdam and the Final Decision to Use the Bomb," Department of Energy Archives (http://www.cfo.doe.gov/): "During the second week of Allied deliberations at Potsdam, on the evening of July 24, 1945, Truman approached Stalin without an interpreter and, as casually as he could, told him that the United States had a 'new weapon of unusual destructive force.' Stalin showed little interest, replying only that he hoped the United States would make 'good use of it against the Japanese.' The reason for Stalin's composure became clear later: Soviet intelligence had been receiving information about the atomic bomb program since fall 1941."

[376] Stalin's black propaganda hoax: Interview with EG&G engineer.

[377] "a warning shot across Truman's bow": Interview with EG&G engineer. The engineer says this information was relayed to him by his EG&G boss, who had been given the information by a government superior. One cannot rule out the possibility that the elite EG&G engineers were given false information as a means of coercing them into participating in a morally reprehensible program; in 1951, there was no greater enemy to the free world than Joseph Stalin. Until Russia opens its UFO archives, Stalin's side of the story will remain unknown, but since the collapse of the Soviet Union, Stalin's interest in UFOs has come to light. In *Korolev,* Professor James Harford discusses an incident where Stalin asked his chief rocket designer, Sergei Korolev, to study UFOs (pages 234, 362). In 2002, Pravda.ru ran a story called "Stalin's UFOs," identifying the dictator's Roswell/UFO research team as "mathematician Mstislav Keldysh, chemist Alexander Topchiyev, and physician [sic] Sergey [sic] Korolev." Other ufologists identify Stalin's UFO team as Sergei Korolev, missile designer and inventor of Sputnik; Igor Kurchatov, father of Russia's atomic bomb; and Mstislav Keldysh, mathematician, theoretician, and space pioneer (see photographic insert).

[377] "Hitler invented stealth," says Gene Poteat: Interview with Gene Poteat. Also from Poteat's participation in the CIA's Oxcart panel discussion at the National Air and Space Museum, Smithsonian Institution, Steven F. Udvar-Hazy Center, September 24, 2010.

[377] Whatever happened to the Horten brothers: Interview with David Myhra.

[377] captured by the U.S. Ninth Army on April 7, 1945: Myhra, *The Horten Brothers and Their All Wing Aircraft,* 229.

[378] London high-rise near Hyde Park: Ibid., 230.

[378] Theodore von Kármán: National Aviation Hall of Fame, biography, Theodore von Kármán. http://www.nationalaviation.org/von-karman-theodore/. Myhra, *The Horten Brothers and Their All Wing Aircraft,* 230.

[378] tapes can be found: National Air and Space Museum, Archives Division, Reimar and Walter Horten Interviews, Accession No. 1999-0065.

[378] "Reimar had me agree to two restrictions": Interview with David Myhra.

[378] 2010 Freedom of Information Act request: Letter, October 29, 2010, to Ms. Annie Jacobsen from Nathan L. Mitchell, Assistant to the General Counsel, Department of the Army, Office of the General Counsel, 104 Army Pentagon, Washington DC.

[379] another [important] engineer: The name of this engineer and his employment with EG&G during the 1950s have been verified with other former EG&G employees.

[379] empty lot of asphalt: The lot is adjacent to the buildings identified as EG&G's original Las Vegas headquarters in a film about the history of the Nevada Test Site, funded by the National Nuclear Security Administration, Nevada Site Office: "When EG&G first moved to Las Vegas, their headquarters were located on 'A' Street now called Commerce."

[379] "Little wooden discs": Interview with Ed Lovick.

[380] sworn affidavit: "Dead Airman's Affidavit: Roswell Aliens Were Real." Fox News.com, July 3, 2007. http://www.foxnews.com/story/0,2933,287643,00.html, accessed December 30, 2010.

[381] "It's difficult": Written correspondence with Bob Lazar, 2010.

[382] hidden inside secret "Restricted Data" files: Interview with EG&G engineer.

[382] Vannevar Bush: To further understand Vannevar Bush, I reviewed his papers, letters, and hand-edited drafts of his articles, books, and monographs from three major collections: Vannevar Bush, "A Collection of His Papers in the Library of Congress," Manuscript Division, Library of Congress, Washington, DC; Vannevar Bush, "Office of Scientific Research and Development," National Archives and Records Administration, College Park, Maryland; Vannevar Bush Papers, Carnegie Institute, Washington, DC.

[382] human experiments to study the effects: The trials involved high concentrations of lewisite and mustard gas. *Advisory Committee on Human Radiation Experiments, Final Report,* 98; *Veterans at Risk: The Health Effects of Mustard Gas and Lewisite,* 66–69.

[382] "Although the human subjects": Ibid., 66.

[383] Dixon Institute...Feeble-Minded: *Advisory Committee on Human Radiation Experiments, Final Report,* Chapter Seven, Nontherapeutic Research on Children, 320–351. Dr. Susan Lederer, *Military Medical Ethics,* Volume 2, "The Cold War and Beyond: Covert and Deceptive American Medical Experiments," 514. Lederer, a Clinton committee staff member, cites D. J. Rothman, *Strangers at the Bedside: A History of How Law and Bioethics Transformed Medical Decision Making,* Basic Books, 1991.

[383] letter-number designation of S-1: Gosling, *The Manhattan Project: Making the Atomic Bomb,* 10.

[384] JT3: From the company Web site (http://www.jt3.com/), accessed October 18, 2010. "The Department of Defense (DoD) has merged the engineering and technical support management of several western ranges into one organization to streamline support for test and training customers. In response to this challenge, URS (URS) and Raytheon Technical Services Company (RTSC) formed JT3, a Limited Liability Company (LLC) dedicated to supporting Joint Range Technical Services (J-Tech) requirements. We are experts at assisting our customers and other contractors in the planning, preparation, and execution of test projects and training missions."

Author Interviews and Bibliography

PRIMARY INTERVIEWS

The individuals listed below, by birth year, did many things in their long careers. Noted are topics we discussed during our interviews. All military officers and intelligence agency personnel are retired.

Helen Kleyla (1913–   ). Longtime secretary to CIA deputy director Richard Bissell.
CIA, Richard Bissell, Area 51, Bay of Pigs.
Interviews: Written correspondence, fall 2009

Colonel Richard S. Leghorn (1919–   ). The father of peacetime overhead espionage.
Army Air Forces, USAF, CIA, World War II, Korean War; U-2, MiG, Corona satellite system, reconnaissance over Normandy, overhead espionage, Operation Crossroads, General Curtis LeMay.
Interviews: July 21, 2009; July 24, 2009; February 10, 2010; written correspondence: July 2009–October 2010

Edward Lovick Jr. (1919–   ). The father of stealth technology.
Lockheed Skunk Works, U-2, A-12 Oxcart, SR-71 Blackbird, D-21 drone, Harvey, Have Blue, F-117 Nighthawk, Project Kempster-Lacroix, radar testing, and pole testing at Area 51.
Interviews: January 5, 2008; February 7, 2008; March 6, 2008; April 3, 2008; April 18, 2008; April 29, 2008; May 29, 2008; June 6, 2008; June 18, 2008; July 2, 2008; July 10, 2008; July 23, 2008; July 30, 2008; August 6, 2008; August 13, 2008; August 21, 2008; August 28, 2008; September 4, 2008; November 18, 2008; December 9, 2008; January 6, 2009; January 20, 2009; March 17, 2009; March 30, 2009; June 11, 2009; June 28, 2009; August 1, 2009; February 28,

*2010; April 22, 2010; September 5, 2010; written correspondence: February 2008–
October 2010*

Ray Goudey (1919–   ). Flew U-2 "Ship One" at Area 51.
Lockheed test flights, U-2, Burbank to Area 51 flights.
Interviews: June 12, 2009; July 8, 2009; October 8, 2009

Fred White (1921–   ). Wrote the flight manuals for Lockheed U-2, A-12,
and SR-71.
Lockheed Skunk Works, U-2, A-12, YF-12, SR-71, engineering projects at
Area 51.
*Interviews: October 3, 2009; October 8, 2009; written correspondence: October
2009–May 2010.*

Colonel Hugh "Slip" Slater (1922–   ). Base commander at Area 51.
Army Air Force, USAF, CIA, A-12, YF-12, D-21 drone, commander of
the U-2 Chinese Black Cat Squadron, commander for Operation Black Shield,
the 303 Committee.
*Interviews: November 13, 2008; December 20, 2009; January 7, 2009; March 4,
2009; April 25, 2009; June 25, 2009; July 14, 2009; October 7, 2009; October 8,
2009; January 13, 2010*

Alfred O'Donnell (1922–   ), early Manhattan Project member. Armed,
wired, and fired 186 nuclear bombs at the Nevada Test Site and the Pacific
Proving Ground.
Nuclear weapons, World War II, Battle at Okinawa; timing, wiring, and firing system on atomic bombs; timing, wiring, and firing system on thermonu-
clear bombs; Operation Crossroads, Operation Greenhouse, Operation Ivy,
Operation Castle, Operation Plumbbob, Operation Hardtack, Nevada Test Site.
*Interviews: May 9, 2009; May 25, 2009; May 27, 2009; June 24, 2009;
June 25, 2009; July 15, 2009; September 7, 2009; September 8, 2009; October 6,
2009; October 7, 2009; November 17, 2009; December 14, 2009; December 15,
2009; December 16, 2009; January 13, 2010; January 14, 2010; February 11, 2010;
March 6, 2010; June 28, 2010, June 29, 2010; written correspondence: May 2009–
October 2010*

Colonel Hervey S. Stockman (1922–2011). First man to fly over the
Soviet Union in a U-2.
Army Air Forces, USAF, U-2 pilot, atomic-sampling pilot, fighter pilot in
World War II, Korea, and Vietnam; POW at the Hanoi Hilton and other pris-
ons from June 12, 1967–March 4, 1973.
Interviews: August 24, 2009; September 17, 2009; March 24, 2010

Colonel Sam Pizzo (1922–   ). Navigation expert for the A-12 at Area 51 and escort to Nikita Khrushchev from Moscow to America in 1959.

Strategic Air Command, USAF, A-12 Oxcart, Operation Home Run, celestial navigation, General Curtis LeMay.

Interviews: April 22, 2009; April 24, 2009; May 19, 2009; May 21, 2009; October 3, 2009; October 7, 2009; December 2, 2009; written correspondence: April 2009–September 2010

General Hsichun "Mike" Hua (1926–   ). Flew with U-2 Chinese Black Cat Squadron.

CIA U-2 pilot, CIA air base at Taoyuan, Taiwan.

Interview: March 12, 2010; written correspondence: winter/spring 2010

Ralph James "Jim" Freedman (1927–   ). Procurement manager at Area 51, EG&G weapons test engineer, and nuclear explosion photographer.

EG&G, CIA, nuclear test liaison to Howard Hughes from Area 51, Nevada Test Site, Operation Greenhouse, Operation Ivy, Operation Castle, A-12 Oxcart, Project Aquiline.

Interviews: May 7, 2009; May 8, 2009; April 25, 2009; June 24, 2009; September 8, 2009; October 8, 2009; December 15, 2009; June 28, 2010; August 4, 2010; November 30, 2010.

Brigadier General Raymond L. Haupt (1927–   ). The only man to fly all three models of the Oxcart at Area 51.

USAF, U-2, A-12 Oxcart, YF-12, SR-71 Blackbird, Blackbird flight manuals, Lockheed pilots, Area 51 operations.

Interviews: October 3, 2009; October 8, 2009

Major General Patrick J. Halloran (1928–   ). Squadron operations officer for the U-2, wing commander for the SR-71 Blackbird.

USAF, U-2, SR-71 Blackbird, U-2 shoot-downs over China.

Interview: June 12, 2009

Dr. Albert D. "Bud" Wheelon (1929–   ). CIA's first deputy director of Science and Technology, also known as the mayor of Area 51.

Project Palladium, A-12 Oxcart, Cuban missile crisis, satellites, early missile systems, TRW, defense contracting, MIT, President Kennedy, James Killian, General Ledford, John McCone, Richard Helms, Lyman Kirkpatrick.

Interviews: May 29, 2009; November 9, 2009

Colonel Kenneth B. Collins (1930–   ). A-12 Oxcart pilot for the CIA.

USAF, CIA, A-12 Oxcart pilot, SR-71 Blackbird pilot, Korean War, Vietnam War, Operation Black Shield, Jack Weeks, Walt Ray.

Interviews: October 29, 2008; January 20, 2009; March 17, 2009; April 14, 2009; April 28, 2009; May 19, 2009; June 1, 2009; June 13, 2009; August 4, 2009; October 20, 2009; December 2, 2009; January 20, 2010, April 4, 2010, August 6, 2010; written correspondence: October 2008–October 2010

Lieutenant Colonel Francis J. "Frank" Murray (1930–   ). A-12 Oxcart pilot for the CIA.

USAF, CIA, A-12 Oxcart pilot, F-101 pilot, Vietnam War, Operation Black Shield, USS *Pueblo*, General Ledford, Walt Ray.

Interviews: March 4, 2009; March 5, 2009; April 28, 2009; October 6, 2009; October 7, 2009; January 6, 2010; January 13, 2010; written correspondence: March 2009–May 2010

Lieutenant Colonel Roger W. Andersen (1930–   ). Area 51 command post operations for Area 51 and Kadena Air Base during Operation Oxcart.

USAF, CIA, Nevada Test Site, atomic tests, Operation Black Shield.

Interviews: March 5, 2009; May 26, 2009; October 7, 2009; September 24, 2010; written correspondence: May 2009–September 2010

Robert "Bob" Murphy (1930–   ). Lockheed Skunk Works engineer and project airplane manager at Area 51.

U-2, A-12 Oxcart, D-21 drone, U-2 missions out of Asia, Have Blue, F-117 Nighthawk.

Interviews: July 4, 2009; July 20, 2009; September 24, 2010

William "Bill" Weaver (1930–   ). Lockheed test pilot for the A-12, YF-12, SR-71, and the only pilot to survive a Mach 3 bailout at 78,000 feet in an SR-71 Blackbird.

SR-71 Blackbird, high-speed bailouts, parachutes.

Interview: June 13, 2009

Captain Donald J. Donohue (1930–   ). Crew captain for A-12 Oxcart at Area 51.

USAF, A-12 Oxcart.

Interviews: May 8, 2009; December 9, 2009

Frank Micalizzi (1930–   ). Warehouse supervisor at Area 51.

USAF, CIA, Kadena Air Force Base, A-12 Oxcart camera film storage.

Interview: May 8, 2009

Florence DeLuna (1930–   ). Area 51 transport pilot.

USAF, C–47, Walt Ray, Dreamland airspace and air traffic control.
Interview: May 8, 2009

Ernest "Ernie" Williams (1930–   ). Atomic Energy Commission motor pool and food services coordinator, escorted the Apollo astronauts around the Nevada Test Site.
AEC, Nevada Test Site, astronaut training.
Interviews: October 7, 2009; December 14, 2009

S. Eugene "Gene" Poteat (1930–   ). Pioneer of electronic countermeasures, first CIA officer assigned to the National Reconnaissance Office.
CIA, NRO, Project Palladium, Area 51 radar tests, U-2 and A-12, Caspian Sea Monster, Project Aquiline.
Interviews: September 27, 2010; September 28, 2010; September 30, 2010

Richard Mingus (1931–   ). Area 51 security, Nevada Test Site Security, and Lawrence Radiation Laboratory operations manager.
Atomic Energy Commission, Department of Energy, Lawrence Radiation Laboratory, Federal Services, Inc., Wackenhut Security, Inc., U-2 security guard, Area 51 security, Area 52 security, Nevada Test Site, Tonopah Test Range, Project 57, Operation Plumbbob, underground nuclear testing.
Interviews: September 9, 2009; October 8, 2009; November 18, 2009; December 14, 2009; December 15, 2009; December 16, 2009; January 14, 2009; February 10, 2010; February 12, 2010; June 28, 2010; June 29, 2010

Harry Martin (1931–   ). In charge of the million-gallon fuel farm at Area 51.
USAF, CIA, fuels, A-12 Oxcart.
Interviews: November 13, 2008; March 5, 2009; May 26, 2009

Lieutenant Colonel Tony Bevacqua (1932–   ). Youngest pilot to fly U-2 at Area 51.
USAF, U-2 pilot, SR-71 Blackbird pilot, Vietnam War, Kadena Air Force Base, Gary Powers.
Interviews: June 12, 2009; June 13, 2009; October 8, 2009; written correspondence: June 2009–October 2010

Colonel Charles E. "Charlie" Trapp (1933–   ). Area 51 helicopter search-and-rescue pilot.
USAF, C–47, Walt Ray, Dreamland airspace and air traffic control.
Interview: June 4, 2010; November 18, 2010; November 24, 2010

Troy Wade (1934–   ). Longtime Nevada Test Site official, former assistant secretary of energy for defense programs, ran Operation Morning Light for the Department of Energy, Nevada Test Site Historical Foundation.

Atomic Energy Commission, Department of Energy, Nevada Test Site, Operation Morning Light, underground nuclear testing.

Interviews: September 9, 2009; October 8, 2009; December 15, 2009

Wayne E. Pendleton (1935–   ). EG&G radar expert.
Lockheed Skunk Works, EG&G radar range, National Reconnaissance Office, Have Blue, Howard Hughes.

Interviews: October 3, 2009; October 7, 2009; April 22, 2010

Thornton "T.D." Barnes (1937–   ). Radar expert on multiple Area 51 projects.

CIA, EG&G, Atomic Energy Commission, NASA, Project Palladium, A-12 Oxcart, MiG, X-15 rocket plane, Apollo 1, NERVA, Nike missile system, Hercules missile system, Have Blue.

Interviews: November 3, 2008; November 13, 2008; December 20, 2009; December 21, 2009; January 7, 2009; March 4, 2009; March 5, 2009; March 6, 2009; April 24, 2009; April 25, 2009; May 7, 2009; May 8, 2009; May 26, 2009; June 12, 2009; June 13, 2009; June 24, 2009; June 25, 2009; July 14, 2009; September 7, 2009; September 9, 2009, October 7, 2009; October 8, 2009; October 9, 2009, December 14, 2009; December 15, 2009; December 16, 2009; January 13, 2010; January 14, 2010; February 11, 2010; February 12, 2010; March 6, 2010; June 29, 2010; written correspondence: November 2008–October 2010

Ken Swanson (1937–   ). Electronic warfare, electronic countermeasures expert, Red Dog/Blue Dog ECM System.

Interview: June 17, 2010

Sherre Lovick (1960–   ). Lockheed Skunk Works engineer.
Lockheed Skunk Works, radar signature, defense contracting.

Interviews: February 7, 2008; March 6, 2008; April 3, 2008; April 29, 2008; May 29, 2008; June 6, 2008; July 2, 2008; July 23, 2008; July 30, 2008; August 6, 2008; August 21, 2008; June 28, 2009

Colonel Buzz Aldrin, Apollo 11 astronaut and the second man on the moon

Dr. Robert B. Abernethy, Pratt and Whitney engineer; invented the Oxcart's J-58 engine

Joseph C. Behne Jr.: Former test director, Lawrence Livermore National Laboratory

Arthur Beidler, 67th Reconnaissance Tactical Squadron, Japan

Colonel Adelbert W. "Buz" Carpenter, SR-71 pilot

Harold B. Finger, former manager of AEC–NASA Space Nuclear Propulsion Office

R. Cargill Hall, historian emeritus, National Reconnaissance Office

Milton M. Klein, former manager of AEC–NASA Space Nuclear Propulsion Office

Darwin Morgan: National Nuclear Security Administration, spokesman (current)

Dennis Nordquist, Pratt and Whitney mechanical engineer, J-58 engine

Grace Weismann: Joe Walker's widow

Charles "Chuck" Wilson: U-2 pilot

Changti "Robin" Yeh: U-2 pilot, Chinese Black Cat Squadron

Secondary Interviews and Correspondence

Steven Aftergood

Joerg Arnu

Doris Barnes

Stacy Slater Bernhardt

Tim Brown

Fred Burton

Lee Davidson

Martha DeMarre

Jeanne Donohue

Stanton Friedman

Norio Hayakawa

Bill Irvine

George Knapp

Tony Landis

Eunice Layton

Colonel Ronald "Jack" Layton

Bob Lazar

Ken Leghorn

Jim Long

Dr. Craig Luther

Tom Mahood

Mary Martin

Millie Meierdierck

Peter W. Merlin

Martha Murphy
Mary Jane Murphy
Stella Murray
David Myhra
James Oberg
Ruth O'Donnell
Thomas O'Donnell
Major General Jude Pao
John E. Pike
Gerald Posner
Gary Powers Jr.
Dr. Jeffrey Richelson
Dr. David Robarge
Louise Schalk
P. W. Singer
Barbara Slater
Peter Slater
Peter Stockman
Sharlene Weeks
Stephen M. Younger
G. Pascal Zachary

Current and former employees from the following organizations, agencies, and corporations were interviewed, some on the condition of anonymity.
National Security Agency (NSA)
National Reconnaissance Office (NRO)
National Imagery and Mapping Agency (NIMA)
National Photographic Interpretation Center (NPIC)
Defense Intelligence Agency (DIA)
National Aeronautics and Space Agency (NASA)
Central Intelligence Agency (CIA)
Atomic Energy Commission (AEC)
Department of Energy (DOE)
Defense Nuclear Agency (DNA)
National Nuclear Security Administration (NNSA)
United States Air Force (USAF)
Federal Bureau of Investigation (FBI)
United States Army Air Forces (USAAF)
EG&G Special Projects Group
Lockheed Martin Corporation

Northrop Grumman
Raytheon
General Atomics Aeronautical
Hughes Aircraft Company
Summa Corporation

Books and Monographs

Aldrin, Buzz, with Ken Abraham. *Magnificent Desolation: The Long Journey Home from the Moon*. New York: Harmony Books, 2009.

Anders, Roger M., Jack M. Holl, Alice L. Buck, and Prentice C. Dean. *The United States Nuclear Weapons Program: A Summary History*. Washington, DC: U.S. Department of Energy, 1983.

Ball, Desmond. *Politics and Force Levels, the Strategic Missile Program of the Kennedy Administration*. Berkeley: University of California Press, 1980.

Bamford, James. *Body of Secrets: Anatomy of the Ultra-Secret National Security Agency*. New York: Anchor Books, 2002.

Berlitz, Charles, and William Moore. *Roswell Incident, the Most Important UFO Encounter of Our Century*. New York: MJF Books, 1980.

Bissell, Richard M., with Jonathan E. Lewis and Francis T. Pudlo. *Reflections of a Cold Warrior: From Yalta to the Bay of Pigs*. New Haven: Yale University Press, 1996.

Bower, Tom. *The Paperclip Conspiracy: The Hunt for the Nazi Scientists*. Boston: Little, Brown and Company, 1987.

Bradley, David. *No Place to Hide*. Boston: Little, Brown and Company, 1948.

Broad, William J. *Teller's War: The Top Secret Story Behind the Star Wars Deception*. New York: Simon and Schuster, 1992.

Brugioni, Dino A. *Eyeball to Eyeball: The Inside Story of the Cuban Missile Crisis*. New York: Random House, 1990.

Brzezinski, Matthew. *Red Moon Rising: Sputnik and the Hidden Rivalries That Ignited the Space Age*. New York: Henry Holt and Company, 2007.

Buck, Alice. *History of the Atomic Energy Commission.* Washington, DC: U.S. Department of Energy, 1983.

Burrows, William E. *By Any Means Necessary: America's Heroes Flying Secret Missions in a Hostile World.* New York: Penguin Putnam, 2002.

Coffey, Thomas. *Iron Eagle: The Turbulent Life of General Curtis LeMay.* New York: Random House, 1986.

Coll, Steve. *Ghost Wars: The Secret History of the CIA, Afghanistan and bin Laden, from the Soviet Invasion to September 10, 2001.* New York: Penguin Press, 2004.

Coolidge, Matthew. *The Nevada Test Site: A Guide to America's Nuclear Proving Ground.* Culver City, Calif.: The Center for Land Use Interpretation, 1996.

Cornwall, John. *Hitler's Scientists: Science, War and the Devil's Pact.* New York: Penguin Group, 2003.

Crickmore, Paul F. *Combat Legend: F-117 Nighthawk.* Shrewsbury, England: Airlife Publishing Ltd., 2003.

———. *Lockheed SR-71: The Secret Missions Exposed.* London: Osprey, 1993.

Dewar, James A. *To the End of the Solar System: The Story of the Nuclear Rocket.* Lexington, Kentucky: University of Kentucky Press, 2004.

Dickson, Paul. *Sputnik: The Shock of the Century.* New York: Walker and Company, 2007.

Dolibois, John E. *Pattern of Circles, an Ambassador's Story.* Kent, Ohio: Kent State University Press, 1989.

Fehner, Terrence R., and F. G. Gosling. *Battlefield of the Cold War: Atmospheric Nuclear Weapons Testing 1951–1963.* Washington, DC: U.S. Department of Energy, 2006.

———. *Origins of the Nevada Test Site.* Washington, DC: U.S. Department of Energy, 2000.

Fehner, Terrence R., and Jack M. Hall. *Department of Energy, a Summary History, 1977–1994.* Washington, DC: U.S. Department of Energy, 1994.

Finger, H. B., and W. H. Robbins. *An Historical Perspective of the NERVA Nuclear Rocket Engine Technology Program.* Cleveland, Ohio: NASA Lewis Research Center Group, 1991.

Gates, Mahlon. *Operation Morning Light, Northwest Territories, Canada 1978, a Non-Technical Summary of U.S. Participation*. Nevada: U.S. Department of Energy, 1978.

Goode, Timothy. *Above Top Secret: The Worldwide UFO Coverup*. New York: William Morrow, 1988.

Goodman, Matthew. *The Sun and the Moon: The Remarkable True Account of Hoaxers, Showmen, Dueling Journalists, and Lunar Man-Bats in Nineteenth-Century New York*. New York: Basic Books, 2008.

Goodman, Michael S. *Spying on the Nuclear Bear: Anglo-American Intelligence and the Soviet Bomb*. Palo Alto, California: Stanford University Press, 2007.

Gosling, F. G. *The Manhattan Project: Making the Atomic Bomb*. Washington, DC: United States Department of Energy, History Division, 1999.

Graham, Richard H. *SR-71 Blackbird: Stories, Tales, and Legends*. Minneapolis: Zenith Press, 2002.

Hand, Richard J. *Terror on the Air! Horror Radio in America, 1931–1952*. Jefferson, North Carolina: Macfarland and Company, 2009.

Harford, James. *Korolev: How One Man Masterminded the Soviet Drive to Beat America to the Moon*. New York: John Wiley and Sons, 1997.

Hathaway, Robert M., and Russell Jack Smith. *Richard Helms as Director of Central Intelligence, 1963–1973*. Washington, DC: CIA Center for the Study of Intelligence, 1993.

Heaps, Leo. *Operation Morning Light: The True Story of Canada's Nuclear Nightmare*. New York: Ballantine Books, 1979.

Helms, Richard, with William Hood. *A Look Over My Shoulder: A Life in the Central Intelligence Agency*. New York: Ballantine Books, 2003.

Hewlett, Richard G., and Oscar E. Anderson. *The New World: A History of the United States Atomic Energy Commission*. Washington, DC: U.S. Atomic Energy Commission, 1962.

Hoffman, David E. *The Dead Hand: The Untold Story of the Cold War Arms Race and Its Dangerous Legacy*. New York: Doubleday, 2009.

Hua, Mike H. *Lost Black Cats: Story of Two Captured Chinese U-2 Pilots*. Bloomington: AuthorHouse, 2005.

Hunt, Linda. *Secret Agenda: The United States Government, Nazi Scientists, and Project Paperclip, 1945 to 1990*. New York: St. Martin's Press, 1991.

Jenkins, Dennis R. *Hypersonics Before the Shuttle: A Concise History of the X-15 Research Airplane*. Washington, DC: National Aeronautics and Space Administration, Monographs in Aerospace History, 2000.

Johnson, Clarence L., "Kelly," with Maggie Smith. *Kelly: More Than My Share of It All*. Washington, DC: Smithsonian Institution Press, 1985.

Johnson, Leland. *Sandia Report: Tonopah Test Range Outpost of Sandia National Laboratories*. Washington, DC: U.S. Department of Energy, 1996.

Johnson, Loch K., ed. *Strategic Intelligence*. Santa Barbara, Calif.: Praeger Security International, 2006.

Jones, R. V. *The Wizard War: British Scientific Intelligence, 1939–1945*. New York: Coward, McCann and Geoghegan, 1978.

Jung, Carl. *Flying Saucers: A Modern Myth of Things Seen in the Skies*. Princeton: Princeton University Press, 1979.

Kaplan, Fred. *The Wizards of Armageddon*. New York: Simon and Schuster, 1983.

Keegan, John. *Intelligence in War: The Value and Limitation of What the Military Can Learn About the Enemy*. New York: Vintage Books, 2004.

Killian, James R. Jr. *Sputnik, Scientists and Eisenhower: A Memoir of the First Special Assistant to the President for Science and Technology*. Cambridge: MIT Press, 1977.

Kirkpatrick, Lyman B. *The Real CIA*. New York: Macmillan Company, 1968.

Korda, Michael. *Ike: An American Hero*. New York: HarperCollins, 2007.

Kozak, Warren. *LeMay: The Life and Wars of General Curtis LeMay*. Washington, DC: Regnery, 2009.

Khrushchev, Nikita. *Khrushchev Remembers*. Translated and edited by Strobe Talbott. Boston: Little, Brown and Company, 1970.

Mallick, Donald L., with Peter W. Merlin. *The Smell of Kerosene: A Test Pilot's Odyssey*. Washington, DC: National Aeronautics and Space Administration, 2003.

Marks, John. *The Search for the "Manchurian Candidate": The CIA and Mind Control*. New York: Norton, 1991.

McAuliffe, Mary S., ed. *CIA Documents on the Cuban Missile Crisis 1962*. Washington, DC: CIA History Staff, Central Intelligence Agency, 1992.

McPhee, John. *The Curve of Binding Energy*. New York: Farrar, Straus and Giroux, 1973.

Merlin, Peter W. *Mach 3 + NASA/USAF YF-12 Flight Research, 1969–1979*. Washington, DC: U.S. Government Printing Office, 2002.

Michels, Juergen, and Olaf Przybilski. *Peenemuende und seine Erben in Ost und West*. Bonn: Bernard and Graefe, 1997.

Miller, Richard L. *Under the Cloud: The Decades of Nuclear Testing*. New York: Free Press, 1986.

Moran, Barbara. *The Day We Lost the H-Bomb: Cold War, Hot Nukes, and the Worst Nuclear Disaster*. New York: Presidio Press, 2009.

Myhra, David. *The Horten Brothers and Their All-Wing Aircraft*. Atglen, Pennsylvania: Schiffer Publishing Ltd., 1998.

Narducci, Henry M. *Strategic Air Command and the Alert Program, a Brief History*. Nebraska: Office of the Historian, Offutt Air Force Base, 1988.

Neufeld, Michael J. *Von Braun: Dreamer of Space, Engineer of War*. New York: Alfred A. Knopf, 2007.

Newman, James R., and Byron S. Miller. *The Control of Atomic Energy*. New York: McGraw-Hill Book Company, 1948.

Oberg, James. *UFOs and Outer Space Mysteries*. Virginia Beach: Donning Press, 1982.

O'Keefe, Bernard J. *Nuclear Hostages*. Boston: Houghton Mifflin Company, 1983.

Pechura, C. M., and D. P. Rall. *Veterans at Risk: The Health Effects of Mustard Gas and Lewisite*. Washington, DC: National Academy Press, 1993.

Peebles, Curtis. *Dark Eagles: A History of Top Secret U.S. Aircraft Programs*. Novato, Calif.: Presidio Press, 1995.

————. *Watch the Skies: A Chronicle of the Flying Saucer Myth.* New York: Berkley, 1995.

Pizzo, Sam. *As Good As It Gets: A Man of Many Hats.* New Orleans: Tommy Towery, 2008.

Plaskon, Kyril. *Silent Heroes of the Cold War: The Mysterious Military Plane Crash on a Nevada Mountain Peak—and the Families Who Endured an Abyss of Silence for Generations.* Las Vegas: Stephens Press, 2008.

Pocock, Chris. *Dragon Lady: The History of the U-2 Spyplane.* Shrewsbury, England: Airlife, 1989.

Posner, Gerald L., and John Ware. *Mengele: The Complete Story.* New York: Cooper Square Press, 1986.

Powers, Francis Gary, and Curt Gentry. *Operation Overflight: The U-2 Spy Pilot Tells His Story for the First Time.* New York: Holt, Rinehart and Winston, 1970.

Quist, Arvin S. *Security Classification of Information.* Oak Ridge, Tenn.: U.S. Department of Energy, 1989.

Rhodes, Richard. *Dark Sun: The Making of the Hydrogen Bomb.* New York: Simon and Schuster, 1995.

————. *The Making of the Atomic Bomb.* New York: Simon and Schuster, 1986.

Rich, Ben R., and Leo Janos. *Skunk Works: A Personal Memoir of My Years at Lockheed.* Boston: Little, Brown and Company, 1994.

Richelson, Jeffrey T. *Spying on the Bomb: American Nuclear Intelligence from Nazi Germany to Iran and North Korea.* New York: W. W. Norton and Company, 2006.

————. *Civilians, Spies and Blue Suits: The Bureaucratic War for Control of Overhead Reconnaissance, 1961–1965.* Washington, DC: National Security Archive Monograph, 2003.

————. *The Wizards of Langley: Inside CIA's Directorate of Science and Technology.* Boulder: Westview Press, 2002.

Robarge, David. *Archangel: CIA's Supersonic A-12 Reconnaissance Aircraft.* Washington, DC: Central Intelligence Agency, 2007.

Saler, Benson, Charles A. Ziegler, and Charles B. Moore. *UFO Crash at Roswell: The Genesis of a Modern Myth.* Connecticut: Konecky and Konecky, 1997.

Samuel, Wolfgang W. E. *American Raiders: The Race to Capture the Luftwaffe's Secrets*. Jackson: University Press of Mississippi, 2004.

Schwartz, Stephen I., ed. *Atomic Audit: The Costs and Consequences of U.S. Nuclear Weapons Since 1940*. Washington, DC: Brookings Institution Press, 1998.

Singer, P. W. *Wired for War: The Robotics Revolution and Conflict in the Twenty-first Century*. New York: Penguin Press, 2009.

Smyth, Henry DeWolf. *Atomic Energy for Military Purposes; The Official Report on the Development Under the Auspices of the United States Government, 1940–1945*. Princeton: Princeton University Press, 1945.

Spitz, Vivien. *Doctors from Hell: The Horrific Account of Nazi Experiments on Humans*. Boulder, Colorado: Sentient Publications, 2005.

Stone, I. F. *The Best of I. F. Stone*. Edited by Karl Weber. New York: Public Affairs, 2006.

Taubman, Philip. *Secret Empire: Eisenhower, the CIA, and the Hidden Story of America's Space Espionage*. New York: Simon and Schuster, 2003.

Taubman, William. *Khrushchev: The Man and His Era*. New York: W. W. Norton and Company, 2003.

Thomas, Evan. *The Very Best Men: Four Who Dared, the Early Years of the CIA*. New York: Simon and Schuster, 1995.

Wallace, Lane E. *Flights of Discovery: Sixty Years of Flight Research at Dryden Flight Research Center*. Washington, DC: National Aeronautics and Space Administration, 2006.

Weiner, Tim. *Legacy of Ashes: The History of the CIA*. New York: Anchor Books, 2008.

Wells, H. G. *The Island of Dr. Moreau*. 1896. Reprint, New York: Dover, 1996.

———. *The War of the Worlds*. 1898. Reprint, New York: Dover, 1997.

Wiesner, Jerome B. *Vannevar Bush, Biographical Memoirs*. Washington, DC: National Academies Press, 1979.

Wilcox, Robert K. *Scream of Eagles: The Dramatic Account of the U.S. Navy's Top Gun Fighter Pilots and How They Took Back the Skies Over Vietnam*. New York: Pocket Star Books, 2005.

Wills, Gary. *Bomb Power: The Modern Presidency and the National Security State*. New York: Penguin Press, 2010.

Zachary, Pascal G. *Endless Frontier: Vannevar Bush, Engineer of the American Century*. New York: Free Press, 1997.

Government Documents and Publications

Advisory Committee on Human Radiation Experiments. "Final Report." Washington, DC: U.S. Government Printing Office, 1995.

"Agreement Between Secretary of Defense and the Director of Central Intelligence on Responsibility of the National Reconnaissance Office." May 2, 1962.

"Army Air Forces Operation Crossroads: A Complete Pictorial Record of Task Unit 1.52 Which Had for Its Job the Biggest Photographic Assignment in History." Planographed by John Swift and Co., Inc., St. Louis, n.d.

Army Intelligence, G-2 Paperclip, Memorandum for the AC of S G-2, Intelligence Summary, Captain Paul R. Lutjens, 6 June 1947, RG 319, Washington National Records Center (WNRC), Suitland, Maryland.

Army Intelligence, G-2 Paperclip, Memorandum for the AC of S G-2, Intelligence Summary, Captain Paul R. Lutjens, 20 June 1947, RG 319, Washington National Records Center (WNRC), Suitland, Maryland.

Army Ordnance Department, Fort Bliss Rocket Project, "Report on Hermes Missile Project," RG 156, Washington National Records Center (WNRC), Suitland, Maryland.

Army Records, Assistant Chief of Staff, Intelligence (ACSI) G-2 (Intelligence), Entry 47F, Project Decimal File, 1949–50, Project Paperclip, Box 55, National Archives, College Park, Maryland.

Army Records, Assistant Chief of Staff, Intelligence (ACSI) G-2 (Intelligence), Entry 47GF, Project Decimal File, 1951–52, Project Paperclip, Boxes 38–40, National Archives, College Park, Maryland.

Army Staff, Assistant Chief of Staff, Intelligence (ACSI), G-2, Entry 1019: Records Relating to the Exploitation of German and Austrian Scientists and Technicians, 1945–1946, Box 1, National Archives, College Park, Maryland.

"Black Shield Reconnaissance Missions, 31 May–15 August 1967. DST-BS/BYE/67-1, Central Intelligence Agency, Directorate of Science and Technology. September 22, 1967.

Bush, Vannevar. "A Collection of His Papers in the Library of Congress." Manuscript Division, Library of Congress, Washington, DC.

Central Intelligence Agency. "Biographic Profile, Albert Dewell Wheelon." NARA, MRB, RG 263, May 10, 1966.

Central Intelligence Agency. "R. V. Jones Intelligence Award Ceremony Honoring Dr. Albert Wheelon." December 13, 1994.

Charyk, Joseph V. "A Summary Review of the National Reconnaissance Office." February 25, 1963.

"Chronology of Events Concerning the Seizure of the USS Pueblo." Central Intelligence Agency Memorandum, January 24, 1968.

Chuykov, V. "Military Thought, Intelligence to the Level of Modern Tasks." Memorandum for the Director of Central Intelligence, January 23, 1962.

Civilian Saucer Investigations. "Minutes of the Meeting of Civilian Saucer Investigations, Wednesday, April 2, 1952, 8:00 p.m." Mayfair Hotel, Los Angeles, California.

"Debriefing of Francis Gary Powers." February 13, 1962 NARA. RG 263, Box 230. CIA Release, 1997.

"Defense's Nuclear Agency 1947–1997." Defense Threat Reduction Agency. Defense Technical Information Center, 2002.

Director of Central Intelligence. Classified Message, 2219Z. Oxcart Secure Ops, May 15, 1962.

Director of Central Intelligence. "Soviet Capabilities and Probable Programs in the Guided Missile Field." NIE 11-6-54. October 1954.

———. "Main Trends in Soviet Capabilities and Policies, 1957–1962." NIE 11-4-57. November 12, 1957.

———. "Main Trends in Soviet Capabilities and Policies, 1959–1964." NIE 11-4-59. February 9, 1960.

———. "Soviet Capabilities for a Long Range Attack." NIE 11-8-61. June 7, 1961.

Dunning, Gordon. "Protective and Remedial Measures Taken Following Three Incidents of Fallout." Washington, DC: United States Atomic Energy Commission, 1968.

EG&G, Inc., Las Vegas Operations. "An Aerial Radiological Survey of the Three Mile Island Station Nuclear Power Plant." Washington, DC: U.S. Department of Energy, 1977.

"First History of AFSWP 1947–1954." Defense Nuclear Agency, 1.941025.002. Declassified October 18, 1994.

Foreign Scientist Case Files, "Riedel, Walther," RG 330, Box 135, 190/900 (A)/24/6, National Archives, College Park, Maryland.

Haines, Gerald K. "CIA's Role in the Study of UFOs, 1947–90." *Studies in Intelligence.* Semiannual unclassified edition 1 (1997): 67–84.

"History of the Air Force Special Weapons Center, 1 January–30 June 1957." Defense Nuclear Agency. Department of Defense, 1995.

Hoerlin, Herman. "United States High-Altitude Test Experiences: A Review Emphasizing the Impact on the Environment." Los Alamos Scientific Laboratory of the University of California Monograph. U.S. Energy Research and Development Administration, October 1976.

Johnson, Clarence L. "History of the Oxcart Program: As Recorded by the Builder." Burbank: Lockheed Aircraft Corporation, Advanced Development Projects, July 1968.

Knaack, Marcelle Size. *Encyclopedia of U.S. Air Force Aircraft and Missile Systems, Post–World War II Bombers, 1945–1973.* Volume 2. Washington, DC: Office of Air Force History, United States Air Force, 1988.

Lowenhaupt, Henry S. "Mission to Birch Woods." *Studies in Intelligence* 12 (Fall 1968).

———. "The Decryption of a Picture." *Studies in Intelligence* 11 (September 1995).

McLean, David R. "Cranks, Nuts and Screwballs." *Studies in Intelligence* 9 (Summer 1995).

National Photographic Interpretation Center. "Chronological Developments of the Kapustin Yar/Vladimirovka and Tyuratam Missile Test Centers, USSR, 1957 through 1963." November 1963.

————. Black Shield Mission X-001. May 31, 1967, June 1967.

————. Black Shield Mission BX-67051. June 20, 1967, June 1967.

Nazi War Crimes & Japanese Imperial Government Records. Interagency Working Group. Final Report to the United States Congress. April 2007.

Nevada Test Organization. *Background Information on Nevada Nuclear Tests.* Las Vegas: U.S. Atomic Energy Commission, Office of Test Information, July 15, 1957.

Notorious Nazi Files, Entry UD-2, Mengele, Josef, Vols. 1–2, Box 3, RG 263, National Archives, College Park, Maryland.

Odarenko, Todos M. Office Memorandum, United States Government, From: Chief, Physics and Electronics Division, SI. Subject: Current Status of Unidentified Flying Objects (UFOB) Projects, 17 December 1953.

————. Office Memorandum, United States Government. To: Acting Assistant Director for Scientific Intelligence: From: Chief, Physics and Electronics Division; Subject: Responsibility for "Unidentified Flying Objects" (UFOBs). August 8, 1955.

Office of Special Projects, 1965–1970. Vol. 1. Washington, DC: CIA, 1973.

Orlov, Alexander. "The U-2 Program: A Russian Officer Remembers." *Studies in Intelligence* (Winter 1998–1999).

Palomares Summary Report. Kirtland Air Force Base, New Mexico: Field Command Defense Nuclear Agency Technology and Analysis Directorate, January 15, 1975.

Parangosky, John. "The Oxcart Story." *Studies in Intelligence* 26 (Summer 1982).

"Path to the F-117A Stealth Fighter: Section II—Have Blue." Advanced Development Programs, Lockheed Martin Aeronautics Company, n.d.

Pedlow, Gregory W., and Donald E. Welzenbach. *The Central Intelligence Agency and Overhead Reconnaissance: The U-2 and OXCART Programs, 1954–1974.* Washington, DC: Center for the Study of Intelligence, 1992.

Poteat, Gene. "Stealth, Countermeasures, and ELINT, 1960–1975: Some Beginnings of Information Warfare." *Studies in Intelligence* (1998).

"Project Crested Ice, the Thule Nuclear Accident (U) Volume 1." SAC Historical Study #113. History and Research Division, Headquarters Strategic Air Command, April 23, 1969.

"Proposed Operation Against Cuba, Top Secret (TS) #176622." CIA Top Secret, March 1961.

"Report of the Defense Science Board, 2008 Summer Study on Capability Surprise, Volume II: Supporting Papers." Washington, DC: Office of the Undersecretary of Defense for Acquisition, Technology, and Logistics, January 2010.

"Report on Conclusion of Powers Trial." USSR International Affairs, August 22, 1960; CIA approved for release, September 1985.

"Results of a Search for Records Concerning the 1947 Crash Near Roswell, New Mexico." GAO/NSIAD-95-187. General Accounting Office, July 1995.

Rogovin, Mitchell. *Three Mile Island, a Report to the Commissioners and to the Public.* Vol. I. Nuclear Regulatory Commission Special Inquiry Group, January 1980.

Rollins, Eugene M. "Nevada Test Site — Site Description," Oak Ridge Associated Universities TEAM, Dose Reconstruction Project for NIOSH, Document Number: ORAUT-TKBS-0008-2, Effective Date: 5/27/2008.

"Scientific Advisory Panel on Unidentified Flying Objects, 14–17 January 1953." Central Intelligence Agency.

Secretary of Defense, OSD Policy Files on JIOA and Paperclip, 1950, Box 1, Box 338, RG 330, National Archives, College Park, Maryland.

SHAEF [Supreme Headquarters Allied Expeditionary Force], Entry 13D, CIOS, Horten Tailless Aircraft, Item-25, RG 331. File No. XXIII-6, Box 92, 290/7/8/2, National Archives, College Park, Maryland.

Taube, L. J. *B-70 Aircraft Study, Final Report.* Vol. 1. SD 72-SH-0003, North American Rockwell, Space Division, April 1972.

Taylor, Leland B. *History of Air Force Atomic Cloud Sampling.* AFSC, Historical Publication Series 61-141-1. Air Force Special Weapons Center, Air Force Systems Command, January 1963.

Tenet, George J. "The U-2 Program: The DCI's Perspective." *Studies in Intelligence* (Winter 1998–99).

"Thirty and Thriving: The National Photographic Interpretation Center." Washington, DC: *Studies in Intelligence* (1991).

U.S. Air Force. "Biography: Major General Paul N. Bacalis," n.d.

———. "Biography: Brigadier General Jack C. Ledford." Died Nov. 16, 2007.

———. "Biography: Lieutenant General Robert Bond. Died April 26, 1984.

U.S. Air Force. Project Grudge and Blue Book Reports 1–12. Washington, DC: National Investigations Committee on Aerial Phenomena, 1968.

U.S. Air Force Air Materiel Command. "Unidentified Aerial Objects; Project Sign," No. F-TR 2274, IA, Records of the U.S. Air Force Commands, Activities and Organizations, Record Group 341, National Archives. Washington, DC, February 1949.

United States Army Intelligence and Security Command, "Horten Brothers / Operation Harass," regraded unclassified, 6 July 1994, CDR USAINSCOM FO1/PO Auth para 1-603 DOD 5200.1R, 358 pages.

"United States Atomic Energy Commission, Annual Report to Congress for 1965." Washington, DC: United States Government Printing Office, 1965.

"United States Atomic Energy Commission, Annual Report to Congress for 1966." Washington, DC: United States Government Printing Office, 1966.

"United States Nuclear Tests July 1945 through September 1992." DOE/NV– 209-REV 15. Department of Energy. Nevada Office Operations, December 2000.

U.S. Congress, Office of Technology Assessment. *The Containment of Underground Nuclear Explosions*. OTA-ISC-414. Washington, DC: U.S. Government Printing Office, October 1989.

U.S. War Department, War Crimes Office, Judge Advocate General's Office, #770475.

Varenstov, S. "The Problem of Combat with the Nuclear Means of the Enemy and Its Solution." CIA, August 1961.

Vaughn, Harold. "Summary of Research of Rocket Programs." Sandia, SCTM34-59(51). Declassified Case No. 409.10, February 5, 1959.

Warner, Michael. "The CIA's Internal Probe of the Bay of Pigs Affair, Lessons Unlearned." *Studies in Intelligence* (Winter 1998–1999).

Weiss, Gus W. "The Life and Death of Cosmos 954." *Studies in Intelligence* (Spring 1978).

Welzenbach, Donald E. "Science and Technology: Origins of a Directorate. Killian and Land Influence." *Studies in Intelligence* (Summer 1986).

"Wernher Magnus Maximilian von Braun aka Freiherr von Braun," Department of Justice, FBI File 116-13038, 297 pages.

Wheelon, Albert D., and Sidney Graybeal. "Intelligence for the Space Race." *Studies in Intelligence* (Fall 1963).

White, M. G., and P. B. Dunaway. *Selected Environmental Plutonium Research Reports of the Nevada Applied Ecology Group, Plutonium Valley.* Vol. 2. Nevada: U.S. Department of Energy, June 1978.

Williams, Michael R. "Ground Test Facility for Propulsion and Power Modes of Nuclear Engine Operation." Savannah River National Laboratory, Department of Energy, 2004.

Wycoff, Runore C. "International Technology Corporation, Record of Technical Change, Area 25 R-MAD Decontamination Facility, Nevada Test Site, Nevada." Project/Job No. 799417.00050010. Division Director, Environmental Restoration Division, January 2000.

Articles

Absher, Kenneth Michael. "Mind-Sets and Missiles: A First Hand Account of the Cuban Missile Crisis." Strategic Studies Institute, United States Army War College, 2009.

Adams, Eric. "Rods from God: Space-launched Darts That Strike Like Meteors." *Popular Science* (June 1, 2004).

Alford, Matthew. "Steven Spielberg." *Cinema Papers* (1978).

Anderson, Jack. "US Heard Russians Chasing U-2." *Washington Post,* May 12, 1960.

"Atomic Tests: The Blast at Lop Nor." *Time* magazine, October 6, 1964.

Barrett, D. M. "Doing 'Tuesday Lunch' at Lyndon Johnson's White House: New Archival Evidence on Vietnam Decisionmaking." *Political Science and Politics* (1991).

Bergen, Peter, and Katherine Tiedemann. "The Drone War: Are Predators Our Best Weapon or Worst Enemy." *New Republic,* June 3, 2009.

————. "The Year of the Drone: An Analysis of U.S. Drone Strikes in Pakistan, 2004–2009." *New America Foundation,* February 24, 2010.

Black, Edwin. "Eugenics and the Nazis: The California Connection." *San Francisco Chronicle,* November 9, 2003.

Burrows, William E. "How the Skunk Works Works." *Air and Space* (April 1994).

————. "The Oxcart Cometh." *Air and Space* (February 1999).

"Congress Reassured on Space Visits." *New York Times,* April 6, 1966.

Cook, Joan. "Kenneth Germeshausen, 83, Dies; Was Nuclear and Radar Pioneer." *New York Times,* August 21, 1990.

Corea, Gordon. "Mystery of Lost US Nuclear Bomb." BBC News, November 10, 2008.

"Cosmos 954: An Ugly Death." *Time* magazine, February 6, 1978.

Darrach, H. B., and Robert Ginna. "Have We Visitors from Space?" *Life* magazine, April 7, 1952.

Edwards, Travis. "First MQ-9 Reaper Makes Its Home on Nevada Flight-line." *U.S. Air Force Public Affairs,* March 14, 2007.

Eger, Christopher. "Secret MiGs flown by the USAF: The US Flew Dozens of MiG Fighters in a Classified Cold War Project." *Air Combat Suite 101,* April 9, 2007.

Epstein, Edward Jay, and Susana Duncan. "The War of the Moles." *New York* 11 (January/February 27, 1978).

Fulghum, David A. "MiGs in Nevada." *Aviation Week and Space Technology,* November 27, 2006.

Garamone, Jim. "Navy to Shoot Down Malfunctioning Satellite." American Forces Press Service, February 14, 2008.

————. "Predator Demonstrates Worth Over Kosovo." American Forces Press Service, September 21, 1999.

Geller, Doran. "Inside the Israeli Secret Service: A History of Its Growth and Missions." *Jewish Virtual Library,* n.d.

Griggs, Brandon. "Could Moon Landings Have Been Faked? Some Still Think So." CNN, July 17, 2009.

Grundberg, Andy. "H. E. Edgerton, 86, Dies, Invented Electronic Flash." *New York Times,* January 5, 1990.

Gup, Ted. "The Ultimate Congressional Hideaway." *Washington Post,* May 31, 1992.

Hambling, David. "Mysteries Surround Afghanistan's Stealth Drone." *Wired,* Danger Room Blog, December 4, 2009.

Hawkes, Terrence. "William Empson's Influence of the CIA: Counterintelligence, Argued James Angleton, Called for the Kind of Practical Criticism He Learned at Yale." *London Times Literary Supplement,* June 10, 2009.

Hayes, Ron. "H-bomb Incident Crippled Pilot's Career." *Palm Beach Post,* January 17, 2007.

Hersh, Seymour M. "Manhunt: The Bush Administration's New Strategy in the War Against Terrorism." *New Yorker,* December 23, 2002.

Hoffman, Carl. "China's Space Threat: How Missiles Could Target U.S. Satellites." *Popular Mechanics* (July 2007).

Hoffman, Fred S. "Allies Help Pentagon Obtain Soviet Arms." Associated Press, May 7, 1984.

Hosenball, Mark, and Evan Thomas. "The Opening Shot." *Newsweek,* November 18, 2002.

Hutcheson, John. "Balad Predator Strikes Insurgents Placing Roadside Bomb Near Balad." *Red Tail Flyer,* 332nd Air Expeditionary Wing, Public Affairs, Balad Air Base, Iraq, March 31, 2006.

Jacobsen, Annie. "The Road to Area 51." *Los Angeles Times Magazine,* April 5, 2009.

Jelinek, Pauline. "U.S. Releases Nazi Papers." Associated Press, November 2, 1999.

"John Parangosky Dies; Helped Manage Spy Satellite System." *Washington Post,* September 26, 2004.

Kirschbaum, Erik. "Cloning Wakes German Memories of Nazi Master Race." Reuters, February 27, 1997.

Lake, Anthony. "Lying Around Washington." *Foreign Policy* 2 (Spring 1971).

Mahnaimi, Uzi. "Stolen Iraqi Jet Helped Israel Win Six-Day War." *Sunday Times of London,* June 3, 2007.

May, James. "Riding the Caspian Sea Monster." *BBC News* magazine, September 27, 2008.

Nelson, Robert. "Low-Yield Earth-Penetrating Nuclear Weapons." *Journal of the Federation of American Scientists* 54 (January/February 2001).

Pincus, Walter. "Yuri I. Nosenko, KGB Agent Who Defected to the U.S." *Washington Post,* August 27, 2008.

"Rise of the Machines." ArmyTechnology.com, May 21, 2008.

Robarge, David S. "Richard Helms: The Intelligence Professional Personified." *Studies in Intelligence,* April 14, 2007.

Sanger, David E., and Thom Shanker. "White House Is Rethinking Nuclear Policy." *New York Times,* February 28, 2010.

Smucker, Philip. "The Intrigue Behind the Drone Strikes." *Christian Science Monitor,* November 12, 2002.

"Stalin UFOs," Pravda.ru, November 19, 2002. http://english.pravda.ru/news/russia/19-11-2002/14700-0/#, accessed January 2, 2011.

Thomas, Evan. "Wayward Spy." *Civilization* (September–October 1995).

Tolip. "Black Ops: American Pilots Flying Russian Aircraft During the Cold War." MilitaryHeat.com, October 4, 2007.

"U.S. Dumps Bunker Buster or Not?" *Jane's Defence,* November 17, 2005.

"U.S. Missile Strike Kills al Qaeda Chief," CNN, November 5, 2002.

Weber, Bruce. "Dina Babbitt, Artist at Auschwitz, Is Dead at 86." *New York Times,* August 1, 2009.

Welsome, Eileen. "The Plutonium Files: America's Secret Medical Experiments in the Cold War." *Albuquerque Tribune,* November 1993.

Whitehouse, David. "NASA Pulls Moon Hoax Book." BBC News, November 8, 2002.

Wilber, Del Quentin. "Hell Hath a Jury." *Washington Post,* October 8, 2009.

Winthrop, Thornton. "Science Discovers Real Frankenstein." *Boston Herald,* June 4, 1939.

Wolverton, Mark. "Into the Mushroom Cloud." *Air and Space* magazine, August 1, 2009.

Oral Histories

Oral history interview with Richard M. Bissell Jr. by Theodore A. Wilson and Richard D. McKinzie, East Hartford, Connecticut, July 9, 1971 (Harry S. Truman Library and Museum).

Oral history interview with Robert Thomas, Los Alamos National Laboratory, Headquarters DOE, 09/22/81. Box No. JNSOO36 I-3. National Radiobiology Archives Project.

Oral history interview with Air Force Colonel John Pickering, for the Advisory Committee on Human Radiation Experiments, by John Harbett and Gil Whittemore, New Mexico, November 2, 1994.

Oral history interview with Al O'Donnell, by Colleen M. Beck and Hilary L. Green. Desert Research Institute, University of Nevada, 2004.

Oral history interview with Roger Andersen by Mary Palevsky. Nevada Test Site Oral History Project, University of Nevada, Las Vegas, September 20, 2005.

Oral history interview with T. D. Barnes by Mary Palevsky. Nevada Test Site Oral History Project, University of Nevada, Las Vegas, January 12, 2007.

Oral history: Conversations with Colonel Hervey Stockman, by Ann Paden and Earl Haney, 2004–2005.

Web Sites

- Central Intelligence Agency archives (http://www.foia.cia.gov/)

- Department of Energy archives (http://www.osti.gov/opennet/index.jsp)

- U.S. Air Force Archives (http://www.archives.gov/research/guide-fed-records/groups/342.html)

- G-2 Intelligence Archives (http://www.dami.army.pentagon.mil/)

- Office of the Deputy Assistant to the Secretary of Defense for Nuclear Matters (http://www.acq.osd.mil/ncbdp/nm/nuclearchronology1 .html)

- The National Security Archive (http://www.gwu.edu/~nsarchiv/)

- Federation of American Scientists (http://www.fas.org/)

- GlobalSecurity.org (http://www.globalsecurity.org/)

- Roadrunners Internationale (http://roadrunnersinternationale.com/)

- The Long War Journal (http://www.longwarjournal.org/)

- JT3 NTTR — Nevada Test and Training Range (http://www.jt3 .com/ne_range.asp)

Documentary Films and Television

The Day After Trinity, 1981.

Return with Honor: American Experience, 1999.

Forgiving Dr. Mengele, 2006.

The Search for Dr. Mengele, 1985.

Vietnam: A Television History, PBS, 1983.

America's Atomic Bomb Tests, 1997.

Hearts and Minds, 1974.

The Nuremberg Trials: American Experience, 2005.

Radio Bikini, 1987.

Atomic Journeys: Welcome to Ground Zero, 2000.

Modern Marvels: The Manhattan Project, History Channel, 2002.

The Fog of War: Eleven Lessons from the Life of Robert S. McNamara, 2003.

The Living Weapon: American Experience, 2006.

"Peter Jennings Reporting: UFOs in American History." ABC, February 24, 2005.

Walter Cronkite. "UFO: Friend, Foe or Fantasy?" CBS News, May 10, 1966.

Index

ABOUT THE AUTHOR

Annie Jacobsen is a contributing editor at the *Los Angeles Times Magazine* and an investigative reporter whose work has also appeared in the *National Review* and the *Dallas Morning News*. Her two-part series "The Road to Area 51" in the *Los Angeles Times Magazine* was widely read. A graduate of Princeton University, Annie Jacobsen lives in Los Angeles with her husband and two sons.

Map 1

Map 2

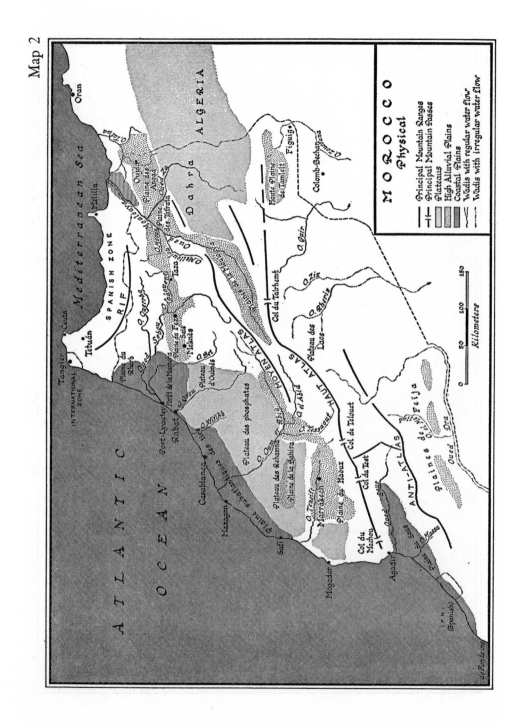

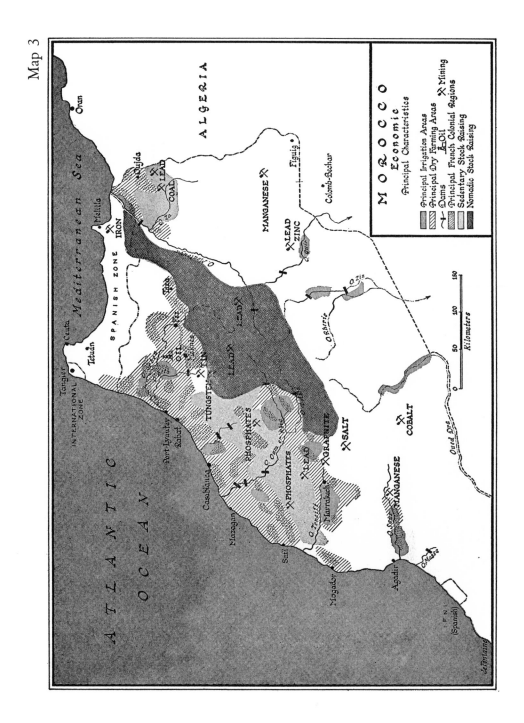

Map 3

Map 4

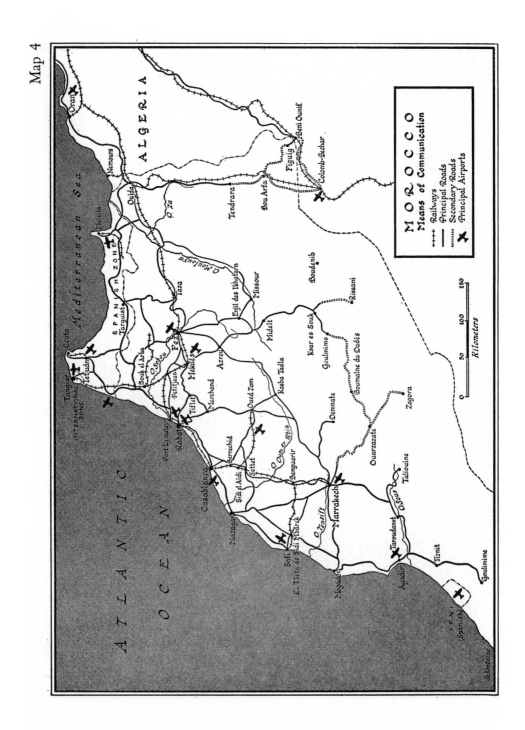

MOROCCO
Means of Communication

+++ Railways
――― Principal Roads
・・・・・ Secondary Roads
✈ Principal Airports

Kilometers
0   50   100   150

Map 5

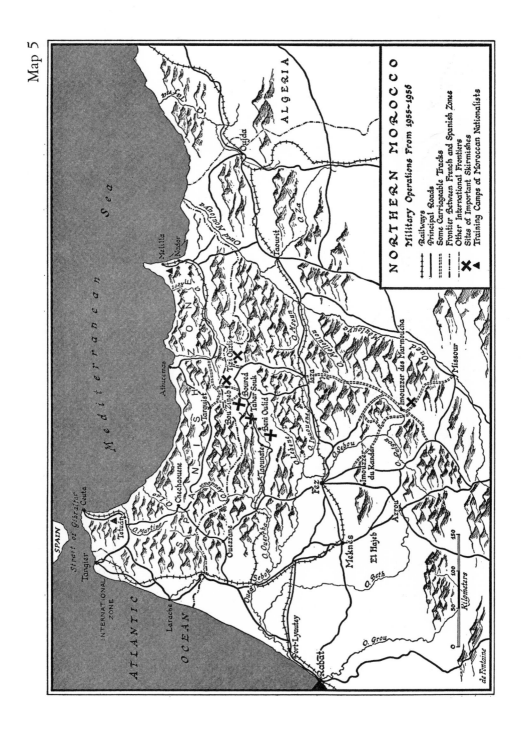

INDEX

667